DATE DUE

JY 5 '91	OC 20 05		
JY 19 '91			
RENEW			
AG 16 '91			
DE 4 '92			
AP 19 '93			
MY 21 93			
RENEW			
MR 11 '94			
AP 21 '95			
OC 20 '95			
MR 1 '96			
MY 7 '98			
OC 10 02			

GOVERNING
An Introduction
to Political Science

fifth edition

Austin Ranney

The University of California, Berkeley

PRENTICE HALL, ENGLEWOOD CLIFFS, NEW JERSEY 07632

Library of Congress Cataloging-in-Publication Data

RANNEY, AUSTIN.
    Governing: an introduction to political science/Austin Ranney.
—5th ed.
        p.   cm.
    Bibliography: p.
    Includes index.
    ISBN   0-13-361833-1
    1. Political science.   I. Title.
JA66.R298 1990
320—dc19   89-4721
                    CIP

Editorial/production supervision: *Edith Riker/Debra Ann Thompson*
Interior design: *Marjorie Shustak*
Cover design: *Diane Saxe*
Manufacturing buyer: *Peter Havens*
Photo Research: *Barbara Scott*

© 1990 by Prentice-Hall, Inc.
A Divison of Simon & Schuster
Englewood Cliffs, New Jersey 07632

Printed in the United States of America

10   9   8   7   6   5   4   3   2   1

ISBN   0-13-361833-1

Prentice-Hall International (UK) Limited, *London*
Prentice-Hall of Australia Pty. Limited, *Sydney*
Prentice-Hall Canada Inc., *Toronto*
Prentice-Hall Hispanoamericana, S.A., *Mexico*
Prentice-Hall of India Private Limited, *New Delhi*
Prentice-Hall of Japan, Inc., *Tokyo*
Simon & Schuster Asia Pte. Ltd., *Singapore*
Editora Prentice-Hall do Brasil, Ltda., *Rio de Janerio*

Contents

CHAPTER 12: **THE EXECUTIVE PROCESS**

\

Preface

This book is a lineal descendant of two earlier books. The older ancestor is *The Governing of Men*, which was first published in 1958 and revised in 1966, 1971, and 1975. The younger forebear is *Governing: A Brief Introduction to Political Science*, which was first published in 1971 and revised in 1975 and 1982. *Governing* began as a considerably shortened and somewhat rearranged version of *The Governing of Men*, consisting of thirteen of its twenty-four chapters. This book's content, as well as its structure, differ considerably from both of its ancestors, and with good reason.

First, in the years since the earlier books last appeared—to say nothing of the decades since the first edition of *The Governing of Men* was published—political events have continued to march at a dizzying pace, and many old truths have been replaced with new understandings, questions, and doubts. The world of 1971 was a world of Nixon-Agnew, Heath, Brandt, Pompidou, and Mao Zedong (in those days we spelled it Mao Tse-tung); of détente with the Soviet Union and implacable hostility between the United States and the People's Republic of China; of the war in Vietnam and college campuses racked with protest. The world of 1975 was a world of Ford-Rockefeller, Wilson, Schmidt, and Giscard d'Estaing; of history's first resignation by a president of the United States; of a beginning thaw in Chinese-American relations; of oil shortages and escalating inflation; of quiet campuses, crowded libraries, and worry about getting jobs. The world of 1980 was a world of Carter-Mondale, Reagan-Bush, Thatcher, Brezhnev, Sadat, Begin, Indira Gandhi, and the Ayatollah Khomeini; of border wars between Vietnam, Cambodia, and China; of Bakke and battles over affirmative action; of the suspension and restoration of democracy in India, and the rise of new democracies after decades of dictatorships in Spain and Portugal.

In 1987, Reagan, Thatcher, and the Ayatollah were still in the headlines, but they were joined by new stars such as Gorbachev, Deng Xiaoping, Mubarak, Shamir, Mulroney, and Rajiv Gandhi. The Reagan and Thatcher "revolutions" had been in place for two terms, and many believe they had permanently transformed their respective countries' politics. New regimes in the Soviet Union and the People's Republic of China seemed to offer great new possibilities and dangers. Inevitably, then, we have already forgotten much of what concerned us most in the fifties, sixties, seventies, and even the eighties.

In the world of the 1990s, Prime Minister Thatcher and President Mitterand are still leading figures, and they have been joined by President George Bush. But as the decade opens, perhaps the most towering new figure is Mikhail Gorbachev and the greatest potential for major changes not only in the Soviet Union but in world politics lies in his efforts to bring *glasnost* (openness) and *perestroika* (restructuring) to the economic practices, political institutions, and foreign policies of the Soviet Union. I can testify personally that President Gorbachev's efforts have already had a significant impact on some textbooks in political science, for I have found it necessary to rewrite to some extent most sections of this book that deal with the Soviet Union.

Second, not only have political events marched a long way, but some of the ways in which political scientists interpret and explain them have changed as well. Consequently, I have made many changes in the discussion of the topics carried over from the earlier books, and have added a number of new topics. These changes reflect not only the recent changes in political science but also the fact that studying how people are governed in the 1980s takes place in an atmosphere very different from that of the sixties, seventies, or eighties.

Politics and government are among the oldest and most universal of human activities and institutions. Many of the greatest minds in history have pondered their nature and possibilities and have enriched us with their reflections. But today the study of governing has acquired a new and terrible urgency. By the calendar, it was not long ago that most people, at least in the "developed" nations of the West and particularly in the United States, were confident that their political systems were the best yet devised. Perhaps they were not perfect, we felt, but they were perfectible, and, if used widely, they were fully capable of achieving humanity's highest goals of personal freedom, social justice, racial and sexual equality, and international peace. Moreover, we assumed that they constituted proper models for new and backward nations, and when we spoke of "developing nations" we meant nations in the process of becoming more like ours.

Then, for a decade or more, we were not so sure. Political conflict in the United States and in every other Western nation seemed to grow uglier every year. Some blacks said that our most cherished institutions—our courts, our leaders, indeed our whole political system—were nothing more than devices to perpetuate white racism. Some young people said that Middle America and its political institutions added up to an Establishment intent on forcing middle-aged, middle-class materialism and hypocrisy on a new generation seeking a better, more meaningful way of life. Some persons of all ages and races insisted that the true result of our great material wealth is not a life of richness and satisfaction, but a world of foul air, stinking streams, dead lakes, urban blight, and noise. And if all this were not enough, over us all, black and white, men and women, young and middle-aged alike, hovered the shadow of The Bomb and thermonuclear World War III.

As the 1990s begin, the big war has still not happened, although plenty of smaller wars are being fought in the Middle East, Indochina, Central America, and elsewhere. But some things have changed. The polls (and the evidence of our own senses) show that most of us are in better civic spirits than we were in the 1970s. We have more faith in the basic soundness of our political institutions and the quality of our leaders; we are more optimistic about the future of our nation, our world, and ourselves; and we are more likely to believe that it is in humanity's power to make things even better. But one thing has not changed: physical scientists and ecologists tell us that humanity now possesses the technical means either to destroy all life on earth or to build a new life of undreamed richness. How we can get people to make the right choices, they tell us, is a *political* problem. And so it is. For amid all the doubts and uncertainties about the future one thing is clear: the most crucial choices humanity makes will emerge from political conflict and be implemented by government action.

Most American colleges and universities, and an ever-growing number of schools in other nations, recognize the crucial role of politics for the human future by giving the study of politics and government a prominent place in their curricula. In most American schools the study of these matters is primarily, although not exclusively, the province of departments variously called "political science," or "government," or "politics." Each such department perennially faces the pedagogical problem of introducing students to this vast, complex, and challenging subject. Two approaches are most commonly used. The first is the detailed study of American government. The second, which may be called the "principles-of-political-science" approach, seeks to identify the properties universal to the governing processes in all human societies and to understand the nature and consequences of the major variations in these processes among different nations.

For a number of years I have taught an introductory undergraduate course using the second approach. My experiences have sensitized me to certain problems arising from its use, and this book, like the successive editions of its predecessors, represents my changing judgments about how best to deal with them.

During the 1950s and early 1960s, strange as it seems today, the main problem appeared to be that of giving students some sense of the relevance of politics and government to their own personal lives, and for students even now it remains a problem. Often students begin with the belief that politics are a dirty game played by other people and that government is something remote from the important concerns of life. For them I have tried to take as my points of departure certain situations that all students have experienced and have tried to show, step by step, how these situations affect and are affected by what happens in such apparently remote places as Washington, London, Paris, Moscow, Beijing—and even in the students' own state capitols and city halls. I have drawn most of my illustrations from current political conflicts in an effort to emphasize the concrete activities and interrelations of real human beings underlying the necessary but highly abstract terms as *political culture, political socialization, separation of powers,* and the like.

In the mid-1980s, many beginning students of political science will have no doubt that the subject matter of the discipline is highly relevant to their lives. Some, indeed, will feel that what is irrelevant is the way political science treats its materials. "Drop all this scientific pseudo-objectivity," some will say, "and talk about the evils of racism, sexism, poverty, and war, about the power structure that sustains them, and about how we can destroy them." However, an accurate understanding of how and why political systems work as they do and produce the policies they do is a necessary, although not sufficient, condition for any effective effort to change those policies and make a better world. In its present state, the contribution of political science is best qualified to provide us with such an understanding; and in a general way that is what I have tried to do in this book.

There is one other respect in which the fifth edition of this book differs from the previous editions: I have come to agree with many of my students and colleagues that an introduction to political science should recognize that the discipline does and should deal with factual descriptions of how modern governments make their policies and the kinds of policies they actually make; it also does and should consider the great clash of ideas about how governments *should* make policies and *what kinds* of policies they should make. Accordingly, I have added an entirely new chapter (Chapter 4) on Modern Political Ideologies.

Like the author of any textbook, I am indebted to many colleagues and friends. I realize that whatever merit it may have, I owe much to their help, and I am grateful for the opportunity traditionally provided by the preface to make public my thanks to those of whom I am most deeply in debt. In addition to my general thanks to the authors of the many works cited in the text for the insights and information they have provided, I wish to make the following acknowledgments of help directly received and greatly valued: to my good friends and generous colleagues, Dr. Jack W. Peltason, Chancellor of the University of California, Irvine, and Professor Emeritus Charles B. Hagan of the University of Houston, each of whom not only read and improved a number of chapters, but in the process greatly contributed to my education; to those colleagues, present and, sadly, departed, who cheerfully read and perceptively criticized particular chapters—Professor Valentine Jobst III, Benjamin B. Johnston, Philip Monypenny, Charles M. Kneier, and Clyde F. Snider, all of the University of Illinois; Charles S. Hyneman of Indiana University, Gillian Dean of Vanderbilt University, Joseph G. LaPalombara of Yale University, Warren E. Miller of Arizona State University, James N. Murray of the University of Iowa, Richard L. Park of the University of Michigan, Fred R. von der Mehden of Rice University, Professor Phillip Abbott of Wayne State University, Professor Nikolaos A. Stavron of Howard University, Professor James F. Ward of the University of Massachusetts-Boston, Professors Charles W. Anderson, Bernard C. Cohen, Jack Dennis, Leon D. Epstein, David Fellman, and M. Crawford Young, all of the University of Wisconsin at Madison, Sigmund Neumann of Wesleyan University, and Professor Jeane J. Kirkpatrick, again of Georgetown University and the American Enterprise Institute after a tour of duty as United States Permanent Representative to the United Nations. I am also grateful to the State Data Program of the University of California and its director, Professor Raymond E. Wolfinger, and to Karlyn Keene, Managing Editor of *Public Opinion*, for furnishing me with up-to-date polling information. My cherished friend and mentor, Evron M. Kirpatrick, Executive Director Emeritus of the American Political Science Association, who guided me through the early stages of creation of this book's first ancestor and has never given up on my political education. Professor John W. Smith of the Henry Ford Community College helped me to understand the special needs of today's students, and Stan Wakefield and Karen Horton have made Prentice Hall a welcome new home for the book. And finally, my thanks go to Joseph A. Ranney of the law firm of Ross and Stevens, who gave great help at various stages in the preparation of the book in all of its stages and versions.

Austin Ranney
Berkeley, California

1 Governments and Governing

> *I must study politics and war, that my sons may have liberty to study mathematics and philosophy . . . in order to give their children a right to study painting, poetry, music [and] architecture. . . .*
>
> *John Adams, 1789*

This book is an introduction to political science, so we will begin by saying what the field is about and why people study it. **Political science** is usually defined as *the systematic study of political and governmental institutions and processes.* It is about why in 1988 the American voters elected Republican George Bush president, but increased the already-substantial majorities of Democrats in both houses of Congress. It is about Mikhail Gorbachev's massive effort to reform the economic and political systems of the Soviet Union through *perestroika* (new thinking) and *glasnost* (openness). It is about the struggles of President Bush and Congress to find ways of balancing the budget without raising taxes and ways of controlling the AIDS epidemic without interfering with people's rights of privacy. It is about the long hot-and-cold war between Israel and the Arab nations in the Middle East over the formation of an independent Palestinian state and perhaps over the very existence of Israel itself. It is about what, if anything, the United Nations is doing to prevent World War III. Things like that.

Well, most of us would say, newspapers and television newscasts are full of such things, so they must be important. Yet let's admit that many of us really feel that such subjects are pretty remote from the things that truly matter in our lives—things like making friends, getting through school, getting a job, making a living, getting married, raising children, staying healthy, enjoying life.

But however remote government actions may *seem* to us, the sad first lesson of political science is that they are just about the most important forces in our lives. Let us see why.

THE OMNIPRESENCE OF GOVERNMENT IN MODERN LIFE

WHAT GOVERNMENTS DO

1. In Primitive Societies

We should begin by recognizing that there are a lot of people in the world for whom government, as we know it in the United States, hardly exists and plays no role of any importance in their day-to-day lives. Many anthropologists and some political scientists specialize in studying such societies,[1] and they report that most of them are run more or less like the Eskimo societies of North America.

The political system of the Eskimo is among the simplest known. The Eskimo peoples are scattered from the Bering Straits to Greenland in small communities, each numbering around a hundred inhabitants, with most of the members of each community related by blood or marriage. There are only two specialized roles that are politically significant—those of the headman and the shaman—and both are mixed roles. The shaman is the religious leader, but he (in Eskimo society the shaman is never a woman) may also punish those who violate taboos. In the extreme case he may order an offender exiled, which in the Arctic may mean death. The headman is a task leader who is influential in making decisions about hunting or the selection of places for settlement. But if the other members of the community disagree with his recommendations, he has no authority or power to impose his choices.

Violations of order are handled mostly through fist fights and "song duels" or, in extreme cases, through family feuds. An individual who threatens the community by repeated acts of violence, murder, or theft may be dealt with by an executioner, who assumes the responsibility for the execution with the approval of the community.[2]

2. In "Advanced/Industrialized" Societies

For better or worse, the readers of this book, like its author, do not live in societies like the Eskimos'. We live in nations such as most of those in North and South America, Western Europe, many in Asia, and some in Africa—societies that political scientists call "industrialized" (because their economies are based on division of labor, mass production, and the heavy use of machines) or "advanced" (presumably because such societies are further up on some historical ladder of progress).

The role of government is very different in such societies. Most of us who live in them are born in government-regulated hospitals and are delivered by government-licensed physicians. (Government protects us against abuse by our parents. Government makes us go to school whether we like it or not until we reach the age of 16. We marry and divorce according to rules made by government. We take and leave jobs, set up businesses or go bankrupt, engage in professions, buy and sell property, and retire according to rules and regulations laid down by government. Every year we pay a sizeable part of the money we earn to government in taxes. We may be ordered by government to serve in the armed forces and even to kill or die at the orders of government officials known as military officers. And when we have finally filled out our last government forms and paid our last tax bills, we are buried in government-licensed cemeteries, and our savings and property—minus portions siphoned off by governments in inheritance taxes—are handed on to our heirs by probate courts with the participation of government-licensed lawyers.

There is no escaping it: Governments play a major role in the lives of just about everyone who lives in the United States and the other advanced/industrialized societies. And since an introductory textbook like this one cannot possibly give equal attention to all kinds of societies and governments, we will concentrate mainly on the political and governmental institutions and processes of the society in which we live and others like it.

WHY GOVERNMENT IS SO PERVASIVE IN MODERN LIFE

Government has not always been as pervasive in people's lives as it is in ours. Before the early nineteenth century, most people in the United States and elsewhere lived out their lives with only occasional contacts with police magistrates and tax collectors and no contacts at all with draft boards and Social Security cards. Since the early 1800s, however, both the number and the variety of government activities in all modern nations have increased enormously. Why?

Most political scientists believe that the answer is rooted in the changing nature of society itself. Before the early nineteenth century, societies everywhere were predominantly rural, and most relationships among people were conducted directly, person to person. Most of our great-great-grandfathers lived on farms or in small hamlets. They personally knew, face-to-face, most of the people who directly affected their lives: their neighbors, the people who bought their produce, the people who sold them their equipment, seed, drugs, clothing, and so on. To protect themselves against being cheated or injured by others, they relied mainly on self-help. If they were harmed by others, they usually sought redress on their own without appealing to government officials to protect them.

But for most people in the 1990s life is very different. The societies in which we live are mainly urban, and most of our dealings with others are indirect and impersonal. We almost never see face to face most of the people who directly affect our lives, and we often do not even know the names of the people in the next apartment. Most of the people who make our cars, compound our drugs, pay our salaries, and bank our money live hundreds and even thousands of miles away, and most of them remain anonymous and faceless to us. This impersonality of modern life results not only from the large numbers of people who live in most cities, states, and nations but also from the complexity and high degree of labor specialization that characterize modern societies and economies.

To illustrate this point, let us consider an episode in the life of John Doe, a typical American living in 1830, and compare it with a similar episode in the life of his great-great-great-great grandson, John Doe VI, living in 1990. John Doe I feels a little out of sorts one day and decides that he needs a spring tonic to pick him up. He goes over to the next farm to see Ezra Roe, who sells him a bottle of Roe's Homemade Tonic. After a few swallows, Doe becomes sick, and he knows that Roe has cheated him. He returns, demands his money back, and, when Roe refuses, uses his fists to convince Roe that he had better return the money if he wants to stay healthy. Doe sees no reason to ask Judge Solon down at the general store to intervene, for he is used to handling such matters himself.

Six generations later, John Doe VI feels under par and goes to the corner drugstore to buy a bottle of Roe's Scientific Blood Conditioner. He takes a couple of swallows, becomes sick, and learns from his doctor that he has a mild case of poisoning from impurities in the conditioner, which is useless anyway. He feels like hitting the man who caused him this trouble, but the person who compounded the particular bottle of conditioner is one of 4,000 workers employed by the Roe Drug Corporation in a city 800 miles away, and the person who produced the television ad that persuaded Doe to buy the stuff works for an even bigger advertising agency even farther away. John Doe VI simply cannot get even solely by his own efforts, and it never occurs to him to try. Living as he does in an impersonal society, he turns instead to government. He sues the Roe Corporation for damages and writes to his congressman, urging that the pure-food-and-drug laws be tightened to prevent such damage in the future.

This little parable illustrates why government has come to be so pervasive in Western life. Few of us ever identify, let alone know personally, most of the people whose activities directly affect the quality of our lives. We therefore, as a matter of course, turn to government to bridge the gap between ourselves and most other people. We are so accustomed to having government intervene between us and them that we hardly give it a thought.

Take, for example, the act of faith that we commit when we swallow an aspirin tablet. We ask the druggist for aspirin, pay our money, and take the pill. But how many of us are analytical chemists skilled enough to be sure merely by looking at and tasting the pill that it in fact contains aspirin, as the label says, instead of arsenic or some other poison? Not many. How, then, do we dare to take the risks involved in swallowing it? The answer is that we know, without even bothering to think about it, that the people who make the tablets are checked by government inspectors and that the firms that manufacture and sell them are required by law, under threat of heavy penalties, to state on the label the contents of each pill and to warn us if it is dangerous. We do not have to be analytical chemists to take aspirin safely, for the government protects us from our ignorance and from the impersonality of life in our society.

In short, government is pervasive in nations such as the United States because the conditions of life in those nations demand that it be so. It may still be true, as Samuel Johnson wrote two centuries ago,

How small of all that human hearts endure

That part which Laws or Kings can cause or cure.

The fact remains, however, that modern industrialized nations and the people who inhabit them have turned to "Laws or Kings"—that is, governments—for putting into effect cures for a good part of "all that human hearts endure." That is why a whole field of study called political science has been developed to study and explain why governments do what they do. And that is why it makes sense to begin the study of political science by considering what kinds of institutions governments are and how they resemble and differ from other kinds of institutions people have established.

WHAT IS GOVERNMENT?

GOVERNMENT AND OTHER ORGANIZATIONS

In some respects, learning what it means to be a human being is not pure joy. From birth we become increasingly involved with an increasing number of social organizations, and as we get involved, we learn that each organization claims the right to make and enforce rules governing our behavior. We are born into a family, and our parents tell us that we must drink our milk, brush our teeth, keep our rooms neat, and not draw on the walls or swear. We go to school, and our teachers tell us that we have to attend class, pass examinations, and say no to drugs. We join a church, and our clerics tell us that we should attend services, say our prayers, and live according to the right moral principles. We get a job, and our bosses tell us that we must get to work on time and do a day's work for a day's pay. And so it goes all the days of our lives.

Furthermore, each organization backs up its rules with **sanctions**—*penalties that a group can impose on those who break its rules.* Parents can spank us and "ground" us on weekends; teachers can keep us after school; college professors can fail us; deans and presidents can throw us out of school; churches can expel us from membership; bosses can fire us.

The older we grow, however, the more we become aware of the rules and sanctions of another organization that claims even greater authority over us: "the government." It orders us to stay in school until we are 16, requires us to pay part of our incomes in taxes, tells us where we can and cannot park our cars, and generally surrounds us with more rules than we can count. And, if "the government" catches us violating its rules, it can fine us or imprison us or even put us to death. So government rules have a standing different from the rules of the other organizations in our lives.

THE RULES PEOPLE LIVE BY

No person acts completely randomly without rhyme, reason, or pattern. To be sure, our behavior patterns may be hard to figure out and may change as we grow older, move, acquire new friends, enter new occupations, and so on. But there is always *some* pattern at every stage of our lives.

Every society, moreover, has certain "normal" behavior patterns—that is, particular ways in which most members behave in particular situations. Most Americans, for example, wear *some* clothes, even on hot summer days when we might be more comfortable without them. Most wear "modern" clothes, not togas, loincloths, or sarongs. Most eat with knives and forks rather than chopsticks or fingers, pay money for what we buy, drive on the right-hand side of the road, and do not eat human flesh or kill rambunctious children. Some of what we do is governed by habit, and it never occurs to us to do otherwise. Much, however, is governed by *rules;* that is, most Americans consciously believe that we ought to act in certain ways, and we also know that if we break the rules, our associates will disapprove and we will be punished. Some of the rules people live by are closely associated with government; others are not. There are three main types: moral precepts, customs, and laws.

Moral Precepts

Every person's behavior is guided to some extent by **moral precepts**— *rules of behavior based on ideas of right and wrong.* We may try to obey such Judeo-Christian commandments as "thou shalt not kill," "honor thy father and mother," and "do unto others as you would have them do unto you." Or we may adhere to such non-Christian commandments as "never give a sucker an even break" and "let's do it to them before they do it to us."

Some or all of a person's moral precepts may come from religious sources. The commandments may be laid down by a religious institution and have behind them some sort of supernatural sanction, such as a priest's warning that sin offends God and may condemn the sinner to the eternal fires of hell. Part or all of a person's moral precepts may also come from nonreligious sources. The commandments may emanate from the person's philosophy of the good life and have behind them such nonsupernatural sanctions as the inner conviction that "virtue is its own reward" and that living immorally will make it tough to face yourself in a mirror.

Whatever their sources, moral precepts differ from other kinds of social rules in that people obey them because they believe it is good to do so, not because they fear some kind of earthly retribution from other people.

Customs

Our behavior is also guided to some extent by what we think others expect of us. For example, neither men's churches nor their private moral philosophies require them to wear business suits instead of togas or monks' habits to the office, to leave tips for waiters at restaurants, or to begin their letters "Dear ___" and close them "Sincerely yours." Yet most men regularly follow these rules because they know that if they don't, most of their associates will regard them as peculiar—and few people want to be pointed out or stared at as peculiar.

Customs are *rules of behavior based on long-established and widespread ways in which most people actually behave.* They are powerful regulators of behavior in all societies. According to anthropologists, in most primitive societies customs are the most powerful regulators of all, and even in the more developed modern nations they play an important role.

The fact that different groups have different customs should not blind us to the fact that customs in general are powerful shapers of human behavior. For example, many college students grow their hair long, wear blue jeans, and regard themselves as rebels against conformity. Many insurance executives have short haircuts, wear pin-striped suits, and regard themselves as upholding the sartorial decencies. But how many insurance executives have long hair and wear blue jeans regardless of what their friends and associates think, because it expresses *their* individuality? By the same token, how many college students have short haircuts and wear pin-striped suits, regardless of what their friends and associates think, because that expresses *their* individuality? Look around you and see. The fact is that all of us, however we feel we are doing our own thing, conform more or less faithfully to *some* group's customs.

Laws

The third kind of rules that limit our behavior are laws. In Chapter 14 we will examine in detail the nature, sources, and types of law. We note here that **law** is *the body of rules emanating from government and enforceable by the courts.* Law differs from customs in that it emanates from a specific source, the government. It differs from moral precepts in that it is enforceable by the courts.

Above all, its rules are made by governments, and in the kinds of societies we consider in this book, governments differ from all other rule-making organizations in a number of significant ways.

A DEFINITION OF GOVERNMENT

The term *government* is often used in two related but distinct senses. Sometimes it refers to a particular collection of *people,* each with individual idiosyncrasies, faults, and virtues, who are performing certain functions in a particular society at a particular time. And sometimes it refers to a particular set of *institutions,*— that is, a series of accepted and regular procedures for performing those functions, procedures that persist over time regardless of who happens to be operating them.

Both senses are incorporated in the definition of government we will use in this book: **Government** is *the body of people and institutions that make and enforce laws for a society.*

Defined thus, government is undoubtedly one of humanity's oldest and most nearly universal institutions. Some political philosophers, to be sure, have speculated about what life would be like in a state of **anarchy**—that is, in *a society with no government.* Yet there is no recorded instance of an actual society, past or present, that has operated for long with no government whatever (unless we count "world society"—more on that in Chapter 17). Evidently, people at all times and in all societies have felt that some sort of government is necessary for the way they wish to live their lives.

However, humanity's universal desire for government has by no means led all people at all times and in all societies to establish the same *kind* of government. Indeed, one of the most striking facts about actual governments, past and present, is their enormous variety. They have varied in complexity all the way from the simple headman-shaman systems of the Eskimos to the highly complex systems of the advanced/industrialized nations. They have varied in the treatment of their peoples all the way from the mass executions and brutality of Nazi Germany to the mild and permissive "welfare state" of Denmark.

Evidently, then, different societies require different kinds of governments to satisfy their special needs. But no matter how much some governments may differ from others, they all share certain characteristics that make them different from all other forms of human organization.

HOW GOVERNMENT DIFFERS FROM OTHER SOCIAL ORGANIZATIONS

In some of the world's more primitive societies—for example, the Eskimos in the Arctic and many Indian tribes in the remote Amazon jungles of Brazil— there is no sharp distinction between the leaders and rules of government and the leaders and rules of families or religions. But in advanced/industrialized societies, government differs significantly from all other social organizations in a number of respects:

COMPREHENSIVE AUTHORITY

Rules made by any social organization other than government apply, and are intended to apply, only to members of that organization. For example, when the University of California rules that all freshmen must take a course in English composition, no one expects this rule to apply to freshmen at Yale or Oxford or Slippery Rock. If General Motors decides to split its stock four for one, no one thinks that Ford or Coca Cola must do the same.

On the other hand, the rules of the government of the United States apply, and are intended to apply, to *all* members of American society. When Congress rules that every American with an annual income above a certain amount must pay a portion of that income in taxes, no one imagines that this rule does not apply to people who disapprove of income taxes, or who cannot afford both to pay the taxes and to buy new cars, or who let payment slip their minds. When Congress says *every* American, we all understand that it means precisely that; for Congress, along with the president and the Supreme Court, have governmental **authority**—*the acknowledged power to make binding decisions and issue obligatory commands.*

INVOLUNTARY MEMBERSHIP

Membership in most social organizations other than government is voluntary; that is, people become members of such an organization and place themselves under its rules only by conscious choice. One does not automatically become a Presbyterian at birth because one's parents are Presbyterian or because one is born in a Presbyterian hospital. One can officially join the church only by going through certain formal procedures, such as baptism and confirmation. Membership in a nation, however, is largely involuntary; that is, most people *initially* become citizens of a nation and subject to its rules without any deliberate choice or conscious act. All nations officially regard as citizens either all persons born in their territories or all children born of their citizens, or some combination of both. Most nations also have procedures for noncitizens to acquire citizenship (a process generally called "naturalization") and for citizens to renounce it; but initial membership of a nation is involuntary.

AUTHORITATIVE RULES

Rules made by some private (that is, nongovernmental) organizations often conflict with those made by other private organizations. For example, a labor union may order its members to use clubs and fists to keep strike breakers from crossing picket lines, yet the church to which some of the union members belong may teach that physical violence should never be used. In most societies there is no clearly defined and generally accepted hierarchy among organizations and therefore no automatic way to determine which organizations' rules should prevail and which should be overridden in situations of conflict. There is no universal agreement, for example, that a church is more important than a labor union or vice versa, and so each union member who is also a church member must decide individually whether to obey the church's rules or the union's.

The rules of government are quite another matter, however, for in every nation those rules are generally recognized as **authoritative**—that is, they are generally considered to be *more binding upon all members of a society than the rules of all other organizations*. In any conflict between the laws of government and the rules of a private organization, there is general agreement that government laws should prevail. For instance, if a religious sect decrees human sacrifice as part of its ritual but the government forbids the taking of human life by any organization other than itself, most members of the society will regard the government's prohibition as more binding than the religious sect's ritual requirement. If the local building code stipulates that brick walls must be at least 12 inches thick and local engineers think that 8 inches is enough, most of the town's citizens—including most of its engineers—will obey the 12-inch requirement, however misguided they think it is.

LEGITIMATE MONOPOLY OF OVERWHELMING FORCE

Of course, all government rules are not always obeyed by all the members of any society. After all, every human organization has to deal with people who disobey its rules, and government is certainly no exception. All organizations impose sanctions on rule breakers, but government differs from other organizations in the kind of sanctions it is authorized to impose. Private organizations are generally authorized to withhold certain privileges, impose fines, and require certain penances. Their ultimate legitimate weapon, however, is expulsion. If a member of a labor union or a church refuses to pay the union's dues or do the church's penances, the most extreme penalty either organization can impose is to expel the delinquent from membership. Government can not only impose all these sanctions as well, but it can also impose two additional sanctions that are forbidden to private organizations: It can send law breakers to prison, and it can take their lives.

It is important to recognize that governments are not the only organizations that *in fact* impose life-and-death sanctions, for that is clearly not so. Gangsters of the Mafia sometimes kill people who violate their rules, and terrorists sometimes kidnap airline passengers and randomly kill patrons of airports and restaurants. The point is that government alone has the *legitimate*

Government's Ultimate Sanction
(Source: AP/Wide World Photos.)

power to execute rule breakers. The concept of **legitimacy** is crucial here, and it means *the general belief of the members of a society that the government's powers to make and enforce rules are proper, lawful, and entitled to obedience.* In every political system, most people believe that if any agency may rightfully use the ultimate sanction of execution, government is the only one. Any private organization or person that uses it is committing murder, perhaps the worst of all crimes.

All social organizations can muster some physical force to enforce their rules, and many, on occasion, use it. At the very least they can use the fists of their members, and many also use rocks, bricks, clubs, razors, knives, and perhaps even firebombs, pistols, rifles, and submachine guns. No American needs to be told that some private organizations sometimes actually use violence to promote their causes: Anyone who reads our newspapers knows that some people who oppose abortion sometimes set fire to abortion clinics, and some students who protest their colleges' business investments in South Africa occupy administration buildings and trash administrators' offices. But there is nothing peculiarly American about such behavior. No nation, sad to say, conducts its internal political conflicts entirely without violence.

Government differs from other social organizations not in the fact that it occasionally uses force to enforce its rules, but in the sheer amount of force it can muster. The rocks and pistols that private organizations can use are feeble indeed compared with the armed police, military forces, intercontinental ballistic missiles, and hydrogen bombs available to governments.

THE HIGHEST STAKES

These special characteristics of government make political stakes the highest that people play for. Controversies among Roman Catholics about the permissibility of birth control and the ordaining of women as priests are very important to Roman Catholic clergy and laity, but less so to Protestants, Jews, and Muslims. The struggles among ABC, CBS, and NBC for viewers and advertising may dominate the lives of all who work in television, but they are, at most, of merely spectator interest to the United Mine Workers or the American Medical Association. But a major confrontation between the United States and the Soviet Union over the Arab–Israeli conflict in the Middle East could quite conceivably escalate into thermonuclear World War III, and the conflict within each of the two "superpowers" over what policy it should follow in the Middle East involves no less a stake than the survival of humanity.

As any poker player knows, when the stakes rise, the nature of the game changes. The processes of politics and government have some instructive similarities to their counterparts in private organizations, but they operate in such a different atmosphere and for such greater stakes that they are very different from the processes in private organizations. It is well to remember this point whenever we are tempted to think of decision making in the White House or the Kremlin as just another version of what goes on in our families or faculty meetings or corporations.

THE BASIC TASKS AND TOOLS OF GOVERNMENT

As government authorities in most nations see it, the basic duty of any government, whether democratic or authoritarian, is to ensure the nation's survival. And that involves two fundamental tasks: defending its independence against external enemies, and keeping its internal conflicts from becoming so bitter that they lead to secession and civil war. To accomplish the second of these tasks, the government must satisfy the people's needs that made them decide to accept a government in the first place. It must sift through the many political demands constantly deluging it, blend them into public policies, and enforce those policies in such a way that no major group of citizens feels compelled to tear the nation apart. National survival is thus the ultimate test of any government.

There is no universal or infallible method for accomplishing this basic task, no surefire way to prevent civil wars or win foreign wars. Throughout this book we will review the wide range of policies actually pursued by modern governments. But we should note here that all governments rely upon combinations, varying in emphasis from time to time and from government to government, of a few basic "tools," which can be noted only briefly here.

INTEREST ARTICULATION

As we will see in Chapter 2, every society's population is divided into many groups distinct from one another in one or more significant respects—for example, in gender, racial and ethnic identity, education, occupation, income, and so on. Just about every one of these groups and the people who compose them have a **political interest**—a concept which plays a leading role in political analysis, and which we will define as *the stake of a person or group in government policy, something of value to be gained or lost by what government does or does not do.* The essence of the political process is that all these groups make certain *demands* that the government do something to help them or refrain from doing something that hurts them. And the essence of governing is responding to these demands in one way or another.

If a nation's government simply does not know what demands its people are making, it can hardly deal with them effectively. If it is dimly aware of the demands but unaware of their variety or intensity, it is not likely to deal with them very well. And if it does not cope effectively with the most urgent and widely supported demands, it risks anger, alienation, and perhaps even rebellion from the groups it ignores.

Consequently, governments need effective methods for the articulation of interests. **Interest articulation,** as political scientists use the term, means *the process of forming and expressing demands by political interest groups and transmitting them to government authorities.* In later chapters we will consider some of the principal devices by which interests are articulated in modern nations—for example, lobbying, propaganda, protest, mass communications, public opinion polls, and campaigns and elections. Here we note only that every political system needs effective ways for its authorities to know and understand its citizens' strongly felt political demands.

INTEREST AGGREGATION

In Chapter 2 we will consider the fact that some political demands inevitably conflict with others and that there is no way a government can fully satisfy each and every demand made on it. It can hope to deal with the demands adequately only if they are "aggregated" in some way. The term **interest aggregation** means *the process of combining the demands of different interest* *groups into general programs of public policy.* Essentially, the aggregating process consists of adjusting the demands to one another so that they do not automatically cancel out one another and so that each major group is reasonably happy with what it gets. As we will see, many aggregating processes commonly occur outside formal government, in discussions among individuals and in negotiations and deals within and among pressure groups and political parties. Considerable aggregation also takes place in the legislative, executive, and administrative agencies of government. But however interest aggregation is achieved, it is a necessity for any political system and a vital tool of any government.

COERCION AND COMPROMISE

Every government, democratic or authoritarian, perpetually faces the key question of how to achieve acceptance of its policies and compliance with its laws. One obvious and important answer, of course, is government **coercion,** *the threat or imposition of sanctions.* Governments can apply many kinds of sanctions to law breakers—physical, economic, psychological, violent, nonviolent. They can deny a license to engage in a business or profession, take away the right to vote and hold public office, withdraw financial aid or expel from school, or even exile. And, of course, they can fine, imprison, "brainwash," torture—and kill. As we noted earlier, government's legitimate monopoly on the ultimate sanction of the death penalty is a prime difference between it and all other social organizations. Governments generally use coercion to achieve one or both of two main objects: (1) to "make examples," which, it is hoped, will convince potential lawbreakers that the consequences of breaking the law will be worse than any likely gains; and (2) to take out of circulation any person who, undeterred by these threats, breaks the law anyway. No doubt there is often an element of revenge as well, but the principal justification for government coercion is deterrence.

Yet no government can rely on coercion alone. It is plainly impossible to execute or imprison massive numbers of citizens; hence large-scale and resolute resistance to a law simply cannot be overcome by coercion alone. Nor is open defiance the only form of resistance that government has to worry about. A policy that receives only sullen, foot-dragging, minimal compliance is not likely to do much good. Accordingly, willing compliance by most people is necessary for any policy to be effective, and enthusiastic popular support can make up for a good many technical deficiencies and miscalculations in any policy. Any government, however brutal and ruthless it is prepared to be, depends upon this kind of voluntary compliance for most of its policies most of the time.

How do governments obtain voluntary compliance? There are myriad

Political Action by Civil Disobedience. Police removing anti-apartheid protestors, 1985. (Source: Ken Karp.)

ways, but to some degree they are all variations on the basic theme of compromise. Given the inevitability of conflicting interests and incompatible demands, for every "winner" in political conflict there is bound to be a "loser." No government can escape this hard fact of life, but it can strive to shape the content and impact of each policy so that the "losers" will feel that continuing to live under the existing regime, though perhaps far from ideal, is at least bearable. A government can best keep its competing interest groups satisfied enough not to rebel by giving each *something* of what it wants, so that no group experiences total "defeat" or the despairing feeling that the whole system is rigged against it so that its wishes and needs will never receive serious consideration. But to do that the government must deny total victory to the "winners" by watering down the maximum demands of all opposing interests.

The resulting policies are likely to contain some logically inconsistent provisions and may even appear downright ridiculous when judged by the canons of logic. But a government is more concerned with preserving its society than with being logically consistent, and if a policy helps to do the job, no one will care much about its lack of neatness or logical symmetry.

Some Politics Involves Conflict among Groups. Prolife demonstrators in Washington, D.C.

AN ILLUSTRATION: THE AMERICAN CONFLICT OVER ABORTION

THE BACKGROUND

Since the early 1970s, the question of in what circumstances, if any, women should be permitted to have abortions has been perhaps the most bitter and hotly contested domestic issue bedeviling the government of the United States. It provides a vivid illustration of the tough choices governments must make in the modern world.

History and anthropology tell us that in just about all societies, ancient and modern, some women have sometimes had abortions (artificially induced terminations of pregnancies) to prevent the birth of unwanted children. In the United States, as in most Western societies, the practice was for centuries generally disapproved, but it was restrained mainly by religious precepts and social customs rather than by laws. In the nineteenth-century United States, however, the new and rising profession of medicine, organized politically by the American Medical Association, took the view that abortion is medically so dangerous that it must be made illegal; and many churches joined forces with the physicians by declaring that abortion is so immoral that the decision to have one must not be left to custom or to the consciences of individual women.

Consequently, most states enacted laws making abortion a crime, punishable by imprisonment, although some states made exceptions for abortions prescribed by physicians as necessary to save mothers' lives.

Since the early 1960s, however, things have changed radically. As we will see in greater detail in Chapter 16, one of the most powerful new forces in American life is the women's rights movement. This movement has fought for a number of changes in government policy, such as requiring that women have the same access to jobs as men and that women receive equal pay for equal work. But one of the changes for which they have fought hardest has been the decriminalization of abortion—that is, the repeal of all laws restricting women's right to have abortions when they wish. And their well-organized political campaign has been sharply contested by an equally well-organized countercampaign by people who feel that abortion is murder and must be prohibited by law. We will look briefly at the arguments and strategies of both sides.

THE PROLIFE SIDE

One side of the struggle, usually called the "antiabortion" or "prolife" movement, is a coalition of Roman Catholic church leaders, such as the National Conference of Catholic Bishops, leaders of Evangelical Protestant churches, such as the Reverend Jerry Falwell and the Reverend Jimmy Swaggart, and leaders of conservative political organizations, such as Paul Weyrich and Phyllis Schlafly. They are conducting an all-out political drive to recriminalize abortion by making it permanently and unequivocally illegal except, perhaps, when necessary to save the mother's life.

The prolife forces make both secular and religious arguments against abortions. Life, they say, begins at conception; hence a fetus at any stage of its development is in every sense a person, with the same right to life as any other person. Thus to take the life of a fetus by abortion is the same as taking the life of an adult without due process of law: that is, fetuses are not accused of a crime or tried for a crime or sentenced to death as a penalty for a crime; they are simply put to death summarily. And that is plain murder.

Moreover, the religious prolife organizations avow, each fetus has an immortal soul from the moment of its conception, and any soul destroyed before it is baptized is eternally lost to salvation. Human bodies do not belong to the people who occupy them or to the parents who beget them, and they certainly do not belong to society. They belong to God, and God alone has the right to decide what happens to them.

The prolife groups believe these arguments deeply, and they feel that their efforts to outlaw abortions are dedicated to the most sacred and important cause in politics: the preservation of innocent human beings and their

Some Politics Involves Conflict among Groups. Prochoice demonstrators in Washington, D.C.

immortal souls from murder and eternal damnation. But their antagonists, the prochoice forces, are committed just as passionately to quite a different set of beliefs.

THE PROCHOICE SIDE

Though they have considerable support from a number of liberal male leaders and organizations, the prochoice forces are led mainly by such feminist writers and activists as Bella Abzug, Betty Friedan, Germaine Greer, Eleanor Smeal, and Gloria Steinem, and spearheaded by such organizations as the National Organization for Women and the National Abortion Rights Action League.

The core of their position is the moral argument that the basic choice as to whether or not a woman should bear a child belongs to that woman alone, for it is one of her basic rights as a woman and a human being. After all, they argue, only women can bear children. In our society the many personal consequences—physical, psychological, economic, and social—of bearing a child are far greater for mothers than fathers. It is therefore the most intensely personal choice that any member of our society can make, and basic justice demands that she who must bear the consequences should have the right to decide

Government Is Compromise. President Bush meets with congressional leaders of both parties.

whether or not she will bear a child whom she does not want because she feels it will cause great economic hardship or do great psychological or social damage to herself or her marriage or her other children. This most personal of all decisions should never be made for any woman against her will by any organization, profession, or person who is not and cannot be as deeply involved as she—not by physicians, not by biological fathers, and certainly not by government legislators or bureaucrats.

The prochoice forces also make a pragmatic argument: The fact is, they say, that most pregnant women who do not want to bear children are going to have abortions anyway. They used to do so by the tens of thousands in the many years when abortions were illegal, and they will do so again if they are made illegal again. The only difference is that when abortions are illegal they are expensive and dangerous, performed in secret by quacks, often under unsafe conditions highly dangerous to the woman's health. Those who do not believe that it is morally wrong to have abortions are not going to obey laws against them any more than the millions of people who did not think it was morally wrong to drink liquor obeyed the law imposed by the Eighteenth Amendment's prohibition of alcoholic beverages from 1919 to 1933. Prohibition, they say, did not keep people from drinking; it only forced them to drink illegally, and the net effect of clinging to that unenforceable law was to promote disrespect for law in general and a great increase in lawlessness. By the same token, recriminalizing abortions will not keep women from having abortions; like prohibition, it will only give rise to massive violations of the law and increasing contempt for law.

WHERE THINGS STAND

In the 1960s and early 1970s, the women's movement persuaded 12 states and the District of Columbia to repeal their antiabortion laws, but the prolife forces responded by working to prevent other states from following suit. Neither side was happy about having such a crucial matter decided on a state-by-state basis, and each urged agencies of the federal government, especially the Congress and the courts of law, to make a final and authoritative ruling that would be binding on all the states. That ruling finally came in 1973 in the U.S. Supreme Court's decision in the case of *Roe* v. *Wade* (1973) declaring unconstitutional a Texas law prohibiting all abortions except those necessary to save the life of the mother.[3] The Court did *not,* however, say that no state could ever under any circumstances limit a woman's right to have an abortion. Rather, they declared that pregnancies progress by three-month stages, or trimesters, and made a different rule for each: (1) In the first trimester, states may not interfere with a woman's right to obtain an abortion if it is recommended by her physician; (2) in the second trimester, states can make reasonable regulations about where and when abortions can be performed, although they still cannot ban them altogether; and (3) in the third trimester, the state's interest in protecting the unborn child becomes so important that it can constitutionally prohibit all abortions except those necessary to save the mother's life.

The *Roe* v. *Wade* decision remains one of the most controversial the Supreme Court has ever made, and it touched off a political struggle that continues to rage in the 1990s. The prolife forces are trying hard to get the decision overridden, either by putting more conservative judges on the Court and getting them to reverse the 1973 decision, or by amending the Constitution so as to outlaw abortions or at least give the states the power to outlaw abortions. The prochoice forces are for the moment taking a mainly defensive position, on the ground that the *Roe* decision, while far less satisfactory than an unequivocal affirmation of women's rights to have abortions whenever they wish, is still preferable to the outlawing of all abortions sought by the prolife forces. But at the beginning of the new administration and Congress in 1989, neither side had won a total victory over the other, and the *Roe* decision continued to be the law of the land.

SOME LESSONS FOR THE STUDY OF GOVERNING

The struggle between the prolife and prochoice forces is surely one of the most bitter and fiercely fought political struggles of our time. It will not be settled one way or the other in the next few years; indeed, it probably will never be settled to the complete satisfaction of one side or the other.

I have not chosen it as an illustration for this chapter because I enjoy writing about it (which I certainly do not). I have chosen it because most readers are likely to feel strongly about the issue and to see it as highly relevant to their personal lives and political ideals, and because thinking about the issue and how the government has handled it up to now teaches us some important lessons about what governing is like in the modern world. What lessons?

The first is one of the most important points to be made in this entire book, and it must be understood by everyone who wants to understand what real-life politics and government are like. One way of putting the point is to say that "in politics there is no free lunch." Another way is to say that for every benefit that government gives to some people, it exacts a cost from other people. To the degree that the Supreme Court, the Congress, or any other government agency allows some women to have abortions under some conditions, it outrages the prolife people because, in their view, it is condoning murder. By the same token, to the degree that government prohibits some women who want abortions from having them, it enrages the prochoice people because it strips those women of their right to decide whether or not they will bear unwanted children.

The struggle over abortion, like so many political conflicts, is what some political analysts call a "zero-sum game"—that is, a contest, like table-stakes poker, in which whatever some players win is inescapably balanced by what other players lose. There is no poker game and no political conflict in which *everyone* wins. The issue in every government decision is never how to give everyone everything they want; it is who will win, who will lose, and how much. Indeed, one of the greatest political scientists of the twentieth century put the point precisely and succinctly when he entitled his book about the basic nature of governing *Politics: Who Gets What, When, How.*[4]

The second lesson from the abortion struggle is that government resolutions of political conflicts—including many that are widely (though never universally) praised—almost always fall far short of being ideal dispensations of justice or models of clarity and logic. Certainly the major premise of the *Roe* case—that there is some fundamental change in kind, not just in degree, in the nature and rights of a fetus when it passes from one trimester to the next—has no basis in logic or in the science of embryology or in philosophies of religion or ethics. The most that can be said for it is that so far it has enabled the nation to deal with this bitter and divisive issue without resorting to some final Armageddon in which one side wins a total victory by utterly destroying the other. Perhaps from the standpoint of government that is all the justification it needs. One who understands why already understands a good deal about governing.

FOR FURTHER READING

In this chapter, as in the rest of the book, I have not attempted the impossible task of trying to tell readers everything they may ever want to know about politics and government. I have tried to write an *introduction* to political science, and I hope it will whet the reader's intellectual appetite rather than satisfy or kill it. What follows is a brief annotated list of some leading books on the topics we have covered in this chapter; similar lists will follow each of the chapters to come. Readers eager for more may turn to them with profit. The lists are, of course, far from exhaustive. They are intended only as samplings of the rich literature on politics and government in today's world and as starting points for further exploration. Asterisks before the authors' names indicate that the books are available in paperback.

By far the most comprehensive recent coverage of the main approaches, theories, findings, and bibliographies of contemporary political science is Fred I. Greenstein and Nelson W. Polsby, eds., *Handbook of Political Science* (Reading, MA: Addison-Wesley, 1975), eight volumes. Other useful readings on the matters covered in this chapter include the following:

BENTLEY, ARTHUR F. *The Process of Government.* Chicago: University of Chicago Press, 1908. Reprinted Evanston, IL: Principia Press, 1935. The classic statement of the group structure of politics and managing group conflict as the essence of the process of government.

FINER, HERMAN. *Theory and Practice of Modern Government,* rev. ed. New York: Holt, Rinehart and Winston, 1949. Though now outdated in many details, this book remains one of the most comprehensive surveys of political conflict and government institutions in modern nations, both democratic and dictatorial.

FINIFTER, ADA W., ed. *Political Science: The State of the Discipline.* Washington, D.C.: American Political Science Association, 1984. Essays by leading political scientists on the present state and future directions of research and knowledge in the main fields of political science.

FRIEDRICH, CARL J. *Man and His Government: An Empirical Theory of Politics.* New York: McGraw-Hill, 1963. An influential theoretical analysis of the basic nature of government.

HELD, DAVID, et al, eds. *States and Societies.* New York: New York University Press, 1983. Essays on the role of government in various societies.

*MACIVER, ROBERT M. *The Modern State.* New York: Oxford University Press, 1964. Study by a leading political sociologist of how government differs from other social institutions.

*___. *The Web of Government,* rev. ed. New York: Free Press, 1965. A classic theoretical statement on the nature and role of government.

MILIBAND, RALPH. *The State in Capitalist Society.* New York: Basic Books, 1969. A Marxist analysis of the nature of government and its relationship to other social organizations.

PLATO, *The Republic* and *The Laws.* Many editions of these works have been published. They and Aristotle's *Politics* were the first systematic studies of the idea and the actual in politics and government, and they continue to hold far more than historical interest for modern students.

*TRUMAN, DAVID B. *The Governmental Process,* 2nd ed. New York: Knopf, 1971. An updating of Arthur Bentley's conception of politics and government, with special attention to the operation of American groups and institutions.

NOTES

[1]We will often encounter the term *society* in the rest of this book, so let us be clear at the outset that a **society** is *a broad grouping of people living in a common environment and having common traditions, institutions, activities, and interests.*

[2]See Gabriel A. Almond and G. Bingham Powell, Jr., *Comparative Politics: A Developmental Approach* (Boston, MA: Little, Brown, 1966), pp. 42–43.

[3]The full citation of the case is *Roe* v. *Wade,* 410 U.S. 113 (1973). Since there are a number of such citations in this book, readers may find it useful to understand what each element of the citation means: The first name is the name of the plaintiff, and the second is the name of the defendant. The numbers tell us that the Court's decision is reprinted in volume 410 of the *United States Reports,* beginning at page 113. And the year in parentheses is the year in which the decision was handed down.

[4]Harold D. Lasswell, *Politics: Who Gets What, When, How* (New York: Meridian Books, 1936).

2 Politics in Human Life

Before we begin our account of the nature of politics in human life, a word of explanation is in order. In the pages to come, some version of the phrase "most political scientists believe" will appear frequently. This usage is intended to alert the reader to the fact that the beliefs described are not shared by every political scientist in the world. There is probably no single statement about political reality on which *all* political scientists would agree, and there are a number of important matters in which we are quite divided. Accordingly, when a particular view on a subject is widely held in the relevant literature of political science, it will be presented in this book as the position of "most political scientists." When there are several competing views, none of which predominates, each will be summarized, and whatever position I may have will be stated, along with my rationale. With that in mind, let us begin.

WHAT IS POLITICS?

"POLITICS" IN EVERYDAY CONVERSATION

We all know *something* about "politics." The word and its derivatives pop up again and again in everyday conversation and reading. When a classmate tells us that "X was picked for editor of the school paper because of politics, not because she deserves it," or a university president charges that "politicians are interfering with higher education," or a newspaper columnist declares that a tax increase to balance the budget is "politically impossible," most of us think that we know what such statements mean. Indeed, we are likely to nod sagely and perhaps add a sigh for the imperfections of human nature.

These and similar statements give some hints about what politics means to most of us. For one thing, it has something to do with distributing desirable things in scarce supply, with deciding who gets the lion's share and who gets the mouse's. For another, it operates not only in the "the government" but in private groups as well—for example, in a school paper as well as in Congress. And it often suggests selfish squabbling for private gain rather than states-manlike cooperation for the common good.

There is no doubt that as a group, politicians have a poor reputation. Recent Gallup polls show that the only kinds of people who are thought to have even lower ethical standards than politicians are labor union leaders, advertis-ers, and car salespeople; and only 23 percent of Americans would like to see their children go into politics as a life's work.[1] And Roget's trusty *Thesaurus* lists such unflattering synonyms for *politician* as *grafter, spoilsmonger, influ-ence peddler, wheeler-dealer, finagler,* and *wire-puller.*[2] On the other hand, while most people look down on "politicians," they admire "statesmen." The only trouble is that they can never agree on which public figures deserve which label. To some, for example, Franklin D. Roosevelt was a "great statesman," but to others he was a "lying politician." Similar disagreements have existed about almost every other president from John Adams to Ronald Reagan. (Only George Washington seems to have had nearly unanimous approval, and even he lost some ground toward the end of his career.)

Some observers suspect that for most people, a statesman is simply a government leader they like and a politician is one they dislike. This suspicion has led some commentators to say that "a statesman is a dead politician," and others that "a statesman is a politician held upright by pressures from all

---

Public life is...the crown of a career, and to young men it is the highest ambition. Politics is still the greatest and most honorable adventure.

John Buchan, 1940

Politics are almost as exciting as war, and quite as dangerous. In war you can only be killed once, but in politics many times.

Sir Winston Churchill, 1920

Politics is the science of who gets what, when and why.

Sidney Hillman, 1944

A politician is an arse upon which everyone has set except a man.

e. e. cummings, 1944

sides." It has also inclined most political scientists to use the terms *politics* and *politicians* in the more neutral senses we will use in this book.

POLITICS AS POLICY MAKING

In its broadest sense, politics includes the decision-making and decision-enforcing processes in any group that makes and enforces rules for its members. Several political scientists have studied these processes in nongovernmental groups such as labor unions, business corporations, and medical associations. But most political scientists have concentrated on the processes of governments rather than on those of private associations,[3] and it seems desirable to use the same focus in an introduction to political science.

As the word will be used in this book, accordingly, **politics** is *the process of making government policies.* Let us see just what is involved in this definition.

When government officials are called upon to take some course of action (or inaction) on a particular matter, they are always faced with a number of alternatives they *might* pursue. They cannot, however, pursue all the alternatives simultaneously, if only because some would cancel out others. They have to select from among the alternatives available the few that they intend to put into effect. The courses of action thus chosen become government *policies;* and the process by which policy makers choose which actions they will and will not take is, according to our definition, politics.

There are countless illustrations of the point, but let us take just one that was much in the headlines in the late 1980s: U. S. policy toward General Manuel Antonio Noriega, the head of the armed forces and de facto[4] dictator of Panama. Since the late 1970s, many U.S. government agencies have declared a "war on drugs"—a commitment to wiping out the production, sale, and use of drugs such as cocaine, heroin, and PCP, which many fear are poisoning our people and destroying our system of law and order. One major strategy in that war has been to try to get the Latin American countries, such as Colombia and Peru, where many of the drugs originate, to help us stamp out production of these drugs and prevent them from being smuggled into the United States.

In the mid-1980s, some agencies began to pick up information that General Noriega was personally engaged in drug trafficking, but they were told that since Noriega was useful in the effort to help the U.S.-supported "contras" overthrow the Communist government of Nicaragua, nothing should be done to undermine his position in Panama.

However, the war against the contras cooled, the war against drugs escalated, the evidence of Noriega's drug-running activities piled up, and by 1988 most leaders of the U.S. war on drugs had decided that Noriega had to go. The question became, what was the best way to get rid of him?

A number of possibilities were considered, most involving unilateral action (that is, action by the United States alone). At one extreme was the "soft" option: doing nothing more than making public statements deploring Noriega's activities in the hope that the Panamanians would be shamed into throwing him out. At the other extreme were the "hard" options: having Noriega assassinated or driving him from office by an armed invasion of Panama. In between were a number of less extreme options. One was to bring criminal charges against Noriega and get him tried and convicted by U.S. courts. Another was to offer the "carrot" of economic aid by promising the Panamanians a generous package of economic benefits in return for ousting Noriega. Yet another was using the "stick" of economic sanctions—for example, freezing Panama's assets in American banks, withholding U.S. payments for the use of the Panama Canal, prohibiting trade with Panama—that would make Panamanians' lives so difficult that they would throw him out. Yet another was to make a deal with Noriega: We would drop the drug charges if he would resign his office and leave the country. And finally there was the multilateral option of keeping a low U.S. profile and asking other Latin American countries to take the lead in inducing the Panamanians to expel Noriega, thereby avoiding charges of "Yanqui imperialism" and interference in the internal affairs of the hemisphere's other nations.

Clearly the United States could not do *all* of these things at the same time, for some would cancel out others. (For example, assassinating Noriega would make it difficult to cut a deal with him.) So the particular option we chose at a particular time became, in this book's terminology, our *policy* toward Noriega. Like all government policies, it was and is subject to repeated revisions; and in the late 1980s a lot of revisions were made, because none of our policies seemed to work.

Successful or not, that is what politics is about. Each of the world's countries has its own special ways of conducting politics, and yet there are some respects in which politics in all countries is essentially the same. In this chapter and the next, we will consider some universal characteristics of politics; later, especially in Chapter 5, we will take up some of the main variations.

SOME UNIVERSAL CHARACTERISTICS OF POLITICS

POLITICS IS CONFLICT

Politics, as we use the term in this book, is the process of making government policies (or *public policies,* which is another way of saying government policies). But what is the process like? What are its main characteristics? The first we will note is that politics everywhere involves **conflict**—that is, *some form of struggle among people trying to achieve different goals and satisfy opposing interests.* A basic, though perhaps painful, first step toward understanding the governing process is thus to face the fact that political conflict is not an unfortunate and temporary deviation from the normal state of perfect cooperation and harmony. It arises from the very nature of human life itself.

Conflict in Human Life

One basic fact of human life is that people live together, not in isolation from one another. Social scientists generally call the largest unit in which people live together a **society** —that is, *a broad grouping of people living in a common environment and having common traditions, institutions, activities, and interests.* When we reflect upon our lives and try to understand what has happened to us, we realize that our stories must be told largely in terms of our relationships with other people—parents and teachers, boyfriends and girlfriends, supporters and opponents, bosses and dependents, and so on. To be human is to interact with—to affect and be affected by—other human beings every day of our lives. And to interact with others is, to some extent at least, to be in conflict with them. Why?

Although all people are alike in certain respects, no person is exactly like any other in every respect. One of the most significant ways in which people differ from one another is in the values that each holds. A **value,** as the term is used here, is *an object or situation deemed to be of intrinsic worth and esteem, something to be sought.* It is something someone thinks is important and desirable, whether it be a Mercedes-Benz, passing grades, social prestige, peace of mind, or a brave new world. Social scientists agree not only that different people have different values but also that every person acts in some way to realize some of his or her values. Wherever people come into contact with each other, their values are bound to conflict to some degree. And in a world of limited resources, to the extent that some values are satisfied, other values must go unsatisfied. For example, if taxes are increased to support higher welfare payments, some taxpayers will be unhappy; if affirmative-action programs reserve certain jobs for African-Americans and women, some white males will be unhappy; and so on.

Accordingly, we all find that to some extent we are in competition with our fellow human beings. As we live our daily lives and try to enter the college of our choice, study what interests us, and then find a good job, we discover that other people also want those good things and that not everyone has equal success in getting them. That is true of even our most lofty aims: We all want a better, more just world—but we do not all agree on the best way to achieve it. We all strive in many ways—working and resting, studying and practicing, speaking and demonstrating, voting and abstaining, telling the truth and lying, obeying the rules and breaking them—to achieve our goals in competition with others, who pursue different goals or the same goals in different ways. Conflict, then, is an essential and inescapable consequence of the fact that most people live together in societies, not in isolation from one another.

Political Conflict in Society

Wherever people live together in a society, most of them feel that some values can be fully satisfied only by rules that bind everyone in the society. For example, most Americans who believe that racial segregation in public schools must be ended will not be satisfied with the tokenism of entering a few African-American children in unsegregated schools while all others are forced to attend all-black schools. They demand that any African-American child whose parents wish him or her to attend an unsegregated school must be allowed to do so, and they will settle for nothing less, even if it means busing some children to schools distant from their homes. In other words, they have a **political interest** in desegregation—*the stake of a person or group in public policy; something of value to be gained or lost by what government does or does not do.*

In most societies, then, most people regard government action as the best

---

Physicians and lawyers are among the best-educated, most-respected, and highest-paid professionals in the United States. It is therefore especially unsettling to learn that in the 1990s they are locked in a tough political struggle with each other over the issue of medical malpractice law suits. Under the present malpractice laws of most states, if patients believe that their physicians' actions or inactions in treating them have made their physical condition worse rather than better, they can sue the physicians for damages in personal injury suits. And if their lawyers can use the testimony of expert witnesses and other evidence to convince juries that the physicians' treatments indeed failed to meet accepted standards of sound medical practice, the juries are likely to award large damages, often amounting to several hundred thousand dollars. Moreover, the patients need not assume all the legal costs. Lawyers usually take such cases on a contingency-fee basis—that is, if they win they will be paid an agreed percentage of the jury's award (usually one-third and sometimes more); and if they lose, there is no charge.

To protect themselves against financial disaster, physicians take out malpractice insurance, with annual premiums now running as high as $100,000 for such high-risk specialists as obstetricians and neurosurgeons.

In recent years the number of malpractice suits has increased, the damages awarded by juries have soared, and the annual premiums for malpractice insurance have nearly doubled. As a result, the American Medical Association has mounted a major campaign to induce state legislatures to put ceilings on the amounts juries can award, reduce attorneys' fees, and set up arbitration procedures for such suits.

The lawyers have not been quiet in the face of the physicians' move. The Association of Trial Lawyers of America (ATLA) has launched a strong countercampaign to block it. They argue that physicians, like lawyers or any other professionals, should be held accountable for the damage they do by slipshod professional behavior. "There is no medical malpractice insurance crisis," ATLA leaders say. "The cause of medical malpractice legislation is medical negligence." And bumper stickers on physicians' cars retort, "Feeling sick? See a lawyer" and "Help support a lawyer: Send your daughter to medical school."

High levels of education, skill, and prestige, it seems, do not keep our top professionals out of political conflict.

way to obtain authoritative and binding rules. Conflict over what the rules should be is thus, according to our definition, *political* conflict. To be sure, many conflicts in any society are fought outside the political arena, in such other areas of life as economics, academics, sports, and marriage. The point is that no society—traditional or modern, more advanced or less advanced, democratic or authoritarian—is entirely without political conflict; and as we will see repeatedly throughout this book, in modern societies most conflicts over values sooner or later, for good or ill, become political conflicts.

GROUP CONFLICT IN POLITICS

Many political scientists emphasize a second universal characteristic of politics: the fact that the antagonists are rarely isolated individuals acting without reference to or support from other people. In most conflicts, a number of people on both sides feel that they have a stake in the outcome and join forces with others who feel the same way. Most political conflict is thus best seen as conflict among groups rather than among individuals. For example, the contest among Michael Dukakis, Richard Gebhart, Albert Gore, Jesse Jackson, and Paul Simon for the Democratic party's presidential nomination in 1988 was much more than a contest among those five men alone. Each was supported, opposed, and influenced by particular labor unions, ethnic groups, and business associations and also by majorities of such unorganized but potent groups as African-

Politicians Deal with People in Groups. U.S. Rep. Steny Hoyer (D-Md) greets constituents. (Source: Art Stein/Photo Researchers.)

Americans, whites, women, the middle class, workers, "yuppies" (young urban professionals), and retired people. To describe the contest solely in terms of what the five individuals said and did would present only a partial and misleading picture. For another example, the bitter fights in a number of American metropolitan areas over whether suburban white children should be bused to predominantly African-American inner- city schools and African-American inner-city children bused to predominantly white suburban schools to achieve racial balance have involved not only the children, parents, and school officials directly concerned but also many national pressure groups, both national political parties, and ultimately the president, Congress, and the Supreme Court of the United States.

Defendants in murder trials may appear at first glance to have no group support or interest behind them. Certainly the standard title of such a trial— *The People of the State of New York* versus *John Doe*—seems to suggest that the contest is taking place between Mr. Doe on the one hand and everyone else in New York on the other. If so, it is a highly unequal contest, and Mr. Doe would appear to have absolutely no chance of winning. The fact is, however, that he has considerable support from others. For example, many people in the community believe that every person accused of a crime should be given a fair trial, and as a result the state constitution contains such protections as the guarantee of a lawyer paid for by the state if Mr. Doe cannot afford to hire one himself, the power to subpoena witnesses, and the right to prevent persons who are prejudiced against him from becoming jurors. Neither Mr. Doe nor any other person engaged in political or governmental conflict is entirely alone.

Politics, then, is the conflict among individuals and groups over the formation of public policy. Let us now consider the different kinds of groups that participate in politics.

Categoric Groups

A **categoric group** (or social stratum, as some call it), is *a number of individuals sharing one or more common characteristics:* for example, people under 21 years of age, people earning more than $5,000 a year, residents of Illinois, tool-and-die makers, blondes, tight ends. The individuals in any particular categoric group may or may not be conscious of their common characteristics, regard them as important, and direct their behavior accordingly. Few brown-eyed people, for example, feel strong bonds with other brown-eyed people or are acutely aware of a wide gulf between their interests and the interests of blue-eyed people; they are not likely, therefore, to unite with other brown-eyed people to advance the cause of brown-eyedness against the blue-eyed peril. Most African-Americans, on the other hand, are well aware of their differences from whites, and they form organizations like the National Association for the Advancement of Colored People (NAACP) or the National Urban League to improve their condition. Any particular categoric group thus may or may not be socially or politically significant.

Pressure Groups

Political scientists often speak of a person's or a group's *political interest* in a matter, meaning, as we have seen, the stake of that person or group in what government does or fails to do. When people take action to protect or advance a common interest, they become a social force that has to be reckoned with. And when one of their main activities becomes trying to induce government to do something they want or refrain from doing something they don't want, they become the kind of group on which we will concentrate in this book: a **pressure group**—*an organized interest group that acts to achieve some of its goals by influencing government officials and policies.*

TACTICS OF POLITICAL ACTION

Politics, then, is a many-sided conflict among individuals and groups taking action to get government to help them or keep government from doing harm. Political action is never easy. The stakes are high, the opposition is tough, and each competitor has to decide what combination of the following main tactics is most likely to bring success: lobbying, mass propaganda, litigation, demonstrations, strikes and boycotts, nonviolent civil disobedience, and violence. Let us see what is involved in each tactic.

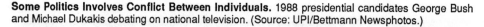

Some Politics Involves Conflict Between Individuals. 1988 presidential candidates George Bush and Michael Dukakis debating on national television. (Source: UPI/Bettmann Newsphotos.)

Lobbying

Many legislative chambers have adjoining rooms, called *lobbies,* in which legislators and their guests meet and talk informally. From this practice has emerged the term **lobbying,** which refers to *direct efforts by representatives of pressure groups to influence public officials to act as the groups wish.* Legislators are the main targets of lobbying, but executives, administrators, and even judges are also frequently approached.

The first prerequisite for successful lobbying is **access** —*the ability to get a hearing from government authorities.* Any group that cannot get a serious hearing from even one such authority can hardly expect much success. A group's access depends on several factors: its general prestige and social position, the reputation and skill of its lobbyists, and so on. For example, a Roman Catholic cardinal is more likely to have access to committees of the Massachusetts legislature than is a representative of the Jehovah's Witnesses, and a lobbyist whom the legislators have long known as reasonable, knowledgeable, and trustworthy is more likely to get a hearing than is one who is thought to be too aggressive, too careless with the facts, or too likely to talk out of turn.

Having gained access to one or more decision-making authorities, lobbyists can use various techniques of persuasion. They can make a formal presentation of their group's position, marshaling facts, figures, and arguments to show it in the most favorable light. They can threaten the legislator or executive with defeat at the next election, and they can reinforce their threat by stimulating a flood of telegrams, postcards, and letters from the official's constituents. They can offer to trade their group's support of some pet project of the legislator or executive for his support of their proposal. They can even offer bribes, either directly, in the form of cash, or indirectly, in the form of promises of well-paid jobs in private industry after the public official has retired from office. Bribery, however, has become so generally disapproved, so hard to keep secret, and therefore so dangerous that it is used far less frequently today than it was a century ago. Campaign contributions are much better: They are legal; all elected officials have to have them; and elections are held frequently.

Working Inside Political Parties

Lobbying is likely to be far more successful with favorably predisposed public officials than with those who are indifferent or hostile. And since political parties nominate most candidates for public office and thereby largely determine what people holding what views occupy the key positions, no major pressure group can afford to ignore the internal operations of the important parties. In Great Britain and in most European democracies, most pressure groups are closely associated with particular parties and make little effort to influence the policies and candidates of opposing parties. In the United States, however, the relatively loose and undisciplined nature of the Democratic and Republican parties (see Chapter 10) has traditionally tended to keep the major interest groups from completely identifying themselves with either party.

In 1984, the main labor organization in the United States, the American Federation of Labor–Congress of Industrial Organizations (AFL–CIO), for the first time in its history, endorsed one of the aspirants for the Democratic party's presidential nomination, Walter Mondale, and its considerable financial and volunteer-worker support played a major role in Mondale's ultimate triumph over Gary Hart and Jesse Jackson. Mondale was also endorsed by several teachers' associations, and the National Organization for Women (NOW) announced that if a woman were not chosen as the Democratic vice-presidential candidate, they might desert the party altogether. Many people felt that NOW's threat had a good deal to do with Mondale's selection of Geraldine Ferraro as the first woman ever nominated on a major party's national ticket. And the Reverend Jerry Falwell's Moral Majority worked hard and successfully to make the Republican party's platform reflect its views on abortion, school prayers, and pornography. Even so, no group is totally identified with either U.S. party, and it is quite common for many special-interest groups to give campaign funds to powerful congressmen of both parties to ensure continuing access to them.

Rather, they have tried to secure the nomination of sympathetic candidates and the adoption of favorable planks in the platforms of *both* parties.

However, no pressure group can "deliver" the votes of *all* its members to any particular candidate or party. There are many illustrations of this rule, but one of the most striking comes from the recent electoral failures of the British Labour party. That party was founded in 1900 as an alliance between labor

Television is the Main Battleground for Modern Election Campaigns. A Bush "spot" advertisement in the 1988 presidential campaign. (Source: Erich Hartmann/Magnum Photos.)

unions and socialist intellectuals. It has always proclaimed itself to be the party of the workers, standing for their interests against the interests of the landowners and businessmen who control the Conservative party. Most of Britain's labor unions are integrated into the British Labour party: They are formally affiliated with the party, they cast 30 percent of the votes that elect the party leader, and they provide most of the money that finances the party's operations. Moreover, part of the union dues of every member of the affiliated unions goes directly into the Labour party's treasury unless the member specifically requests otherwise. Surely, then, the overwhelming majority of the union members always vote for *their* Labour party and shun the Conservatives? Surely not. Studies of British voters show that in recent general elections only slightly over one-third of union members and their families have voted for Labour, while almost as many have voted for the Conservatives![5] The same can be said of almost every other pressure group that publicly supports particular parties and candidates: They can give the orders and blow the trumpets, but they can never get all of their troops to charge.

Mass Propaganda

Lobbying and working inside political parties are tactics aimed mainly at persuading political insiders, such as elected officials, bureaucrats, and party leaders. In the nineteenth century, most pressure groups in most democratic countries concentrated on the inside game and paid little or no attention to mass opinion. In the 1990s, however, the opinions of the general public—whether they are pro, con, or don't care—have a powerful influence on the success of all political groups.

Most modern pressure groups are well aware of this influence. Consequently, they cultivate mass public opinion through a wide variety of public relations operations and spend millions of dollars every year to create favorable climates of opinion for their political objectives. We are all familiar, for example, with the institutional advertising of organizations such as the Mobil Oil Company, whose full-page newspaper and magazine advertisements are not intended to sell Mobil gasoline and oil products over those made by rival oil companies, but rather are meant to promote the political philosophy of laissez faire (see Chapter 4). Similarly, both unions and employers often use full- page newspaper advertisements to plead their causes during strikes.

The old-fashioned lobbyist and "wire-puller" have thus been joined, and in many instances superseded, by the modern public relations counsel.

Litigation

Litigation is *the process of conducting a law suit,* in which one person or group, called the plaintiff, asks a court of law to order another person or group, called the defendant, to do something or to stop doing something (see Chapter 14). Bringing such suits has long been a favorite tactic for U.S. pressure groups, particularly those that are having little success with the executive, legislative, or administrative agencies and the general public.

One prime example has been the movement for equal rights for African-Americans since World War II, a story we will tell in detail in Chapter 16. Essentially the story is this: For decades before the 1960s, the NAACP and other civil rights groups had little success in persuading Congress to pass laws prohibiting racial segregation and discrimination in education, employment, access to public facilities, and other matters. So they adopted a new tactic of bringing suits against school boards, employers, managers of theaters, and other defendants, charging that the rules against African-Americans using the same facilities as whites were violations of the provision in the U.S. Constitution guaranteeing every citizen "the equal protection of the laws." They won a tremendous victory when the Supreme Court, in the 1954 case of *Brown* v. *Board of Education,* ruled that racial segregation in public schools is unconstitutional. The civil rights movement subsequently won many other victories in both Congress and the administrative agencies, but litigation in the courts brought their first great breakthrough.

Many other groups use litigation as a prime tactic. Environmental groups sue electric power companies to prevent them from operating nuclear power plants. Women's groups sue employers for sexual discrimination in hiring and promotion. Gay and lesbian groups sue school boards for dismissing teachers who are homosexuals. Disgruntled state parties sue their national committees for unfairly allocating votes in national nominating conventions. And so on.

Some observers view the high volume of political litigation as a serious threat to American democracy. They argue that it gives the final word in too many political conflicts to courts and judges, who are appointed for life and are therefore not accountable, as elected legislators and executives are, for their actions. Whatever may be the rights and wrongs of the matter, however, the fact is that litigation has become—and is likely to remain—one of the most effective and widely used of all the tactics employed by pressure groups, especially in the United States.

Demonstrations

For many years some pressure groups, especially those known as "protest groups," have relied heavily upon the tactics of demonstrations. They include such operations as picketing, mass marching, chanting slogans, heckling opponents, blocking roads, and occupying public buildings. In the late 1960s and early 1970s, for example, college students protesting the Vietnam War disrupted classes, occupied classrooms and laboratories, staged mass walkouts at graduation ceremonies, and howled down speakers who tried to defend the government's policies. Similar methods have been used by groups with quite different political goals: In the United States, civil rights groups have used freedom marches, white-supremacy groups have used "white power" marches, and both prolife and prochoice groups have picketed Congress and the Supreme

Court. In Great Britain and West Germany, thousands of people marched in protests against the placement of U.S. nuclear missile bases in their countries. In the United States and many European countries, environmental groups and "green parties" staged sit-downs and blockades to protest the building and operation of nuclear power plants. And so on.

Despite the widely different political objectives for which demonstrations have been mounted, they have the same traits as a mode of political action. First, they involve direct and active participation by group members, which is quite different from the more indirect and passive participation involved in paying dues and signing petitions. Group members who demonstrate often have an emotionally stirring experience that intensifies their devotion to group goals, and the leaders thereby gain a more dedicated and effective group of followers.

Second, demonstrations sometimes provoke overreactions from opposing groups and from the police, which may arouse sympathy for the group from outsiders who care little about the group's issues but dislike anything that smacks of repression or brutality. And third, most demonstrations are planned to attract public attention, and many succeed by getting exposure on television. Television broadcasters, to be sure, charge far more than protest groups can afford for broadcasting advertisements presenting the groups' views; but the broadcasters often find in a rousing demonstration just the kind of exciting visual material that gets the attention of their viewers ("fender-bender footage" it is called in the trade), and they often give the demonstrating groups coverage on prime-time newscasts without charging a penny.

Because of their low cost and their power to raise group morale, arouse sympathy, and attract free publicity, demonstrations are likely to continue to be widely used, especially by protest groups.

Strikes and Boycotts

The term *strike* usually means a collective work stoppage by industrial workers for economic goals, but strikes can also be used for political purposes. In the United States most strikes are conducted for such nonpolitical objectives as forcing employers to grant higher wages, shorter hours, better working conditions, job security, and union security. In many European democracies, on the other hand, strikes are sometimes used for political purposes, such as forcing the government to adopt or reject certain policies or even attempting to overthrow the existing form of government. In France, for example, the Communist-dominated CGT labor organization has called a number of strikes since 1945 for the avowed purpose of preventing the French government from participating in such anti-Communist organizations as the Marshall Plan, the European Defense Community, and the North Atlantic Treaty Organization. In some nations—for example, Panama and South Korea in 1988—general strikes have been used in efforts to drive certain public officials, and sometimes whole governments, out of power.

A less familiar variation is the "speedup" strikes that government employees (who are usually prohibited from striking—see Chapter 13) sometimes conduct. Customs inspectors, for example, enforce to the letter every last law and regulation, carefully inspect every piece of every tourist's luggage, and make the tourists so irate that they take their business to other countries. Postal workers, for another example, follow to the letter (so to speak) every rule for inspecting the interior of every mailbag to make sure that it has been emptied of letters, and hand-inspect every letter to make sure that it has the proper postage and return address. This can delay mail delivery by many days. In such cases it is ironic but true that paying government workers more money is the only way government leaders can get the workers to stop doing everything the law requires!

A *boycott* is a concerted refusal by a group of people to deal with another private group or public agency in order to achieve an economic or political goal. A historic American political boycott began in 1955 in Montgomery, Alabama, when Rosa Parks, in protest against the city's laws requiring racially segregated seating on public transportation, refused to give up her seat on a bus to a white man and move to the back. This refusal touched off a general boycott of the Montgomery bus system by African-Americans, organized and led by Dr. Martin Luther King, Jr. The bus system found that it could not survive without its African-American patrons, and eventually the city repealed its segregated-seating laws.

Nonviolent Civil Disobedience

In his leadership of the movement for Indian independence from British rule in the 1930s and 1940s, Mohandas K. ("Mahatma") Gandhi developed a technique for political action that has had a major impact on the Western world. He called it *satyagraha,* and its Western version is **nonviolent civil disobedience**—*the refusal to obey certain laws or government orders for the purpose of influencing government policy.* Its leading American theorist and practitioner was Dr. King, and during the early 1960s it provided the philosophy and guided the tactics for much of the American civil rights movement (see Chapter 16).

As Gandhi and King practiced and preached it, civil disobedience requires a protest group first to explore all the possibilities for negotiation and arbitration with its opponents and with the government. If that fails, the group issues an ultimatum explaining exactly what it will do next and why. It then employs various tactics to make things inconvenient for its opponents without using violence or doing them bodily harm. The tactics include economic boycotts and noncooperation with government authorities (such as refusal to pay taxes or send children to school) and peaceful disobedience of some laws—for example, traffic regulations or prohibitions against parades or picketing. A tactic familiar to television viewers in many nations is what Gandhi called *dharna*—sitting down in streets, corridors of public buildings, airport runways, and other public channels of movement. When the authorities enforce the laws by arresting and imprisoning members of the group, they must not resist so that they can, in Dr. King's words, "testify with their bodies" to the justice of their cause. The ultimate objective is not only to win support from neutral outsiders but eventually also to convert the opponents themselves.

The tactics of civil disobedience have scored many impressive victories. They contributed much to the winning of Indian independence in 1947. And there is no doubt that in the 1960s television's gripping pictures of the contrast between the African-Americans' peaceful demonstrations for their rights and the often brutal measures of repression taken by southern sheriffs and police touched the hearts of many previously apathetic northern whites and won their wholehearted support for the African-Americans' cause.

Violence

Abraham Lincoln, the sixteenth president of the United States, was shot and killed in 1865 by John Wilkes Booth, a southern actor avenging the Confederacy's defeat in the Civil War. Since Lincoln's assassination there have been 25 more presidents. Serious attempts have been made on the lives of seven—almost one-third—and three have succeeded. President James Garfield was killed in 1881 by a disappointed office seeker. President William McKinley was killed in 1901 by an anarchist. Former president Theodore Roosevelt was shot while campaigning for reelection in 1912, but survived. After his election in 1932, president-elect Franklin Roosevelt was shot at and missed, but a bullet intended for Roosevelt killed Mayor Anton Cermak of Chicago. In 1963 President John Kennedy was killed by Lee Harvey Oswald, and a few days later Oswald was killed in a Dallas jail by a local nightclub owner. In 1975 there were two attempts on the life of President Gerald Ford, both unsuccessful. And in 1981 President Ronald Reagan was shot and wounded by a demented drifter named John Hinckley, Jr., who was trying to impress a movie star.

These presidents constitute only a fraction of the prominent American political figures killed or wounded in the line of duty. I will mention only a few other prominent recent instances. In 1968, Dr. Martin Luther King, Jr., Nobel Peace Prize laureate and apostle of nonviolent civil disobedience, was shot and killed by James Earl Ray. The shock of the assassination touched off a wave of rioting and looting in more than 125 cities in 29 states across the nation. Within a week at least 46 people were killed, more than 2,600 injured, and more than 21,000 arrested. Two months later Senator Robert Kennedy was killed by Sirhan Bisra Sirhan, a young Jordanian living in Los Angeles. In 1972, Alabama governor George C. Wallace was shot and crippled for life while campaigning for the Democratic presidential nomination.

The King and Kennedy assassinations led President Lyndon Johnson in 1968 to appoint the National Commission on the Causes and Prevention of Violence. The reports it commissioned constitute the most thorough study yet made of the role of violence in American politics. They stress two main points that we would do well to heed. First, violence—the use of physical force to eliminate or terrorize political opposition—is not a new phenomenon in American life, nor is it caused by some national sickness peculiar to our time. It is, as African-American militant H. Rap Brown correctly said, "as American as cherry pie." The United States was born in a violent revolution against Great Britain. Although we have had only one full-scale civil war, it was the bloodiest war in our history; indeed, more Americans were killed in the 1861–65 war than in all of our foreign wars put together. Much of our continental territory was violently taken from its Indian inhabitants. Vigilante actions, in which private citizens execute suspected criminals without benefit of legal authority or procedures, first occurred in the 1760s and have recurred many times since. In our own time, the white-supremacy violence of the Ku Klux Klan is countered by the violence of African-American urban rioters, and some opponents of abortion attack abortion clinics with fire bombs. And to all this private political violence we must add the violence, ranging from night sticks to atomic weapons, sometimes used by such government agencies as the police and armed forces to carry out our domestic and foreign policies.

It is quite a record. Yet the second point stressed by the research is that the United States has no monopoly on either political or nonpolitical violence: For example, in the 1980s a number of leaders of other countries were killed, including the presidents of Liberia and Lebanon, Indian Prime Minister Indira Gandhi, and Swedish Premier Olof Palme; and in 1981 even Pope John Paul II was shot and wounded by an escaped Turkish murderer in St. Peter's Square in Rome. As sociologist Charles Tilly puts it, "As comforting as it is for civilized people to think of barbarians as violent and of violence as barbarian, Western civilization and various forms of collective violence have always been close partners."[6] Terrorism, riots, rebellions, coups d'etat, violent strikes and strike breaking, sabotage, assassinations, kidnaping, airplane and ship hijacking, massacres of airport patrons, and other forms of violence have been used frequently by many political groups in many parts of the world to try to bring about, or to prevent, social and political change.

Any group's decision of whether or not to use violence involves several questions. Is it right to use violence in *any* circumstance? Pacifists say no, but many political groups say yes. What political price must be paid for using violence? There are many possibilities: little or no price; losing present or potential allies in other groups; alienating the less militant members of one's own group; triggering counterviolence by opposing groups; touching off repressive measures by the government; and injury and death to innocent people. Will the members regard anything less than violence as a "cop- out"? Finally, are violent tactics more likely than nonviolent to achieve the group's goals?

To the extent that a political group's main purpose is to influence government policy—as distinguished from satisfying its members' psychic hungers—this last question seems the most important to be considered in deciding whether or not to use violence. But it is all too clear that few political groups totally reject violence as a tactic never to be used in any circumstance.

TABLE 2.1.　Self-Reported Modes of Political Participation, 1981 (in percentages)

	United States	Great Britain	West Germany	France
Voted in last election	68	73	90	81
Signed petitions	61	63	46	44
Contacted public officials	27	11	11	na
Convinced others how to vote	19	9	22	na
Worked for party or candidate	14	5	8	na
Participated in boycotts	14	7	7	11
Participated in lawful demonstrations	12	10	14	26
Participated in unofficial strikes	3	7	2	10
Occupied buildings	2	2	1	7
Damaged property	1	2	1	1
Personal violence	2	1	1	1

Source: Russell J. Dalton, *Citizen Politics in Western Democracies* (Chatham, NJ: Chatham House, 1988), Table 3.4, p. 47, and Table 4.1, p. 65.

WHO USES WHICH TACTICS?

It is clear, then, that people who want to put some kind of pressure on government to do good things or to refrain from doing bad things have a wide range of tactics they can use. Which ones do most people in fact use most? The answer, at least for people in four advanced/industrial democracies, is given in Table 2.1.

The figures in Table 2.1 show some interesting differences among the four nations. For example, the British are the least likely and the French are most likely to use such "unconventional" political actions as demonstrations, boycotts, unofficial strikes, and occupying buildings, and Americans are much more likely than the others to make direct contacts with public officials. We will consider some of the reasons for these differences in our discussion of political cultures in Chapter 3, but the principal message of Table 2.1 is that in all four nations the great majority of the people depend mainly on the peaceful and personally undemanding political actions of voting and signing petitions.

SOME CHARACTERISTICS OF POLITICAL CONFLICT

Political conflict in every human society displays to some degree the following main characteristics: multiplicity, opposition, overlapping membership, and imperfect mobilization.

MULTIPLICITY

Every distinction among human beings—whether based on race, religion, age, occupation, educational level, or anything else—generates categoric groups, some of which become political interest groups. The more complex the society, the more distinctions there are among its members, and the more likely it is to contain large numbers of political interest groups. Each of the highly complex societies on which political scientists focus contains more categoric groups than we can ever count, let alone describe here. But we can at least get some hint of their multiplicity by listing a few of the political cleavages that are most prominent and persistent, not just in the United States but in all advanced/industrialized nations:

Economic class: rich v. poor; workers v. owners; government employees v. taxpayers.

Occupation: farmers v. industrial workers and owners; some businesses (e.g., buses, newspapers) v. other businesses (e.g., airlines, television); physicians v. lawyers; physicians v. chiropractors and faith healers.

Gender: women v. men

Ethnicity: blacks v. whites; Hispanics v. anglos; blacks v. Asians; Flemings v. Walloons (Belgium); Irish v. English (Northern Ireland); Scots and Welsh v. English (United Kingdom); Armenians and Latvians v. Russians (Soviet Union).

Religion: Catholics v. Protestants; Baptists v. Congregationalists; Christians v. Jews; Jews v. Muslims; Muslims v. Hindus; Shi'ite Muslims v. Sunni Muslims.

Morality: prolife v. prochoice; antipornographers v. libertarians; "straights" v. gays and lesbians.

Ideology: communists and socialists v. capitalists; communists v. socialists; liberals v. conservatives; democrats v. authoritarians.

Quality of life: conservationists v. economic growth proponents; smokers v. nonsmokers; public transportation v. private automobiles.

In addition, of course, there are the cleavages in international politics that we will consider in Chapters 17 and 18: between nation and nation (e.g., the United States v. Libya, Iran v. Iraq, Israel v. Syria); between alliances and blocs (e.g., NATO v. the Warsaw Pact, East v. West, the "third world" v. the advanced/industrialized nations); and so on.

Hence if politics is a contest among political interest groups, then the United States, like all other advanced/industrial nations, has an almost infinite number of active and potential contestants.

OPPOSITION

Every political interest group has opposition—that is, some group or combination of groups seeking conflicting goals. No proposal for public policy therefore ever enlists all the members of society in its support. The closest a nation comes to unanimity is usually in time of war, when the overwhelming majority of its citizens unite behind a win-the-war policy. Even then, however, there is opposition from pacifists, who oppose all war measures, opposition from people who oppose the particular war (no one who lived through the Vietnam War can doubt that), and even opposition from people who want the enemy to win (traitors, they are usually called). So if even wartime does not produce political unanimity in a nation, we can be sure that every political group encounters some opposition in its efforts to induce the government to adopt the policies it wants.

There are many variations in the kind of opposition that particular groups encounter in particular situations. Opposing groups may be organized or unorganized, large or small, powerful or weak, and so on. The degree of hostility between opposing groups ranges all the way from the mild disagreement between groups favoring and opposing free mail service for members of Congress to the bitter and violent disagreements that result in civil war. To be sure, as we noted earlier, not all group conflict is fought out by political means; but most of the disagreements about which people feel most strongly in modern societies are conducted at least partly in the political arena.

OVERLAPPING MEMBERSHIPS

The more complex a society is, the less likely are its political interest groups to have mutually exclusive memberships—that is, to include people who are members of one particular group and no others (see Figure 2.1a). Political interest groups in complex societies relate to one another as shown in Figure 2.1b, sharing some of their members with other groups. Seldom do two groups claim identical membership, however.

This produces the phenomenon of *overlapping membership of political groups*—the fact that members of every political group are also members of several other groups. It is seen in every society that has many distinctions among its members and thus many bases for group formation. Each person belongs to many groups at the same time, and few individuals belong to exactly the same groups (see Figure 2.1b). Readers can check the validity of these

FIGURE 2.1. Membership in political groups.

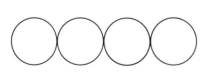

a. Mutually Exclusive Membership

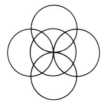

b. Overlapping Membership

generalizations by comparing their group memberships with those of their close friends. They are likely to find, for example, that friend X is a college student, a Protestant, of Scottish descent, a fraternity member, a Republican, and a member of Young Americans for Freedom; friend Y is a college student, a Protestant, of German descent, an independent, and a member of the Young Democrats; and friend Z is a college student, a Unitarian, of English descent, an independent, and a member of the Young Socialists.

IMPERFECT MOBILIZATION

One direct consequence of overlapping membership of interest groups is the important fact that no group can induce all of its members to undertake the highest degree of activity in support of any particular cause. It results from the overlapping membership of interest groups, and it means that the degree of support that any particular group can muster is likely to vary widely from one issue to another in at least two respects. First, the number of members who support the group changes. Recent studies of voting behavior, for example, show that all the major voting groups studied—older and younger people, Protestants and Roman Catholics, rich and poor, whites and blacks, and so on—are divided among themselves in their voting preferences and activities. Figure 2.2 illustrates the point by showing how some American population groups were split in the 1988 presidential election.

The point to note about Figure 2.2 is that while some groups voted strongly for one candidate or the other (African-American and low-income people for Dukakis, business people and college-educated people for Bush), in every group except the African-Americans there was a large minority that voted contrary to the group's majority.

The 1988 election was one instance of an important general rule: Labor, farmers, business people, youth, Roman Catholics, and other such groups are far from being disciplined political armies ready to spring into action whenever their leaders give the command. The members of each group also belong to other groups. On any particular issue some—but not all—of each group's members will approve of its political activities; and of those who do approve, some will participate actively and enthusiastically, while others will not lift a finger.

In certain societies under certain conditions, a few political interest groups may appear to approach 100 percent mobilization. In the modern Republic of South Africa, for example, nearly all the Afrikaners (white residents of Dutch descent) seem to support enthusiastically the policy of *apartheid* (total segregation of whites from blacks and complete white supremacy—see Chapter 16). But some Afrikaners are opponents of apartheid, and so even their political mobilization never reaches 100 percent.

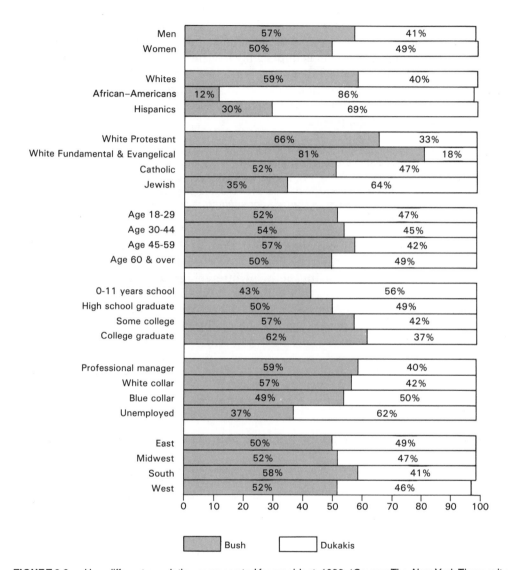

FIGURE 2.2.   How different population groups voted for president, 1988. (*Source:* The *New York Times* exit poll, November 8, 1988 (11,645 respondents) reported in *The New York Times,* November 10, 1988.) Copyright 1988 by the New York Times Company. Reprinted by permission.

POLITICS AND GOVERNMENT

Up to this point we have focused upon the universality and inevitability of political conflict in human society. But this focus should not mislead us into viewing politics solely as a kind of permanent jungle warfare, red in tooth and claw, in which every person is implacably hostile toward every other person. To depict politics as unrelieved conflict is no less a distortion of reality than to depict conflict as an unfortunate deviation from normal peace and harmony.

The crucial point was put forcefully by the eighteenth-century philosopher Jean Jacques Rousseau:

> What made the establishment of societies necessary was, if you like, the fact that the interests of individuals clashed. But what made their establishment possible was the fact that these same interests *also* coincided. *In other words*: It is the overlap among different interests that creates the social bond, so that no society can possibly exist save as there is some point at which all the interests concerned are in harmony.[7]

The fact is that in our time no less than in Rousseau's, every society has both politics and government. Politics, as we have seen, consists of *people acting politically*—organizing political interest groups and trying to induce governments to act in ways that will promote their interests over those of their opponents. To understand politics, therefore, we have to begin by knowing something about how people acquire their political beliefs, values, and notions about how they can and should act politically. That is the task of the next chapter.

FOR FURTHER READING

SCHOLARLY STUDIES OF THE ROLE OF POLITICS IN HUMAN LIFE

*BAILEY, F. G. *Strategems and Spoils: The Social Anthropology of Politics.* New York: Schocken Books, 1973. The political process as viewed by an anthropologist.

*DAHL, ROBERT A. *Modern Political Analysis,* 4th ed. Englewood Cliffs, NJ: Prentice-Hall, 1984. A short but rich introduction to the nature of politics by a distinguished political scientist.

*DEWEY, JOHN. *The Public and Its Problems.* Chicago: Swallow Press, 1927. Difficult but influential early analysis of the nature of politics.

*EDELMAN, MURRAY. *The Symbolic Uses of Politics.* Urbana, IL: University of Illinois Press, 1964. Stimulating analysis of the role of symbols in political conflict and resolution.

*HOROWITZ, DONALD L. *Ethnic Groups in Conflict.* Berkeley, CA: University of California Press, 1985. Detailed analysis of ethnic groups in American lobbying and electoral politics.

*KREML, WILLIAM P. *A Model of Politics.* New York: Macmillan, 1985. Presents an analytical model of politics combining political theory and institutions.

LASWELL, HAROLD D., and Abraham Kaplan. *Power and Society.* New Haven, CT: Yale University Press, 1950. Abstract and difficult but important and influential theory of politics based on power as the key concept.

MERKL, PETER H., JR. *Political Violence and Terror.* Berkeley, CA: University of California Press, 1986. Survey of role of violence and terrorism in modern politics.

POLSBY, NELSON W. *Political Innovation in America: The Politics of Policy Initiation.* New Haven, CT: Yale University Press, 1984. A new look at the policy-making process in the United States, based on eight case studies of recent policy innovations.

*RIKER, WILLIAM H. *The Art of Political Manipulation.* New Haven, CT: Yale University Press, 1976. Distinguished political analyst uses twelve case studies to illustrate how people make political decisions and achieve political goals.

*SCHLOZMAN, KAY LEHMAN, and JOHN T. TIERNEY. *Organized Interests and American Democracy.* New York: Harper & Row, Pub., 1986. Detailed survey of organized interest groups in American national politics.

*WEBER, MAX. *The Theory of Social and Economic Organization,* trans. by A. M. Henderson and Talcott Parsons. New York: Free Press, 1947. Useful collection of much of the work on society and politics by one of the most influential modern social thinkers.

POLITICAL NOVELS

Few of us can personally participate in politics at the highest levels, but we can all acquire a "feel" of what it is like by reading good novels focused on political conflict. Here is a short list of novels dealing with politics in a variety of settings.

*BURDICK, EUGENE L. *The Ninth Wave.* New York: Dell, 1985.

*CAMUS, ALBERT. *The Plague,* trans. by Gilbert Stuart. New York: Modern Library, 1965.

*DOSTOYEVSKY, FYODOR. *The Possessed,* trans. by Constance Garnett. New York: Modern Library, 1936.

*FORSTER, E. M. *A Passage to India.* New York: Harcourt Brace, 1965.

*KOESTLER, ARTHUR. *Darkness at Noon,* trans. by Daphne Hardy. New York: Bantam, 1970.

*O'CONNOR, EDWIN. *The Last Hurrah.* New York: Bantam, 1970.

*ORWELL, GEORGE. *1984.* New York: Signet Classics, 1971.

*PATON, ALAN. *Cry, the Beloved Country.* New York: Charles Scribner's Sons, 1948.

*SCOTT, PAUL. *The Raj Quartet.* New York: Avon, 1979, four volumes.

*SAFIRE, WILLIAM. *Full Disclosure.* New York: Ballantine, 1978.

*SNOW, C. P. *The Masters.* New York: Crowell-Collier and Macmillan, 1951.

SPRING, HOWARD. *Fame is the Spur.* New York: Viking, 1949.

*TROLLOPE, ANTHONY. *Barchester Towers.* New York: Signet Classics, 1950.

———. *The Palliser Novels.* New York: Oxford University Press, 1975, six volumes.

*WARREN, ROBERT PENN. *All the King's Men.* New York: Bantam, 1950.

NOTES

[1]The Gallup Poll, September 22, 1977, and July 12, 1973.

[2]*Roget's International Thesaurus,* 4th ed., ed. by Robert L. Chapman (New York: Thomas Y. Crowell, 1977), p. 594.

[3]See Chapter 1 for the distinctions between governments and private organizations.

[4]Political analysts often use a distinction between *de jure* and *de facto* situations. Generally speaking, **de jure** means *the state of affairs according to the law but not necessarily according to the facts.* **De facto** means *the state of affairs according to the facts but not necessarily according to law.* In this case the de jure head of the government of Panama was the elected president, Eric Arturo Delvalle, but the man who really ran things was General Noriega, and so he was the de

facto head of the government. We will encounter many comparable differences in the rest of the book.

[5]See, for example, Richard Rose and Ian McAllister, *Voters Begin to Choose: From Closed-Class to Open Elections in Britain* (Beverly Hills, CA: Sage, 1986), pp. 58–59.

[6]Charles Tilly, "Collective Violence in European Perspective," in Hugh Davis Graham and Ted Robert Gurr, eds., *Violence in America: Historical and Comparative Perspectives* (New York: Bantam, 1969), p. 4.

[7]Jean Jacques Rousseau, *The Social Contract*, trans. by Willmoore Kendall (Chicago: Henry Regnery, 1954), Book 2, Chapter 1; italics in the original.

3 Political Psychology, Socialization and Culture

"Oh, well," said Mr. Hennessy, "we are as th' Lord made us." "No," said Mr. Dooley, "lave us be fair. Lave us take some iv th' blame oursilves."

Finley Peter Dunne, Observations by Mr. Dooley

We have met the enemy, and they are us.

Walt Kelley, Pogo

POLITICAL PSYCHOLOGY: WHAT FORMS PEOPLE'S POLITICAL BELIEFS AND BEHAVIOR?

This book is basically about *people*. Yes, as the reader already knows, it is filled with discussion of groups and institutions. But a group, after all, is only some people who have one or more common characteristics, and an institution is only a shorthand expression for a set of well-established and recurring ways in which some people behave in particular circumstances. Democratic leaders like George Bush and Margaret Thatcher are people, and so are the citizens who vote them into office; and, however, diabolical they may sometimes seem, dictators like Nicolae Ceausescu and Mu'ammar al-Qadaffi are also people, and so are the subjects who obey their orders.

So the first step to understanding governing is to learn something about how people think and behave politically. Political scientists have learned a great deal about political attitudes and behavior from biology, psychology, psychiatry, and other disciplines focused on the individual, and we now briefly review some of their findings that are most useful in understanding why people think and behave politically as they do.

BIOLOGICAL NATURE AND NEEDS

A good place to begin is with psychologist Kurt Lewin's well-known formula for explaining how people acquire their opinions and calculate their behavior:

$$B = f(PE).$$

In ordinary language, the formula means that "behavior or any kind of mental event . . . depends on the state of the person and at the same time on the environment."[1]

Let us look first at the person, then at the environment. One of the most powerful drives shaping people's behavior is their desire to live rather than die, although it is by no means their only desire. To satisfy this desire even at the level of bare subsistence they must eat, sleep, clothe and shelter themselves, defend themselves against attack by animals and other people, and protect themselves from such onslaughts of nature as floods, fire, hurricanes, and earthquakes. Most people also wish to enjoy sexual relations, reproduce, and protect their mates and children. Furthermore, most people want to achieve these goals at levels of some comfort and pleasure. They are thus likely to favor policies that they believe will help them to achieve good things for themselves and their families, and they are likely to oppose policies that they believe will prevent or hinder their achievement.

PSYCHOLOGICAL PROCESSES AND COGNITIVE MAPS

Lewin's formula for describing human behavior emphasizes the *interaction* of the situation and the person. Accordingly, one critical factor in behavior is the individual's neurological-mental apparatus for receiving, ordering, and interpreting the signals she receives from the outside world and translating them into action. One useful way to picture this apparatus is as a "cognitive map" that each of us has of the physical and social world in which we live and operate—a mental picture of what those worlds are like and how we relate to them. There is a great deal of variation in the cognitive maps of different individuals and groups, but they all have three main elements: perception, conceptualization, and affect.

Perceptions and "Perceptual Screens"

Psychologists define a **perception** as *an awareness of an aspect of reality derived from sensory processes.* Students of political psychology have found that people do not invariably perceive the outside world by receiving and recording visual and auditory signals as photographic film receives and records light waves. Rather, those signals must pass through people's "perceptual screens" before they can become part of their cognitive maps.

For example, suppose that in 1988 voter A supports Michael Dukakis for the presidency mainly because he thinks Dukakis is a much better bet than Bush to keep the country out of war. Suppose also that A is strongly opposed to imposing special tariffs and import quotas on Japanese cars that will protect the American automobile industry but increase everyone's car prices. Then suppose that A hears that Dukakis is enthusiastically advocating just such trade barriers. She is likely to be upset when she learns that the candidate she admires is advocating a position she rejects. How does she deal with it?

This is where A's "perceptual screen" comes in. She may, by "selective exposure," simply close her eyes and ears to television and newspaper stories about Dukakis's protectionism and give her full attention only to stories about Dukakis's devotion to peace and about Bush's sabre rattling. Or she may tell herself that Dukakis does not really believe in protectionism (he is just saying so because he needs labor union votes), but he really does believe in disarmament and peace—even though Dukakis speaks as often and as fervently about protection as about peace.

Whatever A may do about her problem, it is clear that most of us have similar problems. As a result, our cognitive maps are not photographically exact reproductions of what is going on in the political world; they are often perceptually "touched up" a bit to make them easier to live with.

Levels of Conceptualization

Perceptual signals of any kind cannot *by themselves* tell us what is going on in the world or serve as a basis for action. We must first give them meaning by putting them into what we think are their appropriate categories in our **conceptual frameworks**—*the mental categories into which people sort perceptions of the world and relate them to one another to give them meaning.*

Political scientists and psychologists have long been interested in how people conceptualize their political signals. The pioneer work was done by the Center for Political Studies (CPS) of the University of Michigan in the 1950s. They asked their respondents a series of open-ended questions about what they liked and disliked about the parties and presidential candidates in the elections of 1952 and 1956. On the basis of their answers, CPS concluded that people conceptualized on one or another of four main levels. The first level was *ideology,* where people evaluated the parties and candidates in terms of whether they espoused "liberal" or "conservative" policies agreeable to the respondents' own philosophies; only 12 percent were put in this category. The second level was *group benefits,* where people liked or disliked parties and candidates because they thought they were good or bad for a group with which the respondents identified—farmers, working people, middle-class people, and

TABLE 3.1. Levels of Ideological Awareness in Eight Democratic Countries, 1974–75 (in percentages)

	Active Use of Ideology	Recognition/ Understanding Left and Right	Left/Right Placement
Austria	19	39	75
France	na	na	81
Great Britain	21	23	82
Italy	55	54	74
Netherlands	36	48	90
Switzerland	9	39	79
West Germany	34	56	92
United States	21	34	67

Source: Russell J. Dalton, *Citizen Politics in Western Democracies* (Chatham, NJ: Chatham House, 1988), Table 2.2, p. 25.

so on; 42 percent conceptualized at this level. The third level was *nature-of-the-times,* where the respondents said "times are good, so why change?" or "Republicans cause depressions"; 24 percent fit this category. The fourth level had *no issue content,* where people said "I like Ike" or "I'm a Democrat"; 22 percent conceptualized at this level.[2]

More recent studies show that since the CPS studies in the 1950, the proportion of ideological conceptualizers has risen not only in the United States but in other democratic countries, as is demonstrated by the figures in Table 3.1, which show the proportions of people in eight democratic countries in the 1970s who understood the meaning of the terms *Left* and *Right,*[3] used the ideological categories to sort out political leaders and policies, and were willing to place their own political philosophies on a Left/Right scale.

Table 3.1 shows that in all eight countries over two-thirds of the people interviewed were able to locate their own political outlooks on a Left/Right scale. On the other hand, only in Italy and West Germany were more than half able to give a reasonably clear and accurate explanation of what *Left* and *Right* mean, and only in Italy did over half say that their general preferences for the Left or Right play an important role in their preferences for leaders and policies. On all three counts this kind of ideology was less important for Americans than for the citizens of the other countries.

Affect

The third element of a person's political cognitive map is **affect**—*the emotion or feeling attached to an idea or object;* the quality that makes people support or oppose a particular party, candidate, or policy.

In short, our political attitudes and behavior are based upon our particular cognitive maps, and each of our maps consists of our *perceptions* of what is going on in the political world, the *conceptualizations* by which we sort out and

Charisma Counts. Jessie Jackson becomes the first serious black presidental candidate. (Source: AP/Wide World Photos.)

give meaning to those perceptions, and the *affective connotation* we give them that make us decide to act in certain ways rather than in others. We compile our particular maps in part because of our particular biological natures and needs, in part because of our particular psychological processes, but also in part because of our membership in particular social groups. We look next at the role of group memberships.

GROUP MEMBERSHIPS AND PRESSURES TO CONFORM

The Nature of the Process

In Chapter 2 we noted that every person in an advanced/industrial society belongs to many categoric groups—that is, groups of people who share at least one characteristic, such as gender, age, race, occupation, or religion. We further noted that some categoric groups are also interest groups—that is, groups whose members are conscious of their shared characteristics, regard themselves as having certain common goals arising from those characteristics, and to some extent direct their behavior accordingly. Finally, some interest groups become pressure groups because they pursue their goals at least partly by seeking to influence government policy.

Several social psychologists have investigated the influence of groups on the attitudes and behavior of their members. Some have focused mainly upon the influence of **primary groups**—that is, *groups whose members have regular face-to-face interactions,* such as families, friends, and work associates. Others have studied the broader and more impersonal categoric groups. These investigators have concluded that primary groups generally have a more direct and powerful influence on the opinions of their members than do larger and more impersonal groups but that the latter do have considerable influence on the opinions of most people.

Perhaps it would be useful to descend for a moment from the dizzying heights of theory to check these generalizations with our own experience. If we think of the people with whom we have the most daily contact—our parents, schoolmates, boyfriends, girlfriends, and so on—we can ask ourselves, "Are our opinions about most things, including politics, pretty much like their opinions—or do we disagree about a lot of things?" All who ask and honestly answer this question will realize that the social psychologists are talking not only about "other people" but also about *us!*

Just how does this agreement come about? By what processes do we form pretty much the same opinions as the other members of our primary groups? Investigations and experiments by social psychologists suggest some answers.

In every social group, and particularly in every primary group, certain pressures work for uniformity of opinion among the members, pressures that operate on each person and powerfully affect his opinions, political and otherwise. This pressure arises from several sources. First, membership in particular groups to some extent limits the signals the members receive and therefore affects their ideas of what the world is like. For example, a white male with a high school education applying for a firefighter's job in Memphis is likely to be confronted with somewhat different facts about affirmative action and job qualifications than is a female African-American Ph.D. applying for an assistant professorship of sociology at Berkeley. The white male and the African-American female are thus likely to have different opinions about such matters as the intelligence of African-Americans and for whose benefit the job-getting system is rigged.

Second, most people want to be regarded as "okay" or even "cool" rather than as "out of it" or "weird"—*especially in the eyes of the people and groups that matter to us.* Many social psychologists believe that the desire for the approval of one's peers, far more than patriotism or national ideals, accounts for the great courage shown under fire by so many soldiers of so many different nations and ideologies.

Third, if a person values highly her membership in a particular group, such as her family, sorority, church, or the National Organization for Women, and derives real personal satisfaction from it, she may well feel that if she voices opinions sharply different from those of the other members, the group might shun her or even break up, thereby depriving her of its satisfactions and support.

Sometimes these group pressures are exerted by certain members of the group who serve a kind of sergeant-at-arms function. Sometimes they are applied through informal communications among members of the group holding no official position. The strength of the pressures applied to any particular individual depends upon several factors, including the importance of group membership to the individual's own personal satisfactions and the number and strength of the counterpressures exerted by other groups with conflicting goals of which he is also a member.

Types of Influential Group Memberships

Social scientists generally agree that primary groups have more influence upon the political opinions of their members than the more impersonal categoric groups. However, most primary groups are segments of particular categoric groups. One useful way to describe the more influential types of group membership is thus to consider pairs of related primary and categoric groups. Table 3.2 illustrates the point by showing the views on some current public issues held by the members of various categoric groups.

Families and ethnic groups. The first group of which most of us become aware is our family. We get many of our values, reality perceptions, opinions, and behavioral patterns from parents, brothers, and sisters. Indeed, we often hear that most people "inherit" their party affiliations and political attitudes from their parents.

TABLE 3.2. **Differences in American Groups' Political Opinions (in percentages)**

Group	1988 Vote		Abortion			Reduce Deficit by		
	Bush	Dukakis	Pro-choice	Middle	Prolife	Cut Defense	Cut Social Programs	Raise Taxes
Men	57	41	21	59	20	64	46	25
Women	50	49	22	54	24	59	37	21
White	59	40	23	57	21	60	45	23
African-American	12	86	15	51	34	72	20	23
Protestant	66	33	18	58	23	na	na	na
Catholic	52	47	16	57	27	na	na	na
Jewish	35	64	na	na	na	na	na	na
Some college	57	42	27	60	13	68	44	31
High School graduate	50	49	17	55	28	55	42	20
High School non-graduate	44	56	na	na	na	59	35	15
Age 18–29	52	47	21	57	22	56	38	18
Age 30–44	54	45	24	56	21	62	40	23
Age 45–59	57	42	19	57	24	64	47	24
Age 60+	50	49	na	na	na	na	na	na

Source: The Gallup Poll.

Most families are based largely or exclusively on blood relationships and are therefore parts of particular ethnic groups. Social scientists define an **ethnic group** as *a group of people who share a common ancestry and a common and distinctive culture.* The ethnic groups most often discussed are the presumably genetically- based "races" (Caucasoid, Negroid, Mongoloid, and so on), but the term also includes groups associated with particular areas, ancestries, and cultures (Irish Americans and Hispanic Americans in the United States, Sikhs in India, Flemings in Belgium, Bretons in France, Scots and Welsh in Great Britain, and so on). Social scientists believe that the political opinions of most people are influenced to some extent by membership in particular ethnic groups, but that such influence is weaker than that of families. Ethnic group influence appears to be strongest among members of minority groups (for example, African-Americans, Hispanics, and Jews in the United States, Afrikaners in South Africa, Armenians in the Soviet Union) that feel threatened by larger groups.

Friends and age groups.　The second group of which most of us become aware is our circle of friends and playmates. Most of us want the approval of our friends and are strongly influenced by their opinions, not only in childhood and adolescence but in adult life as well.

Who are our friends? The old maxim "Birds of a feather flock together" applies to most of us. Most of our friends are people like ourselves. They live in the same kinds of neighborhoods, attend the same kinds of schools, belong to the same churches, come from similar economic levels and social classes, and often work at the same kinds of jobs. Most of our friends are also close to us in age. Moreover, as everyone knows, younger people often see some social and political matters quite differently from older people. Indeed, much of our literature is focused on the conflict between the young and the old ("between callowness and senility," as one cynic has put it). Most social scientists agree that membership in particular age groups has some influence upon most people's opinions, and the data in Table 3.2 support that conclusion.

Congregations and religious groups.　Many of us attend Sunday school as young children and later join church or synagogue youth organizations and become members of congregations. Most religions are deeply concerned with values and conceptions of the universe, and most try to indoctrinate their members in both. There is no doubt that many people's attitudes on many matters are powerfully influenced by their membership in particular congregations and religious denominations.

Moreover, many churches make official pronouncements on some political issues and have some direct influence on the political opinions and behavior of their members; witness, for example, the role of the Roman Catholic church in the abortion controversy described in Chapter 1. Nations that encourage particular religions or restrict others (for example, Spain and certain Latin American nations) thereby give the favored religions particularly influential roles in the formation of political opinions and public policy. But even in nations, such as the United States, that have no officially "established" or favored religion (that is, no particular faith or denomination that is officially favored by the government), religious leaders have considerable influence upon the political opinions of a great many people. The recent campaigns by certain "born-again" Protestant groups, such as the Moral Majority, in favor of prayers in the public schools and by the Roman Catholic church against abortions are cases in point.

Schoolmates and educational groups.   Modern nations vary greatly in the amounts of formal education their citizens receive, but in most nations both the proportion of those attending school and the average time spent in school are increasing year by year. The U.S. census estimated that in 1986, 34 percent of the population of the United States had had at least some college education, 79 percent were high school graduates, and nearly everyone had had some high school education. All three figures were higher than those in the 1980 census reports, and those in the 1990 reports will doubtless be higher still. The opinions of most Americans, therefore, are exposed to the influence of both schoolmates and school authorities—and with some impact, as is shown by the figures in Table 3.2.

The purposes of education in all nations, democratic and authoritarian alike, include instructing the young in some of the skills and techniques they need to perform useful roles in society— for example, reading, writing, counting, and perhaps driving automobiles and operating word processors—and also indoctrinating them in the nation's special political values and beliefs. In the United States the schools are committed to educating their pupils in the principles of democracy and capitalism, just as in Iran the schools are committed to educating Iranian youth in the principles of the Shi'ite version of Islam and the doctrines of the Ayatollah Khomeini's Islamic Republic. In most nations the schools are considered to be such important shapers of opinion that they are perennial subjects of political controversy. We are all familiar with the frequent clashes in this or that part of our country over whether the schools are teaching our young people the proper values and beliefs. We often hear charges from American conservatives that our schools are teaching "sexual immorality," "socialism," and "atheism"; we also hear charges from liberals that our schools are "apologists for big business" or "racist." Since most schools in most modern nations, democratic and authoritarian alike, are owned and operated by governments rather than by private organizations, what they do and how they do it are always political issues, sometimes hot ones, and the schools are subject to constant powerful and often conflicting pressures from public officials, parents, students, teachers, religious groups, and economic pressure groups.

Work associates and occupational groups.   Most adults spend half or more of their waking hours at work. In terms of sheer frequency of face-to-face contact, the people we see at work every day constitute one of our most important primary groups, and social scientists have discovered that such groups frequently have high degrees of agreement in their political opinions.

Small groups of work associates are also segments of larger and more impersonal occupational groups—college professors, retail merchants, carpenters, unskilled laborers, farm managers, business executives, white-collar workers, and so on. As we will see in Chapter 6, however, the evidence suggests that membership in this kind of categoric group has less influence on people's political opinions than their membership in many of the other kinds of groups we have discussed.

Neighbors, income groups, and social classes. The remaining primary group important to most of us is our neighbors—the people who live in our immediate residential areas. Social scientists have long noted that most neighborhoods are composed mostly of people of the same or similar ethnic groups, religious groups, educational levels, and income levels.

They are also likely to be members of the same social classes— a concept that requires some definition and explanation. According to Karl Marx and his Communist disciples, a social class means only one thing: a group of people holding the same position in the production process. There are only two social classes, Marx said: the capitalists, who own the instruments of production; and the workers, who operate but do not own the instruments. The Marxist doctrine of class struggle proclaims that there is an inevitable war to the death between capitalists and workers, and all politics is simply a manifestation of that war.

Non-Marxist social scientists, however, define a **social class** simply as *a group of persons who share the same socioeconomic status*. They view society as divided into several more than Marx's two classes, and they believe that each class is based upon a number of distinctions from other classes—for example, ethnic identity, length of family residence in the nation and in the local community, educational level, income, and occupational prestige. Most of these factors are difficult to measure precisely, so the boundaries between one class and another are usually indistinct, and identifying the class memberships of particular persons is often difficult. The criteria of class membership used most often are income and educational level, but few, if any, non-Marxist social scientists consider them to be the *only* factors determining social class. Nevertheless, even though they differ on exactly what characteristics should be used to classify people by class, most social scientists believe that class membership has a significant influence upon the political opinions of most people.

The Variable Impact of Group Membership

It is important to remember that no social group has exactly the same political impact on each and every one of its members. This is made clear by the facts we examined in Chapter 2 about the internal division of every social group in elections. As Table 3.2 shows, in the 1988 election, 86 percent of African-Americans favored Michael Dukakis, but even so, 12 percent voted for George Bush. Even more striking is the fact that in the 1980 presidential election, despite Jimmy Carter's well-known status as a "born-again" Baptist and Ronald Reagan's divorce and spotty church attendance, Protestants split 56 to 37 for Reagan, while Catholics gave Reagan a smaller but still useful 51 to 40 margin.

Most social scientists believe that the impact of membership in a particular social group upon a person's political views and behavior depends upon several factors, including the following:

The group's importance for the individual. Some people regard their status as, for instance, women, African-Americans, Roman Catholics, or union members as the most important thing in their lives, and the particular group membership has a powerful effect on their attitudes and behavior. However, other women, African-Americans, Roman Catholics, and union members do not see these group affiliations as that important, and they get their political views from a greater variety of sources. Social psychologists tell us that the more strongly a group's members identify themselves with a group, the more likely they are to think and behave in ways that make that group different from other groups. There is also a good deal of evidence that in most cases the strength of a person's identification with a group is closely related to how long the person has been a member of that group. For example, people who have been raised in Democratic families and have always thought of themselves as good Democrats are more likely to be strong partisans than are people who were raised as Republicans but have recently switched parties.

Perceived political relevance of the group. Strong identification with a group is not enough by itself to shape a person's politics completely. For example, some union members who strongly identify with their union may nevertheless see it as strictly an organization that helps them get better wages, hours, and working conditions; they may not know or care much about its political activities and stands. Their political attitudes and behavior are much less likely to be influenced by their union's politics than are those of unionists who identify strongly with the union in all its activities, including politics.

Transmission of group political standards. The leaders of some social groups —including organizations as varied as the American Medical Association, the National Organization for Women, and the National Conservative Political Action Committee— make regular efforts to "sell" their members on the organization's views and favored candidates. Leaders of other groups, on the other hand, make weak efforts or none at all, and the evidence suggests that the organization's importance and political relevance for its members increase as such "transmissions" from the leadership increase. This tendency is one aspect of the general phenomenon of political communication, which we will consider in detail in Chapter 7.

POLITICAL SOCIALIZATION

THE CONCEPT

While our memberships in a number of primary and categoric groups have an important impact on our political attitudes and behavior, there is nothing automatic or mindless about it. We know from the studies of political attitudes in children that a boy born to upper-middle class white Republican parents living in an expensive suburb does not say as soon as he begins to talk that he is a conservative or that he favors prayer in the schools or that he admires Ronald Reagan. As an adult he may well say all those things, but he, like the rest of us, was not born with those attitudes; we have all acquired our political outlooks the old-fashioned way: We have *learned* them. Political scientists call this learning process **political socialization**—*the developmental processes by which people acquire their political orientations and patterns of behavior.* It is the main process by which people's primary and categoric group memberships are translated into their political attitudes and behavior. How does it work?

PROFILE OF THE DEVELOPING POLITICAL SELF

For most people, political socialization begins early in life and continues until old age or death. There are, of course, many variations in the content and pace of socialization from one person to another, one social group to another, and one nation to another. But there are enough similarities among people in the United States and other developed nations that we can outline the socialization cycle in the following general terms.

Beginnings

Political socialization begins as early as the third or fourth year of life, when children first perceive a few basic political objects—such as the president, the police, and "the government"—as somehow different from their families or the people next door. At about the same time, they also learn that they are part of some groups larger and more remote than their families—that they are Americans, African-Americans, Jews, female, and so on. By the age of seven, many children even say unhesitatingly, "We are Democrats" or "We are Republicans" (note the plural form). In these early stages the children's identifications have more emotional than cognitive content; that is, they know that they are Democrats or Republicans but they are not very clear about how Democrats differ from Republicans or about why they are one rather than the other. But many of the knowledge gaps are filled in quite soon.

Childhood

From ages 6 to 18, most children live at home and attend public schools through the twelfth grade (legally they must attend until age 16). From their parents, teachers, and increasingly from television, they not only acquire such basic skills as reading and arithmetic but also learn a good deal about the political world. They move from highly personalized conceptions of "the government" as synonymous with "the police officer" and "the president" to more abstract and general notions of its group character and ideals. They perceive with increasing clarity the different identities and activities of the president, the police officer, the mayor, the governor, and eventually the legislature and the courts. This process of development is well illustrated by the summary of proportions of children of various ages in New Haven, Connecticut, who gave "reasonably accurate" answers to questions about selected political objects.

Table 3.3 shows that almost all the younger children could name the president of the United States and the mayor of New Haven. But, although considerably fewer than half of the fourth graders (average age 9) could say anything reasonably accurate about the more abstract and general matter of these and other public officials' duties, much higher proportions of eighth graders (average age 13) could. This difference illustrates the proposition that political knowledge in children generally develops from the individualized and personalized to the more general and abstract. The process continues, and by age 14 children's political perceptions are nearly as sharp and as clear as they will ever be, and their affective responses to many political objects (for example, the political parties) are well established.

TABLE 3.3. "Reasonably Accurate" Responses to Selected Political-Information Items, by School Year (in percentages)

Information asked	School Grade				
	4th	5th	6th	7th	8th
President's name	96	97	90	99	100
Mayor's name	90	97	89	99	97
President's duties	23	33	44	65	66
Mayor's duties	35	42	50	66	67
Governor's duties	8	12	23	36	43
Role of state legislature	5	5	9	24	37
N	111	118	115	135	180

Source: Fred I. Greenstein, "The Benevolent Leader: Children's Images of Political Authority," *American Political Science Review*, 54 (December 1960), 937, Table 2.

Adolescence

Adolescence, according to the dictionary, is "the period of life from puberty to maturity terminating legally at the age of majority": that is, from age 13 or 14 (younger for girls) to age 18 in most nations. Many secondary-school teachers say that the period starts horribly (eighth and ninth grades, consisting mainly of 13- and 14-year-olds, are said to be the most difficult of all) but ends better. Parents say that one doesn't know what problems are until one has tried to live with an adolescent.

Most psychologists believe that adolescence is the most painful and difficult period in personal development. Sexuality emerges, the "silver cord" binding child to parents is frayed or severed, the first independent decisions are made, and so on. The psychic maladjustments often produced by these personal crises sometimes find political outlets, particularly in support for sweeping proposals to clear away the corrupt institutions and hypocritical attitudes of the adult establishment and replace them with a brave new society cleansed of war, greed, exploitation, racism, and all the other evils that adults perpetrate.

Thus most students of political socialization find that there is a considerable spurt in political learning between the ages of 11 and 15, especially in the growth of understanding of the larger political world beyond individuals and their families, and by mid-adolescence most teenagers begin to resemble adults politically.

Yet studies of adolescent psychology and behavior suggest that only a small minority express their rebellion in active political ways—for example, by becoming members of partisan organizations such as the Young Republicans or the Young Democrats. From the mid- 1960s to the early 1970s, to be sure, there was a great wave of active student protest at many colleges and universities not only in the United States but also in Great Britain, Italy, France, Scandinavia, and Japan. Even at its height, however, that protest involved only a minority of students, and in recent years it has largely disappeared.

Perhaps the clearest evidence of the relatively low level of young people's political involvement is shown by voting turnout figures. All Americans over the age of 18 were guaranteed the right to vote by the adoption of the Twenty-sixth Amendment to the U.S. Constitution in 1971, but the figures in Table 3.4 show that in presidential elections since then, younger people have voted in far lower proportions than older people.

Adulthood

Table 3.4 shows that the older people become the more likely they are to vote. (They also participate more in other ways.) There are good reasons for this development. After reaching the legal minimum age of adulthood, most people begin to acquire an ever-greater stake in their society and therefore in what government does or fails to do. They complete their formal educations, take jobs or open businesses; marry; acquire houses, automobiles, television sets, and debts. As a result of these and other changes in their lives, they

TABLE 3.4. Voting Turnout by Age Groups, 1972–84

Age Group	Percentage Voting for President				
	1972	1976	1978	1984	1988
18–24	23.6	41.8	39.4	40.8	36.2
25–44	42.2	58.7	58.7	58.4	54.1
45–64	56.9	68.7	69.3	69.8	67.9
65 & older	51.4	62.2	65.1	67.7	68.8

Source: The figures for 1972–84 are taken from the *Statistical Abstract of the United States 1988* (Washington, D.C.: Bureau of the Census, 1988), Table 418, p. 249. The figures for 1988 are from a preliminary Census report.

become more politicized. That is, they grow more concerned about political affairs; they know more about them; their preferences grow more intense; their group affiliations, such as their party identifications, become stronger and more intense; and as a result they are more likely to vote and to participate in politics in other ways.

For most people, politicization in the adult years does not mean switching the party preferences and issue positions they used to hold; it means intensifying their original preferences and positions. Most adults, for example, do not switch parties; rather, they move from being "independents" or "weak identifiers" toward being more strongly identified Democrats or Republicans, although, as we will see in Chapters 7 and 8, this tendency has weakened in recent years.

Old Age

When does political old age begin? If changes in the proportions of voters to nonvoters are an indication, then it appears that in the United States, political old age begins in the early 60s. Voting studies such as those summarized in Table 3.4 show a steady increase in voter turnout at each higher age level from 18 to about 65 and a decline thereafter. This decline no doubt results partly from increasing physical infirmities, but it also suggests that the decline in general social and economic involvement (especially after retirement) produces some depoliticization that is the opposite of the politicization that takes place from the early 20s to the early 60s. Seventy-year-olds still vote substantially more than 25-year-olds, but not as much as people between the ages of 30 and 60.

AGENTS OF SOCIALIZATION

We noted earlier that people's political orientations and behavior patterns are not fixed at birth. They are learned. Political socialization, like all forms of learning, is a process of interaction between the learners and certain elements of their environment, generally called *socializing agents.* Among the agents to which political scientists have paid most attention are families, schools, peer groups, and the mass communications media.

Families

The nuclear family—particularly parents but also to some degree brothers and sisters—is for most people the most powerful single socializing agent in their lives. It is the first group of which they become aware. During the psychologically crucial formative years from birth to age 5 or 6 they are in far closer contact with it than with any other group or social influence. One fascinating exception to this general truth is the *kibbutzim* (collective settlements) of Israel, in most of which children are raised in communal centers rather than in their parents' homes. This has political consequences: Several studies have shown that kibbutz children are more "ideological" and more like one another in their attitudes than are children raised in their parents' homes in the rest of Israel. But for most people in most nations, the psychological pressures toward conformity in primary groups, which we considered earlier in this chapter, are strongest of all in the family.

Thus it is not surprising that there is a widespread tendency for children's political attitudes, preferences, and levels of interest and activity to resemble those of their parents, as is shown by the data about the party identifications of parents and their children in Table 3.5.

Table 3.5 shows that in all three countries, parents' party identifications are a good—but far from infallible—basis for predicting their children's identifications. Parent–child agreements are stronger when both parents have the same identification and weaker when they are divided. They are also stronger when one or both parents have often discussed political questions with, or at least in front of, their children and weaker when the parents have shown little or no political interest or activity.

We should note, however, that parents' influence on their children's partisanship has weakened noticeably in recent years. Studies conducted since the late 1960s tend to show that people under 30 today are significantly less likely than were people under 30 in the 1960s to have the same party preferences as their parents. Moreover, many of these young people have abandoned their parents' Democratic or Republican affiliations, not to join the other party or even a third party, but to become self-styled "independents." We will consider these developments further in Chapter 9.

The strength of these factors, in turn, depends partly upon the society's and the parents' ideas about what kind of conversations, if any, parents should have with (or in the presence of) their children. For example, a well-known comparative study of French and American political attitudes revealed, surprisingly, that the French are generally less involved in politics than Americans. The authors explained that the reason is suggested by the fact that 86 percent of the American respondents, but only 26 percent of the French, could

TABLE 3.5.   Indentifications of Parents and Children in Three Nations (in percentages)

Child	Parent			
United States	Democrat	Independent	Republican	
Democrat	70	40	25	
Independent	20	40	21	
Republican	10	20	54	
	100	100	100	
Great Britain	Labour	Liberal	Conservative	None
Labour	51	17	6	29
Liberal	8	39	11	6
Conservative	1	11	50	6
None	40	33	33	59
	100	100	100	100
West Germany	SPD	FDP	CDU/CSU	None
SPD	53	8	14	19
FDP	4	59	1	3
CDU/CSU	9	—	32	12
None	34	33	53	66
	100	100	100	100

Source: Russell J. Dalton, *Citizen Politics in Western Democracies* (Chatham, NJ: Chatham House, 1988), Table 9.1, p. 182.

describe their fathers' party preferences. Why this strikingly low figure for the French? Probably because, as the French respondents often said of their fathers, "Il ne disait rien a ses enfants (He doesn't say anything to his children)"; "il n'en parlait jamais (he never talks)."[4] If Papa does not discuss politics with or in front of his children and if they do not know how he feels about politics, then the socialization process will be much more indirect and the family less influential in it. But even in France the family is still the earliest and one of the most powerful of the socializing agents.

Schools

All governments try to instill at least some political attitudes and behavior patterns in their citizens. All, for example, try to maximize national patriotism and obedience to law. Some (such as the democratic countries) try to encourage voter turnout and other forms of popular political participation. Others (such as Saudi Arabia) try to encourage the belief that political affairs are best left to the few people who are especially qualified to rule. Still others (like the Soviet Union and the People's Republic of China) try to encourage popular support of the leaders' policies by training all citizens to perform their assigned duties energetically and enthusiastically.

Political Socialization in Schools. A high school social studies class. (Source: Laimute E. Druskis.)

Whatever their objectives, governments rely heavily on the public schools to implant the desired attitudes. For one thing, it is difficult to monitor and control what parents tell children. Even in the Soviet Union of Stalin and Brezhnev, for example, "the family [acted] as an impediment to full and enthusiastic acceptance of the official system of beliefs, especially of those which stress[ed] militancy, total conformity, and instant adaptation to shifting public demands."[5]

For another thing, the public schools are organized, financed, staffed, and programmed by the government, and children are required to attend school from ages five or six until middle adolescence. The schools thus provide the government's most effective direct channel for shaping young people's political attitudes and behavior.

Formal education is certainly powerful in children's political socialization. Perhaps the best evidence is the nearly universal tendency for the most educated people to have the strongest sense of *political efficacy* (that is, the feeling that public officials can be influenced by their ideas and wishes), to be the most politically interested and informed, and to take the most active roles in political affairs. Many people regard education as the last and best hope for curing social ills; war, they say, will never disappear until people have been educated to understand its futility and horror, racism will never disappear until whites are educated to recognize blacks as full equals, and so on. But formal education is certainly not an absolute, irresistible weapon for forming children's—or adults'—attitudes. When children hear one thing in the classroom and quite another at home or from their playmates, there is no reason to think that they will believe teachers and textbooks rather than parents and peers. Laurence Wylie tells how the civics textbooks used in the school of the French village he studied discoursed eloquently and at length on the democratic ideal of trust in others, the high mission of government, the important contributions of political parties, and so on. But, he writes, *outside* school the children

> *constantly hear adults referring to Government as a source of evil and to the men who run it as instruments of evil. There is nothing personal in this belief. It does not concern one particular Government composed of one particular group of men. It concerns Government everywhere and at all times—French Governments, American Governments, Russian Governments, all Governments. Some are less bad than others, but all are essentially bad.*[6]

In France as elsewhere, schools and families working together are a good deal more effective than either is working at cross purposes with the other.

Peer Groups

In addition to parents, siblings, and teachers, most people spend much of their lives in the company of "peer groups"—people who have certain important characteristics in common, such as age or social status, and derive cues from one another about how to behave. Schoolmates are one important peer group, work associates are another, and friendship "cliques" are yet another. What do we know about the role of such groups in political socialization?

We know that at least in such developed societies as the United States and Sweden, the socializing influence of parents and teachers begins to wane in early adolescence and that from then on peer groups become increasingly important in shaping political attitudes and behavior. As people grow older, some peer groups that were highly influential in their adolescence (for example, classmates, sorority sisters, and perhaps radical student organizations) are superseded by others made salient by their new life circumstances: work associates, neighbors, and, above all, husbands and wives. One proof is the political homogeneity of various primary groups. Several studies of American voting behavior have shown that the most politically homogeneous of all American groups, primary or secondary, are husband–wife pairs, followed by friendship groups and then by groups of work associates.

In primitive and traditional societies, on the other hand, most people have many fewer contacts and much less involvement with people outside their families, and such peer groups as do exist are much less powerful socializing agents at any age than in the advanced/industrialized nations. It seems likely, however, that one significant effect—and cause—of political modernization in these societies will be a sharp decrease in the family's traditional near-monopoly of socialization and a parallel increase in the influence of the schools, peer groups, and the mass communications media.

Mass Communications Media

In Chapter 7 we will consider at some length how mass communications media (television, radio, newspapers, and so on) influence public opinion. Here we note only that in all nations with technologically advanced mass communications, the media play a major role in shaping the cognitive maps, as well as the specific opinions, of most people.

How could it be otherwise? Most American children begin watching television at the age of 3 months. By the time they finish high school, they have spent less than 12,000 hours in classrooms but more than 22,000 hours in front of television sets! Americans over 18 spend more time watching television (4 hours a day on the average) than doing anything else except sleeping and working. Moreover, most Americans say they get more political information from television—and trust its accuracy more—than from any other source, including their families and friends. And so it is in the other technologically advanced countries.

The media can potentially play an even greater role in the developing nations, for there they provide the government's best tool—far better than the schools—for modernizing their citizens' traditional outlooks and behavior. After all, schools affect mainly the young, but the leaders often feel that they must change adult orientations immediately without waiting for the new generation to take over. The mass media can reach the largest number of people—adults *and* children—in the shortest time. Leading illiterate masses out of their ancient ways into new ones is tricky at best, and the communicators must be careful not to attempt too sharp a break too quickly. But socialization through the mass media is the best short-run technique available, and many scholars—and leaders of developing nations—believe that it is crucial to political modernization.

To summarize: Every political system operates as it does largely because of the kind of people, both elites and masses, who make the demands and constitute the targets for its policies. Their basic beliefs about the way things are, their convictions about the way things should be, and their accustomed modes of political behavior all fix very real limits on whether and how government can achieve its goals—whether the goals are racial equality or discrimination, peace or world conquest, cutting taxes or putting astronauts on the moon. People's beliefs and values are not congenital or instinctive; they are *learned* through the process we call political socialization. Some socializing agents, particularly the schools and the mass media, are directly controlled to some degree by governments in order to instill "desirable" attitudes and behavior patterns in their citizens. Other agents, particularly families and peer groups, are much freer from direct government control. Many families and peer groups thus preserve and pass on attitudes that differ significantly from those that governments want their people to absorb.

Whatever their sources, the dominant beliefs and values in any nation constitute what political scientists call political culture— the social-psychological climate that shapes and constrains its political system. We turn now to a closer look at its components and consequences.

POLITICAL CULTURE

COMPONENTS

As we use the term in this book, a nation's **political culture** is *a broadly shared set of ways of thinking about politics and government,* a "pattern of orientations to political objects." It provides the psychological environment within which political conflict is conducted and public policy is made, and it has two main components: *cognitive orientations* (knowledge and awareness of political objects) and *affective orientations* (feelings and emotions about the objects).

Cognitive Orientations

Cognitive orientations are what people believe about how things really are in the political world. Scholars of political culture are often struck by the low levels of information ordinary people have about political affairs; just how low those levels are in the United States is suggested by the scores in Table 3.6.

Levels of information make a difference. For example, a study of popular attitudes toward business regulation demonstrated that when people are asked how high business profits are, their answers average between 25 and 30 percent of each dollar of revenue (the correct answer is about 5 percent). Moreover, many more of those whose estimates are high than of those whose estimates are low favor strong regulation of business.[7]

TABLE 3.6.   What American Adults Know About American Government

Question	Percentage Answering Correctly
How many times can an individual be elected president?	74
How long is the term of office for a member of the U.S. House of Representatives?	32
How long is the term of office for a U.S. senator?	30
Who is your U.S. representative?	50
Which political party now controls the House of Representatives?	25
Which nations are involved in what are known as the SALT talks?	37
Which of these nations—the United States or the Soviet Union—is a member of the NATO alliance?	47
Which two nations, aside from the United States, were involved in the Camp David peace talks?	45
Where is El Salvador?	25

Data compiled from the University of Michigan Center for Political Studies, 1972 National Election Study; and Barry Sussman, "How Can Americans Display Such Ignorance of Public Affairs?" *Washington Post*, January 2, 1983.

Political Preferences

People, of course, not only believe that certain things are true about politics and government, but they also like some things and dislike others. For one thing, they have different values and priorities: Some judge things mainly according to whether they seem to promote "law and order" and "stability," while others place the highest value on "social justice" and "fairness." For another thing, different people can look at the same political objects and have very different likes and dislikes. For example, in the contests for the 1988 presidential nominations, some people saw Jesse Jackson as an inspiring fighter for oppressed minorities and poor people, while others saw him as an anti-Semitic admirer of third-world dictators such as Fidel Castro and Yasir Arafat. By the same token, some people saw Michael Dukakis as a smart and resourceful solver of problems, while others saw him as an over-cautious technocrat with no inspiration and no vision.

It is important to note that the factual beliefs and political preferences that together make up a nation's political culture do not have to be logically consistent with one another. Indeed, the evidence suggests that most political cultures, particularly those in the "advanced" nations, fall far short of logical consistency. In the United States, for example, most of us endorse such sentiments as "Love thy neighbor as thyself" and "Help those less fortunate than yourself"—but we also hold to such quite different sentiments as "The Lord helps those who help themselves" and "The wheel that squeaks the loudest gets the grease." Most of us believe in "efficient" and "businesslike" government— but we also believe in separation of powers and checks and balances, which inevitably cause a great deal of inefficiency by making it difficult for any one leader or party to take charge.

Do these inconsistencies in political cultures prove that we are fools and knaves—or do they simply show that we are human beings acting like human beings? Without choosing any of these labels, we can observe that every nation's political culture contains some anomalies—and that, however inconsistent and illogical, every nation's political culture constitutes one of the most powerful influences shaping its political system.

SOME DIFFERENCES AMONG POLITICAL CULTURES

Patriotism: Identification with the Nation

Political scientists agree that one of the most powerful determinants of a nation's political stability and governmental effectiveness is the extent to which its citizens give their primary political loyalties to it rather than to one of its classes or regions or tribes or religions. For example, many new African and Asian nations have faced "crises of identity" shortly after achieving indepen-

Nationalism is the Basic Political Loyalty. Construction
workers in New York City hold a patriotic rally. (Source:
Charles Gatewood.)

dence. Some, like Ghana, Burma, and Tunisia, have weathered them well
enough, though not without some scars, while others, like India, Nigeria, and
Pakistan, have had much rougher going. There are also significant variations
among the developed nations. National identity is very strong, for example,
in Japan, Norway, and Sweden. It is strong in the United States, though
challenged by some African-American separatism and by some echoes of the
Confederate loyalties of a century ago. It is strong in Great Britain, though
challenged by Welsh and Scottish nationalism. On the other hand, it is greatly
diluted in Italy by *campanalismo* (loyalty to the home town or the region rather
than to the nation); and most West Germans still identify with prepartition
Germany, long for the reunification of West and East Germany, and have
developed only limited identification with West Germany as it is presently
constituted. But pure or diluted, strong or weak, the degree of citizens' identification with their nation powerfully affects the stability and effectiveness of its
political system.

Trust in People

A second component of political culture is trust in other people, and it too
varies widely from nation to nation. For example, a pioneering comparative

study of the United States, Great Britain, Germany, Italy, and Mexico showed, among other things, that most Italians feel that only members of their own immediate families can be trusted and that everyone else is a potential enemy, to be watched and guarded against but never trusted. When people in each nation were asked to agree or disagree with the statement, "Most people can be trusted," only 7 percent of the Italians agreed, compared with 55 percent of the Americans, 49 percent of the British, 30 percent of the Mexicans, and 19 percent of the Germans.[8]

Confidence in Institutions

No government can rely entirely on physical force to ensure obedience to its laws. Realistically speaking, it can shoot or torture or imprison only a small fraction of its citizens, and when a large number of citizens resolutely refuse to obey, the authorities are authoritative no longer. Thus every government, authoritarian as well as democratic, has no choice but to rely mainly on most citizens' *voluntary* compliance with its laws. The first prerequisite for such compliance is the prevalence of popular confidence that the authorities have won their posts rightfully, that they make and enforce their decisions by proper procedures, and that their decisions affect matters that are the government's proper business and do not encroach on what is rightfully private and personal. Where such confidence is high, governments need only minimum force to deal with law breakers. Where the authorities' legitimacy is widely questioned, however, law breaking is a major problem, and even revolution is possible. Table 3.7 shows the levels of confidence in five major democratic nations.

Since the mid-1960s, many America-watchers have been concerned over the evidence from a number of public opinion polls showing a sharp decrease in the number of people who say that they have a great deal of confidence in the

TABLE 3.7. Popular Confidence in Institutions in the United States and Europe

Institution	Percentage Expressing "A Great Deal" or "Quite a Lot" of Confidence				
	U.S.	G.B.	Germany	France	Italy
Parliament/Congress	53	40	53	48	31
Civil service	55	48	35	50	28
Legal system	51	66	67	55	43
Education system	65	60	43	55	56
Armed forces	81	81	54	53	58
Police	76	86	71	64	68
Church	75	48	48	54	60
Major companies	50	48	34	42	33
Press	49	29	33	31	46
Labor unions	33	26	36	36	28
Average	59	53	47	49	45

Source: Study by Gordon Heald reported in *Public Opinion,* February/March 1984, p. 11.

leaders of our principal public and private institutions. Confidence was generally high in the early 1960s, and even the Congress and the presidency commanded high confidence from over 40 percent of the people. But then came a series of disasters. The Vietnam War became worse and worse while three administrations said it was getting better and better. As the war escalated, so did protest against it. Universities became arenas for political fighting as well as for teaching and research. The forced busing of school children escalated racial conflict in the North as well as the South. Senator Robert Kennedy and Dr. Martin Luther King, Jr., were assassinated. In 1973–74 the "Watergate" scandals about the illegal activities of the Committee to Reelect the President were exposed, and in 1974 Richard Nixon, about to be impeached, became the first president in history to resign. President Jimmy Carter's administration (1977–81) was relatively scandal-free, but inflation soared and Iran held 60 American diplomats hostage for over a year, while a military rescue mission failed ingloriously as American helicopters crashed into each other on the Iranian desert. As a result, the people's confidence in the leaders of the government—and in the leaders of every other major institution as well—declined sharply from 1966 to 1972, and stayed low throughout the 1970s. Indeed, in 1979 President Carter, in a nationally televised speech, told the American people that the nation was suffering from a "malaise" of feeble civic spirit and economic confidence.

Many observers thought that the decline was permanent and that it was bound to shake the political system to its very foundations. Yet during Ronald Reagan's first term as president (1981–85), popular confidence in all institutions except the press rose. How much of this upsurge can be credited to President Reagan's upbeat personality and the success of his policies is still very much a matter of dispute, but it is undeniable that the American people are expressing considerably more confidence in their major institutions in the 1990s than they were in most of the 1960s and 1970s.

Political Efficacy

A fourth component of political culture is the feeling of **political efficacy**—*the belief that one's political views and actions can affect the political process.* To see how feelings of efficacy are distributed among and within the five nations they studied, Almond and Verba asked respondents what, if anything, they might do to try to change an unjust or harmful local regulation or national law and how likely it was that they would succeed if they tried. Some of the replies are summarized in Table 3.8.

The most striking message conveyed by the data in Table 3.8 is not that Great Britain and the United States have higher levels of political efficacy than West Germany, Italy, and Mexico. It is that the differences among the educational groups *within* each nation are, with one exception, greater than the overall differences *among* the nations. The overall difference between Britain and the United States at one end of the range and Italy and Mexico at the other

TABLE 3.8.   Levels of Subjective Civic Competence, by Nation and Education

| Nation | Total | Percentage of Respondents Who Say They Can Do Something about an Unfair Local Regulation | | |
		Primary Education or Less	Some Secondary Education	Some Collge Education
United States	77	60	82	95
Great Britain	77	74	83	88
West Germany	62	58	83	85
Italy	53	45	62	76
Mexico	53	49	67	76

Source: Taken from data in Gabriel A. Almond and Sidney Verba, *The Civic Culture: Political Attitudes and Democracy in Five Nations* (Princeton, NJ: Princeton University Press, 1962), p. 186. Reprinted by permission of Princeton University Press.

is 24 percentage points; but the differences between the most and least educated groups are 27 percent for Germany and Mexico, 31 percent for Italy, and 35 percent for the United States; only in Great Britain is the difference among educational groups as low as 14 percentage points. Furthermore, the differences among the five nations grow smaller in each higher educational group: Among those with primary education or less there is an internation spread of 29 percentage points; among those with secondary education it declines to 21 percentage points; and among those with college education it declines to 19 percentage points.

Comparable findings in other studies have led most political scientists to suspect that many significant differences among the political cultures of modern nations reflect variations not so much in unchanging and unchangeable "national characters" as in certain processes—especially education—that operate differently in different nations.

Citizens' Obligations

We noted in Chapter 1 that all governments can and sometimes do enforce their laws by *sanctions,* including fines, imprisonment, and even death. We also learned that every government, democratic or authoritarian, in fact depends much more on voluntary compliance than on sanctions.

That being the case, one of the most important elements in every political culture is the sense of *citizens' obligations* —what people think they owe the government. Most political philosophers have said that the citizen's first obligation is *loyalty* or *patriotism*—putting the security and welfare of their own nation and government above those of all other nations and governments. Closely tied to this is *obeying the law*—doing what the authorities have required and not doing what they have forbidden regardless of whether they agree with the wisdom or fairness of the authorities' decisions. Not many people enjoy paying taxes and even fewer enjoy being drafted into military service, but governments depend upon the willingness of most citizens to do both, voluntarily if not cheerfully. Many democratic theorists argue that citi-

Paying taxes is a prime example of a citizen's obligation to government. Governments cannot do anything for very long unless people pay their taxes. Yet they simply cannot hire enough tax collectors and auditors to check on more than a small fraction of the tens of millions of people who owe taxes, so they have no choice but to depend upon most people's voluntarily filling out the complicated forms (no one knows what being a citizen *really* involves until they have filled out their first Form 1040) and sending in the checks. Withholding some taxes from people's paychecks helps, but government still depends mainly upon voluntary payments.

That means that every nation offers great opportunities for people to cheat on taxes. They can fiddle their income tax returns by reporting that they earned less money than they actually did. They can claim exemptions to which they are not legally entitled. They can even bypass the tax system altogether by bartering with others for goods and services with no cash changing hands and no records being kept.

Thus every nation is concerned with tax evasion and the reasons for it. Although we have no hard evidence on the matter, it is said that in the political cultures of some countries, notably Italy, France, and a number of Latin American countries, the idea that the citizen has the right to evade taxes is at least as strong as the idea that good citizens should pay what they owe.

Most Americans used to think that such attitudes were part of the general shoddiness of Latins' characters, but in recent years we have come to worry more and more about how much tax evasion there is in the United States and what kind of popular attitudes underlie it. Accordingly, in 1984 the federal government's Internal Revenue Service hired the polling firm of Yankelovich, Skelly, and White to undertake a study of taxpayer attitudes about compliance. They found that about one-third of their respondents believed that under certain circumstances it is okay to pay less in taxes than the government says you owe, and 19 percent admitted that they had on occasion actually cheated on their taxes. Only about half of the respondents said that it is morally wrong to evade taxes under any circumstances![9] What does this say about the state of American political culture and civic virtue?

zens also have the obligation to *participate* in the nation's political processes, not only by voting but also by signing petitions, writing letters to their elected representatives and newspapers, attending political meetings, joining organizations involved in politics, and the like. In Chapter 9 we will examine the evidence on how many people feel an obligation to participate, and how much and in what ways they actually do so.

A nation's political culture, then, provides the general psychological environment within which the political system must work. But governments are much more conscious of and influenced by the day-to-day pressures of public opinion on particular issues. Those pressures are our concern in the next chapter.

FOR FURTHER READING

POLITICAL PSYCHOLOGY

*FESTINGER, LEON. *A Theory of Cognitive Dissonance.* Stanford, CA.: Stanford University Press, 1957. A leading study of how people's likes and dislikes affect their factual perceptions and understandings.

*FINIFTER, ADA W., ed. *Alienation and the Political System.* New York: John Wiley, 1972. Collection of essays on aspects of one important dimension of political psychology.

GREENSTEIN, FRED I., "Personality and Politics," in Fred I. Greenstein and Nelson W. Polsby, eds., *Handbook of Political Science,* vol. 2, pp. 1–92. Reading, MA: Addison-Wesley, 1975. Useful survey.

LAU, RICHARD R., and David O. Sears, eds. *Political Cognition.* Hillsdale, NJ: Lawrence Erlbaum, 1986. Essays on how people form their views of what the political world is really like.

SNIDERMAN, PAUL M. *Personality and Democratic Politics.* Berkeley: University of California Press, 1975. Use of data to analyze relationship of personality components to "democratic personality."

TAJFEL, HENRI. *Human Groups and Social Categories.* Cambridge: Cambridge University Press, 1981. A probing study of the impact of membership in social groups on human attitudes and behavior.

POLITICAL SOCIALIZATION

COLEMAN, JAMES S. *The Adolescent Society.* New York: Free Press, 1961. Study of developing political attitudes in teenagers.

*DAWSON, RICHARD E., and KENNETH PREWITT. *Political Socialization,* 2nd ed. Boston: Little, Brown, 1977. General survey of research findings about the nature of political socialization.

EASTON, DAVID, and JACK DENNIS. *Children in the Political system.* New York: McGraw-Hill, 1969. Report of a major survey of the development of children's political attitudes in the United States.

*GREENSTEIN, FRED I. *Children and Politics,* rev. ed. New Haven: Yale University Press, 1967. Early study of political socialization.

*JENNINGS, M. KENT, and RICHARD G. NIEMI. *The Political Character of Adolescence: The Influence of Families and Schools.* Princeton, NJ: Princeton University Press, 1974. Use of survey data to analyze the role of families and schools in forming adolescents' political attitudes.

*———. *Generations and Politics: A Panel Study of Young Adults and their Parents.* Princeton, NJ: Princeton University Press, 1981. Study of changes in attitudes of parent–child pairs over time.

NIEMI, RICHARD G. *How Family Members Perceive Each Other: Political And Social Attitudes in Two Generations.* New Haven, CT: Yale University Press, 1974. Use of survey data to analyze political conflict and accord within families.

*VERBA, SIDNEY. *Small Groups and Political Behavior.* Princeton, NJ: Princeton University Press, 1961. Examines political influence of primary-group membership.

POLITICAL CULTURE

*ALMOND, GABRIEL A., and G. Bingham Powell, Jr. *Comparative Politics: A Developmental Approach.* Boston: Little, Brown, 1966. Study of politics in a number of countries emphasizing the impact of various political cultures on the development of political institutions.

*ALMOND, GABRIEL A., and SIDNEY VERBA. *The Civil Culture: Political Attitudes and Democracy in Five Nations.* Boston: Little, Brown, 1965. Comparative sample survey of political attitudes in the United States, Great Britain, West Germany, Italy, and Mexico.

DI PALMA, GIUSEPPE. *Apathy and Participation: Mass Politics in Western Societies.* New York: Free Press, 1970. Comparative study of major aspects of political culture in Western democracies.

ECKSTEIN, HARRY. *Theory of Stable Democracy.* Princeton, NJ: Princeton University Press, 1965. Fullest statement of the concept of political culture and examination of its nature and role in ten nations.

*HUNTINGTON, SAMUEL P. *American Politics: The Promise of Disharmony.* Cambridge, MA: Belknap Press of Harvard University Press, 1981. Exploration of American political culture, emphasizing the clash between liberal-democratic ideals and actual political practices.

JACKMAN, MARY R., and Robert W. Jackman. *Class Awareness in the United States.* Berkeley: University of California Press, 1983. Analysis of the extent and role of class divisions in American political culture.

McCLOSKY, HERBERT, and John Zaller. *The American Ethos: Public Attitudes Toward Capitalism and Democracy.* Cambridge, MA: Harvard University Press, 1984. Magisterial study using survey data and historical materials to trade the evolution of important components of American political culture.

*PYE, LUCIAN W., and Sidney Verba, eds. *Political Culture and Political Development.* Princeton, NJ: Princeton University Press, 1965. Examination of the nature and role of political culture in ten nations.

*SMITH, HEDRICK. *The Russians.* New York: Ballantine Books, 1977. Illuminating account of the life-styles and attitudes of ordinary Russians by a former *New York Times* Moscow correspondent.

*WYLIE, LAURENCE. *Village in the Vaucluse,* 3rd ed. Cambridge, MA: Harvard University Press, 1974. Classic study of the political culture and politics of a small town in the south of France.

NOTES

[1]Quoted in Fred I. Greenstein, "Personality and Politics," in Fred I. Greenstein and Nelson W. Polsby, eds., *Handbook of Political Science* (Reading, MA.: Addison-Wesley, 1975), vol. 2, p. 6.

[2]Angus Campbell, Philip E. Converse, Warren E. Miller, and Donald E. Stokes, *The American Voter* (New York: John Wiley, 1960), Chapter 10.

[3]The terms *Left* and *Right* are widely used all over the world to label the two sides of what many people see as the most important ideological cleavage in politics. Although neither term has a precise definition on which everyone agrees, *Left* generally means a favorable attitude toward the interests of the working classes and *Right* generally means a favorable attitude toward the interests of proprietors and capitalists. For a more extended discussion, see Vernon Bogdanor, ed., *The Blackwell Encyclopaedia of Political Institutions* (London: Basil Blackwell, 1987), pp. 324–25. See also Chapter 4 of this book.

[4]Philip E. Converse and Georges Dupeux, "Politicization of the Electorate in France and the United States," in Angus Campbell, Philip E. Converse, Warren E. Miller, and Donald E. Stokes, eds., *Elections and the Political Order* (New York: John Wiley, 1966), pp. 279–81.

[5]Frederick C. Barghoorn, *Politics in the USSR* (Boston: Little, Brown, 1966), p. 109.

[6]Laurence Wylie, *Village in the Vaucluse* (New York: Harper & Row, Pub., 1964), p. 208.

[7]Seymour Martin Lipset and William Schneider, *The Confidence Gap: Business, Labor, and Government in the Popular Mind* (New York: Free Press, 1983), pp. 176–84.

[8]Gabriel A. Almond and Sidney Verba, *The Civil Culture: Political Attitudes and Democracy in Five Nations* (Princeton, NJ: Princeton University Press, 1963), Table 4, p. 267.

[9]Reported in Madelyn Hochstein, "Tax Ethics: Social Values and Noncompliance," *Public Opinion,* February/March 1985, pp. 11–14.

4 Modern Political Ideologies

The invasion of armies can be resisted, but not an idea whose time has come.

Victor Hugo, Histoire d'un Crime (1852)

Ideas won't keep. Something must be done about them. When the idea is new, its custodians have fervor, live for it, and, if need be, die for it.

Alfred North Whitehead, Dialogues (1953)

It is not the consciousness of men that determines their existence, but on the contrary it is their social existence that determines their consciousness.

Karl Marx, Critique of Political Economy (1859)

Don't watch what we say. Watch what we do.

Edwin Meese, Counselor to President Reagan (1981)

In Chapter 3 we learned that what people think, say, and do in politics is shaped by their "cognitive maps." That phrase is a metaphor for the basic mental structures by which people receive and interpret signals from the outside world and form their beliefs and determine their actions or inactions. There is, however, a much older tradition in the study of politics, one that goes back to Greek philosophers centuries before the birth of Christ. That tradition (some call it "political philosophy") considers people's political values and behavior in terms of their ideologies. There are similarities between the concept of "cognitive map" and the concept of "ideology," but there are also enough significant differences to warrant this separate chapter on modern political ideologies. We will begin by considering the nature of ideologies in general, and then review the main doctrines of the most prominent modern political ideologies.

THE NATURE OF IDEOLOGIES

WHAT IS AN IDEOLOGY?

The most obvious (though perhaps not the significant) characteristic of most ideologies appears to be that their labels end in *-ism,* as in *liberalism, socialism, fascism,* and the like.[1] But we can do better than that. The first point to note is that an ideology is not the same as an idea; it is rather a *set* of ideas that are in some logical way related to one another. For example, one of the most powerful ideas in economics is the belief (assumption? observation?) that everyone's sole purpose in economic life is to acquire as much material wealth as possible. But that belief is only one part, albeit an important part, of a much larger set of ideas making up the doctrine that the best way to organize an economic system is to base it on the private ownership of the production and distribution of goods and services. And that larger set of ideas constitutes the economic ideology people call *capitalism.*

Political scientist Roy C. Macridis suggests that there are four main criteria for distinguishing ideologies from ideas:[2]

Comprehensiveness. A full-fledged ideology includes ideas about many great matters, such as the place of human beings in the cosmos, their relationship to God or history or some other superhuman causal force, the highest goals for society and government, the basic nature of human beings, and the best means for achieving the highest social and political goals. These ideas are more or less consistent with one another logically, and there is often a major organization—a party such as the Communist Party of the Soviet Union or a movement such as the women's rights movement—that is rooted in those ideas and dedicated to realizing them.

Pervasiveness. The ideology's particular set of ideas has not only been known for a substantial period of time but has shaped the political beliefs and actions of many people. For example, people have been talking about democracy, oligarchy, and autocracy since the fifth century before Christ (see Chapter 5), and great movements mobilizing millions of people have fought over them for over 2,000 years.

Extensiveness. The set of ideas is held by a large number of people and plays a significant role in the political affairs of one or more nations.

Intensiveness. The set of ideas commands a strong commitment from many of its adherents and significantly influences their political beliefs and actions.

THE INTELLECTUAL COMPONENTS OF AN IDEOLOGY

Every ideology, as we have seen, is a set of ideas that fit together and also in some respects significantly differ from those of other ideologies. Yet every full-fledged ideology has ideas about at least the following five basic matters:

Values

In Chapter 2 we defined a *value* as an object or situation deemed to be of intrinsic worth and esteem, something to be sought. Every ideology is rooted in the conviction that some values are more important than others, and the highest values provide the criteria by which all other ideas, beliefs, and actions should be judged.

Thus democracy, as we will see in Chapter 5, rests in part on the conviction that the full realization of each person's human potential is one of the highest goals of society, and it can be realized only in a political system in which each citizen has the same ultimate power over the making of government policies as every other citizen. By contrast, the "national socialist" ideology of Adolf Hitler and his Nazi party rested in part on the conviction that the world would be properly run only when the Aryan (white, non-Jewish, Nordic) race controlled all its affairs, and the greatest good the Third Reich could do for mankind was to exterminate the Jews and place its *gauleiters* in absolute power over all other inferior races.

Vision of the Ideal Polity

Every ideology is inspired by a vision of what a polity[3] would be like if it were organized and managed in the best possible manner. Marxism, for example, foresees a time when there will be no private property, no class distinctions, and no opportunity for one class to coerce another; then the state will "wither away," and human affairs will be conducted entirely by voluntary cooperation among the members of the all- inclusive working class. For another example, Shi'ite Islamic fundamentalism as preached by Iran's Ayatollah Khomeini envisions a time in which the world is ruled by devout Shi'ite Muslims, who live their lives according to the rules laid down by the Koran in preparation for eternal life in paradise, and all vestiges of Western materialism and unrighteousness are stamped out forever.

Conception of Human Nature

Every ideology contains beliefs about what makes people, societies, and governments behave as they do. Marxism, for example, holds that capitalists exploit workers, not because they are innately evil persons, but because their position in the economic system as owners of the tools of production forces them to exploit the workers who use the tools. Therefore, the only way to get capitalists to treat workers decently is to abolish the institution of private property altogether and thereby destroy the capitalist system that by its very nature compels all owners to exploit all workers.

Classical liberalism,[4] on the other hand, holds that every citizen wants to choose the best possible candidates and policies for the very good reason that all citizens will have to bear the consequences of poor leadership and ill-conceived policies. If all the facts and all the arguments for and against every possible leader and policy are put before the people, they will make the right choice because it is in their interest to do so. The great mistake is to censor or conceal some facts and arguments so that the people will not have all the materials they need to make the right choices.

Strategy of Action

In military terminology, the *strategy* of a nation or an army is its comprehensive basic plan for winning ultimate victory. Similarly, every ideology has a strategy for changing the existing polity into the ideal polity. Thus, Marxism seeks to raise the workers' "class consciousness" (their awareness that they will always be exploited under capitalism) to the point where they will overthrow capitalism and replace it with socialism. The "libertarianism" advocated by the American Libertarian party seeks to convince American citizens that they are best off when government interference in private affairs is kept to an absolute minimum, and the party tries to persuade voters to elect public officials who will not try to govern people's business dealings, labor contracts, sexual behavior, smoking, drinking, taking of drugs, or any other aspect of their private lives.

Political Tactics

Tactics, in military terminology, means the maneuvers that a nation or an army uses to carry out its basic strategy. In a similar sense, every ideology chooses and uses certain modes of political action (see Chapter 1) but not others.

One of the most striking illustrations is provided by the differences in the tactics advocated and employed by organizations professing different brands of socialism. All socialist ideologies aim at abolishing the institution of private property and replacing it with a society in which all property is owned in common, and production and distribution are governed by the principle "from each according to his abilities, to each according to his needs." But ever since the mid-nineteenth century there have been deep schisms among socialists about the best tactics for overthrowing capitalism. Karl Marx said that *any* tactics that will do the job are acceptable and appropriate. Many of his disciples, then and now, believe that capitalists will never voluntarily surrender their privileges merely because they have lost a democratic election, so the violent overthrow of capitalism is not only morally permissible but tactically necessary. However, many other socialists—for example, the Christian Social-ists and Social Democrats of Western Europe—reject violence and have faith in the institutions of democracy and the good sense of ordinary people; accord-ingly, they hold that the only acceptable tactic for ending capitalism is to persuade popular majorities to elect socialist governments that will, by peace-ful and constitutional methods, pass laws abolishing private property.

Thus, in ideological politics as in any kind of politics, there are significant disagreements not only about what is the promised land but also about how to get there.

TYPES OF IDEOLOGIES

The modern world contains a large number and rich variety of political ideolo-gies. Indeed, in canvassing the literature of political science in preparation for writing this chapter I have come across at least 55 distinct ideologies, and I am confident there are more. Obviously we cannot discuss them all in this limited space, so we will have to bypass such nontrivial ideologies as communitarian-ism, corporatavism, guided democracy, Islamic fundamentalism, militarism, pacifism, primitive communism, social Darwinism, syndicalism, Trotskyism—but why go on listing ideologies that we are not going to discuss?

Moreover, I find that it soon becomes confusing if ideologies are discussed one after another as though each were entirely different from all the others. That is because all political ideologies do not address all of the same questions; indeed, they often in some respects cut across and/or combine with one another. A quick illustration: Most of the British people believe in *monarchism;* that is, they believe that it is right and proper that the official, ceremonial leadership of their government be vested in a monarch, Elizabeth II, who holds her position because she inherited it from her father, not because she was elected to it. By contrast, most Americans believe in *republicanism;* that is, we believe that the official, ceremonial head of our government, like all high officials, should be elected to office, and our counterpart to the British queen is the president we elect every four years. But do the two people's devotion to these different ideologies make us deadly enemies? Hardly. Almost all British *and* Americans also believe in democracy—that the ultimate decision-making power of government should be vested in all the people, not in one of them or a small class of them (see Chapter 5). So political scientists sometimes say that Americans believe in a democratic republic while the British believe in a constitutional monarchy.

Consequently, our purposes in this chapter are best served by arranging the main modern political ideologies into groups that offer different answers to the same questions—in other words, into directly competing ideologies that are concerned with the same basic problems but advocate significantly different answers.

As I see it, the principal groupings of modern political ideologies are: (1) those mainly concerned with the proper limits on the power of government; (2) those mainly concerned with the proper role of government in economic affairs; and (3) those mainly concerned with the proper location of the ultimate power to make political decisions. For most political scientists, including me, the third grouping is the most important, and we will devote Chapter 5 to a detailed exploration of each of its main ideologies. In the remainder of this chapter we will outline the principal doctrines and a bit of the history of the main ideologies in the other two clusters.

IDEOLOGIES OF LIMITS ON GOVERNMENT

CONSTITUTIONALISM

The Meaning of Constitutionalism

Constitutionalism is *the ideology that government power should be limited so as to protect human rights.* Although the two usually go hand in hand in actual polities, the ideology of constitutionalism is different from the ideology of democracy. Constitutional governments, as we will see in Chapter 15, are governments in which constitutional guarantees protect human rights from abridgment by either public officials or private groups. Such governments are called "constitutional" or "free" because of how the *substance* of their policies affects those rights. Model democratic governments, as characterized in Chapter 5, are governments in which political decisions are made according to the principles of popular sovereignty, political equality, popular consultation, and majority rule. Thus a democratic government is defined by the *processes* by which all its decisions are made, while a constitutional government is defined by how the *contents* of its decisions affect human rights.

It is therefore theoretically possible for a benevolent despot to exercise absolute decision-making power in such a way that all the people have full freedom of speech, press, and religion and are guaranteed all other individual rights. The despot might even promulgate a constitution formalizing these limitations on his activities, while reserving to himself the exclusive power to make all other political decisions. Such a government would certainly be free and even constitutional, but it would not, according to the definition used here, be democratic. A democratic government, on the other hand, might have no written constitution and no formal guarantees of civil rights (which is substantially the case in Great Britain) and yet still be a democracy.

However, this distinction between democracy and constitutionalism is more important logically than practically. Most of the nations that non-Communists generally call democratic would certainly also appear on any list of constitutional nations, and none of those generally called authoritarian or dictatorial would win a place on such a list. It therefore appears that most modern democracies have decided that one—though not the only—useful way to maintain their democratic decision-making processes is to have constitutional guarantees protecting the personal freedoms and immunities that make possible genuine political equality and popular consultation.

The Case for Constitutionalism

Many scholars use the terms "classical liberalism" and "nineteenth-century liberalism" as more or less equivalent to "constitutionalism," so we should be clear that the word *liberalism* has had two quite different meanings. People first began to use the word in the late eighteenth century, and until the mid-1930s it meant the ideology advocating maximum freedom for the individual from regulation by the government. However, since the mid-1930s, many people, mostly Americans, have converted the term to mean an ideology that favors not only personal freedom but also government regulation of economic activity and government guarantees of minimum standards of living, health, and employment.

Perhaps the most famous succinct statement of the "classical liberal" case for constitutional freedoms is the following:

> *We hold these truths to be self-evident, that all men are created equal, that they are endowed by their Creator with certain unalienable Rights, that among these are Life, Liberty and the Pursuit of Happiness—That to secure these rights, Governments are instituted among Men, deriving their just powers from the consent of the governed—That whenever any Form of Government becomes destructive of these ends, it is the Right of the People to alter or abolish it, and to institute new*

Founders of Classical Liberalism.

John Locke. (Source: New York Public Library.)

Thomas Jefferson. (Source: New York Historical Society.)

Government, laying its foundation on such principles and organizing its powers in such form, as to them shall seem most likely to effect their Safety and Happiness.

These winged words are, of course, taken from the opening sentences of the American Declaration of Independence, drafted mainly by Thomas Jefferson and adopted by the Congress of the rebel American colonies on July 4, 1776. People who believe in constitutionalism generally base their stand on one or a combination of two premises: First, human rights are ends in themselves, and their preservation is the justification for the very existence of government and therefore its main function. Second, human rights, though not necessarily ends in themselves, are indispensable means for establishing a good government, a good society, and a good life for its citizens. Let us briefly examine each premise.

Rights as Ends.   Nearly everyone who argued and fought for human rights in the seventeenth and eighteenth centuries did so out of a deep commitment to the idea that rights are ends in themselves. Perhaps the most influential exponent of this view was the English political philosopher John Locke. In the brilliant and widely read two treatises *Of Civil Government* (1690), Locke raised one of the most basic questions of political philosophy: What moral obligation, if any, do citizens have to obey the commands of government? The answer, he said, must be based on the fact that people join together in polities and establish governments for only one reason: to secure more firmly the rights to life, liberty, and property that naturally belong equally to all people simply because they are human beings. As Locke put it, "The great and chief end . . . of men uniting into commonwealths, and putting themselves under government, is the preservation of their property [that is, their basic rights]."[5] When a government fails to preserve these rights and thereby ceases to serve the end for which it was created, Locke continued, the citizens have the right—indeed, the duty—to overthrow it:

> *Whenever the legislators endeavor to take away and destroy the [rights] of the people . . . they put themselves into a state of war with the people, who are thereupon absolved from any further obedience, and . . . have a right to resume their original liberty, and by the establishment of a new legislative (such as they shall think fit) provide for their own safety and security, which is the end for which they are in society.*[6]

Locke's convictions were known and shared by most of the eighteenth-century American revolutionists and became the basic rationale for their Declaration of Independence: "Governments are instituted among Men," the Declaration proclaims, "to secure these rights...whenever any Form of Government becomes destructive of those ends, it is the Right of the People to alter or to abolish it."

Since 1776 there have been many statements of these Lockean ideals, and one of the most recent is the Universal Declaration of Human Rights adopted by the United Nations in 1948. Articles 1 and 2 of that document proclaim:

All human beings are born free and equal in dignity and rights. They are endowed with reason and conscience and should act towards one another in a spirit of brotherhood. Everyone is entitled to all the rights and freedoms set forth in this Declaration, without distinction of any kind, such as race, color, sex, language, religion, political or other opinion, national or social origin, property, birth or other status. . . .[7]

Rights as Means.   Many modern advocates of human rights base their case on the more pragmatic argument that rights are indispensable means for other, higher ends. They start from their belief in the supreme value of the individual person. Springing from such diverse sources as ancient Greco-Roman Stoicism (c. 300 B.C.) and more recent developments in Judaism and Christianity, this doctrine holds that all human beings, whatever their individual differences and backgrounds, are equally precious and that each has immense potential for good. A prime goal of all human societies should therefore be to encourage the realization of each person's potential to the fullest possible extent. All institutions, including governments, should be judged by the degree to which they help or hinder achievement of this highest of all social goals. And fully guaranteed human rights are necessary, though not by themselves sufficient, conditions for full human development.

There is another sense in which human rights are a necessary means for the highest social ends. Every nation tries to pursue policies best calculated to achieve the values it holds most dear. Discovering just which of the many policy proposals put forth are the best for those purposes is the greatest problem facing any government. Experience has shown that the most effective way to discover the best policies is to let advocates of each proposal argue their ideas freely and let the people choose among them; for in the long run true ideas and good proposals will win public acceptance over false and bad ones.

This seminal idea was eloquently stated by the English poet and pamphleteer John Milton in his famous pamphlet *Areopagitica* (1644), in which he attacked efforts by the royalist government of England to suppress the printing of writings critical of Charles I and his ministers. Milton argued:

And though all the winds of doctrine were let loose to play upon the earth, so Truth be in the field, we do injuriously, by licensing and prohibiting, to misdoubt her strength. Let her and Falsehood grapple; who ever knew Truth put to worse, in a free and open encounter?...She needs no policies, nor strategems, nor licensings to make her victorious; those are but the shifts and defenses that error uses against her power.[8]

TOTALITARIANISM

A constitutional regime, as we have seen, protects human rights from abridgment by either public officials or private groups. The essence of a totalitarian regime is the government's effort to direct all aspects of all citizens' lives so that they will become the kind of people the nation needs—hard workers, fierce fighters, fecund and uncomplaining mothers, and totally committed, fanatical patriots. Indeed, the very idea that *any* part of a citizen's life is private and therefore not a proper concern of government is morally outrageous and politically subversive.

This philosophy is carried to an imaginative extreme in the society depicted by George Orwell's frightening novel *1984.* Most political scientists believe that the closest approximations to thoroughgoing totalitarian dictatorships in recent years have included Adolf Hitler's Germany, Joseph Stalin's Soviet Union, Mao Zedong's People's Republic of China, Mu'ammar al-Qadaffi's Libya, and the Ayatollah Khomeini's Iran.

Modern totalitarian dictatorships, many observers believe, are twentieth-century inventions quite different from the older forms of authoritarianism, such as the mad despotism of Caligula, the oriental satrapy of Genghis Khan, the renaissance tyranny of Cesare Borgia, and the absolute monarchy of Louis XIV. Each of those premodern autocracies had relatively limited political objectives and made demands only on those aspects of the subjects' lives and thoughts that the dictators thought were necessary to accomplish their goals. But modern totalitarian regimes set no limits on either their objectives or on individual citizens' duty to sacrifice friends, religion, family, and privacy to the leaders' demands.

A leading study has listed the essential characteristics of modern totalitarian regimes:

1. An official ideology covering all aspects of human existence to which every member of the society must adhere, not only by outer form but also by inner conviction.
2. A single mass party, often led by one person and consisting of a relatively small proportion of the total population, which acts as the official ideology's priesthood.
3. A system of terroristic police control making full use of modern technology for spying and surveillance.
4. Nearly complete monopoly of control by the leader and party of all media of mass communication.
5. Nearly complete monopoly of all means of effective armed combat.
6. Central control of the entire economy through bureaucratic coordination of all previously private business organizations.[9]

In strict logic, dictatorship and totalitarianism are as distinct as democracy and constitutionalism. In theory, there could be a totalitarian democracy. (Indeed, it seems to be what advocates of the limited majority-rule position outlined in Chapter 5 seem to fear from unchecked popular majorities.) In fact, however, there is no recorded instance of a government that is both democratic and totalitarian. And, although all totalitarian governments have been dictatorships of the most ruthless sort, some dictatorships, like their ancient and medieval predecessors, are not very totalitarian. Some, indeed, appear to be well characterized by the description of Turkey's Ottoman Empire before the 1920s as "despotism tempered by anarchy." But no one would say that of Stalin's Russia, Hitler's Germany, Qadaffi's Libya, or Khomeini's Iran. The continuing clash between the ideologies of constitutionalism and totalitarianism are thus fought for stakes of great importance and their outcomes have great consequences for the people who live under the ideology that triumphs.

IDEOLOGIES OF ECONOMIC CONTROL

Probably the oldest and most disputed ideological clashes in human history have been over the question of who should have the ultimate power to make government policies, and we will devote Chapter 5 to examining the principal ideologies involved in those clashes.

Probably the second most hotly debated ideological issue in modern politics is the question of what role government should play in the ownership and management of the economy. In most modern nations the debate over this issue has revolved around three main ideologies: *laissez faire* (or, as some mistakenly call it, capitalism), *socialism*, and *modern liberalism*. Let us review each one.

CAPITALISM AND LAISSEZ FAIRE

Some Definitions

As we are using the term in this book, *capitalism* is an economic system, not a political ideology. That is, it is a way of making and distributing goods and services, not a way of making governmental decisions. There is also, however, a political ideology premised on capitalism that is generally called "laissez faire," and that is what we will discuss here.

It is said that Louis XIV's finance minister, Jean Baptiste Colbert (1619–83), once asked a meeting of French entrepreneurs what the state could do to help them. One answered, "Laissez-nous faire!" ("Leave us alone!") He thus gave a name, **laissez faire,** to *the ideology which holds that there should be minimum government intervention in economic affairs.*

All advocates of laissez faire start from the conviction that capitalism is by far the best economic system, and they believe that a capitalist economy will function best if the government confines itself strictly to providing the basic conditions for free economic competition: maintaining law and order, enforcing contracts, protecting private property, and defending the nation against attacks by other nations. Other than that, government should allow free competition among private persons and businesses so that all decisions will be made by market forces and governed only by natural economic laws. Ideally, government should neither hold back the successful nor help the unsuccessful. As Thomas Jefferson put it in his first inaugural address in 1801:

> *A wise and frugal government, which shall restrain men from injuring one another,*
> *which shall leave them otherwise free to regulate their own pursuits of industry and*

Adam Smith. (Source: The Bettmann Archive.)

Friedrich von Hayek. (Source: UPI/Bettmann Newsphotos.)

Milton Friedman. (Source: Austrian Press & Information Service.)

Apostles of Laissez Faire.

improvement, and shall not take from the mouth of labor the bread it has earned. This is the sum of good government, and this is necessary to close the circle of our felicities.[10]

Laissez faire, then, is an application to economic affairs of the doctrine that "that government is best which governs least," which was first proclaimed in the seventeenth and early eighteenth centuries by John Locke and a group of French economists known as the physiocrats. Its most famous and influential exposition was *The Wealth of Nations,* a book published in 1776 by the Scottish economist Adam Smith.

The case for laissez faire may be summarized as follows. Society, like the physical universe, is a rationally designed, orderly mechanism governed by natural laws. These laws of social order can, like the laws of physical order, be discovered by human reason, and some of them—for example, the law that prices in a free market are determined by the interplay of supply and demand—are already well known. A nation that ignores or flouts these laws will encounter economic disaster as surely as a person who ignores and flouts the law of gravity will encounter physical disaster. If government attempts to regulate and restrict economic competition, penalize the efficient and successful, or subsidize the inefficient and unsuccessful, it can only upset the balance of the natural economic system, and the whole nation will be the poorer for it. The best economic policy for government, therefore, is to leave the economy entirely unregulated except by the free market.

Some advocates of laissez faire have carried the doctrine to the logical extreme of anarchy. After all, if that government is best which governs least, then the best government of all must be one that governs not at all. This position was, indeed, advocated by the nineteenth-century British reformer Thomas Hodgskin and the twentieth-century American novelist and essayist Ayn Rand. And the modern American Libertarian party comes quite close to this position, although it stops short of advocating total anarchy.

On the other hand, Adam Smith, like many other champions of laissez faire, was perfectly willing to accept some deviations from the strict hands-off rule. He believed, for example, that government should not let any citizen, no matter how inefficient, starve. He also believed that government should regulate production and consumption in whatever ways are necessary to ensure adequate defense against foreign attack. He added, however, that such deviations can be justified only on humanitarian and nationalistic grounds; from the standpoint of strict *economic* efficiency, they are indefensible and should therefore be undertaken only when absolutely necessary to achieve such noneconomic goals as keeping people from starving and defending the nation against foreign enemies.

SOCIALISM

The Meaning of the Term

The term *socialism* has been widely used in political discourse since the early nineteenth century. Unfortunately, it is like such terms as *democracy* and *freedom* in that, even in a purely descriptive sense, it means different things to different people, and for most it has a high emotional charge. To many people in many parts of the world, *socialism* means equality, justice, the end of exploitation of the poor by the rich, and other equally noble things. To many Americans, on the other hand, *socialism* means government confiscation of property, regimentation of personal life, red tape, inefficiency, coddling the lazy and incompetent, and a lot of other bad things.

In this book, however, **socialism** is used as most political scientists use the term, to denote *an economic system in which the means of production, distribution, and exchange are publicly owned and operated.* So, strictly speaking, the opposite of socialism is **capitalism**—*an economic system in which a society's means of production, distribution, and exchange are privately owned and operated.*

The Case for Socialism

There are several varieties of socialist ideology, and some socialists work harder at denouncing the ideological errors and organizational sins of rival brands of socialism than at attacking laissez-faire capitalism. Despite many,

Karl Marx. (Source: New York Public Library Picture Collection.)

V. I. Lenin. (Source: The Bettmann Archive.)

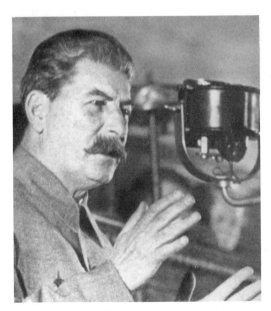

Joseph Stalin. (Source: Sovfoto.)

Mao Zedong. (Source: AP/Wide World Photos.)

Founders of Classical Communism.

and often bitter, disagreements among themselves, however, all socialists have a sufficient number of beliefs in common that we may speak of socialism as one general ideology.

All socialists believe that the main cause of economic suffering and injustice is capitalism's basic institution of **private property:** *the legal right of private persons to exclusive control over the possession and disposition of goods and services.* All socialists, to a greater or lesser degree, argue that the only cure for the evils of capitalist exploitation, fear, and misery is to have most or all of the means of production, distribution, and exchange be owned by society and operated by government. They all propose that the government take over (some say by purchase, others say by confiscation) the "commanding heights" of the economy and distribute economic goods to individuals in accordance with their human needs, not their economic productivity.

Socialism versus Communism

During most of the twentieth century, the main schism in modern socialism has been between socialists and Communists. The main disagreement between them has been over the question of *how* private property should be abolished and government ownership and operation of the economy should be established and maintained.

The socialists—including adherents of such organizations as the British Labour party, the French and American socialist parties, and the West German and Scandinavian Social Democratic parties—place a high value on democracy as well as on socialism. They believe that socialism should be brought about only by such democratic and peaceful means as the organization of socialist political parties, their victory in elections and consequent control of democratic governments, and the peaceful adoption and enforcement of socialist policies. In recent years, indeed, their fervor for the abolition of private property has often yielded to less doctrinaire and more pragmatic programs of piecemeal social reform.

For many decades most Communists have had quite a different view. From its origins in the writings of Karl Marx and Friedrich Engels in the mid-nineteenth century to the death of Leonid Brezhnev in 1965, orthodox Communist doctrine consistently held, first, that true socialism can be established, as it was in Russia in 1917, only by violent revolution and the liquidation of unrepentant capitalists; second, that it can be maintained only through the "dictatorship of the proletariat" established by the monopoly of all political power by a Communist party; and third, that the Soviet Union must be the center, and the Communist Party of the Soviet Union the commander, of the world Communist movement, and all Communist parties and policies in other nations must unquestioningly follow the Soviet leaders' "line." Hence **communism** is usually defined as *a political-economic system in which a single authoritarian party controls the means of production, distribution, and exchange.*

Socialists and Communists have sometimes collaborated with each other against a common enemy, as, for example, in the early years of the government of French Socialist president Francois Mitterand (1981–), but even that alliance was eventually destroyed by bitter disagreements between the two factions). Most of the time socialists and Communists have been in sharp conflict, for each has seen the other as the betrayer of true socialism. Some of the Communists' toughest opponents have been socialists, such as former Chancellor Helmut Schmidt of West Germany, leader of the German Social Democratic party in the 1970s and early 1980s, Hugh Gaitskell, leader of the British Labour party from 1955 to 1963, and eventually, Mitterand himself.

Perestroika and *Glasnost* in Soviet Communism Today

This is the first of several places in this book in which we will consider in some detail the ideology and practice of communism, especially in the Union of Soviet Socialist Republics (USSR) and the People's Republic of China (PRC). In the book's various editions since its initial publication in 1958, I have tried to describe the ideology and practice of communism in those countries in such matters as public opinion, mass communications, political parties, and criminal justice because it was important that readers understand something of the principal adversary to the ideologies and institutions operating in the United States and other Western democracies. And as one edition succeeded another there was little need to make substantial changes in the descriptions of communist ideas and practices in either the USSR or the PRC because they changed very little.

Today that is no longer the case, and it is important to understand that since the mid-1980s, major changes have been taking place in both countries. It is too early to be sure just how far those changes will go in the 1990s and beyond, but we must take account of what has happened so far.

Change began first in China. Under the iron-handed leadership of Mao Zedong, the Communist Party seized control of the country in 1949, and for the next 30 years the PRC adhered rigidly to the doctrines of classical Marxism-Leninism-Stalinism just outlined. After Mao's death in 1976, however, a new group of leaders headed by Deng Xiaoping began to institute a number of sweeping reforms. Most were economic reforms allowing a substantially greater role for private property, individual business enterprise, and economic cooperation with American and other Western business corporations and governments. But there were doctrinal and political changes as well. Public criticism of the content as well as the execution of the Communist Party's policies were allowed far more freely than under Mao, many Chinese students were sent to study in Western universities, and Western scholars, students, and ordinary tourists were allowed to travel freely in China.

In the early 1990s, the PRC is still far from being a political democracy. The Communist Party is still the only legal party; only one Party-approved candidate is allowed to run for each office in elections; and public criticism of the Party's monopoly over public affairs is still out of bounds. But the PRC of today has moved a long way from the communist doctrines of Mao, and most observers think it will move further still.

The changes in the USSR began later but in many respects have gone further. The Communist Party of the Soviet Union (CPSU) took control of the country in 1917, and under the leadership of the charismatic and iron-handed dictators V. I. Lenin (1918–24) and Joseph Stalin (1924–53), the Soviet system featured near-total Party control of the economy, education, communications, art and literature, and all other aspects of society in a system that was called "Marxism-Leninism" or "Stalinism" or simply "communism."

Stalin has had three main successors. Nikita Khrushchev (1958–64) cracked the ice by publicly condemning some of Stalin's more brutal practices and trying to institute some reforms in the USSR's stagnant economy. He was deposed by Leonid Brezhnev (1964–82), who rolled back most of Khrushchev's economic reforms and continued most of the repressive institutions and policies instituted by Lenin and Stalin.

Great changes began in 1985 when Mikhail Gorbachev became the General Secretary of the CPSU and the nation's leader. From the start he made clear his belief that the Soviet economy is disastrously inefficient and unable to produce the goods and services the Soviet people need, and it is falling further and further behind Western economies in its ability to manufacture good products and develop new products. Gorbachev believes that the main reason for this economic failure has been not only the ossified and inefficient economic structure of Stalinism but also the uncreative, unresponsive, and bureaucracy-ridden political institutions that make the economy what it is.

Accordingly, Gorbachev has preached from many platforms a call for changes in both the economic and political systems. His message has two key ideas, which he mentions repeatedly. One is *perestroika* ("restructuring"), which means a need to reconsider all Soviet institutions, economic and political, and reform those that do not work. The other is *glasnost* ("openness"), which means that there should be free public discussion of all aspects of Soviet society as the best way for the leaders and the citizens to find out what is wrong with the system and put it right.

At the present writing the most extraordinary manifestation of *perestroika* and *glasnost* was the 1988 meeting in Moscow of the first general conference of the Communist Party to be held since 1941. Even the most veteran and cynical Kremlin-watchers were astonished by what took place. For the first time in memory, conference delegates lined up at the podium to give fifteen-minute speeches, many of which were highly critical of various aspects of both the economic and political systems. Almost nothing was out of bounds for discussion, including public suggestions that Andrei Gromyko, the 78-year-old president of the country and an old henchman of Stalin, Khrushchev, and Brezhnev, should retire. Even more startling, the debates were broadcast live on national television, and tens of millions of Soviet citizens for the first time in

Architect of *Glasnost* and *Perestroika*. Mikhail Gorbachev.
(Source: Reuters/Bettmann Newsphotos.)

their lives witnessed sharp disagreement and debate among their leaders. As one citizen put it to a Western reporter, "I am hearing things on television that weeks ago I would never have whispered over the telephone."[11]

Gorbachev proposed, and the conference approved, a number of sweeping changes in the structure of the government's legislative and executive agencies. We will consider these changes in some detail in later chapters, but the point to note here is that there is today such ferment in both the PRC and the USSR that a good deal of what most Western political scientists, including me, have been saying about the ideology and institutions of communism is already out of date and may become more so. No one knows, of course, whether Gorbachev can get his reforms adopted or even how long he can remain in power. Perhaps most important of all, no one knows whether his reforms will produce the economic benefits by which ordinary Soviet citizens will ultimately judge their desirability.

One thing is clear, however: Things have already changed a great deal in the ideology and institutions of the Soviet Union and the PRC, and we must take account of them not only here but in the chapters to come.

POLITICAL IDEOLOGIES, AMERICAN STYLE

Many foreign America-watchers believe that the United States has no doctrinal disagreements worthy of being called "ideological cleavages." They correctly point out that public opinion polls show that only tiny fractions of our people are Socialists or Communists or Fascists. On all the great ideological questions of the twentieth century, they say, Americans are almost unanimous: We believe in capitalism instead of socialism, constitutionalism instead of totalitarianism, and democracy instead of oligarchy or autocracy. Above all, some say, Americans believe most of all in **pragmatism:** *the philosophy that judges institutions and policies by whether they work.* This philosophy was developed in the early twentieth century by the American philosophers William James and John Dewey and its essence was succinctly put by James:

> *The pragmatic method . . . is to try to interpret each notion by tracing its respective political consequences. What difference would it practically make to anyone if this notion rather than that notion were true? If no practical differences whatever can be traced, then the alternatives mean practically the same thing, and all dispute is idle.*[12]

Most Americans, however, would not agree that there is *no* ideological conflict in American politics. Judging from what we read in the newspapers, see on television, and hear in our classrooms and personal conversations, there is a very important cleavage in American politics between an ideology called *liberalism* and an opposing ideology called *conservatism.*

Accordingly, I will set aside the question of whether American liberalism and conservatism in the 1990s have the sharply opposed sets of values, visions of the ideal polity, conceptions of how the world works, consistent programs of actions, and concerted tactics set forth earlier as the defining characteristics of full-fledged ideologies, and outline what I think Americans mean when they use the two terms.

MODERN AMERICAN LIBERALISM

As we have already noted, one of the confusing things about the word *liberalism* is that, in the twentieth-century United States, it has come to mean something quite different from what it meant in Europe in the eighteenth and nineteenth centuries. The earlier "classical" liberalism was what some scholars have called "negative liberalism": That is, it was a philosophy that sought to liberate individual human beings from the economic, political, religious, and moral shackles by which they had been bound through centuries of absolute monarchs, feudal economies, and official religions. As Roger H. Soltau summed it up:

> *Originally to be free was not to be a slave, to have legal guaranteed control over one's person, and this is still its essential meaning. To be free is not to be prevented from doing what one wants to do, and not being forced to do what one dislikes doing. Any limitation of this two-fold power is an interference with freedom, however excellent its motives, however necessary its action.*[13]

In the 1930s, however, Franklin D. Roosevelt and his New Deal followers argued that in the twentieth century, true liberalism must become "positive liberalism." It is meaningless, they declared, to guarantee people's freedom of speech and religion if they cannot feed their families or get a decent education or have good health. Thus true liberalism must not only prevent government from interfering with people's basic liberties; it must also require government to act positively to protect people against life's worst economic and physical vicissitudes so that they can be free to enjoy their intellectual liberties.

New Deal liberals argued that these protections should be guaranteed by converting the old do-nothing state into a **welfare state**—*a system in which the government guarantees to every citizen the minimum conditions of a decent life.* Since the 1930s, liberals have argued that every citizen is entitled to the minimum conditions of a decent life as a matter of right and justice, and no citizens should be denied them because they cannot finance them themselves— even less because their parents cannot finance them. Liberals do not all agree, of course, on the exact type and level of benefits that ought to be guaranteed. Some, for example, would include complete medical care "from the womb to the tomb," whereas others would include only hospitalization insurance. Some would include free public education for qualified students from kindergarten right through the Ph.D. degree, whereas others would limit the guarantee to the high school diploma. All welfare-state advocates agree, however, that the proper function of government is to provide every citizen with *some* degree of formal education and medical care even if it requires—as it usually does—that the rich be taxed to provide benefits for the poor.

In noneconomic matters, most modern liberals continue the traditions of individual freedom and choice cherished by their nineteenth-century forebears by holding that government intervention in people's moral, religious, and intellectual lives should be kept to an absolute minimum. For example, liberals generally hold that government should maintain an absolute separation between church and state. It should not in any way favor one religion over another or religion-in-general over atheism or agnosticism; hence any kind of organized prayer should not be allowed in any public school's curriculum. For another example, liberals believe that it is every woman's right to decide for herself whether she will have an abortion to prevent the birth of an unwanted child, and that government should not interfere with that right (see the discussion in Chapter 1). For yet another example, liberals contend that government should not decide what people can read in books and magazines and see on television or at the movies; hence there should be no suppression of pornography or any other form of expression. And for a final example, liberals hold that people's sexual preferences are entirely their own private business, and government should in no way try to dissuade them from homosexuality or lesbianism; nor should it penalize people who have such preferences.

Finally, modern liberalism has a strong strain of *egalitarianism;* that is, liberals generally believe that, while some differences in people's achievements and statuses are probably inevitable, they should be kept as small as possible. For example, most liberals believe that government action to prevent white male majorities from discriminating against women, African-Americans, and other minorities, while desirable, is not enough. We must make up for the discrimination practiced against minorities in the past, and to that end government must impose "affirmative action" rules for employment and "comparable worth" rules for determining salaries (see Chapter 16). For another example, liberals believe that taxes should be progressive; that is, persons with higher incomes should pay higher percentages of their incomes than people with lower incomes. Not only is this fairer than taxing everyone at the same rate, but it helps to redistribute income from the rich to the poor, which is one of the main purposes of taxation. Also, while liberals do not love taxes for their own sake, they feel that taxes must be kept high enough to fund welfare-state benefits at decent levels.

In short, modern American liberalism favors considerable government intervention in people's economic affairs and minimum intervention in their moral, religious, and intellectual affairs.

MODERN AMERICAN CONSERVATISM

Modern American conservatism resembles modern American liberalism in that it constitutes a considerable revision of certain European ideas of the eighteenth and nineteenth centuries. Traditional conservatism (in Great Britain it was called *Toryism)* meant conserving society's traditional values and institutions against the radical changes urged by the classical liberals. Nineteenth-century conservatives believed that society should be run, as it had always been run, by royalty and the aristocracy rather than by the newly rising business class, and that it was the obligation of the upper classes (called *noblesse oblige)* to make sure that factory workers and farm laborers were secure in their jobs and that their moral lives were guided by religion and traditional values, not left to the anything-goes laxity advocated by such liberals as John Stuart Mill. The good society was one in which each person was, by tradition and perhaps even by divine plan, given a particular place in the social hierarchy; everyone "knew his place"; and aristocrats and peasants alike took pleasure in meeting the obligations, as well as enjoying the benefits, of their particular places.

Conservatism meant substantially the same thing in the United States until the 1930s, when the label came to be applied to all the people who for various reasons opposed the New Deal and its welfare-state philosophy. In the 1990s, American conservatism includes two distinct, sometimes even divergent, themes:

Economic Laissez Faire. Almost all conservatives follow the lead of such economists as Milton Friedman and Friedrich von Hayek in arguing that government should regulate private business minimally or not at all. It should enforce the basic rules of free competition by enforcing contracts and preserving private property, but it should neither limit the winners' profits nor ease the losers' losses. Creative and dynamic people develop and market new and appealing products so that they can make money. If they are allowed freedom of enterprise, they will improve old businesses, form new businesses, and thereby create jobs and prosperity for others. But when they are hampered by government regulations and their success is penalized by high taxes, investment dwindles, production drops, and jobs vanish. So the first object should be to "get the government off people's backs."

Preserving Traditional Moral and Religious Values. Unlike classical liberalism, modern conservatism does not mean minimum government interference in all aspects of people's lives. Quite the contrary. Such evangelical Christian conservatives as the Reverend Jerry Falwell and the Reverend Jimmy Swaggart believe that government's highest obligation is to make sure that all aspects of Americans' lives are guided by traditional American values and institutions, such as stable marriages and families, parental authority over children, regular church attendance, monogamous sexual relations and heterosexual practices, and clean and decent magazines, movies, and television. Hence government has not only the right but the duty to require children to pray as part of their regular public school curriculum. Government has the right and duty to prohibit abortions except, perhaps, where absolutely necessary to save the mother's life. It has the right and duty to make sure that pornographic magazines, movies, and television are prohibited or at least kept from children. Some conservatives say that government also has the right and duty to deny jobs, especially in education, to persons with deviant sexual beliefs and practices.

In short, modern American conservatism favors minimum government intervention in people's economic affairs and considerable intervention in their moral, religious, and intellectual affairs.

However, on what many political scientists believe is the most important ideological cleavage of the twentieth century or any other time—the conflict between democracy and other forms of government—almost all Americans, liberals and conservatives alike, are on the same side. We turn next to an examination of that cleavage.

FOR FURTHER READING

ON IDEOLOGIES IN GENERAL

HAGOPIAN, MARK N. *Ideals and Ideologies of Modern Politics.* New York: Longman, 1985. A short introduction to modern ideologies, with special emphasis on their European intellectual roots.

HOOVER, KENNETH R. *Ideology and Political Life,* 2nd ed. New York: Brooks/Cole, 1987. A survey of modern ideologies and their role in political life.

*MACRIDIS, ROY C. *Contemporary Political Ideolo-* gies, 4th ed. Glenview, IL: Scott, Foresman/Little, Brown, 1988. A useful introduction to the main ideologies of our time.

McLELLAN, DAVID. *Ideology.* Minneapolis: University of Minnesota Press, 1986. Analysis of the concept of ideology and its role in modern politics.

RIFF, M. A. *Dictionary of Modern Political Ideologies.* New York: St. Martin's Press, 1988. Brief summaries of leading political ideologies.

CONSTITUTIONALISM AND TOTALITARIANISM

ARENDT, HANNA. *The Origins of Totalitarianism.* New York: Meridian, 1958. Influential philosophical analysis of totalitarianism.

FRIEDRICH, CARL J., and Zbnigniew Brzezinski. *Totalitarian Dictatorship and Autocracy,* 2nd ed. Cambridge, MA: Harvard University Press, 1965. Analysis of ideas and institutions in both Fascist and Communist dictatorships.

*MCILWAIN, CHARLES H. *Constitutionalism, Ancient and Modern.* Ithaca, NY: Cornell University Press, 1958. The classic study of the history of the idea of limited government.

*MILL, JOHN STUART. *On Liberty.* London: Penguin, 1982. Modern edition of a classic nineteenth-century defense of the idea of limited government.

CAPITALISM, SOCIALISM, AND COMMUNISM

BOWLES, SAMUEL, and Herbert Gintle. *Democracy and Capitalism.* New York: Basic Books, 1986. Analysis of the ideologies of democracy, liberalism, and Marxism.

*FRIEDMAN, MILTON. *Capitalism and Freedom.* Chicago: University of Chicago Press, 1981. Argument by a Nobel Laureate in economics that a free capitalist economy is the basis for civil liberties.

*HARRINGTON, MICHAEL. *The Twilight of Capitalism.* New York: Touchstone, 1977. Case for socialism put by today's leading American socialist theorist.

*HAYEK, FRIEDRICH A. *The Road to Serfdom.* Chicago: University of Chicago Press, 1956. Influ-ential statement of the view that economic freedom is the basis for all other freedoms.

HOWE, IRVING. *Socialism in America.* New York: Harcourt Brace Jovanovich, 1985. A leading American socialist's presentation of the case for socialism.

MARX, KARL. *Capital,* 3 volumes. New York: International Publishers, 1967. A recent edition of the fountainhead of "scientific socialism" and modern communism.

*MILIBAND, RALPH. *The State in Capitalist Society.* New York: Basic Books, 1978. Critique of governing institutions in capitalist democracies by a leading British Marxist.

AMERICAN LIBERALISM AND CONSERVATISM

*GRAY, JOHN. *Liberalism.* Minneapolis: University of Minnesota Press, 1986. A survey of modern American liberal ideas and policies.

KIRK, RUSSELL. *The Conservative Mind,* 6th ed. Chi-cago: Henry Regnery, 1986. Survey of the intellectual roots and present doctrines of American liberalism by one of its foremost advocates.

*NISBET, ROBERT. *Conservatism: Dream and Reality.* Minneapolis: University of Minnesota Press, 1986. Survey of the main strands of contemporary conservative ideology by a distinguished social theorist.

NOZICK, ROBERT. *Anarchy, State, and Utopia.* New York: Basic Books, 1977. Influential statement of minimum- government position.

*RAWLS, JOHN. *Theory of Justice.* Cambridge, MA: Belknap Press of Harvard University Press, 1971. Much-discussed argument for social and economic equality as the proper goal of society and government.

NOTES

[1]Two experts on American English usage say that *"Ism* is a suffix, forming a noun of action. In addition to this it came to indicate the name of a system, whether in practice or theory. . . . When the suffix was detached to become a word in itself, denoting some unspecified system or peculiarity, it connoted scorn and disparagement *(God knows what ism he's embraced now. I can't keep track of 'em)."* Bergen Evans and Cornelia Evans, *A Dictionary of Contemporary American Usage* (New York: Random House, 1957, p. 257.

[2]Roy C. Macridis, *Contemporary Political Ideologies* (Glenview, IL: Scott, Foresman/Little, Brown, 1988), Chapter 1.

[3]The reader will often encounter the term **polity** in these pages. I use it, as most political scientists do, to mean *a politically organized society*—that is, a society with some kind of government.

[4]For reasons set forth later in this chapter, it is necessary to distinguish the ideology of "classical liberalism" or "nineteenth-century liberalism" from the kind of "modern liberalism" that competes with "conservatism" in modern American politics.

[5]John Locke, *Two Treatises of Civil Government* (London: J. M. Dent, 1924), p. 180. Regrettably, Locke, like other seventeenth-century philosophers, used the term *men* as synonymous with the term *people.*

[6]*Ibid.,* p. 229.

[7]From the Universal Declaration of Human Rights, which is reprinted in the *UNESCO Courier,* December 1963, pp. 16–17.

[8]John Milton, *Areopagitica and Other Prose Works,* (London: J. M. Dent, 1927), pp. 36–37.

[9]Carl J. Friedrich and Zbigniew Brzezinski, *Totalitarian Dictatorship and Autocracy,* 2nd ed. (Cambridge, MA: Harvard University Press, 1965), pp. 9–10.

[10]*The Works of Thomas Jefferson,* ed. by Paul Leicester Ford (New York: Putnam's, 1905), vol. 9, p. 197.

[11]Quoted in *Time,* July 11, 1988, p. 29.

[12]William James, *Pragmatism* (New York: Meridian, 1959), p. 42.

[13]Roger H. Soltau, *An Introduction to Politics* (New York: Longman, 1951), p. 127.

5 Models of Democracy and Authoritarianism

For the first time in the history of the world, no doctrines are advanced as antidemocratic. The accusation of antidemocratic action or attitude is frequently directed against others, but practical politicians and political theorists agree in stressing the democratic element in the institutions they defend and the theories they advocate. This acceptance of democracy as the highest form of political or social organization is the sign of a basic agreement in the ultimate aims of modern social and political institutions. . . .[1]

Italian Fascism is the realization of true democracy.

Benito Mussolini

Germany under National Socialism is the most ennobled form of a modern democratic state.

Joseph Goebbels

People's democracies are new, higher forms of democracy as compared to the old, bourgeois-parliamentarian democracy.[2]

It would appear from the foregoing statements that just about everyone in the world "believes in" democracy. Fascists believe in it. Communists believe in it. Conservatives believe in it. Liberals believe in it. Only a handful of old-fashioned absolute monarchs like King Fahd of Saudi Arabia and the Sultan of Oman scorn to call their regimes democratic.

But what do these statements mean? Nothing more, really, than the fact that the *word* "democracy" arouses strongly positive emotions in most people, who apparently find it psychologically necessary to claim the label for whatever set of political institutions they prefer. Many, indeed, insist that *only* the particular set of institutions they favor are truly "democratic."

Some political observers are not impressed by the near-universal popularity of "democracy." Instead, they are appalled by the fact that it seems to be "a kind of conceptual Gladstone bag which, with a little manipulation, can be made to accommodate almost any collection of social facts we may wish to carry about in it."[3] Most political scientists, however, believe that, whether we like it or not, the word is here to stay and will continue to play an important part in talk about politics. Accordingly, perhaps the best we can do is to identify its principal meanings and specify which one we are using. In this book the term will be used in constructing models of democracy and authoritarianism that will help us to compare and contrast actual governments. We begin by considering the nature and uses of models in social science.

THE NATURE AND USES OF MODELS IN SOCIAL SCIENCE

MEANING

Modern social scientists use intellectual models as tools to help them understand the complexities of the real world. Among these tools are *semantical models*. And as the term is used in this chapter, each **semantical model** of democracy and authoritarianism is *an intellectual construct of a government organized in perfect accord with a particular principle*. Perhaps the best-known example of a semantical model is one widely used in economic analysis: the model of the free market. The free market is a mental picture of an economic system in which all exchange takes place through free bargaining between sellers and buyers in the marketplace, the only motive influencing human behavior is the universal desire to buy cheap and sell dear, and the price of any commodity or service is determined solely by the interplay of supply and demand.

Now, everyone, including economists, knows that no actual economic system has ever operated in perfect accordance with free-market principles. People are in fact influenced by many motives other than their desire to buy cheap and sell dear—for example, their desire to be in fashion. Furthermore, sellers often agree among themselves to set prices at certain levels regardless of supply and demand so that every seller can make a larger profit than would be possible under conditions of unrestricted competition; and every nation's government interferes to some degree with the free interplay of supply and demand.

USES

Why, then, do economists talk about the free- market economy when no such thing has ever existed in pure form? The answer is that they find it useful in isolating certain aspects of actual economies and studying them apart from all other aspects. To illustrate: Economists ask, "If an economy *were* organized as a perfect free market, what would be the effect on prices of variations in supply and demand?" They then observe what actually happens in a real economy when supply or demand changes. The difference between the effects they predict on the basis of the model and the effects they actually observe gives them a rough measure of the actual nature and influence of supply and demand relative to other factors.

Using models is thus one way in which social scientists can achieve something comparable to the results that physical scientists obtain through controlled experiments. Chemists in their laboratories, for example, can hold certain variables[4] (such as molecular structure, volume, weight, and density) constant, vary another (such as temperature), and then observe the outcome. Changes in the results, they conclude, are caused by changes in the particular variable under inspection, for all the others have been held constant. Economists, however, cannot manipulate human economies in this fashion. But they can *imagine* what would happen in a free-market economy when supply is increased, and by comparing the two sets of results increase our understanding of the operation and influence of supply and demand relative to other factors.

NORMATIVE AND DESCRIPTIVE MODELS OF GOVERNMENT

In ordinary conversation we often use the word *model* to mean something worthy of imitation, an ideal to live up to. "He is a model boy" or "Her paper is a model of how to write an examination." Social scientists call this the *normative* use of the term, for it equates the model with good and its opposite with bad.

However, in this discussion we are using the term in a purely *descriptive* sense: It means simply an idea of what a government would be like if it were totally democratic or totally authoritarian. Most of us no doubt believe that governments *should* follow the democratic model. Fine—but that moral belief should not cloud our factual observations that some governments *do* follow the authoritarian model rather than the democratic model.

COMPARING POLITICAL REALITY WITH A MODEL

Let us see how a model can be used to understand and evaluate some aspect of political reality. One essential principle of the model of democracy outlined later in this chapter is political equality, defined in the model as equal access to political power for every member of the community. The model requires that each adult citizen must have the same right to vote as every other adult citizen, and each vote must count for as much as every other vote.

So much for the model; now for the reality. In the American states before 1962, most legislatures were elected from districts of widely varying populations. In Vermont, for example, each town, regardless of its population, elected one state representative. The town of Stratton, with 24 inhabitants, elected one legislator, and so did the city of Burlington, with 35,531 inhabitants. Thus each Strattonite's share of the power to determine the legislature's membership was 1,480 times greater than that of each Burlingtonian! In California the smallest state-senatorial district had a population of 14,294 and the largest had 6,038,771—that is, 422 times as many people. Comparable disparities existed in most other states.

In a series of decisions from 1962 to the present, however, the U.S. Supreme Court has considered whether or not such disparities are consistent with the principle of political equality and has decided that they are not. It has also considered the constitutional-normative question of whether or not such disparities should be eliminated in obedience to the requirement of the Fourteenth Amendment that "no State shall . . . deny to any person within its jurisdiction the equal protection of the laws" and has decided that the disparities must be abolished. The political equality part of the model, then, has provided both a benchmark for measuring aspects of reality and a goal for political change.

Matters become more complicated, however, when we use models to classify actual governments.

SPECTRUM CLASSIFICATION OF ACTUAL GOVERNMENTS

One more problem remains. If no actual government fully measures up to a particular model, how can we legitimately call any such government democratic or authoritarian? The answer is simple. If we think in terms of two mutually exclusive categories—democracies (all governments that completely correspond to our model in every detail) and nondemocracies (governments that in one or more respects fall short of the model)—then all the governments in the world have to be placed in the nondemocracy category. But if we think in terms of a *spectrum,* we can quite legitimately describe some actual governments as more democratic than others, as pictured in Figure 5.1.

The familiar categories of "rich" and "poor" illustrate the principle of spectrum classification. We all use these categories every day, and nobody thinks that we are talking nonsense when we call this person poor and that person rich. Yet consider for a moment the reasoning underlying these classifications. We could rank each person in the United States in increasing order of net worth. We could agree that those at the top of the list were rich and those at the bottom were poor. But exactly where would we draw the line between rich and poor? At $10,000? If so, would we say that a person worth $9,999.99 was poor and that acquiring one more penny would make that person rich? Clearly not. Yet the lack of an arithmetically precise dividing line between the categories should not prevent us from using the categories at all. They are, to be sure, gross categories, in the sense that they are not as precisely defined as

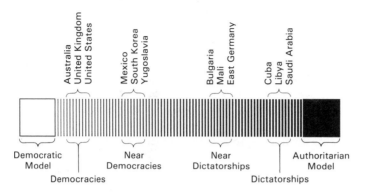

FIGURE 5.1. Spectrum classification of democracies.

those in mathematics, but most of us find them useful all the same, particularly in describing people at the two extremes of the spectrum. If your net worth is $1,000,000, you are rich; if it is $1,000, you are poor; if it is, say, $50,000, you are somewhere in between.

This same kind of reasoning, with all its advantages and limitations, underlies the classification and labeling of actual governments in this book. Our spectrum may be shown graphically as in Figure 5.1. But how do we construct such a spectrum and decide which nation belongs where on it? Essentially, we begin by fixing one extreme of the scale with a particular model of democracy—a mental picture of what a government would be like if it were organized in complete and perfect accordance with what we regard as the quintessential principles of democracy. Some writers also fix the opposite extreme with a model of authoritarianism—a mental picture of what a government would be like if one or a few persons had exclusive control of all government machinery and policies. When the spectrum is thus anchored, we ascertain as best we can how each actual government measures up to the principles of our model of democracy or authoritarianism. From these data we can compile a "score" for each government and place it on the spectrum relative to the scores assigned to other governments.

Several social scientists have ranked the "democratic-ness" of actual governments by such procedures. One attempt was made by Arthur K. Smith, Jr., in 1969. He combined the scores of 110 nations on each of 19 variables measuring various aspects of his model of democracy with their scores on an index of stability and change in democratic institutions during the period from 1946 to 1965. The composite scores enabled him to rank nations from the most democratic (Australia, New Zealand, Denmark, and Norway) to the least democratic (Afghanistan, Sudan, Laos, and Libya).[5] Smith's rankings did not correspond exactly with those of other scholars, and a number of nations (for example, Spain and Portugal) have become much more democratic since 1965. The point is that the differences between Smith's rankings and rankings by other scholars arise from differences in the models used as well as differences in the facts about the countries ranked.

Whether a particular government is called democratic or authoritarian thus depends largely upon the model against which it is assessed. And, as we will see, there are plenty to choose from.

COMPETING MODELS OF DEMOCRACY

We began this chapter by noting that whatever comfort we might gain from knowing that nearly everyone in the world "believes in" democracy is likely to evaporate when we recognize the endless confusion and disagreement about what democracy is. Despite this semantic mess, however, it seems unlikely that the word will disappear from political talk. Thus it may help if we at least try to understand what others mean by it—and make clear to others what we mean when we use it. Before outlining this book's particular model of democracy, let me briefly review some of the leading alternatives.

THE COMMUNIST MODEL OF LENIN, STALIN, AND MAO

We noted in Chapter 4 that in recent years great changes have been taking place in the political thinking and institutions of many communist nations, particularly the PRC under Deng Xiaoping and the USSR under Mikhail Gorbachev. It is too early to tell what permanent changes will be made in the prevailing conceptions of democracy in either country; but they may well be significantly different from the conception that prevailed in the two countries and their satellites during most of the twentieth century under the ideas of V. I. Lenin, Joseph Stalin, and Mao Zedong. It is the older conception we will outline here.

Disciples of Marxism-Leninism-Stalinism insisted that only the Soviet Union and the "people's democracies," whose regimes were modeled on the Soviet Union's, were true democracies. They were aware, of course, that most of us in the West regard the regimes of nations like Norway, Switzerland, and Sweden as democratic, but they insisted that all such non-Communist regimes are merely false fronts erected by capitalists to conceal the naked realities of their exploitation of the toiling masses.

The core of the traditional Communist conception was the conviction that true democracy is a regime in which government advances the *real* interests and welfare of the masses; that is, government does what is "objectively" good for the masses whether the masses want it or not. Accordingly, democracy is essentially a matter of what government does, not of how government decides what to do. It is a government *for* the people (the workers) but not necessarily government *by* the people. From the old Communist point of view, the kind of spectrum between democracy and authoritarianism shown in Figure 5.1 is meaningless: To Stalinists and Maoists, dictatorship was not the opposite of democracy; it was a necessary means for achieving democracy.

The pre-Gorbachev model of democracy did, however, have a few procedural elements worth noting. One was the notion of the Communist party as "the vanguard of the proletariat." During the present stage of historical development, it was held, the highly trained and dedicated elite of the party knows far better than the masses what is best for them and how to achieve it. To permit freedom of organization and expression for non- or anti-Communist opponents of party policies—and, even worse, to allow them to run candidates against those approved by the party—would, by definition, be undemocratic. It would allow "capitalist exploiters," "imperialist saboteurs," "deviationist adventurers," and other enemies of communism to sabotage the party's programs and therefore the masses' welfare. The regime therefore permitted only one political party to exist—the Communist party; it allowed only one party-approved candidate to run for each elective office; and it suppressed all forms of opposition to the Communist system and the party's policies. All these institutions—one-party rule and the suppression of opposition—were, in the Stalinist-Maoist view, the only truly democratic modes of conducting government, for anything else might permit the adoption of policies that would work against the welfare of the masses.

Soviet leaders from Lenin to Brezhnev were well aware, of course, that their policies could be truly effective only if they had the masses' enthusiastic support. Mere sullen, foot-dragging acquiescence would cripple any policy, however enlightened. Accordingly, the Stalinist system included devices for discovering the masses' reactions to party policies and for whipping up mass approval and enthusiasm. But that did not alter the fact that while the welfare of the toiling masses remained the government's proclaimed paramount end, decisions about what measures would best achieve that end remained strictly the monopoly of the Communist party.

There was a Maoist variation on these Stalinist themes. In the 1950s and 1960s, Mao Zedong and his disciples made increasingly bitter attacks on their former Soviet comrades. These attacks did not reflect any explicit Chinese departure from the principles of Marxism-Leninism. The main cause of their quarrel with the Soviets, they said, was the desertion by the Russians of true Communist principles. Consequently, the Maoist model of democracy was very similar to the Soviet version.

There were, however, a few differences in language and emphasis. The most noteworthy was the Maoist doctrine of the "mass line"—the integration of the party's leadership with the physical power of the masses in order to build true communism. The mass line was said to involve a two-way interaction: leadership by the party's cadres in farm, village, city, and factory to mobilize, inspire, and energize the masses to do what the party had decided must be done; and sensitivity of the party, through its cadres, to the masses' aspirations and feelings.

But in Mao's China, as in Stalin's Russia, the question of who should decide what is best for the masses was clearly answered by Chairman Mao himself:

> *All the experience the Chinese people have accumulated through several decades teaches us to enforce the people's democratic dictatorship, that is, to deprive the reactionaries of the right to speak and let the people alone have that right. . . . To sum up our experience and concentrate it into one point, it is: the people's democratic dictatorship under the leadership of the working class (through the Communist Party) and based upon the alliance of workers and peasants.*[6]

And a Western scholar adds:

> *The masses, the Communists [held], are not as farseeing as the vanguard, the masses are more contaminated by reactionary ideologies and counter-revolutionary elements. . . . The ordinary Chinese, Mao implied, have neither the duty to create the mass line relationship nor the right to reject it. They cannot turn against the vanguard because they cannot reverse the tide of their own historical movement which creates the vanguard.*[7]

NON-COMMUNIST MODELS

The non-Communist world has never had a single model of democracy to set against the Leninist-Stalinist model and its Maoist variant. Rather, there have been and still are several non-Communist models, no one of which has won, or is likely to win, universal acceptance as the one with the only rightful claim to the label "democracy." These models share significant areas of agreement, but they are sufficiently different to warrant brief separate descriptions of the two most influential.

The Participatory Model

Most present-day political theorists believe that widespread direct popular participation in day-to-day government is impossible in modern nations, all of which include millions of people. Some theorists argue, however, that a valid model of democracy must provide for the maximum possible degree of direct popular participation. The basic moral purpose for which democracy exists is to develop the potential of every person in the community to its fullest. The only way to work toward this goal is to encourage maximum participation by all the people in the making of all the decisions, public and private, that affect their lives. Anything less demeans their humanity and cripples their intellectual and moral growth.

But how can such participation be brought about? For one thing, these theorists reply, a true democracy should permit and encourage greater popular participation in smaller nongovernmental decision-making bodies, such as political parties, labor unions, neighborhood associations, small businesses, schools, and churches. In addition, it should delegate a larger share of public

A town meeting in New England. (Source: Robert Houser/Photo Researchers.)

A cantonal meeting in Switzerland. (Source: Paolo Koch/Photo Researchers.)

Direct Democracy.

power to government units small enough to permit effective and meaningful mass participation in decision making, such as small municipalities and neighborhoods within big cities.

Many other devices are also needed, these theorists say, but the first and most important step is to recognize that the development of people is the best way to achieve participation. When people generally understand and accept these basic principles, they can get on with the lesser technical job of thinking up new and better means for increasing popular participation.

The Accountable-Elites Model

Most, though not all, social scientists agree that, as a matter of observed fact, in almost no human organization do all members participate all the time with equal energy, commitment, and influence. In every organization a few members are more committed, more willing to work, more likely to take initiative, and as a result more likely to have influence than the more passive majority. Social scientists usually speak of an organization's **elite** as *people* *who are most interested, active, and influential in making an organization's decisions.*

Does the prevalence of influential elites in human groups mean that democracy is impossible? Not at all, say some political theorists. The essence of democracy lies not in the absence of elites but in the popular control of elites. In their model, control is exercised through the *competition* of elites for office and power, popular *selection* of the winners by the people in periodic elections, *limitations* on the power that any elite can exercise while in office, and *removal* of the incumbent elite whenever it fails to perform to the people's satisfaction—in short, through the *accountability* of the elite in power at the moment to the people.

To these theorists, a properly organized representative and accountable government is in principle every bit as democratic as the participatory kind. Rather than wasting our energies in hopeless searches for ways to bring about universal popular participation in modern governments, they say, we should focus on the more fruitful quest for ways of establishing effective popular control of such governments. Town-meeting democracy may be a fine model for the small city-state of ancient Athens, the rural cantons of Switzerland, or the small towns of New England, but the accountable-elites model is equally democratic and a good deal more appropriate for a modern nation.

PRINCIPLES FOR A WORKING DEFINITION OF DEMOCRACY

We are about to consider the basic principles of the working definition of democracy we will use in this book. Before we do, let us recognize that neither science nor logic can prove that any particular conception of democracy (including the one set forth here) is the only correct one—that is, the one to which all people must adhere if they are not to be considered irrational or immoral. The proper meaning of *democracy,* like that of any other word, depends upon the degree to which it is generally understood and accepted. Let us further recognize that many people, both non-Communists and Communists, do not use *democracy* in exactly the same sense in which I use it here.

Recognizing these differences does not, however, exempt us from the obligation to select a particular definition. The term *democracy* cannot be avoided in discussing certain aspects of governing. Throughout this book we consider the political and governmental agencies and processes of "the democracies"— the nations that cluster toward the model-democracy end of a spectrum such as the one shown in Figure 5.1. Our analysis of modern government is likely to be clearer and more useful if we understand from the outset what the model includes and why it has been chosen over others. But I certainly do not insist that this particular conception is the only one that is logically possible or morally permissible.

As the term is used in the book, **democracy** is a *form of government organized in accordance with the principles of popular sovereignty, political equality, popular consultation, and majority rule.* In order to understand the definition, let us briefly examine what is involved in each of its four principles.[8]

POPULAR SOVEREIGNTY

Briefly stated, the principle of **popular sovereignty** requires that *the ultimate power to make political decisions is vested in all the people rather than in some of them or one of them.* This principle, which is the nucleus of the conception of democracy outlined here, has several major aspects.

Sovereignty: The Ultimate Decision-Making Power

Political scientists have long argued about the proper meaning and usefulness of the concept of sovereignty. For our purposes it is unnecessary to summarize or take sides in this debate. As we will see in Chapter 17, one characteristic of any modern nation that sets it apart from all other forms of political organization is that it is sovereign; that is, it has the full and exclusive legal power to make and enforce laws for the people within its territory and under its jurisdiction. And in every sovereign nation the ultimate power over its political decisions is located somewhere in its political-governmental structure. In a democracy it must be vested in all the people, not in one of them or a small group of them.

Vestment in the People

The principle of popular sovereignty does not logically require that all the people directly make all the daily decisions of government. Democracy does not require that every dog license and every parking ticket be issued only when all adult citizens specifically and individually consent to it—any more than a dictatorship requires that the dictator must personally issue every license and ticket. The people in a democracy, like the dictator in a dictatorship, may lend, or "delegate," part of their decision-making power to legislators, executives, administrators, judges, or anyone else they wish. The people are sovereign as long as they, and not their delegates, have the *ultimate* power—the final word beyond which there is no appeal—to decide which decision-making powers they will keep for themselves and which they will delegate to whom, under what conditions of accountability, and for what periods of time.

"The People" = All Adult Citizens

If democracy means government by the people, then we may reasonably ask, who are "the people"? Are they, for instance, all persons physically present within the nation's borders at a given moment—including infants, aliens, lunatics, criminals in prison, and so on? I have implied an answer to this question by stating that in a democracy, power rests in all adult citizens rather than in all persons who happen to be around.

The criteria for determining who may share in this power are thus citizenship and adulthood. As we will see in Chapter 17, every nation distinguishes between the people who are its citizens and the people who are not. In Chapter 8 we will note that every nation requires its citizens to attain a minimum age (most commonly, age 18) before they can vote. No one argues that it is undemocratic for, say, Denmark to exclude 6-month-old infants or citizens of the United States from voting or holding office in Denmark. Some may feel that the minimum age should be lower (or higher) than 18, and it is said that some Europeans feel that they should have a right to vote in U.S. presidential elections, since who is president of the United States is more important for their well-being than who is prime minister of their own countries! But these are quarrels about the applications of the principle; no one argues that everyone in the world should vote in the elections of every nation.

Sovereignty of All the People

When ultimate power is vested in one person, the government is a dictatorship. When it is vested in a few persons, they constitute a ruling elite, and the government is what political scientists call an oligarchy or aristocracy. Only when it is vested in all the people is the government a democracy.

POLITICAL EQUALITY

The second principle of democratic government, **political equality,** requires that *each adult citizen has the same opportunity as every other adult citizen to participate in the political decision-making process.* This principle clearly means "one person, one vote," but it includes other matters as well. For instance, all citizens of the Soviet Union over age 18 have the legally guaranteed right to vote, but they have never had true political equality. The fact that up to now they have been allowed to vote for only one Communist-approved candidate for each office has deprived them of genuine choice. Their right to vote, accordingly, has carried with it no real power over political decisions. Thus the Soviet Union has until recently embodied the principle stated by George Orwell in *Animal Farm:* "All animals are equal, but some animals are more equal than others." Certainly the Communist party leaders who have chosen the candidates are "more equal" than ordinary Soviet citizens, who have been able only to rubber-stamp the official candidates or, at some risk, "scratch" their ballots.

Political equality thus requires free elections, as described in Chapter 8: All the people must be able to vote and have their votes counted and given equal weight with all other votes cast. Genuine alternatives must be put before them so that they may make meaningful choices. All voters must have an equal chance to find out what the alternatives are and to hear the arguments for and against each alternative. They must also have an equal opportunity to persuade others and to be persuaded by them. And whatever candidates or party lists get the required number of votes must win the offices.

The principle of political equality is, of course, a logical consequence of the principle of popular sovereignty. If some members of the community have greater opportunities than others—if, for example, their votes are given double or triple weight, or if only they are eligible for public office—then they become a specially favored ruling class, which according to the principle of popular sovereignty is permissible only in an oligarchy, not in a democracy.

Let us be clear that the principle of political equality means genuinely equal *opportunities* for all adult citizens, not actual equal participation. Democracy guarantees the right to abstain as well as the right to vote. In no known or imaginable democracy does every person actually participate to exactly the same degree as every other person. As long as each adult citizen has a genuinely equal opportunity to participate to the degree that he or she wishes, the requirements of political equality are satisfied.

POPULAR CONSULTATION

The principle of popular consultation requires two arrangements. First, a democratic nation must have some kind of institutional machinery through which public officials learn what public policies the people wish adopted and enforced. Second, having ascertained the people's preferences, public officials must then put them into effect whether they approve or not. This principle, like political equality, is a logical consequence of popular sovereignty. When officeholders do what they, rather than the people, wish and do so without any accounting or danger of losing office, they, and not the people, are sovereign.

This principle is the most obvious point of difference between this conception of democracy and that of the communism of Lenin, Stalin, and Mao Zedong. Those Communists, as we have seen, regard democracy as government *for* the people—government in which a special all-wise elite, the Communist party, decides what policies will best promote the "real" interests of the people—much as parents decide what is best for their small children. Popular approval of those policies is desirable, but it is not as important as making sure that the *right* policies are followed whether the people like them or not.

The conception presented here, on the other hand, defines democracy as essentially government *by* the people. The principle of popular consultation requires that the decisions about which public policies will best promote the people's interests ultimately must be made *by the people themselves,* and not by any permanent or nonaccountable ruling class of party leaders, scientists, priests, military leaders, business people, or college professors. According to this conception, the claim of a particular policy to the title *democratic* is determined by *how it is made,* rather than by its content. A policy's content is relevant only when it directly affects the nature of the decision-making processes themselves.

MAJORITY RULE

The Principle

The final principle of this model of democracy is probably the most controversial of the four, and I will take special pains to explain its meaning and the reasons for including it.

When the people in a democracy agree unanimously that a particular policy should be adopted, the principle of popular sovereignty clearly requires that the government must follow that policy. But in real life such unanimity is almost never achieved. Thus most political decisions in a democracy eventually become choices among alternative policies, each of which has some supporters among the sovereign people. In every such situation only one group can have its way, and the other group or groups must "lose." So the problem is, how should a democratic government, which rests on the principle that the basic decision-making power must be vested in *all* the people, determine *which* of the disagreeing groups of people should carry the day?

This model of democracy answers: All decisions should ultimately be made by popular majorities rather than minorities. Thus the principle of **majority rule** requires that *when the people disagree on an issue, the government should act according to the wishes of the larger rather than the smaller number.*[9] Note that this principle does not require that each and every government action be undertaken only after all the people have been consulted and a majority has specifically approved. It is up to popular majorities to decide how they want various kinds of decisions made. A majority may, for example, wish to reserve for itself and future majorities all government decisions, however minor—though no actual popular majority has ever done so. Or a majority may wish to leave all such decisions to certain elected and appointed public officials and confine itself to deciding in periodic elections whether or not those officials should remain in office. Or it may leave some decisions to public officials and reserve others for direct popular decision by such means as initiatives and referendums (see Chapter 8). As long as the *procedures* used to make government decisions are approved by at least 50-percent-plus-1 of the people and as long as the same proportion of the people can at any time revise those procedures, the principle of majority rule is satisfied.

Limited Majority Rule?

Some political theorists argue that this kind of "unlimited" majority rule is incompatible with true democracy. In a true democracy, they say, popular majorities must not take certain kinds of action. For example, they must not destroy any of the other principles of democracy by transferring sovereignty from the people to a dictator; they must not give certain people extra voting power; they must not prohibit certain people from expressing their political views; and they must not abolish free elections. Bare popular majorities must also not destroy the liberties and guarantees of due process of law described in Chapters 15 and 16. Any nation in which bare popular majorities do any of these things, these commentators insist, cannot legitimately be called a democracy.

Self-Limited Majority Rule?

People like me, who believe that unlimited majority rule must be a principle of democracy, have no quarrel with the arguments in the preceding paragraph—as far as they go. But the critical question is, *how* are popular majorities to be prevented from destroying other democratic principles? Some opponents of unlimited majority rule do not answer this question directly, but they imply two kinds of answers. First, popular majorities in a true democracy must voluntarily restrain themselves from stepping over the line, and, second, when a popular majority in a particular polity fails to restrain itself and destroys essential institutions and guarantees, then that polity is no longer a democracy. Yet both propositions are entirely compatible with the principle of unlimited majority rule presented here, for they assume that in a democracy, popular majorities are *self*-limited only.

Other opponents of unlimited majority rule, however, say that self-limitation is not enough. They insist that bare popular majorities must be limited by some agency beyond their control. They argue that there must be some restraining institution, such as judicial review (see Chapter 14) or requiring extraordinary majorities (that is, majorities of two-thirds or three-quarters, rather than merely 50-percent-plus-1) for certain kinds of action. In other words, a minority must be able to veto any majority action that the minority considers a threat to the privileged institutions and guarantees.

In this debate, the issue between the advocates of self-limited and externally limited majority rule is most clearly joined. Those who, like me, favor self-limited majority rule argue that such external limitations are incompatible with the principles of popular sovereignty and political equality. To give minorities the power to veto, we believe, is to give them the power to rule. Why? Because in any decision-making situation there are always a number of possible alternatives that might be chosen, and one of them is always to "do nothing"—that is, to continue the status quo. A minority with veto power can, to be sure, choose *only* the status quo, but if it is large enough (if it commands, for example, one-third plus one of the votes of the Congress or a majority of the U.S. Supreme Court), it can force continuation of the status quo over any alternative policy desired by the majority.

Such minority veto power is, in my view, incompatible with the principles of popular sovereignty and political equality. When a two-thirds vote is required to pass a measure, a person who votes no counts for twice as much as one who votes yes, and that violates the principle of political equality. Under such a requirement, each person who opposes change and prefers the status quo has more political power than a person who wants change. Thus those who prefer the status quo become a specially favored class, and that violates the principle of popular sovereignty.

For these reasons, then, the conception of democracy outlined here demands that popular majorities have the power to take any government action they wish and insists that that power be subject to no limitations other than those that are imposed—and can be removed—by popular majorities. But what if a popular majority chooses to give all power to a dictator or to abolish freedom of speech or to deprive minorities of the right to vote? The answer is, of course, that in such cases the polities would immediately cease to be democracies. Locating full *power* to take such actions in popular majorities, however, is not in itself inconsistent with democracy; for surely even the power to commit suicide as a democracy must be part of the all-inclusive sovereign power that democracy, as conceived here, vests in the people.

We may also ask, What if a particular majority establishes judicial review or some other device to restrain future majorities? Under this conception such a decision is perfectly compatible with majority rule and the other principles of democracy *provided* that any future majority can at any time abolish judicial review or any other restraining device by the same simple-majority procedures by which the device was initially established. In short, the majority of today cannot bind majorities of tomorrow—unless the later majorities want to be bound.

The debate over the appropriateness of unlimited majority rule has to some extent been obscured by both sides' apparent assumption that there is such a thing as *the* majority—a single identifiable group that sticks together on issue after issue and continually beats down *the* minority. The opponents of unlimited majority rule, for instance, have sometimes argued that the majority is composed of the most ignorant, prejudiced, and selfish members of the community, who cannot be trusted to rule wisely in the interests of all. The defenders of unlimited majority rule have sometimes fallen into the same trap, arguing that the majority is composed of sturdy working citizens, like Henry Wadsworth Longfellow's village blacksmith, who may not read books or use fancy words but make their decisions on the much sounder grounds of "practical experience" and "common sense."

Both sides are, of course, talking about something that does not exist. As we will see in Chapter 6, every time one issue is succeeded by another in the center of the political stage, there is always some reshuffling of the various "opinion groups." Neither the majority nor the minority on any particular issue is made up of exactly the same people as the majority or the minority on any other issue. When, for example, the issue of who should be elected president of the United States in 1988 had been settled and was succeeded in 1989 by the issue of whether there should be substantial cuts in the defense budget, many of the 1988 Bush voters continued to support his stand for the expensive

Strategic Defense Initiative (SDI), but some of them opposed it. By the same token, most of the 1988 Dukakis voters also opposed Bush on the SDI issue in 1989, but some supported him.

Thus actual majorities and minorities are specific to particular issues rather than being permanent bodies whose members always side together on all issues. That is why I have specified that the only restraints on popular majorities (not *"the* majority") compatible with democracy are those imposed by majorities on themselves and removable at any time by any majority without any minority having a veto power.

I repeat: I do not insist that this conception of democracy is the only one that is logically possible or morally acceptable. I have described it at such length because, however defined, *democracy* is a concept of great importance in the study of governing, and the reader is entitled to know what I mean by it and why. It should be clear, then, that wherever the term appears in this book, *democracy* means a form of government organized in accordance with the principles of popular sovereignty, political equality, popular consultation, and majority rule.

AUTHORITARIANISM AND DICTATORSHIP

Authoritarianism is *a form of government in which the ruling authority imposes its values and policies on society irrespective of its members' wishes.* The authority may be one person, such as Adolf Hitler in Nazi Germany (1933–45), Joseph Stalin in the Soviet Union (1922–53), Mu'ammar al-Qadaffi in Libya (1969–), and Fidel Castro in Cuba (1959–); or it may be a small ruling clique, often called an *oligarchy,* such as the Soviet Union's Politburo after Stalin's death or the military juntas that have ruled various Latin American nations at various times.

In our time, many people use the term *authoritarianism* as synonymous with the term *dictatorship,* though some prefer to preserve the older usage in which *dictatorship* meant rule by one person and *oligarchy* meant "rule by a small elite." Even the term *dictator* has not always meant arbitrary and unlimited rule by one person, however. It originated in the republic of ancient Rome. When the city was threatened by foreign invasion or domestic rebellion and the Senate determined that regular governing procedures were inadequate to meet the danger, they appointed a *dictator* and gave him, for a limited period, absolute power to use all of Rome's resources as he saw fit in order to save the city. When the danger had passed, the dictator's power reverted to the Senate, and he returned, as the great Lucius Quinctius Cincinnatus did, to his former status of ordinary citizen. In the republic's later years, however, ambitious politicians seized the title and power of dictator through armed rebellion or intimidation of the Senate, and for many centuries thereafter, a dictator was generally thought to be one who seized and held absolute power illegitimately,

Dictator of the Left. Fidel Castro of Cuba. (Source: UPI/ Bettmann Newsphotos.)

in contrast to an autocrat, who also had absolute power but achieved it by such legitimate means as inheriting a throne.

Political scientists have long since dropped these ancient distinctions and most now use the more general term *authoritarian* to denote all nondemocratic forms of government. Constructing a model of authoritarianism should take less time and argument that constructing a model of democracy. The reason is clear. As we have seen,the word *democracy* kindles such a pleasant emotional glow in most people the world over that they feel compelled to insist that it applies best—perhaps exclusively—to whatever systems or policies they favor. Any effort to claim it for other systems or policies usually encounters resistance and often resentment.

The words *authoritarianism* and *dictatorship* carry neither the popularity nor the confusion. For most people they mean something bad. The much rarer disputes over their usage therefore usually hinge not on what they mean but on whether this or that actual government deserves the insult.

In any event, as political scientist *Samuel E. Finer* points out, whether an authoritarian government's decisions are made by one man or a small clique, all such governments have three main characteristics:[10]

Dictator of the Right. Mu'ammar al-Qadaffi of Libya. (Source: UPI/Bettmann Newsphotos.)

1. The techniques of making decisions by public discussion and voting are largely or wholly supplanted by the decisions of those in authority.
2. The ruler(s) are not restrained by constitutional limitations and can impose whatever policies they choose.
3. The authority the ruler(s) claim does not necessarily nor usually derive from the consent of the government but rather from some special quality—some unusual personal charisma or special knowledge—that they alone are thought to possess.

The dictator or dictatorial elite may acquire power by inheritance, as King Hassan II did in Morocco; by overthrowing an established regime in a civil war, as Fidel Castro did in Cuba and Mao Zedong did in China; or by using the procedures of a democracy to gain a foothold and then destroying all opposition, as Adolf Hitler did in Germany. Authoritarianism is the opposite of democracy. Its essence lies not in the manner in which power is acquired but in who holds power. Its basic principles are sovereignty concentrated in one person or a small group, political inequality, no popular consultation, and minority rule.

Dictator of a Theocracy. Ayatollah Ruhollah Khomeini of Iran.
(Source: UPI/Bettmann Newsphotos.)

Authoritarianism is thus a model in the same sense that democracy is a model: a full intellectual realization of a particular organizational principle, not a complete and precise description of any actual government. Just as there are degrees of democracy (degrees of approximation to the model), so there are degrees of authoritarianism. In no actual government has one person or a small elite actually single-handedly controlled *all* decisions. From Tiberius of ancient Rome to Fidel Castro of present-day Cuba, all authoritarian rulers have had to rule through subordinates who have interpreted and carried out their orders; as we will see in Chapters 13 and 14, any interpretation or implementation of an order necessarily creates an area of discretion effectively controlled by subordinates, whatever the organizational charts may say.

Actual dictatorships, like actual democracies, are thus matters of more or less, not of all or none. They come in many varieties: the traditional absolute monarchies of Saudi Arabia and Oman, the fundamentalist theocracy of the

Ayatollah Khomeini, the military regimes of Chile and Panama, and what might be called the "people's dictatorships" of Nicolae Ceaucescu in Romania and Fidel Castro in Cuba.

CLASSIFYING REAL GOVERNMENTS

Any classification of actual governments as democratic or authoritarian is likely to be tentative and imperfect. Given the present state of political science, it could hardly be otherwise. Yet in a book such as this, which attempts to describe the main processes of politics and government the world over, I can hardly avoid talking about democratic and authoritarian regimes, nor would I wish to do so.

Anyone who talks of the form of an actual government must necessarily abstract part of its total reality, and the particular parts on which one chooses to concentrate are determined by one's conception of a model, or perfect example of such a form. For example, we often hear the governments of the United States and Great Britain called democratic and those of Romania and Libya called authoritarian. Let us consider for a moment what those labels mean and what they do not mean. They do not mean that the governments of the United States and Great Britain are exactly alike, for we know that certain British public officials (for example, the Queen and some members of the House of Lords) inherit their posts, whereas all American public officials are either elected or appointed to their jobs. Nor do the labels mean that the governments of the United States and Great Britain are *completely* different from the governments of Romania and Libya, for we know that all four governments make laws, punish those who break the laws, maintain armed forces, collect taxes, and so on.

We know that to some extent the governments of all nations are alike, yet no two governments are *exactly* alike. How, then, can we justify calling some democratic as if they were identical, and calling others authoritarian as if they too were identical but completely unlike the democracies? The answer is that *in certain respects* the governments of the United States and Great Britain are essentially alike, and *in those same respects* both are significantly different from the governments of Romania and Libya. The label of a particular nation's government reflects a form that we discern among certain items *selected* from its unique mixture of laws, customs, and institutions. When we have labeled the government democratic or authoritarian, we have described it only partially, and many other valid statements can also be made about it.

The items we select as the basis for our classifications are derived from our models of both forms of government. My purpose in this chapter has been to make as clear as I can the nature of the models of democracy and dictatorship I use and by what reasoning I call some actual governments democratic and others authoritarian.

FOR FURTHER READING

ABOUT DEMOCRACY

*ARROW, KENNETH. *Social Choice and Individual Values.* 2nd ed. New York: Wiley, 1963. Influential exposition by a Nobel laureate in economics of the "paradox of voting"— the logical impossibility of choosing among several alternatives the one most preferred by most voters.

*BACHRACH, PETER. *The Theory of Democratic Elitism.* Boston: Little, Brown, 1967. Short exposition of participatory model.

BARBER, BENJAMIN R. *Strong Democracy: Participatory Politics for a New Age.* Berkeley: University of California Press, 1984. Argument for maximizing participatory grassroots democracy by devolving power to smaller, local units of government.

COOK, TERENCE E., and PATRICK M. MORGAN, eds. *Participatory Democracy.* San Francisco: Canfield Press, 1971. Collection of essays on theory and practice of participatory democracy.

*DAHL, ROBERT A. *Polyarchy.* New Haven, CT: Yale University Press, 1982. View of democracy as competition among accountable elites.

*———. *A Preface to Democratic Theory.* Chicago: University of Chicago Press, 1956. Develops the "polyarchy" model of democracy and analyzes alternative models.

*———. *Democracy, Liberty and Equality.* New York: Oxford University Press, 1987. An examination of the tension between liberty and equality in the theory of democracy.

*HELD, DAVID. *Models of Democracy.* Stanford, CA: Stanford University Press, 1987. Analysis of competing models of democracy.

KENDALL, WILLMOORE. *John Locke and the Doctrine of Majority Rule.* Urbana: University of Illinois Press, 1941. Explanation of origins and content of the absolute-majority-rule doctrine.

O'DONNEL, GUILLERMO, PHILIPPE C. SCHMITTER, and LAURENCE WHITEHEAD. *Transitions from Authoritarian Rule.* Baltimore: Johns Hopkins University Press, 1986. Study of recent transitions from authoritarian to democratic regimes in Spain, Portugal, and several Latin American countries.

PATEMAN, CAROLE. *Participation and Democratic Theory.* New York: Cambridge University Press, 1970. Most thorough defense of participatory model.

*RIKER, WILLIAM H. *Liberalism Against Populism: A Confrontation between the Theory of Democracy and the Theory of Social Choice.* San Francisco: W. H. Freeman, 1982. Analysis by a leading political theorist of theories of democracy and some of their alternatives.

*SARTORI, GIOVANNI. *The Theory of Democracy Revisited,* 2 vols. Chatham, NJ: Chatham House, 1987. Updated and reconsidered version of the most comprehensive and analytical discussion of the various meanings of democracy.

*SCHUMPETER, JOSEPH. *Capitalism, Socialism, and Democracy,* 3rd ed. New York: Harper Torchbooks, 1950. Influential analysis of democracy as competition among accountable elites.

*SPITZ, ELAINE. *Majority Rule.* Chatham, NJ: Chatham House, 1983. Most recent analysis of argument over status of majority rule in democratic theory.

ABOUT AUTHORITARIANISM

ARENDT, HANNA. *The Origins of Totalitarianism.* New York: Meridian, 1958. Influential philosophical analysis of totalitarianism.

FRIEDRICH, CARL J., and ZBIGNIEW BRZEZINSKI. *Totalitarian Dictatorship and Autocracy,* 2nd ed. Cambridge: Harvard University Press, 1965. Analysis of ideas and institutions in both Fascist and Communist dictatorships.

PERLMUTTER, AMOS. *Modern Authoritarianism: A Comparative Institutional Analysis.* New Haven, CT: Yale University Press, 1981. Study of ideas and institutions of modern authoritarian regimes.

NOTES

[1]Richard McKeon, ed., *Democracy in a World of Tensions: A Symposium,* prepared by UNESCO (Chicago: University of Chicago Press, 1951), pp. 522–23.

[2]Soviet journal quoted in Zbigniew R. Brzezinski, *The Soviet Bloc,* rev. ed. (Cambridge, MA: Harvard University Press, 1967), p. 31.

[3]Carl L. Becker, *Modern Democracy* (New Haven, CT: Yale University Press, 1941), p. 4.

[4]*Variable* is a technical term often used in political science as well as in many other disciplines. As we are using the term, a **variable** is *a characteristic of a social situation or institution that may appear in different degrees or forms in different situations and institutions.*

[5]Arthur K. Smith, Jr., "Socio-Economic Development and Political Democracy: A Causal Analysis," *Midwest Journal of Political Science,* vol. 13 (1969), pp. 104–105.

[6]Quoted in Lucian W. Pye, *China: An Introduction,* 3rd ed. (Boston: Little, Brown, 1984), p. 173.

[7]J. W. Lewis, *Leadership in Communist China* (Ithaca, NY: Cornell University Press, 1966), pp. 75, 83. Copyright 1966 by Cornell University. See also Pye, *China,* Chapter 10.

[8]The definition of democracy presented here is a somewhat revised version of that set forth in detail in Austin Ranney and Willmoore Kendall, *Democracy and the American Party System* (New York: Harcourt Brace Jovanovich, 1956), Chapters 1–3. I have borrowed heavily from these chapters for the present analysis.

[9]In strict arithmetical terms, a popular *majority* is 50-percent-plus-1 of the people voting; hence when there are only two choices, yes or no, and 51 votes are cast for Yes and 49 votes for No, 51 is a majority and wins. In some situations, however, there are more than two choices and no one of them may receive a majority: For example, there are three candidates for office, and A gets 40 votes, B gets 35 votes, and C gets 25 votes. Under the principle of majority rule, this can be handled in several ways, but the most common are (1) to drop C and have the majority choose between A and B; or (2) to use the derived principle of *plurality* rule and give the win to the alternative that has more votes than the others even though those votes are not a majority of the while. Under the *plurality rule,* A would win the election because 40 votes are more than either 35 or 25.

[10]Samuel E. Finer, "Authoritarianism," in Vernon Bogdanor, ed., *The Blackwell Encyclopeadia of Political Institutions* (Oxford, England: Basil Blackwell, 1987), p. 34.

6 Public Opinion in Democratic Systems

Governments must concern themselves with the opinions of their citizens, if only to provide a basis for repression of disaffection. The persistent curiosity, and anxiety, of rulers about what their subjects say of them and their actions are chronicled in the histories of secret police. Measures to satisfy each curiosity by soundings of public opinion are often only an aspect of political persecution; they may also guide policies of persuasion calculated to convert discontent into cheerful acquiescence. And even in the least democratic regime, opinion may influence the direction or tempo of substantive policy. Although a government may be erected on tyranny, to endure it needs the ungrudging support of substantial numbers of its people.[1]

Although this chapter will focus mainly on public opinion in democratic systems, it is a mistake to believe that public opinion plays a significant role only in the democracies. As the preceding quotation makes clear, authoritarian regimes also have an important stake in knowing whether their policies are going to receive sullen acquiescence or enthusiastic cooperation.

For these reasons, the cultivation of public opinion is a major preoccupation of most political groups in both democratic and authoritarian systems. In the democracies, political parties, candidates, and pressure groups spend millions of dollars bombarding ordinary citizens with television "spots," billboard displays, newspaper advertisements, bumper-sticker slogans, and the like, all intended to nudge public opinion in the desired direction. A public relations counsel sits at the elbow of many public figures, advising them on how to cultivate good public images. Commercial polling organizations are hired by newspapers to report on how the public views the parties, candidates, and issues of the moment.

Public Opinion Counts in Diplomacy. Soviet General Secretary Mikhail Gorbachev "working a crowd" in Poland (Source: Bernard Bisson & Thierry Orban/Sygma.)

But authoritarian regimes are also vitally concerned with public opinion. Their ministries of propaganda (or "public education" or "public information") employ thousands of functionaries to whip up enthusiasm for the rulers' policies. And most use a variety of devices—including even public opinion polls—to learn how the masses feel about current policies and how they are likely to react to contemplated future policies.

All governments and most political actors thus treat public opinion as a mighty force. But exactly what *is* it? What forces shape it? How can we be sure what public opinion demands, permits, or rejects on this or that matter of public policy? These questions have long fascinated students of politics, and in this chapter we will review some of their findings.

THE NATURE OF PUBLIC OPINION

As an introduction, let us sketch the opinion processes in an imaginary democracy and then call attention to some of their main characteristics. Let us imagine a New England town with a population of 15 adults. Citizens A, B, and C have farms on the town's north road and propose that the town pave it; A and B feel very strongly about it, but C is less intense. Citizens D, E, and F, who own farms on the south road, feel discriminated against and oppose the move, although F is less angry about it than the other two. Citizens G, H, and I are merchants who believe that paving the road will mean higher taxes, and they plan to oppose it—unless opposition means the loss of A's, B's, and C's business. Citizens J and K are widows living on income from real estate, and they too oppose the proposal because of the higher taxes it will bring, but they consider it unladylike to be too openly political. Citizens L and M, the town's odd-job men, own no farms, pay no property taxes, and could not care less about the issue. Citizens N and O, the town's ministers, have parishioners on both sides, see no moral or religious issue involved, and decide it would be prudent to stay out of the fight.

At the town meeting, A moves that the north road be paved. A, B, and C vote yes; D, E, F, G, H, I, J, and K vote no; L and M have not bothered to attend the meeting; and N and O, though present, do not vote. A's motion is defeated, 8 votes to 3. Then A has an inspiration. He moves that *both* the north and south roads be paved and that one of them be officially named after the late husband of J. On this second proposal, A, B, and C again vote yes and are joined not only by D, E, and F, but also by J and by N (the late Mr. J was one of N's favorite parishioners). Only G, H, I, and K vote against it, and the proposal carries by a vote of 8 to 4.

What can we say about public opinion in this imaginary democracy? For one thing, on neither issue did *all* the town's members express opinions. For another, not all the members of any side felt equally strongly about the matter. For yet another, when the first issue was replaced by the second there was a reshuffling of the individuals composing the pro and con sides. Although both issues may be said to have been decided in accordance with public opinion, it is misleading to picture "*the* public" as consisting of all 15 members of the community, all holding views on all issues of public policy. How, then, should we picture public opinion in real-life situations?

A DEFINITION

The nineteenth-century British politician Sir Robert Peel doubtless spoke for many political leaders then and since when he referred to "that great compound of folly, weakness, prejudice, wrong feeling, right feeling, obstinacy, and newspaper paragraphs, which is called public opinion."[2] Most present-day political scientists would reject Sir Robert's unflattering definition and use instead, as we will, V. O. Key's definition: "**Public opinion** consists of *those opinions held by private persons which governments find it prudent to heed.*"[3] In other words, public opinion is the sum of all private opinions of which government officials are aware and take into account in making their decisions.

According to this definition, then, public opinion is the cutting edge of a nation's political culture (see Chapter 3). It is specific to particular political situations and issues; it is not a body of ideas on *all* issues held by *all* the members of the community known as *the* public. Each issue produces its particular combination of opinion groups, always including one that expresses no opinion whatever. (Every public opinion poll on a political issue discovers that some responses must be classified as "don't know" or "don't care".) From issue to issue there is always some reshuffling among the individuals composing the various opinion groups, some of the pros and cons on one issue reverse sides or become "don't cares" on the next, and some of the previous "don't cares" take sides.

DIMENSIONS OF PUBLIC OPINION: PREFERENCE AND INTENSITY

Political scientists find it useful to think of public opinions as having two dimensions: *preference* and *intensity*. The preference dimension measures the property of being for or against some party, candidate, or policy; the intensity dimension measures how strongly people feel about their preferences. In terms of actual political conflict, each dimension is as important as the other. For example, if 60 percent of the electorate prefer Michael Dukakis, 40 percent favor George Bush, and all feel strongly enough to vote, Dukakis wins by a margin of 3 to 2. But if only half of Dukakis's supporters and all of Bush's care enough to vote, then Bush wins by a margin of 4 to 3. History, indeed, records many victories of small but intensely motivated groups over large but more apathetic oppositions.

Political candidates and public officials thus need to know not only what people prefer but how strongly they prefer it. Pollsters often try to measure the intensity of people's preferences by arraying their answers on scales rather than lumping them into pro and con catchalls. For example, in 1984 the *ABC/Washington Post* poll asked a national sample of Americans this question: "Do you tend to agree or disagree with this statement: A woman should be able to get an abortion if she decides she wants one?" Of the 1,524 respondents, 610 (40 percent) strongly agreed; 335 (22 percent) agreed somewhat; 107 (7 percent) disagreed somewhat; and 472 (31 percent) disagreed strongly. Presented graphically, as in Figure 6.1, this distribution of opinion constitutes a classic example of what opinion analysts call a U-shaped curve, which reveals a state of intense disagreement. Most people have opinions, most of those who have opinions hold them strongly, and those who feel strongly are more or less evenly divided between the two extreme positions. Proposals for government funding of abortions for poor women will thus be pressed strongly and opposed strongly, and the capacity of the political system to resolve the disputes will be tested more than if most persons were clustered in the middle categories of preference and intensity.

Other issues, however, produce J-shaped curves because most people cluster at one end of the scale. For example, in 1984 the Center for Political Studies of the University of Michigan asked a national sample of American adults this question: "Which do you think—schools should be allowed to start each day with a prayer, or religion does not belong in the schools?" Sixty-five

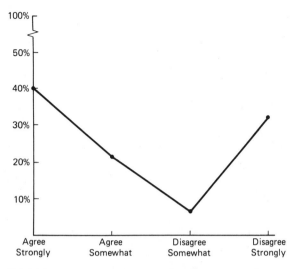

FIGURE 6.1. U-shaped curve of opinion distribution on statement: "A woman should be able to get an abortion if she wants one," 1984. (*Source*: *ABC/Washington Post* poll reported in *Public Opinion,* April/May, 1985, p. 25. Used by permission of the American Enterprise Institute.)

percent of the respondents said that schools should be allowed to start the day with prayers, 26 percent said that religion does not belong in the schools, and 9 percent gave some other response. Shown graphically, as in Figure 6.2, this yields a classical J-shaped curve. Clearly such a distribution of opinion has very different consequences for policy making than the U-shaped curve shown in Figure 6.1.

MEASUREMENT BY PUBLIC OPINION POLLS

The Problem

(Measuring public opinion is a major concern for every democratic government. Democracy, after all, means government acting in accordance with the desires of popular majorities (see Chapter 5). If a political system seeks to realize the ideal, there must be some way of learning how popular majorities feel about political issues; for if the government does not and cannot know those feelings, it can hardly act in accordance with them.)

Some democratic philosophers, notably Jean Jacques Rousseau, have dreamed of "plebiscitary" democracy, in which the majority's wishes on each and every issue are always clear and, through some kind of continuous popular consultation, control whatever action the government takes. No actual democratic system, including the famed New England town meetings and the Swiss

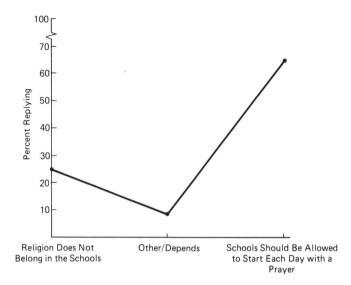

FIGURE 6.2.   A J-shaped curve of opinion distribution on the question: "Which do you think—schools should be allowed to start each day with a prayer, or religion does not belong in the schools?"(*Source*: Center for Political Studies, University of Michigan, 1984, reported in *Public Opinion*, June/July, 1985, p. 36. Used by permission of the American Enterprise Institute.)

cantonal *landsgemeinden,* has ever been organized along these lines. The principal official devices for discovering public opinion in modern democracies have been either indirect and periodic, like representation and elections, or direct and intermittent, like the initiative and referendum (see Chapter 8).

The Rise of the Polls

Modern social science has developed a device that some think is capable of both direct and continuous measurement of public opinion. It is the **sample survey,** which is *a study of the opinions of a population conducted by asking questions of a representative sample of the population.* (Such surveys are also, though more loosely, called "public opinion polls.")

No government has yet adopted sample surveys as part of its official policy-making apparatus (although many government agencies conduct polls regularly to learn "how the land lies"). Nevertheless, polls have come to occupy an important position in the analysis and measurement of public opinion all over the democratic world, in part because commercial polling businesses survey public opinion and publish their findings in newspapers. They include such famous American firms as the American Institute of Public Opinion (founded by George Gallup) and Louis Harris and Associates in the United States, Market and Opinion Research International (MORI) in Great Britain, and the *Société Française pour Études Sondages* (SOFRES) in France; and such newspaper-television combinations as the *New York Times/CBS News* poll and the *Washington Post/ABC News* poll. Some of the most sophisticated work is done by academic organizations, such as the Center for Political Studies of the University of Michigan (CPS), the National Opinion Research Center of the University of Chicago (NORC), and the Survey Research Center of the University of California, Berkeley (SRC).

Polls have become big business in many democratic nations. In the United States alone, commercial polling organizations together now gross well over $100 million a year, and they are comparably profitable in Great Britain, France, West Germany, Japan, and many other advanced/industrial democracies. In most of these nations, most of their research is financed by contracts with manufacturers and concentrates on consumer reactions to their products and advertisements. Some of the pollsters' revenues come from polling opinion on political questions and selling the results to newspapers, and it is this aspect of the polls that concerns us here. Polling has also become an important campaigning device for political parties and candidates in every modern democracy, where the major parties regularly use public opinion experts to analyze published polls and to conduct private polls.

How the Polls Work

All national sample surveys work more or less alike. They first draw samples of the adult population, and in the United States those samples number from 3,000 to 6,000 persons. What makes a sample good is not its size but its *representativeness*—how faithfully it reflects the divisions of opinions among all adults. Most pollsters now believe that the best way to get such a sample is to make a "random" or "probability" sample—one in which each member of the population is just as likely to be chosen as any other member. For example, for its final survey for the 1988 presidential election the Gallup organization interviewed 4,089 adults and sorted out 2,626 of them as likely voters, whose preferences provided the data for their final prediction of the outcome (which turned out to be within two points of the actual result—see Table 6.1).

The next step is to draw up a set of questions that will enable the pollsters to find out how the members of the sample feel about things, and the trick is to avoid biasing the questions in such a way as to elicit particular answers. Then the pollsters' interviewers put the questions to the people in their samples; nowadays they do so largely by telephone, although a few studies still use personal interviews in the respondents' homes. Finally, the answers are entered in computers and analyzed, and the pollsters make their reports to whatever clients are paying the freight—newspapers, television networks, political parties, and candidates.

The most recent wrinkle in polling are the "exit polls" now widely used by the newspaper-television polls such as the *New York Times/CBS News* poll

Exit Polls Forecast Election Results. Voters marking cards for CBS's exit poll in November, 1984. (Source: Bobbie Kingsley/Photo Researchers.)

and the *Washington Post/ABC News* poll. The pollsters select a small group of representative voting precincts across the nation and station their agents at each precinct. As the voters leave the polls, the agents ask them to mark a secret "ballot" telling how they voted and giving their age, sex, ethnicity, income, and the like. The results are telephoned to the organization's national headquarters, where they are immediately computerized and analyzed. These polls are especially good for making quick analyses of elections because all their interviews are with people who actually voted, and there is no problem in sorting out the likely voters from the likely nonvoters as in preelection polls.

How Accurate Are They?

Perhaps the most frequent question asked about the polls is whether they accurately report the state of public opinion. So far no entirely satisfactory method has been developed to check the accuracy of their reports of public opinion on issues— questions of whether the government should follow this or that policy. However, preelection polls on how people intend to vote have the great advantage of being checkable by actual election results, and although such unpredictable factors as the weather on election day may influence the actual voting figures, most people believe that the best method yet developed

TABLE 6.1.   Record of the Presidential Polls, 1936-88 (in percentages)

	Actual	Vote Predicted for Democratic Candidate by						
Year	Democratic Vote	Gallup	Roper	Crossley	Harris	ABC/WP	CBS/NYT	NBC/AP, WSJ
1936	60	54	62	54	—	—	—	—
1940	55	55	55	—	—	—	—	—
1944	54	53	54	52	—	—	—	—
1948	49.6	45	37	45	—	—	—	—
1952	44	46	43	47	—	—	—	—
1956	42	41	40	—	—	—	—	—
1960	49.7	49	47	—	—	—	—	—
1964	61	61	—	—	—	—	—	—
1968	43	40	—	—	43	—	—	—
1972	37.5	38	—	—	39	—	—	—
1976	50	49.5	—	—	48	—	—	—
1980	41	45	—	—	43	—	45	41
1984	41	41	43	—	43	40	37	34
1988	46	44	—	—	48	45	45	47

Sources: The figures for 1936–60 are reported by permission from James MacGregor Burns and Jack Walter Peltason, *Government by the People: The Dynamics of American National, State, and Local Government,* 11th ed., p. 217.

Reprinted by permission of Prentice-Hall, Englewood Cliffs, NJ. Figures for 1964–88 have been added by the author.

for checking the accuracy of polls is to examine their record in predicting the popular vote in elections.

By this standard, how accurate are they? Their record in predicting the outcomes of American presidential elections is shown in Table 6.1.

The figures in Table 6.1 show that in the period from 1936 to 1988, the major polls made a total of 54 predictions. Deviations from the actual outcomes ranged from 0.1 points (Gallup in 1964) to 12.5 points (Roper in 1948). The average deviation was 1.6 points for Gallup, 1.5 for Harris, 3.8 for Roper, 4.0 for Crossley, 1.0 for *ABC/Washington Post,* and 3.0 for *CBS/New York Times* (the last two made predictions only in 1980–88). Forty-six of the 54 predicted winners actually won— an 85.2 percent record of success. Moreover, 4 of the 8 failures came in 1948, when none of the polls correctly forecasted President Harry S. Truman's reelection—a failure that has had about as much publicity as all the polls' successes put together.

Most observers agree that such evidence shows that the polls have been far more accurate in predicting election results than have news commentators or politicians. However, some of the polls' critics argue that success in predicting election results is no sign that polls are equally capable of revealing public opinion on issues. Their main criticism is that the way in which the questions

TABLE 6.2.   Public Opinion on Spending for Lower-Income Groups, 1968, 1982

Question: "For each group described, tell me whether you feel the government should do more than it now does, or whether the government should not get involved, or whether you think the government is doing just about enough." (in percentages)

Group	Should Do More for		Is Doing Just About Enough for		Should Not Get Involved with	
	1968	1982	1968	1982	1968	1982
The poor	61	59	33	34	6	7
People on welfare	32	25	57	56	11	18

Source: Survey by Yankelovich, Skelly and White for the American Council of Life Insurance, reported in *Public Opinion,* June/July, 1985, p. 28.

are asked has a powerful effect on the answers. And there is a lot of truth to their charge. There are many examples of this effect, but the following is typical: In 1968 and again in 1982, the polling firm of Yankelovich, Skelly and White asked their respondents this question about government help for each of a number of groups in the population: "[Please tell us] whether you feel the government should do more than it now does, or whether the government should not get involved, or whether you think the government is doing just about enough." Two of the groups asked about were "the poor" and "people on welfare." The respondents' answers in both years are shown in Table 6.2.

The answers in Table 6.2 seem to show that the American people want government to do more for "the poor" but not for "people on welfare"—even though most social scientists would say that the two are one and the same. Clearly, then, the results of polls about the desirability of welfare programs depend in part upon which phrase the pollster uses to describe people at the bottom of the economic ladder. Comparable effects can be found in almost any other set of questions. The pollsters are well aware of the problem, and most of them try to phrase their questions so that there will be minimum bias in the answers; even so, the problem is far from solved, and perhaps it never will be to the satisfaction of all concerned.

How Much Influence Do They Have?

Ever since modern pollsters began to achieve their present prominence, people have asked how much influence the polls have on the making of public policy. They have asked two main questions. First, do public officials read poll results and make policy accordingly? There is every reason to believe that most public officials in most democracies do read the results, but it is hard to say just how much what they read influences what they do. Most observers believe that poll results are for most public officials one, but by no means the only, factor influencing their decisions. Second, do poll results have a "bandwagon effect"

Polls Are News. A New York Times story on presidential popularity. (Source: Copyright © 1986 by The New York Times Company. Reprinted by permission.)

on the voters? That is, do a lot of undecided or weakly committed voters read preelection polls and decide that they might as well vote for the winner? Are people on the West Coast of the United States discouraged from voting by the television networks' forecasts that, based on results in the East, South, and Midwest, so-and-so has already won? Again there is no definitive evidence, but what there is suggests that while there is little or no "bandwagon" effect (vote for the winner) or "sympathy" effect (vote for the loser), some weakly motivated citizens may decide not to bother voting if the polls—or the television networks' election-night "calls" of the probable winners—tell them, in effect, that it is all over and their votes won't make any difference.

Despite these criticisms, however, most political scientists, like most politicians and managers of the mass communications media, believe that public opinion polls are here to stay, not as the key element of democratic government but as a valuable aid in grappling with the problem of one of democracy's most difficult problems: finding out what the people want their government to do so that government can respond to the popular will.

OPINION DISTRIBUTIONS IN WESTERN DEMOCRACIES

WHAT CONCERNS PEOPLE? WHAT DO THEY KNOW?

It seems appropriate to conclude this chapter with a brief survey of the state of public opinion on some leading issues in the United States and other Western democracies at the end of the 1980s, for it should tell us quite a bit about the environment in which candidates will have to fight campaign elections and in which governments will have to make policies in the 1990s.

The obvious place to begin is to ask: What are people most concerned about? What do they see as the most important values governments should promote? Political scientist Russell J. Dalton has assembled the answers given by American, British, French, and West German respondents to these questions, as shown in Table 6.3.

Table 6.3 shows a number of important similarities in public opinion among the four Western democracies. For example, in all four nations, achieving and maintaining economic health, fighting crime, and maintaining law and order are the most important concerns, and aesthetic values, such as more beautiful cities, rank low. The table also shows some intriguing differences. For example, only Americans put a high value on maintaining strong defense forces, and only the French put a high value on making a "friendlier, less impersonal society."

As we would expect, the salience of the various concerns varies not only from one country to another but also from time to time in any particular country. This is well illustrated by Figure 6.3, which shows the changing responses of Americans during the Reagan years to the Gallup poll's standard question, "What do you think is the most important problem facing this coun-

TABLE 6.3. The Most Important Goals for Government (in percentages)

Goal	U.S.	G.B.	F.R.G.	France
Fighting crime	43	32	23	22
Maintaining a stable economy	51	23	33	11
Fighting rising prices	29	25	25	33
Economic growth	18	29	26	13
Maintaining order	27	18	23	15
Giving people more say at work and in their community	25	12	8	21
Protecting freedom of speech	14	16	12	18
Maintaining strong defense forces	39	11	5	3
A friendlier, less impersonal society	6	9	11	31
More beautiful cities	4	3	7	6

Each respondent could give several answers; the entries are the percentages ranking each goal as the most important or second-most important.

Source: Russel J. Dalton, *Citizen Politics in Western Democracies* (Chatham, NJ: Chatham House, 1988), Table 5.1, p. 83.

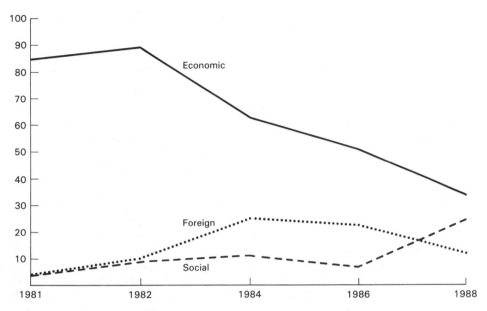

FIGURE 6.3. "What do you think is the most important problem facing this country?" 1981–1988. (*Source*: The Gallup Poll, reported in *Public Opinion*, July/August, 1988, pp. 34–35.

try?" As the figure shows, they consistently expressed more concern with economic matters (inflation, unemployment, government spending, taxes) than anything else, but the number doing so declined significantly from 85 percent in 1981 to 34 percent in 1988—no doubt reflecting the fact that in 1988 unemployment was the lowest since World War II and inflation was still well under control. Moreover, foreign policy concerns (fear of war, arms control, terrorism) declined from a peak of 26 percent in 1984 to 12 percent in 1988; while, in 1988, social concerns (drugs, morality, and AIDS) concerned more people than did foreign policy issues.

IDEOLOGY

Left and Right in Western Nations

In Chapters 4 and 5, we reviewed the doctrines of the modern world's leading political ideologies, but one may well ask how much they really matter in shaping public opinion. Most political scientists have measured the importance of ideology in a country's public opinion by noting how many of its people (1) show some understanding of what the ideologies of Left and Right mean (for our definition, see Chapter 4), (2) are willing to place themselves in one category or the other, and (3) use their ideological loyalties as important bases for forming opinions on specific issues and deciding how to vote in elections.

Table 3.1 in Chapter 3 shows how the people in each of eight Western democracies score on each of those questions.

Liberals and Conservatives in the United States

The figures in Table 6.4 show that ideology is least important to the general public in the United States and Switzerland and most important in West Germany and the Netherlands. But that does not mean that it is of no importance whatever in American thinking about politics. Since the 1970s the Gallup poll has been asking its respondents, "In politics, would you say that you are a liberal, a moderate, a conservative, or what?" Their replies are shown graphically in Figure 6.4.

Figure 6.4 shows that since the 1970s, approximately 90 percent of Americans have been willing to place themselves on a scale with "liberal" at one end, "conservative" at the other end, and "moderate" in the middle; and most people have called themselves moderates. Other studies have shown that people in different social categories tend to identify themselves somewhat differently: For example, men are generally more conservative than women; whites are more conservative than African-Americans; older people are more conservative than younger people; Protestants are more conservative than Catholics, both are more conservative than Jews, and all three are more conservative than people who say that they have no religious preference; and, least surprisingly,

FIGURE 6.4. Americans' self-identifications as liberals, conservatives, and moderates, 1976–86. (Source: R. S. Erikson, N. R. Luttberg, and K. L. Tedin, *American Public Opinion,* 3rd ed. (New York: Macmillan, 1988), Table 3.11, p. 69.

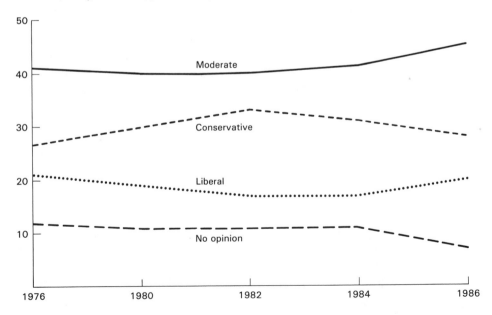

the higher people's annual incomes are, the more likely they are to be conservative (the proportions of people calling themselves conservatives is about one-third among people earning less than $10,000 per year and over half among those earning over $50,000).[4]

But how much do such self-applied labels mean? The answer from dozens of sample survey studies seems to be, something but not everything. For example, when respondents were asked to say what the liberal or conservative position is on particular issues (such as "getting tougher on the subject of crime" and "increasing federal programs to help the poor"), an average of 30 percent said that they did not know, and another 20 percent consistently identified the liberal or conservative position incorrectly (that is, not as the scholars designing the studies identified them). Moreover, only about 20 percent of Americans appear to evaluate parties, candidates, and issues mainly in terms of whether they are liberal or conservative. Accordingly, the following summing-up by a leading study of American public opinion seems to be correct:

> *While the American public displays some familiarity with the terminology of liberalism and conservatism, most people cannot be said to order their political viewpoints by means of a general ideological anchor. . . . the fact that there is little consistency among people's viewpoints—especially when the opinions cut across issue areas—demonstrates that few people use their ideological position as a cueing device to arrange their responses to the political world. The kind of attitudinal constraint that motivates people toward consistently liberal or moderate viewpoints is reserved mainly for a small politically active segment of the American public.*[5]

Does College Make a Difference?

Conservative parents, alumni, and pressure groups sometimes say that American colleges and universities are hotbeds of liberalism, where radical faculty members preach left-wing political views in their classes and thereby convert their students away from the conservatism they learned from their parents. Let it be confessed that, in a perverse way, many college professors are secretly flattered by this charge, because it rests on the belief that what professors say in class has a major impact on their students' outlooks (thereby refuting the old canards that college teaching is "talking in someone else's sleep" or "casting false pearls before real swine.") But is it true?

The answer is complex, but some parts of it are clear. Certainly the faculties of most colleges have higher proportions of liberals than in the population at large, although their liberalism varies with the subjects they teach. For example, one study showed that 64 percent of college social science teachers consider themselves liberals, while only 20 percent call themselves conservatives—compared with the general population, which, as Figure 6.4 shows, divides itself into 22 percent liberal, 29 percent conservative, and 44 percent moderate. Teachers of business, engineering, and agriculture are much more likely to be conservative.[6] But college students in general are substantially more conservative than their teachers, as is shown by the figures in Table 6.5.

TABLE 6.4.   Political Ideologies of College Students and
             Faculty, 1976–85 (in percentages)

Year	Liberal*	Middle of the Road	Conservative†
1976			
Students	38	39	23
Faculty	44	28	28
1984			
Students	25	39	36
Faculty	42	27	31

*Comprised of responses to "Left" and "Liberal"

†Comprised of responses to "Moderately Conservative" and "Strongly Conservative"

Source: Ernest L. Boyer, *College: The Undergraduate Experience in America* (New York: Harper & Row, Pub., 1987), p. 189. Copyright © 1987 by the Carnegie Foundation for the Advancement of Teaching.

Table 6.4 shows that in both 1976 and 1984, college teachers were more liberal than college students. The table also shows that from 1976 to 1984, faculty members became only slightly more conservative, while students became a good deal more conservative. So evidently there are more powerful forces than indoctrination by their teachers affecting the ideologies of college students. It is true that college students, today as in the past, are substantially more liberal than people of college age who do not go to college, but the evidence shows that most young people who go to college are already more liberal in high school than their classmates who do not go to college. In short, there is some evidence that going to college has some effect on making some students more liberal, but there are many other, more powerful forces that make some people more liberal in their twenties than they were in their teens.[7]

Accordingly, perhaps we can get a better understanding of public opinion by looking at people's views on specific issues rather than at their general political ideologies, as in the following discussion.

DOMESTIC POLICY: THE ECONOMIC AND SOCIAL RESPONSIBILITIES OF GOVERNMENT

For decades now, one of the messages delivered most often and most fervently by President Ronald Reagan and most American conservatives is that government in the United States is too big, that government is "part of the problem, not part of the solution," and that in order to get a better America we have to "get the government off people's backs." The polls show that most Americans agree: For example, in 1986, 62 percent agreed with the statement that "the federal government creates more problems than it solves"; and when asked in

1985 whether big government, big business, or big labor is the biggest threat to the country's well-being, 50 percent named big government as compared with only 22 percent for big business and 19 percent for big labor.

Before we conclude that Americans have become confirmed "Reaganauts," however, let us also note that in 1985–86, some 85 percent also said that "there must be substantial government involvement to handle the problem of poverty," while only 15 percent said that "the problem of poverty can be handled mainly by volunteer efforts"; 85 percent also agreed that the federal government should help finance long-term care for the elderly rather than leaving it up to private action; and 87 percent said that "government should make a major effort to help American business become more competitive in foreign markets" rather than leaving it up to businesses to do it by themselves.[8]

Similarly, when people are asked whether the government is spending too much money, three-quarters or more say yes; but when they are asked whether government is spending too much or too little in a number of specific areas the answers are quite different, as is shown in Table 6.5.

It is especially instructive in this regard to compare American public opinion with that in other Western democracies. In the late 1970s, political scientist Samuel Barnes and his colleagues asked national samples in the United States, Great Britain, and West Germany whether they thought that government had a responsibility for dealing with a variety of problems. Their answers are shown in Table 6.6.

Compared with people in other Western democracies, then, Americans are substantially less supportive of the idea that government has the prime responsibility for managing the economy. There has never been much support in the United States for the socialist ideal of public ownership and operation of major sections of the economy, while much larger portions of European publics support it. Moreover, as we will see in Chapter 10, most European nations have at least one political party pledged to socialism as its basic program, while hardly any of the leaders or supporters of the American Democratic and Republican parties advocate or favor socialism.

TABLE 6.5. **Attitudes Toward Government Spending in Particular Areas, 1986 (in percentages)**

Area	Government is Now Spending		
	Too Much	About Right	Not Enough
Improving and protecting the environment	8%	281%	56%
Improving the nation's education system	4	34	62
Improving and protecting the nation's health	6	34	60
Improving public transportation	9	41	36

Source: Public Opinion, March/April, 1987, p. 22.

TABLE 6.6.   Government Responsibility for Dealing with Problems (in percentages)

Problem Area	United States	Great Britain	Federal Republic of West Germany
Fighting pollution	56	69	73
Fighting crime	53	56	78
Providing good medical care	42	74	63
Providing good education	47	68	55
Looking after old people	41	58	51
Guaranteeing jobs	34	55	60
Providing adequate housing	25	60	39
Equal rights for minorities	33	24	20
Reducing income inequality	13	25	29
Equal rights for sexes	24	19	27
Average	37	51	49

Samuel Barnes, et al. *Political Action* (Beverly Hills, CA: Sage, 1979).

In all countries, most people think taxes are too high; but when they are faced with the choice between cutting taxes and maintaining government services, they choose the services. How can they be so inconsistent? They say there is no inconsistency: If governments will just cut out "waste and fraud," they can cut taxes *and* maintain services. The fact that no government seems to manage that very well does not keep people on both sides of the Atlantic from thinking that it is a splendid idea.

As we will see later in the book, until recently, questions about equal treatment of the races and the sexes have been more prominent in American politics and public opinion than in most European democracies. Since the 1960s, however, Great Britain and France have faced mounting problems resulting from the sharply increased flow of black and brown immigrants from their former colonies in India, Pakistan, the West Indies, and North Africa, and their native white populations have had to face up to problems of equality in jobs, housing, public accommodations, and the like. The women's movement began earlier and has become politically more powerful in the United States than in European countries, but political issues concerning equality of the sexes are steadily becoming hotter in Great Britain and its European neighbors.

In the United States as in the European democracies, there has been what one scholar calls "a phenomenal growth in racial tolerance" since the 1950s. In the 1940s, most white males believed that women, African-Americans, and other racial and ethnic minorities were not entitled to any government help to improve their positions, but in the late 1980s almost everyone, including white males, believed that sexual and racial discrimination is wrong and that government has an obligation to prevent it. As we will see in Chapter 16, there is still a great deal of disagreement over whether the goal should be equality of opportunity or equality of condition, and over whether programs such as affirmative action and comparable worth are proper means to reach the desired ends. But the ideas cf ending racial segregation and providing equal opportunities for all races are now strongly supported by public opinion in all democratic nations.[9]

FOREIGN POLICY

A leading survey of public opinion notes that "because issues of foreign policy are quite removed from everyday experience, 'foreign policy' attitudes are generally held less firmly than opinions on domestic policy."[10] On a few occasions, foreign policy has become highly salient because of a war, whether it is an all-out war such as World War II or a limited war, such as that in Korea (1950–53) or Vietnam (1962–73), that produces casualties without victory. But political elites are much more likely than mass publics to have strong and enduring opinions on the more specific foreign policy questions that fill the newspapers, such as American aid to the "contra" rebels in Nicaragua or continued American membership in the United Nations Educational, Scientific, and Cultural Organization (UNESCO); (see Chapter 18).

TABLE 6.7. Attitudes on Foreign Policy Issues (in percentages)

Issue Area	United States	Great Britain	Federal Republic of West Germany	France
Threat of war most important issue	45	31	28	44
Main cause of international tensions				
Soviet military power	37	47	50	31
American military power	19	37	41	20
Leader in military strength				
Soviet Union	42	52	35	30
Equal	39	27	33	38
United States	11	11	18	16
Best way to improve security				
Strengthen NATO	na	31	21	18
Push arms control	na	40	35	50
Best policy toward Soviet Union				
Conciliatory policy	34	na	67	52
Policy of firmness	57	na	28	35
Better to fight than submit to Russian domination	83	75	74	57

Source: Russell J. Dalton, *Citizen Politics in Western Democracies* (Chatham, NJ: Chatham House, 1988), Table 6.8, p. 117.

In this respect, American public opinion is very much like that in other democratic countries; but there are also noteworthy differences. Table 6.7 displays some of them.

The figures in Table 6.7 show that the Americans and the French are considerably more concerned about the possibility of war than the British or the West Germans. In all four countries, Soviet military power is considered a greater threat to peace than American military power, and pluralities of all three European publics feel that arms control is a better bet than strengthening the North Atlantic Treaty Alliance (NATO) for maintaining their security. And popular majorities in all four countries feel that it would be better to fight a war than to submit to the Soviet Union, although many more Americans than French feel that way. Perhaps the most striking information in the table is its showing that most Americans believe that a policy of firmness toward the Soviet Union is the best bet to ensure national security, while most German and French believe that a conciliatory policy is better.

CONCLUSION

The foregoing discussion sets forth some of the opinions that the governments of the United States and some other democratic polities "find it prudent to heed." In Chapter 7 we will consider some of the ways in which people communicate their political ideologies and policy preferences to each other and to their governments, and consider whether the modern revolution in mass communications technology has basically altered the nature of democratic government.

FOR FURTHER READING

ABRAMSON, PAUL R. *Political Attitudes in America: Formation and Change.* San Francisco: W. H. Freeman & Company, Publishers, 1983. Detailed study, using survey data, of current state of public opinion in the United States.

*ASHER, HERBERT R. *Polling and the Public: What Every Citizen Should Know.* Washington, D.C.: Congressional Quarterly Press, 1987. Useful brief summary of the techniques, uses, and impact of public opinion polls.

CONVERSE, PHILIP E. "Public Opinion and Voting Behavior," in Fred I. Greenstein and Nelson W. Polsby, eds., *Handbook of Political Science.* Reading, MA.: Addison-Wesley, 1975, vol. 4, pp. 75–169. Thoughtful review of the state of knowledge on the formation and content of public opinion.

*DALTON, RUSSELL J. *Citizen Politics in Western Democracies.* Chatham, NJ: Chatham House, 1988. A comparative study, based on survey data, of public opinion in the United States, Great Britain, West Germany, and France.

ERIKSON, ROBERT S., Norman R. Luttberg, and Kent L. Tedin, *American Public Opinion,* 3d ed. New York: Macmillan, 1988. Up-to-date review of American political attitudes based on extensive survey data.

KEY, V. O., JR. *Public Opinion in American Democracy.* New York: Knopf, 1961. A distinguished political scientist's analysis of public opinion.

*LIPPMANN, WALTER. *Public Opinion.* New York: Free Press, 1965. First published in the 1920s, a classic philosophical study of the origins and nature of public opinion.

LIPSET, SEYMOUR MARTIN, and WILLIAM SCHNEIDER. *The Confidence Gap: Business, Labor, and Government in the Public Mind.* New York: Free Press, 1983. Over-time study of changing American levels of confidence in major institutions.

*NIEBURG, H. L. *Public Opinion.* New York: Praeger, 1984. Survey of the formation, content, and impact of public opinion in the United States.

In addition to these books, two magazines are useful in presenting up-to-date information from the polls about the current state of public opinion in the United States and some other countries: *Public Opinion,* published five times a year by the American Enterprise Institute; and *Public Opinion Quarterly,* published four times a year by the American Association for Public Opinion Research.

NOTES

[1] V. O. Key, Jr., *Public Opinion and Democracy* (New York: Knopf, 1961), p. 3.

[2] Quoted in Bernard C. Hennessy, "Public Opinion and Opinion Change," in James A. Robinson, ed., *Political Science Annual,* vol. 1 (Indianapolis: Bobbs- Merrill, 1966), p. 245.

[3] Key, *Public Opinion,* p. 14.

[4] See the summaries of studies by the Roper organization and the National Opinion Research Center in *Public Opinion,* April/May, 1985, pp. 37–40.

[5] Robert S. Erikson, Norman R. Luttberg, and Kent L. Tedin, *American Public Opinion,* 3rd ed. (New York: Macmillan, 1988), p. 90.

[6] Everett Carll Ladd, Jr. and Seymour Martin Lipset, *The Divided Academy* (New York: McGraw-Hill, 1975), pp. 57–60.

[7] See the review of the evidence in Erikson, Luttberg, and Tedin, *American Public Opinion,* pp. 152–56.

[8] The poll results are taken from *Public Opinion,* March/April, 1987, pp. 21–29.

[9] For a detailed review of many public opinion polls in the United States and Europe underlying these conclusions, see Russell J. Dalton, *Citizen Politics in Western Democracies* (Chatham, NJ: Chatham House, 1988), Chapter 6.

[10] Erikson, Luttberg, and Tedin, *American Public Opinion,* p. 62.

7 Political Communication

Whatever one or more men can and do talk about, but which is not amenable to direct sensory contact by them, has no reality beyond what can [be] and is said about it.[1]

Let us begin with some facts about American life in the 1990s. Ninety-eight percent of all American households have at least one television set, and 57 percent have two or more sets. Ninety-nine percent have radio sets, and the average number of sets per household is 5.4. By the time they reach the age of 18, American children have spent more time watching television than going to school. The average adult American spends more time watching television than doing anything else except working and sleeping. Most American adults read some part of a newspaper every day, and even more read a Sunday paper.

While attention to the mass communications media is probably a bit higher in the United States than elsewhere, mass communications play a critical role in the politics of all industrialized nations, democratic or authoritarian. Take an obvious example: In 1988 about 23 million people, by voting in primaries and caucuses, decided that the Democratic presidential nominee would be Michael Dukakis and another 12 million decided that George Bush would run for the Republicans. And in November, about 92 million voted on the final-election choice between Dukakis and Bush. But how many of us actually *knew* Dukakis or Bush or any of the other hopefuls? How many of us had talked with the candidates or worked with them or seen first-hand how they behave in a crisis? Obviously only a tiny fraction, perhaps one-tenth of 1 percent. Where, then, did the rest of us get the information about the candidates' experience, characters, and stands on issues that provided the basis for our choices?

Since we could not possibly acquire it first-hand, we got our information the only way we could—by having it *communicated* to us, either in personal conversations with friends or from what we saw on television, heard on the radio, or read in newspapers. And which of those were the most important? When asked in a national survey in 1987, "Where do you usually get most of your news about what's going on in the world," 66 percent of American adults said television, 36 percent said newspapers, 14 percent said radio, and 4 percent said "other people."[2] (The figures sum to more than 100 percent because some people gave multiple answers.)

As Walter Cronkite used to say in closing his nightly newscasts for CBS, "That's the way it is." Hence, political communication is without question one of the most important aspects of governing in the modern world. Let us begin by seeing what it involves.

THE NATURE OF POLITICAL COMMUNICATION

WHAT IS COMMUNICATION?

In its most general sense **communication** is *the transmission of meaning through the use of symbols.* It is the process by which a person or group tries to make another person or group aware of its feelings about something. In this broad sense, communication occurs in many different ways—through pictures, music, mathematical symbols, gestures, facial expressions, even physical blows. The most common form of communication in human society, however, is the system of oral and written symbols that we call language.

It is easy to see that communication is *the* basic social process. A society, let us recall, is a grouping of people who live in a common environment and have common institutions, activities, and interests. But if they do not communicate with each other in any way, they cannot even be aware of their common interests let alone take any purposeful common action. So the conclusion is simple: *no communication, no society.*

Communication plays an especially significant role in politics, for it is the basic process by which political groups are formed and try to influence public policy. For example, the fact that some people are poor and others are rich has no political significance in itself. But by watching, listening, talking, and reading, poor people learn that some other members of their society are also poor and some are rich. They learn that they are members of a particular economic group that is different from and, to some extent, opposed to another economic group. After talking and reading about these matters, some members of each group decide that they want the government to follow policies favorable to their interests. And through speaking and writing—and perhaps also through cartoons, billboards, protest marches, and other less verbal means—

they try to induce public officials to adopt those policies. Thus communication is the basic process by which political action and political conflict take place.

THE ELEMENTS OF POLITICAL COMMUNICATION

The nature and role of political communication are best understood if we begin by briefly describing the nature of each of its main elements.

Communicators

Any person or group that acts to influence government policy is a political communicator. The main types of such communicators in modern democratic polities are political parties and pressure groups, whose organization and activities are described in Chapters 2 and 10. In addition, however, in every democracy many government agencies use "handouts," "backgrounders," and "leaks" to try to influence the opinions of persons in other agencies and the general public. For example, most of the executive departments and other agencies of the U.S. government maintain public relations bureaus that print and distribute pamphlets, send out speakers, produce radio and television programs, and in other ways try to create public support for their programs. Authoritarian regimes have total control of all the media of mass communications and use them extensively to get their subjects in the right frame of mind to do what the rulers want them to do. They also try to shape the content of all

News Media are Critical for Politicians in Democracies. Senator Edward M. Kennedy (D-Mass.) facing cameras, microphones, and reporters. (Source: Chris Cross/Uniphoto.)

direct personal communications, although they find that much more difficult than controlling what their people see on television, read in newspapers, or hear on radio.

Messages

Communicators begin the communication process by sending out messages. Each message consists of the symbols—words, pictures, gestures, and so on—by which the communicators try to convey the ideas in their minds to the minds of their targeted receivers—the people they especially want to receive their messages.

Media

Communicators must use some kind of medium—some way of transmitting their messages so that their targeted receivers can become aware of the messages. There are, of course, many different "media"[3]—personal conversations with family, friends, and government officials; television and radio broadcasts; columns and editorials in newspapers and magazines; signs carried in protest marches; stones thrown through windows; and so on. We will consider the organization and impact of the various media later in this chapter.

Receivers

A receiver is a person who becomes aware of a communicator's message. Some receive it directly from the original communication, while others receive it indirectly, through second-hand reports from other people. In either case the knowledge, level of interest, and cognitive maps (see Chapter 3) of the receivers, as we will see, are among the major factors that determine the message's impact.

Responses

Every political communication is intended to produce some kind of response from its receivers. To illustrate, let us say that a communicator makes a speech advocating the right of women to have abortions when they wish. The speech, like any communication, may not evoke any response at all, or it may even increase the receivers' hostility to the speaker's position. But the speaker, like all communicators, intends it to produce one or another of at least four kinds of favorable response: initiation, conversion, reinforcement, and activation.

> *Initiation.* The receivers have not previously thought much about the issue. Hence the speaker "initiates" their views on the question.
>
> *Conversion.* Before the speech, the receivers were to some degree prolife, but the speaker's presentation is so effective that it persuades them to abandon their previous views and support the prochoice position.

Reinforcement. Before the speech, the receivers were mildly prochoice, but their beliefs were shaken by prolife sermons delivered in their churches, and some considered switching sides. However, the prochoice speech refutes the points made in the sermons and gives the audience new prochoice arguments, and the audience leaves the hall supporting the prochoice position more strongly than before.

Activation. Before the speech, the audience was mildly prochoice and never seriously considered changing their minds, but they were not excited about the issue and did nothing to advance the prochoice cause. However, the speaker stirs them up so that they contribute money, volunteer to pass out leaflets, and picket speeches by prolife advocates.

Many studies have been made on each of the five basic elements of communication, but in the rest of this chapter we will focus mainly on two aspects: the organization and operation of the mass media, and the impact of political communication on people's political views and behavior.

THE MASS COMMUNICATIONS MEDIA

Communications media are usually divided into two types. **Face-to-face media** are *media that transmit their messages by direct personal contact between communicators and receivers;* they include personal conversations, personal letters, and the like. **Mass media** are *media that "broadcast" their messages to large numbers of receivers with whom they have no face-to-face contact.* The most prominent media in this category are television, radio, newspapers, movies, magazines, and books. In all industrialized nations, democratic and authoritarian, television, newspapers, and radio (in that order) have by far the greatest audiences and political impact, so we will concentrate on them in this chapter.

TELEVISION

Ownership, Organization, and Regulation

In the United States, most television broadcasting is privately owned and operated, and most broadcasters receive most of their revenues from the sale of time for broadcasting advertisements. But American broadcasters are very far from having a completely free hand in broadcasting about politics. The political content of their programs is, in fact, much more closely regulated than the political content of newspapers, magazines, and books. Their main regulator is the Federal Communications Commission (FCC), whose main weapon is its licensing power. Every broadcasting station must obtain a license from the FCC before it can operate, and its license comes up for renewal every five years. In order to qualify for a new or renewed license, each broadcaster must comply with a number of FCC standards and rules, some of which apply to the content

---

AMERICAN TELEVISION FACTS, 1987–88

Number of broadcasting stations

Commercial:	968
Public:	303
Total:	1,271

Number of cable systems: 7,900
Annual revenues from advertising: $22.6 billion
Number of stations receivable by percentages of population

1 to 4:	3
5 to 6:	5
7 to 8:	9
9 to 10:	9
11 to 14:	29
15 to 19:	16
20 or more:	29
	100

Percentage of households with television sets

At least one:	98
Two or more:	57

Percentage of television households subscribing to cable: 45
Average hours per week watching television

Children 2–5:	28
Children 6–11:	27
Teenagers:	22
Adults 18–34:	29
Adults 35–54:	30
Adults 55 and older:	40
Men:	30
Women:	36

Sources: Statistical Abstract of the United States 1988 (Washington, D.C.: Bureau of the Census, 1988), Table 878, p. 52, and Table 887, p. 526; and *Nielson Reports on Television* (A. C. Nielson Co., 1984 and 1985).

---

of broadcasts about politics. For example, the "equal opportunities rule" requires that if a station sells or gives time to a particular political party or candidate, it must make available on the same terms an equal amount of time to any competing party or candidate. The FCC also controls such matters as the operating frequencies and power of broadcasting transmitters, the legal and financial relationships of broadcasting stations with the networks, and the number of stations that can be owned by one person or corporation. It has exercised little if any political censorship, but it has had considerable (not enough, according to some critics; too much, according to others) effect upon the

> *The mass media in America are business, whether big or little; they are, as George Gerbner has said, "the cultural arm of American industry." That is the primary fact about the mass media in the United States, oriented as they are to marketing. One must understand that fact to grasp the essential meaning of the media and their relationship to the American social order. A similar understanding is necessary for analysis of the Soviet communication system. To grasp the essential meaning of the Soviet mass media and their relationship to Communist society, one must first recognize that the Soviet communication system is an arm of the political order, as it is in any authoritarian society.*[4]

content of programs and upon the financial and legal structure of the broadcasting industry.

There are various patterns of ownership and regulation in other democratic countries. In Belgium, Denmark, Ireland, and Norway, for example, all radio and television stations are owned and operated by the government. In Sweden, broadcasting is also controlled by a monopoly, but one in which both the government and private interests participate. In most other democracies, there is, as in the United States, a mixture of privately owned commercial television and publicly owned noncommercial television. The systems of greatest interest to Americans are probably those of France, Great Britain, and Canada, and we will look at them in a bit more detail.

For many years, all radio and television broadcasting in France was, as in Denmark, a government monopoly. In 1982, however, the system was radically changed. The government retained its monopoly over television transmissions, but all programming was put in the control of seven independent but government-financed companies under the overall supervision of the nine-member Haute Autorité de la Communication Audovisuelle. Each company has its own budget and administrative council made up of two representatives of the government and one representative each from parliament, the press, and its own staff. All three television channels are financed partly by private advertising but mainly by public funds.

Great Britain has a mixture of publicly and privately owned broadcasting. The British Broadcasting Corporation (BBC) was chartered as a "public corporation" by Parliament in 1927 but has never been directly owned or controlled by the government. The BBC's board of governors is appointed by the Queen on the advice of the prime minister, but its members are not political in a partisan sense, and they make policy without supervision by any government agency. Every owner of a radio or television set must purchase a license, and the revenue from the license fees is assigned to the BBC. The rest of BBC revenue comes from the sale of its weekly publication, *Radio Times,* and from the sale of its programs to foreign broadcasters. Most BBC programs are planned and broadcast centrally and relayed over a series of local and regional stations, although some local and regional programs are also broadcast. The BBC now operates two television channels.

Parliament has also authorized commercial television (1954) and radio (1972) for private profit. It has created a body somewhat comparable to the American FCC, the Independent Broadcasting Authority (IBA). The IBA owns and operates the transmitting stations, but the programs are produced by private companies under contract to the IBA. There are now 17 such companies for television and 21 for radio, most of them organized on regional bases. Some are controlled by motion picture interests, others by newspapers, others by general investors. Advertisers do not directly sponsor programs as in the United States but purchase time between programs when a series of advertisements are broadcast—singing commercials and all. IBA also operates two television channels.

The Canadian system is an interesting hybrid of American, British, and European practices. The Canadian Broadcasting Corporation (CBC) was created and is periodically renewed by acts of Parliament. The Canadian Parliament directly controls the CBC's finances, whereas the British Parliament has no such control over the BBC's finances. The CBC used to be supported entirely by receiver license fees on the British model, but since the 1950s it has been financed by a combination of commercial revenue and annual parliamentary grants and loans. Privately owned broadcasting stations are also licensed and

Accountability by Television. President Bush answers questions at a nationally televised press conference. (Source: AP/Wide World Photos.)

regulated by an entirely separate agency, the Canadian Radio-Television and Telecommunications Commission (CRTC), which is analogous to the American FCC. These arrangements result in three parallel and separate broadcasting groups: the CBC's national network, the privately owned CTV national network, and a number of independent private stations. Some of the latter are affiliated with the CBC and use some CBC programs at no cost, while the CBC shares in any commercial revenues raised by the stations in connection with CBC programs. The net result is that although the Canadian system was originally fashioned on the British model, it now more nearly resembles the American model.

Presentation of Political News and Information

In all democratic countries, television broadcasters present political news and information mainly through their regular newscasts, which feature short accounts of the important political events (as selected by their news producers) that have taken place since the previous newscast. They usually include pictures and words about what political candidates and officeholders have been doing, and they often emphasize interviews of the political leaders by television correspondents and "anchors."

From the politicians' standpoint, this kind of coverage has several advantages and one great disadvantage. On the plus side, the coverage is free and the viewing audience tends to believe that what they are seeing is what has really happened—probably because it comes as news, not as advertisements trying to sell them something. But there is also a negative side: The television producers and correspondents control the content of each broadcast; hence they, and not the candidates, select the 15- or 20-second segments ("TV bytes" they are called) of the candidates' speeches that will appear on the air, and their objective is to make interesting news stories, not to make the candidates look good.

That disadvantage has two consequences. One is a constant drumbeat of complaint by supporters of particular leaders, parties, and ideologies that television's news coverage is biased against them. And the other is a demand by politicians for free and unedited access to the airwaves so that they can present their issue-stands and personal characters in *their* way, not the networks' way.

The Western democracies meet such demands by some mixture of two devices. One is permitting candidates and parties to purchase air time just like commercial advertisers and use it to present their own political advertisements, usually in 30-second or 1-minute "spot" advertisements shown, like nonpolitical advertisements, during regular entertainment programs. The other is giving the political parties some free air time in which they can present their cases any way they wish without interference by government authorities. These are generally called "party political broadcasts."

Thus in the United States, political parties, candidates, and pressure groups are allowed to buy television time for political advertisements, although in presidential elections there are limits on the total amount of money they can spend on campaigning and therefore on how much they can spend on television. Some public stations provide the equivalent of "party political broadcasts," but local commercial stations and national networks will not give the parties free air time in which they, and not the broadcasters, control the contents.

The status of political advertising and party political broadcasts varies considerably among Western democracies. In Great Britain, no party or candidate can purchase time from either the BBC or the IBA for broadcasting political advertising. The only broadcasts whose contents are controlled by the parties are the free "party political broadcasts." In the 1959 general election, the BBC and the Independent Television Authority (the IBA's predecessor) jointly proposed to the leading parties that the free time made available for party-controlled telecasts be divided into a ratio of 4 parts for Conservatives, 4 for Labour, and 1 for the Liberals (presumably reflecting the parties' respective voting strengths); and the parties were delighted to accept. In subsequent elections from 1964 to 1979, the ratio was changed to 5:5:3, reflecting increased Liberal strength; in the 1983 and 1987 elections it was changed again to 5:5:4, with the increased share going to the new alliance between the Liberal and Social Democratic parties. In each party political broadcast, the party decides for itself what to do with its allotted time, and the stations broadcast whatever it has prepared. In addition, the BBC and ITN (Independent Television News, the private news-producing company) broadcast their own debates, forums, interviews, talk shows, and other political programs and try—not entirely to the satisfaction of the party leaders—to divide the attention they give to each party's candidates and programs by the same 5:5:4 formula. This British variation on the American equal-time rule is now well established and is likely to persist.

Canada allows political parties to purchase air time for political advertising but limits the total amount they can purchase and allocates it among the parties according to their electoral support and seats in Parliament. In French presidential and parliamentary elections, some free air time is given to each of the presidential candidates and political parties, but no one can purchase air time for political advertising. In West Germany, parties are granted free time on television to broadcast a number of 150-second spot broadcasts *(Wahlspots)* corresponding to their shares of the popular votes. Italy also provides free broadcast time to all eligible parties during election campaigns but requires that some of it be used for press conferences.

In summary, then, the United States is one of the few countries in the world (Venezuela is another) in which parties and candidates can purchase as much television time as they can afford for political advertising and also one of the few in which no air time is given free to the parties or candidates to use as they see fit. In most democracies it is now possible for businesses to purchase air time for broadcasting commercial advertisements, but most of them prohibit parties and candidates from buying air time for broadcasting political advertisements. Of course, in the United States, as in all democratic countries, there are many broadcaster-controlled newscasts, discussion programs, interviews, call-in shows, and the like covering not only election campaigns but many other aspects of public policy and policy making. Most scholars agree that this free television exposure is far more important than paid political advertisements in shaping the way the viewing public feels about candidates, parties, and causes.

Political and Structural Bias in Television News

Ever since television became the preeminent medium of political mass communications, a considerable debate has raged about whether or not the broadcasters' news coverage of political events and issues is biased. The debate has been especially noisy in the United States, where quite a few political partisans have charged that the broadcasters, especially those in the news divisions of the three national networks (ABC, CBS, and NBC), have a strong *political* bias—that is, they deliberately slant their coverage so as to help certain candidates and causes and harm others. The most familiar version of this charge is made by a number of conservative organizations and critics, ranging from Reid Irvine and his Accuracy in Media organization and former Vice President Spiro T. Agnew to Pat Buchanan, the chief communications aide to President Reagan in his second term. They accuse the network newscasts of consistently and deliberately favoring liberals over conservatives, Democrats over Republicans, prochoice advocates over prolife advocates, and opponents of prayer in the schools over its proponents.

Much less well-known is the mirror-image charge by left-wing critics, such as David Altheide, Robert Cirino, and the organization Fairness and Accuracy in Reporting, that the network newscasters are hired guns for the bosses of big business and use their broadcasts to glorify the establishment and suppress news of how the power structure is crushing and alienating the masses.

There is a third view: Many scholars of television's coverage of politics—including, among others, Edwin Diamond, Edward Jay Epstein, Doris Graber, Richard Hofstetter, and Michael Robinson—conclude that television's bias is not political but *structural*. Their studies of political programming have convinced them that there is no systematic favoring of liberals over conservatives or Democrats over Republicans; rather, there is consistently more sympathetic coverage of people who challenge the establishment than of people in power, of "mavericks" than of "party bosses," of candidates running behind than of front-runners, of dark horses than of favorites, of new faces than of old ones, and, perhaps most important of all, of nonpoliticians than of politicians.

This structural bias, they believe, grows from the very nature of the television medium itself—the legal constraints on how it operates, the fierce competition among the networks, the need to attract and keep huge audiences by featuring vivid pictures instead of boring "talking heads," the need to squeeze everything into 24-minute broadcasts (30 clock minutes minus 6 min-

Dan Rather of CBS.
(Source: AP/Wide World Photos.)

Tom Brokaw of NBC.
(Source: AP/Wide World Photos.)

Peter Jennings of ABC.
(Source: AP/Wide World Photos.)   **The Anchors: America's Most Powerful Men?**

utes for commercials), and above all the need not to overtax the short attention spans of their viewers, most of whom are quickly bored by political stories.

The networks, of course, heatedly deny that they have *any* kind of bias. One producer for NBC News says, "The news is not a reporter's perception or explanation of what happens; *it is simply what happens*"; and a former head of CBS News has described television as an "electric mirror" that simply shows what is going on in the world just as a glass mirror shows what is standing in front of it.[5]

Regulation of Political Broadcasting in the United States

Whatever may be the merits of the charges of bias, we should be clear that the political contents of television broadcasts are regulated far more closely than their counterparts in newspapers, magazines, and books. The First Amendment to the U.S. Constitution declares that "Congress shall make no law . . . abridging the freedom of . . . the press." The Supreme Court has interpreted this prohibition very strictly. For example, in *New York Times* v. *Sullivan* (1964), the Court held that neither public officials nor public figures can collect damages for defamatory remarks made about them unless they can prove that the remarks were made with malicious intent and with reckless disregard for the truth. Consequently, the print media are free to print just about anything they wish about politics; they are constrained very little by libel laws, and they have no legal obligation to be "fair" or "balanced" in what they say about political issues or personalities.

Television and radio broadcasters, on the other hand, operate under much tighter legal restraints. The Supreme Court has repeatedly upheld the constitutionality of these restraints on the basis of the "scarcity doctrine." That doctrine notes that there are only a limited number of frequencies available for broadcasting television and radio signals, and two stations cannot operate in the same area on the same frequency. Hence the frequencies have to be assigned to particular stations by the FCC, and the Supreme Court has declared that in return for allowing those stations to use such a limited and precious national resource, Congress and the FCC have the right to impose certain rules on how the stations operate.[6] And Congress has stipulated that the basic purpose to be served in assigning and renewing broadcasting licenses is "the public interest, convenience, or necessity"—*not* the broadcasters' right to make money or propagandize for their personal political preferences.

In carrying out this mandate, Congress and the FCC have imposed several rules on the broadcasting of political materials. The most important are the following:

The Requirement to Broadcast Public Affairs Programs. The Federal Communications Act (FCA) requires that every station must broadcast a reasonable number of programs on public affairs. The exact ratio of such programs to other programming is never spelled out, but broadcasters understand that it had better be at least 15 percent or so. The rule is satisfied mainly by regular broadcasts of national and local news, including political news, although some broadcasters air a few "documentaries" dealing with public problems and political issues in greater depth than in the short news broadcasts.

The Fairness Doctrine. Until recently the FCC required that whenever a station broadcast material on a controversial issue of public interest, it was required to broadcast—then or later—presentations of contrasting views on that issue. The broadcasters usually discharged this obligation by including in the initial program statements by advocates of both the "pro" and "con" positions on each issue, and occasionally they also provided short periods of free time for replies by advocates of opposing views.

At the present writing the Fairness Doctrine is suspended, perhaps permanently. During most of the Reagan administration, Mark Fowler, the chairman of the FCC, contended that broadcasters should be as free as newspapers, books, and magazines to present whatever political news stories and commentaries they wish in any manner they wish. The scarcity-doctrine argument no longer makes sense, he argued, because the great expansion of cable television, direct satellite broadcasting, videocassette recorders, and other new technologies have given television viewers even more alternative sources of information than newspaper readers, and it is therefore time to make broadcasting as free as the print media. Many people—both liberals and conservatives (the issue seems to cut across the usual ideological lines)—do not agree. They fear that cancelling the Fairness Doctrine will open the floodgates for broadcasters to slant the news any way they wish to promote their favorite candidates and causes; and the fact that television has a much stronger impact than newspapers on people's information and understanding means that slanted television will distort our democratic system much more than slanted newspapers, books, and magazines do.

In 1987, a federal court of appeals unexpectedly ruled that Congress had not *mandated* the Fairness Doctrine but had merely authorized the FCC to impose it. Fowler and the FCC seized the opportunity and suspended the doctrine. Congress then amended the legislation to *require* the FCC to enforce the rule, but President Reagan vetoed the bill and the Senate could not muster the necessary two-thirds vote to override the veto. At the end of the 1980s it was not clear what President Bush and the new Congress would do about restoring the Fairness Doctrine, but it was clearly destined to be one of the major issues of communications policy in the 1990s.

The Equal-Opportunities Rule. As we have seen, the FCC requires that if a station gives free time to a candidate for public office, it must give an equal amount of free time to all other candidates running for that office. Under recent rulings, however, this does not apply to the coverage of candidates on news programs. Hence there is no need for the stations and networks to give as much news time to minor-party candidates as to major-party candidates, and they are perfectly free to broadcast the debates between the Democratic and Republican presidential candidates without including third-party candidates so long as the broadcasters, and not the candidates, control the debates' formats.

NEWSPAPERS

Since the 1960s, television has replaced newspapers as the preeminent mass communications medium. Nevertheless, it is important to recognize that while

AMERICAN NEWSPAPER FACTS, 1950–87

	1950	1960	1970	1987
Number of Newspapers				
Daily	1,894	1,854	1,838	1,646
Semiweekly	337	324	423	510
Weekly	9,794	8,979	8,903	6,750
Total	12,115	11,315	11,383	9,031
Newspaper circulation (in millions)				
Daily	53.8	58.9	62.1	62.5
Sunday	46.6	47.7	49.2	58.9
Daily circulation (per capita)	.354	.327	.305	.260
Broadcasting stations owned by newspapers and/or magazines				
Television	161	191	191	272
AM radio	412	318	318	232
FM radio	147	248	248	226

The figures are taken from the *Statistical Abstract of the United States 1988,* Table 892, p. 528; Table 893, p. 528; and Table 889, p. 527.

people now turn to newspapers less than to television for their political information and trust what they get less than what they get from television (see Table 7.1), newspapers are still very important elements in the communications systems of most countries, including the United States. As the figures in the box show, the number of American newspapers has declined since 1950, and so has their readership. Yet people regard them as their second most important and second most trusted source of political information. Equally important and less obvious, most scholars of communication believe that newspapers—especially the wire services and the top-quality national papers such as the *New York Times, Washington Post, Wall Street Journal, Los Angeles Times,* and a few others—set the agenda and perform the basic news-gathering function for the network news shows. We are told that the first thing the network news producers do every morning is to read carefully the *Times, Post, Journal,* and perhaps one or two other papers. That is how they find out what is going on in the world and what they need to feature on that night's newscasts. If the top papers give a story big headlines and a lot of space, the networks will think that it must be important, and they will give it a prominent place on their newscasts. The networks may go their own way on lesser news stories and particularly on the weather reports and human-interest stories that are so prominent in their newscasts; but basically they rely on the "news consensus" as printed by the major newspapers to tell them what is happening and what is important. Hence newspapers deserve our attention, if not as much attention as we have given to television.

In authoritarian systems, such as those of Iran and North Korea, all mass media, including newspapers, are government-owned and government-operated monopolies. Their mandate is to persuade the people to support government policies with enthusiasm, not to tell them what is really going on. In the democracies a few newspapers, such as *L'Humanité* of Paris and *L'Unità* of Rome, are owned and operated by political parties (in these instances Communist parties), mainly as agencies for drumming up electoral support. Most newspapers, however, are privately owned and operated and are run mainly for the same purpose for which other private businesses are mainly run: to make profits for their owners.

In the United States, newspapers obtain their revenues partly from subscriptions but mainly from advertising, which accounts for 65 to 90 percent of their total income. Increased circulation is therefore a prime goal of all American papers, for it not only brings in more direct revenue but also attracts more advertisers. This goal inclines editors to print material that they think will interest readers and yet not unduly offend present and potential advertisers. No commercial newspaper can afford to print only what its editors think readers ought to read; it must print what they think readers *want* to read, and this objective plays a great part in determining what is regarded as news. In addition to news, most papers print many "features," such as comic strips, recipes, fashion notes, bridge columns, and so on.

Most newspapers also print material explicitly intended to influence the political opinions of their readers, mainly in the form of unsigned editorials and signed "columns." The evidence suggests that such material affects the political opinions of readers relatively little. In both the United States and Great Britain, for example, almost every voter regularly reads some part of a newspaper, and the great majority of American and British newspapers editorially favor the Republican and Conservative parties, respectively; yet the Democratic and Labour parties, despite their usual lack of editorial support, continue to win quite a few elections.

Newspapers have a larger audience than any other mass medium except television. In the United States, for example, approximately 90 percent of all adults regularly read at least some part of a daily newspaper. Elsewhere in the world the largest numbers of newspapers and the largest audiences are found in nations with the highest rates of per capita wealth, industrial development, and literacy. More than 80 percent of the total newspaper circulation in the entire world is in Europe and North America.

RADIO

The advent of the television age has certainly not driven radio broadcasting out of business, even in the United States. In 1950, at the beginning of television's growth, the average American household had 2.1 radio sets; in 1985, 25 years after television had become the leading mass medium, the average household had 5.4 radio sets, the number of commercial radio stations had increased from 5,949 to 8,556, the number of FM stations doubled, and there were also 1,194 educational FM stations.

Radio has adapted to the dominance of television, especially in the United States, by changing from "broadcasting" to "narrowcasting." That is, prior to 1950, most stations and the national networks with which they were affiliated sought, like television broadcasters today, to attract the largest possible audiences, and so their programs were designed to appeal to everyone. In the 1980s, however, most radio stations cater only to particular segments of the population and broadcast only programs designed to appeal to them. Hence the radio sections of most big-city newspapers identify each station's specialty—hard rock, soft rock, country and western, classical, "beautiful music," all-news, news-and-talk, and so on. As Table 7.1 shows, radio is now a distant third to television and newspapers as a source of information for most people. Even so, it continues to play a political role of some significance: For instance, shortly after leaving the governorship of California in 1974, Ronald Reagan began broadcasting weekly political commentaries. He built up a substantial audience that was very helpful in his drive for the presidency and he continued his broadcasts during his tenure as president.

Radio is probably somewhat more important in the other developed countries than in the United States. It is certainly much more important in the less developed countries of Africa and Asia, where it reaches many more people than television and is the principal medium of mass communications.

THE POLITICAL IMPACT OF MASS COMMUNICATIONS

ON MASS PUBLICS

Since the late 1950s, several national polling organizations have been asking respondents where they get their information about what is going on in the world and what sources of information they trust the most. Their answers over a 15-year span are shown in Table 7.1.

From the evidence we have reviewed so far, there is no doubt that in the 1990s most people in the advanced/industrialized countries learn most of what they know about politics from watching television and reading newspapers rather from conversations with family and friends, reading books and magazines, or participating directly in politics. There is also no doubt that most of us are voracious consumers of the mass medias' messages, and even though only a small fraction of those messages have much political content, they are bound to have some impact on our political beliefs and actions. The question is, what kind of impact and how much?

Some people regard modern advertising as an irresistible weapon for making people do what the advertiser wants. They view people as bundles of

TABLE 7.1.   Use of and Trust in News Sources, 1959–84

"I'd like to ask you where you usually get most of your news about what's going on in the world today—from the newspapers or radio or television or magazines or talking to people or where?" (more than one answer permitted)

Source of Most News	1959 (%)	1968 (%)	1974 (%)	1978 (%)	1984 (%)
Television	51	59	65	67	64
Newspapers	57	48	47	49	40
Radio	34	25	21	20	14
Magazines	8	7	4	5	4
People	4	5	4	5	4

"If you got conflicting or different reports of the same news story from radio, television, the magazines and the newspapers, which of the four versions would you be most inclined to believe—the one on radio or television or magazines or newspapers?" (only one answer permitted)

Most Believable	1959 (%)	1968 (%)	1974 (%)	1978 (%)	1984 (%)
Television	29	44	51	47	53
Newspapers	32	21	20	23	24
Radio	12	8	8	9	8
Magazines	10	11	8	9	7
Don't know, no answer	17	16	13	12	9

Source: Burns W. Roper, "Trends in Attitudes Toward the Media: A 26-Year Review," *Public Attitudes Toward Television and Other Media in a Time of Change* (Roper Poll, Television Information Office, 1984), pp. 3, 5.

psychological "knee-jerk" reflexes, and they are convinced that if a skilled advertiser taps the correct reflexes in the correct ways, people can be made to do anything, from buying a particular brand of toothpaste to voting for a particular candidate. Thus, for instance, such people believe that Ronald Reagan was elected president in 1980 and reelected in 1984 solely or mainly because he was "the great communicator"—an experienced and professional motion picture, radio, and television performer who knew just how to use the mass media to beguile people into seeing things his way.

Let us admit that the great success of the advertising industry and the ability of dictators like Adolf Hitler and the Ayatollah Khomeini to mobilize the masses fanatically behind them lend a certain credibility to this view. Nevertheless, social science research has shown it to be wrong. Michael J. Robinson, for example, points out that in the 1984 election, the television networks and major newspapers consistently gave Reagan much more unfavorable treatment than they gave Mondale—not, he emphasizes, because they were liberal Democrats trying to beat a conservative Republican but because Reagan was both the "establishment candidate" and the front-runner. Yet Reagan won reelection by a large margin, and Robinson's research shows that the more unfavorable the networks' treatment of Reagan became, the larger his lead grew. As Robinson put it, the "good news" that the media reported—the booming economy, the low rates of inflation and unemployment, and the fact that the United States was not at war anywhere—simply overshadowed the "bad press" and the "negative spin" the media consistently gave Reagan by emphasizing his age and his vagueness on the issues.[7]

What, then, *is* the political impact of the mass media? The answer, I think, was best stated by the distinguished political sociologist Bernard Berelson:

> Some kinds of *communication* on some kinds of *issues,* brought to the attention of some kinds of *people* under some kinds of *conditions* have some kinds of *effects.*[8]

Each of the italicized words in Berelson's formulation identifies a significant variable in the process, and each may operate quite differently in different circumstances.

Kind of Communication

A communication may have reportorial or editorial content or both. Reportorial content simply *presents* the known facts about what has happened. Editorial content *evaluates* what has happened and *speculates* about what might happen in the future. Although most attention has been directed to "editorializing," the evidence suggests that reportorial content is more effective in influencing opinions. If we tell people, "Arab terrorists want to intimidate American leaders," they may or may not be impressed; but if we tell them, "Arab terrorists have just killed over 200 U.S. marines in Lebanon with a truck bomb," we are likely to get a more intense and active response.

Another aspect of communication that has long interested social scientists is the fact, shown repeatedly by their research, that television clearly has the greatest impact of all the mass media. Why? As I have written elsewhere:

> *For most of us an important part of any communication is not only what the communicator says but what kind of human being he or she seems to be. That information is conveyed far more vividly by television's combination of words, voice, and pictures than by the faceless voice of radio or by the faceless and voiceless words of newspapers. Perhaps that explains why most Americans consume more political news from television than from newspapers and why they rely more on the accuracy of what they see on television than on what they read in newspapers.*[9]

Kind of Issue

Communication is most effective when it deals with new and unstructured issues on which no strong opinions already exist. Most of us are more likely to accept the judgments, favorable or unfavorable, of people and groups about whom we know little than of those that we know well. For example, if we tell a railroad president, "All politicians are crooks!" he may well agree; but if we tell him that "X railroad is the most inefficient in the world," he will probably reply that the situation involves too many complex factors to justify such an extreme statement. On the other hand, if we make both statements to a politician, he will probably enter qualifications and reservations about politicians and heartily agree about the railroad.

Communication is likely to be more effective on issues that the receivers regard as relatively unimportant than on those they see as crucial. They may have views on both kinds of issues, but their opinions on what they see as the important ones are likely to be far stronger (and therefore less changeable) than their opinions on issues that seem relatively unimportant.

Kind of Audience

Obviously, communicators can affect the opinions only of those who receive their messages. Thus people who watch a lot of television, read only the comics and sports pages of their newspapers, and never read a book are more likely to be affected politically by what is broadcast on television than by what is printed in newspapers or books. Conversely, people who do a lot of reading as well as viewing are likely to be better informed and less easily influenced by television alone. By the same token, as we have seen, people who already have strong views on a matter are much less likely to be influenced by the mass media, including television, than people with weakly held or no views.

Conditions

A communicator who controls all the communications media is obviously in a better position to influence opinion than is one who must worry about competing messages. That, of course, explains why the rulers in authoritarian regimes are careful to control the communications media as completely as they possibly can. It also explains why the model of democracy outlined in Chapter 5 requires free access to communications media, and it accounts for the concern that some observers have expressed over the tendencies toward increasing concentration of ownership and control of the mass media in modern democracies. Most observers agree, however, that this tendency has not yet become full-fledged monopoly; and in any case the effectiveness of mass communications is limited by the other factors we are considering here.

Effects

Berelson argued that the long-range effects of communication are more significant than the short-range effects. Among the long- range effects he included such matters as giving meanings to key political terms, furnishing basic pictures of what the world is like, and emphasizing and perpetuating certain social values.

Communications, especially as they affect political campaigns, appear to have the following kinds of effects on their receivers. The least frequent is *conversion*—inducing people to switch preferences from one candidate or policy to another. More frequent is *initiation*—establishing attitudes on issues that have previously had little or no visibility for the mass public, and on which most people have no prior opinions. Still more frequent is *reinforcement*—bolstering the preferences that receivers already have and providing them with arguments to counter both their own doubts and unsettling propaganda from the other side. The most frequent effect is *activation*—making supporters feel that the issue is so important and their side is so right that they will act to advance it, by voting, attending meetings, contributing money, and so on.

Most directors of political campaigns are well aware of these probabilities. As a result, most campaigns are designed not to win people away from the opposition, but to keep people already on their side faithful to the cause and to ensure that they go to the polls when it counts.

ON POLITICAL AND GOVERNMENTAL LEADERS

In Election Campaigns

The people who organize political campaigns in modern democracies know that most voters get most of their information about the candidates' personalities and stands on the issues from the mass media, especially television. Consequently, the management of campaigns has largely passed from party leaders with backgrounds in party politics and public office to professional "campaign consultants" with backgrounds in advertising and television production.

The main object of every political campaign is to send favorable messages about the candidate's personality and issue positions over television—messages that the voters will see and believe. They have two ways of doing this. One is to get favorable coverage by the "free media." We noted earlier that in all democratic countries, both private and public television stations and networks broadcast a great deal of material about electoral politics, in their newscasts covering campaign speeches and rallies, televised debates between candidates, interviews with candidates, call-in talk shows, and the like. Free media coverage has two great advantages: Air time costs nothing; and viewers are more likely to believe what they see because they know that the broadcasters, not the candidates or the parties, control what comes over the air. It also has one great disadvantage: The broadcasters control the broadcasts' contents, and if they portray candidates negatively, they can do great damage and there is nothing the candidates can do about it.

Hence every campaign organization does all that it can to get as much and as favorable coverage from the free media as it can. But it also puts out its own "paid media"—mainly political advertisements that present their candidates in the best possible light and/or their opponents in the worst. Paid media have one great advantage: Their contents are controlled by the candidates and can be produced to make them look as good as possible. But paid media also have one great disadvantage: They are advertisements trying to sell the voters something, and the voters know it. Most of those voters have spent much of their nonpolitical lives being bombarded by thousands upon thousands of commercial advertisements trying to sell them countless products, and they are wary of any media message that they know is trying to sell them something.

That being the case, no candidate organization can afford to rely entirely on either paid media or free media. They do their best to get their candidates frequently and favorably covered by the broadcasters, and they spend hundreds of thousands of dollars in preparing persuasive political advertisements and buying air time to show them. But the point to remember is that the mass communications media, especially television, are the main sources of information for most voters; most candidates and their organizations are well aware of this; and consequently the main tactic of every modern political campaign is to use both free media and paid media to get the best exposure they can.

In Government: Handouts, Backgrounders, and Leaks

The mass communications media are at least as important for public officeholders and other policy makers between elections as they are for candidates during elections. They know that their chances of getting their getting their policies adopted and improving their personal status and power depend mainly on what other policy makers—and ultimately the general public—know and feel about what they are doing.

Consequently, every major elected official and every major administrative agency has some kind of "public relations" office charged with "getting out their story" through the mass media in the most favorable light. For example, every president of the United States has a press secretary and dozens of assistants whose job is to make sure that the 5,000 newspaper and television correspondents assigned to cover the White House publish and air stories that are as favorable as possible. Every cabinet member, every executive department, and every administrative agency has its equivalent, though none draw more than a small fraction of the president's coverage. Every senator and representative has a press secretary with a similar job, and the Senate maintains three and the House six recording studios in which the members can make audiotapes or videotapes for free broadcast by stations in their states and districts. The main products of press secretaries and public relations bureaus are official "handouts" and semiofficial "backgrounders." Handouts are prepared documents, often hundreds of pages long, in which the official or agency sets forth in detail defenses of past actions and arguments for proposed actions. Backgrounders are more informal occasions in which press secretaries or perhaps their bosses meet with members of the press and tells them "off the record" what is really going on so that the correspondents will write the story knowing the "true facts"—and therefore, it is hoped, put the policy maker in a good light. The correspondents cannot attribute their information to a public official by name, so they attribute them to such sources as "a high White House official" or "an authoritative source in the State Department."

Both handouts and backgrounders are important sources of information for the news media, but perhaps even more important, and certainly more controversial, are the never-ending flow of "leaks"—one of the most widespread, influential, and deplored processes of modern democratic government. Strictly speaking, a **leak** is an *officially unauthorized transmission of confidential government information to the news media.* There are countless examples, but let me mention two prominent instances in the Reagan administration. In November 1982, the administration was looking for ways to cut the budget deficit, and one possibility under consideration was taxing unemployment benefits on the same basis as regular income. A staff aide to the secretary of the treasury was strongly opposed to the idea, and he secretly told a reporter for the *Washington Post* that it was under serious consideration. The *Post* headlined the story the next day, a storm of protest broke from labor unions, and after a few days the president's press secretary announced that the idea had never been seriously considered and would not be pursued. The leak thus killed the policy, as the leaker intended.

In 1984 there was a struggle inside the administration over how to handle the matter of the Soviet Union's violations of past arms control treaties. The hard-liners wanted the president to make a speech about the violations so as to create an atmosphere hostile to any new arms control treaty with the Soviets, which they feared would weaken America's defenses. The soft-liners wanted the violations to be discussed only with the Soviets and only in secret so that neither side would lose face and a new treaty could be signed. The hard-liners leaked the information about the violations through friendly members of various congressmen's staffs to the Washington *Times,* which then ran a series of stories, complete with maps and charts, reporting the secret information about the violations. As a result, the signing of the treaty was delayed for nearly four years until the administration could satisfy enough members of the Senate that new inspection systems would force the Soviets to live up to the proposed new agreement on limiting intermediate-range ballistic missiles in Europe. In this instance the leaks did not kill the treaty, but they delayed it four years.[10] Perhaps most famous of all are the leaks by a still-unknown official in the Nixon administration, code-named "Deep Throat," to *Washington Post* reporters that provided much of the information about the Watergate scandals that ultimately led to President Nixon's 1974 resignation.[11]

Every president since George Washington has deplored leaks and sought ways of preventing them. In recent administrations, Richard Nixon established a secret "plumbers' unit" to "fix the leaks" by tapping the telephones of persons suspected of passing secret information to reporters. In November 1985, Ronald Reagan signed a secret directive ordering the random use of mandatory lie-detector tests on 182,000 federal employees and defense contractors with access to secret information; but someone who opposed the policy leaked the directive to a reporter for the *Los Angeles Times*. The *Times* immediately published the story, which evoked the comment from Secretary of State George

Shultz that "the minute in this government I am told that I'm not trusted is the day that I leave," and the next day the president cancelled the order.

Not only was this one more of a great many instances in which a leak has killed a policy, but it confirmed the fact that leaks are a permanent and inescapable part of the mass communications process in modern democratic governments. Why are they so inevitable? One reason is the news media's eagerness to "scoop" their competitors by publishing exclusive and accurate stories based on leaked information about what is *really* going on behind government's closed doors. Most journalists consider it part of their professional obligation to report all the facts that they can dig up and verify. Moreover, they know that most of their viewers and readers enjoy such stories. Perhaps even more important is the fact that all policy makers on occasion find that a leak to the right reporter at the right time can be very helpful in accomplishing their political purposes. Indeed, some of the greatest leakers of all have been cabinet members, agency heads, and even presidents.

So long as that continues to be the case, and so long as the Constitution of the United States stipulates that "Congress shall make no law abridging the freedom of the press," policy makers from the president on down will continue to deplore leaks—and use them when they seem likely to help put over a policy they favor or kill a policy they oppose.

In a society where mass communications have become perhaps *the* basic social process, it can hardly be otherwise.

THE COMMUNICATIONS REVOLUTION, PAST AND FUTURE

What some call the communications revolution has already radically transformed just about every aspect of human life, certainly including politics. For example, only the few thousand people who made their way to the towns where they were held heard the famous Lincoln–Douglas debates in 1858. But in 1988, about 100 million people, most of them sitting in their own homes, watched the televised debates between George Bush and Michael Dukakis. For another example, before the 1950s, most political campaigns were planned and conducted by the candidates and their lieutenants, almost all of whom were veteran party politicians. In the 1990s, almost every campaign is planned and conducted not by the "old pols," but by a new breed of professional election consultants—some call them hired guns—who head teams of pollsters, speech writers, television "spot" producers, media analysts, and other high-priced technicians to conduct modern media-dominated, "scientific" campaigns. For yet another example, diplomatic communications were so slow in 1815 that the Battle of New Orleans was fought in the United States several weeks after the peace treaty had been signed in Europe. In the 1990s, every nation's ambassadors can, and are expected to, consult with their superiors back home—it can be done in seconds—before making any commitments, and the White House and the Kremlin are directly connected by the famous hot line.

Thus politics, like almost every other aspect of life, has changed a great deal since the end of World War II because of the communications revolution. But a number of recent technological advances mean that the revolution still has a long way to go. For instance, cable television can now provide any viewer in any place with 80 or more separate channels, in contrast to the 12 or so provided in most areas by over-the-air stations. This is bound to have a considerable impact on the present near-monopoly of televised news and political discussion that ABC, CBS, and NBC used to enjoy. Indeed, the networks' share of the viewing audience has declined from 90 percent in the 1970s to 80 percent in the 1980s and is likely to decline further in the 1990s. In Columbus, Ohio, experiments are well along with the "Qube system," a form of interactive or audience-participation TV that enables cable viewers to send signals from their receivers back along the cable to the studio and thus to express their opinions on what they are seeing and even to vote electronically on policy questions put to them after televised political discussions (much the same way selected viewers made minute-by-minute evaluations of President Ford's performance in the 1976 presidential debates). Some say that there is no technical reason why we cannot extend the Qube system into a national "town meeting."

No one can say with certainty what the impact of these and other new technologies will be on the politics of the future in the United States or

---

The Ford campaign [in 1976] used . . . data from an instant response analysis of a panel of registered voters. The panels consisted of approximately fifty voters from the Spokane, Washington, area. . . . Each member of the panel was equipped with a dial mechanism labeled from zero to one hundred. Zero indicated that the respondent was feeling much closer to Governor Carter and one hundred indicated that they were feeling much closer to President Ford. A value of fifty was an indication that the panelist was not leaning toward either man. . . . The panelists were to move the dial toward zero in response to positive feelings about Governor Carter and toward one hundred for positive feelings about President Ford.

The dial mechanisms were tied in with a computer, and throughout the broadcast [of the first debate] the responses were summed continuously and [average scores] calculated for the entire group as well as for . . . those who at the beginning of the broadcast had been identified as leaning toward the governor or toward the President. Finally, these continuous average scores were superimposed on a video tape of the debate for later viewing and analysis. This system provided useful information on the reaction of a group of uncommitted voters to the arguments and presentations of the two candidates. It was helpful in shaping our approach to later debates and enabled us to highlight those issues on which the President scored most heavily against the governor, and vice versa.

Source: Richard B. Cheney, "The 1976 Presidential Debates: A Republican Perspective," in Austin Ranney, ed., *The Past and Future of Presidential Debates* (Washington, D.C.: American Enterprise Institute, 1979), pp. 120–21. Copyright American Enterprise Institute.

anywhere else. But if the communications revolution of 1990–2015 has anything like the impact of the communications revolution of 1945–80, then a few decades from now much of the political landscape will look very strange indeed to people who were brought up in the 1970s.

FOR FURTHER READING

ARTERTON, F. CHRISTOPHER. *Media Politics: The News Strategies of Presidential Campaigns.* Lexington, MA: Lexington Books, 1984. Study of how mass media cover presidential campaigns and how politicians try to use the media for their own ends.

*CIRINO, ROBERT. *Don't Blame the People.* Los Angeles: Diversity Press, 1971. An attack on the mass media as apologists for big business and special interests.

COMSTOCK, GEORGE. *Television in America.* Beverly Hills, CA: Sage, 1980. Perceptive analysis of the impact of television on American society and politics.

*DEUTSCH, KARL W. *The Nerves of Government: Models of Political Communication and Control.* New York: Free Press, 1963. Stimulating general theory about government as a series of interconnected communications processes.

DIAMOND, EDWIN. *The Tin Kazoo: Television, Politics, and News.* Cambridge: MIT Press, 1975. Analysis of network news broadcasting by a leading scholar.

*EFRON, EDITH. *The News Twisters.* Los Angeles: Nash Publishers, 1971. An attack on the mass media as being the mouthpieces of the "liberal establishment."

*EPSTEIN, EDWARD JAY. *News from Nowhere: Television and the News.* New York: Random House, 1973. One of the best scholarly analyses of the nature of network news broadcasting and the economic and legal constraints on it.

*GANS, HERBERT J. *Deciding What's News: A Study of CBS Evening News, NBC Nightly News, Newsweek and Time.* New York: Random House Vintage Books, 1980. Thoughtful analysis of the reporting and editing ideas dominating the mass news media.

*GRABER, DORIS A. *Mass Media and American Politics,* 3rd ed. Washington, D.C.: Congressional Quarterly Press, 1989. A comprehensive introduction to the topic.

IYENGAR, SHANTO, and DONALD R. KINDER. *News That Matters: Television and American Opinion.* Chicago: University of Chicago Press, 1987. Uses survey data to measure the powerful impact of television's presentation of news on American public opinion.

*KRASNOW, ERWIN G., and LAWRENCE D. LONGLEY. *The Politics of Broadcast Regulation,* 2nd ed. New York: St. Martin's Press, 1978. Analysis of congressional acts and FCC regulations affecting broadcasting.

*KRAUS, SIDNEY, and DENNIS DAVIS. *The Effects of Mass Communications on Political Behavior.* University Park, PA: Pennsylvania State University Press, 1978. Useful summary of the major empirical studies of the effects of mass communications on political behavior.

*MARTEL, MYLES. *Political Campaign Debates: Images, Strategies and Tactics.* New York: Longman, 1983. Comprehensive description of candidate debates in presidential and other elections.

*MCLUHAN, MARSHALL. *Understanding Media: The Extensions of Man.* New York: McGraw-Hill, 1966. Still one of the most stimulating sets of ideas about the essential natures of the various mass media and the constraints they impose on who does well or badly with them.

*PATTERSON, THOMAS E. *The Mass Media Election.* New York: Praeger, 1980. Informative study, based on sample survey evidence, of the role of newspapers and television in the 1976 presidential election.

*RANNEY, AUSTIN. *Channels of Power: The Impact of Television on American Politics.* New York: Basic Books, 1983. Analysis of impact of television on parties, campaigns, voters, and governing processes.

*RIVERS, WILLIAM L. *The Other Government: Power and the Washington Media.* New York: University Books, 1982. Study of impact of mass media on policy making.

*ROBINSON, MICHAEL J., and MARGARET A. SHEEHAN. *Over the Wire and on TV.* New York: Basic Books, 1984. Detailed study of content and impact of coverage of the 1980 presidential election by the network news and the wire services.

SEYMOUR-URE, COLIN. *The Political Impact of Mass Media.* London: Constable, 1974. Analysis by a leading British scholar, with references to experience in several countries.

*TANNENBAUM, PERCY H., and LESLIE J. KOSTRICH. *Turned-On TV/Turned-Off Voters.* Beverly Hills, CA: Sage, 1983. Analysis of impact of

TV election-night projections of winners on west coast voters.

WESTIN, AV. *Newswatch: How TV Decides the News.* New York: Simon & Schuster, 1983. Description of how network news operates by a former head of a network news division.

NOTES

[1]Lee Thayer, "Communication—*Sine Qua Non* of the Behavioral Sciences," in D. L. Arm, ed., *Vistas in Science* (Albuquerque: University of New Mexico Press, 1968), p. 54.

[2]Burns W. Roper, "Trends in Attitudes Toward the Media: A 26-Year Review," *Public Attitudes Toward Television and Other Media in a Time of Change* (Roper Poll, Television Information Office, 1984) p. 3.

[3]I am well aware that many Americans use the term *media* as a single noun, as in the phrase "the media is biased." However, in this book we will cling to the tradition of many centuries and the stipulations of all the dictionaries that the word *media* is the plural form of the word *medium.*

[4]Theodore Peterson, Jay W. Jensen, and William L. Rivers, *The Mass Media and Modern Society* (New York: Holt, Rinehart, & Winston, 1965), p. 25.

[5]Roan Conrad, "The News and the 1976 Election: A Dialogue," *Wilson Quarterly* (Spring 1977), p. 84; and Sig Mickelson, *The Electric Mirror* (New York: Dodd, Mead, 1972).

[6]The leading case upholding the "scarcity doctrine" and the greater regulation of the electronic media is *National Broadcasting Company* v. *United States,* 319 U.S. 190 (1943).

[7]Michael J. Robinson, "Where's the Beef? Media and Media Elites in 1984," in Austin Ranney, ed., *The American Elections of 1984* (Durham, NC: Duke University Press, 1985), Chapter 6.

[8]Bernard Berelson, "Communications and Public Opinion," in Wilbur Schramm, ed., *The Process and Effects of Mass Communications* (Urbana, IL: University of Illinois Press, 1954), p. 345, italics in the original.

[9]Austin Ranney, *Channels of Power: The Impact of Television on American Politics* (New York: Basic Books, 1983), p. 16.

[10]Both examples are drawn from the informative discussion of leaks in Hedrick Smith, *The Power Game* (New York: Random House, 1988), pp. 437–46.

[11]The story of "Deep Throat" and (his? her?) leaks is told in rich (and rather self-serving) detail in a book by the two reporters, Carl Bernstein and Bob Woodward, *All the President's Men* (New York: Warner Books, 1976).

8 The Electoral Process

Elections still remain the primary way of achieving popular goals....Elections in democracies allow a change of rule in ordinary ways and without awaiting extraordinary occasions. In such systems, therefore, officials avoid not only the extremely unpopular action but even the uncomfortable....[Responsiveness of rulers to the people's wishes] has not been provided by depending on the good will of rulers, on the presumed identity of interests between governed or governors, or on institutional controls, such as a federal structure or supervision by a monopolistic political party. To the ancient question, "Who will guard the guardians?" there is only one answer: those who choose the guardians.[1]

ELECTIONS IN DEMOCRATIC SYSTEMS

Abraham Lincoln's Northern political opponents—and there were many—called him a dictator. Why? Because, in clear defiance of the Constitution, he had suspended the writ of habeas corpus, clapped some of his political adversaries in jail, raised an army, taken money out of the Treasury, and started a war, all without even asking Congress for permission.

Lincoln's supporters replied that while he had certainly used the emergency powers of the presidency to their fullest, he was no dictator. Why not? Because in the elections of 1862 and 1864, the voters had had a chance to throw first his supporters in Congress and then Lincoln himself out of office. Any public official who can be turned out of office in a free election, they said, is no dictator. As long as such elections are held, the people, not the president or any other public official, hold the ultimate ruling power, as democracy demands.

Just about every non-Communist theorist of democracy (see Chapter 5) would agree. Free elections are certainly not all there is to democracy; but in every modern nation that is generally called democratic, free elections are, as they always have been, the basic device that enables the people to control the rulers. In short: *No free elections, no democracy.*

We should be clear, however, that many nations in the modern world do not hold elections at all and that many of those that do hold elections do not hold *free elections* as we are using the term. For instance, in 1988 over 30 nations—including Chad, Cuba, Ethiopia, Nepal, and Saudi Arabia—had not held elections for many years if ever, and had no intention of holding elections in the foreseeable future. For another instance, elections for a great many offices have been held in the Soviet Union, and usually well over 90 percent of the adult population have cast votes in them. Yet, until very recently, Soviet voters have had no choice: In each election for each office there has been only one candidate on the ballot, and the voters could either vote for that candidate or not vote at all—though the system may be changing, as we will discuss later.

Some Campaigning Is Personal. Democratic vice-presidential and presidential candidates Lloyd Bentsen and Michael Dukakis at an airport rally, 1988. (Source: UPI/Bettmann Newsphotos.)

It is appropriate, therefore, to begin our analysis of the democratic electoral process by setting forth the main characteristics that most political scientists think an election must have in order to qualify as a free election.

ESSENTIAL CHARACTERISTICS OF FREE ELECTIONS

Regular Elections

Elections must take place regularly within prescribed time limits and may not be postponed indefinitely by public officials whenever they wish.

Meaningful Choices

In order to exercise effective control of public officials, voters must have a choice between at least two candidates for each office to be filled. Clearly this requirement rules out the single-candidate elections that have long been held in the Soviet Union. Some observers say that it also rules out the "Tweedledum versus Tweedledee" contests supposedly characteristic of American elections, elections that provide no real choice on such important issues as capitalism versus socialism, militarism versus pacifism, or black power versus white racism. Others reply that although a choice between Michael Dukakis and George Bush does not provide alternatives at the absolute extremes of these ideological spectrums, it does provide a significant choice between two quite different points along each spectrum—and, equally important, between two quite different human beings. But all agree that a truly free election must furnish the voters meaningful choices, however defined.

Freedom to Put Forth Candidates

No substantial group in the population is denied the opportunity of forming a political party and putting up candidates.

Freedom to Know and Discuss the Choices

If two candidates for an office are allowed to run but only one is permitted to make public speeches or have his name on the ballot, then he is effectively the only candidate. There must be full freedom for all candidates and their supporters to publicize their names and policy positions so that the voters can hear what they have to say. Some observers would add that if this requirement is to mean anything, every candidate must be guaranteed at least some financial support and free radio and television air time so that all candidates, rich and poor alike, have at least minimum opportunities to present their views and appeal for popular support.

Universal Adult Suffrage

Substantially the entire adult population has the right to vote.

Equal Weighting of Votes

We noted in Chapter 5 that one of the four basic principles of democratic government is *political equality*—the principle that each adult citizen must have the same opportunity as every other adult citizen to participate in the political decision-making process. Applied to elections, the principle means not only that all adults must have an equal opportunity to register their choices by voting but also that each person's vote will have the same weight as every other person's vote. If some people's votes are weighted more heavily than other people's, the principle of political equality is violated, and the favored voters constitute a kind of oligarchy or ruling elite.

Free Registration of Choices

Voters must be able to go to the polls without any obstruction or fear of subsequent reprisal. They must be able to vote without coercion or fear of reprisal, which in turn requires that they be able to cast their votes *secretly*.

Accurate Counting of Choices and Reporting of Results

The voting procedures—whether they consist of marking a paper ballot or pulling levers on a voting machine or punching holes in an IBM card—must permit voters to register their choices accurately and unambiguously. The counting procedures must provide accurate totals of the preferences registered for each alternative. And reporting procedures must guarantee that the totals, which control who wins the contested office, are honestly published. If any of these principles is ignored, the others are rendered meaningless.

From these eight essential characteristics of free elections we turn to a survey of some of the problems that democratic nations have encountered in trying to satisfy them.

QUALIFICATIONS FOR VOTING

The Principle of Universal Suffrage

One of our requirements for a free election is what is often called universal suffrage—that is, the rule that all adults have an equal opportunity to vote. However, this principle has never been interpreted to mean that *everyone* in the community must have the right to vote. No democratic nation has ever permitted 10-year-old children to vote, and no democratic theorist has ever called their exclusion undemocratic. Most democratic nations also exclude aliens, people confined to mental institutions, and criminals in prison, and few people think this violates the principle of universal suffrage.

As a democratic ideal, in other words, the principle of universal suffrage requires that every *member of the community,* rather than every person who happens to be present in the community on election day, has the right to vote. Generally, only adults who have demonstrated their inability (for example, by confinement in a mental institution) or their unwillingness (for example, by conviction for a felony) to assume the obligations of loyalty to the nation and obedience to its laws are considered not to be full-fledged members of the community and therefore are not entitled to vote in its elections.

Qualifications for Voting

The main qualifications for voters in modern democratic polities are the following:

Citizenship. Most democratic nations permit only their own citizens to vote but make no distinction between native-born and naturalized citizens. This requirement rests upon the conviction that only people loyal to the nation, who prefer it to all others, should be permitted to vote in its elections. Citizenship is generally regarded as the best formal indication of such loyalty.

Age. Just about every society requires its members to attain a certain minimum age before being admitted to full participation in community affairs, on the ground that infants and children are incapable of such participation. Most primitive societies, for example, have special rites for the induction of young people into adulthood and full membership. Every modern democracy requires that its citizens reach a certain minimum age before they can vote.

Every such age limit is, of course, arbitrary in the sense that it does not reflect different levels of maturity among different individuals. In all democratic nations, however, the difficulty of conducting individual "maturity examinations" is regarded as greater than the possible injustices resulting from applying one minimum-age requirement to all. As late as the 1960s, the most common minimum age was 21 years, but in the 1970s a number of countries— for example, Italy, the United States, and Great Britain—lowered it to 18, and that is now the most common minimum age.

Residence. Most democratic systems also require voters to live in the nation and in their particular voting districts for certain periods of time before they can vote. For example, in Illinois, voters must live in the state for 30 days before the election in which they wish to vote.

Registration. In order to prevent election frauds, most democratic systems supply officials at each election district with a full roster (usually called a register) of all eligible voters, against which the names of those asking for ballots can be checked to make sure they are eligible and have not already voted. Some registration systems are permanent, in that once the roster is compiled it is kept up to date by eliminating ineligible individuals and adding eligible ones. Others are periodic, in that at regular intervals the entire register is scrapped and a new one is drawn up.

The most significant distinction among registration systems lies in who takes responsibility for getting citizens registered. At one end of the scale stand the European democracies, which require public officials to take the initiative by making periodic door-to-door canvasses of each district and registering every eligible person who is not already registered. The United States stands at the other end. Most states require each would-be voter to take the initiative by coming to the registration office and formally applying; only a few permit or encourage door-to-door canvassing and registration in the home. In addition, people who are registered in one state and move to another are not automatically re-registered. They must go to the registering officials in the new state and launch the process all over again, and many Americans move and many forget to re-register amid the many other strains and demands of moving. Thus in the United States new voters and voters who have moved must take the initiative on two occasions: first, during the registration period, and second, on election day. In other democracies the voters must take the initiative only on election day. Most analysts believe that this explains why there are many more unregistered but otherwise eligible citizens in the United States than in other democracies. And many believe that registration laws are one of the main causes for lower voting turnouts in the United States (see Table 8.1 and the following discussion).

NONVOTING AND COMPULSORY VOTING

John Locke, Jean Jacques Rousseau, Thomas Jefferson, and other early advocates of democracy assumed that once members of a community were given the legal right to vote, they would eagerly exercise it at every opportunity. The evidence indicates, however, that actual voting participation in modern democratic nations does not measure up to their expectations. Table 8.1 shows the average percentage of legally eligible voters actually voting in recent national elections. It reveals that a nation's turnout rate depends on the counting method used. Most countries figure the rate as the number of persons voting divided by the number of persons on the register (remember that nearly every person of voting age is automatically placed on the register by the authorities). In the United States, on the other hand, voting turnout is customarily calculated by dividing the number of persons voting by the number of persons of voting age—which includes aliens, people in prisons and mental institutions, and, most important, persons who are not registered. When turnout rates are figured by these two very different methods, as in the first column of Table 8.1, the United States has one of the lowest turnout rates in the world—a fact that

TABLE 8.1. Voting Turnouts in Democratic Nations According to Two Measures*

Rank	Traditional Measure of Turnout	Rank	Vote as Percent of Registered Voters
1. Belgium**	94.6	1. Belgium**	94.6
2. Australia**	94.5	2. Australia**	94.5
3. Austria	91.6	3. Austria	91.6
4. Sweden	90.7	4. Sweden	90.7
5. Italy**	90.4	5. Italy**	90.4
6. Iceland	89.3	6. Iceland	89.3
7. New Zealand	89.0	7. New Zealand	89.0
8. Luxembourg	88.9	8. Luxembourg	88.9
9. West Germany	88.6	9. West Germany	88.6
10. Netherlands	87.0	10. Netherlands	87.0
11. France	85.9	11. *United States*	86.8
12. Portugal	84.2	12. France	85.9
13. Denmark	83.2	13. Portugal	84.2
14. Norway	82.0	14. Denmark	83.2
15. Greece**	78.6	15. Norway	82.0
16. Israel	78.5	16. Greece**	78.6
17. Great Britain	76.3	17. Israel	78.5
18. Japan	74.5	18. Great Britain	76.3
19. Canada	69.3	19. Japan	74.5
20. Spain**	68.1	20. Canada	69.3
21. Finland	64.3	21. Spain**	68.1
22. Ireland	62.2	22. Finland	64.3
23. *United States*	52.6	23. Ireland	62.2
24. Switzerland	48.3	24. Switzerland	48.3

*Most recent national election prior to 1981.

**Compulsory voting laws.

Source: David Glass, Peverill Squire, and Raymond Wolfinger, "Voter Turnout: An International Comparison," *Public Opinion,* December/January 1984, pp. 49–55.

is often commented on in the United States and elsewhere. However, when turnouts are compared by using the *same* measure—percent of registered voters who vote, as in the second column of Table 8.1—the United States has one of the highest turnout records in the world. The key to this paradox is simple: In the United States, well over 80 percent of the registered voters usually vote in presidential elections, but only about 60 percent are registered. Thus the problem in increasing U.S. voting turnout is not getting registered voters to the polls; it is getting eligible people registered.

The most thorough recent study of nonvoting in Western democracies was made by political scientist Robert W. Jackman, who used a number of advanced analytical techniques to estimate the relative weight of various causes for different turnout rates in nineteen Western democracies. He found that very little can be explained by political culture factors, for although Americans generally score higher than the citizens of the other countries on such measures as belief that voting is a civic duty and confidence that it makes a difference who wins elections, the United States still has a lower turnout rate than any other country except Switzerland, where cultural factors also favor voting. He concluded that, in addition to the differences in registration laws, the main influences on turnout are as follows:

> *Competitiveness:* The closer the elections and the greater the likelihood that the party in power might be defeated, the higher the turnout.
>
> *Proportionality:* The closer the proportion of the offices won by each party is to its share of the popular votes, the higher the turnout (we will say more about proportionality in a moment).
>
> *Clear winners:* The more likely elections are to produce a clear winning party or candidate with full power, the higher the turnout; conversely, the more likely elections are to produce coalitions with no clear single winner, the lower the turnout.
>
> *Unicameralism:* Turnouts are higher in countries where the parliament has only one house with real power, and lower in countries, such as the United States, where power is divided between two houses.[2]

Many of democracy's well-wishers regard failure to register and vote as both a disgrace and a threat to democratic survival. Many political scientists have therefore sought not only the legal but the social and motivational causes of nonvoting and have recommended such remedies as European-style registration, reducing the frequency of elections and the number of elective offices, television get-out-the-vote advertisements by civic organizations and advertising councils, and—the great cure for all social ills—more and better civic education.

Table 8.1 shows, however, that some nations have turned to a more radical solution: compulsory voting. In Australia, for example, any person on the register who fails to vote in any election is required by law to submit an explanation. If the authorities regard the excuse given as inadequate, the nonvoter is fined. Compulsory-voting laws work very well: They increased turnout from 64 percent to 95 percent in Australia and from 70 percent to 93 percent in Belgium. Even so, there is no general agreement among political scientists—or, for that matter, among Australians and Belgians—on whether compulsory voting is a good idea. Some commentators argue that the right to abstain is just as precious as the right to vote, and if the right to vote is guaranteed, the decision about whether to use it in any particular election should be left entirely to the individual. Others argue that in Australia and Belgium, compulsion has greatly increased the number of irresponsible and "automatic anti" votes. Still others believe that by increasing voting turnout, compulsory voting has increased participation and thus strengthened democracy.

The most we can say here is that in the few democratic nations that have compulsory voting, there is no powerful sentiment to abolish it; but most democracies do not want to go that route and continue to depend upon other agencies, notably political parties (see Chapter 10), to motivate voters to go to the polls.

NOMINATIONS AND CANDIDATE SELECTION

The Meaning of the Terms

Most free elections involve choices among competing candidates—persons legally eligible for the offices contested whose names are printed on official ballots. The first step in the conduct of free elections is thus the process by which a few of the many citizens eligible for office actually get their names on the ballot. This process has two major parts:

Nomination means *the legal procedures by which election authorities certify certain persons as qualified candidates for office and print their names on the official ballot.*

Candidate selection is *the mainly extralegal process by which political parties decide which persons will be designated on the ballot and in election communications as their recommended candidates.*

Significance of Candidate Selection

In a democracy, all voters have the legal right to vote for any person eligible for any office. In practice, however, they do not have any such complete freedom and could not use it if they had. In the United States, for example, about 105 million people presently fulfill all the legal qualifications for the presidency. But if all voters had been required to choose among all 105 million in 1988, to be fair to all they would have had to learn the personal qualifications and positions of each one! That is obviously impossible. No human being can have even the dimmest notion of the nature of each of 105 million alternatives, let alone make an intelligent choice among them. But no such impossible task actually confronted the voters in 1988. The various political parties, through their nominating processes, reduced the alternatives from 105 million to the 19 candidates who appeared on the ballots of one or more states. Since most people were accustomed to voting for either the Democratic or Republican candidate, most voters were faced with choosing between only Dukakis and Bush. The major parties' candidate selections thus reduced the alternatives from 19 to an even more manageable 2.

Most of us can learn quite a bit about the personal qualifications and political opinions of two candidates and can make a meaningful choice between them. The reduction process therefore makes meaningful choice possible for us. Surely it is as significant a part of the total election process as is the final election in which the voters reduce the alternatives from 2 to 1.

Formal Nominating Procedures

The formal nominating procedures of most democratic nations are much simpler than those used in the United States. Two principal methods are now used.

Petitions.   The formal procedure for becoming a candidate for the British House of Commons is simplicity itself. Any British subject over 21 years of age is eligible, with the exception of members of the nobility, judges of the High Court, members of the permanent civil service, convicted felons, and clergy of the Church of England, the Church of Scotland, or the Roman Catholic Church. Would-be candidates go to the election offices and get an official nomination paper, on which they state their name, address, occupation, and the constituency in which they wish to "stand." The form must also be signed by two voters from that constituency acting as proposer and seconder and by eight other such voters acting as assenters. The completed form must be filed with the authorities, along with a deposit of £500. This deposit will be forfeited to the Treasury if the candidate fails to poll more than 5 percent of the votes cast in the constituency in the ensuing election. (The purpose of this requirement is to discourage frivolous and "nuisance" candidates.) When these minimal requirements have been met, the candidate's name is placed on the ballot—but only since 1969 has Britain allowed the candidates' party labels to be printed by their names. Approximately the same procedure is followed in such other democratic countries as Canada, France, Japan, and New Zealand.

Party-list designations.   In most nations that use some form of the party-list system of proportional representation, the authorized agent of each recognized political party draws up a list of candidates for each constituency and presents it to the election authorities. When the authorities have verified the eligibility of the names on each list, they are placed on the ballot without further ado. In some countries (for example, Israel) this is the only procedure by which a candidate can be placed on the ballot. In other nations (for example, Denmark and Finland) a hundred or so independent voters can also nominate a single candidate or list of candidates by petition. In general, however, the initiative rests mainly or exclusively with party officials and agencies.

The Unique American Direct Primary.   Perhaps the sharpest contrast between nominating procedures in the United States and those in other democratic countries is provided by U.S. use of the direct primary. The **direct primary** is *a procedure in which candidates are selected directly by the voters in government-supervised elections rather than indirectly by party leaders in caucuses and conventions.* It was first adopted by the state of Wisconsin in 1903, and since then every one of the 50 states has adopted it for nominations for some offices, and most states require it for nominations for all offices. Note that it is unique to the United States; no other country in the world uses it.

In general, the direct primary is designed to ensure that nominations are made as nearly as possible in the same way in which regular elections are conducted. Any qualified person who wishes to receive a particular party's nomination for public office may file with election officials a petition containing her name, address, the nomination desired, and the signatures of a legally designated number of voters registered as members of the party whose nomination is sought. When the filing period has elapsed, the election authorities print ballots for each party including the names of all who have petitioned for each office. On primary-election day, the voters go to the polls and mark their preferences for each office. The person who receives the largest number of votes for each office on each party's ballot is certified as that party's official nominee, and the nominee's name and party designation are then printed on the ballot for the ensuing general election.

The only major differences among the direct primary systems of the various states relate to who is eligible to vote in a particular party's primary: In *closed primaries* (25 states), only persons pre-registered as members of a particular party can vote in its primary; persons registered as independents have no party and thus cannot vote in any party's primary. *Crossover primaries* (14 states) are the same as closed primaries, except that on election day all voters, including independents, can vote in the primary of either party after publicly declaring which party they have chosen. In *open primaries* (9 states), there is no party registration or declaration of any kind, and on primary day voters are allowed to vote in either party's primary (but not both) without any public statement of the party they have chosen. In *blanket primaries* (2 states), there is no party registration or declaration, and on primary day voters can vote in the primaries of both parties, although they are restricted to voting in only one party's primary for any particular office. Finally, in *nonpartisan primaries* (only Louisiana for state offices but in many states for local offices), there is no party registration or public declaration, and all candidates for each office are put on the same ballot. Each voter votes for one candidate per office, and the candidate who receives a majority of the votes for that office is elected; if no candidate receives a majority, a later (or run-off) election is held between the two candidates with the largest numbers of votes, and the one who receives a majority in the second election wins the office.

I repeat that the United States is the only country in the world that uses the direct primary. Many commentators believe that it is one of the main reasons why American political parties are so different from the parties in other democracies. We will consider this further in Chapter 10.

PRINCIPAL DEMOCRATIC ELECTORAL SYSTEMS

In setting up their electoral systems, all democratic countries have tried to satisfy the requirements of free elections outlined at the beginning of the chapter, but they have chosen a wide variety of means for doing so. No nation's

New Technology Makes New Politics. Richard Viguerie, whose organization raises millions for conservative causes by computerized direct-mail solicitations. (Source: UPI/Bettmann Newsphotos.)

system is exactly like any other's in all its details, and the variations are so numerous and often so complicated that we will not even try to list them all here. We will note the main types of systems and the principal differences among them.

SINGLE-MEMBER-DISTRICT SYSTEMS

"First-Past-the-Post" Plurality Systems

Most readers are probably familiar with the "first-past-the- post" system, since it is used for elections to the United States House of Representatives, both houses of most American state legislatures, the British House of Commons, the Canadian House of Commons, and many other legislatures and parliaments, especially in the English-speaking world. The basic principles are simple. The nation is divided into a number of *districts* (the American term) or *constituencies* (the British term) or *ridings* (the Canadian term). Each district elects one member of the legislative assembly at each election, and the voter votes for one candidate. When the votes are counted, the candidate receiving the largest number of votes (a plurality) in each constituency is elected. It is called first-past-the-post because, as in a horse race, the winner is the contestant who leads the others across the finish line, and the margin by which she leads does not matter.

Absolute Majority Systems

A few polities have felt that electing candidates by only a plurality violates the basic democratic principle of majority rule (see Chapter 5), and so they have installed devices for ensuring that the winner has at least 50 percent plus 1 (a majority) of all the votes. One such device is the run-off election: If no candidate receives an absolute majority in the first election, a second election is held between the two top candidates, and the one who wins a majority in the second election is the winner. The most notable use of the absolute-majority system at present is in elections for president of France. For example, in April 1988, the first round of the presidential election was held with nine candidates on the ballot; their vote shares were as follows:

Mitterand	34.1%
Chirac	19.9
Barre	17.0
Le Pen	14.4
Lajoinie	7.0
Waechter	3.7
Juquin	1.5
Laguiller	1.4
Boussel	1.0

Two weeks later the second, or "run-off," ballot was held between the two top finishers, and the results were as follows:

Mitterand	54.0%
Chirac	46.0

Another device is the preferential ballot, which is now used in elections to the Australian House of Representatives and to four Australian state parliaments. This system requires voters to mark each of the candidates in order of preference by placing numbers beside their names. If no candidate receives a majority of first-place preferences on the first count, the candidate with the fewest first-place preferences is dropped and his ballots are redistributed according to the second-place preferences on each ballot. Such redistributions are continued until one candidate's ballots constitute an absolute majority of all those cast. That candidate is then elected.

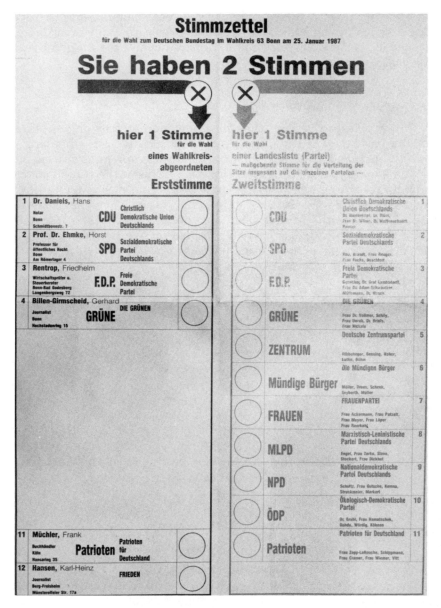

Ballots in Majority and Proportional Systems. The West Germany Bundestag election of 1987. (Source: German Information Center, and Eric Bouvet/Gamma-Liaison.)

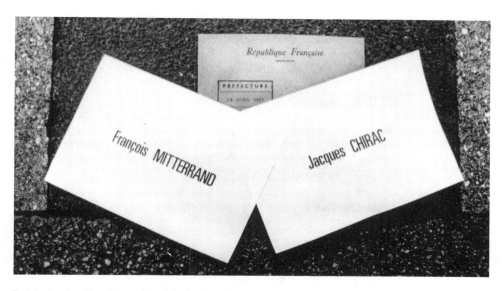

Ballots for the French presidential election of 1988. (Source: German Information Center, and Eric Bouvet/Gamma-Liaison.)

MULTIMEMBER-PROPORTIONAL SYSTEMS

Their Rationale

Since the mid-nineteenth century, some democratic theorists have argued that the single-member-plurality systems make truly democratic representation impossible and have proposed that all such systems be replaced with some form of proportional representation (PR). Their arguments can be briefly summarized as follows:

A truly democratic representative assembly should be to the nation's political divisions as a map is to its territory. Thus it should ensure that every point of view held by members of the community has a number of advocates in the assembly proportionate to its adherents in the community.

The first-past-the-post system cannot produce such an assembly. Wherever it operates, the majority party has more assembly seats than its share of the popular vote warrants, and all other parties have fewer seats than their vote shares warrant. Furthermore, the majority system forces a two-party system on the population, for third and fourth parties have little or no chance of electing assembly members. The legislatures that result from this kind of party system cannot accurately express the many shades of public opinion any more than a black-and-white photograph can accurately represent the many colors of reality.

Also, the argument continues, in a truly representative system every citizen should be directly represented in the assembly. That is, each voter should be able to point to at least one member of the assembly and say, "My vote helped to put her there, so she represents me." But under the majority systems, all those who vote for losing candidates have no such member, and so their votes are wasted.

For these reasons, PR advocates believe that the single-member district systems should be replaced with some kind of proportional representation—a system in which no votes are wasted and in which all points of view are represented according to their relative strengths in the electorate. The proportional systems now used in modern democratic nations are variations on two basic types: party-list systems and the single transferable vote.

Party-List Systems

In all party-list systems, political parties are the basic units of representation. The systems all have multimember constituencies, each of which elects from two to twelve or more members (in Israel the entire nation consists of one constituency, which elects all 120 members of the Knesset). The ballots contain lists of candidates nominated by the leaders or executive committees of the various parties, and the voter votes for one or another of these lists. The counting process is designed to distribute seats in the legislative assembly as nearly as possible in accordance with each party's share of the total popular vote.

Party-list systems differ from one another only in the degree to which voters can vote for individual candidates as well as for whole party lists. Some systems, like that in Israel, allow the voters to vote only for one party's entire list, and voters have no way of expressing a preference for any individual candidate on that list. Some, like that in Belgium, permit voters to change the order of the candidates on the list of the party they vote for, but those voters cannot vote for candidates on any other party's list. Some, like that in Switzerland, allow the voter to vote for one party's list and also for an individual candidate on that list or on another party's list.

Essentially, however, all party-list systems operate on the assumption that voters are most interested in supporting particular political parties that best express their political philosophies; hence the party, not the individual, is the main unit of representation.

The Single-Transferable-Vote System

The single-transferable-vote system operates from a very different premise. It assumes that voters are more interested in individual candidates than in parties and should be given maximum freedom to indicate their preferences for individuals.

The most notable use of this system is in elections for members of the *Dail* (parliament) of Ireland. In Ireland, each constituency elects several members to the legislative assembly, and any individual can obtain a place on the ballot by petition, with or without a party designation. Voters indicate their orders of preference among the various candidates by marking numbers in the boxes beside their names. The ballots are first sorted according to the first-place choices for each candidate. Then the "electoral quota" of total votes needed to be elected is figured according to one of several possible formulas, all too complicated to be described here. If a candidate's first-preference votes exceed the quota, the excess votes are distributed to the second-choice candidates marked on the ballots. When no surpluses remain and there are still seats to be filled, the candidate with the fewest first-place choices is dropped, and her ballots are redistributed according to the second-place choices on each. Transfers of surpluses of elected candidates and of votes for eliminated candidates is continued until a sufficient number of candidates have satisfied the quota and all the seats are filled.

Approval Voting: A New Twist

In recent years a few political scientists, notably Steven J. Brams, have advocated a new kind of electoral system called "approval voting." They propose a system in which each voter is not confined to casting one vote for one party or candidate; rather, the voter can vote for as many candidates or parties as he approves—that is, finds acceptable—without ranking the candidates as to which are more acceptable. If only one candidate is to be elected, then the candidate with the most approval votes wins; if two candidates are to be elected, then the two top votegetters win; and so on.

The advocates of approval voting say that in elections such as presidential primaries in the United States where there are large numbers of candidates, there is often one candidate on the Left, one candidate on the Right, and several candidates in the Center. Left-wing and right-wing voters are usually only small minorities of the electorate, but they often elect their candidates because each votes for its side only; the centrist majority, on the other hand, scatters its votes among several candidates, none of which has enough votes to win. But under approval voting, each centrist voter can vote for several candidates, which means that one or more of them are much more likely to accumulate enough approval votes to be elected. This not only prevents extremist candidates from winning, but also results in a more accurate representation of the centrists, who are usually the largest single group in any electorate.[3]

No major governmental agency has yet adopted approval voting, but it has been used for elections in a number of private organizations such as professional societies, colleges, and universities.

POLITICAL EFFECTS OF ELECTORAL SYSTEMS

Both the first-past-the-post and proportional systems have strong partisans among modern democratic theorists. We have already surveyed the main arguments for PR, but we should note here that its critics declare that wherever it has been tried, it has encouraged the development of splinter parties, deepened ideological divisions, and intensified political conflict. It has also, they say, made governments into weak coalitions of quarreling and mutually suspicious parties, and it has failed to produce popular mandates on immediate and pressing political issues.

In a survey of this sort, I cannot present the full argument for each side, let alone declare which is correct. But political science research has provided considerable evidence that can provide the basis—if not the conclusions—for this debate. Political scientist Douglas Rae's systematic study of the political consequences of various electoral systems came to the following conclusions.[4]

First, every electoral system tends to give parties with large shares of the popular votes more than their proportional shares of parliamentary seats. And the other side of that coin is that small parties get even smaller shares of the parliamentary seats than their shares of the popular votes. The party with the largest single share of the popular vote profits most from this tendency, but it also helps the number two party in the sense that it discriminates strongly against third and fourth and even smaller parties. This charge is quite correct, as is shown in Table 8.2 by the typical seats-to-votes ratio produced by the British general election of 1987.

Second, single-member-district systems tend to produce two-party systems except where minority parties are especially strong in particular areas.

Third, proportional systems discriminate against small parties without strong sectional bases less than majority systems do, and consequently they tend to produce multiparty rather than two-party systems.

Fourth, in order to achieve a legislative majority capable of ruling, more parties willing to join coalitions are necessary in proportional than in single-member district systems.

Finally, the most important single factor affecting the degree of proportionality—that is, the closeness between the shares of the popular vote and the shares of the legislative seats—is the size of the electoral districts. The more

TABLE 8.2.   Vote and Seat Shares in the 1987 British General Election

Party	Popular Votes	Percentage of Votes	Seats	Percentage of Seats	Difference
Conservative	13,763,134	42.3	374	57.5	+15.2
Labour	10,033,633	30.8	227	34.9	+4.1
Alliance					
Liberal	4,165,091	12.8	17	2.6	−10.2
S.D.P.	3,174,821	9.8	5	0.8	−9.0
Scot. Nat.	416,873	1.3	3	0.5	−0.8
Plaid Cymru	123,589	0.4	3	0.5	+0.1
N.I. Unionists	400,430	1.2	13	2.0	+0.8
Other	457,086	1.4	8	1.2	−0.2

Source: Keesing's Record of World Events, 1987 (London: Longmans, 1987), p. 35,269.

members elected from each district, the more proportional are the seat shares to the vote shares. Israel and the Netherlands, both of which elect all the members of their most important legislative house at large from nationwide constituency rather than from districts, have the highest proportionality of any electoral system. They also have very large numbers of parties with one or more seats in their parliaments.

These are some of the most notable facts. It may also be mentioned that most of the democratic electoral systems adopted since World War II—for example, in Japan, Italy, Portugal, and Spain—employ some form of PR. On the other hand, most of the English-speaking nations now use first-past-the-post systems, and few are seriously considering adopting PR. The one major exception is Great Britain, where the system's discrimination against the new and rising Liberal-Social Democratic Alliance, shown in Table 8.2, is so great that adopting proportional representation has become the top item in the alliance's program. Otherwise, whatever the respective merits of the two systems may be, it is clear that in the foreseeable future, neither is likely to become the sole democratic method for electing public officials.

THE WEST GERMAN HYBRID

The debate over the respective merits of proportional representation and first-past-the-post systems has been going on since the early nineteenth century, and most democratic polities have chosen one or the other. The only major exception is the Federal Republic of Germany (West Germany). In reconstructing the electoral system in their new, post-Nazi constitution after World War II, the West Germans decided to establish a combination of both systems in an effort to maximize the benefits and minimize the drawbacks of each. The resulting hybrid has fascinated many students of electoral systems, and some regard it as the model that all democracies ought to follow.

It works as follows: For purposes of electing members to the Bundestag, (the lower and more powerful house of the nation's parliament), the nation is divided into 248 constituencies. Each constituency elects one member directly to the Bundestag, and 248 additional members are allocated on the basis of the lists of candidates put up in each of the ten *lander* (the German equivalent of states) by the political parties. Each election has the following main steps:

1. Every voter casts two ballots. On the first ballot he marks his preference for one of the individual candidates running for the Bundestag in his district. On the second ballot he marks his preference for the political party he would most like to see in control of the Bundestag.
2. In deciding how many seats each party will get in the Bundestag, the first step is to add together all the second-votes each party has won everywhere in the nation. The authorities then drop from all further consideration those parties that have won less than 5 percent of the second votes and have elected two or fewer individual

candidates in the constituencies. The second-vote totals for the parties thus eliminated are subtracted from the total cast to provide the figure on which the national allocations are made.

3. On the basis of this new figure, a calculation is made of how many of the national total of 496 seats each party deserves based on its share of the national total of second-votes.

4. The national allocation for each party is then distributed among each of the parties in each of the ten *lander.*

5. In each of the ten *lander,* the number of seats won by individual candidates for each party is subtracted from the total number of seats that it has been allocated in step 4. The remaining seats to which it is entitled are awarded to the candidates on each party's list in the order in which they are listed by the parties.[5]

This rather complicated blend of single-member districts and proportional representation has typically produced national allocations of seats that are quite proportional to the parties' shares of the second votes, as is shown by the results of the 1987 election summarized in Table 8.3.

New Technology Makes New Voting Methods. A U.S. voter studies the Choices on a voting machine. (Source: Irene Springer.)

TABLE 8.3.   Vote and Seat Shares in the 1987 West German Bundestag Election

Party	Number of Seats	Percentage of Seats	National Percentage of Second Votes
SPD	186	37.3	37.0
CDU	174	35.0	34.5
CSU	49	9.9	9.8
FDP	46	9.3	9.1
Greens	42	8.5	8.3
NDP	0	0	0.6
OOP	0	0	0.2
Others	0	0	0.4

Source: Kessing's Record of World Events, 1987 (London: Longman's, 1987), pp. 35,014–15.

APPORTIONMENT OF ELECTORAL DISTRICTS

As we have seen, every democratic nation except Israel and the Netherlands is divided into a number of geographical subdivisions known as districts or constituencies, each of which elects one or more members of the national legislature. **Apportionment** is *the process of assigning to local areas the number of representatives each will elect to the central legislature.* And in political reality it is also the process of allocating political power among the nation's interest groups as well as regions. The problem of achieving fair apportionment is greatest in nations that use single-member districts, but it also exists in those using multimember districts.

PROBLEMS

Fair apportionment is difficult, especially among single-member districts, because a number of competing principles have legitimate claims and it is impossible to satisfy them all. The most obvious and most basic is the principle of "one person, one vote," which, in apportionment terms, means the principle of equal electorates. Any deviation from this standard means a violation of the basic democratic principle of political equality (see Chapter 5). If district A has 500,000 people and district B has only 250,000, but each elects one legislator, then each resident of B has twice as large a share of the nation's law-making power as each resident of A. In the "reapportionment revolution" that it has brought about since 1962, the U.S. Supreme Court has held that the principle of equal electorates must be the primary rule governing the apportionment of both houses of all state legislatures and also of the U.S. House of Representatives. Even minor deviations are constitutionally permissible only when "based on legitimate considerations incident to the effectuation of a rational state policy" (*Reynolds* v. *Sims*, 377 U.S. 533, 1964).

Exactly what qualifies as "legitimate considerations"? The Court has yet to spell it out, but in most modern democracies there are at least three. First, it is easier and cheaper for local authorities to administer elections if national district lines coincide with the boundaries of local government units. Hence congressional districts and parliamentary constituencies are usually formed by combining counties or metropolitan wards rather than by creating entirely new subdivisions without regard to existing local government boundaries.

Second, because the new boundaries are drawn up by incumbent legislators, they are usually drawn so as to minimize the number of incumbents whose districts will be radically changed.

Third, no matter how equal the districts' populations may be, it is always possible for the dominant political party to draw the boundaries in such a way as to make the most effective use of its own votes and to waste those of the opposition. The basic technique is to concentrate large blocs of opposition voters in a few districts and distribute large blocs of favorable voters more broadly. This is generally called **gerrymandering**—*the drawing of electoral district boundaries so as to advantage a particular political party or interest group.* Successful gerrymandering may result, for example, in two opposition candidates regularly elected by margins of 10 to 1 along with five of the dominant party's candidates regularly elected by margins of 3 to 2. The most faithful application of the other principles will not prevent gerrymandering. The main safeguards against it are the dominant party's sense that it had better show some restraint lest the opposition take revenge at some future time and, above all, the voters' insistence that apportionment not be used to give one party too much of an unfair advantage over the others.

PROCEDURES

The power to make and revise apportionment rules and to draw and redraw district lines is of considerable importance in any democratic government. In the United States, the Constitution stipulates that each state, regardless of population, shall have two members of the Senate and at least one member of the House of Representatives but leaves it up to Congress to apportion the other seats in the House among the states. Under the present law, after each national census (taken every decade beginning in 1790), Congress determines how many representatives each state will have. Then the legislature of each state establishes the districts from which each of its allotted national representatives will be elected as well as the districts for electing members of the two houses of the state legislature. Thus the key role in apportionment in the United States is played by the state legislatures, not Congress. However, since the case of *Baker* v. *Carr* (1962), the federal and state courts have kept such a close watch on the legislatures' apportionment activities that they no longer have the free hand they once enjoyed.

In Great Britain, Parliament periodically establishes four nonpartisan boundary commissions (one each for England, Scotland, Wales, and Northern Ireland) to review constituency boundaries and recommend revisions. The commissions' recommendations are usually accepted (though sometimes revised) by the ruling political party and enacted by Parliament. The most recent "redistribution" raised the total number of constituencies from 635 to 650 and went into effect for the general election of 1983.

In France *decoupage* (districting) usually results from an ad hoc agreement between the minister of the interior and the prefect of each *departement;* partisan considerations—for example, minimizing the number of Communist deputies elected—have played an important role. In both Switzerland (1962) and West Germany (1963), national supreme courts have voided as unconstitutional apportionments that strayed too far from the principle of equal electorates. And in all democratic nations apportionment controversies, though seldom as dramatic or as flagrantly partisan as in the United States, are nevertheless frequent and sometimes hotly contested.[6]

REFERENDUM ELECTIONS

RATIONALE

Most elections in modern democratic nations are candidate elections; that is, they are contests between candidates for elective public offices. But there is another class of elections, generally called **referendums**—*elections in which questions of public policy are voted upon directly by ordinary citizens.*

The rationale for referendums is rooted in the belief of some democratic theorists that any system of representative government that depends entirely upon the election of public officials is bound to be a poor way of translating the people's will into government action. Rousseau, for example, argued that representation in any form inevitably distorts public opinion to some degree, for when one person's ideas are passed through the mind of a second person, what comes out is always somewhat different from what went in. (Anyone who has ever read a set of examination papers will heartily agree with this observation.) For this reason, Rousseau argued, we cannot permit elections to office to be the sole method of finding out what the people want. At the very least we must supplement it with some device that expresses the popular will directly and without interpretation or alteration by any intervening agency.

Many people believe that the New England town meeting or the Swiss *landsgemeinde* (face-to-face meetings of all the citizens of some rural cantons, government subdivisions roughly comparable to American states) is the ideal device for this purpose, and some people believe that public opinion polls can do the job. But town meetings are possible only in small communities, and too many people have too many doubts about the accuracy and reality of public opinion polls. Consequently, most people who have doubts about representation believe that it must be supplemented by some form of the referendum. Few argue that referendums should replace entirely the election of representatives, but many believe that they should be available for use whenever the elected representatives are unable to figure out—or to carry out—what the people want.

ORGANIZATION

Approximately 80 nations—by no means all of them democracies—have occasionally used one or another of four basic forms of referendums:

Government-Controlled Referendums

In this form, the government—that is, the leaders of the party or coalition of parties controlling the legislature and the executive—has sole control over when a referendum will be held, on what issue it will be held, and how the proposition put to the voters will be worded. Most national referendums have been of this type.

Constitutionally Required Referendums

Some countries' constitutions require that certain matters—especially constitutional amendments—be finally adopted only by direct votes of the citizens. The government decides upon the wording of the amendment, but it must be approved by the voters before it becomes law.

Referendums by Popular Petitions

A few political systems—Switzerland and a number of American states for example—allow ordinary voters to challenge an act of the legislature by submitting a petition demanding a referendum vote on that act. If the required number of signatures are gathered, a vote must be held; and if a majority vote against the act, it is repealed even though the government wishes to retain it.

Popular Initiatives

Ordinary voters are allowed to file a petition demanding that a certain measure that the government has not adopted be referred to the voters. The petitioners, not the government, determine the wording of the proposition, and if they secure the required number of signatures, their measure must be set before the voters at the next election. If it receives a majority in the referendum, it becomes law even though the government may think it unwise.

RESULTS AND EVALUATION

Switzerland has been by far the heaviest user of nationwide referendums. From 1866 to 1986, the Swiss held 401 referendums of one type or another, followed by Australia with 41, France with 20, Denmark with 14, Italy with 13, and Ireland with 12.

The United States and the Netherlands are the only two democracies that have never held a national referendum, but a number of the American states have held many statewide referendums. As of 1988, every state except Delaware requires popular referendums for the final approval of constitutional amendments; 39 states have some form of referendum on ordinary legislation; 14 have popular initiatives for constitutional amendments; and 22 have some form of popular initiative for adopting ordinary laws. All told, the states have held well over a thousand referendums since 1778, when Massachusetts held the first modern referendum on adopting its new constitution. (The voters turned it down.)

Dictators have also used referendums. In 1936, for example, Adolf Hitler received 98 percent approval for his policies in a national referendum, and in 1938 he received 99 percent approval for his *anschluss* (uniting) with Austria. More recent examples include the 99 percent approval of the peace treaty with Israel by Egypt in 1979 and the 99 percent approval of the new Islamic Republic constitution in Iran in 1979. Western observers may wonder why the authoritarian regimes bother with such referendums, and the answer seems to be that they do so for many of the same reasons (to be discussed in a moment) that the Soviet Union holds candidate elections: The dictators or ruling oligarchies believe that the legitimacy and acceptance of their policies will be enhanced if they use the forms of democracy even though the substance violates all democratic principles of free elections. Our main interest here, however, is with democratic referendums and with the question of their impact on other institutions and policies.

Campaigns for and against most referendum measures in the democracies are conducted mainly by organized interest groups rather than by spontaneous citizens' opinion groups. The evidence suggests that, contrary to a belief cherished by editorial writers, newspaper endorsements have little effect upon the outcomes. Occasionally political parties take strong stands on particular measures. When they are on the same side, the measure usually passes. When they are on opposite sides, the voters' party loyalties usually exert strong, but not all-powerful, influences on their voting. Similarly, although measures

A SAMPLE OF RECENT REFERENDUMS

Country	Date	Subject	Percentage Voting Yes	Turnout
(California)	1978	Cut property taxes (Prop. 13)	65	55
(Massachusetts)	1986	Prohibit abortions	42	29
(Oregon)	1986	Allow growing and possession of marijuana for personal use	26	50
Poland	1987	Economic reforms	66	67
		Limited political liberalization	69	67
Iran	1979	Approve new Islamic constitution	99	65
Ireland	1986	Remove constitutional prohibition of divorce	36	59
(Quebec)	1980	Start negotiations for separation from Canada	41	85
Switzerland	1971	Allow women to vote	66	58
Switzerland	1986	Approve full Swiss membership in the United Nations	32	48
Spain	1986	Remain in NATO	53	59
Chile	1988	Approve another 8-year term for President Pinochet	45	99

Sources: The national referendum results are taken from *Keesing's Record of World Events;* the referendum results for American states are taken from *Public Opinion.*

initiated by government agencies by no means win all the time, they do considerably better than measures proposed by citizens' groups. Referendum elections usually attract fewer voters than elections for public office, but occasionally the turnout for a hotly contested referendum on a highly controversial measure—for example, the 1978 vote in California on Proposition 13—will match or even exceed that for candidate elections.

But what most people want to know is, Is the referendum basically a device for conservative policies or for liberal policies? The evidence from Switzerland and the American states, the heaviest users of referendums, appears to show that it is neither inherently conservative nor inherently liberal. It is a politically neutral device that generally produces outcomes favored by the current state of public opinion, and public opinion is seldom liberal or conservative on all measures. In the American states in the 1970s and 1980s, for example, referendums generally had liberal outcomes on questions of government spending, conservation of natural resources, and a "freeze" on nuclear

Entering the polling booth on Tuesday, November 3, 1964, the typical California voter found himself confronted with an immense sheet of finely printed green paper, a dirty black rubber stamp, a tiny ink pad, and thirty decisions to render. A few minutes later (the legal maximum is ten) he emerged and numbly surrendered to a clerk his ballot, now slightly embellished, like the fingers of his decision hand, with black ink stains.

Most of his decisions were made on a lengthy array of [referendum] propositions. In these, questions on an assortment of issues were posed, each couched in language tedious and obscure—as only minds trained in the finest law schools could devise.[7]

weapons, and generally conservative outcomes on questions of dealing with crime, limiting use of handguns, and taxation (tax-cutting propositions mostly won in the late 1970s but lost in the mid-1980s).

Political scientists do not agree on whether referendums are good or bad. Some argue that legislative decision making has two critical advantages over referendums. First, the legislative process encourages competing interest groups to retreat from their initial non-negotiable demands and work out compromises that will give all groups something of what they want and avoid total defeat for any. But a referendum, such as one on outlawing abortions, poses only two choices: Either allow any woman to have an abortion whenever she wishes, or make all abortions a crime. Referendum results thus often mean near-total victory for one side and near-total defeat for the other—which it may not peacefully accept if it feels sufficiently outraged.

Closely related, these critics say, is a second advantage for legislative policy making. Legislatures typically weigh the *intensity* of demands as well as the number of people making them; but in a referendum each voter's preference is equal to any other voter's, and there is no way to register different intensities. Thus a white majority fairly strongly opposed to compulsory open housing for African-Americans can—as they did in California in 1964—defeat an African-American minority passionately convinced that they are entitled to open housing as a basic human right. Such results, the critics conclude, produce neither justice nor social peace nor government stability.

The defenders of referendums reply that all such considerations are less important than the fact that the device enables the voters to express their policy preferences directly, without distortion and dilution by legislative interpretation and compromises.

Whatever may be the merits of referendums, they are widely used only in Switzerland and in some American states. Consequently, elected public officials remain the sole or principal decision makers in every modern democracy, and the candidate elections by which they are put into or turned out of office remain by far the most important institution for keeping modern democratic governments responsible to their citizens. But while democratic countries are the only ones that hold free elections, they are not the only ones that hold elections of any sort.

NOMINATIONS AND ELECTIONS IN THE SOVIET UNION BEFORE PERESTROIKA[8]

In Chapter 4 we noted that since Mikhail Gorbachev became the leader of the Soviet Union in 1985, he has urged a series of radical reforms in the Soviet economic system intended to make it competitive with the much more productive, efficient, and innovative economies of Japan and the Western democracies. Even more interesting from our point of view is the fact that he has also advocated a number of major changes in the nation's political system, for only thus, he argues, will the Soviet Union acquire the kind of social and political system that alone can make possible the economic improvements. All Soviet institutions, he has been saying, need *perestroika* ("restructuring").

In Chapter 4 we also recognized that it is too soon to be confident that Gorbachev's reforms will all be adopted or, if adopted, that they will produce the economic results he seeks. But whatever finally happens, it is clear that the Soviet system of the 1990s is likely to differ in many important ways from the system that Lenin, Stalin, Khruschev, and Brezhnev commanded from 1917 to 1965.

One of the most radical political reforms Gorbachev has pressed is the introduction—in some places and to some degree—of competition in elections to public office. In a moment we will briefly summarize his proposals, but let us begin by describing the Soviet electoral system as it operated in the period before Gorbachev.

FORMAL PROCEDURES

At first glance the formal nominating and electing procedures in the Soviet Union before 1985 appeared to justify Joseph Stalin's famous boast that the Russian Constitution is "the most democratic constitution in the world." Article 96 of the 1977 version, for example, guarantees the suffrage to "all citizens of the USSR...with the exception of persons who have been legally certified insane."[9] The members of all national, regional, and local legislative bodies were elected, and they added up to a total of over 2,200,000 elected officials. Moreover, just about every eligible Soviet voter voted, and in elections to the Supreme Soviet from 1961 to 1984, the average turnout was a staggering 99.98

percent! Even the most optimistic get-out-the-vote organizations in the Western democracies despair of ever matching that figure.

When Western observers looked more closely at the formal procedures and actual conduct of Soviet nominations and elections before 1985, however, they could only conclude that Soviet elections corresponded very little to the standards of free elections outlined earlier in this chapter.

Nominations

All Soviet elections have had only one candidate for each office on the ballot; hence the critical stage has been the nominations, not the elections. The election laws stated that nominations of candidates for all elective offices could be made by a number of organizations: branches of the Communist Party of the Soviet Union (CPSU), trade unions, military units, youth organizations, and such work units as factories and collective farms. In fact, however, the CPSU party branches apportioned the right to nominate among the various enterprises and institutions in their areas: This trade union could name four, that university division could name one, that farm collective could name five, and so on. Each agency informed the local election commission of its choice, and the commission decided which of the various people proposed would go on the ballot. What could be simpler or more democratic?

Yet these procedures never produced from any agency more names than it had been allotted. In the conversations that took place in a trade union or a university before its official nominating meeting, the party members in the unit—and there were always party members in every unit—let it be known that a particular person would really be the best choice and the other names suggested would not do for one reason or another. So at the nominating meeting one name was publicly proposed for each allotted slot, everyone voted for that name, and it went forward to the election commission, where it was duly ratified and put on the election ballot.

The evidence strongly suggests that the CPSU exercised close control over nominations. For example, its membership is only about 9 percent of the whole population, but more than 80 percent of the nominees for the Supreme Soviet were party members. Even nonparty nominees were carefully selected to represent such major elements as workers, farmers, the old, the young, women, the intelligentsia, and so on. And no nonparty candidates, we may be sure, were *anti*party!

Until Gorbachev, Soviet leaders were neither furtive nor apologetic about their single-candidate system. As one Soviet writer put it:

> *During the nomination of candidates for Deputy many meetings name several candidates. Why does only one candidate's name remain on the ballot? Back in 1936, M. I. Kalinin, speaking at the pre-election rally in Leningrad, said: "If in our country in a number of places candidates withdraw their names in favor of a single*

candidate, this is the consequence of their social kinship and the community of their political goals. After thorough discussion, tens and thousand of voters have agreed on a single candidate. This is also a hallmark of socialism, a sign that there is no, and cannot be any, discord among our laboring masses, the kind of inner discord that exists within bourgeois society."[10]

Elections

After the nominations were made, extremely active campaigns were mounted lasting at least two months. Especially ardent and articular party members formed *agitpunkti* (agitation centers) in just about every work place and led frequent discussions about the party's great programs and the importance of voting in the election. There were also many public rallies, parades, and programs on television and radio, and in other ways the campaigns were at least as busy as those in any democratic country.

Elections were always held on Sunday, a legal holiday. Voters went to the polls and received ballots from the local election official. The law gave them two choices. If they approved the candidate listed on the ballot, they merely folded the ballot, unmarked, in front of everyone in the room and dropped it in the ballot box; if they wished to they could retire to a screened voting booth, cross out the official candidate's name, fold the ballot, and drop it in the ballot box—with everyone knowing exactly what they had done. They could not write in the name of another candidate but were restricted to voting against the official candidate. It is not surprising that only tiny fractions of the voters (estimated at 1 to 5 percent by Western observers) took their ballots into the screened booths. When almost every voter in the nation had performed this ritual (in the 1984 election the official turnout figure was announced as 99.95 percent!), the polls were closed, the ballots were counted, and the newspapers and radio and television stations (all, of course, government owned and managed by the CPSU) announced the outcome—yet another glorious triumph for the CPSU.

WHY DID THEY BOTHER?

To those of us accustomed to Western democratic procedures, the whole elaborate pre-Gorbachev Soviet system of nominating, campaigning, and electing seems pointless, even ridiculous. That is because we think of nominations and elections as methods by which a truly sovereign electorate chooses among many rivals for public office and political power; it is difficult for us to understand why the Soviets bothered to go through the motions of democracy when they knew that they had—and *wanted* to have—rule by the party elite rather than by the masses.

When we view the matter from the traditional Leninist-Stalinist-Brezhnevian point of view, however, it made a kind of sense. Elections were regarded as a useful device for mobilizing the masses' approval and even enthusiasm for party policies while giving them the feeling—however spurious it may seem to democratic eyes—that they were participating in the nation's governing processes. They gave the party's leaders a good way of checking on the devotion, energy, and skills of its local members in leading the *agitpunkti*. They helped to socialize new voters into the ways of the system. They reinforced the regime's legitimacy by parading its apparent enthusiastic support by 99.95 percent of the people. Above all, they were an ideal occasion for generating and renewing the enthusiasm that party leaders needed for themselves and their programs. And even the tiny variations in the numbers of abstentions and negative votes provided a useful barometer for detecting changes in public opinion.

The purpose of democratic candidate recruitment and elections is to establish popular *control* over public officials. The purpose of Soviet nominations and elections before Gorbachev was to create popular *support* for policies and leaders already determined by the party oligarchs.

GORBACHEV'S PROPOSALS FOR ELECTION REFORM

Soon after he took office in 1985, Mikhail Gorbachev said on a number of occasions that it might be a good idea if the Soviet Union tried some truly contested elections—elections in which at least two candidates for each public office would appear on the official ballot, and the voters would be able to make genuine choices by marking their ballots in private election booths so that no one can know whom they have chosen. He proposed that this radical change in Soviet ways first be tried on an experimental basis in some elections for local offices, and if it seemed to work well, as he believed it would, it could be extended to elections for the Supreme Soviet. He greatly extended the idea in the 1988 Communist party conference (see Chapter 4) by proposing that local elected government councils should take over a good deal of local economic and administrative management from the CPSU's local branches, that the members of those councils be elected in multicandidate elections, and that officials of the CPSU would be excluded from council membership. He also proposed that henceforth there should be multiple-candidate, secret-ballot elections for the national parliament and for all regional and local councils, and he specifically said that these elections should permit nonparty groups to nominate and campaign for candidates. Finally, he proposed that a limit of two five-year terms should be imposed on all top officials, elected and appointed—presumably including himself.

The election of March 27, 1989 for the new national Congress of Deputies was the first held under Gorbachev's new rules, and Western observers called it the freest election held in the Soviet Union since the Communists took power in 1917. About three-fourths of the districts had real contests between two or more candidates, and even in the uncontested districts a record number of voters drew lines through the names of the single candidates. There were a number of dramatic results: Boris Yeltsin, who had been deposed as Moscow Communist Party leader for being too enthusiastic about *perestroika*, was elected over a candidate backed by the Moscow party organization. Many high Communist leaders were defeated, including the mayors of Leningrad and Kiev and the president of Lithuania. When Soviet television asked Gorbachev how he felt about all these defeats of Communist Party leaders, he replied, "I am in favor of competition and competitiveness, and at every stage." In the 1989 election, he got it.[11]

As I have said before, it is too early to tell how well these reforms will work, and whether they will indeed produce the economic payoffs that Gorbachev expects. But this much we can say: If the statement in the fourth edition of this book was correct that not only were the nominating and electing institutions in the Soviet Union almost completely different, in substance if not in form, from those in the democratic countries—and that "in few other institutional comparisons is the contrast and distance between the Western and Communist conceptions of democracy so apparent"—then, perhaps more than any of the other elements of *perestroika,* Gorbachev's proposals for radical changes in the Soviet electoral system will lead to radical changes in every other aspect of the whole Soviet polity. We will see.

FOR FURTHER READING

SUFFRAGE AND CANDIDATE ELECTIONS

BOGDANOR, VERNON, and DAVID BUTLER, eds. *Democracy and Elections: Electoral Systems and Their Political Consequences* (New York: Cambridge University Press, 1983). Essays on the political impact of various electoral systems.

*BUTLER, DAVID, HOWARD R. PENNIMAN, and AUSTIN RANNEY, eds., *Democracy at the Polls.* Washington, D.C.: American Enterprise Institute, 1981. The most recent comprehensive comparative study of the conduct of elections in twenty-eight selected democratic nations.

CAIN, BRUCE E. *The Reapportionment Puzzle.* Berkeley: University of California Press, 1984. Analysis of political consequences of reapportionment and gerrymandering, with special reference to California.

DUMMET, MICHAEL. *Voting Procedures.* New York: Oxford University Press, 1985. Description of leading electoral systems and their political impacts, with emphasis on strategies of voting.

*GROFMAN, BERNARD, and AREND LIJPHART, eds. *Electoral Laws and Their Political Consequences.* New York: Agathon Press, 1986. Essays on electoral systems and their political consequences in a number of democratic countries.

LAKEMAN, ENID. *How Democracies Vote.* London: Faber & Faber, 1970. Survey of various electoral systems by a leading advocate of proportional representation.

*RAE, DOUGLAS W. *The Political Consequences of Electoral Laws,* rev. ed. New Haven, CT: Yale University Press, 1971. A lucid and well-documented analysis of how various electoral systems affect the number and strength of political parties.

SMITH, T. E. *Elections in Developing Countries.* New York: St. Martin's Press, 1960. General survey of procedures and problems of elections in developing nations.

PROPORTIONAL REPRESENTATION

HOAG, CLARENCE G., and GEORGE H. HALLETT. *Proportional Representation*. New York: Crowell-Collier and Macmillan, 1926. For many years the standard exposition of the case.

LIJPHART, AREND, and BERNARD GROFMAN, eds.

Choosing an Electoral System: Issues and Alternatives. New York: Praeger, 1984. Essays on the costs and benefits of proportional and first-past-the-post electoral systems.

NOMINATIONS AND CANDIDATE SELECTION

BARTELS, LARRY M. *Presidential Primaries and the Dynamics of Public Choice*. Princeton, NJ: Princeton University Press, 1988. Analysis of "momentum" in presidential nominations caused by media coverage of sequential primaries.

RANNEY, AUSTIN. *Pathways to Parliament*. Madison: University of Wisconsin Press, 1965. Study of how British parties choose their candidates for Parliament.

GALLAGHER, MICHAEL, and MICHAEL MARSH, eds., *Candidate Selection in Comparative Perspective*. Beverly Hills, CA: Sage, 1988. Essays on the selection of parliamentary candidates in Belgium, Great Britain, France, West Germany, Ireland, Italy, Japan, the Netherlands, and Norway.

REFERENDUMS

*BUTLER, DAVID, and AUSTIN RANNEY, eds. *Referendums: A Study in Practice and Theory*. Washington, D.C.: American Enterprise Institute, 1978. Studies of conduct and impact of referendums in various democratic nations, with appendices listing results of all nationwide referendums held up to the middle of 1978.

CRONIN, THOMAS E. *Direct Democracy: The Politics of Initiative, Referendum, and Recall*. Cam-

bridge, MA: Harvard University Press, 1989. Discussion of the uses and potential of initiatives and referendums in the United States.

MAGLEBY, DAVID B. *Direct Legislation*. Baltimore: Johns Hopkins University Press, 1984. Detailed study of the initiative and referendum in the United States, describing their use, financing, and impact on voters.

NOTES

[1]Gerald M. Pomper, *Elections in America* (New York: Dodd, Mead, 1968), pp. 262–63.

[2]Robert W. Jackman, "Political Institutions and Voter Turnout in the Industrial Democracies," *American Political Science Review*, vol. 81 (June 1987), pp. 405–23.

[3]See Steven J. Brams and Peter Fishburn, *Approval Voting* (Cambridge, MA: Birkhauser Boston, 1983).

[4]Douglas W. Rae, *The Political Consequences of Electoral Laws,* rev. ed. (New Haven: Yale University Press, 1971), especially Chapters 4–10. See also Bernard Grofman and Arend Lijphart, eds., *Electoral Laws and Their Political Consequences* (New York: Agathon Press, 1986).

[5]The system is described in detail in Max Kaase, "Personalized Proportional Representation:

The 'Model' of the West German Electoral System," in Arend Lijphart and Bernard Grofman, eds., *Choosing an Electoral System: Issues and Alternatives* (New York: Praeger, 1984), pp. 155–64.

[6]For a comparative analysis of reapportionment in the United States and Great Britain, focusing on why the process is so political and controversial in the United States and so technical and consensual in Britain, see David Butler and Bruce E. Cain, "Reapportionment: A Study in Comparative Government," *Electoral Studies,* vol. 4 (December 1985), pp. 197–213.

[7]John E. Mueller, "Voting on the Propositions," *American Political Science Review,* vol. 63 (December 1969), pp. 1,197–1,212.

[8]This discussion is drawn mainly from Theodore H. Friedgut, *Political Participation in the USSR* (Princeton, NJ: Princeton University Press, 1979), Chapters 1–2; and Stephen White, "Noncompetitive Elections and National Politics: The USSR Supreme Soviet Elections of 1984," *Electoral Studies,* vol. 4 (December 1985), pp. 215–29.

[9]From the English translation of the 1977 Soviet Constitution in *Keesing's Contemporary Archives,* December 9, 1977, p. 28,705.

[10]P. Tumanov, quoted in John A. Armstrong, *Ideology, Politics, and Government in the Soviet Union,* rev. ed. (New York: Praeger, 1967), p. 111.

[11]*New York Times,* March 3, 1989, p. A1.

9 Voting Behavior

The nation blessed above all nations is she in whom the civic genius of the people does the saving day by day, by acts without external picturesqueness; by speaking, writing, voting reasonably; by smiting corruption swiftly; by good temper between parties; by the people knowing true men when they see them, and preferring them as leaders to rabid partisans or empty quacks.

William James, Memories and Studies

Most of us become upset, frightened, or angry at times about what our government is doing or not doing. Some of us are concerned about the nuclear arms race and demand that our government conclude a nuclear freeze agreement with the Soviet Union. Some of us are concerned about the rising amount and easy availability of pornography in magazines, movies, and videocassettes, and we demand that government stamp it out. Some of us are concerned about the rapid deterioration of our physical environment and demand drastic anti-pollution measures before it is too late. And so on.

There comes a time for most of us when we feel that mere talk is no longer enough, that it is time for action—now! But what kind of action? "I'm only one person," we often hear people say. "What can *I* do?"

In a democratic system there are many answers to that question. We can join one of the existing political parties or form a new one and try to elect new public officials. We can join a pressure group to "put the heat" on incumbent officials to make them do something or stop doing something. We can file law suits against the officials. We can demonstrate, boycott, and strike. The physical means are readily at hand to assassinate the president or start a revolution.

That is what we *can* do, but what do most of us *actually* do to advance our political goals? The answers for the citizens of four Western democracies are shown in Table 9.1.

TABLE 9.1.   **Levels of Peaceful Political Participation in Four Western Democracies**

Form of Participation	Percentage Reporting Activity, 1981			
	United States	Great Britain	West Germany	France
Voted in last election	68	73	90	81
Sign petitions	61	63	46	na
Contact officials	27	11	11	na
Convince others how to vote	19	9	22	na
Attend meeting or rally	18	9	22	na
Work for party or candidate	14	5	8	na
Participate in demonstrations	12	10	14	26
Join in boycott	14	7	7	11
Participate in unofficial strike	3	7	2	10
Occupy building	2	2	1	7

Source: Russell J. Dalton, *Citizen Politics in Western Democracies* (Chatham, NJ: Chatham House, 1988), Table 3.4, p. 47, and Table 4.1, p. 65.

The data in Table 9.1 show that most people in all four nations find most forms of political action too demanding, too costly, too dangerous, or morally wrong. Hence voting for or against particular parties and candidates in periodic elections is for most citizens of democracies the most-used way of trying to influence government policies, and for many of us it is the only way.

Voting may or may not be the most effective way for ordinary citizens to make governments do as they wish, but in every modern democratic system votes are the basic units of political power. When all is said and done, the groups that mobilize the largest numbers of voters in support of the public policies and officials they favor get the largest shares of what they want out of politics. If some people have every quality necessary to be, say, great presidents except the ability to make people vote for them, their other qualities will not make them *any* kind of president. A political party may have the most intelligent and progressive program possible, but if it cannot attract enough voters, its program will never become public policy. A pressure group may lobby so skillfully that it lines up everyone in the legislature on its side, but if the voters throw these legislators out of office at the next election, its lobbying efforts will go for naught. Even the power of money, sometimes mistakenly regarded as an irresistible force in politics, ultimately depends upon its ability to produce votes.

So the question of what makes voters vote as they do is of great concern to every party politician and lobbyist. It is of equal concern to every student of democratic politics, and in the past forty years so many excellent studies have been made of voting behavior that today it is generally considered to be one of the most advanced areas in political science. In this chapter we will review the principal findings of those studies so that we may better understand how and why this basic coin of political power is distributed among parties and candidates.

High Turnout in European Elections. Miners voting in a West German national election. (Source: AP/Wide World Photos.)

INTERVENING VARIABLES IN VOTING BEHAVIOR

In any democratic system, the aspect or voting behavior that first concerns both participating politicians and political scientists is the *result*—how many people vote and which way—because it is at that point that voters have their most direct and powerful impact on the governing process. Hence most political scientists have taken two dimensions of voting behavior as their main *dependent variables*—that is, the kinds of behavior they are trying to explain.[1] The first dimension is *preferences*—what makes people prefer one party or candidate over other parties and candidates. And the second dimension is *voting and nonvoting*—what makes people decide to vote or not vote.

The studies of voting behavior typically regard voting behavior as one special form of public opinion, and as we saw in Chapters 3 and 6, many independent variables help to shape most political attitudes and behavior, including voting behavior. These variables include voters' biological natures and needs, their psychological makeups, their membership in primary and secondary social groups, the communications they receive, and so on. Should we, then, simply assume that these independent variables explain all public opinion, including voting behavior, and let it go at that?

The authors of the classic study of American voting behavior say no.[2] They point out that when we ask people why they voted as they did in a particular election, few are likely to reply, "Because I have a high socioeconomic status" or "Because I live in a suburb" or "Because my husband told me to." Most people will probably say, "Because I am a Republican" or "Because I don't want my taxes raised" or "Because Bush has the experience we need." In other words, most people think that they vote the way they do because of how they feel about the political parties, the issues, and the candidates. Hence these feelings *intervene* between the basic independent variables (people's socioeconomic status and primary group memberships) and the dependent variables (voting and nonvoting, voting for Dukakis or Bush). In this sense, they are *intervening variables*.

If that is the case, then the first step in understanding how and why people vote is to understand how they feel about the parties, issues, and candidates.

PARTY IDENTIFICATION

Meaning

Party identification is *the sense of attachment a person feels to a political party*. It is thus an inner psychological feeling or attitude, not an outward formal dues-paying attachment to a party such as party *membership* (see Chapter 10). Political scientists usually measure the direction and intensity of people's party identifications by asking a standard question that the Center for Political Studies (CPS) at the University of Michigan has asked American respondents in its surveys every two years since 1948. The question is, "Generally speaking, do you usually think of yourself as a Republican, a Democrat, an independent, or what?" If a person answers "independent," they ask the follow-up question, "Do you think of yourself as closer to the Republican or Democratic party?" If a person answers to the first question "Democrat" or "Republican," the follow-up question is, "Do you think of yourself as a strong Democrat (Republican) or not so strong?" Their responses are then classified in the seven categories shown in Table 9.2.

Development

Party identification is the first attitude that most people acquire in their political socialization. As we saw in Chapter 3, by age 7 or 8 most Americans will tell an interviewer, "We [that is, the respondent's family] are Republicans (or Democrats)." Evidently we acquire our initial party identifications, as aspects of our identifications with our families. The more united the parents are in their party preferences and the more vocal they are about them, the more likely their children are to have the same preferences for the rest of their lives. In many people these early preferences are likely to grow stronger through life

TABLE 9.2. Party Identification in the United States, 1960–86 (in percentages)

Year	Democrats				Republicans			
	Strong	Weak	Ind.	Ind.	Strong	Weak	Ind.	Other
1960	21	25	8	8	14	13	7	4
1964	27	25	8	8	11	13	6	2
1968	20	25	9	11	10	14	9	2
1972	15	26	10	13	10	13	11	2
1976	15	25	12	14	9	14	10	1
1980	18	23	11	13	9	14	10	2
1984	17	20	11	11	12	15	12	2
1986	18	22	10	12	15	10	11	2

Source: Robert S. Erikson, Norman R. Luttberg, and Kent L. Tedin, *American Public Opinion* (New York: Macmillan, 1988), Table 1.6, pp. 9–10.

as a result of the general principle, noted in Chapter 3, that the longer one maintains identification with any group, the more intense the identification becomes. On the other hand, where, as in France, the usual family relationship does not allow for political discussion by parents with or in the presence of children, fewer people have stable long-term party identifications.

Fluctuation

Another reason for the lower incidence of stable party identifications in France is that the parties themselves have been less stable than in many other democracies. The parties of the Third Republic (1870–1940) disappeared under the Vichy regime (1940–44), reappeared in somewhat altered form and with some new names under the Fourth Republic (1946–58), and have undergone more reshuffling in the Fifth Republic (1958–). Furthermore, under the Fourth Republic some parties (the Rassemblement du Peuple Français, Social Republicans, and Poujadists) were purely "flash" parties: They emerged, fought one or two elections, and disbanded. In recent years France has offered fewer durable parties with which the French people could form lasting identifications than most other democracies have provided for their citizens.

In the United States, however, the present party alignment has lasted since 1854, in Great Britain and Norway since 1900, in Switzerland since 1919, in Canada since 1918, and so on. In these countries, party identifications tend to be noticeably stronger and more stable than in France, but some fluctuations occur nevertheless. According to the CPS, some Americans switch parties for personal reasons: A person's spouse has an opposing party loyalty and he or she switches to keep peace at home; a person achieves a socioeconomic status higher than that of his parents or moves to a new neighborhood and switches to the party predominant in the new environment; and so on.

Politically, however, the most significant fluctuations are those in which massive numbers of voters switch from one party to another and thus change the balance of electoral power. Such a shift certainly occurred in the United States between 1930 and 1936, when many Republicans became Democrats, and some commentators believe that in the 1980s similar shifts—especially from strong party attachments to weaker attachments to all parties (to be discussed further in a moment)—have been taking place in the United States and other Western democracies.

Impact

As we have noted previously, in most modern democracies the most visible contestants in electoral politics today are the same political parties—or at least parties bearing the same names—that have been prominent for periods ranging from sixty years to more than a century. In such nations the parties are about the only political objects that are recognized by almost everyone. Party identification thus serves many people as their main device for making sense of the political events, issues, personalities, charges, and countercharges flooding them from the communications media. Put another way, the one political fact that most of us are sure of is that we are Democrats or Republicans; when in doubt—as we often are—about this issue or that candidate, we can still choose by simply going along with our parties' positions or candidates.

It is therefore not surprising that political scientists have consistently found powerful associations between intensity of party identification and most other aspects of voting behavior. For example, the most partisan people are also the most interested in, and best informed about, political affairs, the most likely to vote, and the most likely to try to influence others to vote.

The least partisan are quite different. We are all familiar with the inspiring picture of "independents" as ideal citizens—people who are deeply concerned with civic affairs, acquaint themselves with the facts about the issues and candidates, and make their decision on each according to the merits, their thinking uncontaminated by loyalty to party labels. Without commenting on whether or not good citizens *should* be this way, we must recognize that the voting studies have found only a small fraction of self-styled "pure independents" who fit the ideal. Quite the contrary: Typical pure independents are far less interested in politics than strong partisans, know much less about issues and candidates, care little about how elections come out, and are much less likely to vote. Their independence, in short, results from apathy rather than from a high-minded rejection of partisanship.

Remember, though, that the previous paragraph applies only to the pure independents—that is, people who express no preference of any kind for one party over the other. There are also the **independent leaners**—*people who call themselves independents but have some preference for a particular party.* Such people are quite different from the pure independents in several respects: They are much more interested in politics; they know much more about the issues and the candidates; they care much more about how elections come out;

and they are far more likely to vote. Indeed, recent studies have shown that they score higher on all these counts than the "weak Democrats" and "weak Republicans."

In short, in terms of political involvement, knowledge, and activity, the strong party identifiers rank first, the independent leaners are second, the weak party identifiers are third, and the pure independents are a distant last.

Realignment or Dealignment?

Several developments in the 1980s led a number of commentators to declare that American politics is in the midst of a party realignment, in which the Republicans are replacing the Democrats as the country's majority party. They point to these facts: Since 1968, the Republicans have won five of the six presidential elections—two (1972 and 1984) by landslides—and have accumulated a grand total of 265 million votes (55 percent) to the Democrats' 216 million. Moreover, in 1980 the Republicans won a majority in the Senate for the first time since 1954, and they held it in 1982 and 1984. Finally, in 1984 and 1985, the Gallup Poll and other polls showed that the Republicans had almost as many identifiers as the Democrats.

Other commentators argued that a *de*alignment, not a realignment, is taking place not only in the United States but in many other Western democracies. They point to the fact, made evident in Table 9.2, that the proportion of Americans identifying with *neither* party has risen from 27 percent in 1964 to 37 percent in 1986.

Moreover, over half of American voters now regularly split their tickets— that is, they vote for Democrats for some offices and Republicans for other offices. In a 1986 study, respondents were asked, "Would you describe yourself as a loyal Republican who votes mostly for Republican candidates, a loyal Democrat who votes mostly for Democratic candidates, or as switching between the two parties?" The results are shown in Table 9.3.

Such large-scale ticket splitting explains why, despite Republican Ronald Reagan's large victories in the 1980 and 1984 elections, the Democrats retained a sizeable majority in the House of Representatives throughout his eight years

TABLE 9.3. Ticket Splitting in the United States 1986 (in percentages)

	Party Identification		
	Democrats	Republicans	Independents
Stay loyal to party	50	47	9
Switch between the parties	48	53	87
Neither, not ascertained	2	0	4

Source: Survey by *Time*/ Yankelovich, Clancy, and Shulman, September 8–10, 1986, reported in *Public Opinion* (January/February 1987), p. 34.

Campaigning in a Parliamentary Democracy. Progressive-Conservative party leader Brian Mulroney campaigning in the 1988 Canadian general election. (Source: Canapress Photo Service.)

and won control of the Senate in 1986 and 1988. Clearly, millions of voters who voted for Reagan and Bush also voted for Democratic candidates for Congress.

Voters in Western European democracies cannot split their tickets in national elections because they vote only for the members of parliament from their districts, and the leader of the party that wins a majority of the seats automatically becomes the prime minister—or, if no party wins a majority, the prime minister is selected by a coalition of parties (see Chapter 12). Even so, many analysts believe that those countries are undergoing a substantial erosion of party loyalty and that voters switch back and forth between the parties from one election to the next more than they formerly did. In most democracies, then, party identifications have never been the only factors influencing people's votes, and in the 1980s and 1990s they seem to be growing steadily weaker.[3]

We will see. But even in its heyday before 1968, party identification was obviously never the sole determinant of voting behavior. If it had been, the Republicans would never have won a presidential election, when in fact they have won more than half of the elections since 1948. This record can be explained in part by the countervailing effects of the two other intervening variables—both of which may now be growing even more important as party identification weakens.

ISSUE ORIENTATION

A **political issue** is *a disputed question about what government should or should not do.* Much of what we hear about politics in our newspapers and on television—especially during election campaigns—describes conflict between (and often within) the parties over issues. Senator A says that the United States should impose import quotas and taxes to keep the Japanese from selling us so much more than they buy from us, while Senator B says that prices should be kept free from government meddling and find their true economic level. Some people (perhaps even some readers of this book) who pay considerable attention to discussions of politics in the mass media assume, quite erroneously as we saw in Chapter 3, that everyone else is as interested in politics as they are and knows as much about issues as they do. Consequently, many students of political science, like many political commentators, tend to exaggerate the influence of issues and ideology on the mass electorate.

Why *exaggerate?* The authors of *The American Voter* correctly point out that in order to have a measurable impact on voting behavior, an issue must fulfill three conditions. First, the voters must be aware of its existence and have some opinions about it. Second, it must concern them enough to influence how they vote. And third, they must perceive that the position of a particular party or candidate on the issue is nearer to their own position than the opposition's. Only when an issue fulfills all three of these conditions for large numbers of voters can it exert significant influence on the outcome of an election.

Studies of voting behavior demonstrate that the more ideological the parties and the more the voters strongly identify with them, the more likely people's stands on issues are to be predictable from their party identifications. This association has generally been weaker in the United States than in other Western democracies, mainly because the American major parties have usually advocated less clear and consistent ideologies than do the parties in the other democracies. Since the 1950s, issue voting has noticeably increased in all democratic polities including the United States.[4]

Public opinion studies have consistently shown that from the mid-1960s on, increasing numbers of American voters have perceived significant differences between the policy positions of the Democratic and Republican parties and candidates, and those perceptions have played increasingly influential roles in their voting choices. This has been especially noticeable in the case of at least two issues of overriding importance in the voters' minds. One instance was the role of the Civil Rights Act in the 1964 presidential election. As we will see in Chapter 16, that legislation had given the national government great new powers in guaranteeing all races equal access to public accommodations, education, and job opportunities. Most voters knew that Democratic presidential candidate Lyndon Johnson was strongly in favor of the legislation, while Republican presidential candidate Barry Goldwater had opposed it. A significant number of Democrats who opposed the legislation voted for Goldwater, while an even larger number of Republicans who favored it voted for Johnson.

Another instance occurred in 1972: Most voters were very concerned with the issue of whether or not the United States should immediately withdraw from the war in Vietnam; most of them also correctly perceived that Democratic presidential candidate George McGovern favored withdrawal and Republican candidate Richard Nixon opposed it; among strong Democrats, McGovern received nearly two-thirds of the "dove" vote but only a small fraction of the "hawk" vote. There were relatively few Republican doves, but many more of them than the Republican hawks voted for McGovern. In both instances, then, issue considerations clearly overrode party loyalties for a great many voters, and the same can be said for a growing number of other issues.[5] But the impressive electoral victories of Ronald Reagan in 1980 and 1984 and George Bush in 1988 show that issue voting, while on the rise, is still far from being the only important factor that determines American election outcomes.

CANDIDATE ORIENTATION

Candidate orientation means *voters' opinions of candidates' personal qualities considered apart from their party affiliations or stands on issues.* For example, when one votes for George Bush mainly because he is the Republican candidate, party identification is the prime factor; when one votes for him mainly from a conviction that he will stand firm against the Communist government in Nicaragua, issue orientation is most prominent; and when one votes for him because he is seen as an experienced and strong leader, then candidate orientation is the prime factor.

Contrary to what we sometimes read or hear, candidate orientation is never the only consideration in voting and often not even the most important one. Its power varies with several circumstances—the conspicuousness of the office, the type of election, whether things are going well or badly, and so on. It is strongest when the voters vote directly for the occupant of the office, when they choose between well-publicized candidates, and when the incumbent is so often in the news that the office is prominent in most voters' minds. It is thus probably at its strongest in elections for the chief executives of presidential democratic systems.

This is clearly shown in the case of the United States by the comparison, shown in Figure 9.1, of three different measures of the Democratic party's voting strength in the period from 1952 to 1984. In those 32 years, the Democrats' share of voters' party identifications varied between a low of 47 percent in 1984 and a high of 61 percent in 1964—a difference of 14 points. Their share of the total national vote for U.S. representatives varied even less, from a low of 50 percent in 1952 and 1984 to a high of 57.5 percent in 1964—a difference of 7.5 points. But in presidential voting their share fell as low as 37.5 percent for George McGovern in 1972 and rose as high as 61 percent for Lyndon B. Johnson in 1964—a difference of 23.5 percentage points! Clearly, then, many

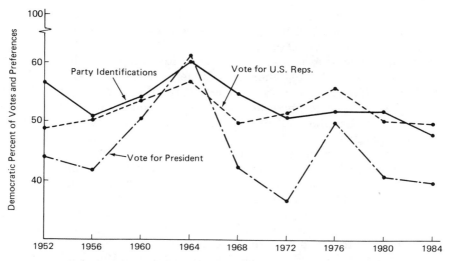

FIGURE 9.1. Democratic Shares of party identifications and votes, 1960–84.(Source: The data on party identifications are taken from William Schneider, "The November 6 Vote for President: What Did It Mean?", in Austin Ranney, ed., The American Elections of 1984. (Durham, NC: Duke University Press, 1985), Chapter 7. The data on vote shares are taken from Nelson W. Polsby, "The Democratic Nomination and the Evolution of the Party System," in ibid., Chapter 2.)

voters' choices in presidential elections are strongly affected by how they feel about the personal qualities of the candidates.

The great electoral success of Ronald Reagan illustrates the importance of candidate orientation. Reagan is arguably one of the great vote-getters in American history: In 1980 he defeated incumbent president Jimmy Carter by the impressive margin of 51 percent of the popular votes to Carter's 41 percent; and in 1984 he was re-elected by the landslide margin of 59 percent to Democrat Walter Mondale's 41 percent. What accounts for his great success? Certainly party identifications played a minor role, because in both elections Reagan ran as the candidate of the minority party. What about issue orientation? Certainly, as we saw in Chapter 6, American public opinion was turning more conservative in the 1980s, and perhaps Reagan merely rode the crest of the wave. Yet a good deal of the evidence shows that substantial majorities of the public consistently opposed many of Reagan's most cherished policies, so issue orientation is certainly not the whole explanation.

Thus candidate orientation—the fact that a lot of Americans liked Reagan the man, as distinct from his Republican affiliation or his conservative policies—had a lot to do with it. Just how much is suggested by the results of an interesting *ABC News/Washington Post* poll taken in May 1984 just before Reagan started his re-election campaign. They asked their respondents two questions: Do you like Reagan personally? Do you approve of his policies?

Thirty-nine percent said they liked *both* Reagan and his policies; 18 percent said they both disliked Reagan and disapproved his policies; 11 percent said they disliked Reagan personally but approved of his policies; and 28 percent—the second-largest group—said they liked Reagan personally but disapproved of his policies. Added together, only 50 percent approved of his policies, while 67 percent liked him personally.[6] Clearly, then, a good many people who voted for Reagan did so because they liked him personally (candidate orientation), not because they liked all Republican candidates (party identification) or because they agreed with all his conservative policies (issue orientation).

Candidate orientation is said to be less significant in the parliamentary democracies, where the prime ministers are not directly elected but achieve office as a result of their parties' winning majorities of the seats in parliament (see Chapter 12). In some of these nations, however, the personalities of party leaders appear to be growing more and more prominent in election campaigns—the "Americanization of politics" some call it. For example, most analysts believe that the British Labour party did better in the 1987 general election than in the 1983 election mainly because its 1987 leader, Neil Kinnock, projected a much more attractive image than his predecessor, Michael Foot; and in both elections one of the Conservative party's main assets was the widespread admiration of prime minister Margaret Thatcher as a strong and determined leader (some called her "the iron maiden"). Other indirectly elected prime ministers whose personalities have notably attracted voters to (or repelled them from) their parties have included Pierre Elliott Trudeau in Canada, Menachem Begin in Israel, Helmut Schmidt in West Germany, and Indira Gandhi in India. Although candidate orientation probably remains more powerful in the presidential than in the parliamentary democracies, it appears to be growing steadily more important in many of the latter.

But direct election does not in itself guarantee high candidate orientation, for the less prominent the office, the less important are the candidates' personal qualities in affecting the outcome. In many American states, for example, the voters first choose—usually with some confidence—their candidates for president, Congress, governors, and state legislatures. But usually they are also called upon to choose among candidates for state secretary of state, treasurer, comptroller of public accounts, attorney general, and superintendent of public instruction. And when they have made those choices they still are not finished: They have to vote for county supervisor, clerk, treasurer, sheriff, auditor, clerk of the circuit court, coroner, superintendent of schools, justices of the peace, sanitary commissioners, park commissioners, and recorder of deeds.

By the time voters get down to the contest for recorder of deeds, even the most conscientious are likely to say to themselves, "I don't know either of these candidates, I don't know what the recorder of deeds does, I can't imagine that it makes much difference which candidate gets the job, and I'm tired!" So they either leave that part of the ballot unmarked or, more likely, simply vote for the candidate of their party. Direct elections for such minor offices, we can say with confidence, seldom feature high candidate orientation for anyone except the candidates' relatives. As elsewhere, party identification remains the most powerful psychological variable intervening between the voters' behavior at elections and the wider context of political events, institutions, and communications.

A NEW LOOK AT AMERICAN VOTERS

In recent years some political scientists and more newspeople have become dissatisfied with the usual ways of dividing American voters into their main component groups. For instance, they feel that party identification today is so weak and ticket splitting is so common that classifying voters as Democrats, Republicans, and Independents tells very little about them. By the same token, they find in public opinion polls that on quite a number of issues "liberals" and "conservatives" take very similar stands, so that typology[7] is not very useful either. They have similar objections to such typologies as upper class, middle class, and working class; and northerners, southerners, easterners, and westerners.

In 1987 the Times Mirror Company, publishers of the *Los Angeles Times* and a number of syndicated features, decided to try something new. They hired the Gallup organization to do an extensive new survey of a representative national sample of 4,244 adults. They then used statistical techniques known as regression analysis and cluster analysis to classify their respondents into the most homogeneous voting groups possible, and they came up with eleven distinct groups.[8] By no means haves all political scientists or newspeople accepted all of the study's methodology or findings, but it is worth briefly summarizing here.

According to the Times Mirror, the main voting groups in the United States are the following:

1. *Enterprise Republicans* (10 percent of the adult population, 16 percent of the likely electorate). They are white, affluent, well educated. They are very likely to vote, and they vote mainly Republican. They are very conservative on economic issues (for example, they want to balance the federal budget by cutting welfare spending, not by tax increases), but they are more liberal on social questions (for example, they oppose restrictions on abortion and quarantine of AIDS patients).

2. *Moralist Republicans* (11 percent of the population, 14 percent of the likely voters). They are white, middle-income people, somewhat less well educated, living in suburbs and small cities, with a heavy concentration of southerners and many "born-again" Christians. They are somewhat more liberal on economic matters and are inclined to favor social spending except when it is targeted to minorities. They strongly oppose abortion and favor prayer in the schools and quarantining AIDS patients. They too vote mainly Republican.

3. *Upbeats* (9 percent of the adult population and the likely electorate). They are young, white, middle-income people, most of whom have high school educations. They are economically conservative but socially liberal. They vote mainly Repub-

lican, but John F. Kennedy is one of their great heroes. Unlike the first two Republican groups, they are not critical of government's role in society.

4. *Disaffecteds* (9 percent of the adult population, 7 percent of the likely voters). They are mainly middle-aged, middle-income white people who are strongly antigovernment *and* anti–big business, but promilitary. They support government welfare except when it is targeted to minorities, and they favor a strong defense and vigorous foreign policy. Most of them and their families began as Democrats but in recent years have been voting mainly Republican.

5. *Bystanders* (11 percent of the adult population, 0 percent of the likely electorate). They are mainly young, poorly educated, and have almost no interest in political affairs. They are of little significance politically, and if there is to be a major increase in voting turnout much of it will have to come from this group.

6. *Followers* (7 percent of the adult population, 4 percent of the voters). This group is composed mainly of young, poorly educated blue-collar workers. They have only a limited interest in politics; they split about evenly on Reagan and have strongly supported Senator Edward Kennedy. They favor government spending to reduce unemployment, but on most other issues they split evenly.

7. *Seculars* (8 percent of the adult population, 9 percent of the likely electorate). The only group in the United States that professes no religious belief. They are well educated, white, and middle-aged; they have mainly professional occupations, and they are especially liberal on questions of personal freedom, though they are more conservative on economic questions.

8. *Sixties Democrats* (8 percent of the adult population, 11 percent of the likely voters). They are generally upper-middle class, college educated, and disproportionately female. They identify strongly with the peace, civil rights, and environmental movements of the 1960s, and they favor most forms of social spending, oppose large military spending, and feel that the United States is too suspicious of the Soviet Union. They vote strongly Democratic.

9. *New Deal Democrats* (11 percent of the adult population, 15 percent of the likely voters). These people are mainly older, blue-collar union members with moderate incomes. They generally favor social spending measures, but are conservative on issues such as school prayer and abortion. They defected to Reagan in large numbers but have stayed with the Democrats in congressional, state, and local elections.

10. *God-and-country Democrats* (7 percent of the population, 6 percent of the electorate). They are less well educated, disproportionately southern and African-American, and have lower incomes. They favor all forms of social spending and are more supportive of tax increases than any other group, but they oppose abortion and favor school prayer and a strong military. They are strongly religious, and many defected to Reagan while voting Democratic for other offices.

11. *Partisan poor* (9 percent of the population and the likely voters). They have very low incomes and are strong advocates of all forms of social spending, but they oppose tax increases. They favor school prayers but are divided on abortion. They favor cutting defense spending as the best way to deal with the budget deficit. They are the most solidly Democratic of all the groups, and only a few voted for Reagan.

Those are the groups. The Times Mirror analysts found that the core of support for Republican candidates for most offices is provided by the first four groups, while the last five groups provide the base for Democratic candidates. Much of Reagan's success resulted from his ability to attract support from the disaffecteds and the followers, but most of them did not also support

Republican congressional candidates. If the Republicans are to continue their success in presidential elections, their candidates must continue to hold the same groups, which together made up the "Reagan coalition." If the Democrats are to do better in presidential elections, they must hold the last five groups and win back most of the disaffecteds and followers. And if the Republicans are to become the true majority party, not just in presidential elections but in congressional, state, and local elections, they must win across-the-board loyalty from the disaffecteds and followers that matches what they already have from the enterprisers and moralists.

There is nothing in the Times Mirror analysis that suggests that either party will have any easier a time of it in the 1990s than they had in the 1980s.

FOR FURTHER READING

*BERELSON, BERNARD, PAUL F. LAZARSFELD, and WILLIAM N. MCPHEE. *Voting.* Chicago: University of Chicago Press, 1954. Pioneer sample survey study of the 1948 presidential election in Elmira, New York, and summary of findings from other studies of determinants of voting behavior.

*BUTLER, DAVID, and DONALD STOKES. *Political Change in Britain,* 2nd ed. New York: St. Martin's Press, 1974. The authoritative study of British voting behavior.

CAMPBELL, ANGUS, PHILIP E. CONVERSE, WARREN E. MILLER, and DONALD E. STOKES. *The American Voter.* New York: John Wiley, 1960. Still generally regarded as the leading work on American voting behavior, based on sample surveys for the 1952 and 1956 presidential elections.

*CAMPBELL, BRUCE A. *The American Electorate.* New York: Holt, Rinehart & Winston, 1979. Useful introductory survey of American voting behavior.

*DALTON, RUSSELL J., SCOTT C. FLANAGAN, and PAUL ALLEN BECK, eds. *Electoral Change in Advanced Industrial Democracies.* Princeton, NJ: Princeton University Press, 1984. Analysis of recent changes in voting patterns in a number of Western democratic nations.

*DEVRIES, WALTER, and V. LANCE TARRANCE. *The Ticket Splitter: A New Force in American Politics.* Grand Rapids, MI: William B. Eerdmans, 1972. Analysis of increase and impact of split-ticket voting in the United States.

*FLANIGAN, WILLIAM H., and NANCY ZINGALE. *Political Behavior of the American Electorate,* 5th ed. Boston: Allyn & Bacon, 1983. Useful analysis of current patterns in U.S. voting behavior.

KEY, V. O., JR. *The Responsible Electorate.* Cambridge, MA: Harvard University Press, 1966. Early emphasis on importance of issue voting.

*LIPSET, SEYMOUR MARTIN. *Political Man.* Baltimore: Johns Hopkins University Press, 1981. Reprint of a comparative survey of preference and participation patterns in many democratic countries.

MILLER, WARREN E., and TERESA E. LEVITIN. *Leadership and Change.* Cambridge, MA: Winthrop, 1976. Uses survey data to argue that the American electorate is changing in basic ways.

*NIE, NORMAN H., SIDNEY VERBA, and JOHN R. PETROCIK. *The Changing American Voter.* Cambridge, MA: Harvard University Press, 1976. Uses survey data to update *The American Voter,* with emphasis on the rise of issue voting since the 1950s.

NIEMI, RICHARD G., and HERBERT F. WEISBERG. *Controversies in Voting Behavior,* 2nd ed. Washington, D.C.: Congressional Quarterly Press, 1984. Detailed examination of data and theories dealing with American voting behavior.

*ORNSTEIN, NORMAN, ANDREW KOHUT, and LARRY MCCARTHY. *The People, the Press, and Politics.* Reading, MA: Addison-Wesley, 1988. A major new look at the structure of the American electorate based on a massive public opinion survey sponsored by the Times Mirror Company.

*POMPER, GERALD M. *Voter's Choice: Varieties of American Election Behavior.* Washington, DC: University Press of America, 1983. Analysis of electorate stressing rise of issue voting.

ROSE, RICHARD, ed. *Electoral Behavior.* New York: Free Press, 1973. Essays on elections and voting behavior in twelve Western nations.

NOTES

[1]The reader should understand the meanings of the following technical terms often used by political scientists: **Variable:** see Chapter 5, footnote 4. **Dependent variable:** *a variable whose characteristics are thought to be affected by other variables;* roughly equivalent to an *effect* in a cause-and-effect relationship. **Independent variable:** *a variable whose characteristics are thought to affect the status of a dependent variable;* roughly equivalent to a *cause* in a cause-and-effect relationship. **Intervening variable:** *a variable whose characteristics are thought to be the channel through which an independent variable affects a dependent variable;* see the discussion in the text.

[2]Angus Campbell, Philip E. Converse, Warren E. Miller, and Donald E. Stokes, *The American Voter* (New York: John Wiley, 1960), Chapter 2.

[3]For evidence of "partisan dealignment" in European democracies, see the articles in Ivor Crewe and D. T. Denver, eds., *Electoral Change in Western Democracies* (New York: St. Martin's Press, 1985).

[4]For the rise of issue voting in European as well as American elections, see Russell J. Dalton, *Citizen Politics in Western Democracies* (Chatham, NJ: Chatham House, 1988), pp. 192–200.

[5]For a detailed survey of the evidence on the rise of issue voting in the United States since the 1950s, see Robert S. Erikson, Norman R. Luttberg, and Kent L. Tedin, *American Public Opinion* (New York: Macmillan, 1988), pp. 252–71.

[6]*ABC News / Washington Post* poll quoted in Austin Ranney, ed., *The American Elections of 1984* (Durham, NC: Duke University Press, 1985), Table 1.4, p. 34.

[7]As social scientists use the term, a *typology* is a set of categories for classifying people, in which all the people in each category, or type, share one or more significant characteristics.

[8]The most complete summary of the Times Mirror study's methodology and findings is Norman Ornstein, Andrew Kohut, and Larry McCarthy, *The People, the Press, & Politics* (Reading, MA: Addison-Wesley, 1988). Since the publication of this book, the Times Mirror syndicate has continued to report new findings from the study in a series of special stories published by the *Los Angeles Times* and other subscribers.

10 Political Parties and Party Systems

[P]olitical parties created democracy and...modern democracy is unthinkable save in terms of the parties.... The most important distinction in modern political philosophy, the distinction between democracy and dictatorship, can be made best in terms of party politics. The parties are not therefore merely appendages of modern government; they are in the center of it and play a determinative and creative role in it.[1]

POLITICAL PARTIES IN DEMOCRATIC SYSTEMS

WHAT IS A POLITICAL PARTY?

Political parties are a special kind of political organization. How can we distinguish them from the other kinds, particularly pressure groups? In both democratic and authoritarian regimes, political parties have at least the following fundamental characteristics:

1. They are groups of people to whom *labels*—"Republican," "Communist," "Liberal," and so on—are generally applied by both themselves and others.
2. Some of the people are *organized*—that is, they deliberately act together to achieve party goals.
3. The larger society recognizes as *legitimate* the right of parties to organize and promote their causes.
4. In some of their goal-promoting activities, parties work through the *mechanisms of representative government.*
5. A key activity of parties is thus *selecting candidates* for elective public office.

By these criteria, then, a political party differs from a group like consumers because it is organized. It differs from a group like the American Medical Association because it nominates candidates and puts them forth in elections with its own label. Pressure groups, as we learned in Chapter 2, resemble political parties in many respects. They often take part in elections by endorsing candidates, raising money, issuing campaign propaganda, and ringing doorbells. But most of them are concerned mainly with what government *does,* while parties are equally or more concerned with who holds office. The "who" and "what" of government are not completely separate, of course, but parties generally put greater emphasis on the "who" aspect, as demonstrated by the fact that candidates run for office with official party labels. Pressure groups do not provide this kind of sponsorship, and are more concerned with the "what" aspect of government.

PARTY IDENTIFICATION AND MEMBERSHIP

Identifiers, Supporters, and Members

In Chapter 9 we saw that most citizens in most modern democratic nations have some party identification; that is, they have some sense of belonging to a particular political party. We also noted that most people acquire their party identifications early in life; that the identifications tend to grow stronger as people grow older; and that, while in recent years they have weakened in many Western democracies, they are still a major influence on voting behavior and constitute one of the most stable and powerful factors affecting the outcomes of free elections.

Being a *member* of an organization usually means something different from being an identifier or a supporter, however. The loyal Green Bay Packers fan who attends all the games, cheers the team, jeers the opposition, and offers free (though unheeded) advice to the coach is a team identifier and supporter, but no one would call the fan a team *member.* Membership implies that one assumes obligations to the organization and at the same time has access to the organization's decision-making processes. Accordingly, a person who tells a Gallup poll interviewer "I am a Democrat" but never contributes money, attends rallies, hands out leaflets, or makes any contribution to the party other than occasionally voting for its candidates is, like our Packers fan, an identifier and occasional supporter but not a member. Hence **party membership** means *formal attachment to a political party, usually involving the assumption of obligations to the party and receiving privileges from the party.*

Party Membership Rules

In most democracies other than the United States, political parties are purely private organizations, like bowling leagues or garden clubs. Few if any laws regulate how they manage their affairs. All matters—including membership requirements and admission procedures—are controlled by the rules each party makes and enforces for itself.

Most parties in most countries other than the United States have at least mildly demanding requirements. They usually require a person to apply formally for membership, and party officials can accept or reject the application (though in fact they are almost always accepted). To continue as a party member in good standing, the person must at least pay annual dues (usually amounting to the equivalent of only $5 or $10 per year) and sometimes also take an oath to support the party's principles and candidates. Moreover, the party can expel a member for nonpayment of dues, deserting the party's principles, supporting the candidates of opposition parties, and the like (although such expulsions are very rare). The number of people willing to make this kind of commitment varies substantially from one nation to another: For example, the parties of Great Britain taken together have only about 1,500,000 dues-paying members, while in Sweden one party alone (the Social Democrats) has 1 million members out of an adult population of about 8 million. In general, however, only 1 to 3 percent of the adults in most democracies are formal party members, and the numbers are declining in many countries.[2]

Political parties in the United States operate quite differently. In most states party membership requirements are defined by law so as to control who can vote in a particular party's direct primary elections (see Chapter 8). To qualify as Republicans in a closed-primary or crossover-primary state, for example, qualified voters must publicly state their preference for the Republican party to registration officials before they can receive Republican primary ballots. The law usually permits a party representative to challenge a voter's declared party choice, but voters need only make sworn statements of their sincerity and there the matter ends. Such challenges are extremely rare, so a simple self-declaration is in fact the only test any American has to pass in order to become a Democrat or a Republican. In open-primary states, citizens may vote in the primary of any party they choose without even having to state their choices publicly. Accordingly, the American Democratic and Republican parties are unique among the world's parties in that the party leaders do not control admissions to party membership, and there is no formal difference between members and supporters.

Many political scientists believe that these wide-open membership rules are the major cause of the weakness of American parties and their lack of clear and consistent programs. Whether this is true or not, in several states (California, New York, and Wisconsin are leading examples) some party activists have tried to overcome the effects of loose legal membership by imitating parties in other democracies. They have established dues-paying party "clubs," which operate outside the legal machinery, support particular candidates in primaries, and take on the main burden of raising funds and campaigning. But in most states party members are simply people who designate themselves as such prior to voting in party primaries.

Members and Activists

Although party membership in most democratic systems involves more than simple self-designation, all the members of any party are never equally active or influential in party affairs. As in any human organization, some members—whom we will call *activists* (in some countries the term is *militants)*—feel especially strongly about the party's goals, devote much time and energy to its affairs, and consequently have the most to say about what it does.

To give just one illustration, membership in the British Conservative party is open to anyone "who declares his or her support of the party's objects," and pays dues equivalent to about two dollars a year to the local Conservative constituency association. The average membership of those associations is around 5,000, but only a fraction—estimated at 1 to 3 percent—are consistently active in association affairs. Most of the time these few dominate the only important business of the local associations, which is selecting parliamentary candidates for their constituencies.

Almost every democratic party's activists differ from its identifiers and members in several significant respects. The most important is the fact that the activists' political philosophies and policy preferences are generally more extreme than those of the party's identifiers in the electorate. This is true not

An American Party Convention in Action. The Republican convention of 1988. (Source: UPI/ Bettmann Newsphotos.)

only of the "missionary" parties but also of the "broker" parties (these terms will be discussed in a moment), such as the American Democrats and Republicans. A recent illustration of this was provided by the *New York Times* in 1988. They asked a sample of the delegates to the Democratic and Republican national party conventions—most of whom fit our activists category—a series of questions about their personal political ideologies and views on the leading issues in the campaign, and then compared their answers with answers to the same questions given by a sample of each party's identifiers (see Chapter 9) and by a sample of all adults. The answers given by each group are presented in Table 10.1.

The figures in Table 10.1 are clear and consistent: Democratic party activists are substantially more liberal than ordinary Democratic identifiers; Republican party activists are substantially more conservative than ordinary Republican identifiers; and partisans on both sides are ideologically more extreme than the general adult population.

This situation is normal for democratic political parties, and it poses a real dilemma for party leaders. On the one hand, they have to satisfy the ideological activists in order to win their leadership posts; on the other hand, they also have to satisfy the more moderate party identifiers and the still more

TABLE 10.1. Convention Delegates, Party Identifiers, and General Public on Issues, 1988 (in percentages)

	Dem. Del.	Dem. Voters	Total Adults	Rep. Voters	Rep. Dels.
Call themselves conservatives	5	22	30	43	60
Call themselves liberals	39	25	20	12	1
Prefer smaller government giving fewer services	16	33	43	59	87
Prefer larger government giving more services	58	56	44	30	3
Favor increased federal spending on education	90	76	71	67	41
Favor increased federal spending on day care and after-school care for children	87	56	52	44	36
Say abortion should be legal, as it is now	72	43	40	39	29
Say government is paying too little attention to needs of blacks	68	45	34	19	14
Favor defense spending at least at current level	32	59	66	73	84
More worried about Communist takeover in Central America than about U.S. involvement in a war there	12	25	37	55	80

Source: New York Times, August 14, 1988, p. 14.

moderate general public if they hope to win elections over the opposition party. Perhaps that is why it is so difficult to become—and remain—a popular and successful party leader.

PRINCIPAL ACTIVITIES OF PARTIES

Selecting Candidates

From the standpoint of democratic government, selecting candidates is the most important activity of a political party. The nominating process, as we saw in Chapter 8, plays a crucial role in the selection of public officials, and because in all democratic countries parties virtually monopolize nominations, they have tremendous power to shape governments and policies. They also accomplish a task that must be accomplished if the voters are to have manageable and meaningful choices.

The process of candidate selection is also important for success at the polls and for internal control of the parties themselves. For one thing, the ability to make *binding* nominations— nominations that are regularly accepted and supported by most of the party's workers and members—is vital to winning elections. For another, control of the party's nominations is the principal source of power in any political party. Those who control candidate selection control who speaks officially for the party before the electorate; the choice and phrasing of official party policies; the distribution of whatever patronage and power may come to the party as the result of winning elections; and the kind of party it is going to be. Most party leaders and activists, accordingly, believe that winning struggles with opposing factions inside the parties over nominations is at least as important as winning contests with the opposition parties for elective office.

On the basis of the studies of candidate selection in a number of democratic countries, we can say that selection processes vary substantially from one nation to another on several dimensions.

Centralization.   At one extreme, all power over the selection of party candidates for all elective offices is centralized in a national party agency; at the other extreme it is spread among regional and local party organizations. A good example of highly centralized selection processes are those of the Israeli parties. In Israel the entire nation is a single parliamentary constituency. Each party submits one national list of up to 120 candidates for the Knesset (the one-house national parliament). Each list is prepared by the party's national executive committee or comparable inner circle, and, although the selectors usually try to achieve reasonable geographic balance in their list, the choice of particular names and of their order on the list is entirely in the hands of the leaders. The order of the names is very important because the party is sure to receive well below half of all the popular votes cast, and it can elect only the number of its candidates that corresponds to its share of the popular votes.

Those successful candidates are taken from the top of the list one at a time until the party has filled all the seats to which it is entitled. Thus if a party wins 36 percent of the popular votes, it is entitled to 43 seats, and they are filled by the top 43 names on the party list (see the box). Hence the party leaders can place candidates they like at the top of the list and, in effect, veto candidates they dislike by keeping them off the list entirely or by putting them so far down on it that they have no chance of election. It is a very considerable power.

At the opposite extreme are the Democratic and Republican parties of the United States. To be sure, each party's presidential candidate is selected at a national convention—but the convention is made up mainly of delegates already pledged to particular candidates and chosen by state direct primaries and conventions. Furthermore, each party's 100 senatorial and 435 congressional candidates are selected in *local* (state or district) direct primaries or (rarely) conventions, and neither the national committee, the national chairperson, nor any other party agency has the power to veto any candidate locally selected.

Somewhere between the Israeli and American extremes are the nominating systems of most other democratic parties. In Great Britain, for example, national agencies of both the Conservative and Labour parties have the power to veto any locally chosen candidate and also have limited opportunities to place people in "winnable" constituencies. However, both parties have rarely used their veto powers, and more often than not their efforts at placing particular candidates in particular constituencies have been blocked by local constituency organizations who indignantly refused to submit to national orders. In Norway, on the other hand, each party's list in each of the 20 parliamentary constituencies is chosen by a provincial nominating convention made up of delegates from the party organizations in the cities, towns, and rural communes of the constituency. The decisions they make are final, and the national party agencies have no power to participate in the nominations or veto the results.

The Likud party of Israel, which won the election of 1977 and formed the government led by Menachem Begin, was a coalition of three former independent parties: Herut, led by Begin; the Liberals, led by Simcha Ehrlich; and La'am, led by Yigal Hurvitz. The three parties agreed to run a combined list of 120 candidates (there are a total of 120 seats in the Knesset), and their best guess was that from 40 to 45 would be elected. So slots 1 through 40 on the list were considered "safe," slots 40 through 45 were considered "marginal," and slots 46 through 120 were considered "hopeless." After delicate negotiations among the three groups' leaders, the candidates were placed on the list as follows: Begin was given slot 1, Ehrlich slot 2, and Hurvitz slot 3; Herut got 18 of the first 40 slots, the Liberals got 12, and La'am got 10. The "marginal" slots were allocated 1 to Herut, 2 to the Liberals, and 2 to La'am. Likud's total share of the popular votes in the election entitled it to 43 seats, so Herut wound up with 19, the Liberals with 14, and La'am with 10.

Participation.   Another important dimension of candidate selection is participation—the degree to which rank-and-file party members are guaranteed the opportunity to participate in selecting the candidates. At one extreme the selection process is controlled by a small party elite operating behind closed doors with no opportunity for other party members to influence the selection. At the other extreme the process is open to all party members; the candidate is selected publicly on the basis of receiving a larger number of all the members' votes than any of the rivals.

No actual selection system falls entirely at either extreme. The Israeli system is probably the most nearly closed, and the American system is the most nearly open. But even in the United States the wide-open selection processes called for by direct-primary laws in many states and localities are sometimes dominated by small groups of party "slate makers," who choose candidates in secret and then push them in the primaries. In most situations, however, it is dangerous to make such a move, for few things can devastate a candidate's chances of winning a primary as being seen as "the candidate of the party bosses." Thus where the formal procedures appear to provide an entirely open process in American parties, the political facts may sometimes make it closed—not often, but sometimes.

Election Campaigning

Once their nominees have been selected, most democratic parties play major roles in conducting and financing the campaigns to get them elected. In this area, as in many others, American parties are increasingly an exception to the rule. Their role in financing and managing presidential and congressional campaigns has all but vanished. They have been largely replaced by a new breed of "political consultants," whose leaders include Joseph Napolitan, Gerald Rafshoon, Matt Reese, and John Deardourff. These professionals, hired by the candidates for substantial fees, organize "high-tech" campaigns that feature such up-to-date (and costly) techniques as raising money by computerized direct-mail solicitations, preparing and buying choice air time for "spot" advertisements on television, and conducting and analyzing polls to determine how the candidate's "packaging" is affecting his popularity with the voters. The "old pols," the national, state, and county party chairpersons and committee members who used to direct campaigns, are now out of the picture almost entirely.

"High-tech" politics has taken over to some degree in all democratic nations, although nowhere as much as in the United States. In most countries, parties continue to play significant roles in political campaigns, and party campaigning is still the principal organized activity that arouses popular interest in elections and stimulates citizens to vote. We learned in Chapter 9 that the more people identify with a party, the more likely they are to vote and to participate in politics in other ways; people with the weakest party identifications are the least active. If maximum participation in the election of public officials is as desirable as most students of democracy think, then political parties deserve a large measure of praise—which they do not always receive—for encouraging such participation more effectively than any other social organization.

Organizing Government

Every modern democratic government requires a great deal of organization. If all of the government's tens of thousands of public officials acted entirely on their own without any mutual consultation or cooperation, chaos would surely result. In Chapters 11 through 14, we will consider some of the main agencies that operate modern democratic governments. We should recognize here, however, that official agencies do not do the job alone. In every modern democratic country, the successful candidates of each political party form some kind of party organization within the government. For example, the legislators belonging to a particular party usually join together in a "caucus" or "group"; they select "policy committees" and "floor leaders"; they determine who will serve on what legislative committees; and they consult on matters of legislative policy and strategy. The parties thus backstop the formal organization of the legislature with informal party organizations and thereby give some order and direction to the legislature's activities. More on this in Chapter 11.

Other Activities

The parties in many democratic countries conduct other activities in addition to the three basic functions just described. They hold social affairs—banquets, picnics, and so on—at which the rank and file can mingle with the leaders. They establish youth organizations to mobilize new voters and to recruit workers and leaders. Some parties sponsor boy scout groups, summer camps, and adult education classes. Some publish daily newspapers and other periodicals. Some even organize and finance the funerals of deceased party members. Indeed, the lives of many Europeans are influenced in almost every major area by their political parties. They are named after party heroes, attend both party and public schools, join party-sponsored children's and youth groups, receive wedding gifts from the party, do most of their socializing at party affairs, join party-sponsored trade unions, and are laid to rest at party-organized funerals. Such close contact is much less common in the United States, but even so, some Americans know that their political parties are more than merely bodies that nominate candidates and campaign for their election.

DIFFERENCES AMONG PARTIES IN DEMOCRATIC SYSTEMS

IN THE NATURE AND ROLE OF IDEOLOGY

Every democratic party adopts some sort of platform or program—some set of statements about how its candidates will use government power if elected. The platforms of some parties in some countries are mainly restatements and elaborations of one or another of the ideologies we reviewed in Chapter 4. The platforms of other parties say relatively little about ideologies and focus mainly on the parties' proposed solutions to specific problems that especially concern voters at the time of the election. Political scientists have found it useful to classify most political parties as belonging to one or another of the following two main types according to the nature of their ideologies and the role those ideologies play in shaping party attitudes, programs, and operations.

Missionary Parties

At one extreme on this dimension are **missionary parties** — *parties whose principal aim is to win converts for their ideologies, not to maximize their votes so as to win elections.* As an example, let us consider the Socialist Workers party (SWP) of the United States. This party is dedicated to "non-communist Marxism." That is, its members believe that true Marxism (as opposed to what they think is its corrupted form in the Soviet Union and the People's Republic of China) is the key not only to understanding what society is now but also to determining goals toward which the society and party should work. As Marxists, they believe that the essence of history and society is the conflict between those who control wealth (the bourgeoisie) and the workers (the proletariat). The ultimate objective is a victory for the proletariat, followed by the establishment of a classless society. The Socialist Workers are convinced that history and truth are on their side. In their electioneering activities they seek not votes but converts. Although the vast majority of Americans do not share its beliefs, the SWP will not change its ideology to become more popular. If the party's ideology is rejected by the voters, then it is the voters who must change, not the ideology. The ideology is believed to be *true,* and no part of it may be changed or softened in an effort to gain popularity. The SWP's strategy for winning power (if indeed it has such a goal) is to convert the masses gradually, over many decades or even centuries if need be. In the 1988 presidential election, the party's presidential candidate, James Warren, polled only 13,338 votes of the national total of 91,585,896 votes cast (one-tenth of 1 percent), but none of the party faithful thought this was any indication of how well the party was doing what it should be doing. In this sense, then, the SWP is a missionary party, as are many European parties and some other American parties, such as the Communist party and the Libertarian party. Some European Social Democratic and Christian Democratic parties are not above occasionally altering their ideologies a bit to make themselves more attractive to the voters, but even so they are much closer to the missionary type than are the major parties in the English-speaking nations.

Broker Parties

At the other extreme stand the **broker parties**—*parties whose main goal is to win elections, and who therefore appeal to as broad a spectrum of interests*

Republicans In Protest. Protesting the awarding of a bitterly contested Indiana seat to Democrat Frank McCloskey, House Republicans march out of the House chamber in anger, 1985. (Source: UPI/Bettmann Newsphotos.)

and ideologies as possible. Leading examples of such parties are the Democratic and Republican parties of the United States. Neither has a full-fledged ideology, comparable to Marxism or even American-style liberalism or conservatism, that is shared by all its members and activists. The Republican party includes more conservatives and the Democratic party includes more liberals (see Chapter 4); but the Democrats also have a significant number of conservatives, and the Republicans also have some liberals (though nowadays they are generally called "moderates"). In the Democratic party, neither the liberals nor the conservatives can accurately claim to be "the *real* Democrats" if for no other reason than the fact that the law stipulates that anyone who wins a Democratic primary, no matter what her philosophy, is every bit as much a Democrat as anyone else who wins such a primary. The same is true for the conservatives and moderates in the Republican party.

Each of the parties appeals to and draws voters from every major interest group in the nation. Rather than trying to convert people to the one true ideology, as the Socialist Workers party does, each major party tries to put together a program that will attract support from the greatest number of voters. The Democratic and Republican parties measure their success, not by whether their programs, leaders, and supporters rigidly follow a particular ideology, but by how many candidates they elect.

Some critics, especially those who are dedicated Marxists or devotees of laissez faire, are contemptuous of the Democrats and Republicans and all other broker parties. They do not stand for anything (as one critic put it, "They are two bottles with different labels, but both are empty"); they paper over the vital political conflicts between rich and poor, African-American and white, male and female; and they provide the voters not with real choices but with meaningless choices between the Tweedledees and the Tweedledums.

This criticism has merit if—and only if—we concede that only a choice between, say, a Communist party and a Fascist party is a real choice. There is strong evidence, however, that many Americans think that there are a number of important differences between the Democratic and Republican parties—more than enough to justify choosing one over the other. A recent illustration of this fact is provided by Figure 10.1, which arrays the answers given by Americans in 1987 to the question of whether one party or the other is best able to tackle a range of national problems.

The other democratic parties of the world can be ranged between these two extremes. The Liberal and Progressive Conservative parties of Canada, for example, are almost as much broker parties as the major American parties. The British, Australian, and New Zealand Conservative and Labour parties have somewhat more clearly defined ideologies, but they too are more broker than missionary parties. The left-wing (Communist, Socialist) and right-wing (Conservative, Monarchist) parties of most European democracies fall nearer the missionary extreme.

IN CENTRALIZATION

Most parties in the democracies maintain organizations at the national, regional, and local election- district levels. They differ sharply, however, in the way in which they distribute power among the various levels. These differences can be most clearly seen by looking at the various methods by which the parties select their candidates.

From this standpoint, the American Democratic and Republican parties, as we saw in Chapter 8, are the most decentralized in the world. Their national conventions nominate only candidates for president and vice president. Moreover, today even the national conventions are dominated by the organizations developed by particular presidential aspirants and by intraparty pressure groups such as the women's caucus, the African-American caucus, and the prolife caucus. Candidates for the U.S. Senate are nominated in state primary elections, and candidates for the House of Representatives are nominated in district primaries. If the national leaders of either party object to a particular person running in a state or district primary because she is not a "true Democrat" or a "real Republican," they are helpless to block the nomination if

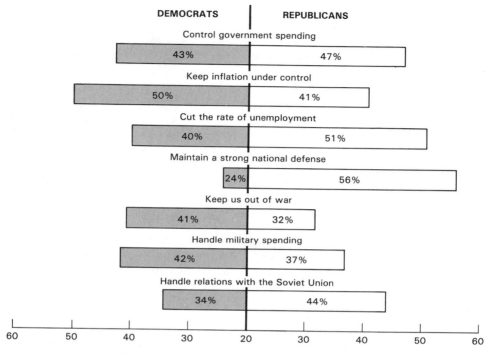

DEMOCRATS | REPUBLICANS

Control government spending
43% | 47%

Keep inflation under control
50% | 41%

Cut the rate of unemployment
40% | 51%

Maintain a strong national defense
24% | 56%

Keep us out of war
41% | 32%

Handle military spending
42% | 37%

Handle relations with the Soviet Union
34% | 44%

60 50 40 30 20 30 40 50 60

FIGURE 10.1. "Tell me whether you think the Republican party or the Democratic party can best tackle the problem."(Sources: The Wirthlin Group, quoted in *Public Opinion*, July/August 1988, p. 32; and survey by Marttila and Kiley for "Americans Talk Security," October 1987, quoted in *Public Opinion*, March/April 1988, p. 28).

the unwanted candidate wins the primary. On a few occasions in the past, a popular national party leader has intervened in local primaries to try to prevent unacceptable local candidates from being nominated, but all have failed. A notable example was President Franklin D. Roosevelt's attempt in 1938 to defeat in the primaries twelve Democratic congressmen who had opposed his New Deal programs; popular as he was, eleven of the twelve were renominated. He failed, as all such efforts have failed, because the national leaders have been unable to win the help of local organizations and because many voters and party leaders have viewed such interventions as outrageous violations of their rights and prerogatives.

Thus in the Democratic and Republican parties, power over nominations—the main objective of the leaders of any major democratic party—is highly decentralized. Instead of being controlled at the national level, candidate selection is in the hands of state, county, and district party organizations as well as pressure groups and temporary candidate organizations. Later we will see to what extent other powers of U.S. parties are also decentralized.

The United States is not the only democratic country with decentralized parties. Many European conservative parties are little more than loose federations of local associations and leading parliamentary personalities. In Switzerland all the major parties, with the possible exception of the Socialists, are organized mainly in the cantons (governing units below the national level, similar to but more powerful than American states). The Swiss national parties are even looser groups of local parties than those in the United States. There are no outstanding national party leaders, but only leading local figures who are generally unknown to most people outside their own areas. In the Scandinavian countries, candidates for the national parliaments are generally selected by district committees or conventions, and national party leaders can only advise on who should and should not be selected.

Most democratic parties are more centralized in their nominating procedures and other activities, however. In Great Britain, for example, the local Conservative and Labour constituency associations select candidates for Parliament, but national party agencies have the power to veto candidates. The Conservatives have used this power very seldom, Labour somewhat more often; still, both are considerably more centralized than most parties in Switzerland and Scandinavia. Canadian parties, despite their federal organiza-

A British Party Conference in Action. The Conservative conference of 1988. (Source: Reuters/Bettmann Newsphotos.)

tions, nominate candidates much as British parties do. And in most European nations, which use the party-list form of proportional representation (see Chapter 8), national party agencies select the candidates for their lists and determine the order in which they will appear.

IN DISCIPLINE

In any human organization, **discipline** means *the leaders' control of the members of a group obtained by dispensing rewards and imposing sanctions.*

The leaders of every democratic political party possess disciplinary weapons, but some are more effective than others. For example, the president of the United States can, if he wishes, give patronage jobs to a few obedient members of his party and withhold them from party rebels and mavericks. He can also make his public support of his party's other candidates dependent on their support of his policies. The president can even try to defeat in party primaries candidates who do not support his programs. None of these weapons is very effective, however. He has very little patronage to hand out. In addition, most candidates for Congress do not need the president's support to be elected; they know it and he knows it. And finally, as we have seen, a president has never been successful in "purging" unwanted candidates by intervening in congressional and senatorial primaries. Presidential discipline in both American parties thus involves little more than persuasion and coaxing. And every president, as even Franklin Roosevelt and Ronald Reagan learned, must expect considerable opposition to some of his policies from members of his own party.

The leader of a British major party is in a much stronger position. All the members of her party in Parliament know that when "the whip is laid on" (that is, when the party leader tells the members that they are expected to vote in a certain way on a particular bill), to disobey is to risk their political careers. The prime minister controls who gets the ministerial offices, and the leader of the opposition party controls who will get them when it wins power. Since the ordinary member of Parliament (MP) cannot, as in the United States, rise to power and influence through seniority, the only road to political success is through the good will of the party leaders (see Chapter 11). Also, as we have seen, the national party organization, which the leader controls, can veto the renomination of MPs who get out of line and thus deny them their parliamentary seats (though the veto is seldom used). But the leader's greatest power comes from the fact that in the British parliamentary system, control of the government is in the hands of the majority-party "team." When that team can no longer muster majority support in Parliament, a new election must be held. Therefore, any MP's vote against his party is, in effect, a vote to put or keep the other party in power. It is not surprising, then, that party discipline in Britain is widely (though not universally) regarded as a good thing.

Most of the missionary parties of Europe and Scandinavia give their national leaders the power to expel from the party members of the national

Not All Party Leaders are Men. Prime minister Benazir Bhutto of Pakistan. (Source: Reuters/Bettmann Newsphotos.)

parliament who refuse to vote the "party line." While expulsion from the party is less likely than in Britain to result in the loss of the individual's seat in the parliament, he may no longer take a part in the party's decision making. As a disciplinary weapon, therefore, this is somewhat less powerful than the British party leaders' vetoes—but it is much more powerful than any weapon available to American party leaders.

IN COHESION

The differences in centralization and discipline are reflected in different degrees of cohesion within various democratic parties. As the term is normally used, a party's **cohesion** is *the extent to which party members holding public office act together on major policy issues.* If a party's legislative members vote alike on every issue, it is said to have perfect legislative cohesion. If a party's legislative members split 50-50 on every issue, it is said to have zero legislative cohesion.

Democratic parties vary widely in cohesion. The major British parties are among the most cohesive, for on almost every issue they can count upon all of their members in the House of Commons to vote as the party leaders desire. On the few occasions on which some members have not supported the leaders' policies, the dissenters have been more likely not to vote at all than to vote against the leaders' wishes. Since the mid-1970s there has been some increase in the number of such occasions; even so, the parties can count on the support of all their members over 90 percent of the time.

At the other extreme, some small parliamentary parties in France split on almost every public issue and therefore have little or no legislative cohesion. The other democratic parties fall somewhere between these two extremes. The larger French, Scandinavian, and German parties, for example, are almost—but not quite—as cohesive as the British parties. The American parties in Congress, though relatively uncohesive, are more cohesive than the smaller French parties. In the various American state legislatures, the parties cover almost the entire range of cohesion, from very high to very low. And in Italy, as we will see in Chapter 11, party cohesion cannot be measured because votes in parliament are cast by secret ballot and it is impossible to say whether the members of a particular party have stuck together or not.

The variations in ideologies, centralization, discipline, and cohesion of each nation's parties have a considerable impact on the way in which they interact with one another in the nation's party *system*. Hence there are also a number of differences among the types of party systems that operate in modern democracies. We now look briefly at the nature and political consequences of each type.

FRACTIONALIZATION OF DEMOCRATIC PARTY SYSTEMS

MEANING

In analyzing and comparing political parties in modern democratic nations, political scientists often speak of *party systems*. The term refers to certain general characteristics of party conflict in particular political environments, which can be classified according to various criteria. On the basis of the factors described in the preceding section, for example, we can speak of missionary and broker party systems or of centralized and decentralized party systems. However, many political scientists are especially interested in the degree of **party fractionalization**—*the degree to which a nation's votes and offices are evenly divided among a large number of parties.* By this standard, the least fractionalized system would be one in which only one political party exists and wins all the votes and offices all the time. At the other extreme, there is no theoretical limit to how high fractionalization can go, but a highly fractionalized system would be one in which a great many parties more or less evenly share both the votes and the public offices. We will consider both levels of fractionalization in the rest of this chapter.

MEASUREMENT: RAE'S INDEX OF FRACTIONALIZATION

Until recently, political scientists generally classified all party systems as either one-party, two-party, or multiparty. However, their techniques for measuring degrees of fractionalization were developed mainly for the analysis and comparison of the party systems of the American states. They were thus of little use in analyzing the many variations among the European party systems, which were usually lumped together as multiparty systems. To fill this void, Douglas W. Rae devised an ingenious index of party fractionalization that can be applied to any party system. Rae's measure taps two dimensions: the *number of parties* receiving shares of the popular vote and seats in the national legislature; and the *relative equality* of their shares. At one end of the scale is a model one-party system, in which one party receives all the votes and seats for an index score of 0.00. As we will see, the party system of the Soviet Union fulfills all these requirements. As the number of parties and the relative equality of their shares of the votes and seats increase, the index score rises. In a theoretically perfect two-party system, two parties would split the votes and seats evenly, for a score of 0.50. If ten parties split the votes and seats evenly, the system would have a score of 0.90.[3]

Table 10.2 presents the fractionalization scores for twenty-five democratic nations using the results in three recent general elections for members of the lower house of their national legislatures.

TABLE 10.2.   **Party Fractionalization in 25 Democracies, 1977–88**

Country	Average Fractionalization Score	Index of Competitiveness*
Belgium	.8464	.3464
Finland	.8340	.3340
Denmark	.8138	.3138
Switzerland	.8041	.3041
Italy	.7357	.2357
Netherlands	.7302	.2302
Israel	.7299	.2299
Portugal	.7191	.2191
Norway	.7175	.2175
Sweden	.6984	.1984
West Germany	.6862	.1862
France	.6527	.1527
Japan	.6447	.1447
Venezuela	.6408	.1408
Ireland	.6152	.1152
Spain	.6152	.1152
India	.5845	.0845
Australia	.5812	.0812
Austria	.5760	.0760
Colombia	.5436	.0436
Greece	.5435	.0435
United Kingdom	.5348	.0348
United States	.4796	.0204
Canada	.4839	.0161
New Zealand	.4931	.0069

*The difference between the average fractionalization score and .5000 (the score for a perfect two-party system).

Source: Calculated by the author from election returns taken from *Keesing's Record of World Events.*

For most of the 25 nations ranked in Table 10.2, the score for legislative fractionalization was a bit lower than the score for electoral fractionalization. These data support Rae's conclusion that all electoral systems—even those using proportional representation—discriminate to some degree in favor of the larger parties.

Figure 10.2 makes the general picture more concrete by showing the vote shares and fractionalization scores in recent elections in each of five party systems, covering the entire range of fractionalization, from an index of .4800

FIGURE 10.2. Fractionalization in Five Democratic Elections

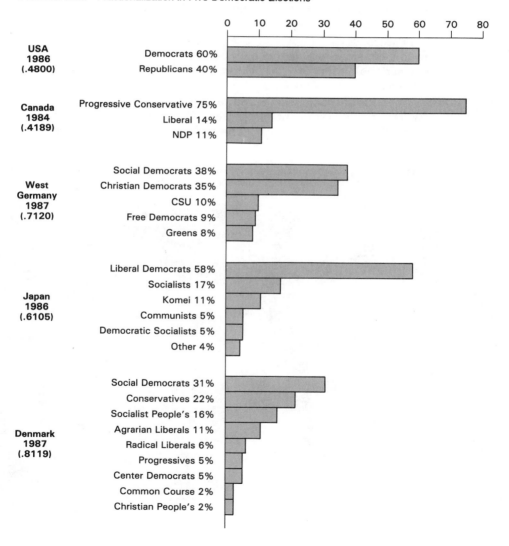

for the American system (close to a perfect two-party system score) to one of .8119 for Denmark's system.

CHARACTERISTICS OF THE MORE FRACTIONALIZED SYSTEMS

What differences does fractionalization make? Let us look at the evidence. The party systems of Western European democratic nations generally rank on the high side of the fractionalization scale. In each of these nations, at least three, and often as many as five or six, parties regularly win enough votes and legislative seats to be called "major" parties. A single party hardly ever wins a majority of the seats, and the cabinets and ministries are composed of coalitions of several parties rather than members of one majority party.

As we saw in Chapter 8, the debate over proportional representation turns to a considerable degree on whether one believes that a high degree of party fractionalization is a good thing. The critics of highly fractionalized party politics say that it produces unstable and ever-changing governments, splits the nations into hostile camps, and fails to mobilize popular majorities either for or against government programs. This, they say, seriously weakens democracy's ability to survive. They often point to the party systems of

Choices in a Highly Fractionalized Party System. An Israeli voter contemplates the posters of over twenty competing parties. (Source: UPI/Bettmann Newsphotos.)

Germany's Weimar Republic (1919–33) and France's Third (1871–1939) and Fourth (1945–58) Republics as examples of the damage that highly fractionalized party systems can do.

The defenders of proportional representation and the more fractionalized systems claim that the wide range of party ideologies accurately reflects the shades of public opinion in their countries and thereby gives the voters truly meaningful choices. Consequently, they contend, such systems come much closer to the ideals of representative democracy than do the oversimplified, all-things-to-all-people parties in the less fractionalized systems.

We cannot decide the merits of this debate here, but some things seem clear. First, since a single party almost never wins a majority of all the seats in the national legislature, the countries are typically ruled by **coalition governments,** which are *arrangements in which the government is managed by an alliance of two or more separate parties, each of which has members in the top ministerial posts.*

Second, government instability does not necessarily result from more fractionalized party systems and coalition governments. For example, the party systems of Finland, Denmark, Switzerland, and the Netherlands usually produce coalition governments that are just as stable as the governments in nations with less fractionalized systems.

Third, the fractionalization of the party systems does not appear to be a prime *cause* of the deep ideological and social divisions in nations like Italy and Belgium. Most students of Israeli politics believe that the large number of parties in that country has resulted from deep ethnic and religious divisions that are far more basic and complex than the particular kind of party system. This is not to say that more fractionalized systems are "better" than less fractionalized ones, but that a nation's party system is only one factor—and in many instances not the most important factor—that determines the nature of its basic political conflict.

CHARACTERISTICS OF THE LESS FRACTIONALIZED SYSTEMS

The party systems of the English-speaking democracies, including the United States, Great Britain, New Zealand, Australia, and Canada, are generally less fractionalized than those of Western Europe (see Table 10.2). The major parties of these nations differ from one another in various ways, but they are also very similar in certain important respects. Among their leading similarities, four are especially noteworthy:

Broker Parties

The major parties tend to be broker rather than missionary parties. Some, like the various labor and socialist parties, have somewhat more distinct ideologies than the others, but all are more concerned with winning elections here and now than with eventually making permanent converts.

General Appeals

The major parties direct their appeals for votes at all major population groups. The American Republicans and the British Conservatives, for example, never say to labor union members, "We stand for business first, last, and always, and if we get into power we intend to destroy the unions!" Rather they say, "We stand for the welfare of *both* labor and business. If you want fair and decent treatment for labor and management alike, vote for us instead of them." Their programs and platforms are not as clear and logically consistent as those of the missionary parties, because they are intended to win as many votes as possible from many, often incompatible, interests.

Moderate Parties

The major parties are moderate: They try to offer programs that will not seriously upset any major group of voters. They also try to avoid or postpone taking clear and uncompromising stands on any issues on which the community is sharply divided. Furthermore, extremists in the ranks of either major party must moderate their views as the price of retaining their positions in the party's inner circles.

Narrow Differences between the Parties

The major parties tend to be a lot alike in their basic views and specific programs. They agree generally on the basic form of government and the general direction of public policy. When one replaces the other in power, there is seldom a drastic shift in government policy. Yet they are not identical, so the voters have real choices. Usually their disagreements concern the details of policies and the *pace* at which certain policies should be adopted or abandoned. Consequently, most voters believe that the parties are sufficiently different to justify a preference for one over the other (for an American illustration, see Figure 10.1).

The major American parties, as we have seen, are considerably more decentralized than those in the other English-speaking nations, but otherwise the major parties in all the less fractionalized systems are essentially similar.

AUTHORITARIAN ONE-PARTY SYSTEMS

Authoritarianism is as old as government itself. But authoritarian rule by means of a single all-powerful political party is an invention of the twentieth century. In fact, one clear difference between the governments of Stalin's Soviet Union, Mao's China, Hitler's Germany, and Mussolini's Italy and older authoritarian regimes was the central role played by the single party. In each case the party had many of the trappings of parties in more democratic systems—but none of their competition.

Yet there are different degrees of authoritarianism, as there are of democracy. Hence it is not surprising that there are significant differences among the party systems of modern authoritarian regimes. Western political scientists have paid some attention to these differences, especially in their studies of party systems in the new nations of Africa and Asia. But a Polish political scientist, Jerzy J. Wiatr, suggests that it is useful to distinguish among three different subtypes of one-party systems. In order of increasing fractionalization, they are (1) **monoparty systems,** in which *only one party is legally permitted to exist;* (2) **hegemonic systems,** in which *several parties are permitted to exist, but they run candidates only when allowed to do so by an officially superior party, and no competition between the parties is permitted;* and (3) **dominant systems,** in which *any party may organize and run candidates, but one party wins almost all of the votes and offices because of its hold on the voters' loyalties.*[4]

Let us briefly examine each type.

MONOPARTY SYSTEMS

Some Common Characteristics

All democratic parties value democratic government as much as they value their particular social and economic aims. Thus they tolerate the existence of opposing parties, use only peaceful and democratic methods to pursue their goals, and peacefully accept the verdicts of the voters in elections. Essential to all democratic party systems is the general acceptance of the principle of *loyal opposition.* This is the principle that a party that opposes a nation's governing party or coalition does so only by constitutionally permitted means, remains—and is recognized as remaining—loyal to the nation and its political system, seeks to overthrow the party in power only by winning elections, and thereby has the right to participate freely in the nation's politics.

The single parties that monopolize the field in communist and fascist regimes resemble democratic parties only on the surface. They are more like combat armies, and many of them, indeed, use military terms (*vanguard, phalanx, spearhead)* to describe themselves and their operations. An even better comparison is that between a totalitarian party and a militant religious order. Every totalitarian party arises from and is committed to a kind of secular religion, each with its sacred texts (*Das Kapital, Mein Kampf),* its prophets (Marx and Lenin, Hitler), its total explanation of the nature of society (dialectical materialism, the genetic superiority of the Aryan race), and its ethical system (the end justifies the means). The party has its "priesthood" and its "missionaries"—and no doubt also its less-than-fanatical members and supporters.

Many of us in the democratic world are puzzled over why communist and fascist regimes bother with democratic trappings of political parties at all.

When we look a little more closely at the authoritarian monoparty systems, however, we can see that they perform several roles that the rulers need performed.

In the nations in which there is a single legal political party, such as Castro's Cuba, these pseudodemocratic trappings make it possible for tightly knit, well organized, and devoted oligarchies (small groups of all-powerful leaders) to operate the formal governing structures more efficiently. Second, they provide useful psychological and organizational bridges between the nations' masses and their rulers—bridges that older, more aristocratic oligarchies lacked, with the result that they were more vulnerable to revolts by the masses. In these and others respects, then, communist and fascist parties are essentially alike. In order to see how they differ, let us briefly examine each type of monoparty system.

Collective Leadership in a Monoparty System. Leaders of the Communist Party of the Soviet Union salute the Moscow May Day parade, 1985. (Source: Reuters/Bettmann Newsphotos.)

The Leninist-Stalinist Prototype

The monoparty, or single-party, system of the Soviet Union is the oldest and still the most powerful of its type. It has served as the model not only for all other communist systems but also for many aspects of the fascist systems. Since 1918 the Communist Party of the Soviet Union (CPSU) has been the only legal party in the Soviet Union, and all attempts to organize rival parties have been officially regarded as treason. The 1977 Soviet Constitution describes the CPSU as "the leading and guiding force of Soviet society and the nucleus of its political system, of all state and public organizations" (Article 6).

How have the Soviet rulers traditionally justified permitting only one party to exist in what they claim is the most democratic government in the world? According to communist theorists, every political party represents a class. In nations where several classes exist, several political parties must also exist, with one or more representing each class; but in the Soviet Union there is only one class, the working class; and therefore only one party—the CPSU—is needed to represent it. Any other party could only oppose the interests and welfare of the proletariat, and that, of course, would be treason. "True democracy" (government in the interests of the workers) can permit only one party.

Structure and Composition of the CPSU.   The CPSU presently has about 25 million members, representing about 9 percent of the total population of the USSR. This small proportion does not mean, of course, that communism is "unpopular" in Russia; the party is *intended* to be an elite rather than a mass organization. A Soviet citizen can become a party member only after having been recommended by three party members of at least three years' standing and after having successfully passed many tests during a year's candidacy. Furthermore, in periodic purges the leadership expels all members whom it deems "inactive" or "politically incorrect" (about 50,000 members are expelled every year). Lenin originally intended the party to be composed mainly of manual workers, but now they make up only about one-quarter of its membership, and nearly half of the party's members are white collar workers.

The primary party organizations, once called *cells,* are set up in work places—factories, farms, military units, and so on. Above them are a series of district, provincial, and republic committees and bureaus. Heading the whole party is the national party congress, an assembly of about 5,000 delegates which is supposed to meet every four years but has not always done so (no congress was held from 1939 to 1952, for example). The congress chooses the central committee, which is divided into several committees; by far the most powerful of these, and the actual ruling oligarchy of the Soviet Union, is the Politburo, which in 1988 had 14 members and 8 alternates. At the top is the general secretary of the party. This is the key office of the entire party and government structure, and whoever holds it is *the* leader of the CPSU and therefore of the government and the nation. After the death of Leonid Brezhnev in 1982, the office was held briefly by Yuri Andropov and Konstantin Chernenko, both in their seventies and in poor health. After Andropov's death in 1984 and Chernenko's in 1985, Mikhail Gorbachev became the new general secretary and, at age 56, the youngest man to hold the office since Stalin in 1922.

The Leninist-Stalinist version of communism made much of the principle of "democratic centralism," which called for free discussion within the party before a decision was made but for closed ranks and no criticism once a policy had been adopted. In practice, however, democratic centralism meant that the party's rulers—Stalin alone before his death in 1953 and the Politburo afterward—make the decisions and that their decisions were binding on all the lower levels of the party organization, whose members could criticize only those few matters permitted by the Politburo.

Closely connected to the party structure were several organizations characteristic of all one-party systems. They included the secret political police (now called the KGB), who were responsible for detecting and punishing those who did not conform. There were also youth organizations to indoctrinate the young in communism and to single out the more able for future party membership and leadership. The main youth organizations were the Little Octobrists (ages seven to ten), the Young Pioneers (ages ten to fifteen), and the Komsomols (Young Communist League, ages fourteen to twenty-eight).

The Changing (?) Role of the Party.   Like all totalitarian parties in power, the CPSU since 1917 has been first of all a ruling oligarchy, "the government of the government," "a state within a state." Each major legislative, executive, administrative, and judicial agency of the formal government has had its parallel party organization and has been supervised by a committee of the central committee, which has controlled and operated the formal agency.

We have spoken several times earlier in the book about the various proposals Mikhail Gorbachev has made since 1985 for *perestroika* (restructuring) Soviet governing institutions. One major thrust of his proposals is to reduce significantly the traditionally dominant role of the CPSU in all aspects of Soviet politics and government. For example, at the famous Party Congress in 1988 (see Chapter 4), Gorbachev proposed that the nation's regional and local areas should be governed mainly by revived local "soviets," or elected government councils, which would *not* have corresponding units of the party at each level and to which the party would provide only the most general ideological guidance rather than day-to-day directions. Moreover, while traditionally the local party officials have also been the leading figures in the local governing units, Gorbachev proposed that for the most part, party officials should be excluded from membership in the soviets. He also suggested that the party should not have a veto power over who is nominated as candidates for elective offices.

In 1988 Gorbachev made a tentative first step toward allowing parties other than the CPSU to operate. An organization called the People's Front was established in the Soviet Republic of Estonia, and its membership soon grew to 40,000. Its platform called for support of Gorbachev's reforms, greater political and economic autonomy for Estonia, and running their own candidates for local public office against those approved by the CPSU. They were allowed to hold large public rallies, and they were widely thought to be a trial run for the creation of similar organizations in other parts of the Soviet Union that would also combine support for *perestroika* with opposition to local CPSU functionaries. Whatever their eventual fate, the fronts were the first cracks in the CPSU's monopoly since Lenin took power in 1917.[5]

Fascist Monoparty Systems

In its pre-1945 Italian and German versions, fascism, like communism, was a kind of secular religion at war with all other ideologies. It had its sacred texts and prophets, its total explanation of society, and its ethical system. It too regarded its single chosen party as a priesthood of true believers dedicated to spreading the doctrine and converting or eliminating the unbelievers. Even though fascism glorified the nation and the race, while communism gloried the Soviet Union and the working class, the two movements were basically similar in their organizations.

The Fascist party in Mussolini's Italy from 1922 to 1945 and the National Socialist German Workers' (Nazi) party in Hitler's Germany from 1933 to 1945 were the only legal parties in their respective nations. The structure of each party paralleled the structure of the formal government and became the de facto governing body. As in Communist one-party systems, the Fascist parties acted both as ruling bodies and as agencies for whipping up mass support for the leaders' policies.

In the organization of Fascist parties, the *Fuhrerprinzip* (leadership principle) was officially more important than it has been in Communist party organization, although in practice neither Hitler nor Mussolini dominated his party or nation more completely than Lenin and Stalin dominated theirs. Both the Fascist and Nazi parties were organized like armies. The Duce and the Fuhrer were absolute commanders-in-chief, and the black-shirted Fasci di Combattimento, the brown-shirted "storm troopers," and the black-uniformed "elite guard" (SS) were the "shock troops."

People became members of the Fascist parties mainly through prior service in their youth organizations—the Italian Balilla and Avenguardia and the German Hitler Youth for people from the ages of 6 to 21. Both parties conducted periodic purges (including the murderous Nazi "blood purge" of 1934) to eliminate all but the most fanatical members. And, like the Communist parties, both were intended to be elite rather than unselective mass organizations.

HEGEMONIC PARTY SYSTEMS

Several Eastern European nations first liberated from the Germans and then occupied by the Red Army during and after World War II have established "people's democracies"—regimes modeled on, but not identical with, the traditional Soviet system. One prominent feature of these "sovietoid" regimes is what Jerzy Wiatr calls their "hegemonic" party systems. The main features of such systems are illustrated by the parties and elections in Poland.

First, more than one political party is legally permitted to exist, organize, and present candidates for public office. There are three legal political parties in Poland: the Polish United Workers (Communist) party (PUWP), the United Peasant party (UPP), and the Democratic party (DP).

Second, the other legal parties are associated with the hegemonic party in a "people's front," which presents a single all-party list of candidates at each election and thus eliminates all electoral competition between the parties. In Poland the PUWP, UPP, and DP have formed a "permanent National Front," which offers a joint list of candidates in each election. Furthermore, Polish law states that, once the national authorities of a party have agreed to present a joint list of candidates, any separate list proposed by any party's local authorities is automatically invalid. The law also allows the joint list of candidates in any constituency to include as many as two-thirds more names than there are posts to be filled. The National Front can thus permit some competition among individual candidates, though none is possible among the parties. The Front has actually allowed a small amount of such competition, and on a few occasions a candidate from the top part of the official list has not been elected. In all elections the PUWP has won about two-thirds of the seats in the Sejm (parliament); the UPP usually wins about 25 percent and the DP about 8 percent.

Third and most important, the "hegemonic" party (the PUWP) is clearly the unchallenged dominant element in the National Front. The other parties have separate identities and even some separate activities, but the UPP and the DP do not decide for themselves what they will and will not do. That is decided for them by the PUWP.

However, in 1989 the Polish system began to change even more radically than Gorbachev's Soviet system. The ruling Communist Party of General Wojciech Jaruzelski not only agreed to recognize Lech Walesa's opposition Solidarity labor union but also opened the way to Poland's first free elections since before World War II. Elections were scheduled for June, 1989 in which 35 percent of the seats in the Sejm were opened to candidates nominated by Solidarity and other organizations without the approval of the PUWP. Moreover, it was agreed that the remaining 65 percent would in the near future also be opened to freely contested elections. It remained to be seen how close and how soon the new reforms would bring Poland to truly free elections among competing political parties, but the break with the traditional system described by Wiatr was clearly fundamental.[6]

DOMINANT PARTY SYSTEMS

In Democratic Systems

From 1854 to the late 1970s, no Republican candidate was elected to any state office in Louisiana. In most elections no Republican even bothered to run, and the few who did rarely received more than 5 percent of the votes. During the same period the Democrats did only a little better in Vermont. After the Republican party was founded in 1854, the Democrats did not win any state office until 1958, and they have never held more than a small fraction of the seats in the state legislature. In Great Britain, the Welsh coal-mining constituency of Ebbw Vale has for decades given Labour candidates majorities of 75 percent or more. In France many working-class districts in Paris, Lyons, and Lille regularly give comparable majorities to the Communists.

In short, every democratic nation has areas with "dominant party systems." But they differ from the monoparty and hegemonic systems of the dictatorial regimes in one vital respect: Rival parties are not outlawed, nor are their ideologies and programs suppressed. They have the same opportunities to win votes and offices as the dominant parties, and over the years they may even gradually increase their support, as the Democrats have in Vermont and as the Republicans have in Louisiana and most of the South.

In Developing Nations

A few developing nations—Nepal and Saudi Arabia, for example—do not pretend to have government by popular election of public officials, so they do not permit political parties of any kind. But most developing nations go through the motions of popular elections, and some honor their substance as well.

About a quarter of the developing nations have monoparty systems based more or less on Communist or Fascist models. Only one party is legally permitted, and efforts to form opposition parties are considered treasonous. The official party is usually a version of the political movement that originally won the nation's independence or overthrew its previous regime. It is usually dominated by one individual—the Arab Socialist Union in Libya by Mu'ammar al-Qaddaffi, for example, and the United Party of the Social Revolution in Cuba by Fidel Castro. The dictator generally uses the party much as Fascists and Communists do: to advance national unity by stamping out opposition, to mobilize popular enthusiasm behind the dictator's program, to give the masses a sense of participation in government, and to keep the ruler informed on how far a program can be pushed before popular resistance makes it unworkable.

When outsiders criticize these systems, the dictators and their party lieutenants usually reply with the classical Fascist and Communist arguments. The official party, they say, represents the whole nation, and opposition to it is opposition to the whole nation—in a word, treason. Quarreling parties and contested elections would only divide the people and make the nation easy prey for its colonialist enemies. And, they conclude, even if party competition might conceivably be tolerated in times of peace, plenty, and security, that time is not now.

In other developing nations, party competition is legally tolerated. Parties other than the National Liberation party organize, nominate some candidates, contest some elections, and win a few seats in the national legislature. But the National Liberation party regularly wins most of the votes and offices and government power. Most conflicts over public policy are thus fought out within the dominant party rather than in contests between it and opposition parties.

Perhaps the leading example of such a party system is that of Mexico. The Mexican Revolution of 1910 was followed by two decades of political confusion and instability, which were finally ended in 1929 with the establishment of a national party that united most of Mexico's major groups and interests. The party underwent several reorganizations and changes of name, but in 1946 it adopted its present name, the Party of Revolutionary Institutions (PRI), and organization. From 1929 to the mid-1980s the PRI was opposed by the Conservative (PAN), Marxist (PPS), and dissident PRI (PARM) parties but won all presidential elections by overwhelming margins and held more than 80 percent of the seats in Congress.

In recent years Mexico's increasing economic difficulties and charges of widespread corruption in the government have resulted in increasing discontent with PRI's dominance and have presented a growing challenge, especially by PAN. In the presidential election of 1988 the PRI's candidate, Carlos Salinas de Gortari, was challenged as never before not only by the PAN candidate, Manuel Clouthier, by also Cuanthemoc Cardenas of the National Democratic Front (FDN). For nearly a week after the votes were cast, no results were announced, and there were widespread charges of fraud. In the end, the official election commission declared the PRI candidate the winner, but with only 47 percent of the vote to 27 percent for Cardenas and 21 percent for Clouthier—the first time since the PRI's founding in 1929 that its candidate received less than half of the votes. Whatever the future would bring, everyone agreed with Salinas de Gortari's declaration that the day of one-party dominance by the PRI has passed in Mexico.

Nevertheless, a number of commentators continue to believe that, despite its recent failures, the Mexican dominant-party system and others like it in Gabon, Malaysia, and elsewhere provide an important third alternative to the full competition of two-party and multiparty democracies on the one hand and the iron monopolies of power in the authoritarian one-party systems on the other. They feel it offers new and struggling nations a way out of what some people see as an impossible choice between too much party competition and none at all. For this reason, if for no other, it deserves to be studied as carefully as the other types of party systems.

Thus political parties and party systems come in many different forms, and they constitute an important—but not universal— device for organizing modern political systems. As we have seen, democratic and dictatorial regimes alike depend upon parties to perform important tasks. In formulating policies, selecting leaders, and arousing popular support, political parties enable governments to operate in densely populated modern nations. The differences among the kinds of party systems that perform these tasks account for many of the differences between democratic and authoritarian systems.

Some commentators have suggested that modern mass communications, and especially the manner in which television permeates every aspect of modern life, have rendered political parties obsolete. That may or may not be so; but if it is, it is far from clear what agencies will replace parties in performing the many functions that have made them vital forces in most modern governments.

FOR FURTHER READING

DEMOCRATIC POLITICAL PARTIES

BOGDANOR, VERNON, ed. *Parties and Democracy in Britain and America.* New York: Praeger, 1984. Essays on the current state of the parties in the United States and Great Britain.

*DUVERGER, MAURICE. *Political Parties.* New York: John Wiley, 1954. Influential work by a French political scientist outlining a general theory of political parties that applies to many nations.

ELDERSVELD, SAMUEL J. *Political Parties in American Society.* New York: Basic Books, 1982. Comprehensive and sophisticated description of the American party system.

*EPSTEIN, LEON D. *Political Parties in Western Democracies.* New York: Praeger, 1967. Covers much the same ground as Duverger's book but in a more empirical and pragmatic manner.

———. *Political Parties in the American Mold.* Madison: University of Wisconsin Press, 1986. An in- depth analysis of the unique character of American political parties and the historical, legal, and political reasons for their peculiar evolution.

*HERRING, PENDLETON. *The Politics of Democracy.* New York: Holt, Rinehart & Winston, 1940. Classic defense of the decentralized American party system.

*LADD, EVERETT CARLL, JR., and Charles D. Hadley. *Transformations of the American Party System.* New York: W. W. Norton, 1975. History of American parties told in terms of both changing institutions and changing bases of electoral support.

*MAZMANIAN, DANIEL A. *Third Parties in Presidential Elections.* Washington: Brookings Institution, 1974. Useful account of nonmajor parties in the United States.

*MICHELS, ROBERT. *Political Parties.* New York: Free Press, 1949. First published in 1915. Exposition of the much-discussed "iron law of oligarchy," based on a study of European Socialist parties in the early twentieth century.

*OSTROGORSKI, M.I. *Democracy and the Organization of Political Parties,* 2 vols. New York: Crowell-Collier and Macmillan, 1902. Classic study of the history and organization of British and American parties up to 1900 and an attack on "permanent parties." Also available in an abridged paperback edition.

*POLSBY, NELSON W. *Consequences of Party Reform.* New York: Oxford University Press, 1983. Thoughtful analysis of the purposes, methods, and impact of extensive party reforms adopted in the United States since 1969.

*RANNEY, AUSTIN. *The Doctrine of Responsible Party Government.* Urbana: University of Illinois Press, 1954. Description of the origins of the idea that American parties should be centralized and disciplined on the British model.

*———. *Curing the Mischiefs of Faction: Party Reform in America.* Berkeley: University of California Press, 1975. Analysis of theory, practice, and consequences of party reform from the 1820s to the present.

*SARTORI, GIOVANNI. *Parties and Party Systems: A Framework for Analysis.* New York: Cambridge University Press, 1976. Broad theoretical analysis of party systems, with special attention to interparty competition, drawing upon experience of many nations.

SCHATTSCHNEIDER, E. E. *Party Government.* New York: Holt, Rinehart & Winston, 1942. Influential exposition of the responsible-parties model and criticism of American parties.

*WATTENBERG, MARTIN P. *The Decline of American*

Political Parties, 1952–1980. Cambridge: Harvard University Press, 1984. Describes the decline of American parties in voter loyalty and organizational strength and functions.

SEMI- AND NON-DEMOCRATIC PARTIES

GEHLEN, MICHAEL P. *The Communist Party of the Soviet Union.* Bloomington: Indiana University Press, 1969. General description.

HUNTINGTON, SAMUEL P., and CLEMENT H. MOORE, eds. *Authoritarian Politics in Modern Society.* New York: Basic Books, 1970. Essays on the nature and problems of leading contemporary one-party systems.

*LAPALOMBARA, JOSEPH, and MYRON WEINER, eds. *Political Parties and Political Development.* Princeton, NJ: Princeton University Press, 1966. Comprehensive survey of the role of parties in developing nations.

MCINNES, NEIL. *The Communist Parties of Western Europe.* London: Oxford University Press,

1975. Comparative description of their organization, operations, and relations with Moscow.

WALLER, MICHAEL. *Democratic Centralism: An Historical Commentary.* New York: St. Martin's Press, 1981. Examination of origins and present meaning of a key principle of communist government.

*ZOLBERG, ARISTIDE R. *Creating Political Order: The One-Party States of West Africa.* Skokie, IL: Rand McNally, 1966. Sophisticated analysis of monoparty states with general theoretical applications.

NOTES

[1]E. E. Schattschneider, *Party Government* New York: Holt, Rinehart & Winston, 1942), p. 1.

[2]See Leon D. Epstein, *Political Parties in Western Democracies* (New Brunswick, NJ: Transaction Press, 1980), pp. 98–129, 233–60, 369–77.

[3]Douglas W. Rae, *The Political Consequences of Electoral Laws* (New Haven, CT: Yale University Press, 1967), pp. 53–58. For mathematically inclined readers who may want to make their own index scores, Rae's formula for calculating the index is as follows:

$$F_e = 1 - \left(\sum_{i=1}^{N} \tau_i^2 \right)$$

where T_1 = any party's share of the legislative seats, expressed as a decimal fraction.

[4]Jerzy J. Wiatr, "One-Party Systems: The Concept and Issues for Comparative Studies," in Erik Allardt and Yrjo Littunen, eds, *Cleavages, Ideologies, and Party Systems,* vol. 10 (Turku, Finland: Westermarck Society, 1964), pp. 281–90.

[5]*New York Times,* June 21, 1988, pp. 1, 5.

[6]*Newsweek,* April 17, 1989, p. 36. The freest Polish election in 40 years was held on June 5, 1989, and the Communist Party suffered an amazingly disastrous defeat. All but a handful of the 100 Senate seats were won by candidates from Lech Walesa's Solidarity movement. Moreover, by agreement with Solidarity, 35 top Communist government candidates ran unopposed for the Sejm and needed only to be approved by at least 50 percent of the voters to be elected; but so many of the voters crossed out so many of Communist candidates' names that only 2 of the 35 were elected: *New York Times,* June 6, 1989, pp. A1, A4.

11 The Legislative Process

No political truth is certainly of greater intrinsic value, or is stamped with the authority of more enlightened patrons of liberty than that...the accumulation of all powers, legislative, executive, and judiciary, in the same hands, whether of one, a few or many, and whether hereditary, self-appointed, or elective, may justly be pronounced the very definition of tyranny.

James Madison, *The Federalist*, Number 47

[In a parliamentary democracy] the executive consists of those members of the legislature chosen by the elected legislative majority. The majority elects a premier or prime minister from among its number, and he selects other leading members of the majority as the members of his cabinet. The majority as a whole is responsible for forming and conducting the "government." If any key part of its overall program is rejected by the legislature, or if a vote of "no confidence" is carried, the "government" must resign and either a new "government" must be formed out of the existing legislature, or a new legislative election must be held. If the program is legislated, the public can judge the results and can decide at the next regular election whether to reelect the majority or turn it out. At all times the voting public knows who is in charge, and whom to hold accountable for success or failure.[1]

In this and the next four chapters we will consider the principal official policy-making institutions of modern governments—"official" because they are formally established by constitutions and laws and generally regarded as parts of the government—in contrast to unofficial agencies outside the government, such as political parties and pressure groups.

In the course of this survey we will see that the legislatures, executives, civil services, and courts of the Western democratic nations are substantially alike in many ways. But we will also see that some democratic systems differ significantly from others in certain respects, particularly those relating to the official status and interrelationships of legislative and executive agencies. These differences are so important that we begin our survey of the official institutions by briefly describing and contrasting the two major forms of modern democratic governments—presidential democracies and parliamentary democracies.

PRESIDENTIAL AND PARLIAMENTARY DEMOCRACIES

Presidential democracies differ from parliamentary democracies mainly in that they are organized according to the principle of **separation of powers**—the principle of *the division of government power among coequal legislative, executive, and judicial branches.* It is therefore important to understand why some democracies have embedded the principle in their constitutional systems and others have rejected it altogether.

THE DOCTRINE OF SEPARATION OF POWERS

James Madison's quotation, which opens this chapter, forcefully states a view of government and human rights held by almost all of the 55 men who drafted the Constitution of the United States in the summer of 1787. They believed that in constructing a government that is truly just and free, people must steer between two very different but equally great dangers. On the one hand, government, with its great legal powers and physical force, is a permanent threat to people's liberties, and we must always be vigilant against its inherent tendencies to tyranny. On the other hand, the lawlessness and anarchy that result when government is too weak are equally dangerous to human rights. The great problem of statecraft is therefore to establish a government that is strong enough to maintain law and order but sufficiently restrained to keep it from becoming tyrannical. But how?

The answer, Madison and the other framers believed, is to vest each of the government's three basic powers in a separate and independent branch of government. When all three branches act in concert, government can do what it must, but no executive, legislature, or court should ever be able to use the whole power of government to work its way heedless of restraint. *Any* concentration of powers in a single branch is tyrannical, no matter whether that agency is an elected and responsible representative assembly, or an irresponsible hereditary monarch. Only true separation of powers protects the liberties of the people against the aggressions of government.

SEPARATION OF POWERS IN PRESIDENTIAL DEMOCRACIES

Presidential democracy is the term that political scientists generally apply to *any democratic government organized according to the principle of separation of powers.* The government of the United States is the oldest government organized in this way, but the category also includes such nations as Colombia, Costa Rica, Mexico, and Venezuela—all of whose governments are modeled more or less closely on the United States prototype. In all presidential democracies the three types of power are kept formally separate by two main devices.

Separation of Personnel

The Constitution of the United States specifically prohibits any person from holding office in more than one of the three branches of government at a time. Article I, Section 6, declares that "no Person holding any Office under the United States, shall be a Member of either House during his Continuance in Office." If the attorney general wishes to be a senator from New York, he must resign his executive position, as Robert Kennedy did in 1964. If a senator from Maine wishes to be secretary of state, he must resign his Senate seat, as Edmund Muskie did in 1980. If the assistant attorney general wishes to become a justice of the Supreme Court, he must resign his executive post, as Byron White did in 1961. If a justice of the Supreme Court wishes to become U.S. ambassador to the United Nations, he must resign his seat on the bench, as Arthur Goldberg did in 1965.

Checks and Balances

The U.S. Constitution does not try to isolate the three branches of government from one another completely; rather, each is given a number of "checks" with which it can keep the others in proper "balance." Thus Congress is empowered to check the president by refusing to pass bills that he requests, withholding appropriations for executive and administrative agencies, denying approval of his appointments to the other top executive posts, and even impeaching him and expelling him from office. Congress is empowered to check the Supreme Court by limiting its appellate jurisdiction and by withholding approval of the appointment of new judges. The president is empowered to check Congress by vetoing its acts and to check the Supreme Court by his initial appointment of its judges. And the Supreme Court can check both Congress and the president through its power of judicial review (see Chapter 14).

FUSION OF POWERS IN PARLIAMENTARY DEMOCRACIES

Most of the world's democratic nations neither accept the doctrine of separation of powers nor use checks and balances in the American pattern. They have, instead, what political scientists generally call **parliamentary systems**—

Parliamentary Democracy at Work. A plenary session of the West Germany Bundestag. (Source: German Information Center.)

governments organized according to the principle of fusion of powers. Great Britain, the British Commonwealth nations, the nations of Western Europe and Scandinavia, and such non-European democratic nations as India and Japan fall into this category.

The essential principle of all parliamentary democratic systems is what some analysts call the **fusion of powers**—that is, *the concentration of all powers in the parliament.* The powers are fused by two devices, each of which is the direct opposite of its counterpart in the presidential democracies.

Overlap of Personnel

With rare exceptions, the constitutions of the parliamentary democracies require that everyone who holds a top executive position—a minister or a subminister (see Chapter 12)—*must* be a member of the parliament. Thus the top layers of the executive branch, such as the cabinet and the ministry, are in effect "committees of the parliament to preside over the executive agencies."

Formal Supremacy of Parliament

The ministers' authority to direct the executive agencies in a parliamentary system is granted to them by the parliament. Any time the parliament of "no confidence" in them. When that happens, either the ministry must resign and be replaced by another acceptable to the parliamentary majority, or a general election must be held to elect a new parliament—which may then reappoint the old ministry or replace it with a new one. In short, disagreement and deadlock between the legislature and executive, which are so common in presidential systems, cannot be tolerated in a parliamentary system and must be resolved by changing the membership and behavior of either or both branches of government so that agreement between them can be restored.

CROSSING BOUNDARIES

Most present-day political scientists believe that the eighteenth-century three-way classification of the powers of government is inadequate and misleading. They recognize that in all modern democratic systems no agency sticks exclusively to the job formally assigned to it. Legislative bodies often engage in executive activities (for example, their investigations of wrongdoing in government, schools, and labor unions). Courts often "make" laws (as in their interpretations of constitutions and laws). Executive and administrative agencies often make and interpret laws (for example, making administrative regulations and holding hearings to determine whether licenses for television broadcasting stations should be renewed or revoked).

A few political scientists have attempted to preserve the traditional conception by calling the judicial activities and powers of executive agencies "quasi-judicial." Most, however, have concluded that the adjectives *legislative, executive,* and *judicial* should be used only as convenient tags for identifying particular government agencies. They do not constitute complete and accurate descriptions of what the agencies actually do.

In this chapter, accordingly, we will focus on those agencies generally called *legislatures.* According to Nelson W. Polsby, legislatures can be distinguished from executives and courts by six special characteristics: (1) they are *official* government agencies, in the sense we discussed in Chapter 1; (2) they are *multimembered;* (3) their members are *directly elected* by the citizens; (4) their *members are formally equal*—that is, the vote of each legislator has the same formal weight as the vote of every other legislator; (5) they arrive at their decisions by *deliberating on alternatives;* and (6) they register decisions by *counting the votes* of their members.[2]

In examining the legislative process, we will deal with the principle activities of these bodies, but we will not be concerned with the question of whether or not these activities are truly legislative in the eighteenth-century sense of the term. For our purposes, *any* function performed by an agency called a legislature is a legislative function. We will proceed from similar premises in subsequent chapters on the executive, administrative, and judicial processes.

FUNCTIONS OF LEGISLATURES

STATUTE MAKING

The first function of legislatures in modern democratic systems is making statutes. I use the term *statute making* rather than *law making* because it more accurately describes what legislatures actually do. *Law* means any rule of behavior that officially emanates from any authorized government agency, while a **statute** is *a law formally enacted by a legislature*. Statutes constitute an important segment of any democratic system's total body of law, but that body of law also includes such elements as common law and rules of equity determined by the courts as well as the more significant executive and administrative decrees and regulations. Legislatures thus monopolize the making of statutes but not the making of laws.

CONSTITUENT FUNCTIONS

The legislatures in most democratic systems have certain powers over the establishment and amendment of their nations' constitutions. Many constitutions are originally drawn up by legislative bodies, and every legislature is authorized to play some role in making formal amendments. In some democratic countries, such as Great Britain and New Zealand, the national legislature is the sole agency authorized to amend the constitution. In many others, such as Australia, Switzerland, and France, the legislature normally proposes amendments and the voters ratify or defeat their proposals in referendums. In still others, such as the United States, amendments are proposed by the national legislature and ratified by state legislatures or conventions. Most democratic legislatures have also added to their constitutions by enacting certain kinds of statutes; in the United States, for example, Congress has adopted statutes establishing the executive departments, the regulatory commissions, and the courts under the Supreme Court. (The Supreme Court is explicitly established by the Constitution.)

ELECTORAL FUNCTIONS

Most democratic legislatures play an important role in selecting some or all of the top executives. The outstanding instances are the indirect "elections" of prime ministers by the legislatures of the parliamentary democracies. These legislatures do not always directly cast ballots for various candidates for this office, of course; yet every time a legislature votes on a motion of no confidence (see Chapter 12), it is, in effect, re-electing or defeating the incumbent prime minister.

Even in the presidential democracies the legislatures have some electoral powers. The Constitution of the United States, for example, provides that if no candidate for president or vice president receives a majority of the votes in the Electoral College, the House of Representatives will choose the president from among the top two or three candidates, and the Senate will choose the vice president in a somewhat different way. No president or vice president has been selected by these procedures since 1824, but Congress retains its electoral powers against the day when they may be needed again.

FINANCIAL FUNCTIONS

In every modern democracy the legislature holds the basic "power of the purse." It determines the nature and amount of taxes, and the only funds that governments can legally spend are those appropriated by the legislature. As in the case of many other legislative functions, the main initiatives in government finance have passed from the legislatures to the executives in most democratic systems. Most legislatures now merely revise budgets proposed by executives, rather than drawing up their own from scratch. How much revision particular legislatures make depends upon the degree of control the executives have achieved— a matter we will consider later in this chapter.

EXECUTIVE FUNCTIONS

In addition to acting upon executive budgets, most democratic legislatures also pass upon some other kinds of executive proposals. In most democratic countries, for example, international treaties are negotiated by the executives but must be approved by the legislatures before they become effective. In the United States the president appoints various officials (federal judges, cabinet members, heads of administrative agencies, and ambassadors) "by and with the Advice and Consent of the Senate" (Article II)—that is, the appointments are only provisional, or "interim," until approved by a majority of the Senate. Anyone who watched the Senate in 1988 reject President Reagan's nomination of Robert H. Bork for membership on the Supreme Court knows that the performance of this legislative function occasionally becomes front-page news and has serious consequences.

JUDICIAL FUNCTIONS

Some democratic legislatures also perform judicial functions. The Constitution of the United States, for instance, provides that the House of Representatives may impeach any civil officer of the national government (including the president, the vice president, cabinet members, and judges). An impeachment, remember, is not a conviction; it is a formal accusation of crime, comparable to a grand jury's indictment in an ordinary criminal case. Any officer so

Many economists believe that by far the worst problem the United States faces in the 1990s is the huge national debt, which by the end of the Reagan administration in 1988 totalled well over $225 *trillion* and was increasing by $175 billion or more every year. Already in 1980, some 12.7 percent of all federal outlays were spent on paying interest on the debt, and in 1986 it grew to 18.9 percent. Almost everyone, liberals and conservatives, Democrats and Republicans alike, now agrees that the government must do something drastic before the whole economy is wrecked.

But what? One solution, of course, is to raise taxes; but Ronald Reagan consistently refused to consider anything but tax *cuts,* and Walter Mondale's 1984 campaign proposal to raise taxes was widely regarded as one of the main causes for his landslide loss to Reagan. In 1988, Bush vowed that he would never raise taxes under any conditions (one of his best-remembered campaign statements was, "Read my lips: No new taxes!"); and Dukakis said that he would do so only as a last resort. So if we can't raise taxes, we must drastically cut expenditures so that they will match the amount of money we take in with our present taxes.

That seems obvious and sensible, and yet each year of his administration, Reagan proposed budgets calling for much greater expenditures than anticipated tax revenues, and Congress not only went along but often increased the expenditures. So the executive and the legislature alike agree that expenditures must be cut, but no one seems to do anything about it.

Many observers have come to believe that it is impossible for elected politicians, both the president and the members of Congress, to cut expenditures. The benefits of expenditures are immediate and obvious and therefore very pleasing to voters. The benefits of cuts in expenditures are obscure and come years down the road; hence they are displeasing to voters and likely to lead to electoral defeat for people who cut programs. Thus the only hope such observers see is to have some kind of *automatic* expenditure-control system that will cut the deficits without putting particular politicians on the spot.

That approach was adopted in 1985 when Congress passed the Balanced Budget and Emergency Deficit Reduction Act (generally known as the Gramm-Rudman-Hollings act after its three main sponsors in the Senate). The bill set mandatory maximum limits on the allowable size of the deficits for the next five years, with the goal of a balanced budget by 1991. If in any year the president and Congress could not in the regular budget process agree on expenditures that would meet the mandatory limits, the comptroller general would inform the president by what percent expenditures would have to be cut to meet the overall limits, and those cuts would be automatically made without any vote by Congress. Specifically exempted from the automatic cuts were outlays on Social Security, Aid to Families with Dependent Children, food stamps, Medicaid, and federal pension funds; and the automatic cuts would come 50 percent from defense appropriations and 50 percent from nonprotected domestic expenditures, such as those for education, highways, environmental protection, and the like.

However, in 1986 the Supreme Court declared that giving the comptroller general the power to stipulate the level of the mandatory cuts gave him, an employee of the Congress, a power that belonged to the president and was therefore a violation of separation of powers. This decision, in effect, eliminates the mandatory–automatic cuts feature of the new bill, and puts expenditure-cutting and budget-balancing right back where it has long been—in the ability of the president and Congress to agree what expenditures should be cut and by how much. They were notably unsuccessful in doing this prior to Gramm-Rudman-Hollings, and most observers believe that, without the act's mandatory features, they will have little more success in the 1990s.

impeached must be tried by the Senate, where a two-thirds vote is necessary for conviction. The House has impeached a total of thirteen officers since 1789: ten judges, one president (Andrew Johnson), and one cabinet member. Only five, all judges, have been convicted and removed from office, but President Andrew Johnson escaped conviction in 1868 by the bare margin of one vote; and in 1974, President Richard Nixon resigned when it became clear that the House was going to impeach him.

Similarly, the French national assembly can indict the president of the Republic and the ministers for treason and other crimes and misdemeanors, although indicted officers are tried by the high court rather than by a legislative body. The British House of Lords has lost most of its other powers but continues to be the nation's highest court of law. Most of the Lords' judicial work, and all of its work as a court of appeals, is performed in the name of the whole chamber by a small group of ten to fifteen legal experts, including the lord chancellor, the nine lords of appeal in ordinary (the "law lords"), and other members of the House who have held high judicial office (for example, former lord chancellors).

INVESTIGATIVE FUNCTIONS

Legislative investigations often receive considerable publicity, especially in the United states. Congressional probes, such as those by the Ervin Select Committee on Presidential Campaign Activities in 1973 and by the 1988 joint House–Senate committee on the secret efforts of National Security Adviser John Poindexter and his aide Oliver North to sell arms to Iran and use the proceeds to finance aid to the Nicaraguan "contras," are the best-known recent examples. American legislatures have no monopoly on this kind of activity, however. The British House of Commons establishes a number of "select committees" for the purpose of digging up information desired by the House on matters not covered by its standing committees. The select committees hold hearings, subpoena witnesses and records, and then submit reports that sometimes stimulate changes in existing legislation, administrative practices, or both. Although the British, unlike the Americans, conduct much of their governmental investigations through royal commissions (bodies composed of both legislators and outsiders), the select committees nevertheless have a significant role in the development of legislative and administrative policy.

INFORMATIONAL FUNCTIONS

Some legislative investigations are conducted mainly to collect information necessary for new legislation. Many, however, are intended mainly to inform other government agencies and the general public about what is going on. For example, the Ervin committee's investigations of the Watergate scandals in 1973 were intended only in part to provide the basis for new legislation regulating campaign finance and practices; in addition, they were designed to determine whether or not the legislation already on the books had been violated by President Nixon or members of his administration and campaign organization. For other examples, in the late 1970s both houses of Congress created committees to investigate the assassinations of President John F. Kennedy in 1963 and Martin Luther King, Jr., in 1968 to see whether they were the acts of individual assassins, as earlier investigations had concluded, or were the results of conspiracies.

Legislative investigations are one way of informing the public, and legislative debates are another. In many legislatures, party lines are so strong that legislative debate hardly ever changes a member's vote. Yet debate provides the main forum in which the pros and cons of issues are aired. It thus serves much the same function of informing and activating public opinion that election campaigns are supposed to perform. Debates in the British House of Commons, although they almost never change legislative votes, sometimes change the opinions of voters, and some observers describe them as a continuing election campaign. If an informed and enlightened citizenry is indeed a prime requisite for healthy democracy, then informing the public is far from the least significant of the legislature's functions.

STRUCTURE AND PROCEDURES OF LEGISLATURES

NUMBER OF HOUSES

Approximately two-thirds of all modern democratic nations have bicameral (two-house) legislatures, and one-third have unicameral (one-house) legislatures. Although there are several variations in the structure of the bicameral legislatures, most are organized in substantially similar fashion. One of the two houses (or chambers), generally called the lower house, has the larger membership and the shorter term of office, and is elected (under one of the electoral systems described in Chapter 8) by the widest franchise. Examples of such chambers are the American House of Representatives, the British House of Commons, the French Assemblé National, and the Swiss Nationalrat. The other chamber, generally called the upper house, has the smaller membership and longer term of office, and is selected in various ways. The members of the American Senate, for example, are elected by the voters in statewide constituencies for 6-year terms; some members of the British House of Lords inherit their positions, and others are appointed for life on the advice of the prime minister (none are elected); the members of the Canadian Senate are appointed for life by the governor-general on the advice of the prime minister; and the members of the Austrian Bundesrat are elected by the legislatures of the various *lander* (provinces).

Why should a nation establish two legislative chambers rather than one? Historically there have been two main reasons. First, some federal democracies have thought it necessary to give their subnational units (states, provinces, *lander)* equal representation in the national legislature: For example, the U.S. Senate has two members from each state, regardless of its population or wealth. Perhaps even more important has been the desire to provide an internal check on legislative action. The lower houses have been thought to be closely in tune with popular appetites and passions and have therefore been regarded as dangerous to national stability and welfare. Many nations, accordingly, have at one time or another established higher property and age qualifications for people who elect members of the upper houses than for those who elect members of the lower houses, and a few nations still retain these special franchise requirements.

In recent years a number of democratic nations have formally or informally abandoned bicameralism, mainly on the ground that it dilutes the power of the chamber most representative of the people. A few nations, such as Denmark and New Zealand, have officially abolished one of their chambers. Other nations have reduced the powers of one chamber so drastically that they are now little more than advisory bodies, and the other houses have become, for all practical purposes, unicameral legislatures. For example, until the nineteenth century the British House of Lords was in every respect as powerful as the House of Commons. After the democratization of the Commons in 1832, however, the powers of the Lords began to slip away. The Parliament Act of 1911 stripped it of all but a few delaying powers, and an act of 1949 reduced these powers still more. Accordingly, today the House of Lords is merely an advisory and delaying body, with little or no legislative power. Most observers believe that it performs useful advising and revising functions, but Parliament has become a de facto unicameral legislature. The same thing has happened to a greater or lesser degree in almost all unitary democracies. Only in some of the federal democracies (for example, the United States and Switzerland but not Canada and Australia) do the upper houses retain powers equal or superior to those of the lower houses.

MAIN STEPS IN HANDLING BILLS

Despite differences in procedural details, the legislatures of most democratic regimes put bills through similar steps before they become law.

Introduction

In most legislatures, any member may introduce a bill either by giving it a "first reading" on the floor and moving for its adoption or, as in both houses of Congress, merely by dropping it in the "hopper" at the clerk's or secretary's desk. This formal equality in the right to introduce bills is misleading, however. Many democratic legislatures, such as the British House of Commons, make a formal distinction between government bills (those introduced by ministers on behalf of their ministries or "the government") and private members' bills (those introduced by ordinary members on their own initiative). Only government bills are likely to be passed. The government introduces about 85 percent of all bills in Great Britain, and over three-quarters of the bills passed are government bills. No such formal distinction is made in the U.S. Congress, but a bill generally known to be an administration bill (one backed by the president and pushed by his partisans in Congress) has a much better chance of passing than one that lacks administration backing.

Consideration by Committee

Later in this chapter we will examine the structure, operations, and role of committees in the legislative process. Here the point to note is that in most democratic legislatures, bills are referred to and considered by committees *before* they undergo general consideration and debate by the whole chamber. Committees therefore have a great deal to say not only about the contents of bills but also about which bills have a realistic chance of becoming laws. In the British House of Commons, however, bills are referred to committees *after* general debate and *after* most details have been established by the whole house (which means by the cabinet). Thus British committees, unlike those in most other democratic legislatures, are charged with cleaning up details, and with very little else. The nations of the British Commonwealth, such as Canada and Australia, generally follow British practices in this regard, but the United States and most European democracies assign their legislative committees far more decisive roles, as we will see in a moment.

General Debate

The few bills that survive the screening process in committees are then reported back to the whole house in original or altered form and are given "second readings" (which usually means only that the presiding officer or the clerk announces the number and title of each bill about to be considered, not that anyone literally reads aloud its entire contents). At this point all legislators have a chance to express their views on the basic policy questions involved in the bill and also to offer amendments to it. If the bill survives this stage, its chances of final passage are excellent.

Final Passage

After general debate and after all proposed amendments have been accepted, rejected, or revised, the bill is given its third and final "reading," and the question is put as to whether the whole bill, as amended, should be passed. An affirmative vote means that as far as the particular chamber is concerned, the bill should be law.

Consideration by Conference Committees

In many supposedly two-house legislatures, as we have seen, the upper houses have the power only to suggest amendments and to delay bills passed by the lower houses. After the delaying period has elapsed and after the lower house has accepted or rejected the upper house's amendments, the bill moves on to the next and final stage, regardless of further objections by the upper house. But in the United States and a few other nations, each bill must pass both houses in identical form before it can move on to the final stage. When the two houses disagree on the final wording of a bill, whether on a minor detail or on a major policy question, and neither is willing to accept the other's version, the differences must be ironed out and the bill worded in a manner that will be approved by majorities in both houses. This problem arises with 30 to 50 percent of all the bills that pass both houses of Congress, including almost every major bill.

In a genuinely bicameral legislature, the necessary ironing-out activities are conducted by some version of the American conference committees, which operate as follows. In each case in which the two houses have passed somewhat different bills on similar subjects, the presiding officer of each house appoints from three to nine members to represent the house as conferees. The two sets of conferees constitute a conference committee, which tries to work out a version of the bill on which all or most of the conferees can agree. Conference committees usually produce compromises between the versions of the two houses, but on rare occasions they write substantially new bills. When the conferees have reached agreement, they report to their respective houses. Their reports cannot be amended by either house but must be accepted or rejected in their entirety. They are usually accepted, for the very good reason that most members of both houses know that if a conference committee's version is not accepted, there will probably be no bill at all.

Conference committees, accordingly, have considerable power over the final content of legislation—so much that some observers call them "the third house of Congress." However, some such institution is indispensable in any genuinely bicameral legislature.

Final Action by the Executive

After the legislature has officially enacted a bill, it is submitted to the executive for official approval and inclusion in the collection of statutes in force.

In the parliamentary systems, the executives—monarchs or presidents—have no choice but to approve the bills and declare them law. In the presidential systems, however, the presidents can veto bills. Thus, if the president of the United States vetoes a bill, it can become law only if repassed by both houses with a two-thirds majority in each. This procedure will be discussed further in Chapter 12.

LEGISLATIVE COMMITTEES

Organization

Every democratic legislative body establishes committees of its members to perform various functions. Committees appear to be a universal response to two main needs. First, the sheer size of most legislatures prevents them from effectively handling questions of detail and wording. Most legislatures have several hundred members, and hundreds of people can deal effectively only with dozens of broad questions of policy, not with thousands of questions of detail. Second, the sheer number of bills introduced requires some way of weeding out the few that will get serious consideration. In an average session of Congress,

Congress Works in Committees. National Security Advisor John Poindexter and his counsel testifying before the joint congressional committee on the "Irangate" affair, 1987. (Source: AP/Wide World Photos.)

for example, 10,000 to 12,000 bills are introduced—obviously far too many to consider seriously. In fact only about 500 to 1,000 survive to final passage.

In the United States and most European democracies, most of the weeding out is accomplished by legislative committees. In the United States each house of Congress maintains a number of *standing committees* (those considered permanent) established according to subject matter: agriculture, appropriations, armed services, foreign affairs, and education and labor are examples. They range in size from 9 to 50 members and include legislators of the majority and minority parties in approximately the same proportions as the two parties' shares of the seats in the whole house. Nominally the members of each committee are elected by the whole house, but actually the leaders of each party (assembled in its "committee on committees") determine which of their members will sit on which committees. In making these selections the leaders are bound by a series of informal but nonetheless powerful rules. For example, all the previous members of a committee must be reappointed if they so desire, and every major area and interest must have a spokesperson on a committee that deals with matters affecting it.

The *commissions* of the French national assembly are in some respects similar to American legislative committees. The principal French variation is the institution of the *rapporteur* (reporter). As each bill is received by a particular *commission,* it appoints one member as the *rapporteur* for that bill. The *rapporteur* then takes the lead in studying the bill, in preparing the *commission's* report on it, and in defending the *commission's* position in the debate before the whole assembly.

The British House of Commons, in contrast to the American and French legislatures, maintains only eight "alphabet" standing committees (so called because they are officially designated committee A, committee B, committee C and so on rather than "armed forces" or "agriculture" and the like). The British and French committees are not specialized by subject matter and are far less powerful than their counterparts in many other legislatures.

Besides standing committees, democratic legislatures from time to time establish *select committees,* which make special inquiries into, and recommendations on, particular questions. The bicameral legislatures sometimes establish *joint committees,* composed of members from each house, to supervise certain matters (for example, Congress's Joint Committee on Atomic Energy, created to supervise the Department of Energy's administration of nuclear energy matters).

Activities and Power

Most legislatures' standing committees have two main activities. The first is disposing of bills referred to them by their chambers. A powerful committee has a wide range of choice in deciding how to dispose of a particular bill. It may simply shelve it—which is what happens to most bills—or it may immediately report the bill in its original form back to the whole house with a recommendation "that it do pass." It may also decide to work the bill over before making any recommendation, in which case it may hold hearings at which representatives of various interested groups are invited to testify. When the hearings are over, the committee may then go into a "mark-up session" and rewrite the bill as little or as much as it sees fit, up to and including deleting everything but the title and substituting an entirely new bill!

Committees are not restricted to acting only on bills referred to them. They may decide to draw up and have members introduce new bills of their own. They may decide to investigate possible wrongdoing in the executive, administrative, or judicial agencies—or for that matter, in schools, labor unions, athletic competition, and the like.

The power of legislative committees over the general legislative process varies considerably among modern democracies. At one extreme stand the committees of the U.S. Congress and state legislatures, which are the most powerful in the world. Not only do they receive bills before general debate and before basic policy decisions have been made, but also they can, and often do, make major decisions on basic policy as well as on matters of detail and wording. "Little legislatures," Woodrow Wilson called them, and the phrase is as apt today as it was when he wrote it in 1885.[3]

At the other extreme stand the committees of the British House of Commons. They do not receive a bill until after its second reading, when the basic policy decisions have already been made. They are authorized to make alterations and amendments only on minor details. They do not specialize in particular subject-matter areas, so they develop no special expertise in any area. Their members are subject to strong party discipline both inside and outside the committees. The committees therefore play a relatively unimportant role in the British legislative process.

Under the Third and Fourth Republics of France, the powers of the French *commissions* were more like those of American committees. However, the Constitution of the Fifth Republic (1958) was written to reduce those powers and thus to reduce the fragmentation of policy making that had tied up the legislatures under the preceding regimes. The number of *commissions generales permanentes* (standing committees) was reduced from nineteen specialized committees on the American model to six unspecialized committees on the British model. It is now the government's bills—not the committees' amendments and counterproposals, as in the old days—that come before the whole assembly for debate and final action.

The power of legislative committees in the other democracies falls between these extremes. On the one hand, committee reports usually serve as the basis for debate and action in the whole legislature, and a committee has considerable power to redraft and amend the bills referred to it. On the other hand, in most parliamentary democracies the government's control of the legislative agenda and the political parties' control of their members' votes are so strong that the committees can rarely do anything against the government's wishes.

PARTY ORGANIZATION

Principal Agencies

Almost every member of every democratic legislature is elected as the candidate of a political party. In every legislature the members of each party form some kind of organization to consult on matters of policy and strategy so as to advance their common cause most effectively. Although these legislative party organizations vary in detail from nation to nation and from party to party within some nations, most include some version of each of the following principal agencies.

Caucus.   In its most general sense, the term **caucus** refers to *a meeting, usually secret, of the members of a political party or interest group to agree on strategy or to select candidates, or both.* A legislative party caucus is an assembly of all the party's members in the particular house. The American versions are called conferences or caucuses; the British versions are called parliamentary parties; the French versions are called *groupes;* and so on. Their main function is to select their parties' legislative leaders, although occasionally

Majority (Democratic) Party Leaders in Congress, 1989. Whip Tony Coelho (California), Speaker Jim Wright (Texas), Majority Leader Tom Foley (Washington state). (Source: UPI/Bettmann, Newsphotos.)

some also decide what stands their members should take on particular legislative issues.

Executive committee.   The caucus usually selects a few of its members as some kind of executive committee and authorizes them to take the lead in setting the party's strategy and tactics. The American versions are called steering committees or policy committees; the British versions are called the leadership or the cabinet (see Chapter 12); the French versions are called the party executive; and so on.

Floor leaders.   Each caucus also selects one of its members as its official leader and main spokesperson. The American versions are called the majority leader and the minority leader; the British equivalents are the prime minister and the leader of Her Majesty's loyal opposition.

Whips.   The caucus or leader selects a few members to act as assistant leaders, generally known as "whips."[4] Their functions are to inform the rank and file of the leadership's decisions about policy and strategy, to keep them from straying from the leaders' line on key legislative issues, and to inform the leaders about any dissatisfactions and resentments the members may have.

Power and Role

We noted in Chapter 10 that the discipline and cohesion of legislative parties vary widely among democratic nations. At the high end of the scale stand the British parliamentary parties. The majority party picks its leader, who automatically becomes prime minister. The prime minister, in turn, chooses the members of the cabinet and ministry; and together they constitute the British executive. Led by the prime minister, the cabinet controls the proceedings and decisions of the House of Commons. Organized opposition is dominated by the second-largest party's leader and "shadow cabinet," which not only continuously criticize the majority party's policies but also expound the alternative policies the opposition intends to adopt when the voters make them the majority party. As a result, British government is *party* government, in the sense that party organizations and operations are the very core of its legislative and executive processes.

Near the low end of the scale stand a few of the smaller center and right-wing parties in democratic nations with high degrees of fractionalization (see Chapter 10). Their members ordinarily feel little obligation and no compulsion to act or vote together. They are thus little more than aggregations of independent legislators who happen to bear the same formal party labels.

The Democratic and Republican parties in the American Congress stand between these two extremes. On matters of personnel (for example, electing the presiding officers and allocating committee positions) they are as cohesive as British parties. On most issues of public policy they are less cohesive than British parties but more cohesive than some French parties. To illustrate:

Since the late 1940s a number of pressure groups have kept scores on how every senator and representative has voted on issues of particular concern to them. Their records show that around 70 percent of the votes cast by Democrats in both houses supported labor and liberal positions, whereas only about 25 percent of those cast by Republicans did so. They also show that some Democrats (for example, Senators David Boren of Oklahoma and John Stennis of Mississippi) were as conservative as were the most conservative Republicans—and that some Republicans (for example, Senators Lowell Weicker of Connecticut and Mark Hatfield of Oregon) were almost as liberal as the most liberal Democrats. On most key issues in Congress, then, majorities of Democrats oppose majorities of Republicans; but each party has some mavericks who vote mostly with the opposition party, and rarely do *all* Democrats vote one way and *all* Republicans vote the other way. The same is true in most state legislatures.

We also noted in Chapter 10 that in centralization, discipline, and cohesion, the dominant parties in most democracies fall somewhere between the British and American major parties. But in every democratic nation the parties' power over their legislative members' votes and actions determines the role of parties in the nation's legislative process. It also sets the conditions for the individual legislator's public life. Let us see how.

LEGISLATIVE WAYS OF LIFE

For our present purposes, legislators in modern democracies may usefully be divided into two general types. The first type is the "party soldier," exemplified by the ordinary members of the British House of Commons (MPs), who are subject to such strict party discipline that except under the most unusual circumstances they feel compelled to vote as their party whips direct. The second type is the "independent operator," exemplified by ordinary members of the U.S. Senate or House of Representatives, who are subject to such weak party discipline that they can, if they wish, feel safe in voting contrary to their whips' requests.

PARTY SOLDIERS

Life on the Back Benches

Most of the members of the British House of Commons are **backbenchers**—that is, *MPs who hold no ministerial office.* As we saw in Chapter 10, while the number of occasions on which MPs have voted against their party leaders' orders have increased in recent years, it is still the case that almost all MPs almost always vote as their party leaders direct, and practically speaking they have no independent power. Accordingly, the only way a backbencher can achieve personal success is to be appointed to ministerial office by his party leaders. If MPs are ambitious—and not all of them are— whatever they do as backbenchers must convince their leaders that they are of ministerial caliber. Even if the backbenchers have no hope of reaching ministerial rank, they have little freedom to use their votes to gain other goals.

When, then, can they do? For one thing, they can speak in parliamentary debates. If they are good at it, they may win the attention and approval necessary for advancement to ministerial office; even if they do not, they may still enjoy the applause of their colleagues and favorable notices in the newspapers. For another thing, they can keep the ministers on their toes by asking sharp questions during "question time" (see Chapter 13). For still another, they can rise to eminence in their parties' committees of backbenchers and through them exert substantial influence on the leaders. They can introduce motions that may cause some public stir. They can introduce private bills, a few of which may pass. And there is always the possibility, however remote, that by abstaining or threatening to abstain from voting in a major crisis they may help to bring down an unwanted government (as in the unseating of Neville Chamberlain's government in 1940) or reverse a disastrous government policy (as in the crisis over the seizing of the Suez canal by Britain and France in 1956).

By American standards, the British backbenchers' position is not impressive. Their votes are not their own; they have little independent power to put pressure on administrators; they are paid very little—the equivalent of about $10,000 a year plus very modest secretarial, living, and travel allowances; and most have to share offices with three or four other members. Yet backbenchers are by no means complete ciphers. They belong to one of Great Britain's most exclusive clubs (about the only one in London that guarantees parking space for its members), they are insiders in the nation's most fascinating game, and their positions as MPs may be highly useful in their careers in journalism, law, or business. Relatively few MPs retire voluntarily, and many who are defeated in general elections try over and over again to win their way back. Evidently, then, even the party soldiers who never rise to ministerial rank find considerable satisfaction in being backbenchers.

Relations with Constituents

Because ordinary backbenchers do not control their own parliamentary votes, they have no meaningful individual voting records for their opponents to attack or their supporters to praise. But in their constituencies they are much more than merely names with party labels. They are expected to provide certain local services, and if they function well they can have significant voices in constituency affairs. Although the institution of ministerial responsibility (see Chapter 12) prevents them from exerting direct pressure on civil servants in the American sense, they can explain local problems and dramatize local needs through speeches in the House and private talks with ministers.

Most MPs hold regular "surgeries" in their constituencies; that is, they have office hours during which they are available to all constituents who care to call on them, express their views, and make requests about such matters as ill treatment by the ministry of pensions or difficulty with the ministry of local government and planning. If the MPs find merit in their constituents' claims, they can at least make sure that the relevant ministries pay attention. Conscientious MPs also grace local festivals, celebrations, and ceremonies with their presence. And at their constituents' request they can provide tickets of admission to the Strangers' Gallery (from which they can watch the House in session, usually a good show) and frequently also invite them to tea on the handsome terrace overlooking the Thames.

MPs who shirk their local duties are more likely to find themselves in trouble with their constituency party organizations than with the voters, but recent research by three American scholars shows that there is some electoral payoff as well: They found that, other things being equal, Labour voters are more likely to vote for an incumbent Labour MP (who presumably has been tending to his constituents' needs) than for a nonincumbent Labour candidate standing in the same constituency; and a higher proportion are likely to vote for an incumbent Conservative MP than a nonincumbent Conservative candidate.[5] Thus the local obligations of British MPs are an important—and often wearying—part of their public life. In some respects, then, the party soldiers have many of the independent operators' burdens but few of their powers.

In 1714 a British member of Parliament, Antony Henry, received a communication from his constituents asking him to vote against an excise (tax) bill. He is said to have replied:

> *Gentlemen: I have received your letter about the excise, and I am surprised at your insolence in writing to me at all.*
>
> *You know, and I know, that I bought this constituency. You know, and I know, that I am now determined to sell it, and you know what you think I don't know that you are now looking out for another buyer, and I know, what you certainly don't know, that I have now found another constituency to buy.*
>
> *About what you said about the excise: may God's curse light upon you all, and may it make your homes as open and as free to the excise officers as your wives and daughters have always been to me while I have represented your rascally constituency.*[6]

INDEPENDENT OPERATORS

Life in the Senate and House of Representatives

Members of the American Congress operate in quite a different setting from British MPs. They owe their nominations to the people who vote in the direct primaries in their districts, and the national leaders of their parties

In 1948 a brilliant and idealistic young liberal was elected to the U.S. Senate from a midwestern state. Justly proud of his speaking ability and burning with zeal to push the liberal legislation for which he campaigned, he made his "maiden" speech a few days after having been sworn in and in the ensuing weeks followed it up with a number of speeches on a wide variety of topics. All his speeches were eloquent and witty and received favorable notice in the press, especially back home. But somehow the other senators did not seem to be persuaded by them, not even the other liberals.

Increasingly frustrated, the young senator began to accept outside speaking engagements, in the course of which he often referred to the stubbornness of the conservative senators, the lack of leadership and gumption among his fellow liberals, and the inertia and sloth of the Senate as an institution. His name appeared in the headlines with increasing frequency, and his mail indicated that the folks back home thought he was just wonderful. But it seemed that the more popular he became outside the Senate, the less able he was to accomplish anything inside the Senate. He introduced many well-conceived and innovative bills, but most of them never even got out of the committees.

Finally, in desperation, he went to his party's floor leader and asked, "Why can't I get anything done in this outfit? What am I doing wrong?" The floor leader replied, "Look, fellow, you're doing just about everything wrong. A couple of days after you got here you made a major speech. During your first six months you sounded off—at length—on every major issue that came up. Then you started shooting your mouth off outside the Senate and had the gall to say a lot of nasty things about some individual senators and the Senate itself. And now you keep introducing bills on every subject under the sun. Frankly, my friend, the boys think that you are a blowhard and a publicity hound. They think you don't know what you're talking about most of the time, and no matter how good the bills you introduce may be, the fact that you introduced them is, as far as most of the boys are concerned, enough reason in itself to dump them. That's the way it is."

The young senator was stunned and angry. But, although he was eager to be a hero to the folks back home, he also wanted to see his liberal legislation pass the Senate—he wanted to get something *done*. So he decided to make a few changes in the light of the floor leader's comments. First, he picked four subjects—agriculture, civil rights, foreign affairs, and taxation—and spoke only on legislation in those areas. Second, he carefully prepared each speech, showed himself to be thoroughly familiar with all the facts and figures in each area, and confined himself to no more than one major speech on each major bill in each of his chosen areas. Third, he sharply reduced his outside speaking engagements and refrained from any direct criticism of the Senate or its individual members. Fourth, he made a point of frequently seeking the advice of a number of senior senators in both parties and did some chores for them. Finally, he introduced only one or two major bills in each session.

After a while the young senator noticed that when he spoke in the Senate, the others not only did listen but some of them even quoted him in their own speeches. His bills began to receive serious and friendly consideration, and most were passed in some form or other. Other senators began to come to him for advice. By the end of his first term in office he felt that he had learned how the Senate really works, and he only wished he had started his education a little sooner.

> The time was the early 1950s, the young senator's name was Hubert Humphrey, and the floor leader who set him straight was Lyndon Johnson. In his succeeding five terms, Humphrey became, by general acclaim, the most effective and creative senator of his time. In 1964 President Lyndon Johnson chose him to be vice president, and in 1968, after Johnson withdrew from the race, Humphrey became the Democratic presidential nominee. Though he was narrowly defeated by Richard Nixon in the general election, he returned to the Senate in 1970 and resumed his influential role there. When he died in 1978 his loss was mourned and he was honored more than any other public figure of his time who had never become president.

cannot keep them from being renominated. In some instances their chances of re-election may be marginally affected by the success and support of their national party leaders, but their political fortunes depend mainly upon what the local voters think of them. Not only do the national leaders have little effective power to punish members of Congress for deviant voting, but also a member's reputation for independence and "refusal to submit to the party bosses" may well be worth thousands of votes to him in many districts. Then too, voting against the "party line" is in no sense a vote to put the other party in control of Congress or the presidency—fixed terms and separation of powers take care of that. The vote of every member of Congress therefore belongs to the member alone. Members may voluntarily decide to "go along" with their parties on most issues; a majority, as we have seen, do just that. But the fact that their parties cannot effectively *make* them to vote this way or that makes their positions very different from those of British MPs.

How do American legislators use this heady independence? Most political scientists have answered this question by identifying the different roles that various legislators choose (or are forced) to play. James David Barber's study of Connecticut first-term legislators, for example, distinguished among "spectators," "advertisers," "reluctants," and "law makers." The pioneering study by John C. Wahlke, Heinz Eulau, William Buchanan, and LeRoy C. Ferguson of legislators in California, New Jersey, Ohio, and Tennessee identified several sets of roles. In their representational functions, legislators were classified as "trustees," "politicos," and "delegates." In their dealings with pressure groups they were "facilitators," "neutrals," or "resisters." Several studies distinguish between members of Congress who are "members of the inner club" and "outsiders." The common theme of all these studies is that legislators are impelled by their own psychological makeups, their perceptions of the legislative process in the capital and of the electoral process in their states and districts, and their goals and ambitions to choose certain roles. And the roles they choose have much to do with both their activities and their effectiveness.

Several recent studies of Congress have concluded that more and more members of Congress are choosing to follow an "outside" rather than an "inside" strategy. As Norman Ornstein points out, prior to the advent of the television age in the 1960s, the ambitious young congressman—like Hubert Humphrey in the boxed story—had no choice but to play the "inside" game of conforming to the norms of behavior prescribed by the old hands. In the famous words of Sam Rayburn, the Speaker of the House from 1940 to 1961, "to get along you have to go along." But in 1960 John F. Kennedy, a relatively minor member of the Senate, used his popular appeal on television to win the presidency, and since then, local and national television newscasters have found that individual members of Congress—especially *colorful* ones— make good copy. So more and more members appear in the interview slots on the networks' national news programs, and the result has meant a significant change in the way in which many members of Congress conduct themselves. As Ornstein sums it up:

> *As media coverage expanded, the number of members of Congress who were brought to public attention mushroomed, and more and more of the publicized members came from the rank and file....This trend toward personal publicity provided, in contrast to the Rayburn era, a range of tangible and possible outside incentives. No longer did a member have to play by inside rules to receive inside rewards or avoid inside setbacks. One could "go public" and be rewarded by national attention; national attention in turn could provide ego gratification, social success in Washington, the opportunity to run for higher office, or, by highlighting an issue, policy success.* [7]

Relations with Constituents

Most U.S. members of Congress, like most British MPs, cannot concentrate solely on their dealings with their fellow legislators, for the voters back home have the final power over their political careers. Hence members of Congress, like MPs, must perform a number of services for their constituents. Furthermore, constituency services are even more important to members of Congress than they are to MPs; for the congressmembers' electoral fortunes are much less tied to those of their parties, and unlike MPs, they *can* exert some pressure on executives and administrators.

Thus failure to provide good constituency services is much more likely to count against members of Congress than MPs at election time. And success is much more likely to keep members of Congress in office regardless of how well or badly their parties are doing in national elections. The most striking proof of this is the fact that during the past two decades, over 90 percent of all incumbents running for re-election have been re- elected—Democrats as well as Republicans, and liberals as well as conservatives. For example, even in 1984, when Republican Ronald Reagan won 59 percent of the votes and carried 49 of the 50 states, 255 Democratic members of the House of Representatives ran for re-election and 242—95 percent—were re-elected. In 1988, incumbent House members did even better: 243 Democratic incumbents ran for re-election, and 241 won; 159 Republicans incumbents ran, and 155 won; altogether, then, 402 incumbents ran for re-election and 396—98.5 percent—won.

There are even greater differences between members of Congress and

MPs. The votes of the British legislators are in most instances controlled by their parties, but the votes of American legislators are almost entirely their own, to be cast as they see fit, not according to orders from the president or their parties' floor leaders in the House or Senate. In deciding how to cast those votes, members of Congress often have to face very difficult issues about whether they should vote as they think best or vote as their constituents want them to vote. Let us look more closely at what is involved in these issues.

THE REPRESENTATIVE–CONSTITUENT RELATIONSHIP

One of the oldest and most debated issues among people who believe in democracy concerns the proper relationship between representatives and their constituents. Two distinct positions on the issue were first fully stated in the eighteenth century, and most subsequent pronouncements on the issue have been restatements of these original positions.

THE MANDATE THEORY

Some early democratic theorists, notably John Lilburne and Jean Jacques Rousseau, argued that the proper function of the representative assembly in a true democracy is not to initiate policies on its own but only to register the policy preferences of the popular majority it represents. They started from the premise that the ideal method of popular consultation is a face-to-face assembly of all community members. But this method is impossible in a large and densely populated nation, so the next best thing is for the members of the community to express their will through their elected representatives. As a member of the American constitutional convention of 1787 put it:

> *What is the principle of representation? It is an expedience by which an assembly of certain individuals chosen by the people is substituted in place of the inconvenient meetings of the people themselves.*[8]

In this view, as long as the representative assembly confines itself to registering its constituents' views, representation involves no significant departure from democratic principles. But when the assembly begins to make policy on its own, in either ignorance or defiance of its constituents' desires, it becomes a kind of oligarchy.

These theorists concluded that individual representatives may rightfully act only on the basis of *mandates* from their constituents—that is, instructions by their constituents to advocate in the assembly whatever views would be advocated by the constituents if they could be there. If the constituents order the representatives to support proposals that the representatives believe are wrong, they must either swallow their objections and vote as they are mandated or resign in favor of representatives who will vote as they are told. Under no circumstances should representatives vote contrary to their mandates. If they do not know their constituents' desires on any issue, they should go home and find out before they vote in the assembly.

THE INDEPENDENCE THEORY

Other theorists have argued that the kind of representative system advocated by Lilburne and Rousseau is neither possible nor desirable in a modern nation. They say that the problems of modern government are so complex and difficult that they can be understood and dealt with effectively only by people who make governing a full-time job. Constituents have to spend most of their time and energy on earning a living and cannot possibly acquire the necessary information and understanding as effectively as their representatives can. The representative assembly must therefore initiate—and not merely register— policies if the nation is to avoid disaster. This way of doing things need not convert democracy into some kind of legislative oligarchy, for the power to decide who sits in the legislature is still the basic power to rule, and that power is retained by the constituents. The classical statement of this view was made by the eighteenth-century British politician and philosopher Edmund Burke:

> *[The constituents'] wishes ought to have great weight with [the representative]; their opinions high respect; their business unremitted attention....But his unbiased opinion, his mature judgment, his enlightened conscience, he ought not to sacrifice to you, to any man, or to any set of men living....If government were a matter of will upon any side, yours, without question, ought to be superior. But government and legislation are matters of reason and judgment, and not of inclination; and what sort of reason is that in which the determination precedes the discussion, in which one set of men deliberate and another decide, and where those who form the conclusions are perhaps three hundred miles distant from those who hear the arguments?*[9]

A logical corollary of Burke's position is the proposition that representatives should exercise their judgment on public affairs independently, without giving the final decisions to their constituents. When representatives' terms end, their constituents should certainly ask whether the representatives have used their powers of independent judgment wisely, and if the constituents' conclusion is negative, the voters can and should throw the representatives out. But so long as the representatives are in office, they should use their own best judgments, not orders from their constituents, in deciding how to vote on legislative issues.

Political theorist Hanna Pitkin has pointed out that the long- standing dispute between the mandate theory and the independence theory arises from their quite different conceptions of true representation. The mandate theorists say that government in which representatives can do the opposite of what their constituents want is not truly representative. The independence theorists reply that representatives who never act on their own and serve merely as conduits for their constituents' preferences are not truly representing. It is hard to disagree with Pitkin's comment that

> *Confronted by two such arguments, one wants to say that both are somehow right. The man is not a representative if his actions bear no relationship to anything about his constituents, and he is not a representative if he does not act at all. Of course, in either case he may still be formally the representative of a certain group, but the substance is missing.*[10]

Pitkin concludes that we should not view representation as a single precise standard that, if rightly understood, will settle the controversy between the mandate and independence theories once and for all. We should view it rather as a set of limits "beyond which we will no longer accept what is going on as an instance of representation." Complete independence, whatever its desirability might be on other grounds, is certainly inconsistent with the conception of democracy set forth in this book, which requires government response to the citizens' desires. On the other hand, complete mandating is simply not possible, because constituents have no clear or strong views on many issues that come before legislators, and the legislators have no effective way of finding out what their constituents want. We should therefore be willing to accept a mixture of both theories, with the proportion of each adjusted by each legislator according to her best judgment of what is needed in particular circumstances.

Indeed, it appears that this position is the one that most legislators in modern democracies actually live by, regardless of what they may say to their constituents and colleagues. In those rare instances in which their constituents hold strong views, the legislators are well advised to go along if they wish to be re- elected. Legislators also need the cooperation of other legislators if they are to accomplish anything. They have friends and supporters in pressure groups whose help they need to continue in office. Even in the United States, legislators have parties to which they feel some loyalty and obligation, though party leaders cannot "purge" them. And the legislators themselves are not mere puppets jerked about by external pressures. They are human beings with values, perceptions, and feelings about right and wrong. Lacking the confining but simplifying all-powerful party constraints of MPs, American legislators have the freedom—and the necessity—to balance the many forces impinging on them. It is seldom easy.

THE CHANGING ROLES OF DEMOCRATIC LEGISLATURES

In the spring of 1988 a select joint committee of the U.S. Senate and House of Representatives held a series of dramatic, nationally televised hearings on what some called the "Irangate affair"—the role of National Security Adviser

Admiral John Poindexter and his aide, Marine Lieutenant-Colonel Oliver North, in using the proceeds of secret sales of arms to Iran for support of the "contra" rebels against the Marxist "Sandinista" regime in Nicaragua. The main argument made by Poindexter, North, and their supporters was that the Congress, by repeatedly changing its mind on how much and what kind of aid should be given to the contras, had made it impossible for the United States to conduct an effective policy in Central America. Accordingly, they said, it was not only the right but the duty of Poindexter and North, as assistants to the president, to do what had to be done to counter the grave threat the Sandinistas posed for other Central American countries and for the security of the United States itself.

This dispute evoked hard feelings and harsh words on both sides, but in the larger perspective, it was only the most recent renewal of one of the oldest, most fundamental, and most difficult issues about the proper extent and limits of the legislature's power in a presidential democracy. Let us see what is involved in that issue.

"TRANSFORMATIVE" VERSUS "ARENA" LEGISLATURES

How much power do modern democratic legislatures have relative to other government agencies? How much power *should* they have? As a baseline for answering these questions, political scientist Nelson W. Polsby suggests that we place actual legislatures along a continuum anchored at each end by a model of the sort discussed in Chapter 5. One model is the "transformative" legislature, which possesses "the independent capacity, frequently exercised, to mold and transform proposals from whatever source into laws." The other model is the "arena" legislature, which serves as a "formalized setting for the interplay of significant political forces in the life of a political system"—forces like the executive, the bureaucracy, political parties, and pressure groups.[11]

The authors of the eighteenth-century conception of separation of powers believed that the legislature should be the main policy-making agency in any properly organized government. After all, they reasoned, statutes and public policy are the same thing. The legislature originates, amends, and adopts all statutes, so it necessarily monopolizes the making of public policy. Thus in the debates on the new Constitution of the United States in the 1790s, most people agreed that the most powerful—and potentially the most dangerous—part of the new government would be the House of Representatives. Not only would it be a legislative body, which automatically made it very powerful, but it would also be the only body directly elected by the people and thus subject to the passions of popular majorities little restrained by consideration for minority interests.

However, political scientists today agree that, setting aside the question of whether or not democratic legislatures *should* be transformative, the fact is that most of them are much nearer the arena model. In almost every modern democratic nation during the past century, the legislature has increasingly lost the initiative in policy making to the executive and administrative agencies. The loss has perhaps been most dramatic in France, where the national assembly dominated the executive and controlled policy making in the Fourth Republic (1945–58) but has played only a minor role in the Fifth Republic (1958–). In almost all parliamentary democracies the prime ministers, cabinets, and ministries not only originate almost all major bills but also control the timing, the agendas, and in most instances the majorities of the legislature's votes.

GROWTH AS CHECKERS, REVISERS, AND OVERSEERS

It would be a great mistake to conclude from the foregoing that the legislature plays *no* significant role in modern democratic government. It certainly does play a role, but a different one from that envisioned in traditional ideas of separation of powers.

Although democratic legislatures have lost their power as initiators of policy to the executive and administrative agencies, they have greatly increased their power and activities as checkers, revisers, and overseers of policies initiated by others. After all, they still retain their formal powers to make statutes, which means that for a great many of the policies most desired by executive agencies (for example, those relating to taxes, appropriations, treaties, and statutes of all types), the legislature's consent must be won. Where, as in Great Britain, the cabinet's control of the legislature through the majority party is at maximum strength, the executive appears able to ram through whatever policies it wishes. Yet a rebellion within the majority party is always possible, and defeat by the voters at the next election is even more possible. No British cabinet can or does totally ignore resentments and discontent among its backbenchers or sharp criticisms by the opposition party—especially those that appear to represent the feelings of substantial portions of the electorate or powerful pressure groups. In Great Britain, although the objections and misgivings of legislators cannot force the executive to change its policies, they can and often do persuade the executive that a certain amount of sail trimming and course altering will make for much smoother passages for the policies they favor.

In countries like the United States and the democratic nations of Europe, where the executives' control over the legislatures is weaker than in Great Britain, the legislatures' functions of revision and criticism are even more prominent. The president of the United States may initiate most major pieces of legislation, but he must expect some of them to lose and most of them to emerge from Congress in somewhat altered form. Furthermore, at any time a congressional investigation may draw public attention to the mistakes of executive officers and administrators, object to various contracts and appointments, and in general resist the notion that the president alone has a mandate to run the government.

If there were ever any doubts that Congress is still important, they have been removed by the events of the 1970s and 1980s. Richard Nixon was re-elected president in 1972 by a landslide, but in less than two years Congress enacted legislation severely limiting presidential power to make war and substantially increasing its own budgetary powers. Then came the "Watergate" crisis. When in 1974 the certainty of impeachment by the House of Representatives and probable conviction by the Senate forced Nixon to become the first president in the nation's history to resign his office, he was succeeded by Gerald Ford. Jimmy Carter was elected in 1976. Ford's and Carter's personal integrity and adherence to the law were never in question; yet neither had much more success than Nixon in getting Congress to adopt presidential programs without major alterations. And even Ronald Reagan, who is widely regarded as one of the most powerful and successful presidents of recent times, was balked by Congress on many occasions—for example, when the House of Representatives refused to vote the money Reagan requested to support the Nicaraguan contras, and when they rejected his proposal for a constitutional amendment outlawing abortion.

American presidents, no less than British prime ministers and European premiers, are always aware that they have to deal with the legislature. And who, after all, is to say that the modern legislature's role of criticizing, revising, and overseeing the executive and the administration does not constitute as valuable a contribution to the health of democracy as the monopoly of policy making originally assigned to it?

FOR FURTHER READING

LEGISLATURES

BOYNTON, G.R., and CHONG LIM KIM, eds. *Legislative Systems in Developing Countries.* Durham, NC: Duke University Press, 1975. Role of legislatures in developing countries.

*DAVIDSON, ROGER H., and WALTER J. OLESZEK. *Congress and Its Members,* 2nd ed. Washington, D.C.: Congressional Quarterly Press, 1985. Knowledgeable description of how members of Congress do their jobs.

*FENNO, RICHARD F., JR. *Congressmen in Committees.* Boston: Little, Brown, 1973. Perceptive analysis of the nature and role of congressional committees.

HUITT, RALPH K., and ROBERT L. PEABODY. *Congress: Two Decades of Analysis.* New York: Harper & Row, Pub., 1969. Collection of essays by two leading students of Congress.

JUDGE, DAVID. *Backbench Specialization in the House of Commons.* Exeter, NJ: Heinemann Education Books, 1982. Study of changing role of nonministerial members of the House of Commons.

KING, ANTHONY, and ANNE SLOMAN. *Westminster and Beyond.* London: Macmillan, 1973. Survey of the life of MPs based on extensive interviews.

MALBIN, MICHAEL J. *Unelected Representatives: Congressional Staff and the Future of Representative Government.* New York: Basic Books, 1980. Analysis of enormous growth in size and influence of congressional staffs.

*MANN, THOMAS E., and NORMAN J. ORNSTEIN, eds. *The New Congress.* Washington, D.C.: American Enterprise Institute, 1981. Essays on the many respects in which Congress has been changing its attitudes and behaviors in recent years.

POLSBY, NELSON W. "Legislatures," in Fred I. Greenstein and Nelson W. Polsby, eds. *Handbook of Political Science.* Reading, MA: Addison-Wesley, 1975, vol. 5, pp. 257–319. Broad survey of main types of legislatures.

*SCHICK, ALLEN. *Making Economic Policy in Congress.* Washington, D.C.: American Enterprise Institute, 1983. Authoritative analysis of new congressional budget process with description of how it has been used by the Reagan administration.

SCHWARZ, JOHN E., and L. EARL SHAW. *The United States Congress in Comparative Perspective.* Hinsdale, IL: Dryden, 1976. Comparative study of legislatures.

SMITH, STEVEN S., and CHRISTOPHER J. DEERING. *Committees in Congress.* Washington, D.C.: Congressional Quarterly Press, 1984. Detailed description of the organization and operation of congressional committees.

WAHLKE, JOHN C., HEINZ EULAU, WILLIAM BUCHANAN, and LEROY C. FERGUSON. *The Legislative System.* New York: John Wiley, 1962. Pioneering study of legislative roles and attitudes in four states, based on extensive interviews.

REPRESENTATIVE–CONSTITUENT RELATIONS

BURKE, EDMUND. "Address to the Electors of Bristol," in *The Works of Edmund Burke.* New York: Harper & Brothers, 1855, vol. 1, pp. 219–22. Classic statement of the "independence" theory of representative–constituent relationships.

CAIN, BRUCE, JOHN FEREJOHN, and MORRIS FIORINA. *The Personal Vote: Constituency Service and Electoral Independence.* Cambridge, MA: Harvard University Press, 1987. Comparative study of legislators' services to constituents in Great Britain and the United States, and the consequences for their support by voters.

*FENNO, RICHARD F., JR. *Home Style: House Members in Their Districts.* Boston: Little, Brown, 1978. American styles of representation based on direct observation by a leading political scientist.

MAYHEW, DAVID R. *Congress: The Electoral Connection.* New Haven, CT: Yale University Press, 1974. Study of impact of districts on behavior of congressmen.

PITKIN, HANNA FENICHEL. *The Concept of Representation.* Berkeley: University of California Press, 1966. The most comprehensive and influential analysis of the leading theories of representation, including the mandate and independence theories.

———, ed. *Representation.* New York: Atherton, 1969. Collection of essays on theories of representation, with a useful introductory paper by the editor.

ROUSSEAU, JEAN JACQUES. *Considerations on the Government of Poland.* Several editions have been published. Classic statement of the mandate theory of representative–constituent relationships.

NOTES

[1]Lloyd N. Cutler, "To Form a Government," reprinted in Donald L. Robinson, ed., *Reforming American Government* (Boulder, CO: Westview Press, 1985), pp. 13–14.

[2]Polsby, "Legislatures," in Fred I. Greenstein and Nelson W. Polsby, eds., *Handbook of Political Science* (Reading, MA: Addison-Wesley, 1975), vol. 5, pp. 257–319.

[3]Woodrow Wilson, *Congressional Government* (Boston: Houghton Mifflin, 1885), p. 57.

[4]The title is said to be derived from the "whippers-in," who, in British fox-hunting, have the job of keeping the hunting dogs from straying from the pursuit of the fox to seek their own prey.

[5]Bruce Cain, John Ferejohn, and Morris Fiorina, *The Personal Vote: Constituency Service and Electoral Independence* (Cambridge, MA: Harvard University Press, 1987).

[6]Quoted in Peter G. Richards, *Honourable Members* (London: Faber & Faber, 1959), p. 157.

[7]Norman J. Ornstein, "The Open Congress Meets the President," in Anthony King, ed., *Both Ends of the Avenue* (Washington, D.C.: American Enterprise Institute, 1983), p. 202.

[8]William Paterson at the American Constitutional Convention of 1787, quoted in Max Farrand, ed., *Records of the Federal Convention of 1787* (New Haven, CT: Yale University Press, 1937), vol. 1, p. 561.

[9]Edmund Burke, "Address to the Electors of Bristol," in Burke, *Works,* (Boston: Little, Brown, 1871), vol. 2, pp. 95–96.

[10]Hanna Fenichel Pitkin, "The Concept of Representation," in Pitkin, ed., *Representation* (New York: Atherton Press, 1969), p. 19.

[11]Polsby, "Legislatures," pp. 277–302.

12 The Executive Process

Most Americans can name the president of the United States, and many can also name the governor of their state and perhaps one or both of the state's U.S. Senators. But the handful who can name their U.S. Representative or the people who represent them in the state legislature can claim to be exceptionally well informed.

The fact that most of us know more about top executives than top legislators does not mean that we are poor citizens. It means that for most Americans, as for most citizens of other democratic nations, executives are the "stars" of government. The people who write our newspapers and produce our television shows pay a lot more attention to executives than to legislators (with rare exceptions, like Congressman Jack Kemp and Senator Edward Kennedy) because they think that executives are more newsworthy; that is, ordinary people are simply more interested in them than they are in legislators or judges.

The fact that executives in most democratic systems normally receive more public attention than other officials is both a result and a cause of the changing roles and positions of the executives and the legislatures. We noted in Chapter 11 that in most democratic countries today, the legislatures have lost their traditional policy-initiating roles and have become mainly checkers, revisers, and overseers of policies initiated by executives. In this chapter we will take up the other side of the story: the general expansion of executive power and prestige that has occurred in just about every democratic nation.

WHAT IS AN EXECUTIVE?

THE EXECUTIVE AS THE CORE OF GOVERNMENT

It is harder to define an executive than a legislature or a court. There are two reasons for this. One is that historically the executive has always been the core of government, and what we today call legislatures and courts are, so to speak, the branches that have grown out from the original executive trunk.

As political scientist Anthony King points out, in the early years of most polities, all government power was exercised by a monarch or a ruling oligarchy. As other centers of economic and social power emerged, they wanted to limit, but not abolish, the power of government. They figured that the best way to do this was to establish new institutions or adapt old ones, make those institutions independent of the sovereign, and give them the power to check and limit the sovereign's powers. Thus, as King writes:

> *...with the passage of time legislative and judicial institutions broke off, so to speak, from the central core of government....Executives did not emerge; being the core of government, they were already there. The executive alone, on this account, does not need to be explained: it is neither more nor less than what is left of government (the greater part, as it happens) when legislatures and courts are removed. If this view is accepted, it follows that there is little point empirically in trying to identify other functions or procedures that are uniquely the executive's: The executive is simply whatever the legislature and the judicature are not.*[1]

THE TWO FUNDAMENTAL EXECUTIVE ROLES

For the foregoing reasons, it is tempting to define "executive" officers and agencies simply as those officers and agencies that are clearly not in the domain of either the legislature or the courts, but it may be a bit neater to define **executives** as *the heads of nonlegislative and nonjudicial agencies who are elected or appointed for limited terms to supervise the making and execution of government policies.* In this chapter we will not try to describe the almost countless activities and functions of the almost numberless officials and agencies that fit this definition. Instead, we will focus on the top executives in modern governments—the presidents, prime ministers, monarchs, dictators, and juntas that, as we have noted, receive so much attention from the news media.

We begin our survey by noting that in modern governments these top executive officials play one or another—and in a few instances both—of two quite distinct roles.

Chief of State

Every government has an official who serves as its **chief of state**—that is, *the official who acts as the government's formal head and spokesperson.*

Head of Government

Every government also has an official who serves as its **head of government**—that is, *the official who leads and supervises the officers and agencies who initiate and enforce the government's policies.*

The head-of-government role has much the greater impact on the making of public policy in modern governments, and so we will devote most of our attention to it in this chapter. The chief-of-state role is by no means insignificant, however, and so we will briefly review what it involves, how it is performed, and who performs it.

THE EXECUTIVE AS CHIEF OF STATE

PRINCIPAL TYPES

Since the executive has always been the core of government and the formal head of every government has been an executive, it is not surprising that several different types of chiefs of state have developed. Four are most common: hereditary monarchs, elected "monarchs," elected heads of government, and collegial executives.

Hereditary Monarchs

In 37 nations today, the chiefs of state are **hereditary monarchs**—that is, *persons who inherit their positions as chiefs of state.* They perform their functions either directly (for example, the British queen, the Belgian and Scandinavian kings, and the Japanese emperor) or indirectly, through official representatives known as governor-generals (for example, in the British Commonwealth nations of Australia, Canada, and New Zealand).

As recently as the nineteenth century, many hereditary monarchs not only served as their nations' chiefs of state but also played prominent roles in policy making, and some were close to being absolute dictators. Even today government in many "constitutional monarchies" is formally conducted in the monarchs' names. The British queen, for example, opens and dissolves Parliament, gives her assent to all acts of Parliament before they become law, appoints all ministers and judges, and awards all titles of nobility and other honors. Yet the queen, like her fellow sovereigns in Belgium, Denmark, Japan, Norway, Sweden, and the other constitutional monarchies, does these things only on the advice of her ministers, who are selected by and responsible to Parliament. Only in a few "monarchical dictatorships," such as Bhutan, Saudi Arabia, and Oman, do present-day monarchs play policy-making roles approaching those of such absolute monarchs of history as Philip V of Spain or Louis XIV of France. Constitutional monarchs, then, are chiefs of state *only;* and in this capacity they perform functions we will consider in a moment.

Elected "Monarchs"

In the twentieth century most absolute monarchs have been toppled from their thrones, and many have been replaced with more democratic regimes. In the constitutional monarchies this change has been accomplished by stripping the monarchs of all policy-making powers and leaving them only the ceremonial functions of a chief of state. Other nations have entirely abolished their monarchies and replaced them with regimes formally headed by officials, usually known as presidents, who are selected by the national legislatures or by special electoral colleges and who perform the chief-of-state functions without having any power over policy making. The presidents of Austria, West Germany, Iceland, India, and Italy are examples of such "elected monarchs."

Directly Elected Heads of Government

A few democratic countries vest the functions of chief of state in directly elected presidents who also act as heads of government. The outstanding instance of such an official is, of course, the president of the United States, but similar dual roles are performed by the presidents of Argentina, Colombia, Costa Rica, Finland, France, and Venezuela. In every such nation, the performance of these two very different roles by a single official generates many complications, some of which we will examine later.

The Swiss Collegial Executive

In only one modern democratic nation are the executive powers and functions neither divided between two officials, as in the parliamentary systems, nor concentrated in one official, as in the presidential systems. In Switzerland they are performed by a seven-member federal council, selected every four years by the two houses of the national parliament meeting in joint session. The parliament also selects a member of the council to serve for one year as president of the Confederation, and the office rotates among the members of the council in order of seniority. Ceremonial functions are performed by the member who happens to be president at the moment, but the policy-directing functions are performed by the whole council.

PRINCIPAL FUNCTIONS

Symbolic and Ceremonial

In Chapters 1 and 2 we noted that one of the greatest problems facing the people of every modern democratic nation is maintaining a society and a government in which the many interest groups can freely pursue their conflicting objectives yet continue to live together as one nation under one government. We observed that every such nation faces the ever-present possibility of civil war and disintegration and that it also contains certain social forces and institutions that encourage national unity and consensus. In the final analysis, we concluded, the citizens of the United States, like those of any democratic nation, will continue to live together in this fashion only so long as they think of themselves as *Americans* as well as African-Americans, Catholics, workers, or whatever.

Every nation has symbols and ceremonies that help to remind its citizens of their common national identity, their common achievements, and their common aspirations. No American needs to be told of the significance of the Stars and Stripes, the Pledge of Allegiance, or the Fourth of July; and every other nation has its equivalents. Most citizens of every democratic nation evidently feel the need to include among these symbols a special person who officially embodies their national identity and on great occasions speaks for the whole nation both to outside world and to the nation itself.

This need is the main reason that every nation, democratic or dictatorial, has an official chief of state (almost always a single official), and it defines the functions the chief of state must perform. When, for example, a member of the armed forces receives the nation's highest decoration—the Congressional Medal of Honor or the Victoria Cross—the president or the queen pins it on. When the nation pays tribute to its war dead, the president or the queen lays the wreath on the unknown soldier's tomb. When the Red Cross, the Boy Scouts, or some other worthy enterprise needs a boost, the president or the queen speaks on its behalf and is photographed with its leaders. In these and many other ways the president and the queen personalize and humanize that sometimes grim abstraction "the government" and remind the citizens of their common heritage and hopes.

Reigning

Constitutional monarchs and elected "monarchs" perform mainly ceremonial and symbolic functions, but they also "reign"; that is, they provide the formal channel through which power is passed in a peaceful and orderly way from one head of government to another.

In any of the parliamentary democracies, for example, when the prime minister leaves office and must be replaced by another, the chief of state formally accomplishes the transfer by summoning the new leader, who is then given the responsibility of forming a new government. On the great majority of such occasions in Great Britain and other parliamentary democracies, the monarch has no option but must summon the leader of the party that controls the national legislature.

Yet British monarchs have occasionally made real choices. The clearest instance was in 1957, when Conservative party leader Prime Minister Sir Anthony Eden suddenly resigned. Because the Conservatives held a majority in the House of Commons, Queen Elizabeth II had to replace Eden with another Conservative, but the party had never decided whether it wanted Eden's successor to be Harold Macmillan or R. A. Butler. After private consultations with her personal advisers, the queen summoned Macmillan, and he became the new prime minister. She is widely believed to have played a similar role in the choice of Sir Alec Douglas-Home over Butler in 1963. Since then, however, the Conservatives (and all other British parties) have adopted procedures that enable them to choose new leaders in a matter of hours, and so it is unlikely that any future British monarch will have as much freedom of choice as Elizabeth II had in 1957 and 1963.

SEPARATION AND MINGLING OF ROLES

During the Korean War (1950–53), President Harry S. Truman was scheduled to award a posthumous Congressional Medal of Honor to an American serviceman through his father, but the father refused to accept it, saying, "Harry Truman isn't fit to honor my son." This episode dramatized the disadvantages of combining in one executive officer the two separate roles of chief of state and head of government. Obviously, the serviceman's father was not saying that the United States itself was unfit to honor his son, but only that the individual Harry Truman—who was not only president of the United States but also the feisty head of the Democratic party, "the man who got us into the war," a Fair Dealer, and many other political things—was objectionable. In other words, the father objected to the head of government, not to the chief of state—but both officials came wrapped in the same Missouri package!

Television and radio networks face a similar problem. When an American president speaks free of charge in a national broadcast on some public issue and the opposition party demands equal free time to reply, the networks must decide whether the president was speaking as chief of state or as head of government. If he was speaking as chief of state, the opposition's demand should be denied, but if he was speaking as a *political* leader, fair play and the Federal Communications Act require that the opposition be given equal time.

It is illuminating to recall in this regard that when the English kings Charles I (1625–49) and George III (1760–1820) played active parts in policy making and strove to become the heads of their governments, they were widely and openly criticized—and indeed Charles I was executed. Now that such monarchs as Olav V of Norway and Elizabeth II of Great Britain are chiefs of state *only*, they are largely beyond public criticism and certainly are in no danger of losing their heads. Occasionally British monarchs and their consorts have been criticized for making political speeches (that is, speeches favoring certain policies), but such criticism means only that particular individuals may have stepped outside their proper roles, not that the roles themselves have become intermingled and confused, as in the United States. Herman Finer has summed up the advantages of assigning the two roles to different officials:

As a father-image, or an impersonation of the romantic, says the psychoanalyst, king or queen stands scatheless, the noble father or mother, while the politicians may be vilified and scourged. This duality is politically comfortable. On the one hand, politics might be red in tooth and claw; on the other, royalty reminds the nation of its brotherhood and their conflicts. The silk gloves are something to be thankful for.[2]

On the other hand, being chief of state is useful to the president of the United States in his role as head of government. And like his counterparts in other democracies, the president in his capacity as head of government has come to play *the* central role in the making and enforcement of public policy.

THE PRESIDENT AS HEAD OF GOVERNMENT

PRESIDENTS AND PRIME MINISTERS

Every modern democratic nation except Switzerland has a single executive officer who assumes the demanding and key role of head of government. However, the manner in which the head of government performs this role is

First among Unequals. President Bush and his new cabinet, 1989. (Source: AP/Wide World Photos.)

greatly affected by whether he or she operates in a presidential or a parliamentary democracy (see Chapter 11).

Most modern democracies, as we have seen, have parliamentary systems. In each of those systems the role of head of government is performed by a leader formally designated by the chief of state for the post but actually selected by a majority of the legislature. In some countries the leader's official title is premier or chancellor, but the most common title is prime minister. In most cases the prime minister has no fixed term of office but depends upon his or her ability to get and keep the support of a legislative majority. When that majority turns down a major bill proposed by a prime minister, or when it passes a motion of no confidence, the prime minister must resign, and the chief of state must either call a new election or appoint a new prime minister whom the legislature will support. In Great Britain, Australia, Canada, New Zealand, and the other parliamentary democracies with strong national two-party systems, the prime ministers are normally the leaders of the parties holding majorities in the main legislative house.

As we observed in Chapter 10, however, a number of democratic countries have highly fractionalized party systems, and therefore no legislator can hope to lead a party that commands a majority of the seats in the legislature, as the British prime minister usually does. In these multiparty democracies the heads of government are chosen because they can put together coalition governments, each consisting of the leaders of several parties and supported by their members in the parliament. When one or two of the participating parties decide to withdraw their support, the prime minister's government falls and is replaced by a new coalition put together by a new prime minister—who may, of course, be the same person as the old prime minister. Prime ministers in the more fractionalized party systems vary widely in the security of their tenure, their power, and their constitutional ability to direct public policy. Near one extreme we can place the Italian prime ministers, whose terms in office have averaged less than one year and who are widely regarded as much weaker than the prime ministers of the two-party nations. Near the other extreme we can place not only the British prime ministers but also the prime ministers of several highly stable though fractionalized systems, such as those of the Scandinavian countries, the Netherlands, and Israel.

A few democracies, however, vest the powers of the head of government in a chief executive called the president—that is, "the one who presides." These officials cannot be members of the legislatures and are elected to office either directly by the voters (for example, in Argentina, Brazil, Colombia, Costa Rica, Ecuador, France, Mexico, and Venezuela) or indirectly by an electoral college (for example, in Finland and the United States). The president holds office for a legally fixed term whether or not she commands the "confidence" of the legislature. As we noted in Chapter 11, the presidency of the United States is the oldest and best-known office of this type and is in many respects the prototype for the others. We turn now to a more detailed examination of its powers and problems.

AMERICAN PRESIDENTIAL ROLES

Chief of State

The first role of the president of the United States is that of chief of state, in which capacity he performs symbolic and ceremonial functions similar to those of all chiefs of state. Although the combination of roles of chief of state and head of government in the presidency generates a certain amount of confusion, it also lends the president a kind of majesty that assists him considerably in his policy-making role. When the leader of the Republican party walks into a room, there is no reason for any Democrats or even most Republicans to pay him more than the most ordinary courtesies. But when the president of the United States walks into a room, every American should stand up out of respect for the nation and the office that symbolizes the nation. Therefore, being president of the United States is bound to help the leader of any party if he knows how to use it in his political campaigns and in his dealings with Congress; and by far the greatest single asset any candidate for the presidency can have is to be the incumbent president—even though, as Gerald Ford and Jimmy Carter can testify, it does not guarantee re-election.

Chief Executive

The president formally heads most of the agencies charged with enforcing and administering acts of Congress and decisions of the national courts. In the 1980s President Ronald Reagan was responsible in one way or another for the work of 13 major departments, more than 100 bureaus, 500 offices, 600 divisions, and a host of other agencies. Together they employed a total of about 3 million people, not counting members of the armed forces. This figure included approximately 1 out of every 65 civilians in the nation, in contrast to the ratio of 1 out of every 2,000 in George Washington's time.

For many years the president's principal assistants in supervising administrative agencies were the heads of his executive departments. There are now 14 such departments: Agriculture, Commerce, Defense, Education, Energy, Health and Human Services, Housing and Urban Development, Interior, Justice, Labor, State, Transportation, the Treasury, and Veterans Affairs. Since the early 1790s, the secretaries of the executive departments have regularly met with the president and have advised him not only on matters of administration but on matters of policy as well. In their collective advisory capacity they are known as the cabinet. Some presidents have been strongly influenced by their cabinets, whereas others have given theirs only a secondary role. Abraham Lincoln, for example, used his cabinet as little more than a sounding board for his own ideas, while Dwight Eisenhower and Ronald Reagan regarded their cabinets as among their most important advisory bodies.

Over the years the cabinet has increasingly become an advisory body on policy rather than an administrative or supervisory agency, and recent presidents have turned more and more to other agencies to assist them in their

A President has a great chance; his position is almost that of a king and a prime minister rolled into one.

Theodore Roosevelt

Measured against the opportunities, the responsibilities, and the resources of others in our political system and in other nations, the powers of the Presidency are enormous. It is only when we measure these same powers against the problems of our age that they seem puny and inadequate.

Nelson W. Polsby[3]

I sit here all day trying to persuade people to do the things they ought to have sense enough to do without my persuading them....That's all the powers of the President amount to.

Harry S. Truman

Before he reached the White House Woodrow Wilson once remarked: "Men of ordinary physique and discretion cannot be Presidents and live, if the strain be not somehow relieved. We shall be obliged always to be picking our chief magistrates from among wise and prudent athletes—a small class."...This formula needs some revision. The strain is vastly greater now, with no relief in sight. If we want Presidents alive and fully useful, we shall have to pick them from among experienced politicians of extraordinary temperament—an even smaller class.

Richard E. Neustadt[4]

mammoth task of overseeing the 3 million civil servants. In 1939 Congress established the Executive Office of the President for this purpose. It now has more than 1,500 full-time employees and includes such agencies as the White House Office, the Office of Management and Budget, the Council of Economic Advisers, the Council on Environmental Quality, and the National Security Council.

Probably even more important than these official aides is the president's "kitchen cabinet"—the small group of his most trusted advisers with whom he can talk most comfortably and those upon whose candid advice he counts, whether they hold official positions or not. Any list of the people most influential in shaping recent presidents' views on policy would include several who have held minor posts or none at all—Clark Clifford and Bill Moyers (Lyndon B. Johnson), H. R. Haldeman and John Ehrlichman (Richard M. Nixon), Richard Cheney and Donald Rumsfeld (Gerald R. Ford), Hamilton Jordan, Jody Powell, Charles Kirbo, and Rosalynn Carter (Jimmy Carter), and Justin Dart, Holmes Tuttle, Joseph Coors, and Nancy Reagan (Ronald W. Reagan).

The presidency is thus no longer—if it ever was—something that the president carries around under his hat. It has become a large, complex network of public officials and private advisers performing in the president's name a wide variety of tasks only a small fraction of which he can supervise personally. In Chapter 13 we will consider further the consequences of this situation.

Chief Diplomat

The president has always dominated the formation and conduct of our foreign policy. He is the sole official channel of communication with foreign nations, and by receiving or refusing to receive official emissaries from foreign nations, he alone determines whether or not the United States formally recognizes their governments. He and his representatives negotiate all international treaties and agreements. The Constitution requires that all treaties be approved by two-thirds of the Senate, but recent presidents have concluded a great many "executive agreements"—international agreements made by the president on his own authority and not referred to the Senate for ratification. The importance of such agreements is shown by the Supreme Court's refusal to decide unequivocally whether or not they are just as binding as treaties ratified by the Senate.

Commander in Chief

The Constitution designates the president as commander in chief of all armed forces. The framers of the Constitution wrote this clause mainly to establish the cherished principle of civilian supremacy and control over the military, and some wartime presidents (such as Abraham Lincoln and Franklin D. Roosevelt) have been very active in planning strategy and even directing troop movements, whereas others (such as James Madison and Woodrow Wilson) have left such matters entirely to professional soldiers. The main significance of the president's position as commander in chief is this: the Constitution gives Congress, not the president, the power to *declare* war; but as commander in chief the president can order the armed forces to go wherever he wants them to go and do whatever he wants them to do, including making armed attacks on other nations.

And since the mid-nineteenth century a number of presidents have done just that. To mention only some recent instances, in 1950 President Truman ordered American armed forces to resist the North Korean attack on South Korea. For two years we fought a "police action" in Korea that was not a war only because Congress had not formally declared it. A decade later, in 1962, President Kennedy ordered the armed forces to "quarantine" Cuba from further shipments of Russian missiles even if it meant sinking Russian ships and starting a thermonuclear war with the Soviet Union. A series of executive decisions by presidents Eisenhower, Kennedy, and particularly Johnson increased American involvement in Vietnam, from the supplying of advice and materiel, to a full-scale war involving more than 500,000 American troops; only Congress's Tonkin Gulf Resolution of 1964 (repealed in 1970) served as a broad after- the-fact authorization. In 1983 President Reagan, at the request of some neighboring countries and in order to rescue American students from possibly being held hostage, ordered an armed invasion of the Caribbean country of Grenada. And in 1986 Reagan ordered U.S. warplanes to bomb targets in Libya to deter the government of Mu'ammar al-Qadaffi from continuing to train and finance terrorists for attacks on American and European civilians.

Until the 1970s, the Supreme Court consistently held that all these presidents were acting properly under their powers as commander in chief. In 1973, however, Congress took the first major step in over a century to limit the president's war-making powers. It passed a law setting a 60-day limit on the president's power to commit troops abroad without a prior congressional declaration of war or specific authorization for the commitment of troops. The law also provides that Congress can at any time pass a concurrent resolution (a congressional act that does not require a presidential signature to take effect) ending any unauthorized presidential commitment of combat troops. President Nixon vetoed the bill, arguing that it would endanger the nation's security by preventing him and future presidents from acting swiftly in emergencies. But Congress was more concerned with recovering its constitutional power over war and peace, and both houses overrode the veto, with consequences first experienced by President Ford (see his boxed comments) and strong objections by Ford and every president since.

Emergency Leader

In the spring of 1861, faced with the secession of a number of southern states and the imminent collapse of the Union, Abraham Lincoln ordered Fort Sumter to be provisioned and reinforced, knowing full well that his action would start a civil war. After Fort Sumter had been fired on, Lincoln—on his own authority and without prior authorization from Congress—proclaimed a naval blockade of southern ports, summoned the South Carolina militia to active service, spent government money on war material, suspended the writ of habeas corpus, and generally ignored constitutional restraints on his power. Lincoln knew that he had violated the Constitution by these acts, but in a letter to one of his critics he explained why he had done so:

> *I felt that measures otherwise unconstitutional might become lawful by becoming indispensable to the preservation of the Constitution through the preservation of the nation. Right or wrong, I assumed this ground, and now avow it. I could not feel that, to the best of my ability, I had even tried to preserve the Constitution if, to save slavery or any minor matter, I should permit the wreck of the government, country, and Constitution all together.*[5]

Lincoln believed that any government must have an emergency power—a power to do whatever is necessary to save the nation in a time of crisis. Because the president can act more swiftly than Congress, this power must necessarily be his. Lincoln's re-election in 1864 and his subsequent elevation to something approaching national sainthood suggest that the American people in his time and since have not only approved his actions in this crisis but have also

Once the consultation process began, the inherent weakness of the War Powers Resolution from a practical standpoint was conclusively demonstrated. When the evacuation of Da Nang was forced upon us during Congress's Easter recess, not one of the key bipartisan leaders of the Congress was in Washington. Without mentioning names, here is where we found the leaders of Congress: Two were in Mexico, three were in Greece, one was in the Middle East, one was in Europe, and two were in the People's Republic of China. The rest we found in twelve widely scattered states of the Union.....

On June 17, 1976, we began the first evacuation of American citizens from the civil war in Lebanon. The Congress was not in recess, but it had adjourned for the day. As telephone calls were made, we discovered, among other things, that one member of Congress had an unlisted number which his press secretary refused to divulge. After trying and failing to reach another member of Congress, we were told by his assistant that the congressman did not need to be reached. We tried so hard to reach a third member of Congress that our resourceful White House operators had the local police leave a note on the congressman's beach cottage door: "Please call the White House."

Gerald R. Ford

Source: Gerald R. Ford, *The War Powers Resolution: Striking a Balance between the Executive and Legislative Branches* (Washington, D.C.: American Enterprise Institute reprint no. 69, 1977). Copyright American Enterprise Institute.

expected his successors to take over in other crises. Subsequent presidents have at various times intervened in strikes, closed the banks, suspended stock market operations, and ordered troops to take military action abroad or suppress disorder at home. There is no doubt that in any future crisis—a great depression, a nuclear war, major domestic violence—most Americans will look to the president rather than Congress to lead them.

Party Leader

The president is also either the chief Democrat or the chief Republican. The American national parties, as we observed in Chapter 10, are mainly devices for nominating and electing presidents, to a lesser degree agencies for staffing the top political positions in the administrative agencies, and to a still lesser degree agencies for making policy in Congress. In all these operations the president is the leader of one of the two major parties. He names the chairman of its national committee, and if he is a candidate for re-election, usually dominates its national convention. Through his power of appointment he is the main dispenser of patronage. Through his appeals to party loyalty and his promises to help re-elect his party's members of Congress he can exert some modest influence over Congress. In none of these capacities is he as powerful as national party leaders in most other democratic nations, but he certainly comes much nearer to being the national leader of his party than any other person. No matter how strongly he may wish to be "nonpartisan" and "the president of all the people," he sooner or later finds himself forced to act in a partisan manner. For example, President Dwight D. Eisenhower (1953–61) at first wished to avoid any partisan campaigning in the 1954 congressional elections, but the pleas of his fellow Republicans for help became so strong that he not only issued a public blanket endorsement of all Republican candidates but also personally campaigned more actively than any president had ever done in an off-year election, at least until President Reagan's efforts in 1982 and 1986.

The party that has *lost* the presidency, however, has no equivalent leader. Its defeated presidential candidate—like the Democrats' Jimmy Carter in 1981, Walter Mondale in 1985, and Michael Dukakis in 1989—may or may not still be liked by his party, but with rare exceptions he is regarded as a political has-been. Even when the "out-party" controlled one house of Congress, as the Democrats did after the defeats of Carter and Mondale, their chief leaders (House speakers Thomas P. O'Neill and Jim Wright) made no claim to be the head of the whole party and would have been ridiculed if they had. The fact is that the out-party has *no* single recognized leader, and does not get one until it nominates its next presidential candidate.

This is in sharp contrast with British practice. After each general election the leader of the largest party in the House of Commons becomes prime minister, and the leader of the second- largest party is automatically named to a salaried official position which has no American counterpart: the Leader of Her Majesty's Loyal Opposition (a position held after 1983 by Neil Kinnock, the leader of the Labour party). It makes a major difference: If Americans want an authoritative statement from the "out-party" (that is, the party other than the one led by the president) about what it would do about tax reform or nuclear arms control, that party simply has no single leader who is authorized to speak for it—and it will not have one until it nominates its next presidential candidate; but when the British want to know the official opposition's position on any issue, Mr. Kinnock is clearly authorized—indeed, paid by public funds—to state it.

Chief Legislator

In his capacity as chief executive the president can make a great deal of law, as the term is defined in this book. He can issue proclamations, directives, regulations, and orders, all of which are legally binding on those to whom they apply and enforceable by the courts. He is generally also regarded as our chief legislator mainly because he now takes most of the initiative in the nation's statute-making process (see Chapter 11). Most of the major public bills passed by Congress are now conceived and drafted by the president's advisers in the cabinet and the administrative agencies and are steered through Congress by the president's supporters there.

Congress does not, of course, supinely comply with the president's wishes—far from it. Congress almost always revises his requests, sometimes drastically, and it not infrequently rejects them entirely. But to the extent that the American system has a single source and supervisor of an overall legislative program, the president is it.

Legislative relations between the president and Congress are more often a contest than an effort at cooperation. Congress retains the formal power to enact statutes and make appropriations, so it is far from helpless in this perennial contest. Over the years, however, various presidents have fashioned weapons to overcome Congress's constitutional advantages. They include the following:

Convincing Congress.   During his service as floor leader of the Senate Democrats (1953–60), Lyndon Johnson won a reputation as one of the most skilled legislative leaders in history. In his first years as president (1963–66) he matched—many think excelled—Franklin Roosevelt's record of inducing Congress to adopt his programs, including such major and controversial measures as the Civil Rights Act of 1964, the Voting Rights Act of 1965, and the War on Poverty. Most observers believe that his basic method was to convince members of Congress that it was in the nation's interest *and* in the members' interest to vote for his programs. He used direct conversation (the White House phone was in constant use), favors and reminders of past favors, and intimate knowledge of the politics and needs of the congressional districts and the states, which permitted him to know whom to press when, how, how hard, and how often. His phenomenal success suggests that the best way to win the legislative contest with Congress is to make them appear to be accommodations of mutual interests rather than tests of strength.

On the other hand, when Ronald Reagan took office in 1981 he not only had never served in Congress but had never held any federal office. Nevertheless, he performed what many observers regarded as a legislative miracle in his first months in office. He proposed massive slowdowns in many long-established federal programs, a massive increase in defense spending, and a substantial reduction in personal income taxes. Despite the fact that the opposition Democrats held a substantial majority in the House of Representatives, Reagan nevertheless got his program through, mainly by winning the support of nearly all the Republicans and adding to them enough defecting Democrats to construct a legislative majority.

Thus skill, not experience, is what gets the job done. But even when Congress refuses to be persuaded, the president still has some other shots in his locker.

The veto and threat of veto.   The Constitution provides that if the president vetoes (refuses to approve) an act of Congress, it can become law only if repassed by a two-thirds vote in each house. Such majorities are usually very difficult to muster. From 1789 to 1986 a total of 2,838 bills were vetoed, and only 99 (3 percent of the total) were overridden by Congress. The veto is thus a powerful negative weapon. It has also become a positive weapon, for many a

The personal touch with members of Congress does not always work for presidents. A classic case in point was the effort by President Eisenhower in 1957 to persuade Congressman Otto Passman (Democrat, Louisiana) to drop his opposition to the 1957 foreign aid bill. Rowland Evans describes what happened:

> *"It was kind of embarrassing, you understand," he told me in his musical southern voice. "I refer to it as the Passman trial. They sent for me in a long black Cadillac, I guess the first time I had ever been in one. I felt real important, which is not my usual way of feeling. When I got to the President's study at the White House, all the big shots were there. Admiral Radford and Secretary Dulles and the leaders of Congress. We had tea and little cakes and they sat me right across from the President. They went around the room asking for comments, one minute each. When they got to me, I said I would need more than one minute, maybe six or seven minutes, to tell what was wrong with their program...."*

Passman's lecture was complete with footnotes and fine print. Figures down to the last thin dime, unobligated balances in the various foreign aid accounts, carryover funds, re-obligated, de-obligated obligations, supplies in the pipe-line, uncommitted balances, and so on—in that mysterious verbal shorthand that only a man who lives and breathes foreign aid could comprehend....After...everyone left, the President turned to his staff and said, "Remind me never to invite that fellow down here again."

Source: Rowland Evans, Jr., "Louisiana's Passman: The Scourge of Foreign Aid," *Harper's Monthly*, January 1962, pp. 78–83. Used with permission.

president has let it be known through his congressional copartisans that if a particular provision is retained in a particular bill he will veto it and has thus often induced Congress to eliminate an objectionable provision.

The effectiveness of the veto is limited, however, by the fact that it is not an item veto such as those enjoyed by the governors of many American states. The president must either approve or veto a bill in its entirety and cannot veto only some items while approving others. Like many of their predecessors, presidents Ronald Reagan and George Bush have repeatedly urged the Congress to give them the power to veto particular items in bills, especially appropriations bills, but the Congresses in their presidencies, like Congresses in all previous presidencies, has refused to give the presidents this major new weapon in the continuing, and apparently permanent, conflict between the two branches.

The absence of such a power makes possible the practice of attaching "riders": Congress includes items that the president opposes in a bill (especially an appropriations bill) that he cannot afford to veto. No doubt that handy way of getting certain items past the president accounts in part for the longstanding reluctance of Congress to give the president the item veto. But even without it his veto power is a strong weapon of legislative leadership.

Party leadership. To some extent every president since William McKinley has used his position as party leader to induce Congress to follow his wishes. Some, notably Woodrow Wilson, Franklin Roosevelt, Lyndon Johnson, and Ronald Reagan, have used it with some success. As we noted in Chapter 10, however, a president can remove a rebellious congressman of his party only by defeating him in a state or district primary election. Only a few presidents have tried to do so, and they succeeded only on the rare occasions when they were able to gain the support of the local party organization. Consequently, the president's party leadership is one of his weaker weapons.

Appeal to public opinion. Wisely used, the president's most powerful weapon against balky legislators is a direct appeal to the people to pressure their representatives to support the administration's program. Most presidents have considered it a weapon of last resort, to be used only when all others have failed. If the president is more nearly in tune with the state of public opinion than Congress, and if his appeal to the people is skillful, Congress can hardly resist him, for such an appeal hits legislators where they are most vulnerable—in the ballot box. But if they have gauged the popular temper more accurately than the president, if his appeal is inept, or if he makes too many appeals on too many issues, he loses his credibility. The trick is knowing when, how, and on what issues to make such appeals. Most observers believe that Ronald Reagan's professional skills and experience as a movie actor and television host—unique in the history of the presidency—enabled him to use this weapon more effectively than any president since Franklin Roosevelt. But even Reagan did not always get the results he hoped for with his appeals on national television.

POWER AND PROBLEMS OF THE AMERICAN PRESIDENT

In trying to be an effective head of government the typical president has a number of advantages over a typical prime minister. For one thing, he is not elected by, or responsible to, the Congress (except for the impeachment device, which has been used only twice in over 200 years). For another, he has a number of independent constitutional powers (as chief executive, sole channel of communications with foreign nations, and commander in chief) that enable him to make and enforce many policies on his own without even consulting Congress, let alone winning its approval. Perhaps most important, his many roles reinforce one another and strengthen his domination of the policy-making process. As Rossiter sums it up:

> He is a more exalted Chief of State because he is also the Voice of the People, a more forceful Chief Diplomat because he commands the armed forces personally, a more effective Chief Legislator because the political system forces him to be a Chief of Party, a more artful Manager of Prosperity because he is Chief Executive.[6]

Yet there are many limitations on the president's power. As Richard Nixon learned the hard way in 1973 and 1974, the constitutional process of impeachment is still more than a quaint historical anachronism. The Constitution limits him to two elected terms in office. And when everyone knows that he cannot be president after a certain date, his legislative and party leadership are inevitably weakened to some degree. Dwight Eisenhower learned this in his second term (1957–61), Richard Nixon was forced to resign partway through his second term (1973–74), and Ronald Reagan learned the same hard lesson in his second term (1985–89), particularly in the last two years.

The Constitution also assigns large independent powers to Congress and the Supreme Court, which means that the president cannot command them; at best, he can only persuade them. When Congress denies him the legislation and appropriations he seeks, he cannot, as a prime minister can, dissolve Congress, force a new election, and get another Congress more to his liking. The Supreme Court can declare some of his acts unconstitutional (as it declared President Truman's seizure of the steel mills in 1952 unconstitutional), and though he may threaten to "pack" the Supreme Court as Franklin Roosevelt did in 1937, the widespread belief in an independent judiciary will frustrate him. He can never count upon either solid or energetic support for all his policies from all the members of his party in Congress or in the country. Despite his formal position as chief executive, as we will see in Chapter 13, he cannot even be sure that his orders to his administrative subordinates will be carried out just as he wishes.

The presidency remains the key institution of American government, but although the system allows the president many opportunities to persuade, it offers him little power to command. Here is testimony from one who knew:

In the early summer of 1952, before the end of the campaign, President Truman used to contemplate the problems of the General-become-President should Eisenhower win the forthcoming election. "He'll sit here," Truman would remark (tapping his desk for emphasis), "and he'll say, 'Do this! Do that!' *And nothing will happen.* Poor Ike—it won't be a bit like the Army. He'll find it very frustrating."[7]

THE PRESIDENCY OF FRANCE

Before 1958 the president of France was an indirectly elected "monarch" of the type described earlier in this chapter. But the Constitution of the Fifth Republic, adopted in that fateful year and still in force, converted the French presidency into a very different kind of office, and it has changed further in the years since.

The 1958 constitution provided France with a form of government that does not fit easily into either the "presidential" or "parliamentary" categories we have been using. President Valery Giscard d'Estaing (1974–81) called it "presidentialist," and most observers think it has become much more presidential than parliamentary.

The French president is directly elected by the voters for a seven-year term, and there is no limit on how many terms he can serve. He appoints the premier, theoretically with a view to the distribution of party strength in the National Assembly but actually as his personal choice. In 1958 President Charles de Gaulle chose as his first premier Michel Debré, a member of the Assembly and second in command of the new Gaullist party, the Union pour la Nouvelle Republique (UNR). But in 1962 the two men disagreed about calling a national election, and Debré resigned—not, be it noted, because the National Assembly voted against him but because *le grand Charles* dismissed him. De Gaulle replaced him with Georges Pompidou, a businessman and longtime loyal supporter, who had never been elected to public office. This choice made it clear that the premier does not hold his position because he is the number-two leader of the largest party in the assembly; he is premier because the president personally chooses him. He is, so to speak, the national commander's chief of staff. When Pompidou succeeded de Gaulle as president in 1969, he in turn selected his own man, Jacques Chaban-Delmas, rather than accepting someone picked for him by his party.

The French president has many other broad powers. He can dissolve the National Assembly and call a general election whether the premier requests it or not. Article 16 of the constitution stipulates that when the nation's independence or institutions are threatened, the president is authorized to suspend regular government procedures and take whatever measures he sees fit—as deGaulle actually did during the 1961 revolt by the French colonists in Algiers. He can submit constitutional amendments directly to the voters for popular referendums without prior authorization by the National Assembly—as de Gaulle did in the referendum of 1962, in which his constitutional amendment providing for direct popular election of the president was approved.

Some observers thought that the Fifth Republic and its presidency were the personal creations of de Gaulle and that when he left the scene both would change radically. Their expectations were put to the test in 1969. De Gaulle resigned after the voters in a referendum rejected his proposals for constitutional reform. A special election to replace him was held, Pompidou was elected, and his presidency differed some in style and policy but very little in executive power from de Gaulle's. The same has been true of the presidencies of Giscard d'Estaing and François Mitterand (1981–).

What kind of government, then, *is* the Fifth Republic? The surest way to answer this question is to ask what would happen if the president and a majority of the National Assembly had an irreconcilable difference on an important policy matter. In a pure presidential democracy each branch would nevertheless serve out its term in office. In a pure parliamentary democracy either the prime minister would resign, or a new election would be called and the new legislative majority would either reappoint the old prime minister or select a new one. What about France?

Events since 1986 have suggested something of an answer. François Mitterand, the leader of France's Socialist party, was elected president in May 1981, his party won a majority in the legislative elections a month later, and for the next five years he named a succession of Socialist leaders to be premier. In the legislative elections of March 1986, however, a coalition of conservative opposition parties won a small majority in the National Assembly. Socialist premier Laurent Fabius immediately resigned, and Mitterand asked Jacques Chirac, the principal leader of the newly dominant conservative coalition, to become the new premier.

In doing so, Mitterand acted just as the chief of state in a parliamentary democracy would act, but his term as president still had two years to run, he still had many constitutional powers independent of the assembly, and the question of whether France's system is parliamentary or presidential could not be answered finally until either the assembly or the president flatly refused to take an action demanded by the other. Such a situation had never arisen before, so no one could say with certainty what the outcome would be.

Though many people expected it, the final confrontation did not come. Both Mitterand and Chirac stopped short of forcing a showdown, and they continued as president and premier in an arrangement the French called "cohabitation" (a wonderfully French word for an informal political truce). In 1988 Mitterand ran for another seven-year term as president against Chirac and won. Chirac resigned as premier and Mitterand appointed a member of the Socialist party, Michel Rocard, as the new premier. In the parliamentary elections a few weeks later, however, the Socialists won only 48 percent of the seats in the National Assembly, so a new form of "cohabitation" began.

Under the new situation Rocard could cobble together majorities to support his legislative proposals only by getting some support from the Communists or the conservatives. The only way Rocard could be removed as premier, other than by Mitterand's dismissing him, would be for an absolute majority of all the members of the National Assembly to vote for a censure motion, which would require total cooperation between the Communists and the conservatives. So it appeared that Rocard would have to negotiate a new legislative majority for each of his proposals, but would remain in office even when he failed. So the question of the French system is closer to the American model or the British model remains unanswered.

OTHER PRESIDENCIES

Although the presidencies of other democratic systems, unlike that of France, have been modeled on the office of president of the United States, most have become even more powerful than the Washington prototype. Most have all the American president's formal powers—position as chief of state, power of appointment, direction of administration, dominance over foreign policy, command of the armed forces, a veto over legislation, and so on. Many also have some additional formal powers, notably the right to introduce bills directly in the legislature.

These other presidents are generally free of some of the American president's handicaps. For example, some have the power to make most or all administrative appointments without having to secure legislative approval. Moreover, in none of these nations does a merit system (see Chapter 13) cover as many offices as in the United States, and the president's appointment powers thus go far beyond those of his Washington counterpart. Furthermore, the legislatures of Argentina, Colombia, Mexico, Venezuela, and the rest generally pass legislation couched in much more general and permissive language than is used by the U.S. Congress. As a result, their presidents have powers to issue *decretos con fuerza de ley* (decrees having the force of law) to carry out general legislative instructions—powers that are far broader than any comparable power of the president of the United States. In some nations, indeed, the president's *potestad reglamentaria* (regulatory power) applies to substantially more of the total policy-making process than does the legislature's statute-making power.

One striking recognition of the executive power in the other presidential democracies is their longstanding limitations on presidential tenure. The United States has had such a limitation only since 1951, and France has none at all. The most common rule in the other presidential democracies is a requirement that the president cannot be re-elected until a specified period of time has elapsed after he leaves office (4 years in Colombia, 10 years in Venezuela, forever in Mexico).

The great formal powers of these other presidents are in every case equaled or exceeded by their informal powers. The presidents are considerably stronger leaders of their national parties than the man in the White House, and their control of extensive patronage enables them to keep potential rebels in line far more effectively than he can. They are no more dictators than he is, for with all their advantages, they must still persuade their legislatures to go along, and in some nations some of the time they are not very successful. Like the president of the United States they have limited tenure in office and little or no influence over the choice of their successors. But while they are in office the presidents of the Latin American democracies enjoy more weapons and fewer handicaps than the president in Washington.

THE PRIME MINISTER AS HEAD OF GOVERNMENT

STRUCTURE OF THE BRITISH EXECUTIVE

The British executive, or "the Government" as it is often called,[8] is composed of three interrelated but distinct sets of officials: the prime minister, the ministry, and the cabinet. It is formed as follows:

First among Equals? British prime minister Margaret Thatcher and her new cabinet, 1987. (Source: British Information Services.)

The Prime Minister

The first stage in the formation of a British executive (or "Government") occurs when the monarch summons one of her subjects and asks her to become prime minister and form a government. In most instances the monarch has no option but must pick the leader of the party holding the largest number of seats in the House of Commons (though, as we noted earlier, on a few occasions when the leading party has not designated a leader the monarch has exercised some choice). The prime minister must be not only a member of Parliament but also, since 1902, a member of the House of Commons. Note the difference between the two systems: in the presidential democracies the chief executive *cannot* be a member of the legislature; in the parliamentary democracies the chief executive *must* be a member of the legislature.

The Ministry

The prime minister automatically becomes First Lord of the Treasury (a paid office with no administrative duties) and then proceeds to fill the other top and secondary executive posts by making recommendations to the monarch, which are invariably accepted. These posts include the top ministers—the heads of the twenty ministries (which are equivalent to American executive departments): for example, the Foreign Office, the Home Office, and the Ministry of Defense. They also include some additional ministers without specific departmental duties, such as the lord privy seal and the chancellor of the

Duchy of Lancaster; and some with duties, such as the economic secretary to the treasury and the minister of state in the Foreign Office. In addition to these top officials there are also the parliamentary secretaries, who serve as deputies to the ministers of the various departments; several law officers (such as the attorney general and the solicitor general); and the whips (see Chapter 11). These top executives, amounting to about one hundred officials in all, plus the prime minister constitute the ministry, or the Government.

In making recommendations to the monarch, however, the prime minister does not have an absolutely free hand. In the first place, with rare exceptions, every member of the ministry must be a member of Parliament, and most important ministers must be members of the House of Commons. In the second place, most members of the ministry and all the important members must be leaders of the majority party—except in coalition or national (all-party) governments such as those established during times of crisis (for example, from 1915 to 1922 and from 1940 to 1945). In the third place, the prime minister must find posts for the other top leaders of the parliamentary party regardless of how she feels about them personally, and must also make sure that no major faction of the party feels left out.

The Cabinet

The ministry never meets or deliberates as a body. That kind of activity is left to the cabinet, which consists of those members of the ministry whom the prime minister regularly invites to consult with her as a group. Its size and composition change from time, in accordance with the prime minister's wishes, but normally it has between 18 and 23 members. (Margaret Thatcher's new cabinet in 1987 had 21 members.) It includes all the top ministers both with and without departmental duties. It has thus been called "a select committee of Parliament" but it is better described as "a committee of the top leaders of the majority party."

THE CABINET'S STATUS, FUNCTIONS, AND POWERS

Some commentators on the British system emphasize the convention according to which the cabinet, like the ministry and the prime minister, remains in power only as long as it "commands the confidence of the House of Commons"—that is, as long as the House does not vote down any measure that the cabinet regards as important and does not pass a motion of no confidence in the whole cabinet or any of its members. This emphasis, however, is misleading. Since 1894 only four prime ministers and cabinets have resigned because of adverse votes in the House (Lord Rosebery in 1895, Stanley Baldwin in 1924, Neville Chamberlain in 1940, and James Callaghan in 1979), and the discipline and cohesion of British parties are so strong that such episodes are highly unusual.

The cabinet cannot and does not totally ignore the feelings of the House, of course, but it can usually count on as much of its full statutory five-year tenure of office as it wishes.

Although a number of its members have administrative and supervisory duties, the cabinet is primarily a policy-making and legislation-designing body. Its members and their advisers conceive, draft, and introduce most of the major public bills in Parliament. They defend government policies in parliamentary debate, guide government legislation through the various parliamentary stages, decide which amendments to accept and reject, and generally control what Parliament does.

The dominance of the cabinet over Parliament is thus far greater than that of the president over Congress. There are many reasons for this, some of which, such as the great cohesion and discipline of British parties, we have already noted. We should add one more: the prime minister's power to dissolve Parliament and force a general election. According to British law, a general election for all the members of the House of Commons *must* be held every five years—but it *may* be held at any time earlier than that chosen by the prime minister. Thus in Great Britain the dates of elections are not fixed by law and known in advance, as they are in the United States. Indeed, one of the favorite games for British politics buffs is guessing when the prime minister is going to call the next general election. When the prime minister asks the monarch to dissolve Parliament, she must do so, and a general election for a new House of Commons must be held forthwith. This requirement means, of course, that should the House kick over the traces and deny the prime minister and cabinet some important piece of legislation, the prime minister need not meekly resign—or carry on in office even though she cannot get her policies adopted. She can call a new election. From the standpoint of the rebel MPs in her party, the trouble with a new election is that the opposition party might win. So a vote against one's party can amount to a vote to put the other party in power. Most MPs are unwilling to go quite that far in their occasional rebellions. Most analysts believe that the powers of the prime minister to withhold the party label from rebellious MPs and, even more, to dissolve Parliament whenever she wishes are the cabinet's basic and nearly irresistible weapons in getting the House of Commons to follow their leadership.

THE PRIME MINISTER AND THE CABINET

Not so long ago it was fashionable to say that the position of the prime minister in the cabinet is that of *primus inter pares* ("first among equals"), much like that of the chairperson of the board of directors of a business corporation. However, most present-day commentators believe that, though this description may have been valid years ago, the modern prime minister has become the dominant figure within the cabinet and therefore within the whole British system of government. The prime minister, and not the cabinet, has the power to ask the monarch to dissolve Parliament and to appoint and dismiss ministers, judges, and diplomats. The prime minister, and not the cabinet, represents Britain at international summit conferences of heads of government. And it is the prime minister who determines who sits in the cabinet; the cabinet does not determine who is prime minister.

The present dominance of the prime minister is the result of three main factors. First, the increasing centralization, discipline, and cohesion of British political parties have given their leaders increasing control not only over the parties' rank and file but also over the second-echelon leaders who make up the cabinet and the ministry. And the majority party's top leader is always the prime minister.

Second, the combination of universal suffrage and modern mass communications has increasingly converted British general elections into contests for the office of prime minister. The campaigns are centered mainly on the personalities and qualifications of the two rival party leaders, who do most of the campaigning for their respective parties. Most people still vote mainly for the party they prefer or against the party they cannot stand. But British voters today are less devoted to parties than they used to be, and so the personal popularity or unpopularity of each party's leader is increasingly important in British voters' decisions about which party to vote for in particular elections. For example, most commentators said that in the 1983 general election the Labour party was severely handicapped by the unprecedented unpopularity of its leader, Michael Foot, while the much better performance by Foot's successor, Neil Kinnock, in the 1987 general election was the main reason for the increased Labour vote.

The prime minister's position is well summed up by Lord Robert Cecil:

> *I should say that if you really looked into the real principal of our constitution now, it is purely plebiscital, that you have really a plebiscite by which a particular man is selected as Prime Minister, he then selects the Ministry himself, and it is pretty much what he likes, subject to what affects the rule that he has to consider— namely, that he must not do anything that is very unpopular.*[9]

Finally, the same kinds of economic and military crises that have, as we have noted, taken power away from the collegial body of Congress and given it to the president as "emergency leader" have also taken power away from the collegial body of the British cabinet and given it to the prime minister as "emergency leader."

The prime minister is thus in some respects even more powerful than the president, particularly in her ability to lead her party and the legislature. But such power is certainly not enjoyed by the heads of government in *all* parliamentary systems, as the following discussion will show.

PRIME MINISTERS IN COALITION GOVERNMENTS

The British prime minister's power is firmly rooted in her leadership of a disciplined and cohesive political party that holds a majority of the seats in the House of Commons. As long as she commands its loyalty, she need not worry about how the opposition votes: It will usually vote against her proposals but will not have enough votes to defeat them. Her main political concern is that the voters will approve her government's policies and performance, and will renew its mandate to govern at the next general election.

In the democratic nations with more fractionalized party systems (see Chapter 10), however, one party rarely if ever wins a majority of the legislative seats, and so the governments are necessarily coalitions of several parties. The prime minister (or premier) of such a coalition cannot rely solely upon his own party's backing, for he needs the votes of the other coalition members to stay in office. His first concern must thus be what his coalition partners, rather than the voters, think of his actions and proposals.

Inside the Revolving Door. Italian premier Ciriaco de Mita, 1988. (Source: Italian Embassey, Washington, D.C.)

How does this concern affect the first prerequisite for effective leadership—the ability to stay in office? The answer evidently depends upon the nature of the other parties in the coalition rather than upon the degree of fractionalization in the party system as a whole. Evidence for this conclusion is presented in Table 12.1, which shows that executive tenure in modern democratic countries is far from a simple reflection of party fractionalization.

For the most part, the figures in Table 12.1 show what we would expect: The most fractionalized party systems (Belgium, Denmark, and Italy) have had the most changes in the heads of government, and the least fractionalized systems (New Zealand, Canada, the United States, Great Britain) have had far fewer. On the other hand, Israel, which ranks fourth in fractionalization, has had fewer changes than Great Britain; and Ireland, which has a lower fractionalization score than Norway or France, has changed its head of government much more frequently. The fewest changes of all have taken place in West Germany, which ranks in the middle of the fractionalization scores.

Since 1960, Italy has had the dubious honor of having the shortest executive tenures. All postwar Italian premiers except two have been members of the Christian Democratic party, but that party is organizationally weak and internally divided by strong ideological disagreements among its various factions. Moreover, as we saw in Chapter 10, all votes in Parliament are taken by secret ballot, and so it is impossible for the Christian Democratic party's leaders to know just which of its parliamentarians are disobeying their orders and voting

TABLE 12.1.   Party Fractionalization and Executive Tenure, 1945–87

Nation	Fractionalization Ranking	Mean Legislative Party Fractionalization, 1945–87*	Changes in Head of Government 1945–87**
Belgium	1	.3464	24
Denmark	2	.3138	15
Italy	3	.2357	30
Israel	4	.2299	6
Norway	5	.2175	8
West Germany	6	.1862	2
France	7	.1527	5
Ireland	8	.1152	12
Australia	9	.0812	4
Austria	10	.0760	4
Great Britain	11	.0348	7
United States	12	.0204	5
Canada	13	.0161	5
New Zealand	14	.0069	5

*Difference between mean party fractionalization score and .5000 (see Chapter 10)

**Changes from one party to another or, in Belgium and Italy, from one faction of a coalition leading party to another; changes within the same party caused by death or resignation rather than by political developments are not counted.

Source: Keesing's Record of World Events.

to throw out their coalitions. The result has been a Byzantine maze of factional struggles within and between parties in the ruling coalition and a resultant rapid-fire succession of premiers and cabinets. The details are given in the box.

The position of the premier in a coalition government seems to depend upon a few basic factors. If the legislative seats are divided among many little parties instead of a few big ones, he will have that many more party leaders to find ministerial offices for and keep happy. If there are deep ideological divisions among the principal parties—and, even worse, among the factions of his own party, Italian-style—he will have to construct his program very carefully. If the party and factional leaders dislike one another personally, he will have to handle them with special tact. Being premier of such a government is not the most desirable executive position in the world, though no nation seems to suffer any shortage of politicians trying to fill it.

THE EXECUTIVE IN NONDEMOCRATIC SYSTEMS

We need not linger long over the similarities and differences between executive roles in democratic systems and those in nondemocratic systems. In almost every Western-style democracy, as we have seen, the executive has become the

Communist Heads of Government.

Deng Xiaoping, Chairman of the Central Advisory Committee of the Communist Party of the People's Republic of China. (Source: AP/Wide World Photos.)

Mikhail S. Gorbachev, First Secretary of the Communist Party of the Soviet Union. (Source: AP/Wide World Photos.)

REVOLVING DOORS IN ROME

From 1979 to 1988, Italy had more changes in its heads of government than any other democratic country. But even that statement does not tell the whole story. The details were these:

January 31, 1979: The five-party coalition government led by Christian Democratic premier Giulio Andreotti falls when the Communists decide to pull out. President Sandro Pertini asks Andreotti to form another government; he tries but cannot get the necessary support in Parliament. Pertini then asks Ugo La Malfa, leader of the small Republican party, to form a government. La Malfa also fails. Pertini next asks Andreotti to try again, and on March 21, Andreotti manages to get enough support for a three- party coalition government of Christian Democrats, Social Democrats, and Republicans.

March 31, 1979: The new Andreotti government loses a vote of confidence and resigns. Pertini dissolves Parliament and calls for new elections. The elections are held on June 3–4; the Christian Democrats get 38 percent of the seats to the Communists' 30 percent; a total of twelve parties get at least one seat.

July 2, 1979: Pertini asks Andreotti to form a new government; he tries but the Socialists refuse to join, so Andreotti gives up.

July 9, 1979: Pertini asks Bettino Craxi, leader of the Socialist party, to form a government; Craxi fails. Pertini then asks Filippo Pandolfi to try, but he also fails.

August 5, 1979: Pertini asks Francesco Cossiga, another Christian Democrat, to form a government, and he puts together a coalition of Christian Democrats, Social Democrats, and Liberals. It is a minority government, but the Socialists agree not to vote against it—for a while.

March 19, 1980: The Cossiga government resigns after the Socialists end their truce. Pertini asks Cossiga to form another government.

April 3, 1980: Cossiga forms a new government, this one including Socialists.

September 27, 1980: The second Cossiga government falls when its economic reform bill is defeated. Pertini asks Arnaldo Forlani, yet another Christian Democrat, to form a new government. Forlani succeeds, putting together a coalition of Christian Democrats, Socialists, Social Democrats, and Republicans.

May 26, 1981: The Forlani government resigns after a scandal about some of its leaders' membership in Masonic lodges. Pertini asks Forlani to form a new government; Forlani tries but fails.

June 28, 1981: After a long hiatus, a new government is formed by Giovanni Spadolini, the leader of the small Republican party; he forms a coalition of Christian Democrats, Socialists, Social Democrats, Liberals, and Republicans and becomes the first non-Christian Democratic premier since 1945.

November 13, 1982: After 17 months in office the Spadolini government resigns when the Christian Democrats and Socialists quarrel. Pertini asks Christian Democrat Amintore Fanfani to form a new government, and he puts together a coalition like Spadolini's but without the Republicans.

April 29, 1983: The Fanfani government resigns when the Socialists withdraw from the coalition. Pertini asks Tommaso Morlino to form a new government; Morlino tries but fails. Pertini calls for new elections.

June 26–27, 1983: In the elections the Christian Democrats drop from 38 to 33 percent of the seats, the Communists keep their 30 percent, and the Socialists rise from 9.8 percent to 11.4 percent. Pertini asks Craxi to form a government, and after weeks of haggling he does so.

August 4, 1983: Craxi takes office as the first Socialist premier since World War II, with a government made up of Christian Democrats, Socialists, Social Democrats, Liberals, and Republicans.

March 3, 1987: After holding office longer (3 years, 7 months) than any Italian head of government since Mussolini, Craxi resigns.

April 4, 1987: After over a month of negotiations, Amintore Fanfani forms a new government.

June 6, 1987: A general election is held, the Christian Democrats increase their percentage of the seats from 35 to 38, the Communists drop from 31 to 28, and the Socialists gain from 12 to 15.

July 29, 1987: After more tortuous negotiations, Christian Democrat Giovanni Goria is sworn in as premier.

February 10, 1988: After losing on several votes on the 1988 budget, Goria resigns, but President Cossiga persuades him to stay on until the budget is finished.

March 11, 1988: After getting the budget through, Goria resigns after losing a vote on nuclear power.

April 13, 1988: After more negotiations, Ciriaco de Mita, leader of the anti-Goria faction of the Christian Democrats, is sworn in as premier.

Final score for the nine years:
Heads of government resigning: 11
Persons asked to form new governments: 17
Persons unable to form new governments: 7
Persons forming new governments: 10
General elections: 3

single most powerful agency for making government policy. But we have also seen that the executive is far from being all-powerful. Even the most powerful democratic chief executive (the president of the United States? of France? of Venezuela?) must operate within very real limits set by legislatures, courts, opposition parties, factions in his own party, pressure groups, and ultimately the electorate.

The nondemocratic political systems have at least one trait in common, whether they be the Communist systems of China and Eastern Europe or the one-party regimes or military dictatorships of Africa, Asia, and Latin America. In each the executive agency *is* the government. Indeed, as we have seen, no fewer than 20 nations in 1985 had no legislatures whatever. In this sense, then, the core agency of *all* governments is the executive, not the legislature; for, while a number of nondemocratic regimes operate with no legislatures, *no* regime, democratic or nondemocratic, operates without an executive. To be sure, the formal constitutional chief executives of some nondemocratic regimes may be only the chief errand boys of the all-powerful parties or ruling cliques. But the point is that, as we saw in Chapter 11, their legislatures are essentially sounding boards and cheering sections for the dictators, party leaders, or ruling juntas. And, as we will see in Chapter 14, their courts of law operate as arms of the executives, not as checks upon them. Accordingly, Western political scientists simply do not bother much with questions of the power of executives relative to the legislatures and courts in the nondemocratic nations.

Perhaps the most interesting comparative observation is that in many modern governments, democratic and authoritarian alike, a great deal of government policy is made in the *name* of the executive or legislature—but in fact the policies are made by "nonpolitical" public employees presumably hired to carry out the wishes of the "political" executives and legislatures. These employees have a number of labels—civil servants, bureaucrats, *apparatchiks*, and the like. But whatever they are called, they play powerful—though often obscure—roles in determining what rules their governments actually impose on the people under their jurisdiction. We will examine their roles in the next chapter.

FOR FURTHER READING

PRESIDENTS

*ANDREWS, WILLIAM G. *Presidential Government in Gaullist France.* Albany: State University of New York Press, 1982. Study of the formative years of the unique French presidency under the Fifth Republic.

*EDWARDS, GEORGE C., III, and Stephen J. Wayne. *Presidential Leadership.* New York: St. Martin's Press, 1985. Comprehensive survey of presidential leadership in the light of Ronald Reagan's first term.

*FENNO, RICHARD F., JR. *The President's Cabinet.* Cambridge: Harvard University Press, 1959. Authoritative study of the cabinet's varying importance under different presidents.

*HARGROVE, ERWIN C., and MICHAEL NELSON. *Presidents, Politics, and Policy.* New York: Random House, 1984. Survey of current operation of the presidency and its role in policy making, with special emphasis on changes under the Reagan administration.

*HESS, STEPHEN. *Organizing the Presidency.* Washington, D.C.: Brookings Institution, 1976. Description and analysis of how various presidents have organized their assistants and advisers.

HERRING, E. PENDLETON. *Presidential Leadership.* New York: Holt, Rinehart & Winston, 1940. Classic study, based mainly on observation of Franklin Roosevelt's presidency.

KELLERMAN, BARBARA. *The Political Presidency.* New York: Oxford University Press, 1986. Study of recent presidents' strategies for getting their policies adopted.

KERNELL, SAMUEL. *Going Public: New Strategies of Presidential Leadership.* Washington, D.C.: Congressional Quarterly Press, 1986. Study of presidential appeals to public opinion, with special emphasis on the Reagan administration.

*KING, ANTHONY, ed. *Both Ends of the Avenue.* Washington, D.C.: American Enterprise Institute, 1984. Essays focusing on the changing relationships between the president and Congress.

LIGHT, PAUL C. *Vice-Presidential Power.* Baltimore: Johns Hopkins University Press, 1982. Exploration of the increasing importance of the vice presidency in governing and as a steppingstone to the presidency.

LOWI, THEODORE J. *The Personal President: Power Invested, Promise Unfulfilled.* Ithaca: Cornell University Press, 1984. Stimulating discussion of the conversion of the presidency into a direct relationship with the people, with adverse consequences for the governing system.

*NEUSTADT, RICHARD E. *Presidential Power: The Politics of Leadership from FDR to Carter.* New York: John Wiley, 1979. An updated version of one of the most influential studies of the presidency.

*PAGE, BENJAMIN I., and MARK P. PETRACCA. *The American Presidency.* New York: McGraw-Hill, 1983. Comprehensive description of the modern presidency, set in a theoretical framework explaining the powers and limitations of the office apart from the persons who occupy it.

*POLSBY, NELSON W. *Congress and the Presidency,* 4th ed. Englewood Cliffs, NJ: Prentice-Hall, 1986. The best short discussion of the relationship between the president and Congress.

*REEDY, GEORGE R. *The Twilight of the Presidency,* rev. ed. New York: New American Library, 1987. Lyndon Johnson's press secretary analyzes changes in the presidency from the Vietnam War era to the Reagan administration.

*ROCKMAN, BERT A. *The Leadership Question: The Presidency and the American System.* New York: Praeger, 1985. Analysis of presidential leadership in the fragmented American political system of the 1980s.

PRIME MINISTERS

CARTER, BYRUM E. *The Office of Prime Minister.* Princeton: Princeton University Press, 1956. Analysis of the prime minister's political positions and governmental powers.

*KING, ANTHONY, ed. *The British Prime Minister,* 2nd ed. Durham, NC: Duke University Press, 1985. Excellent collection of essays on the British executive.

————, "Executives," in Fred I. Greenstein and Nelson W. Polsby, eds. *Handbook of Political Science,* vol. 5. pp. 173–256. (Reading, MA: Addison-Wesley, 1975. Best broadly comparative analysis available, with a useful bibliography appended.

*MACKINTOSH, JOHN P. *The British Cabinet,* 2nd ed. New York: Barnes and Noble, 1968. Analysis stressing the "presidentialization" of the prime minister's position and the weakening of the cabinet's powers.

*ROSE, RICHARD, and EZRA N. SULEIMAN, eds. *Presidents and Prime Ministers.* Washington, D.C.: American Enterprise Institute, 1980. A comparative study of heads of government in Great Britain, Canada, France, West Germany, Italy, Norway, Spain, and the United States.

NOTES

[1]Anthony King, "Executives," in Fred I. Greenstein and Nelson W. Polsby, eds., *Handbook of Political Science* (Reading, MA: Addison-Wesley, 1975), vol. 5, pp. 181–82.

[2]Herman Finer, *Governments of Greater European Powers* (New York: Holt, Rinehart & Winston, 1956), pp. 189–90.

[3]Nelson W. Polsby, *Congress and the Presidency,* 4th ed. (Englewood Cliffs, NJ: Prentice-Hall, 1986), p. 84.

[4]Richard E. Neustadt, *Presidential Power* (New York: John Wiley, 1960), p. 195.

[5]Abraham Lincoln, letter to A. G. Hodges, April 4, 1864, quoted in Louis Brownlow, *The President and the Presidency* (Chicago: Public Administration Service, 1949), p. 58.

[6]Clinton Rossiter, *The American Presidency* (New York: Harcourt Brace Jovanovich, 1956), p. 25.

[7]Neustadt, *Presidential Power,* pp. 9–10, emphasis in the original.

[8]British political commentators customarily use the term "the Government" to denote the entire body of politicians who for the moment control the making of public policy. It includes 20 or so senior ministers who are members of the cabinet, 30 or so senior ministers who are not members of the cabinet, and 50 or so junior ministers. There is no exact American equivalent to the term, but "the Administration" comes close.

[9]Quoted in Herman Finer, *Theory and Practice of Modern Government*, rev. ed. (New York: Holt, Rinehart & Winston, 1949), p. 363. If Lord Cecil were writing today, of course, his pronouns would have to take account of the fact that since 1979 the British prime minister has been a woman.

13 The Administrative Process

For all but a handful of citizens in any advanced industrial society, the *real* government consists of what political scientists call *administrators* or *bureaucrats*, not the top-level legislators, executives, and party leaders we have been discussing up to now. For one thing, 99 percent of all the people who work for the government fall in this class. For another thing, members of Congress, members of Parliament (MPs), presidents, and prime ministers are not real people; rather, they are media figures, like movie stars and television anchors, in the sense that we never meet them face to face or deal with them directly. We know them only from what we see on television or read in the newspapers.

On the other hand, almost all of us have bought stamps at a post office or taken a test for a driver's license, and so we know first hand what post office clerks and driving examiners look like and how they do their jobs. Governmentally speaking, they, and not most of the loftier public officials discussed in this book, are "where the rubber meets the road."

Accordingly, in this chapter we ask: What kind of people work in government jobs? How are they hired and fired? How good are they? Are they merely flunkies who carry out the orders of the higher-ups, or do they make a lot of decisions on their own?

Political scientists usually begin their answers to these questions by making some important distinctions.

THE DISTINCTION BETWEEN EXECUTIVES AND ADMINISTRATORS

IN FUNCTIONS

During the formative period of the U.S. Constitution, most Americans believed in the traditional conception that the governing process is divided into three distinct kinds of activity: law making, law enforcement, and law adjudication. They also believed that power over law enforcement should be assigned exclusively to the executive, and that the executive should confine itself largely to enforcing policies adopted by the legislature.

In Chapter 12 we observed that since the nineteenth century, the executives of most democratic nations have acquired ever-increasing influence over policy. Toward the end of that century a number of political scientists, notably Woodrow Wilson and Frank J. Goodnow, recognized that the traditional description of the executive as an enforcer rather than an initiator of policy no longer fit the facts. Yet they wished to make some kind of distinction between policy-making and policy-enforcing officials, and they also wished to reconcile the ideal of a permanent, professional civil service with the ideal of a responsive democratic government. Consequently, they proposed a distinction between "political" (that is, policy-making) officials, including the president and other top executives, and "administrative" (that is, policy-enforcing) officials.

We will return to the Wilson-Goodnow formula in a moment, but we should note here that it underlies the distinction many political scientists continue to make between executives and administrators: **Executives** are *political heads of executive agencies who are elected or appointed for limited terms to initiate policies and direct the work of administrators.* **Administrators** are *persons appointed to executive agencies to enforce laws and carry out policies and whose tenure and promotion depend on professional merit rather than political affiliation.* We will learn that these distinctions become blurred in real life, but they will do as a place to start.

IN SELECTION AND TENURE

Although some political scientists today continue to distinguish between executives and administrators (or "civil servants," as administrators are often called) in the foregoing manner, most believe that because many administrators play major roles in policy making, the politics–administration distinction is meaningless. However, few go on to argue that *all* public officials should be replaced whenever a majority of the voters transfer their support from one political party to another. Most continue to believe, with Wilson and Goodnow, in a permanent, professional civil service loyally doing the bidding of "political" legislators and executives—but not to be hired, promoted, or fired because of their party affiliations or policy preferences.

WHAT ABOUT BUREAUCRACY?

Many political scientists and sociologists use the term *bureaucracy* in a neutral sense, as a synonym for *civil service*. They follow the great German social theorist Max Weber in thinking of bureaucracy as a large and complex organization with fixed and official areas of jurisdiction, a hierarchical system of centralized authority, and a body of officials with special professional skills who follow systematic general rules and procedures.

But that is not what many people mean by *bureaucracy*. To them, it is a kind of congenital government disease, the leading symptoms of which are the addiction of public officials to tortuous procedures, buck-passing, senseless and rigid rules, rudeness to citizens, and operating at glacial speed—in short,

Government "Red Tape." A line of passport applicants. (Source: AP/Wide World Photos.)

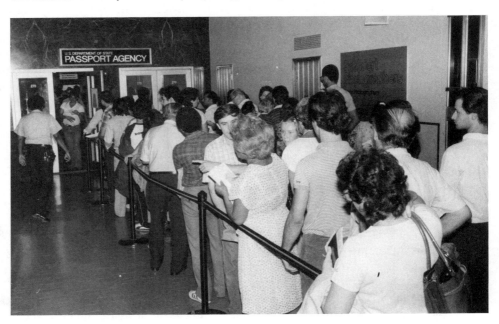

everything summed up in the term *red tape*. We will therefore stick to the more neutral terms *administration* and *civil service* to denote the parts of government with which we are concerned in this chapter.

FORMAL STATUS OF ADMINISTRATIVE AGENCIES

SIZE

In terms of the number of people employed, the administrative agencies constitute by far the largest element of any modern government. Table 13.1 shows the number of civilians (persons serving in the armed forces are excluded) employed in the various branches and agencies of the United States federal government in 1986.

The figures in Table 13.1 show that the overwhelming majority of all federal employees work for the executive branch and that well over half work for just two huge agencies: the Department of Defense and the U.S. Postal Service. The grand total of 3,022,189 federal employees constitutes only 3 percent of all gainfully employed civilians, but when state and local government employees are added the proportion is 16 percent. Some countries with less elaborate structures of regional and local government than the United States employ smaller proportions of their labor forces in civil service jobs; in the early 1980s, for example, government employees constituted only about 6 percent of the gainfully employed in Great Britain and 15 percent in France.

TABLE 13.1.   Civilian Employment in the U.S. Federal Government, 1986

Branch or Agency	Number	Percentage of Total
Legislative branch	36,490	1.2
Judicial branch	18,966	0.6
Executive branch	2,966,773	98.2
Total	3,022,189	100.0
Executive Agencies		
Dept. of Defense	1,067,974	36.1
U.S. Postal Service	790,960	26.5
Veterans Administration	240,423	8.1
Dept. of the Treasury	135,628	4.6
Dept. of Health & Human Services	133,842	4.5
Dept. of Agriculture	113,147	3.8
All others	484,799	16.4
Total executive employees	2,996,773	100.0

Source: Statistical Abstract of the United States 1988 (Washington: D.C.: Bureau of the Census, 1988), Table 501, p. 309.

STRUCTURE

A few decades ago most students of public administration believed in certain principles of organization—certain correct ways of "interrelating the subdivisions of work by allotting them to people who are placed in a structure of authority, so that the work may be coordinated by orders of superiors to subordinates, reaching from the top to the bottom of the entire enterprise."[1] Today most political scientists are dubious about the scientific validity or practical applicability of these principles, but many continue to believe that most administrative agencies should be organized in accordance with two principles: the principle of hierarchy and the principle of separation of staff and line functions.

The Principle of Hierarchy

According to this principle, the people in any administrative agency should be formally related to one another in a clear chain of command reaching from top to bottom and a line of responsibility from bottom to top. All employees know just who their superiors, equals, and inferiors are and therefore to whom they may give orders and from whom they must take them. Often mentioned as models are the organization of any modern army and the clerical hierarchy of the Roman Catholic Church. The principle is illustrated by the organization of the U.S. Department of the Interior shown in Figure 13.1.

The Principle of Separation of Staff and Line Functions

This principle is based on the idea that every agency performs two basic types of functions. The U.S. Department of the Interior, for example, supervises the care of over 500 million acres of federally owned land, monitors health and safety procedures in the nation's mines, promotes the development, conservation, and use of fish and wildlife resources, preserves the nation's scenic and historic areas, supervises the relations with our former trust territories in Micronesia, and so on. These are its "line" functions. But in addition, the department, if it is to be run efficiently, must also perform a number of "staff" or "housekeeping" functions, such as hiring and firing, determining promotions and pay increases, and budgeting. Many writers on public administration believe that these two types of activities should be performed by separate sets of agencies, each reporting to the agency's head but each independent of the other.

The point—and its complications—are also illustrated by the official organization chart of the Department of the Interior shown in Figure 13.1, which shows that the Department of the Interior's organization sticks closely to the two principles. The hierarchy is clear. The secretary is the head, the undersecretary is his chief subordinate, and the staff agency heads, such as those for the Office for Equal Opportunity, the Office of Hearings and Appeals, and the Office of Territorial Affairs, all report directly to the undersecretary. Each of

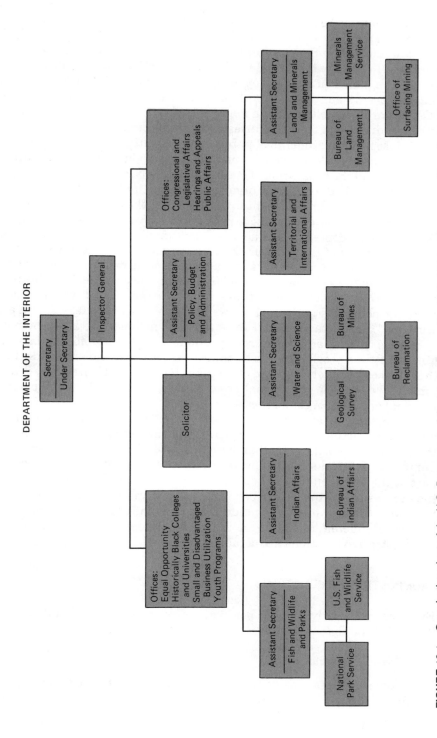

DEPARTMENT OF THE INTERIOR

FIGURE 13.1. Organization chart of the U.S. Department of the Interior(Source: The United States Government Manual 1984/85 (Washington, D.C.: Office of the Federal Register, 1984), appendix C, p. 833.)

the line agencies reports to an assistant secretary, who in turn reports to the undersecretary; for example, the heads of the U.S. Fish and Wildlife Service, the National Park Service, and the Heritage Conservation and Recreation Service all report to the Assistant Secretary for Fish and Wildlife and Parks.

But a glance at almost any of the other organization charts in the *United States Government Manual* will show that the lines between staff and line agencies are often blurred, and many agencies bypass the assistant secretaries to report directly to the secretaries and undersecretaries.

Most modern students of public administration recognize that the practical problems of real-life agencies usually force deviations from the principles of hierarchy and the separation of staff and line functions. And they say that what really matters is the informal organization, not the formal organization.

Let us pause for a moment to see just what they mean. An agency's formal organization is the one publicly prescribed by written acts of Congress and written rules adopted by the agency—for example, the formal organization of the Department of the Interior shown in Figure 13.1. But anyone who closely observes an actual administrative agency soon learns that the *real* relationships among the various subdivisions, assistant secretaries, and bureau chiefs do not correspond exactly to those shown in the official organization chart. Thus the chart in Figure 13.1 shows that assistant secretary A and assistant secretary B are exactly equal in power; but anyone watching them actually work sees that in fact, the secretary thinks that A is stupid and lazy and sees him as little as possible, while he thinks that B is shrewd and works hard, and that he sees her every day and often takes her advice. Hence while A and B are completely equal in the formal organization, B is clearly A's superior in the informal or actual organization.

Accordingly, an agency's formal organization chart is at best a rough guide to its actual organization—and it is the actual organization that gets things done. As this point has become more clearly understood, a growing number of political scientists have chosen to study administrative agencies as part of the broad subject of behavior in all human organizations. Thus, while they are aware of the prescribed legal powers and responsibilities, they focus mainly on the networks of communication and influence among the people who are actually doing the work, for that is where decisions are really made and administrative functions are actually performed.

FORMAL ADMINISTRATIVE FUNCTIONS

Every administrative agency performs one or two, but rarely all, of the following basic functions:

Providing Services

Some agencies provide services for all who wish to use them. For example, the Agricultural Research Service of the U.S. Department of Agriculture conducts an elaborate program of research on such matters as pest control, farm and land management, and breeding and raising livestock. It makes the results available at low cost to farmers who wish to improve their operations. The British National Health Service provides government-subsidized medical care and hospitalization for all who wish them. But in the United States, as in all advanced industrial nations, the greatest services are defense and education, as described in the box.

Regulation

Some agencies regulate the operations of private individuals and businesses to keep them from doing certain bad things and to make sure that they do certain good things. The best-known example of such activity, of course, is the enforcement of criminal laws by the police, but there are many others, as is shown by the following lists:

Government Regulation. A research scientist in the Food and Drug Administration tests a new drug for possible licensing. (Source: FDA consumer).

Regulating Economic Competition

Enforcement of contracts and granting and protecting copyrights and patents

Control of the issuance and sale of stocks and bonds

Prohibition of unfair competitive practices, such as false and deceptive advertising

Prohibition of unfair labor practices by employers or unions

Enforcement of antimonopoly laws, corporation income taxes, excess-profits taxes, and the like, in an effort to prevent excessive concentration of economic power

Control of banking procedures, reserve funds, accounting practices, and so on

Control of the volume of currency, credit, and prices, initiation of public works, and other measures to prevent extreme fluctuations in the business cycle

Regulation of contributions to, and expenditures by, political candidates, parties, and political action committees (PACs)

Regulation of rates charged by power companies, telephone companies, and other public utilities

Prevention of signal interference and maintenance of programming standards by licensing television and radio broadcasting stations

Regulating Safety, Welfare, and Morals

Detection, capture, trial, punishment, and rehabilitation of persons committing crimes

Enforcement of safety standards in the construction and operation of buildings, roads, bridges, harbors, airports, nuclear power plants, automobiles, aircraft, lawnmowers, and so on

Enforcement of health and sanitation standards in the production, labeling, and distribution of food and drugs

Enforcement of professional qualifications through the examination and licensing of doctors, nurses, pharmacists, lawyers, architects, teachers, pilots, and so on

Enforcement of rules governing private exploitation of mineral, forest, wildlife, wilderness, and other natural resources

Prohibition of pollution of air, water, and other aspects of the environment

Enforcement of moral standards in the production and distribution of liquor, drugs, gambling, movies, books, magazines, and television and radio programming

Encouragement of employment of minorities by affirmative action programs

Minimum-wage and maximum-hours laws

Limitation of aliens' access to professions and employment

Control of the spread of infectious and epidemic diseases by such means as quarantines

Zoning and antibillboard regulations to preserve the aesthetic qualities of parts of the environment

Licensing

In most democratic nations, a private person or corporation can legally conduct certain kinds of business only after obtaining a license from some

GOVERNMENT SERVICES: AN EXAMPLE

When we consider all the activities of all the governments—national, state, and local—in the United States, the two greatest services provided by those governments are defense, which is entirely a service of the national government, and education, which is mainly a service of the state and local governments with contributions by the national government.

Educational services by governments in the United States, as in all modern democratic countries, are rooted in the ideal of universal public education—the conviction that all children, whatever their race and sex and economic status, are entitled to, and should be required to have, the kind of education that will enable them to play productive roles in the nation's economy and to participate effectively in the nation's political affairs. Hence, to the extent that private schools, operated by religious denominations or private education corporations, can provide this education, they are allowed to operate under government supervision and even with some government subsidies. But the guarantee of education for all children is fulfilled mainly by public schools—schools owned and operated by governments of one kind or another. In 1986 there were a total of 8,397 private schools of all kinds and 49,312 public schools of all kinds.

Public education is more decentralized in the United States than in any other advanced/industrialized country. Almost all public primary and secondary schools are owned and operated by local school districts (there are now more than 15,000 such districts in the country) under state laws and with considerable financial aid from the state and federal governments. All states require that children attend school, and while the specifics vary from state to state, the laws generally require that formal schooling begin by age 7 and continue to age 16. Every state also operates some postsecondary institutions, including two-year community colleges and four-year and postgraduate colleges and universities; at this level as well there are more public institutions (9,600) than private (2,797).

In 1987, a grand total of $229 billion was spent on public schools in the United States, and another $54 billion was spent on private schools. Of the money spent on public schools, 8 percent came from the federal government, 47 percent from the state governments, and 32 percent from local governments (13 percent came from private foundations, gifts, and other sources). Expenditures for education accounted for 29 percent of all expenditures by state and local governments. Education was by far the largest single item in their budgets, with welfare expenditures second, with 18 percent, and highways third, with 7 percent.

administrative agency. Thus licensing involves not only the performance of a service but also a considerable measure of regulation. This point is illustrated by the description in Chapter 7 of how the Federal Communications Commission uses its power to grant and renew licenses for radio and television stations as a device to control the way broadcasters present political information. Similar regulatory power is involved in any agency's power to grant or withhold licenses.

Adjudicating Disputes

The job of settling disputes by applying the law to particular situations is assigned exclusively to the courts in the traditional allocation of government powers and functions (see Chapter 14). Yet in many democratic nations in recent decades, administrative agencies have undertaken a number of quasi-judicial functions—"quasi" only because they are performed by administrators instead of judges. When, for example, a worker or an employer complains to the National Labor Relations Board (NLRB) that an employer or a union is engaging in an unfair labor practice in violation of the law, the NLRB is empowered to hold hearings, render a decision, and dismiss the complaint or order the challenged practice stopped. For another example, in Great Britain, complaints by workers about the orders of their superiors in the nationalized coal industry are brought before the National Coal Board, which then decides who is right. This growing type of administrative activity has drawn more and more attention to the problem of regular courts' powers to review and reverse administrative decisions, and we will return to the problem later in this chapter.

STATUS AND SELECTION OF ADMINISTRATORS

Political Activity

Most modern democratic systems try to "keep politics out of administration"; that is, they try to insulate civil servants from interference and control by political parties so that they may serve with equal faithfulness and efficiency the leaders of *any* political party that may at the moment control the legislative and executive policy-making agencies. The most common means for achieving this end is to protect civil servants from losing their jobs when one party replaces another in power. A number of democracies have added another means: restricting civil servants' participation in partisan political activities. In the United States, for example, members of the national "competitive" civil service and state and local employees of programs financed wholly or partly by the national government are forbidden by law from taking an active part in partisan politics. They may vote, privately voice their political opinions, and even attend party rallies as spectators. But they may not solicit funds for a party or candidate, make partisan public speeches, hold party office, or work for a party in any other way. In Great Britain the rules prohibit "policy-making" civil servants from engaging in partisan activities, such as canvassing, making partisan public speeches, or standing as candidates, that might conflict with their roles as impartial servants of all parties. In recent years, however, British civil servants with "routine" posts have been permitted more freedom of partisan activity. France is among the few modern democracies that place no restrictions upon such activities, but even in France the ministers and top administrators can and often do use administrative regulations to prevent their employees from supporting extreme antigovernment parties.

Administrative and political career lines are far more blurred in Japan than in most other democracies. Not only are civil servants allowed to engage freely in party and pressure politics, but movement from the civil service into political leadership—very rare elsewhere—is quite common in Japan. Indeed, "parties have always recruited heavily from the bureaucracy both because of the great abilities and prestige of its administrators and [because of] the continued personal links such men have with former colleagues and the outside interests. Probably the surest route to the highest political posts lies in a career with the bureaucracy."[2]

Unions and Strikes

The classic weapons used by workers in private businesses to protect and advance their interests are forming unions and striking. What about government workers? Most modern democratic systems permit their civil servants to form unions but limit or deny altogether their right to strike. For example, employees such as police officers, fire fighters, and postal workers are generally prohibited from striking on the ground that the continuous operation of their services is necessary to avoid national calamity. But these laws are sometimes difficult to enforce: It is impossible, for example, to jail hundreds of thousands of postal workers and school teachers, as the United States has learned from time to time; and strikes or large-scale "sick-outs" by fire fighters, police officers, sanitation workers, and others are by no means unknown. Public employees can also evade the prohibition of strikes in less risky ways. On several occasions, for example, British postal employees have sought higher wages through "work-to-rule" campaigns, in which they rigidly enforce every last postal regulation, with the result that mail delivery is delayed so much that their superiors feel compelled to make concessions. Employees of nationalized railways and coal mines, on the other hand, generally have the right to strike, although every effort is made to avoid such strikes by prior arbitration. Even so, the year-long strike by British coal miners in 1984 and 1985 was one of the longest, costliest, and most bitter strikes by public employees in a long time. The net effect of these rules in most democracies is that civil servants' right to organize unions is almost as well protected as that of workers in private industry, but their right to strike is much more restricted.

Selection

At some period in its history, every modern democratic nation has selected its civil servants for reasons other than merit. For example, in Great Britain before the nineteenth century, most government posts were filled by *patronage*—an arrangement whereby members of the nobility and landed gentry literally owned certain government jobs and, as "patrons," filled them with relatives, friends, and retainers, many of whom were too incompetent to hold any other kind of job. In France's *ancien regime* before the revolution of

STRIKES BY PUBLIC EMPLOYEES: THE CASE OF THE AIR TRAFFIC CONTROLLERS

The heavy traffic by commercial airliners and private planes into and out of most airports has made necessary the services of air traffic controllers—people on the ground who tell airplane pilots when they can land and take off and what routes they must fly. In the United States the controllers are federal employees working for the Federal Aviation Administration (FAA). For many years until 1981 they were allowed to form a union, the Professional Air Traffic Controllers Organization (PATCO), which served as their official bargaining agent with the government; however, the law prohibited them from striking.

In 1981 PATCO demanded a new contract for its members providing for $740 million in wage increases, but the FAA was willing to offer only $40 million. PATCO's president, Robert Poli, put the government's proposal to his members for a vote, and they turned it down by 13,495 to 616. So on August 3 the union went on strike. Federal judge Thomas Platt immediately issued an injunction against the strike and imposed fines of $2.4 million a day on the union for ignoring a back-to-work order, saying that such strikes "are substantially more than merely unfair labor practices—they are crimes."

President Ronald Reagan and Secretary of Transportation Drew Lewis took the same line. They gave the strikers 48 hours to return to work and said that any who failed to do so would be fired and banned from ever again working for the federal government in any capacity. The FAA manned the control towers with military controllers and speeded up the training and certification of nonmilitary controllers, and air traffic continued, although at a reduced rate. Poli said that PATCO was willing to return to the bargaining table, but Reagan and Lewis said the time for that had passed; the strikers had broken the law and thereby forfeited the right to negotiate.

Other unions, including the American Federation of Labor and Congress of Industrial Organizations (AFL-CIO), showed some sympathy with PATCO, but not all unions did. Poli took the line that the air traffic control system had become badly undermanned and very unsafe, but John O'Donnell, the president of the airline pilots' union, said that the system was quite safe, and who would know better than the pilots?

Secretary Lewis then instituted action in the courts to "decertify" PATCO—that is, to revoke its certification as the officially recognized bargaining agent for federal air traffic controllers, and in August the courts made the decertification. This was the first time any American union of public employees had ever been decertified.

On December 31, 1981, Poli resigned as the union's president. The air traffic control system was gradually restaffed, the strikers went into other lines of work, and the strike was completely crushed. The final irony of the episode was the fact that in the 1980 election, PATCO had been one of the few labor unions to endorse and give money to candidate Ronald Reagan!

1789, all but the few highest offices in the kingdom were regarded as a kind of private property, to be sold, bequeathed, or given away by their owners to whomever they pleased. In the United States before the late nineteenth century, most civil-service posts were filled by the **spoils system**—*the award of government jobs to members and supporters of the party in power.*

Prussia (and later united Germany) was the first modern nation to select its civil servants by the **merit system**—*the selection, retention, and promotion of government employees on the basis of demonstrated technical merit.*

Beginning in the late eighteenth century, civil-service reform movements arose in most democratic nations, aimed at abolishing patronage and spoils and replacing them with merit systems on the Prussian model. The movement succeeded earliest in France in the 1790s, when Napoleon Bonaparte installed a professionalized civil service. In Great Britain the reform began in the 1830s when the administrators of British India established a merit system for selecting members of the Indian civil service. It was extended to the whole British civil service after the adoption in 1853 of the Northcote-Trevelyan Commission's report on the organization of the permanent civil service. In the United States, national reform began in 1883 with the passage of the Pendleton Act, which established the Civil Service Commission and provided merit-system rules for the selection and promotion of members of the various administrative agencies.

In most democratic countries today, all or nearly all civil-service employees are selected by some kind of examination, and their tenure is largely or entirely independent of their party affiliations. The United States' national civil service has been somewhat slower in this respect than most, but, as Figure 13.2 shows, it has come a long way since 1883. By 1988 about 97 percent of all the federal government's civilian employees were under the merit system, and in most other democratic nations the proportion was the same or even higher.

At present about 60 percent of all federal civil servants are under what is officially called the *competitive service.* Employees in this classification are appointed after they have passed written examinations drawn up and administered by the Office of Personnel Management (OPM), established in 1978 to succeed the old Civil Service Commission. The remaining 40 percent are under what is called the *excepted service,* in that they do not come under the jurisdiction of OPM. However, all but a handful are also selected on merit-system principles because they have special qualifications and skills needed for the jobs they fill, and the agencies that hire them run their own merit systems. This is the case, for example, with all Postal Service employees, all foreign-service officers in the State Department, and all agents of the Federal Bureau of Investigation (FBI). Only between 1 and 3 percent of the employees can be appointed by the president or his subordinates without any kind of special examination. These include a variety of appointees, such as executive assistants, confidential secretaries, and ambassadors, whose first and most important qualification is that they be loyal to the president and his policy views.

Aside from this handful, almost all civil servants in the United States and

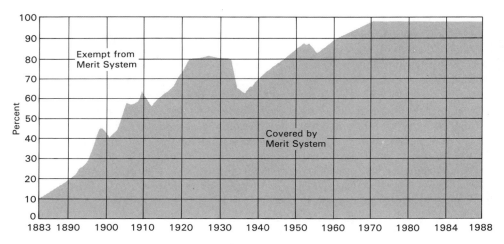

FIGURE 13.2.   Growth of the American merit-system civil service, 1883–1988.(Source: Statistical Abstract of the United States 1988 (Washington, D.C.: Bureau of the Census, 1988), Table 521, p. 322.)

in every other modern democracy are permanent in the sense that their tenure in office is not limited and they are not directly subject to the approval or disapproval of the voters through ordinary electoral processes.

POLITICS, ADMINISTRATION, AND POLICY MAKING

THE DICHOTOMY BETWEEN POLITICS AND ADMINISTRATION

Many nineteenth-century American reformers, as we have noted, valued highly the ideal of government efficiency and believed that a Prussian-type, permanent, professionalized civil service would help to realize it in the United States. Most also valued the ideal of democracy and had no wish to see the entire governmental process "Prussianized." They were reluctant to choose between the two ideals, and therefore for many the most urgent question was: How can a permanent, professional civil service be reconciled with the ideals and institutions of democracy?

Toward the end of the century, some political scientists advanced a doctrine that many believed harmonized the two ideals, and for several decades afterward many analysts of administration believed that this doctrine had settled once and for all the problem of the proper place of permanent administrators in a democratic government. Let us briefly examine its content, consequences, and current status.

Origins and Content

Most students of public administration credit the first statement of the doctrine to an article published in 1887 by a young political scientist at Princeton named Woodrow Wilson. Briefly summarized, Wilson's argument ran as follows: The old classification of governmental powers and functions into legislative, executive, and judicial categories does not fit the facts of modern government. All governments perform only two basic functions: politics, which is the making of general policies and laws; and administration, which is the application of policies and laws to particular individuals and situations. Because administration is so different from politics, Wilson contended, it must be kept nonpolitical; for, in his words, "administrative questions are not political questions. Although politics sets the tasks for administration it should not be suffered to manipulate its offices. The field of administration is a field of business."[3] A quarter-century later, Professor Wilson became the 28th president of the United States and found that political reality is even more difficult than scholarly theory.

Wilson's dichotomy between politics and administration was taken up by another eminent political scientist, Frank J. Goodnow, and elaborated into a broad doctrine of the proper place of administrators in a democracy, which he advanced in his influential book *Politics and Administration* (1900). Like Wilson, Goodnow argued that all government activities are either politics ("operations necessary to the expression of [the government's] will" or administration ("operations necessary to the execution of that will"). Goodnow—unlike many of his followers—believed that these two functions could not be completely separated or exclusively assigned to entirely separate parts of government. He recommended, however, that as much as possible some agencies should be mainly political and others mainly administrative. He concluded that in a democracy, the mainly administrative agencies must be subordinate to, and controlled by, the mainly political agencies. As he put it, "popular government requires that ... the executive authority ... shall be subordinate to the expressing authority, since the latter in the nature of things can be made much more representative of the people than can the executing authority."[4]

Consequences

For four decades after 1900, the politics–administration dichotomy was almost universally accepted by political scientists, and it deeply affected their thinking about the proper role of administrators in democratic government. It had three main consequences. First, for most scholars and reformers it provided a satisfactory theoretical justification for the presence of a permanent, professional civil service in the United States or any other democracy. If administrators only carry out policies assigned to them by political agencies, they reasoned, there is no need to make them directly responsible to the voters.

Second, it provided the theoretical foundations for a new "science of public administration," which first emerged in the United States in the decade after the publication of Goodnow's book. This new branch of political science concentrated on such problems as how to organize administrative agencies and how to recruit and train administrators so that administration can be conducted with maximum efficiency and economy. These problems were similar to those taken up by the new and rising "scientific management" movement in private industry, headed by Frederick W. Taylor, the first of the modern "efficiency experts." The new specialists in public administration did not think that by concentrating on the values of efficiency and economy, they were slighting the values of democracy. The latter, they felt, were the concern of politics, not administration; and civil servants can and should concentrate on how to maximize efficiency and leave to others the problems of maximizing democracy.

Third, it provided a clear and sensible set of principles for organizing governments. All policy-making officials were to be elected or appointed by elected officials for short terms, and all administrators were to be selected by the merit system and were to hold office as long as they remained technically competent and efficient.

Present Eclipse

Since the late 1930s, a growing number of political scientists, led by such scholars of public administration as Luther Gulick, Robert A. Dahl, Charles S. Hyneman, Carl J. Friedrich, and Herbert Simon, have rejected both the politics–administration dichotomy and the revised version of separation of powers based on it. They have abandoned the dichotomy because they believe that it is an inaccurate description of the governing process. The exercise of discretion, they argue, is the essence of policy making; and all public employees, whether they are called politicians or administrators, exercise discretion. If politics means policy making and not merely partisanship, they concluded, it cannot be "taken out of administration" as long as administrators exercise the discretion to interpret the laws they administer and to decide when, how, and how much to enforce them. And there is no way to prevent the exercise of this discretion even if it were desirable to do so.

These scholars have come to this conclusion mainly through observing what administrative agencies actually do. They have found that no matter how professionalized and formally nonpolitical those agencies are supposed to be, they have a great deal to say about what policy is—and in the very nature of things they cannot be confined merely to carrying out policies laid down by legislatures and executives. These scholars are convinced, furthermore, that the policy-making powers of administrators do not result from their hunger for power or contempt for democracy, but are inevitable products of modern government. Let us briefly survey the evidence on which they base these conclusions.

POLICY MAKING BY ADMINISTRATORS

Administrative Influence on Legislative and Executive Policies

In almost every human decision-making organization, the expert—the person who knows the organization's problems inside out and has detailed technical knowledge about the possibilities and practicality of the various proposed solutions—has an enormous advantage over nonexperts, who at best have only a general, partial, and probably shaky technical knowledge. The more complex and difficult the problems, moreover, the greater the expert's advantage. Since the problems of modern government are the most difficult faced by any human organization, the expert administrator in a democracy has a very great advantage indeed.

For many reasons, an administrator has a much better chance than a legislator or an executive to become an expert on a particular subject. For one thing, the administrator's career tends to make her a specialist on *one* subject, whether it be writing military procurement contracts, issuing passports, or regulating airline fares. The legislator and the executive, on the other hand, necessarily deal with all these matters and many more besides. They cannot afford to specialize. What is more, the legislator or the executive is often getting ready for the next election and must therefore spend considerable time raising money, planning strategy, and campaigning.

Administrators, however, are forbidden to engage in such activities and can therefore spend their full time and energy on the policy questions before their agencies. Finally, most legislators and executives are considerably less permanent than merit-system civil servants: It is said that the average assistant secretary stays in office for only two years, while the average civil servant of comparable age and skill stays in office for decades. Thus legislators and executives do not have nearly such long periods in office during which to acquire the detailed knowledge and "feel" that constitute expertise.

In all modern democracies, accordingly, short-term, part-time, and unspecialized political officials often ask advice from long career, full-time, and specialized administrative experts on the relative merits of policies—and far more often than not they follow the advice. Administrators' own policy preferences inevitably enter into and affect their advice. How could it be otherwise? Most of them are intelligent, well-meaning, conscientious people. They spend years pondering the complexities of certain policy questions. As their knowledge and involvement grow, they are bound to develop strong preferences for some policies over others. And they understandably feel that it is their patriotic duty as well as their professional obligation to express their conclusions and to do their best to see that the government follows wise policies and not foolish ones.

Thus when administrators are asked for advice, they can hardly avoid making their views known, and when, as often happens, "political" officials and their constituents have no strong views of their own, civil servants' preferences are likely to become policy.[5]

Occasionally, of course, "political" officials have strong views of their own that run sharply counter to those of the civil servants formally subordinate to them. The Goodnow doctrine requires that the administrators in such a situation set aside their own preferences and loyally carry out those of their political superiors. But government by no means always works this way, as is vividly illustrated by the American "Irangate affair" in the late 1980s, which is outlined in the box.

ADMINISTRATIVE POLICY MAKING: THE "IRANGATE" AFFAIR

The "Irangate affair," which began in the early 1980s and had still not run its course by the end of the decade, involved complex questions about making and carrying out three major foreign policies of the Reagan administration. The first and highest on the administration's agenda was the effort to supply military and nonmilitary aid to help the "contra" rebels overthrow the hard-left "Sandinista" government of Nicaragua. The second was the effort to secure the release of a number of Americans kidnapped in Lebanon and held hostage by Shi'ite Muslim terrorists thought to be controlled by Iran's Shi'ite leader, the Ayatollah Khomeini. The third was the effort to develop contacts with presumed "moderate forces" in Iran as the basis for improving relations with that country after the Ayatollah left power.

From the day of his first inauguration, President Ronald Reagan repeatedly urged the Congress to supply aid to the contras. On some occasions Congress (in which the House of Representatives was controlled by the Democrats) voted both military and nonmilitary aid, on other occasions they approved only nonmilitary aid, and on some occasions they refused to provide any kind of aid. Moreover, in 1982 and 1984, Congress adopted the "Boland Amendment" (named after its author, Representative Edward P. Boland, D-Massachusetts), which prohibited the Defense Department and the Central Intelligence Agency from channeling any aid to the contras. Congress's stop–go actions posed major difficulties for the administration's Central American policy, but Reagan and his National Security Advisor, Robert McFarlane, were also concerned about the kidnapping and possible torture of the hostages in Lebanon and about the possibility that Iran might win its war with Iraq and, because of its hatred for the United States ("the great Satan" in Khomeini's words), would destroy the American strategic position in the Persian Gulf area.

In 1985, McFarlane proposed that secret approaches be made to the Iranian "moderates" so as to build a basis for better relations after the Ayatollah left power. With Reagan's approval, and in close association with his chief aide, Marine Lieutenant Colonel Oliver L. North, McFarlane made a secret trip to Teheran, during which he worked out a deal to show good will toward Iran by selling arms to its leaders in return for Iran's showing good will toward the United States by securing the release of the hostages. In 1986 Reagan directed McFarlane's successor, Admiral John M. Poindexter, to continue the policy, the arms were sold, and the proceeds were placed in a secret Swiss bank account.

One hostage was released (while three more were captured), and nothing much came of the opening to the "moderates." But, fearing that Congress's denial of aid to the contras would destroy resistance to the Sandinistas, North and Poindexter used some of the funds in the Swiss account to purchase military supplies for the contras, and added funds they had secretly solicited from private donors and from some foreign governments.

In late 1986, however, a Beirut newspaper published a story describing the arms sales, and Attorney General Edwin Meese investigated and discovered the diversion of the funds to the contras. Reagan announced that North was relieved of his post, and Poindexter resigned.

That did not end the matter. In 1987, both the House and the Senate appointed committees to investigate the arms sales and the diversion of the funds, and an "independent counsel," Lawrence E. Walsh, was appointed to gather the facts and recommend indictments if the transactions had violated the law. In dramatic, nationally televised committee hearings during much of the summer of 1987, North, Poindexter, and a number of other people involved in what North called "the enterprise" testified about what they had done and why they had done it.

The testimony was far too lengthy and complex to be detailed here, but some highlights are worth noting. For our purposes, the key issue was: Were North and Poindexter carrying out President Reagan's orders, or were they acting on their own? Both men testified that Reagan did not specifically direct the diversion of the funds and did not know about it, but they nevertheless felt that they were doing what needed to be done to carry out his general policy of aiding the contras. As Admiral Poindexter said, "I felt it was within my authority because it was an implementation of a policy that was well understood, that the President felt very strong about. ... So it wasn't a matter of going out and making a secret foreign policy. The policy was clear. This was a way of going about, of carrying out that policy." He also said that he was careful *not* to tell the president what was going on "because I knew very well it would be controversial, and I wanted the President to have some deniability so that he would be protected and at the same time we would be able to carry out this policy and provide the opposition to the Sandinista government."[6]

Two other statements are worth noting. In a nationally televised speech after the hearings concluded, President Reagan said, "Let me put this in capital letters: I did not know about the diversion of the funds. ... Yet the buck does not stop with Adm. Poindexter, as he stated in his testimony; it stops with me. I am the one who is ultimately accountable to the American people. ... I have the right, the obligation to make my own decision."

And at the conclusion of North's testimony, Representative Lee Hamilton (D-Indiana) said to North: "I don't have any doubt at all, Col. North, that you are a patriot. ... For you, perhaps patriotism rested in the conduct of deeds, some requiring great personal courage, to free hostages and fight communism. ... But there's another form of patriotism which is unique to a democracy. It resides in those who have a deep respect for the rule of law and faith in America's democratic traditions. To uphold our Constitution requires not the exceptional efforts of the few but the confidence and the trust and the work of the many."[7]

"Loose Cannot" Bureaucratic Policymaker or Faithful Servant of Elected Policymakers? Lt. Col. Oliver P. North testifying before the congressional committee on the "Irangate" affair, 1987. (Source: AP/Wide World Photos.)

Administrative Rules

One of the many issues raised in the "Irangate" hearings was whether the Boland Amendment prohibited only the Pentagon and the CIA from giving aid to the contras not authorized by Congress, or whether, by not mentioning the National Security Council (NSC), it allowed NSC officials like North and Poindexter to do what they did. North, Poindexter, and some congressmen said it did. Most congressmen said it did not. But this was just one more instance of an inescapable problem in governing modern nations.

Every statute, amendment, and executive order is necessarily written in general terms, in the sense that its language cannot possibly describe in detail every conceivable factual situation that might arise. Legislatures and executives try to make their general intentions clear and set forth general principles that will help administrative agencies carry out their desires. But those agencies have to ascertain the facts in future factual situations and then decide whether those facts are what the legislatures and the executives had in mind when they laid down their general rules. Consequently, no administrative agency can avoid exercising discretion, and most develop their own bodies of **administrative rules**—*rules drawn up by administrative agencies to implement in detail general guidelines laid down by legislatures and executives.* Most students of government are convinced that it is absolutely necessary for administrative agencies to make such rules—and that making them necessarily involves administrators in policy making. The broader and more general the directives handed to administrators, the more important administrative rules become in shaping public policies as they actually affect people.

The implementation of the "fairness doctrine" in regulating the presentation of political issues on television (see Chapter 7) is an excellent example. Section 315a of the Federal Communications Act requires that in presenting news and comment on controversial political issues, a television broadcaster "must operate on a basis of overall fairness, making his facilities available for the expression of the contrasting views of all responsible elements in the community on the various issues which arise."

In carrying out this congressional directive, the Federal Communications Commission (FCC) has adopted a number of its own administrative rules, which give the doctrine its operational meaning. For instance, the FCC has adopted a "personal attack" rule: It requires broadcasters to notify persons or groups attacked during the discussion of a controversial issue and give them an opportunity to respond. But it also makes some exceptions: For example, newscasts and interview shows are exempt from the rule. Also, the FCC has generally taken the position that if every broadcast on a controversial issue presents statements by two different sides—the pro side and the anti side—the fairness doctrine is satisfied. The FCC thus operates as though every issue has two—and only two—sides. Most philosophers would reject that assumption, but broadcasters know that presenting two sides satisfies the FCC; and in their world the FCC's view of political reality is a lot more important than any philosopher's. The point is that in terms of what broadcasters can, must, and cannot do, the FCC's administrative rules implementing the fairness doctrine are at least as important as Congress's original adoption of the doctrine.

Pressure groups in broadcasting, like those in many other fields, have long known this political fact of life. The most successful and powerful among them, accordingly, have never regarded their work as finished when the legislature has passed a bill or the executive has issued an order. They have shifted their attention to the appropriate administrative agencies to ensure that those agencies carry out the statute or directive as the pressure groups wish. For example, the groups supporting restrictive immigration policies have kept a close watch on the Immigration and Naturalization Service to make sure that no undesirable aliens slip through the legal nets. And the National Cooperative Milk Producers' Federation once made sure that the Bureau of Internal Revenue diligently collected the special tax on oleomargarine, a strong competitor of butter. Recent studies of pressure politics in various democratic nations have

shown that administrative agencies are becoming targets of increasing importance for pressure groups.

Administrative Discretion

Administrators also acquire a good deal of policy-making power from the
discretion they *must* have in the enforcement of their own rules as well as the
legislative acts, executive decrees, and court orders of their legal superiors.

Police enforcement of automobile speed limits provides an illustration we
can all understand (but not from personal experience, I trust). Let us say that
the law sets top limits of 55 miles per hour for intercity highways, 40 for
suburban arterial boulevards, 25 for residential streets, and 15 for streets in
business districts. The police know that there are plenty of people who think
these limits are too low and will ignore them whenever they can. The police also
know that the state legislature and the city council will never give them enough
officers and cars to patrol every inch of every road every minute of every day.
No one expects them to do that; so we know that they have to have some
discretion about where to patrol and when, and we expect them to use it wisely.
So the police use their discretionary power, as they must, to *select* patrolling
areas and times. They may even develop their own rules of thumb; for example,
they will stop everyone going over 65 on the highway, but no one going under
60—thereby making the official limit of 55 into an actual limit of 60.

The point is not that some police officers do not enforce the letter of every
law all the time and are therefore derelict in their duty. The point is that no
officer can possibly enforce all of the laws everywhere all of the time, and thus
all officers have no choice but to use discretion in deciding which laws to
enforce, when, where, and against whom. If this is true for the police, it is also
true for, say, the Federal Reserve Board when it considers whether to raise the
discount rate, or the Food and Drug Administration when it considers whether
to allow doctors to prescribe a certain drug, or the Federal Trade Commission
when it considers whether to ban advertisements for tooth-decaying candy on
children's television programs.

For all these reasons, there is no escaping the conclusion that, whatever
their *formal* status and powers may be, administrative agencies make a lot of
public policy in every modern democratic nation. Until recently, most democratic countries have emphasized, and to a large degree have succeeded in,
getting politics (partisan politics, that is) out of administration; but they have
given less attention to the significant fact that administration has gotten into
politics (that is, making policy) in a big way. This fact not only makes the
politics-administration dichotomy of Wilson and Goodnow obsolete, but it has
also poses a grave problem for those nations that wish their governments to be
both democratic *and* efficient. We will conclude this chapter by analyzing the
problem and reviewing some of the efforts that have been made to solve it.

"ADMINISTOCRACY" IN A DEMOCRACY: ATTEMPTED SOLUTIONS

THE PROBLEM: MAKING ADMINISTRATORS RESPONSIBLE

The term **administocracy** was coined by Guy S. Claire to denote an *"aristocracy of administrators—a government effectively run by career civil servants."*[8] The problem of administocracy is this: Citizens of most democratic polities wish their governments to be efficient and are convinced that a permanent, professionalized civil service recruited and promoted according to standards of technical merit is the most likely to be efficient. They have no wish to return to the bad old days of the patronage and spoils systems. Yet most of them also wish their governments to be democratic—that is, to realize the ideal of popular control of government and do what the people want and not what some elite thinks is good for them. Most of us want *both* efficiency and democracy, and we do not wish to sacrifice one ideal to promote the other.

But are the two ideals compatible? Can we pursue them both? These questions have long concerned political theorists. For several generations, as we have seen, most scholars believed that the politics–administration dichotomy solved the problem. But most present-day political scientists believe that this dichotomy is based upon a misconception of what administrators actually do and offers no solution at all.

Accordingly, most political scientists today believe that the solution to the problem of administocracy lies not in any futile attempt to prevent administrators from making policy, but rather in ensuring that administrators are *responsible* in their policy-making activities. When we examine their ideas closely, however, we discover that they use the key word *responsibility* in two distinct senses, and their proposals for making administrators responsible reflect different emphases on the two meanings of the word.

"Responsibility" as Conforming to a Professional Code

A number of political scientists, notably Carl J. Friedrich, have argued that the political responsibility of administrators supposedly reflected in their accountability to elected officials can never be enforced completely. They argue that we must place heavy reliance on developing functional or objective responsibility; that is, we should select and train our administrators in such a way that they will operate according to built-in professional standards and adhere to a professional code of ethics. Ideally, according to Friedrich, administrators should be responsible in the same sense and for similar reasons that judges are responsible:

> *Judicial decisions are relatively responsible because judges have to account for their action in terms of a somewhat rationalized and previously established set of rules. Any deviation from these rules on the part of a judge will be subjected to*

extensive scrutiny by his colleagues and what is known as the "legal profession."
Similarly, administrative officials seeking to apply scientific "standards" have to
account for their action in terms of a somewhat rationalized and previously estab-
lished set of hypotheses. Any deviation from these hypotheses will be subjected to
thorough scrutiny by their colleagues in what is known as the "fellowship of
science."[9]

"Responsibility" as Accountability to Elected Officials

Other political scientists, notably Charles S. Hyneman, have argued that, although administrative responsibility in Friedrich's sense is a fine thing, a democratic government must make its administrators responsible mainly by making them accountable to and controlled by elected public officials. Only thus, they insist, can we establish the popular control of administrative policy making that democratic government demands. As Hyneman put it:

> *Government has enormous power over us, and most of the acts of government are*
> *put into effect by the men and women who constitute the bureaucracy. It is in the*
> *power of these men and women to do us great injury, as it is in their power to*
> *advance our well-being. It is essential that they do what we want done, the way we*
> *want it done. Our concept of democratic government requires that these men and*
> *women be subject to direction and control that compel them to conform to the*
> *wishes of the people as a whole whether they wish to do so or not.*[10]

Both Friedrich and Hyneman thus believe that some kind of external control of administrative policy making is necessary to solve the problem of administocracy, although they do not agree about how important this particular kind of control is. We will conclude our discussion by examining briefly some of the principal methods of external control currently employed by democratic nations.

SOLUTIONS

Making Administrators Representative

Some political scientists have suggested that one of the best ways to prevent administocracy is to have a "representative bureaucracy"—one whose employees are drawn from all the nation's social, racial, religious, sexual, and economic groups—though not necessarily in exactly the same proportions that exist in the whole society. Such a bureaucracy, they argue, is likely to be responsive to the people's desires because it *is* the people, or at least a cross-section of them. Indeed, the bureaucracy may be in some ways more representative than elected officials, for it will include members of some groups slighted by electoral majorities.

Perhaps so, but James Q. Wilson, a leading scholar of the way administrators behave, has concluded that there is little evidence that administrators' social backgrounds affect how they behave in their jobs. He is much more impressed with the impact of their professional training and values—for example, as lawyers or economists—and he illustrates his point with examples from the Federal Trade Commission (FTC):

> *Because of their training and attitudes, lawyers in the FTC prefer to bring cases against a business firm that does something clearly and demonstrably illegal, such as attending secret meetings with competitors to rig the prices that will be charged to a purchaser. These cases appeal to lawyers because there is usually a victim (the purchaser or a rival company) who complains to the government, the illegal behavior can be proved in a court of law, and the case can be completed rather quickly. Economists, on the other hand, are trained to measure the value of a case, not by how easily or quickly it can be proved in court, but by whether the illegal practice imposes large or small costs on the consumer. FTC economists often dislike the cases that appeal to the lawyers. The economists feel that the amount of money such cases save the consumer is often small and the cases are a distraction from the big issues—such as whether IBM unfairly dominates the office-machine business or whether General Motors is too large to be efficient. Lawyers, in turn, are leery of big cases because the facts are hard to prove and take forever to decide (one big case can drag through the courts for ten years). In many federal agencies, professional values such as these help explain how power is used.*[11]

Control by Elected Officials

United States. Political control of administrative agencies in the United States is exercised by the president and Congress, both jointly and separately. Jointly they enact the legislation that creates the administrative agencies, defines their objectives and powers, and establishes standards of performance; they provide the money that administrative agencies spend; they collaborate on appointments to top administrative posts; they establish the procedures by which lesser appointments are made; and they review, criticize, and sometimes stop the actions of administrators.

In addition, the president, as chief executive, formally controls most civil servants. He appoints the heads and chief subordinates of most executive agencies, and they are responsible to him. They, in turn, formally control the employees of their agencies. *Formally,* the president, like any commander in chief, can send orders down the administrative hierarchy, count on having them obeyed, and expect his subordinates to keep him informed about what is going on. But organization charts are one thing and reality is another. Not only are the number of civil servants and the number and variety of their activities far too vast for any one person to keep an eye on, but the more dedicated employees are, as we have seen, the more likely they are to develop strong feelings about what policies ought to be followed—feelings that do not always coincide with those of the president. All patriotic Americans, civil servants or civilians, feel that their highest duty is to work for what they believe is in the nation's best interests, and losing a presidential order in the bureaucratic maze is not difficult. As Jonathan Daniels, a former presidential aide, wrote of cabinet officers:

> *Half of a President's suggestions, which theoretically carry the weight of orders, can safely be forgotten by a Cabinet member. And if the President asks about a suggestion a second time, he can be told that it is being investigated. If he asks a third time, a wise Cabinet officer will give him at least part of what he suggests. But only occasionally, except about the most important matters, do Presidents ever get around to asking three times.*[12]

A perceptive modern student of the presidency, Richard Neustadt, concludes that the president's power over his subordinates is not so much the power to command as the power to persuade—an opportunity "to induce them to believe that what he wants of them is what their own appraisal of their own responsibilities require them to do in their own interest, not his."[13] Presidential control of administrators is thus not enough to keep them strictly obedient to the will of elected policy makers.

Congress, on the other hand, relies mainly on *oversight*—that is, reviewing and checking the activities of administrators. Most appropriations run for only a year or two, and when the agencies' requests for new funds come before Congress, the various subcommittees of the appropriations committees in each house use the occasion—when administrators are understandably very cooperative—to review the agencies' past conduct and future plans, and to offer whatever criticisms committee members think appropriate. Investigating committees, as we observed in Chapter 11, provide another useful means of making administrators toe the line. Congress frequently grants powers to administrative agencies for limited periods of time and uses the occasions of renewing the grants to review not only policy but also the way it has been carried out.

These examples are but a few of the many means used by elected officials in the United States to direct and control administrative agencies. If Congress and the president use them vigorously and intelligently, with a clear understanding of what they are about, administocracy can be kept well within acceptable bounds. Hyneman argued, however, that control of administration in the United States is made more difficult by the constitutional independence of Congress and the president from each other. Because they are elected by different constituencies for different terms of office, more often than not they have conflicting views about what policies administrators should pursue. Other students of the question are skeptical about Hyneman's proposed solution: a joint executive-legislative council to formulate policy and direct administration. But most agree with his judgment that until the problem is solved, the overall control of administrative agencies by elected officials in the United States will continue to be less effective than it should be.

Parliamentary systems.   At first glance the control of administrators by elected officials in parliamentary systems appears to be better organized and more effective than it is in the United States, for in most of them, as we learned in Chapter 11, the legislatures and executives usually speak with one voice, at least formally. The administrators in each executive department are directly responsible to the minister; the minister is responsible to the cabinet; and the cabinet and the parliament are always in formal agreement about both policy ends and administrative means.

When we look closer, however, we learn that matters are not quite that simple or neat. For one thing, many parliamentary democracies have established government corporations that, like the British Broadcasting Corporation (BBC), are not subject to direct ministerial control. For another, members of the parliaments in many of these nations apparently think that ministerial control by itself is not sufficient to prevent administocracy. Consequently, many parliamentary democracies have created such institutions as the British "question time" and the French *interpellation.*

On each of the first four days of every legislative week, any member of the British House of Commons may, after having given the Government one or two days' notice, ask a question of any member of the ministry. The questions are put in both oral and written form. They may be simple requests for information or they may require the ministers to explain and justify actions taken by their departments. Furthermore, the questioner and other MPs may ask supplementary questions arising from the ministers' oral answers to the initial questions. Questions are asked not only by the opposition to embarrass the Government, but also by backbenchers of the majority party.

Question time thus not only offers an arena for conflict between the majority party and the opposition party; it often also provides an opportunity for contests between legislators and administrators without regard to party. Asking questions, indeed, is the principal method by which rank-and-file MPs can review and criticize the actions of the civil service and one of the few areas in which they can participate in the governing process free of the shackles of party discipline and cabinet control. An average of 70 to 100 oral questions are asked each day, a total of about 13,000 each year. Some observers believe that they have proved to be at least as effective as ministerial control in keeping civil servants in line.

The British have adopted another device that has to some extent been copied by the United States. Most acts of Parliament set general objectives and standards and leave the writing of detailed regulations to the appropriate administrative agencies. When an agency has drawn up a set of regulations, they are published in a collection known as a *statutory instrument,* which is then placed before Parliament for a period of 40 days. If no MP objects, the instrument becomes law. But if an MP moves a "prayer for annulment," a vote must be taken; and if a majority of the House of Commons agrees, the whole set of regulations are voided and another must be drawn up. To be sure, the cabinet usually imposes party discipline to preserve the regulations, but having them challenged can be embarrassing, and the procedure makes the administrators try hard to avoid promulgating rules that might antagonize an unduly large number of MPs.

In the Third and Fourth Republics of France, members of the National Assembly also asked questions in a procedure similar to question time in the House of Commons, though the questions were designed mainly to elicit information. Far more formidable was the practice of *interpellations*—requesting ministers to explain and justify the actions of their departments. After a minister had replied to a particular *interpellation,* a general debate was held, ending in a motion either censuring or approving the minister's reply and the action of his department. These practices constituted a powerful weapon for legislative control of administrators.

In the Fifth Republic, however, they have been severely limited. Question time is now restricted to one day a week, and the greater power of the executive makes it extremely unlikely that a minister or the whole cabinet will be turned out because of unsatisfactory answers to legislators' questions.

Authoritarian systems.   Whatever may be the *theory* of authoritarianism (see Chapter 5), the *fact* is that no such system is a perfect hierarchy rigidly controlled by all-knowing and all-powerful leaders who closely scrutinize the lowliest bureaucrat's every move. Even such "absolute" dictators as Adolf Hitler and Mu'ammar al-Qadaffi cannot possibly themselves know and oversee all the actions of all their administrative subordinates, and we know that in all authoritarian regimes the orders from the top are often watered down or slowed up by low-level bureaucrats.

In the Communist nations, most enterprises are owned and operated by the state, and so public employees constitute much greater proportions of their work forces than their counterparts in the Western democracies. And, judging from what their own commentators say, one of the Communists' most acute and recurring problems is controlling bureaucracy—establishing and maintaining an *apparat* (civil service) that is efficient, incorruptible, and quickly responsive to the wishes of the rulers.

Under Lenin, Stalin, and Brezhnev, the Soviet Union attacked the problem mainly by using the Communist party as the watchdog of the state administrative apparatus right down to the level of village governments and individual factories and collective farms. The central ministries customarily issued detailed instructions to regional and local units and enterprises, allowing them only small areas of discretion. Each unit and enterprise had some party members on its staff or overseeing it from local party headquarters—an updated version of the ancient Russian institution of "the inspector."

Furthermore, the party encouraged ordinary nonparty citizens to report and criticize lapses in zeal or performance by local *apparatchiks* (administrators), factory managers, and collective-farm managers. Even so, the managers of the state factories and farms developed a number of tricks for protecting themselves. Knowing that they would be in real trouble if they did not fulfill their assigned production quotas, they sought to have low quotas assigned, underreported plant capacity and current output, or maintained inventories of finished products or raw materials unknown to the central planners. In this way they could be confident of meeting their assigned quotas and even be praised for exceeding them.

Many of the reforms proposed since 1985 by Mikhail Gorbachev as part of his program of *perestroika* (restructuring) are aimed at promoting local and personal initiative by decreasing Moscow's centralized control of economic enterprise and by reducing the party's role as everyone's watchdog. It is significant, ironic—and probably inevitable—that some of the strongest opposition to *perestroika* is coming from the local party *apparatchiks,* who had such a good thing under the old regime.

The People's Republic of China has tried several different control systems. Before the Communist takeover in 1949, China had one of the world's oldest traditions of professional bureaucracy and a distinct administrative class with great prestige. To Mao Zedong and his followers, these administrators epitomized all that was wrong with the old regime, and as a result, under Mao's regime (1949–76) there was great hostility to traditional bureaucracy. At first the Mao regime followed the Russian model of parallel party and management structures, with the party keeping a close eye on the bureaucrats. In the early 1950s it turned to "one-man management" of local enterprises. After that the Communist party leaders sought to eliminate the evils of bureaucracy by weakening or eliminating all centralized structures and encouraging local enterprises and local party groups to carry out central directives without bureaucratic intermediaries. After Mao's death in 1976, however, the new regime of Deng Xiaoping stressed industrial modernization and returned to more traditional bureaucratic ways to achieve their goals.

Control by Courts

In addition to legislative and executive methods of ensuring that administrative agencies adopt and enforce policies in accordance with popular desires, all democratic nations also provide various judicial restraints to prevent them from violating the rights of individuals (see Chapter 15). If private citizens believe that an administrative agency has used its power unreasonably to harm them or their property, or stepped outside its jurisdiction in giving them an order, or exceeded its regulatory powers, or unfairly denied them a license, they can take their complaint to a court. The remedy may take the form of money paid to them in damages, a writ of mandamus (that is, a court order to a public official ordering him to do his duty as the law requires), or a writ of injunction (that is, a court order prohibiting an administrative official from performing a specific action).

Several democratic countries, including the United States and Great Britain, assign all judicial review of illegal administrative actions to their ordinary courts, whereas others, including France, Italy, and Sweden, have established special administrative courts to adjudicate such disputes. The main purpose of judicial control of administration in most nations, whether exercised by regular or special courts, is not to prevent administocracy as the term is used here, but rather to protect the personal and property rights of individuals against violations by administrators.

Intervention by Ombudsmen

For many private citizens, suing an administrative agency in the courts is not easy or even feasible. It is time consuming, costly, and unpleasant—and there is no guarantee of winning. Judicial control, which leaves the initiative to the aggrieved, is thus more a last resort than a device often used for keeping administrators in line.

Recognizing this difficulty as long ago as 1809, the government of Sweden established the special office of **ombudsman** (the term means "parliamentary commissioner")—*an official appointed by a legislature to hear and investigate complaints by private individuals against administrators.* The ombudsman is appointed by the Riksdag (parliament) to investigate and publicize instances in which administrators have used their powers wrongly or failed to act when they should. Any citizen may register a complaint with the ombudsman. He investigates each complaint and, on the basis of his findings, publicly either exonerates or censures the administrators involved. In most instances public censure by an ombudsman is enough to make an erring administrator mend his ways in a hurry, but if he remains adamant, the ombudsman is authorized to direct the public prosecutor to take the matter to court.

In this way most of the initiative and bother and all of the expense of obtaining a remedy are borne by the office of the ombudsman rather than by private citizens, and many observers believe that the institution is one of the most effective devices democracies have for keeping administrators in line. Most democratic nations have now established ombudsmen for investigating complaints about national administrators. The United States, which still has no national ombudsman, is one of the few exceptions, but a number of American states have instituted such positions. No country believes that having an ombudsman solves all the problems of administocracy, but most believe that it helps.

CONCLUSION

It is clear that the great numbers and power of career civil servants have elevated them to positions of enormous influence in all modern political systems, democratic and authoritarian, and their professionalization has given rise to problems of administocracy. Some modern Cassandras, indeed, have cried that all is lost and that administocracy and "the new despotism" are already upon us. However, the evidence presented in this chapter strongly suggests that such lamentations are, to say the least, premature. The fact that career administrators have great influence in the making of public policy does not mean that they have taken over the whole process and become absolute and unchecked despots. The democratic systems' various legislative, executive, and judicial controls can fix definite and firm limits upon what civil servants can and cannot do. As long as those who exercise these controls do so with the confidence that they are doing what their constituents want them to do, administrators will continue to be valuable servants—but not masters—of democratic regimes.

FOR FURTHER READING

ABERBACH, JOEL D., ROBERT D. PUTNAM, and BERT A. ROCKMAN, eds. *Bureaucrats and Politicians in Western Democracies.* Cambridge: Harvard University Press, 1981. Essays on relationships between political executives and top civil servants in several Western nations.

*BRYNER, GARY C. *Bureaucratic Discretion: Law and Policy in Federal Regulatory Agencies.* Elmsford, NY: Pergamon Press, 1987. Four case studies of bureaucratic policy making in the United States and efforts to control it.

BURKE, JOHN P. *Bureaucratic Responsibility.* Baltimore: The Johns Hopkins University Press, 1986. A new statement of the view that bureaucrats' internalized professional standards are the best safeguards for keeping them responsible.

CAMPBELL, COLIN. *Governments Under Stress: Political Executives and Key Bureaucrats in Washington, London, and Ottawa.* Toronto: University of Toronto Press, 1983. Study of relationships between political executives and top bureaucrats in three democratic countries.

GOODNOW, FRANK J. *Politics and Administration.* New York: Crowell-Collier and Macmillan, 1900. Classic statement of the politics–administration dichotomy.

*GRAY, ANDREW and WILLIAM I. JENKINS. *Administrative Politics in British Government.* New York: St. Martin's Press, 1985. Study of the powerful policy-making role of the British permanent civil service.

GRUBER, JUDITH E. *Controlling Bureaucracies: Dilemmas in Democratic Government.* Berkeley: University of California Press, 1987. Analysis of problems and possibilities for controlling "administocracy" in the United States.

*HECLO, HUGH A. *A Government of Strangers: Executive Politics in Washington.* Washington, D.C.: Brookings Institution, 1977. Analysis of conflict between appointed top executives and career civil servants.

HYNEMAN, CHARLES S. *Bureaucracy in a Democracy.* New York: Harper & Row, Pub., 1950. Influ-

ential discussion of the problem and methods of democratic control over permanent civil servants.

PAGE, EDWARD C. *Political Authority and Bureaucratic Power.* Knoxville: University of Tennessee Press, 1984. Analysis of bureaucracies of France, West Germany, Great Britain, and the United States, with emphasis on the problem of control by elected officials.

RABIN, JACK, and JAMES S. BOWMAN, eds. *Politics and Administration: Woodrow Wilson and American Public Administration.* New York: Marcel Dekker, 1984. Essays reconsidering Wilson's politics–administration distinction and its impact on the role of bureaucracy in a democratic system.

RILEY, DENNIS D. *Controlling the Federal Bureaucracy.* Philadelphia: Temple University Press, 1987. Analysis of problems and solutions in control of bureaucratic policy making by elected officials.

ROSEN, BERNARD. *Holding Government Bureaucrats Accountable.* New York: Praeger, 1982. Analysis of problems and possibilities of holding civil servants accountable for policy-making activities.

*ROURKE, FRANCIS E. *Bureaucracy, Politics and Public Policy,* 3rd ed. Boston: Little, Brown, 1984. Survey of the role of permanent civil servants in the making of public policy in the United States.

SHUCK, PETER H. *Suing Government: Citizen Remedies for Official Wrongs.* New Haven, CT: Yale University Press, 1983. Account of use of litigation as a method of keeping administrative agencies accountable.

SIMON, HERBERT A. *Administrative Behavior,* 2nd ed. New York: Crowell-Collier and Macmillan, 1957. Nobel prize winner's influential study of administrative decision making from the point of view of organization theory and social psychology.

TUMMALA, KRISHNA K., ed. *Administrative Systems Abroad.* Washington, D.C.: University Press of America, 1982. Collection of case studies of administrative agencies in Third World countries, especially in Asia.

WILDAVSKY, AARON. *The Politics of the Budgetary Process.* Boston: Little, Brown, 1964. Analysis of a key administrative activity, emphasizing that change takes place in small "incremental" steps, not great leaps.

WILSON, JAMES Q. *The Investigators: Managing FBI and Narcotics Agents.* New York: Basic Books, 1978. Detailed examination of the internal operations of two federal investigating agencies.

YATES, DOUGLAS. *Bureaucratic Democracy: The Search for Democracy and Efficiency in American Government.* Cambridge: Harvard University Press, 1982. A new look at the bureaucracy-in-a-democracy problem.

NOTES

[1]Luther Gulick, "Notes on the Theory of Organization," in Gulick and L. Urwik, eds. *Papers on the Science of Administration* (New York: Institute of Public Administration, 1937), p. 6.

[2]Frank Langdon, *Politics in Japan* (Boston: Little, Brown, 1967), pp. 175–76, 228.

[3]Woodrow Wilson, "The Study of Administration," *Political Science Quarterly,* 2 (1887), pp. 197–222.

[4]Frank J. Goodnow, *Politics and Administration* (New York: Crowell-Collier and Macmillan, 1900), p. 24.

[5]These points are well and truly made with many real-life illustrations in the books listed at the end of this chapter. I confess, however, that I find them made as accurately and much more entertainingly in two long-running British television series, "Yes, Minister" and "Yes, Prime Minister," which feature the repeated and usually successful schemes of Sir Humphrey Appleby, a senior civil servant, to maneuver his presumed political "master," cabinet and later prime minister Jim Hacker, into adopting Sir Humphrey's policies as his own. Readers who have a chance to see the series should not miss them.

[6]*Congressional Quarterly Weekly Report,* July 18, 1987, p. 1,610.

[7]*Congressional Quarterly Weekly Report,* July 18, 1987, p. 1,605.

[8]Guy S. Claire, *Administocracy* (New York: Crowell-Collier and Macmillan, 1934).

[9]Carl J. Friedrich, "Responsible Government Service under the American Constitution," in *Problems of the American Public Service* (New York: McGraw-Hill, 1935), pp. 36–37. Used with permission of McGraw-Hill Book Company.

[10]Charles S. Hyneman, *Bureaucracy in a Democracy* (New York: Harper & Row Pub., 1950), p. 38.

[11]James Q. Wilson, *American Government: Institutions and Policies,* 4th ed. (Lexington, MA: D.C. Heath, 1989), pp. 373–74.

[12]Jonathan Daniels, *Frontier on the Potomac* (New York: Crowell-Collier and Macmillan, 1946), pp. 31–32.

[13]Richard E. Neustadt, *Presidential Power* (New York: John Wiley, 1960), p. 46.

14 Law and the Judicial Process

This I know, my lords, that where laws end, tyranny begins.

William Pitt, the Elder

The law is a sort of hocus-pocus science, that smiles in your face while it picks your pocket, and the glorious uncertainty of it is more use to the professors than the justice of it.

Charles Macklin

The law is the last result of human wisdom acting upon human experience for the benefit of the public.

Dr. Samuel Johnson

Law is a system of social relationships which serves the interests of the ruling classes and hence is supported by their organized power, the state.

Penal Code of the Soviet Union

The prophecies of what the courts will do in fact, and nothing more pretentious, are what I mean by the law.

Justice Oliver Wendell Holmes, Jr.

Some of us may at times be tempted to agree with the more cynical views of what law is all about, especially when we have just received a ticket for overparking or paid a lawyer's bill. But most of us believe, with Dr. Samuel Johnson, that law is one of the great achievements of human civilization and that people's chances of living together peacefully in society depend largely on their willingness to live according to the law.

The writers of the first constitution of Massachusetts in 1778 declared that its purpose was to establish "a government of laws, and not of men." That hope surely still lives in the hearts of most of us, who want our lives, our fortunes, and our sacred honor to be governed, not by the passing whims of a dictator or the prejudices of a ruling class or even the enthusiasms of a momentary popular majority, but by fundamental principles of right and reason. The actual laws that govern us at the moment may not measure up to this dream, to be sure, but in most of us the dream is strong.

Perhaps that is why Americans generally admire judges more than executives or legislators. The evidence from the public opinion polls on this point is quite clear. Since 1966 the Louis Harris poll has regularly asked its respondents, "As far as the people running various institutions are concerned, would you say you have a great deal of confidence, only some confidence, or hardly any confidence at all in them?" Their changing responses are presented in Table 14.1.

The figures in Table 14.1 show that, with the exception of 1984, when Ronald Reagan's popularity was at its highest, the people have consistently held the Supreme Court in higher esteem than the Congress or the presidency, and, indeed, the Court challenges the military, higher education, and television news for the highest esteem of all the institutions listed. (However, the figures also show that law firms are held in much lower esteem, ranking right down at the bottom with organized labor. The poll did not ask about used-car dealers.)

To some extent, of course, these ratings reflect how people feel about the particular judges, presidents, and members of Congress in office at the moment. Beyond this, however, most of us have a mental picture of "the judge" that is close to reverential, even though no actual judge may quite live up to our ideal.

For there she sits on the bench, our ideal judge, listening attentively and impartially to the plaintiff and the defendant, seeing to it that each side

TABLE 14.1.   Popular Confidence in Leaders of Institutions, 1980–88

	Percentage Expressing "A Great Deal of Confidence"				
	1980	1982	1984	1986	1988
Congress	18	13	28	21	15
The White House	18	20	42	19	17
The Supreme Court	27	25	35	32	32
Law firms	13	na	17	14	13
The military	28	31	45	36	33
Colleges, universities	36	30	40	34	34
Major companies	16	18	19	16	19
Organized labor	14	8	12	11	13
The press	19	14	18	19	18
Television news	29	24	28	27	28

Source: The Harris Poll, May 8, 1988.

receives its full rights under the law, and handing down her decision, not to please this political party or that pressure group, but to achieve what the law says is the just settlement of such disputes as the one before her.

There is little doubt that the law, and the judges and courts that interpret and apply it, occupy a place of high prestige in our attitudes toward government. To what extent do actual judges and courts live up to their ideal models? Perhaps we can discover some answers in this chapter, in which we survey the structure and role of law and courts as they currently operate in the democratic nations.

THE NATURE AND TYPES OF LAW

In the first chapter of this book we spoke of the different kinds of rules by which people live, and pointed out a number of respects in which laws differ from moral precepts and customs, defining **law** as *the body of rules emanating from government and enforceable by the courts.* The reader should note that, according to this definition, no particular government agency is regarded as having a monopoly on law making. In Chapters 11 through 13 we considered the law making activities of legislators, executives, and administrators. In this chapter we will examine the law making activities of judges and the procedures by which they apply laws made by themselves and other government agencies.

The courts in modern industrial societies make and apply several types of laws, and the differences among them are important enough to for us to recognize the principal ways in which laws are classified and the main kinds of laws in each classification.

CLASSIFIED BY SOURCE

One familiar way of classifying types of laws is according to the agency that promulgates them. There are six main types: constitutional law, statutory law, administrative law, common law, equity law, and roman and civil law.

Constitutional Law

Every nation has a **constitution**—*a body of fundamental rules, written and unwritten, according to which its government operates.* Though some of the rules consist of unwritten customs, most are, strictly speaking, constitutional law, which includes a basic written constitution, a number of organic laws, and the interpretations made by the courts. Examples include the constitutions of the United States, the Soviet Union, West Germany, and just about every industrial nation (Great Britain is said to have an "unwritten constitution"); legislative acts establishing basic agencies of government, such as the American Judiciary Act of 1789 establishing the lower federal courts, and the British

Parliament Act of 1911 abolishing the power of the House of Lords to nullify bills passed by the House of Commons. This type also includes the decisions of supreme courts authoritatively saying what the written Constitution means in particular cases—for example, the U.S. Supreme Court's decision in *Brown* v. *Board of Education* declaring that the equal-protection-of-the-laws clause of the Fourteenth Amendment prohibits the states from racially segregating the public schools (see Chapter 16).

Constitutional law is everywhere regarded as the most fundamental of all types of law, in the sense that any law that contravenes a constitutional rule is superseded by the constitutional rule. Maintaining constitutional supremacy is the special prerogative of the courts in some nations; in others the job is done by the legislatures. We will say more about this in a moment.

Statutory Law

Statutory law consists of all the rules *enacted by the legislature* that command or prohibit some form of behavior. An example is the American Voting Rights Act of 1965 (see Chapter 16) or the French law prohibiting the publication of any poll results within two weeks prior to any election. In most nations they are collected and published in "codes" or books of "statutes in force."

Administrative Law

In Chapter 13 we noted that in all modern democratic systems, many executive and administrative agencies are authorized by the constitutions or the legislatures to make rules and regulations within certain specified limits. Examples include the American Environmental Protection Agency's rule requiring all cotton textile mills to install major ventilating systems, and the Federal Communication Commission's "fairness doctrine," which they first imposed and later revoked. The total body of such rules is generally called administrative law, and in most Western nations it has grown to considerable size.

Common Law

In twelfth-century England, royal judges began to travel around the country to settle various local disputes according to their understanding of the prevailing "customs of the realm." During the ensuing centuries, these judges and their successors generally followed the principle of *stare decisis* ("let the decision stand"), according to which judges are obligated to "follow precedent." That is, when judges decide a case to which a rule made in an earlier case applies, they must decide according to the old rule rather than formulate a new one each time a new case comes along. As a consequence of their general adherence to *stare decisis,* the English judges over the centuries built up an elaborate body of legal rules that came to be known as "the common law" to distinguish it from the law created by acts of Parliament. Examples include the rule that a person must perform in good faith the obligations of a contract, and the rule that a jury must be composed of twelve persons (recently modified by statutes in some jurisdictions reducing the number to six).

The common law was, of course, also applied by courts in the English colonies around the world. When some of those colonies became independent— such as the United States, Canada, New Zealand, Australia, and India—their courts continued to apply English common law, although in all these nations English principles have been adapted to local circumstances. If a common-law rule contravenes a constitutional or statutory rule, the common-law rule gives way. But in the nations mentioned, common law continues to govern many matters on which the constitutions and statutes are silent.

Equity Law

During the long evolution of the common law in medieval England, an increasing number of British subjects demanded relief from injustices that they claimed resulted from the judges' rulings. The kings turned over such complaints to their chief legal officers, the chancellors, who in turn appointed assistants known as "masters in chancery" to deal with them. Eventually the masters in chancery came to constitute a regular court, the Court of Chancery. The rules developed by this court outside the common law have come to be known as equity law, and they too were exported to the English colonies and revised after those colonies won independence. An example is the "clean hands" maxim, which stipulates that if you seek relief in a court of equity, you yourself must have behaved properly in the matter. Equity law, like common law, is superseded by constitutional and statutory law where there is conflict, but it still governs such matters as the administration of trusts, mortgages, and other financial obligations on which the statutes and common law are silent.

Roman Law and Civil Law

Every modern nation has constitutional law, statutory law, and administrative law, but common law and equity law operate mainly in the English-speaking nations. The nations of Western Europe and Latin America (as well as the American state of Louisiana and the Canadian province of Quebec) supplement their constitutional, statutory, and administrative law with a system of jurisprudence commonly called the civil law. It consists of a body of rules and procedures that, though differing somewhat from nation to nation, is based upon the *jus civile* of ancient Rome, which was rediscovered and adopted by European judges in the early Middle Ages. Its best-known and most influential codification is that made in France by the order of Napoleon I in 1804, which came to be known as the Code Napoleon, or *Code civil*. Modern civil law differs from common law and equity not only in specific rules and procedures but also in its general tone and manner of growth. Common and equity law are largely made by judges and remain pragmatic in tone, whereas civil law consists to a considerable degree of rules expounded by theorists of jurisprudence and has a more rationalistic and deductive tone than the common law.

Various other kinds of law (for example, admiralty and maritime law and international law) are applied by modern courts, but the types we have outlined here are the principal elements of modern democratic legal systems.

CLASSIFIED BY SUBJECT MATTER

One other classification of law is significant for our purposes—that which distinguishes between criminal and civil law.

Criminal Law

Criminal law, of course, deals with crimes. A crime is a wrong committed against the whole community—"an act done in violation of those duties which an individual owes to the community, and for the breach of which the law has provided that the offender shall make satisfaction to the public."[1] Crimes are usually classified as either felonies (more serious) or misdemeanors (less serious) and are punishable by death, imprisonment, fines, compulsory social service, and other penalties.

Civil Law

Civil law deals with wrongs committed against private individuals but not considered to be damaging to the whole community, and the community's only stake is making sure that the issue is settled fairly. (Note the difference between this use of the term and the European system of "civil law" previously noted.) For example, if A spreads malicious stories about B in the hope of ruining B's reputation, he is considered to have slandered B but not to have harmed the whole community. B's remedy is to sue A for damages. But if A shoots and kills B, he is considered to have threatened the basic safety and security of the entire community, and the government will prosecute him for murder. If he is found guilty, he will be imprisoned or executed. Our next concern is the way in which the courts that apply these types of law in modern democratic nations are structured.

COURT STRUCTURES IN DEMOCRATIC NATIONS

SPECIALIZED JUDICIAL FUNCTIONS

For many centuries, organized societies did not make theoretical or organizational distinctions between law making and law enforcing, nor did they establish government agencies specializing in one kind of operation over the other. Kings, as well as their ministers and courts (a "court," after all, was simply a king's retinue) made *and* enforced laws. In the late Middle Ages, however, the idea began to grow that justice is best served by having one kind of agency—which came to be called the executive—specialize in watching over the behavior of the king's subjects and prosecuting those who violated the law, and another kind of agency to specialize in trying the people thus accused. The agencies that tried the cases retained the ancient title of "courts," and by the eighteenth century in most nations they were at least somewhat distinct in both theory and organization from executive agencies and had largely taken over the functions of determining facts and interpreting and applying law. Thus the courts came to perform what are today regarded as the two distinctively judicial functions.

Law Enforcement

Every law is a general rule made by a government agency either commanding or prohibiting a certain kind of behavior. Every government from time immemorial has established certain official agencies to enforce the law—to detect instances in which "persons" (including both flesh-and-blood individuals and corporations, which are considered to be legal persons) have violated these general rules, and then to punish the offenders. Every agency performing this function must conduct a number of basic operations, which may be illustrated by the following hypothetical example:

A nation has a law against murder, which is defined as the taking of life by deliberate intent and "with malice aforethought." One of its citizens, A, is found dead, and some of the people in the neighborhood tell the government (the police and the prosecutor) that they think that B shot A. The first thing the government does is *ascertain the facts:* Is A really dead? Did he die from a gunshot wound? Did B fire the shot that killed A? Did B fire the shot with deliberate intent to kill A, and had she thought about it well in advance of the shooting? And so on. Second, the government must *interpret and apply the law.* It must decide whether or not what B did is an instance of the behavior prohibited by the law against murder. Third, if B is found to have committed murder, the government must *punish the offender.* It must decide how severe a penalty is warranted by the facts and the law, pass sentence on B accordingly, and make sure the sentence is carried out.

Settling Disputes

Every case that comes before a court involves a dispute between two parties. One party, the *plaintiff,* makes a complaint against the other party, the *defendant.* Either or both of the parties may be private individuals, business corporations, labor unions, pressure groups, public officials, government agencies, or whatever. But the essence of any case at law is a dispute over the merits of the plaintiff's complaint against the defendant. The two parties could, of course, settle their disputes with fists or guns, but the damage done to either or both—to say nothing of innocent bystanders—might well be greater than any benefit coming to the winner. And certainly the community has a stake in having the dispute settled peacefully and justly. So there are three distinct sets of interests in every law case: the plaintiff's, the defendant's, and the community's. The community's interest in the peaceful and just settlement of disputes is protected by having its representative, the court, hear the plaintiff's and defendant's arguments and evidence and decide which should win and how much.

Courts, to be sure, are not the only government agencies that settle disputes. Legislatures, executives, and administrators also settle a good many. But settling disputes is only one among many functions performed by legislators and administrators, whereas it is the essence of the role played by the courts in democratic countries. In that sense, then, settling disputes is especially, but not exclusively, a judicial function.

Judicial Review

Judicial review is *the power of a court to render a legislative or executive act null and void on grounds of unconstitutionality.* Although some English judges in the seventeenth century claimed this power, it first became generally established in some of the American states during the late eighteenth century and was made part of the national constitutional system by Chief Justice John Marshall's decision in *Marbury* v. *Madison* (1803). During the nineteenth and twentieth centuries, the institution of judicial review gradually spread to other nations, and the period after World War I was the time of its widest adoption.

At present about 30 nations expressly assign this power to the courts, and in two other nations the Constitutions have been construed by the courts—as in the United States—as giving them this power. In several nations—Nicaragua and Syria are examples—judicial review exists only on paper, for both the courts and the legislatures do whatever the ruling executive authorities order. In other nations (for example, Canada, Italy, West Germany, and the United States), the courts can—and on occasion do—render legislative and executive acts null and void on grounds of unconstitutionality, and their decisions are accepted as authoritative (though people who object to particular decisions sometimes try hard to get them reversed: *Roe* v. *Wade* [1973] is an example; see Chapter 1).

In Chapters 15 and 16 we will observe a number of instances in which the U.S. Supreme Court has used its power of judicial review to play a critical role in the development of rules governing political speech and the status of African-Americans, women, and other minorities.

THE TWO BASIC SYSTEMS OF JUSTICE

Adversarial

Most court proceedings in the United States, Great Britain, and the former British colonies in various parts of the world are based on the premise

Lawyers Differ in More Ways Than One.
British barristers leaving court. (Source:
Robin Laurance/Photo Researchers.)

that justice is best achieved by the **adversarial system of justice**—*a system in which a neutral court hears the arguments and evidence presented by the plaintiff and the defendant and makes its decision on the basis of what it has heard.* The fundamental ideas underlying the adversarial system of justice are the following: The task of the courts is to settle legal disputes. A legal dispute results from a plaintiff's charge that a defendant has in some way damaged him illegally. In a criminal case, the government, through its official prosecutor, accuses the defendant of breaking the law. In a civil case, one private party

One of the oldest jokes told in law schools about the adversary system of justice tells of a bright young lawyer who heard of an isolated, small, but rich mining town that had no lawyers. He set up his practice there, figuring that as the only lawyer in town he was sure to make a lot of money. In fact, however, he got almost no cases and was rapidly going broke. Then a second lawyer moved to town, and within a couple of years they were both rich.

accuses another of illegally harming his person or property. The trial itself is a contest between the two adversaries. Each side presents its arguments, supports them with testimony from witnesses and other evidence, and tries to discredit the other side's case by cross-examining its witnesses, challenging its evidence, and refuting its arguments. The court's function is to umpire the contest and to declare the winner. It makes sure that each side, in presenting its case and attacking that of its adversary, stays within the established rules of the game—rules of proper evidence, argument, demeanor, and so on. And the court hands down the decision according to its perception of the true facts and relevant law that emerge in the contest between plaintiff and defendant.

The criminal-law version of this pattern is the Anglo-American accusatorial system for determining the guilt or innocence of suspects. The police investigate the facts and report to the prosecutor. The prosecutor goes before a grand jury to convince them that there is enough evidence to justify *indicting* (formally accusing) a particular person in order that a full trial may take place. The person thus indicted is the defendant in the ensuing trial, and the government is the plaintiff. The court (a judge, either acting alone or with a trial jury) listens to the arguments and evidence presented by the two adversaries, the prosecution and the defense, and decides whether or not the defendant is guilty as charged. If the verdict is "innocent," the defendant goes free. If it is "guilty," the court fixes the penalty, within limits laid down by the law. But the court itself has little or no power to produce evidence, cross-examine witnesses, or act as anything other than a neutral umpire of the contest between adversaries, hence the label "adversarial system of justice."

Inquisitorial

France and a number of continental European countries use the quite different **inquisitorial system of justice**—*a system in which the court takes an active role in getting evidence and questioning witnesses as the basis for its decisions.*

The French procedure begins when the police notify the public prosecutor (*procureur*) that they believe that a designated person probably committed a particular crime. If the prosecutor agrees, he notifies an examining magistrate (*juge d'instruction*), who proceeds to conduct the important preliminary investigation (*enquete*). This *enquete* goes a great deal further than a hearing before a grand jury. The magistrate examines the accused and the witnesses in private. He is empowered to open mail, tap telephones, commission reports by experts, and take other steps to learn the facts. When faced with conflicting testimony by two or more witnesses, he can question them until he is satisfied that perjury has been eliminated and that discrepancies in testimony have been reduced to a minimum. When the *enquete* is completed, the *juge d'instruction* decides whether or not to send the case to trial. He does so only if

The Inquisitorial System of Criminal Justice. The French court trying Klaus Barbie for war crimes, 1987. (Source: Reuters/Bettmann Newsphotos.)

he is convinced that the accused is guilty, and so the subsequent trial is usually little more than public verification of the record accumulated in the *enquete*. (The award-winning French film *Z* provides a dramatic description of an *enquete* in which the original prosecutors end up as the defendants!)

The inquisitorial system of France differs from the adversarial system of the Anglo-American democracies in three main respects. First, the decision of whether or not to try a person accused of a crime is made by a professional judge representing the Ministry of Justice, not by a grand jury of ordinary citizens. Second, the body of evidence and arguments by which the fate of the accused is determined is controlled by the judges (both in the *enquete* and the later trial, if any) rather than by the adversaries; the judges can take the initiative to get any evidence they need to make a just decision. And, third, the result is less affected than in the adversarial system by the ability or inability of plaintiffs or defendants to hire especially skilled lawyers to represent them.

On the available evidence, however, we cannot say that either the adversarial or the inquisitorial system is clearly more effective in punishing the guilty or protecting the innocent. But it is important to note that these two quite different systems are used by various democracies to achieve the goals of fair procedures and just results they all seek.

HIERARCHIES OF APPEAL

The Principle of Hierarchy in the Process of Appeal

In Chapter 13 we observed how important to many administrative systems is the principle of "hierarchy"—that is, the principle that every agency should be clearly either the superior, the equal, or the inferior of every other agency. Only thus can everyone know which agency has the power to issue orders to which other agencies. The same principle is basic to every court system, especially in the process of appeal.

The court systems of all modern democracies provide a process of appeal—that is, a process whereby the loser of a case can ask a higher court to review the manner in which his trial was conducted. If the higher court conducts such a review and finds that the first trial was improperly conducted in some important respect, it can throw out the first trial and order that a new trial be held. But this is possible only if all the courts are related to each other in a clear hierarchy of appeal. The hierarchy of appeal among the main courts in the United States is shown in Figure 14.1.

Some hierarchy of courts such as the one shown in Figure 14.1 is absolutely essential to any process of appeal, for if it were possible for the loser in *any* case to appeal the decision to some other court, the process of appeal could go on forever, no final decisions could ever be made, and the plaintiffs and defendants would grow poorer and poorer while the lawyers grew richer and richer.

As it is, however, every court system provides a process of appeal from lower to higher courts up to but not beyond a supreme court. When the supreme court has handed down a decision, the only further judicial appeal possible is a request to the supreme court to reconsider and reverse its own decision, a request rarely granted.

General Structure of Hierarchies of Appeal

Although the details of the courts' names and the cases that they are authorized to hear vary considerably from one country to another, most hierarchies of judicial appeal have four main levels, listed in order of increasing power:

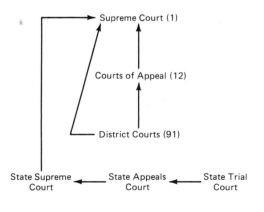

FIGURE 14.1. The hierarchy of appeal among the main American courts (Source: United States Government Manual 1984/85 (Washington, D.C.: Office of the Federal Register, 1984), pp. 59–69.)

Preliminary courts.   In many systems the lowest courts on the judicial ladder are what may be called preliminary courts—including justices of the peace (in Great Britain, Switzerland, and France), *conciliatores* and *praetors* (Italy), *Amtsgerichte* (West Germany), and so on. These bodies have the power to try only small civil cases and misdemeanors, and most refer all major cases to the next level of courts.

General trial courts.   Every system has as the first major rung of its judicial ladder a number of courts authorized to try most civil and criminal cases. In the American national system they are called federal district courts; in Great Britain, county courts for civil cases and crown courts for criminal cases; in France, *tribunaux de premiere instance;* in West Germany, *Landsgerichte;* and so on.

Intermediate courts of appeal.   Most systems provide a level of intermediate courts that mainly hear appeals from the trial courts and rarely or never act as trial courts. In the American system there are regional federal courts of appeal and one for the District of Columbia; in Great Britain there is the national Court of Appeal; in France there are twenty-seven regional courts of appeal; in West Germany there are several *Oberlandesgerichte;* and so on.

Supreme courts.   Every system has a national supreme court. In each nation this court acts as the final court of appeal, and in some nations it also acts as a trial court in a few special cases. These bodies include the Supreme Court of the United States, the British House of Lords, the French and Italian Courts of Cassation, the German *Bundesgerichtshof,* the Swiss Federal Tribual, and so on.

The United States Supreme Court, 1989 (Source: The Supreme Court of U.S.)

A few democracies have established special national tribunals (like Italy's Corte Constituzionale) in addition to their regular supreme courts to pass upon the constitutionality of legislative and executive acts in the process known as judicial review (see the foregoing discussion). However, most of the systems using judicial review vest final reviewing power in their regular supreme courts.

SELECTION AND TENURE OF JUDGES

Lawyers and Judges

Every modern democratic nation has a distinctive legal profession whose members are specially trained in its legal principles and procedures by law schools or as apprentices to established lawyers. Most are required to pass government-administered examinations to become certified as full-fledged members of the legal profession. In the United States all such professionals are called lawyers, and no formal distinctions are made among them because of their specializations within the profession. Great Britain, on the other hand, separates its lawyers into two categories: solicitors, the "office lawyers" who give advice and prepare documents but rarely appear in court; and barristers, the "trial lawyers" who do the actual pleading before the higher courts. The French have three classes of lawyers: *avouets,* who are comparable to British solicitors; *avocats,* who are analogous to barristers; and *notaires,* who specialize in drafting and registering legal documents.

The main difference between the Anglo-American and French systems is that in the Anglo-American the legal profession is regarded as the source not only for legal advisers and advocates but also for all but minor judicial positions. All judges of the higher courts are former lawyers, all have had the same kind of legal training and experience as practicing lawyers, and lawyers and judges alike are regarded as members of one profession pursuing different aspects of a legal career.

In France, however, a sharp distinction is made between the legal and judicial professions. Young French citizens interested in the law decide early in their training whether they want to be lawyers or judges. If they decide on lawyers' careers, they take the appropriate training, pass examinations, and become *avouets, avocats,* or *notaires.* If they choose judicial careers, after finishing legal training they go to the Centre National d'Etudes Judiciaires for four years. The successful graduates become, in effect, civil servants under the Ministry of Justice. They are assigned to courts of first instance and work their way up to the higher judicial posts much as junior civil servants rise in other ministries.

Appointment and Removal of Judges

With a few exceptions, which we will consider in a moment, most modern democratic nations select all their judges, from the lowest justice of the peace to the presiding judge of the highest court, by appointment. The appointing officials vary somewhat from nation to nation, but in many nations all judges are appointed by the chief executive or by the minister of justice or the equivalent; in a few nations judges of some lower courts are appointed by judges of higher courts. Generally speaking, all appointed judges hold office "during good behavior," which means that they can be removed only by a special act of the legislature, called an address of Parliament in Great Britain and impeachment in the United States. This removal power is rarely exercised, however, and most judges in most democratic nations hold their offices for life.

Election and Recall of Judges

Appointment for life tenure is the general rule for judges, but a handful of systems follow different paths. In Switzerland some cantons choose some or all of their judges by popular election for limited terms of office, and the 26 members of the Federal Tribunal, the Swiss national supreme court, are elected by the national legislature for six-year terms. However, the major exception to the appointment-for-life pattern is to be found in the American states.

As of 1986, 14 states elected all their judges; in 12 states most judges were elected and a few minor ones appointed; in 12 states higher judges were appointed initially but later had to win re-election by popular vote; in 9 states all judges were appointed for life; and in 3 states most judges were appointed and a few were elected.

In 4 states, furthermore, judges were subject to "recall." Under this procedure, if a designated number of voters sign a petition asking for the removal of a certain judge, a special election is held to determine whether or not she will remain in office. If a majority of the voters vote to recall her, she immediately leaves office, and her post is filled either by appointment or by a special election. (This is exactly what happened in 1986 to Rose Bird, chief justice of the California supreme court.)

In the American states there is thus far more direct popular control over the selection and tenure of judges than in any democratic nation except possibly Switzerland; for, we should remember, all *federal* judges in the United States are appointed by the president with the approval of a majority of the Senate and remain in office until they die, resign, or are impeached and convicted by Congress (which has happened only 13 times in our entire history).

Does it make any difference? Many political scientists, jurists, and lawyers argue that the popular election of judges is a serious weakness in the states' judicial systems, and they have pressed for the replacement of elective systems with some version of appointment and permanent tenure. They argue that a judge who must worry about re-election will remain more a politician than a judge and cannot develop the calm, detached judicial temperament that every judge should have. They also argue that popular election produces frequent turnover among judges and that few stay in office long enough to acquire the experience necessary to be a good judge. And they contend that when a judge who faces re-election is considering his decision in a case he is likely to pay at least as much attention to what will be popular with the voters as to what the correct decision is under the law.

How valid are these arguments? No one can say with certainty, for while there is plenty of argument on these matters, there are very few careful scholarly studies of them. Indeed, such studies will be very difficult to conduct until we can find an objective method for deciding who is a "good" judge and who is a "bad" one that goes well beyond the simple criterion of whether we like or dislike the decisions they make. For some time to come, this question is likely to be debated on the basis of hunches and general impressions rather than on the basis of systematic scholarly knowledge. One thing is clear, however: There is no indication that many of the states presently using the elective system are likely to drop it in favor of an appointive system, or vice versa.

OFFICIAL RELATIONSHIPS WITH LEGISLATURES AND EXECUTIVES

Separation of Judges from Prosecutors

Many people and nations that do not believe in the doctrine of separation of powers (see Chapter 11) nevertheless strongly support the ideal of an independent judiciary. This ideal calls for organizing the judiciary in accordance with two main principles. The first principle holds that the prosecutor and the judge should never be one and the same person or agency; for if they are, the court loses all semblance of impartiality and becomes merely an arm of the prosecution, a "star chamber" travesty of justice (the Star Chamber was a body established by the English monarchs in the sixteenth century to administer summary "justice" in secret to their political opponents). This evil can be avoided only by making the courts independent of the executive.

This principle is most clearly and firmly established in the Anglophone (English-speaking) democracies. At both the national and state levels in the United States, for example, the prosecuting function is vested in an executive agency headed by an attorney general, who supervises the work of a number of local U.S. attorneys (for the national government) and states' attorneys or district attorneys (for the state governments). In Great Britain the prosecuting function is vested mainly in the director of public prosecutions, who, under the direction of the attorney general, prepares the cases against those accused of crime and engages lawyers to prosecute the cases in court.

The Western European nations, on the other hand, treat judges and prosecutors as different sections of the same public service. In France, for example, there is a single profession—*la magistrature*—which includes three kinds of offices: the "sitting judges," who preside over the courts much as

English and American judges do; the *parquets,* who form a kind of public prosecutor's office attached to each court; and the administrative staff of the Ministry of Justice. All are regarded as civil servants under the same ministry, and any member of the *magistrature* may serve in any of these three offices. It is not uncommon, in fact, for a particular *magistrat* to move from work on the bench in one court to work in the *parquet* of another, from there to a position in the ministry, and perhaps back again to a high judicial post. In any regular French court, both the judge and the prosecutor are officers of the Ministry of Justice, and the two functions are much less clearly separated than in the Anglophone democracies.

Insulation of Judges from Political Pressure

The second principle of the independent judiciary prescribes that the judicial process should operate in an atmosphere of calmness, deliberation, and, above all, insulation from pressures by parties and pressure groups with axes to grind. Thus the courts should be independent of the legislature as well as the executive. In accordance with this principle, the insulation of judges from political pressure is generally sought by securing their tenure from partisan interference. The Constitution of the United States, for instance, provides that all federal judges shall hold office "during good behavior" (that is, until removed by impeachment for "high crimes and misdemeanors") and that their salaries shall not be reduced during their tenure in office. Judges can be removed from office only through impeachment by a majority of the House of Representatives and conviction by a two-thirds majority of the Senate. In Great Britain and other Englishspeaking democracies, judges can be removed from office only by "an address of Parliament"—that is, by resolutions of legislative majorities calling for the removal of particular judges.

In France and most Western European countries before World War II, the tenure, salary, and promotion of judges depended mainly on the decisions of the various ministries of justice. Since 1945, however, some nations have followed France's lead in establishing special bodies to ensure that the status of judges will be somewhat better protected than by ordinary ministerial procedures. France has established a special judicial supervisory body, the Conseil Superieur de la Magistrature, chosen partly by the national assembly and partly by the judicial profession itself, to supervise the corps of judges separately from that of the *parquets* and other civil servants. However, the ministry retains the power of veto over the council's recommendations for the appointment and promotion of judges.

On the basis of these facts, then, it seems that the Anglophone nations come nearer to realizing the ideal of an independent judiciary than most Western European nations do, but the latter appear to be moving in that direction. But however *formally* independent they may be, the *actual* separation of judges from "politics" is a different matter, as we will now see.

THE ROLE OF JUDGES IN GOVERNING

The 1970s and 1980s have produced a series of attacks on the American courts more severe than any since President Franklin D. Roosevelt tried to "pack" the Supreme Court with judges sympathetic to his policies in 1937. These attacks, moreover, have come from both the Right and the Left. Right-wing critics have been outraged by the Supreme Court's decisions in the school-segregation cases in the 1950s; in the cases on school prayer, legislative apportionment, and rights of defendants in the 1960s; and in the cases on capital punishment, abortion, busing of school children, and affirmative action in the 1970s and 1980s. The conservative critics have charged that the Supreme Court, especially under chief justices Earl Warren (1953–69) and Warren Burger (1969–86), acted like a bunch of liberal politicians rather than a body of learned jurists and, worst of all, that they "legislated"—that is, wrote their own ideas of policy into the Constitution rather than interpreting that document "as it really is."

The courts, of course, have not lacked their defenders. In a rather ironic switching of sides, liberals in the 1970s and 1980s made essentially the same argument that conservatives had made in the 1930s to defend the conservative Supreme Court that was throwing out many New Deal programs as unconstitutional: Any attack on the integrity and independence of the courts will violate cherished American traditions and make us "a government of men, not of

---

In the 1980s, the Conservative attack on the Supreme Court increasingly took the form of calling for a new constitutional convention to launch such amendments as forcing the president and Congress to adopt balanced budgets, outlawing abortion, and reinstituting prayer in the public schools. (In fact, economist Herbert Stein suggested that all these proposals be consolidated into one omnibus amendment that would require school children to pray for a balanced budget!) Article V of the Constitution provides that "the Congress ... on the application of the Legislatures of two thirds of the several states shall call a Convention for proposing Amendments. ..." No such convention had ever been called in the nation's history, but by mid-1989, a total of 33 state legislatures—just one short of the necessary 34—had adopted resolutions calling for a convention to consider a balanced-budget amendment.

Constitutional experts were widely divided on a number of questions about such a convention: Do the state resolutions have to be in identical form? How would the members of such a convention be selected? Would the convention be required to consider *only* a balanced-budget amendment, or could it take up any matter and propose any amendments it wished? There were no definitive answers because there were no precedents. Many members of Congress were fearful that such a convention would "run amok" and urged Congress to adopt a proposed balanced-budget measure. No constitutional convention has yet been called, but it remains a live option with a large number of potential complications and consequences.

laws." This switching of sides has led some observers to conclude that the debate over the role of the courts is really a fight between liberals and conservatives over the *content* of the courts' decisions, not about the *procedures* by which the decisions are made. After all, when conservative judges controlled the Supreme Court in the 1930s, liberal critics wanted to reduce its powers, while conservatives praised it as the bastion of American liberty. When liberal judges came to control the court, conservatives wanted to reduce its powers while liberals praised its independence.

Ronald Reagan's election to the presidency in 1980 changed the situation and the sides again. For years before he was elected president, Reagan was one of the most forceful conservative critics of the courts, and when he took office in 1981 he declared his firm intention to fill future judicial vacancies with appointees "who agree with my judicial philosophy," judges who would shun "judicial activism" and practice "judicial restraint"—that is, who would not interpret the Constitution so as to advance liberal policies and sabotage conservative policies (defined about as we defined them in Chapter 4). He was as good as his word. In his eight years in office, almost all of his nominees for the federal courts at all levels were carefully screened to make sure that they were

Judges are Judged for their Policy Views as well as Their Legal Learning.
Judge Robert H. Bork testifying before the Senate Judiciary Committee that voted against his appointment to the U.S. Supreme Court, 1987. (Source: AP/Wide World Photos.)

not judicial activists, and his first nominees to the Supreme Court (Sandra Day O'Connor, Antonin Scalia, and William H. Rehnquist to move from associate justice to chief justice) were strong political conservatives. As the Court grew more conservative, more and more of the attacks on it came from liberals and from groups speaking for the interests of women and ethnic minorities.

The conflict reached its peak in 1987. The Court had become much more evenly balanced between liberal and conservative justices, and the justice who many observers saw as the "swing vote" between the two groups, Lewis Powell, announced his retirement. To succeed him, Reagan nominated Robert H. Bork, a former professor at the Yale Law School, a distinguished scholar of constitutional law, a judge of the federal court of appeals, and the leading exponent of judicial restraint, who struck many moderates and most liberals as a man committed to reversing some key previous Court decisions regarded as great liberal victories. A large and powerful coalition of liberals, women's groups, and African-American and other ethnic groups mounted a major campaign against the nomination, and the Senate finally voted it down by a sizeable majority.

For our purposes, the most interesting aspect of all these debates about the courts from the 1930s to the 1980s is that the fact that the leading advocates of both sides in so many of them talk as though they adhered to a "mechanical" conception of the judicial process, which may be summarized as follows.

THE MECHANICAL VIEW

Judges as Technicians

According to the traditional conception of the proper distribution of governmental powers, as we noted earlier in this chapter, the function of the courts is to interpret and apply, in particular cases, the general rules formulated by law-making bodies. Judges do not *make* the law; they *discover* and *apply* it.

This view of the judicial function stems mainly from the views expressed in perhaps the most widely read and influential of all books among lawyers in the English-speaking world for two centuries: the *Commentaries on the Laws of England* by the eminent eighteenth-century English jurist Sir William Blackstone. To Blackstone (and, apparently, to many of his readers) judges are "the living oracles ... who are bound by an oath according to the law of the land." Even when they reverse earlier rulings on points of law, he wrote, "it is declared not that such a sentence was *bad law,* but that it was *not law.*"[2]

The Blackstonian picture of judges as skilled technicians "declaring" rather than making law is well summarized in the following statement by the nineteenth-century American jurist James C. Carter:

> *That judges declare, and do not make, the law is not a fiction or a pretense, but a profound truth. If courts really made the law, they would have and feel the freedoms of legislators. They could and would make it in accordance with their own views of justice and expedience. ... I need not say that the case is precisely contrary. ... They must decide it consistently with established rules. ... Any judge who*

assumed to possess that measure of arbitrary power which a legislator really enjoys would clearly subject himself to impeachment.[3]

The Ideal of a Nonpolitical Judiciary

According to the mechanical conception, then, judges "declare" law that others have made; they do not make it themselves. Finding out what the law *is* is thus a task for legal technicians, not politicians. It demands a high order of legal skill and training and a "judicial temperament"; therefore, adherents of this conception insist that the courts should be organized so that these difficult technical tasks are performed effectively and so that the judiciary can consider each case strictly on its legal merits without being influenced by political considerations. Four conditions must exist for that ideal to be realized: First, the judiciary must be independent of both legislature and executive, which are necessarily political agencies. Second, the judiciary must be insulated from the selfish and noisy demands of political parties and pressure groups. Third, judges should be selected for their legal skill and judicial temperament rather than for their political preferences. And fourth, judges should refrain from public statements of their policy preferences and should be careful to use only the technical language of the law in writing their decisions.

Judges, in short, should remain completely aloof from politics, and politics must not be permitted to befoul their deliberations. The strength of this ideal is suggested by the fact that until 1941, U.S. state and national judges were allowed to punish for contempt of court any person who sought to influence a judge while a case was in process—and even the Supreme Court decision that struck down this rule was made by a bare majority. And in Great Britain even today, a newspaper can be fined heavily for even discussing a case in any but the vaguest terms while it is *sub judice* ("under judicial consideration").

Description or Ideal?

Many people who uphold this view of the judicial process believe that many judges *do* behave in this fashion, although they usually disagree on *which* judges do. As we have seen, conservatives in the 1930s generally believed that the U.S. Supreme Court was only doing its constitutional duty in throwing out New Deal legislation, whereas the liberals accused the judges of writing their own social and economic views into the Constitution. In the 1960s and 1970s, the tables were turned. Liberals praised the Court for protecting our constitutional liberties, conservatives attacked it for trying to pervert the Constitution with the justices' "left-wing political ideas," and radicals scorned it as a "front for the establishment."

The point is that today, just as in 1937, a great many of *both* the Court's critics and its defenders adhere to the traditional mechanical conception in the sense that they believe that it is the correct standard to apply to actual judges—that it is not only morally right but also an attainable ideal if we can only get and keep the right kind of judges on the bench. In this sense, then, the traditional conception has had a powerful influence upon people's thinking about the role of judges in governing.

JUDICIAL LEGISLATION

An Avoidable Deviation?

The present controversy over whether the Supreme Court is "legislating" its social and economic views or merely "declaring" the Constitution is not unique to the 1930s or our time. Such controversies have flared up over and over again ever since the birth of the Republic. The Jeffersonians, for example, bitterly accused John Marshall's Supreme Court and the rest of the Federalist-packed judiciary of trying to write Federalist party policies into the Constitution. Andrew Jackson and his chief justice, Roger B. Taney, were attacked by the Whigs on similar grounds, and the Taney Court's decision in the Dred Scott case in 1857 was condemned perhaps more violently than any other in history. The conservative justices of the late nineteenth and early twentieth centuries were often charged with trying to write their laissez-faire preferences into the Constitution. And we have already noted the controversies over the Court in 1937 and since 1954.

Complaints about "judicial legislation" have thus been frequent in the United States and are probably a permanent feature of American politics. The scattered evidence available suggests that similar, though perhaps less frequent and noisy, complaints are perennial in every nation with a well-established tradition of an independent judiciary. When we examine the political views of those who attack and those who defend the courts on this score, we find, significantly, that with very few exceptions, people who approve the political effects of a particular line of decisions defend the courts for "enforcing the Constitution," whereas those who dislike those effects claim that the courts are improperly "engaging in judicial legislation." It depends, it seems, on whose ox is being gored.

The point is, however, that most of those who have charged the Court with engaging in judicial legislation seem to believe that it is an *avoidable* deviation from the Court's true function of declaring the law and that the right kind of justices—that is, jurists who are skilled technicians and who accept and adhere to the proper mechanical function of declaring the law—can restore the Court to its proper role in the governmental process.

Inherent in the Judicial Process?

By no means all analysts of the judicial process regard judicial legislation as something that could and would be avoided if all judges had the right attitudes toward their jobs. A growing number of legal scholars, judges, and political scientists argue that judicial policy making is an inherent and inescapable consequence of the very nature of the judicial process itself. Many start

---

SOME RECENT JUDICIAL LEGISLATION IN THE UNITED STATES

Since the early 1950s, the Supreme Court of the United States has not merely waited for Congress and the president to take the lead in all important policy areas and then followed their leads. The court has itself *initiated* a number of major public policies. Among the most important are the following:

> *School desegregation:* voiding all laws requiring that white and African-American children attend separate schools.
>
> *School integration:* requiring that all public schools must have a reasonable mixture of African-American and white children even if that requires busing some white children to predominantly African-American schools and vice versa.
>
> *Legislative reapportionment:* requiring that all congressional and state legislative districts have approximately equal populations, so as to maximize the principle of "one person, one vote."
>
> *Criminal justice system:* guaranteeing a lawyer to every accused person and strengthening limitations on police conduct of questioning and searches.
>
> *State and local antipornography laws:* weakening them to the point where it is now legal to publish and sell just about any kind of book, magazine, or movie that explicitly portrays any and all variations on the sex act.
>
> *Birth control and abortion:* removing restrictions on the sale of birth control devices and on the ability of pregnant women to have abortions on demand.

---

from a premise stated by the eighteenth-century jurist and Anglican bishop Benjamin Hoadly: "Whoever hath an *absolute authority to interpret* any written or spoken laws, it is *he* who is truly the *Law-Giver* to all interests and purposes, and not the person who first spoke or wrote them. ..."[4] They contend that all constitutions, statutes, executive and administrative rules, and other laws are necessarily general to some degree and must therefore be somewhat vague. They have to be interpreted in specific cases, but usually there is no single interpretation that is agreed upon by all people with advanced technical legal training and skills. Lawyers and judges often disagree among themselves about what the law means in particular situations. Previous court decisions rarely settle the question, for some precedent can be found for just about every possible interpretation. Indeed, it is the duty of the lawyers for both sides to bring before the court lists of such precedents, each list calling for an opposite interpretation from that of the other. Every judge is thus continually faced with different— but, judged by any reasonable standard, equally logical— interpretations.

Each interpretation necessarily favors the interests of some groups and damages those of others. The judge cannot help choosing one of the alternatives and therefore cannot avoid promoting the interests of some and hurting those of others. When we look behind the legal jargon, we have to recognize that the process by which a judge chooses one interpretation over the others and makes his decision is, by our definition, *political.* Why? Because whatever decision he makes necessarily satisfies some values and frustrates others.

This observation is true, these writers argue, of *every* court, because every court has the power to "interpret," if not to "strike down," a law. And it will continue to be true until jurists perfect a machine like a cash register on which the judge can punch keys labeled "the facts," pull down a lever called "the law," and read "the decision" that pops out.

To illustrate this characterization of the policy-making functions of the judiciary, let us consider the role that the U.S. Supreme Court has played in the conflict over racial segregation in the schools.

An Illustration: "Equal Protection" and the Schools

The Fourteenth Amendment to the Constitution of the United States declares that "no State shall ... deny to any person within its jurisdiction the equal protection of the laws." Beginning in the late nineteenth century, the southern and border states enacted a series of "Jim Crow" laws prohibiting African-Americans from attending the same schools, riding in the same train cars, using the same public swimming pools and golf courses, and eating in the same restaurants as whites. A number of antisegregationists thought that these laws violated the equal-protection clause; on the other hand, most southern whites and many northerners were segregationists, and they had no doubt that such laws were perfectly in accord with this clause. Certainly the wording of the clause is vague enough so that reasonable people—and even specialists in constitutional law—could and did disagree about whether it prohibits or permits segregation laws.

In the case of *Plessy* v. *Ferguson* (1896), the Supreme Court was called upon to decide whether or not a state law requiring racial segregation on trains was constitutional. It found that under the equal-protection clause, segregation *in itself* is not unconstitutional as long as the accommodations provided for each race are substantially equal to those provided for the other. This ruling came to be known as the separate-but-equal formula.

From then until the late 1930s the Court, following the Plessy formula, upheld all state segregation laws and, indeed, was easily satisfied with what constituted equality of accommodations. In the 1930s, however, the Court began to take a different line. It insisted, for example, that states that would not admit African-Americans to their public universities must provide *really* equal facilities for them. In *Sweatt* v. *Painter* (1950), the Court insisted that Texas either admit an African-American applicant to the University of Texas law school or establish a separate law school for African-Americans that would be its equivalent in every respect—a multimillion dollar project.

Next came the landmark case of *Brown* v. *Board of Education* (1954), in which the Court explicitly overruled the Plessy decision and held that, no matter what accommodations are provided for the two races, segregation in

Every Justice of the Supreme Court has from one to three law clerks to help him or her with the work. Although some effort is made to draw them from various parts of the country, most are recent graduates of the nation's most prestigious law schools. It is a great honor to be chosen as a clerk and a marvelous start for a lawyer's career. The competition is fierce for the few posts available each year, the law graduates chosen rank at the very top of the law schools' classes, and most have been editors of their schools' law reviews.

The clerks do a good deal of the justices' routine but necessary work. They screen thousands of petitions every year by people who want the Court to review their cases, and they recommend to the justices which few should be reviewed. They do research on the facts and legal precedents relevant to the cases before the Court. They often write memoranda for their justices on points of law that have to be decided in the cases. They often try to persuade their justices to vote a particular way on a particular case and to follow certain lines of reasoning in their written opinions. One of the less praiseworthy indications of their importance is the fact that interviews with current and recent clerks about how the justices really behave behind the scenes were the main sources of information used by Bob Woodward and Scott Armstrong in their sensational popular expose *The Brethren* (1980).

However, the most striking testimony to their importance is made by Martin Shapiro, a distinguished scholar of judicial behavior:

> *It is a long-time open secret, although rarely discussed in print, that most of the words in most of the opinions are written by clerks. At one extreme, a justice may tell his clerks which party he wants to win in a given case and then let them do the whole job, merely reading the clerk's finished product and signing it. At the other, a justice may write the entire opinion, asking his clerks only for research assistance on particular points. Some of the justices fall near the first extreme in the handling of nearly every case. Others choose to do a good deal of original writing in certain select cases. There may be a few justices who actually write a majority of the words they sign as their own each year.*[5]

public schools is *in itself* a denial of equal protection for African-Americans, and that therefore all state laws requiring racial segregation in the schools are in violation of the Fourteenth Amendment.

There matters stood until the late 1960s and early 1970s, when the Court decided that equal protection does not mean merely no segregation—it means full integration. It took the position that the ultimate goal is a situation in which there are both African-American and white children in every school, and while every school does not have to reflect the proportions of the races in the whole community and some one-race schools may be permissible in special circumstances, any school system that has ever deliberately practiced racial segregation can be forced to use racial quotas and mandatory busing of children of both races to achieve the proper racial mixture.

Many commentators have bitterly attacked the Court for its role in the school-segregation and busing controversies, and some of the present argument about the proper role of the Court arises from it. The Court's critics charge it with making policy. So it has, beyond a doubt. But some of these critics seem to imply that *all* judicial policy making is highly irregular and wrong, regardless of the content of the policies made. What they forget, or at least do not wish to remember, is that the phrase "equal protection of the laws" is so vague that no single interpretation is clearly preferred by all persons of good will and legal expertise. The point is that the 1896 Court, which declared the separate-but-equal formula, was *also* making policy. In throwing out that formula in 1954 and in developing its later desegregation-is-integration position, the Court was not making policy for the first time; rather, it was reversing policies made earlier.

If present critics of the court, liberals or conservatives, were given complete freedom to amend the Constitution and put on the Court justices whose policy preferences were exactly like their own, they could very likely force it to make the kind of policy they prefer. But there is no conceivable way, short of abolishing courts and judges altogether, to prevent them from making *some* kind of policy. Policy making is inherent in the nature of the judicial process itself.

JUDGES IN THE POLITICAL PROCESS

In recent years a number of political scientists, whose approach was pioneered by Jack W. Peltason in his monograph *Federal Courts in the Political Process* (1955), have viewed the judicial process as simply one aspect of the total political-governmental process and have used many of the same techniques that other political scientists use to study the legislative, executive, and administrative processes. Peltason suggested a number of generalizations, most of which have been borne out by subsequent research.[6]

Peltason contended that the courts are as much involved in political conflict (as the term is used in this book) as any other government agency, for every case that comes before a court involves a conflict of interest between plaintiff and defendant, and many cases involve the interests of groups far broader than just the parties themselves. In deciding each case—for example, ordering this man to go to jail for rioting or that corporation to end its control over other firms or that school board to bus African-American children to white schools—the courts make policies in precisely the same sense that other government agencies do (see Chapter 1). Policies made by courts differ from those made by legislatures, executives, and administrators only in form, not in substance.

This has become even more clear in recent years with the increase in the number of "class-action" suits heard and decided by the courts. A **class-action suit** is *a case brought by a plaintiff on behalf not only of himself but of all other* *persons similarly situated.* The original school desegregation case in 1954 is a famous example. The suit was brought on behalf of Linda Brown, an African-American girl who was required by the rules of the Board of Education of Topeka, Kansas, to attend an exclusively African-American school. But in bringing the suit, the National Association for the Advancement of Colored People (NAACP) asked the court to outlaw forced segregation not only in Topeka but everywhere else, and to allow not only Linda Brown but every other African-American child similarly situated to attend schools with white children. The Court agreed, and the effect of the decision was to outlaw legally required racial segregation in the schools everywhere.

Peltason further suggested that for all the lip service paid to judicial independence, the interests most powerfully affected by court decisions have never refrained from trying to influence their outcomes. Perhaps the main difference between political conflict centered on the courts and conflict centered on the other government agencies is that legal conflict must be conducted in an atmosphere generated by the general acceptance and respectability of the mechanical conception of the judicial process. If a pressure group announces quite openly, "We intend to put pressure on Congress, the president, and the bureaucracy to get our policies adopted," few will think that is improper. But let it announce with equal frankness that "We intend to put pressure on the judges to make their decisions in our favor," and many potential allies will become enemies because they disapprove such efforts to "tamper with the integrity of the courts." Thus while a great many political interest groups *do* try to influence judicial decisions, they rarely *talk* as though that is what they are doing. Rather they talk of "defending the integrity of the courts," "defending the Law against political judges," "making sure that judges with sound views of the Constitution get on the bench," and the like.

This kind of talk does not alter the *fact* of political conflict in the judicial process, but it does mean that such conflict is conducted in a rather special way. Peltason pointed to three main areas of political conflict in the judicial process:

Selection of Judges

When selecting federal judges in the United States, most presidents and senators have *talked* as if they have been selecting only technicians of jurisprudence but have *acted* as if they have been selecting policy makers whose views they wished to be in accord with their own. "Since 1885 over 90 percent of all Federal judges have been filled by members—in most cases active members—of the same party as the President who chose them and most have been supporters of the senator who nominated them."[7] The only president in recent years to fall below this average was Republican Gerald Ford, whose judicial appointments included only 81 percent Republicans. Democrat Jimmy Carter appointed over 90 percent Democrats, however, and Republican Ronald Reagan appointed over 90 percent Republicans.

The American Bar Association (ABA), the national professional association of lawyers, has asked for a greater voice in the selection of judges (after all, the ABA argues, who knows the technical competence of potential judges better than other lawyers?), but the many other interests involved have been reluctant to turn over so much power to what is, in many instances, a rival interest. On the other side of the fence, many judges have clung to their posts long after age and failing health have indicated the advisability of their retirement. Why? Because they have so strongly opposed the political views of the incumbent president and Senate majority that they have not wished the latter to name their successors. Thus in the mid-1980s there were persistent rumors that liberal Supreme Court justices William Brennan and Thurgood Marshall, though old and in poor health, were determined to stay on the Court as long as possible to keep conservative President Ronald Reagan from naming their successors.

Decision Making

Interest groups try to influence the selection of judges whenever they can, but judges' long tenure means that for the most part the groups have to work with and through the judges who are in office. An interest group takes a terrible risk if it tries to influence a judge in the same manner in which it might try to influence a member of Congress or an administrator. Most groups therefore exert direct influence only through such accepted channels as employing expensive and able lawyers, presenting the best possible briefs, and so on. It is interesting to note that in recent decades it has become increasingly common for interest groups to submit *amicus curiae* ("friend of the court") briefs and to offer other legal help to plaintiffs and defendants who represent legal principles that they want established or upheld. Many such briefs were submitted on both sides, for example, in the school-segregation cases of 1954 (see the earlier discussion) and the Bakke case on affirmative action in 1979 (see Chapter 16). The ablest lawyers and the best-drawn briefs by no means always ensure victory, of course—but they help.

Implementation of Decisions

In Chapter 13 we noted that just because a law has been enacted by the legislature and approved by the executive does not necessarily mean that it will be applied by the administrative agencies exactly, or in some instances even approximately, as its authors intended. The administrative process can be as significant a determinant of the policies that government actually follows as the legislative and executive processes.

The same thing can be said of the judicial process. Just because the Supreme Court or any other judicial body has declared what the law is on a particular point does not necessarily mean that every other court and government agency will act accordingly. For one thing, the Court's decision is technically binding only upon the specific parties in the particular case, and if interest groups similar to those represented by the losing party choose to ignore the decision, they can often get away with it. In 1947, for example, the Supreme Court declared that the Board of Education of Champaign County, Illinois, had violated the constitutional separation of church and state in its "released-time" program by allowing teachers to hold classes in religion in the public schools and requiring pupils either to attend the classes or to remain in study hall. After the decision the Champaign school board discontinued its program, but similar released-time programs were continued in many thousands of other school districts throughout the land as if nothing had happened. An even more dramatic illustration occurred in 1955, when the Supreme Court ordered the desegregation of all public schools "with all deliberate speed"; yet for over a decade the schools in many southern states remained almost as segregated as they had been before the 1955 order.

Furthermore, the formal hierarchical structure of court systems is no guarantee that the lower courts will invariably interpret the law exactly as the higher courts wish. As Peltason pointed out:

> *The subordinate judge's task of applying the Supreme Court's mandates is no more mechanical than is the Supreme Court's task of applying the Constitution's mandates. The high court decisions which are supposed to guide and control the subordinates are frequently just as ambiguous as is the Constitution or statute which is supposed to guide the Supreme Court, and they admit of many interpretations. Hence, just as it is said that the Constitution is what the judges say it is, so it can be said that a Supreme Court decision is what the subordinate judges who apply it say it is.*[8]

Finally, groups whose interests are damaged by an adverse Court decision do not have to accept their defeat as final, and they rarely do. They can, for example, try to have the Constitution amended to prevent such rulings in the future (the Eleventh and Sixteenth Amendments were adopted for just such purposes); to persuade the Court to reverse itself (as it did, for example, in the *Brown* case); to induce the lower courts to ignore the decisions; or to pack, or threaten to pack, the Court. Judicial decisions thus do not necessarily settle once and for all the political conflicts with which they deal, any more than legislative acts or executive orders do. But because of the high prestige and officially nonpolitical atmosphere of the judicial process, a favorable court decision is an important victory for any interest group.

THE COURTS AND THE DEMOCRATIC POLITICAL PROCESS

Some readers who may grant that I have presented a reasonably accurate picture of what the courts in the democracies actually do may nevertheless find it depressing. Perhaps they prefer to believe that *somewhere* in the political-governmental process, issues are settled not through conflict between opposing selfish groups, but by real statesmen who are guided only by eternal principles of right and wrong. Perhaps they have given up on legislatures and executives but still hope that they will find such statesmanship in the courts.

Yet there is no reason to be depressed by this picture of the judicial process. After all, democracy is a process in which political conflict takes place among groups that are freely organized and at liberty to express their views—a process that takes the form of discussion and peaceful agitation in a spirit of respect for others' rights to live and "pursue happiness." If there is any validity in this view of democracy, then there is no reason to be either surprised or depressed by learning that judges and courts, like legislators, executives, and administrators, are part of one pervasive democratic decision-making process.

FOR FURTHER READING

LAW AND COURT STRUCTURES

*ABRAHAM, HENRY J. *The Judicial Process,* 3rd ed. New York: Oxford University Press, 1975. Clear and informative description of court structures and procedures in the United States, France, and Great Britain.

DANASKA, MIRJAN R. *The Faces of Justice and State Authority.* New Haven, CT: Yale University Press, 1986. Comparative study of the administration of justice in modern nations.

*JACOB, HERBERT. *Justice in America.* 4th ed. Boston: Little, Brown, 1984. Survey of court structures and legal systems in the United States.

SHAPIRO, MARTIN. *Courts: A Comparative and Political Analysis.* Chicago: University of Chicago Press, 1986. Comparative study of the structure and role of courts in Western democracies.

SOPER, PHILIP. *A Theory of Law.* Cambridge: Harvard University Press, 1984. Discussion of nature of law compared with other types of social rules.

THE JUDICIAL PROCESS

*AGRESTO, JOHN. *The Supreme Court and Constitutional Democracy.* Ithaca, NY: Cornell University Press, 1984. An argument for judicial restraint as the best solution to the perennial problem of reconciling judicial review with democracy.

BERGER, RAOUL. *Government by Judiciary.* Cambridge: Harvard University Press, 1977. Attack on excessive power exercised by courts in American policy making.

BLAIR, PHILIP M. *Federalism and Judicial Review in West Germany.* New York: Oxford University Press, 1981. Useful comparative study of operation of judicial review in a European federal democracy.

*CHOPER, JESSE H. *Judicial Review and the National Political Process.* Chicago: University of Chicago Press, 1982. Analysis by a leading legal theorist of the role of courts and judicial review in the American political system.

FRANK, JEROME. *Law and the Modern Mind.* New York: Brentano's, 1930. Leading exposition of "legal realist" view.

*HOROWITZ, DONALD L. *The Courts and Social Policy.* Washington, D.C.: Brookings Institution, 1977. Analysis of role of courts in making social policy.

*JOHNSON, CHARLES A., and Bradley C. Canon. *Judicial Policies: Implementation and Impact.* Washington, D.C.: Congressional Quarterly Press, 1984. Analysis of what happens to court decisions after they are handed down.

*PELTASON, JACK W. *Federal Courts in the Political Process.* New York: Random House, 1955. Seminal exposition of the conception of the judicial process as part of the political process.

PERRY, MICHAEL J. *The Constitution, the Courts, and Human Rights: An Inquiry into the Legitimacy of Constitutional Policymaking by the Judiciary.* New Haven, CT: Yale University Press, 1982. Analysis of role of courts in civil liberties decisions as an approach to evaluation of judicial review.

STUMPF, HARRY P. *American Judicial Politics.* New York: Harcourt Brace Jovanovich, 1988. Survey of research on how political and legal interpretation interact in the making of American judicial decisions.

NOTES

[1] *Black's Law Dictionary,* 4th ed. (St. Paul, MN: West, 1968), p. 445.

[2] William Blackstone, *Commentaries on the Laws of England,* ed. by Thomas M. Cooley (Chicago: Callaghan and Cockroft, 1871), vol. 1, p. 69, italics added.

[3] James C. Carter, "The Province of the Written and Unwritten Law," (1890), quoted in Fred V. Cahill, Jr., *Judicial Legislation* (New York: Ronald Press, 1952), p. 17, n. 26, italics added.

[4] Quoted in Cahill, *Judicial Legislation,* p. 99.

[5] Martin Shapiro, "The Supreme Court," in Anthony King., ed., *The New American Political System* (Washington, D.C.: American Enterprise Institute, 1978), p. 199.

[6] Jack W. Peltason, *Federal Courts in the Political Process* (New York: Random House, 1955), p. 31.

[7] *Ibid.,* p. 21.

[8] *Ibid.,* p. 14.

15 Human Rights: Principles and Problems

Our reliance is in the love of liberty, which God has planted in us. Our defense is in the spirit which prized liberty as the heritage of all men in all lands everywhere. Destroy this spirit and you have planted the seeds of despotism at your own doors. Familiarize yourselves with the chains of bondage and you prepare your own limbs to wear them. Accustomed to trample on the rights of others, you have lost the genius of your own independence and become the fit subjects of the first cunning tyrant who rises among you.

Lincoln, Speech at Edwardsville, Illinois, 1858

If a nation values anything more than freedom, it will lose its freedom; and the irony of it is that if it is comfort or money that it values more, it will lose that too.

W. Somerset Maugham, Strictly Personal (1941)

A free press can of course be good or bad, but, most certainly, without freedom it will never be anything but bad. ... Freedom is nothing else but a chance to be better, whereas enslavement is a certainty of the worse.

Albert Camus, Rebellion and Death (1950)

PHILOSOPHICAL FOUNDATIONS FOR HUMAN RIGHTS

THE BASIC TERMS

In this and the next chapter, we will consider some of the philosophical issues and practical problems involved in what many people think is the most important of all the areas in which governments relate to people: the area variously called *human rights, civil liberties,* and *civil rights* (in a moment I will try to untangle the terms). As we will see, the philosophical issues are complex, and their applications almost always involve choices between one good thing and another good thing, not between something that is wholly good and something that is wholly bad.

So let us begin by making clear what some of the most basic terms mean. The most basic concept is that of **human rights,** which are *protections to which all human beings are entitled because of their humanity, not their social status or individual merit.* Some of these rights are claimed and enjoyed without regard to the political order, but since this book is concerned with politics and government, we will focus on the two types of human rights that are most closely involved with the actions of governments: civil liberties and civil rights.

As we will use the term in this book, **civil liberties** are *constitutional protections of persons, opinion, and property against arbitrary interference by government.* They include such familiar protections as freedom of speech, freedom of the press, freedom of religious belief, and freedom from arbitrary arrest and punishment.

And **civil rights** are *legally guaranteed benefits provided by a positive actions of government.* They include such guarantees as education, protection against illness and starvation, and financial support in unemployment and old age.

THE EVOLVING IDEA OF HUMAN RIGHTS

Government as the Enemy

The basic idea of human rights is rooted in the two ideologies of constitutionalism and classical liberalism we considered in Chapter 4. For our present purposes we need to recall the beliefs of such seventeenth- and eighteenth-century philosophers as John Locke and Thomas Jefferson that the most precious value in all human society is the individual human being, and the great goal of governments—indeed, the only moral justification for their existence—is to liberate individuals from the economic, political, religious, and moral shackles by which they had been bound through centuries of subjection to absolute monarchs, feudal economies, and official religions. And the best way to do this is by instituting *constitutional* governments—governments whose powers are limited in such ways that they cannot and will not abridge individual liberties (see Chapters 4 and 5).

According to classical liberalism, then, government was the principal potential enemy of human rights, and constitutionalism was the answer. Thus the constitutions of liberal democratic nations written before World War I guarantee only rights of persons *against* government. Their "bills of rights" contain only lists of actions that government is prohibited from taking against individuals, such as abridging freedom of speech and religion, conducting unreasonable searches and seizures, coercing confessions, and the like. The classical meaning of a *civil liberty,* in short, was something that a government may not do to a person. Government was thus viewed as the main enemy of liberty.

This conception of human rights was rooted in the conviction of the constitution makers of the eighteenth and nineteenth centuries (following the ideas of John Locke) that human beings are naturally free and that government is an artificial creation of people rather than a universal creation of nature. As such, government is inherently hostile to human freedom and must be watched suspiciously and restrained resolutely.

Locke and his followers also recognized, however, that people's rights are unsafe in a state of anarchy, for when human aggressions are entirely unrestrained, there is always grave danger that the strong will ride roughshod over the rights of the weak. Some kind of government, they believed, is indispensable to the protection of the rights of *all* humans, weak and strong alike.

Thus they faced a dilemma: Human rights cannot be preserved without government, but government itself is inherently hostile to those rights. The only way they could see out of the dilemma was to organize government so that it would maintain law and order without abridging people's rights; and the only way to do that, they were convinced, was to organize it according to their version of the ancient doctrine of constitutionalism. All rightful governments, they held, must operate within strict limits specified by constitutions. Each constitution, in turn, must firmly restrain government power by listing what government may not do (as in a bill of rights), carefully defining what it may do (as in a list of enumerated powers), and establishing separation of powers—that is, distributing government power among three separate and independent branches of government, the legislative, executive, and judicial (see Chapter 11). In this way, they believed, the power of government could be restrained sufficiently to minimize its inherent danger to human rights.

It is not surprising that Locke and his followers regarded government as the principal enemy of human rights. After all, the governments under which they lived operated according to such principles as the divine right of kings and the privileges of royalty and nobility over peasants and yeomen. The violations of human rights of which they were aware—the suppression of antimonarchy speeches and writings, the secret jailing and torture of the monarch's opponents and dissenters from the official religion—were all committed by agents of authoritarian governments in the name of royal prerogatives and "reasons of state." The only serious and visible threat to human rights in Locke's time was government; as a result his belief in those rights led him logically to the antigovernment doctrine of constitutionalism, the *doctrine that government power should be limited so as to protect human rights.*

In modern times, however, the liberal democratic nations have instituted governments whose decisions are made, not by autocratic monarchs and their lackeys, but by popular majorities and their representatives. Even so, many citizens of modern democracies fear that popular majorities may sometimes try to override the rights of minorities. They believe that constitutional government is just as necessary to the preservation of human rights against popular majorities as it ever was to their preservation against the authoritarian governments condemned by Locke and Jefferson centuries earlier.

The constitutions of the American states and the national government written after 1776 were the first in modern times to attempt to put the ideal of constitutionalism into practice. It soon became apparent that the new systems needed "watchdogs"—that is, agencies whose special duty and power are to determine whether or not any branch of government is exceeding its constitutional limits. In the United States the courts, rather than the legislatures or the executives, took over this role by assuming the power of judicial review—the power of courts to annul legislative and executive acts by declaring them unconstitutional (see Chapter 14). Some nations with constitutional governments have assigned the watchdog function to their legislatures rather than to their courts (and some nations whose constitutions formally establish judicial review have no watchdogs and thus actually have governments that are neither free nor constitutional).

Whether or not they have the power of judicial review, the courts in all free nations have a special role in the protection of human rights, because a great many (though not all) of the conflicts over rights are fought out in cases at law. When a person is tried for a crime, for example, the court must not only determine the defendant's guilt or innocence but must also decide whether or not the defendant's rights to a fair trial and due process of law are respected in the framing of the charges, selection of the jury, admission of evidence, and proper provision for counsel. When a court decides a libel suit brought by plaintiff A against defendant B, it must determine whether or not in the particular circumstances A's right to a good reputation has been unduly damaged by what B has written about A—and whether or not punishing B would abridge B's freedom of speech and press. Only some free nations give their courts the power to void laws as unconstitutional; but the courts of all free nations necessarily have the power to interpret and apply in specific cases the laws and constitutional provisions guaranteeing civil liberties. Court decisions and judicial interpretations thus constitute a significant body of data in discovering the actual status of civil liberties in any free nation, whether or not its courts have the power of judicial review. In Chapter 16 we will review a number of such decisions and interpretations.

The Modern View: Government as Both Enemy and Ally

Most citizens of modern free nations agree with their eighteenth- and nineteenth-century ancestors that human rights must be protected against repressive government actions. Unlike their forebears, however, they do not regard government as the *only* serious threat to those rights. They have come to believe that there are at least three additional threats, each of which is as dangerous as government repression and each of which can be countered only by enlisting the power and authority of government to protect the individual.

National Government v. Subnational Governments.   The first threat is aggression against the rights of national citizens by subnational governments. A good deal of the conflict over human rights in the United States since the Civil War (1861–65) has arisen from efforts by certain state and local governments to impose racial segregation and white supremacy on African-Americans. The Fourteenth Amendment to the U.S. Constitution makes African-Americans citizens of the United States first and citizens of the states in which they reside second. Furthermore, it stipulates that "no State shall make or enforce any law which shall abridge the privileges or immunities of citizens of the United States. ... " To secure their constitutional privileges and immunities, African-Americans, particularly in the southern states, have often turned to the national government as their principal ally against oppression by state and local governments. In Chapter 16 we will examine this conflict in detail, but this brief mention should serve to illustrate the point that many Americans, and certainly most African-Americans, no longer view *all* governments, in pure Lockean terms, as threats to their rights. They have come to see that government has different levels and agencies, some of which may well be the only instruments powerful enough to protect human rights against infringements by other governments and by private persons and groups.

Government v. Mobs.   The second threat is aggression against the rights of private individuals by other private individuals. For example, the right to a fair trial is sometimes threatened by lynch mobs; the most effective protection of that right in such situations lies in the ability and determination of law-enforcement officers to save the accused from the mobs and thereby guarantee their right to fair trials by the courts. The rights of some African-Americans and Jews to live in the neighborhoods of their choice have been violated by "restrictive covenants"—private agreements among property owners to sell only to white gentiles; their right to decent housing can often be protected best by the passage and enforcement of open-occupancy laws prohibiting such agreements. The rights of members of any sexual, racial, or ethnic group to opportunities for jobs and promotions according to ability and training equal to those of "WASPs" (white Anglo-Saxon Protestants) have often been abridged by private employers' policies; such employment rights can sometimes be secured only by the enforcement of fair-employment-practices laws forbidding such discrimination. (I say nothing here of the problems posed by affirmative action plans, which will be discussed in Chapter 16.) The rights of African-American children to attend unsegregated schools may be violated by white mobs trying to overturn the buses carrying them to school; only the intervention of the police can secure the children's rights and perhaps even save their lives. In all these situations, government is far from being the enemy of human rights; it is, in fact, their chief defender.

Government v. Life's Hazards. In Chapter 4 we noted the nearly universal acceptance in modern nations of the ideal of the welfare state, founded on the conviction that people have a right to at least the minimum conditions of a decent life for themselves and their families. The third kind of threat includes such ancient hazards as unemployment, poverty, old age, illness, and above all, ignorance. Here, too, most modern citizens look to government, not as their enemy, but as their main hope for overcoming these hazards.

Whether or not government's obligations to help people have been formally enshrined in their constitutions, all modern democracies have clearly accepted the principle and from time to time have brought new rights under government protection. Indeed, the principle of the welfare state and some of its guarantees, such as universal free public education and protection against starvation, are so firmly established in all industrialized modern nations that any effort to remove them would be considered as drastic an attack on human rights as would a proposal to repeal the constitutional guarantees of freedom of speech and fair trial.

Similar developments have occurred in the first two categories as well. In the United States as early as 1866, for example, Congress enacted laws penalizing anyone who "willfully subjects any person to a deprivation of any rights or privileges secured by the Constitution or laws of the United States." For many years the enforcement of these laws was left in the hands of U.S. attorneys in various localities, and few people were prosecuted for violating them. In 1939, however, Attorney General Frank Murphy established the Civil Rights Section in the Criminal Division of the Department of Justice and charged it with undertaking more vigorous enforcement of the 1866 and 1870 laws. Since then the national government has played a far more active part in protecting human rights. The greatest single advance came when Congress passed the Civil Rights Act of 1964, which commits the national government to positive action to secure for all citizens full equality in their rights to register and vote, to be served by private businesses offering public accommodations, to use public facilities, and to enjoy equal job opportunities. We will examine the act and its impact further in Chapter 16, but it should be marked here as the greatest legislative triumph for modern-style liberalism in the United States since the ratification of the Thirteenth, Fourteenth, and Fifteenth Amendments.

TRADITIONAL COMMUNIST VIEWS OF HUMAN RIGHTS

Since the rise of liberalism in the seventeenth century, its ideas have often been challenged, and liberal institutions have been undermined or overthrown in many countries. Many authoritarian regimes of the twentieth century—Adolf Hitler's Germany, Benito Mussolini's Italy, Francisco Franco's Spain, the Ayatollah Khomeini's Iran, Mu'ammar al-Qaddafi's Libya—have been explicitly antiliberal in philosophy and totalitarian in fact. In the last third of the twentieth century, however, the main challenger to the liberal idea of human rights has been the ideology and institutions of Communism as expounded and practiced by Marx, Lenin, Stalin, and their followers (see Chapter 4).

Formal Guarantees in the 1977 Soviet Constitution.   The 31 separate articles of Chapter 7 of the Soviet Constitution of 1977 enumerate "The Basic Rights, Freedoms, and Duties of USSR Citizens," which include many of the same rights enumerated in the constitutional regimes: for example, freedom of speech, the press, assembly, meetings, street processions and demonstrations (Article 50); separation of church and state, and religious freedom (Article 52); immunity from arbitrary arrest (Article 54); and so on.[1]

Similar guarantees were provided in the Soviet Constitution of 1936, yet all the world now knows what Nikita Khrushchev revealed in his famous speech to the Twentieth Communist Party Congress in 1956: that for 30 years under Joseph Stalin's dictatorship (and 20 years under the 1936 Soviet constitution) secret arrests, torture, and execution without trial were the lot of anyone even suspected of harboring rebellious thoughts against the regime. There was some "thaw" under Nikita Khrushchev (1958–64), but under Leonid Brezhnev (1964–82) the traditional Communist lid was clapped on again, and many novelists, poets, scientists, and pamphleteers were exiled to "corrective labor camps" or committed to mental hospitals or, like the world-famous physicist Andrei Sakharov, exiled to Siberia because of their antiparty and anti-Communist ideas. And when in 1968 the liberal-leaning Communist leaders of Czechoslovakia allowed "dangerous" freedom of expression, resulting in "provocative" criticism of Soviet leaders and the Communist system, Soviet troops and tanks under Brezhnev's orders invaded and efficiently crushed the Czechs' growing liberalism. Soviet troops were poised to do the same thing in Poland in the early 1980s when the rise of the Polish Solidarity labor movement threatened to pull down the Communist regime and replace it with a more liberal one; but Poland's own Communist leader, General Wojciech Jaruzelski, was able to stamp out the dissent enough to keep the Soviets from taking over.

In Chapter 4 and elsewhere we have taken note of Mikhail Gorbachev's efforts to introduce *glasnost* (openness) in the system, and since he took power in 1985, political discussion and dissent has been far more free and open in the Soviet Union than at any time in the Communist regime. Many observers believe that tremendous improvements in human rights have already taken place in the Gorbachev regime, and more are on the way; others say that it all depends on whether Gorbachev's reforms, including *glasnost,* produce soon enough the kind of economic improvements by which their success will be judged. And we should note that some Soviet leaders continue to believe in the conception and practice of human rights expounded by Marx, Lenin, and Stalin.

What the Traditional Communist Guarantees Mean.   What, then, are we to make of the traditional Communist guarantees of freedom as set forth in the

1977 Constitution? Have they been mere verbal smokescreens put up to mask the Soviet leaders' naked and unrestrained power from ordinary Russians and the outside world? Have they been sincere but illogical expressions of what a liberal would regard as very illiberal ideas about human rights? Or what?

The answer for pre-Gorbachev Communism was presented clearly and unabashedly in the following passage from a leading official Soviet explanation of the 1936 constitution's "bill of rights":

> *The fundamental rights of Soviet Citizens are constitutional rights conforming to the interests of the working people of town and country. ... When Soviet power was coming into being, not a single Soviet institution restricted any citizen in his democratic rights. The bourgeoisie and the landlords took advantage of this and utilized the freedoms of speech, assembly and the press, together with all other political rights gained as a result of the October Revolution, for their counter-revolutionary ends. In their speeches and newspapers the enemies of the working people slandered the October Revolution and the Soviet Government. They interpreted the right to free association to mean freedom for all exploiters and traitors to set up their counter-revolutionary organizations. Similarly, the bourgeoisie and the landlords utilized the electoral rights for their anti-Soviet activity. They fraudulently infiltrated into the organs of the Soviet state, trying to undermine and corrupt them from within. The Soviet Government detected these criminal machinations of the enemies of the working people in good time and deprived them of political rights.*[2]

From this and other official pronouncements, it is clear that the Soviet theorists and leaders did not regard guarantees of human rights as protections of the individual's private and personal self against invasion by the government or the Communist party. Like all other Communist political institutions, constitutional rights were explicitly and unequivocally regarded as tools for sustaining the Soviet regime at home and advancing Soviet interests abroad. For example, Article 50 of the 1977 Constitution prefaces its guarantee of freedom of speech and press with this statement of the purpose of such freedoms: *"In conformity with the interests of the working people and for the purpose of strengthening and developing the socialist system,* citizens of the USSR shall be guaranteed freedom of speech, the press, assembly, meetings, street processions, and demonstrations" (emphasis added).

As a leading Western scholar said of similar language in the 1936 Soviet Constitution, "These 'liberties' are reserved for adherents and denied to opponents of the regime. Freedom, in the Soviet constitutional lexicon, is the duty to ratify the policies of the ruling group and not the right to criticize them."[3] Hence it is quite logical that Soviet dissidents who have openly attacked the system and its leaders should be exiled to foreign countries (Aleksandr Solzhenitsyn), placed in house arrest (Boris Pasternak), exiled to Siberia (Andrei Sakharov), stripped of their citizenship (Mstislav Rostropovich), or put in prison (Anatoly Sharansky). In short, under the Communism of Marx, Lenin, Stalin, and Brezhnev, freedom was freedom to express only correct thoughts.

And the Communist party, not any legislature or court, decided what thoughts were and were not permissible.

Under the *glasnost* of Gorbachev, formal freedom may become real freedom. We will see.

RIGHTS FORMALLY GUARANTEED BY CONSTITUTIONS

Every modern constitution contains at least some formal guarantees of human rights. Needless to say, not every formal guarantee in every nation's constitution represents a genuinely protected right of the people living in that nation. But the presence of formally guaranteed rights in any nation's constitution means that the framers, for whatever reasons, deemed it desirable to pay at least lip service—and perhaps more—to the idea of human rights. I therefore list here the main guarantees found in modern constitutions.

LIMITATIONS ON GOVERNMENT

Protections of Belief and Expression

religious worship* (Rights followed by an asterisk are expressly protected by the Constitution of the United States.)
speech*
press*
secrecy of correspondence
preservation of distinct subnational languages and cultures

Protections of Action

assembly*
petition*
suffrage*
secrecy of votes
prohibition of slavery*
practice of chosen profession
privacy of domicile*
movement within and to and from the nation
organization of labor unions and trade associations
strikes
collective bargaining

Protections for Persons Accused of Crime

prohibition bills of attainder*
prohibition of ex post facto laws*

no guilt by association
prohibition of unreasonable searches and seizures*
no trial without indictment*
no double jeopardy for the same offense*
no coerced confessions*
no excessive bail or fines*
no cruel and unusual punishments*
no extradition for political crimes
no capital punishment
no imprisonment for debt
guarantee of the writ of habeas corpus*
general guarantee of due process of law*
guarantee of a speedy and public trial*
trial by an impartial jury*
ability to confront hostile witnesses*
subpoena power for the defendant*

The Accused and His Rights. John Hinckley, Jr., the attempted assassin of President Reagan in 1981, who was held innocent of attempted murder on grounds of insanity. (Source: UPI/Bettmann Newsphotos.)

assistance of counsel*
equality before the law or equal protection of the laws*

Protection of Property

just compensation for private property taken for
public use*
patents and copyrights*
no impairment of the obligation of contracts*

OBLIGATIONS OF GOVERNMENT

To Provide Economic Assistance

work
equal pay for equal work regardless of sex, age, nationality, or caste
minimum wages
maximum hours
unemployment assistance
social security

To Provide Social Assistance

education
prohibition of child labor
protection of families, children, and motherhood
preservation of historical monuments
recreation and culture

CHOICES IN THE IMPLEMENTATION OF HUMAN RIGHTS

There is no divine command or historic inevitability that human rights will
survive in the Western democracies or anywhere else. Certainly human rights
are today cherished and protected in only a minority of countries, as is shown
by a Freedom House survey made in 1988. They rated each nation according to
these criteria: the freedom of its press, radio, and television to criticize the
government; the freedom of its citizens to speak and write what they wish; and
the citizens' ability to sue the government and win in court. Their ratings are
shown in Table 15.1.

If the Freedom House ratings in Table 15.1 are even approximately
correct, then about 38 percent of the world's population today live under
regimes that permit little or no freedom; another 24 percent live in systems
that seek to protect some freedom some of the time; and 38 percent live in
systems under which protection of freedom is a major value. But for people who
value human rights this is a substantial improvement: In 1977, the percent-

TABLE 15.1. Freedom in Modern Nations

Free	Partly Free	Not Free
Antigua & Barbuda	Bahrain	Afghanistan
Argentina	Bangladesh	Albania
Australia	Bhutan	Algeria
Austria	Brunei	Angola
Bahamas	Cape Verde Islands	Benin
Barbados	Chile	Bulgaria
Belgium	China (Taiwan)	Burkina Faso
Belize	Egypt	Burma
Bolivia	El Salvador	Burundi
Botswana	Fiji	Cambodia
Brazil	Gambia	Cameroon
Canada	Guatemala	Cent. Af. Rep.
Colombia	Guyana	Chad
Costa Rica	Haiti	China (PRC)
Cyprus (G)	Hungary	Comoros Isles
Cyprus (T)	Indonesia	Congo
Denmark	Iran	Cuba
Dominica	Ivory Coast	Czechoslovakia
Dominican Republic	Jordan	Djibouti
Ecuador	Korea, South	Equatorial Guinea
Finland	Kuwait	Ethiopia
France	Lebanon	Gabon
Germany, West	Lesotho	Germany, East
Greece	Liberia	Ghana
Grenada	Madagascar	Guinea
Honduras	Malawi	Guinea-Bissau
Iceland	Malaysia	Iraq
India	Maldives	Kenya
Ireland	Mexico	Korea, North
Israel	Morocco	Laos
Italy	Nepal	Libya
Jamaica	Nicaragua	Mali
Japan	Nigeria	Mauritania
Kiribati	Pakistan	Mongolia
Luxembourg	Panama	Mozambique
Malta	Paraguay	Niger
Mauritius	Poland	Oman
Nauru	Qatar	Romania
Netherlands	Senegal	Rwanda
New Zealand	Sierra Leone	Sao Tome & Principe
Norway	Singapore	Saudi Arabia
Papua New Guinea	South Africa	Seychelles
Peru	Sri Lanka	Somalia
Philippines	Sudan	Syria
Portugal	Suriname	Tanzania
St. Kitts & St. Nevis	Swaziland	Togo

(*continued*)

TABLE 15.1.   Continued

Free	Partly Free	Not Free
St. Lucia	Thailand	USSR
St. Vincent	Tonga	Vietnam
Solomon Islands	Transkei	Yemen, South
Spain	Tunisia	Zaire
Sweden	Turkey	
Switzerland	Uganda	
Trinidad & Tobago	United Arab Emirates	
Tuvalu	Vanuatu	
United Kingdom	Western Samoa	
United States	Yemen, North	
Uruguay	Yugoslavia	
Venezuela	Zambia	
	Zimbabwe	

Source: Freedom at Issue, January–February 1988, p. 30. Copyright 1988 by Freedom House, Inc.

ages were 45 percent in the not-free countries, 35 percent in the partly free countries, and only 20 percent in the free countries. Since then major moves toward liberal democracy have been made by Argentina, Brazil, Chile, Grenada, the Philippines, and Uruguay, while moves in the opposite direction have occurred only in Djibouti, Fiji, and Kenya.

Rejection by authoritarian regimes of the Left and Right are by no means the only problems faced by liberalism today. Even if every fascist, communist, and fundamentalist Muslim were to become an avowed liberal, liberalism would still face enormously complex problems in preserving human rights in modern industrial society. We cannot begin to understand these problems until we recognize that they all involve making painful choices among cherished— but competing—values.

The point may be clarified by considering the two main choices that any constitutional government must make when dealing with human rights.

FREEDOM VERSUS SECURITY

The Problem

One apparently permanent dilemma of government in a free society arises from two facts: First, most citizens value *both* freedom and security. They value freedom for the reasons outlined earlier in this chapter; and they value security—government preservation of law and order—for the reasons outlined in Chapter 1. Second, freedom and security are always in conflict, and whatever government does to advance one may well injure the other.

To illustrate, let us consider the conflicting claims of freedom and security in a hypothetical example. A child is kidnapped and later found brutally tortured and murdered. The outraged townspeople demand that the murderer be arrested and punished immediately. The police turn up enough evidence to convince them that a drifter named John Doe is the murderer—but they cannot gather enough evidence to guarantee his conviction under the stringent rules used in American courts. So they arrest Doe "on suspicion" and "grill" him in an effort to make him confess, knowing that a confession added to the evidence they already have will be sufficient to convict him. But Doe refuses to confess and repeatedly claims that he is innocent. The police are convinced that he is lying, and so they give him the "third degree"—beating him with a rubber truncheon, keeping him without sleep for days, and shining bright lights in his eyes while questioning him. Finally the pressure is too much, and Doe breaks down and confesses. The townspeople, meanwhile, are angry about the delay, and they fear that Doe will go free on some "legal technicality" and the hideous crime will go unpunished. Someone suggests dragging Doe out of jail, and hanging him from the nearest lamp post.

Consider what is involved. If security—which means punishing the guilty and deterring potential criminals—were the *only* value held by the townspeople and the police, then the question of what to do would be easily answered. They should beat a confession out of Doe, or just string him up without a trial.

This course of action is, sad to say, no mere theoretical extreme dreamed up to make a point. In Brazil and Argentina, for example, capital punishment was not legal until recently, and no convicted criminal ever served more than 30 years in jail. Some police in both countries felt that this practice amounted to unendurable coddling of the guilty, so they formed small secret "death squads" that tracked down, tortured, and executed criminals who they thought had cheated the law. Nor should North Americans feel self-righteous about such Latino barbarisms. Not long ago in many parts of the South, lynching was the accepted form of instant trial and punishment for African-Americans accused of major crimes against whites. In the North there have been all too many cases in which prosecutors—despite their sworn duty to protect the innocent as well as to prosecute the accused—have concealed and distorted evidence to build up their conviction scores.

In a nation with liberal traditions and values, however, punishing the guilty is only one of the values that people hold. The townspeople and police in our example have no wish to hang Doe if he is innocent. They must therefore choose which they value more: punishing the guilty or protecting the innocent. If they choose the former and torture or lynch Doe, they run the risk of punishing an innocent man; and if they choose the latter and give Doe all his constitutional rights to a fair trial, they run the risk of letting a murderer go unpunished. They cannot have it both ways; they have to take one risk or the other.

Most citizens of the liberal nations, then, are willing neither to sacrifice all security for absolute freedom nor to abandon all freedom for absolute security. In such nations, accordingly, there is always the problem of determining in each situation just where the line should be drawn between the conflicting claims of freedom and security—for conflicting they will always be.

Some American Standards for Drawing the Line

Recognizing that this kind of decision must be made in every case in which government restraint of human activity is involved, most of us would agree that it should be made according to the most just and sensible general standards we can devise. We certainly do not want to leave it entirely to the personal preferences of whatever law-enforcement officer happens to be around or whatever judge happens to be assigned to the case.

Yet we should recognize that such decisions are not and cannot be made in social vacuums in which the decision makers operate entirely free from any kind of political or psychological pressures for particular decisions. They are made by fallible human beings, often operating under great and conflicting pressures. That being the case, we can learn a good deal about how civil-liberties decisions are made—and with what consequences—by focusing on some of the leading decisions made and issues pending in the United States in recent years.

We may begin by noting that the U.S. Supreme Court has evolved several general standards for drawing the line between freedom and security. The best known have been developed in cases involving the question of when, if ever, speech and writing may be suppressed without violating the First Amendment's command that "Congress shall make no law ... abridging the freedom of speech or of the press." The two principal standards may be briefly summarized as follows.

Clear and present danger.   The decision in *Schenck* v. *U.S.* (1919) first ruled that speech and writing can be suppressed only when "the words are used in circumstances and are of such a nature as to create a clear and present danger that they will bring about the substantive evils that Congress has a right to prevent." This **clear-and- present-danger test** holds that *speech can be constitutionally suppressed only when the words said and the circumstances in which they are said are such that the words create an unmistakable and imminent danger for the community's safety.* The presumption is clearly against suppressing speech, and the burden of proof rests with those who would suppress it. This test, with occasional departures, has been generally followed by the Court in free-speech and free-press cases since 1919.

Gravity of evil.   In its opinion in *Dennis* v. *U.S.* (1951) upholding the conviction of eleven Communist party leaders for conspiring to advocate violent overthrow of the government, the Court took a somewhat different tack. It held that freedom of speech can be restricted whenever "the gravity of evil, discounted by its improbability, justifies such invasion ... as is necessary to avoid the danger."[4] Under this "gravity-of-evil" test, the presumption is substantially more in favor of suppressing speech than it is under the "clear-and-present-danger" test. The Dennis standard has been used by the courts in some post–World War II cases involving the advocacy of Communist doctrines. In cases involving speech by people other than Communists, the Court has sometimes followed one standard, sometimes another.

"Preferred Position"

Since the 1940s, some Supreme Court justices have advocated the "preferred position doctrine"—the view that the First Amendment protections of freedom of speech and press have the highest standing among all the values promoted by the Constitution, and any law that limits those freedoms is permissible only under the most extraordinary circumstances. Under this doctrine the burden of proof is always on the government to show that any restriction of expression it wishes to make is absolutely indispensable to the nation's well-being. And any law or act that cannot pass this extremely demanding test should not be allowed.

The judges holding this view have almost always been in the minority, but their opinions have put extra pressure on the other judges and on legislators and executives to justify the restrictions on freedom of expression that they have occasionally attempted. For that reason it has played a significant part in the continuing process of drawing the line between freedom and security in the United States.

THE RIGHTS OF SOME VERSUS THE RIGHTS OF OTHERS

Some people try to escape the hard choices demanded by the conflict between liberty and security by declaring that "we should all be free to exercise our rights so long as we do not interfere with the rights of others." This platitude has a comfortingly plausible air of sweet reasonableness about it, and its popularity is not surprising. The only thing wrong with it is that it seldom works. Why? Because, in most real-life situations, protecting the rights of some citizens inevitably abridges the rights of others.

Consider, for example, one of the most difficult and bitterly disputed civil-liberties issues of the 1970s and 1980s, discussed in Chapter 1: the clash between the right of a woman to have an abortion in order to avoid having an unwanted baby and the right to life of the fetus (or unborn child—even which *term* is proper is very much in dispute). Until the early 1970s most states had laws prohibiting abortions except when deemed necessary by physicians to save mothers' lives. In the 1960s and 1970s, however, one wing of the women's movement (see Chapter 16) challenged the constitutionality of those laws with increasing vigor. They argued that every woman has a fundamental right to the control of what affects her own body, and that right entitles her to terminate an unwanted pregnancy just as much as it entitles her to refuse unwanted sexual intercourse. Their opponents argued, with equal moral fervor, that every human being has just as much right to life between conception and birth as after birth, and that legalized abortion therefore amounts to legalized murder.

As we saw in Chapter 1, it is a tough and painful issue, but one aspect of it, at least, is quite clear: It cannot be resolved by any pat formula that a pregnant woman's rights leave off where her fetus's begin—or vice versa. If we protect the fetus's right to birth, we cannot avoid abridging the woman's right to control what affects her own body; and if we protect the woman's right, we cannot avoid abridging the fetus's right to live. We cannot, sad to say, have it both ways.

Whatever may be the merits of the issue, the Supreme Court ruled in *Roe* v. *Wade* (1973) that the decision to have an abortion in the first three months of pregnancy is strictly up to the woman and her physician, and their freedom to make that decision may not be restricted by any state or national law. The Court added that governments may exercise some limited control over abortions in the second three months of pregnancy, and they may constitutionally prohibit abortions altogether only in the final three months.

Some Americans hailed the Court's decision as a great victory for women's

Court Decisions Have Political Consequences. Demonstration against the Supreme Court's decision in Roe v. Wade (1973). (Source: UPI/Bettmann Newsphotos.)

rights; others denounced it as a grievous blow to unborn babies' right to life. The issue is still far from settled, however. The prolife forces have pressed hard for a constitutional amendment to override the *Roe* decision and allow states to outlaw abortions, and some of the more zealous members of the movement have even set fire to legal abortion clinics. The prochoice forces have battled hard against the proposed amendment, and the bitterness on both sides has escalated alarmingly.

It is no business of a book like this to say who is right on the issue. But it is the business of this book to point out that there is no way that *either* right can be fully protected and freely exercised without to some extent abridging the other. The Supreme Court—like the state legislatures whose laws it overrode—had to choose in 1973, and choose it did. We may agree or disagree with its choice; we may believe that its reasoning was sound or muddled; we may even question the Court's power to have the final word; but we cannot escape the fact that a choice has to be made. And so it is with all questions of human rights.

HUMAN RIGHTS IN THE POLITICAL PROCESS

HUMAN RIGHTS CONFLICTS AS POLITICAL CONFLICTS

We are likely to understand better what is involved in conflicts over human rights if we remember that they are fundamentally political in nature. To be sure, they are often fought out largely (though never entirely) in courts of law, and some people mistakenly regard the judicial process as somehow not political in the same sense that legislative and executive processes are political (we have already considered this issue in Chapter 14). This may obscure their political nature. Yet according to the analytical framework used in this book, these conflicts cannot be other than political. Every conflict over human rights involves the question of government policy. Should government restrict this person's or that group's freedom of action? And as we saw in Chapters 1 and 2, every government action promotes some people's goals and damages the interests of others.

If, for example, government enforces a policy of racial integration in public schools, it promotes some African-Americans' and whites' goal of equal status and frustrates some other African-Americans' and whites' desire for segregation and/or neighborhood schools. If government promotes affirmative action plans for choosing among applicants for medical schools, it improves the chances of African-Americans and other minorities to become doctors, but it also means that some whites with higher grades and test scores will be rejected in favor of some African-Americans with lower grades and test scores. When government enforces open-occupancy laws, it furthers the claims of African-Americans and Jews to equal housing opportunities and thwarts efforts by certain whites and gentiles to keep their neighborhoods "exclusive" for people like themselves.

One Group's Right is Another Group's Crime. Confrontation between prochoice and prolife demonstrators. (Source: AP/Wide World Photos.)

Government decisions on what to do in these and similar situations are thus, in our sense of the term, *political.* We should therefore expect that they will be made as all other political decisions are made—as the result of conflict among competing political actors. Most of these actors will, of course, publicly defend their positions in terms of constitutional rights rather than self-interest, and most will sincerely believe that freedom of speech, due process of law, racial justice, and other lofty ideals demand decisions favorable to their positions. This tendency should not, however, obscure the fact that in matters of human rights, as in all other matters of government policy, someone stands to gain and someone stands to lose. Students of politics and government will better understand the conflicts over human rights if they explore, in addition to the ideological and legal aspects of the conflict, the question of who stands to win what and who stands to lose what.

SOME CONSEQUENCES

Viewing human-rights conflicts as political conflicts may suggest that the processes by which they are conducted and the government decisions affecting them are essentially the same as the processes by which all other political conflicts are conducted and all other government decisions are made. This approach to human-rights conflicts may well provide an understanding otherwise lacking. Some people, for example, think that government policies (including court decisions) on questions of human rights should always be made in conformity with a set of clear and mutually consistent logical principles, and they are disturbed that such decisions often seem to shift logical grounds according to time and circumstances. Perhaps they would be less disturbed if they recognized the political nature of human-rights conflicts, for then they would start with the assumption that particular decisions are the products, not of ill will or temporary aberrations from sanity by judges and legislators, but rather of the decision-makers' estimates of the variations in the nature and fluctuations in the strength of the competing interests involved.

Another consequence of this view is awareness that in any political system the process by which conflicts are conducted and by which the rights of individuals are determined are shaped by the same forces that shape the system's other political conflicts and decisions. The general condition of human rights in a particular system depends largely on such matters as the number and variety of its competing interests, the issues that separate them and bring them into conflict, the degree of overlapping membership among competing forces, the degree to which the competing groups are mobilized, the number and strength of common interests and other unifying forces, the general level of material well-being and its distribution, the degree of security from foreign attack, and all those other general factors affecting politics and government that we have previously examined.

Like everything else in politics (and human life), then, human rights have considerable costs as well as great benefits. What costs are the free nations and their competing groups willing to bear? We will find some of the answers in the next chapter, in which we consider some of the principal challenges to human rights in modern times and some of the ways in which democratic nations have responded to them.

FOR FURTHER READING

BERNS, WALTER. *The First Amendment and the Future of American Democracy.* New York: Basic Books, 1976. Scholarly argument that First Amendment freedoms should have limits, both as a matter of law and as a matter of wise policy.

*BRIGHAM, JOHN. *Civil Liberties and American Democracy.* Washington, D.C.: Congressional Quarterly Press, 1984. Description of current conflicts in civil liberties.

CORBETT, MICHAEL. *Political Tolerance in America: Freedom and Equality in Public Attitudes.* New York: Longman, 1982. Analysis of popular attitudes on civil-liberties issues, using survey data.

*DWORKIN, RONALD. *Taking Rights Seriously.* Cambridge: Harvard University Press, 1977. Strong civil-libertarian view of present controversies over rights.

FLATHMAN, RICHARD E. *The Practice of Rights.* New York: Cambridge University Press, 1976. Balancing of conflicting claims of liberty and order in modern societies.

*KADARKY, ARPAD. *Human Rights in American and Russian Political Thought.* Washington, D.C.: University Press of America, 1982. Comparison of idea of human rights in liberal and Communist political philosophies.

*KRAMER, DANIEL D. *Comparative Civil Rights and Liberties.* Washington, D.C.: University Press of America, 1982. Study of status of human rights in various parts of the world, especially the United States, the Soviet Union, and France.

McCLOSKY, HERBERT and ALIDA BRILL. *Dimensions of Tolerance: What Americans Believe about Civil Liberties.* New York: Basic Books, 1984. Magisterial study in depth of popular attitudes toward civil liberties, based on massive survey studies.

MEIKLEJOHN, ALEXANDER. *Free Speech and Its Relation to Self-Government.* New York: Harper & Row, Pub., 1948. The best modern exposition of the "preferred position" doctrine.

*MILL, JOHN STUART. *On Liberty* (1859). Many editions have been published of this classic defense of free speech and press.

MILTON, JOHN. *Areoopagitica* (1644). Many editions have been published of this early and still influential argument for free speech and free press.

*SCHAUER, FREDERICK. *Free Speech: A Philosophical Inquiry.* New York: Cambridge University Press, 1982. In-depth analysis of the philosophical pros, cons, and limits of free speech.

*SHAPIRO, IAN. *The Evolution of Rights in Liberal Theory.* New York: Cambridge University Press, 1985. Account of the development of theories of individuals' rights from the seventeenth century to the present.

*WOLFF, ROBERT PAUL, BARRINGTON MOORE, Jr., and HERBERT MARCUSE, eds. *A Critique of Pure Tolerance.* Boston: Beacon Press, 1969. New Left attack on liberal ideas of free speech, especially interest for Marcuse's ideas on "repressive tolerance."

NOTES

[1] An English translation of the 1977 Soviet Constitution is printed in *Keesing's Contemporary Archives,* December 9, 1977, pp. 28,701–709.

[2] A Denisov and M. Kirichenko, *Soviet State Law* (1960), quoted in Randolph L. Braham, ed., *Soviet Politics and Government: A Reader* (New York: Knopf, 1965), p. 393.

[3] Merle Fainsod, *How Russia is Ruled,* rev. ed. (Cambridge, MA: Harvard University Press, 1963), p. 378.

[4] *Dennis* v. *U.S.,* 341 U.S. 494 (1961).

16 Human Rights: Challenges and Responses

In all criminal prosecutions, the accused shall enjoy the right to a speedy and public trial, by an impartial jury of the State and district wherein the crime shall have been committed ... and to be informed of the nature and cause of the accusation, to be confronted with the witnesses against him; to have compulsory process for obtaining witnesses in his favor, and to have the Assistance of Counsel for his defense.

Sixth Amendment to the U.S. Constitution

No State shall make or enforce any law which shall abridge the privileges or immunities of citizens of the United States; nor shall any State deprive any person of life, liberty, or property without due process of law; nor deny to any person within its jurisdiction the equal protection of the laws.

Fourteenth Amendment to the U.S. Constitution

The history of liberty has largely been the history of the observance of procedural safeguards.

Felix Frankfurter, McNabb v. U.S. (1943)

There is a danger that, if the Court does not temper its doctrinaire logic with a little practical wisdom, it will convert the constitutional Bill of Rights into a suicide pact.

Robert H. Jackson, Terminiello v. Chicago (1949)

In every nation that values liberty, the problem of preserving human rights in a world of international conflict and nationally racked with clashes among groups and interests is both persistent and enormously difficult. In the

United States and most other such nations, the problem has, in recent years, broken out of the quiet of the scholar's study and the judge's chambers into the forefront of political struggle.

"Moral Majority Denounces Supreme Court's Ban on School Prayer." "Police Claim They Are Handcuffed in Catching Criminals." "School Bus Wrecked in Protest over School Race Balancing." "Abortion Clinic Bombed by Right-to-Lifers." "Affirmative Action Plan Clashes with Union Seniority Rule." Such headlines have been prominent in American newspapers since the end of World War II, and current disputes over civil rights are among the most virulent the nation faces.

The dilemma confronted by every free nation in preserving human rights, as we saw in Chapter 15, cannot be solved by the simplistic formula that we should all be free to do what we wish so long as we do not interfere with the rights of others. Every government action makes some people do something or prevents some people from doing something. Unavoidably, every such action restricts *someone's* freedom to some extent. Guaranteeing a pregnant woman's right to an abortion abridges her fetus's right to life. Protecting Jehovah's Witnesses' right to seek converts by door-to-door canvassing abridges the residents' right to privacy. Protecting a suspected criminal's privacy by prohibiting the tapping of his telephone handicaps police efforts to protect other people's rights to security of life and property. Affirmative action plans to increase the hiring of African-Americans and women makes it harder for whites and men to get jobs. Preserving human rights forces all free nations to make choices—hard choices, *political* choices.

Accordingly, this chapter details some of the situations that pose in their most acute form the great problems—and possibilities—of governing in the last quarter of the twentieth century. It is, of course, impossible in the space of one chapter to describe all the challenges to human rights and all the government responses to those challenges in all modern free nations. So our discussion will be limited to a survey of three areas of political conflict over civil rights that, especially in the United States, get the most attention today: police powers and defendants' rights, the status of women, and the status of African-Americans.

CONFLICT OVER POLICE POWERS AND DEFENDANTS' RIGHTS

CRIME AND THE POLICE

In the United States, as in all constitutional democracies, the critical problems in criminal justice arise from the inescapable conflict between the need to catch, convict, and punish criminals and the need to protect the rights of persons accused of crime. We begin by sketching the extent of crime and the tasks and problems of the police.

Crime, Organized and Unorganized

We noted in Chapter 1 that a political system differs from all other social systems mainly in that it makes authoritative rules—rules that bind all people living in the society and that take precedence over the rules of all other social organizations. Because people are people and not angels, no government's rules are obeyed by all of the people all of the time. The most serious kind of violation is called a crime—that is, "any act done in violation of those duties which an individual owes to the community, and for the breach of which the law has provided that the offender shall make satisfaction to the public."[1] Crimes are usually subdivided into felonies (the more serious) and misdemeanors (the less serious) and are punishable by fines, imprisonment, or death.

Crimes are different from *torts,* which are offenses committed against private individuals but not considered damaging to the whole community. For example, if A spreads malicious stories intended to ruin B's reputation, A is considered to have slandered B but not to have injured the whole community. Hence B's remedy is to sue A for damages, and the community's interest is solely to see that the dispute is conducted fairly and settled equitably. But if A shoots and kills B, A is considered to have damaged not only B but also the basic security of the whole community. Therefore, the government will prosecute A for the crime of murder, not the tort of slander, and if he is found guilty he will be imprisoned or executed.

No one knows precisely how many crimes are committed in each year in any modern nation, for some are always undetected and others are unreported. However, reasonable estimates suggest that crime rates have been fluctuating in many Western democracies in recent years. The most authoritative annual estimates of U.S. crime rates are made by the Federal Bureau of Investigation (FBI), and its figures are summarized in Table 16.1.

A majority of the crimes reported in Table 16.1 were "unorganized"; that is, they were committed by individuals acting alone or in small groups, as in the

TABLE 16.1. Crime Rates in the United States, 1978–86

Year	(Number per 100,000 population)		
	Violent Crime*	Property Crime†	Total Crime
1978	498	4,643	5,140
1980	597	5,353	5,950
1982	571	5,033	5,604
1984	539	4,492	5,031
1986	617	4,863	5,480

*Includes murder, forcible rape, robbery, aggravated assault.

†Includes burglary, larceny-theft, motor vehicle theft.

Source: Statistical Abstract of the United States, 1988 (Washington, D.C.: Bureau of the Census, 1988), Table 263, p. 158.

muggings that have made the streets and parks of so many American cities unsafe at night. But a good many offenses are committed by "organized crime"—large and well-organized criminal "corporations" like Cosa Nostra, which operate for profit both illegal enterprises (narcotics, loan-sharking, extortion, "protection," and so on) and legal businesses (real estate, restaurants, bars and taverns, vending machines, and the like).

Crime ranges from crimes of passion in families to adolescent "joy-riding" in stolen automobiles to such highly organized and profitable businesses as selling narcotics and running the numbers game. Organized or unorganized, crime continues to present a serious threat to everyone living in the United States as well as a massive challenge to the police forces, which bear the main government responsibility for preventing crime and capturing criminals.

The Job of the Police

To ensure that its laws are obeyed, every political system must rely mainly on the willingness of its citizens to obey the law voluntarily—yes, even when they do not believe that a particular law is just. After all, it simply is not possible to put half or three-quarters of the population in jail or to shoot them or exile them. Consequently, as we noted in Chapter 1, any political community in which a substantial portion of the people reject the legitimacy of the government's powers and refuse to obey its laws is no longer a community, but a battlefield for civil war.

Yet no political system depends *entirely* upon voluntary obedience to the law by all its citizens. Every system has some kind of organized police to deal with law breakers. There is wide variation among (and within) modern nations in the organization, specialization, training, methods, and effectiveness of police, but in all nations they are charged with detecting and arresting law breakers and delivering them to the executive and judicial agencies for determination of their guilt or innocence (see Chapter 14). Many totalitarian systems have also relied heavily upon special secret police concerned with such "crimes against the state" as speaking and working against the regime. The best-known examples in recent years have been the Nazi Gestapo, the Savak of the former Shah of Iran, and the Soviet agency known successively as the Cheka, GPU, NKVD, MGB, MVD, and (today) KGB.

We are concerned here only with tasks generally assigned to nonsecret "regular" police. They include preventing violations of law from taking place (patrolling streets and checking stores to discourage muggers and burglars), stopping law violations that do take place (removing political protesters who are blocking public highways), determining who has committed crimes, arresting suspects and delivering them to the prosecuting authorities, and providing evidence at their trials. In a free nation the police have at least one additional major duty: to protect the legal and constitutional rights of all persons, whether they are law breakers or innocent bystanders.

The Lot of the Police

The police officer's job, then, is to enforce the law—but only by the means and within the limits allowed by the law. A character in a Gilbert and Sullivan operetta sings that "the policeman's lot is not a happy one," and it seems that in many modern nations, including the United States, that is indeed the case. The duties of the police are always demanding, and they often risk physical injury and even death. All too often they are underpaid, undereducated, and overworked. Furthermore, they frequently must work among people who distrust and hate them, particularly in urban slum and ghetto areas, where crime rates are high. The most common epithets applied to the police—"pig," "flat-foot," "cossack," "the fuzz"—do not encourage them to feel that they serve in a proud profession respected by all. Even the occasional "Support Your Local Police" bumper sticker or a sympathetic television program like "Hill Street Blues" does not help their morale very much.

At bottom, however, the lot of the police is unhappy because, more than most public officials, they operate on the front lines of the conflict between society's widely held but conflicting values of security and freedom. We can sit in our classrooms and righteously endorse *both* law and order and civil liberties without having to adjust one to the other more than verbally. But the police are charged with fighting crime *and* with protecting the rights of everyone, including law breakers. Depending upon the kind of trouble the police may have in resolving this conflict, they may be charged with brutality, incompetence, laxity, or corruption. To understand the police's dilemma better, let us briefly survey some of the rights they are charged with protecting while fighting crime.

THE RIGHTS OF DEFENDANTS

The Law

Although there are many variations in detail from one nation to another, the main rights of defendants most commonly guaranteed by law in the Western democratic systems include the following.

Pretrial rights.　The law guarantees every person immunity from arbitrary arrest: He may be arrested only in pursuance of a warrant issued by a judge or upon a police officer's belief, supported by some valid evidence, that he may have committed a crime. If his arrest satisfies neither requirement, he can collect damages by suing the arresting officer for false arrest. Shortly after his detention, the suspect has the right to the *assistance of counsel,* and if he cannot afford a lawyer, the government is obligated to provide one for him. During his interrogation by the police he has the *right to remain silent* and his silence cannot be used as evidence against him. The *prohibition of coerced confessions* means that he cannot in any way be forced to give testimony that might help to convict him. Perhaps most important of all, he has the right to a *writ of habeas corpus.* If the police arrest him and jail him, but refuse to charge him formally before a court, he or his lawyer can petition a judge for a court order commanding the jailer to produce the prisoner and show cause for his detention. If the judge decides that the detention is unlawful—that the charges are unspecified or the evidence is insufficient—she orders the prisoner's immediate release. More than any other legal device, the writ of habeas corpus is a safeguard against "preventive detention" and imprisonment without trial—devices which are commonplace in authoritarian methods of law enforcement.

Rights during trial.   The law guarantees a fair trial to every person accused of crime. It requires that *advance knowledge of the specific charges* be given to the accused so that he may prepare his best defense. His right to the *assistance of counsel* means that if he cannot afford a lawyer to conduct his defense, the court must appoint and pay for one for him. There must be an *impartial judge,* an *impartial jury,* or both to decide the case on the basis of law and evidence, without prejudice against the defendant. He can obtain a *change of venue* if he can convince the judge that the climate of opinion at the trial site is prejudicial to his defense. He has the same power as the prosecution to *subpoena witnesses.* He (or his lawyer) has the right to *confront and cross-examine hostile witnesses.* His *immunity from double jeopardy* means that if in a valid trial he is found innocent of a particular crime, he can never again be tried on that same charge. *No ex post facto law* can be applied to him; that is, he cannot be convicted of a crime that was not a crime when he committed it. If convicted, he has the *right of appeal* to a higher court, and if he can convince the appellate court that he has not been allowed full exercise of his rights, his conviction will be set aside. If his conviction stands, *no cruel and unusual punishment* can be inflicted upon him.

In sum, the law in most constitutional systems presumes the defendant's innocence and places the burden of proof upon the prosecution. Insufficient or inconclusive evidence and reasonable doubt are supposed to be resolved in his favor. This legal premise reflects the conviction that it is important to make sure that no innocent person is punished even if the price is that some guilty persons escape punishment.

Issues in the Conflict

Each of the defendant's rights just listed imposes another handicap on police efforts to detect and arrest criminals and on prosecutors' efforts to convict criminals in court. In every democratic system, accordingly, there is always some pressure to attack crime more effectively by giving police and prosecutors more freedom of action. There is also countervailing pressure to make defendants' rights more secure by tightening the restraints on law-enforcement officers. In the United States this perennial conflict between the claims of law and order and the claims of civil liberties has grown more intense in recent years. It has involved mainly the following issues:

Electronic surveillance.   Modern electronics has developed a wide variety of easily hidden "bugging" devices capable of eavesdropping on private telephone conversations and even on unwired conversations in offices and homes. Police naturally find these devices very useful in gathering information about the activities, associations, and plans of suspected criminals, and the width of their electronic net was dramatized by the revelation in the 1973 Watergate hearings that the private telephones of many high officials in the Department of State had been tapped on the orders of President Nixon. Many citizens strongly object to the use of these devices, arguing that they allow government to invade every area of private life, just as totalitarian governments do. Many law-enforcement officials argue with equal vehemence that depriving the police of this tool will benefit only criminals.

The legal phase of the conflict centers upon the Fourth Amendment's prohibition of "unreasonable searches and seizures" and its requirement that investigating officers obtain in advance search warrants "particularly describing the place to be searched, and the persons or things to be seized." A generation ago, the Supreme Court ruled that wiretapping in itself does not violate these rules. A series of recent Court decisions has greatly restricted the circumstances in which police may constitutionally use electronic surveillance devices, however, mainly by requiring that investigators must first get a warrant from a judge, thus satisfying the requirement that places to be searched and the things to be seized must be specified in advance.

After intense pressure to sidestep—and counterpressure to support—the Court's restrictions, Congress included in the Omnibus Crime Control and Safe Streets Act of 1968 an authorization of police wiretapping and "bugging" in investigations of a wide variety of specified crimes. In most instances the police are required to obtain warrants first, but in investigations of organized crime or national-security cases if they find that an emergency exists, they can intercept private communications for 48 hours without a warrant.

This law was a major victory for the police-powers side, but it did not end the war. Most observers believe that many more rounds will be fought in the courts.

Voluntary confessions.   A defendant's confession, unsupported or contradicted by other evidence, is not sufficient to convict him. On the other hand, if the prosecution has some evidence pointing to his guilt but not enough to convince the judge or jury beyond a reasonable doubt, his confession usually provides the clincher. It is therefore not surprising that police and prosecutors try hard to make defendants confess—and that defendants, both guilty and innocent, resist.

As in most constitutional democracies, courts in the United States will admit confessions as evidence only if they are voluntarily given, for, in a famous phrase of the Fifth Amendment, "no person ... shall be compelled in any criminal case to be a witness against himself." "Taking the Fifth" refers to a defendant's exercise of her constitutional right to refuse to answer any question put to her by public authorities if she can convince a court that her answers "may tend to incriminate" her—that is, be used to convict her in the present or some future criminal trial. She has a right to remain silent, and the courts have ruled that her silence may not be used by the prosecution as an indication that she has something guilty to hide. But there is no way of keeping a jury from drawing its own conclusions, and if the defendant voluntarily takes the witness stand, she cannot claim immunity from cross-examination by the prosecution.

In another recent series of controversial opinions the Supreme Court has gone far to ensure that confessions used as evidence in criminal cases are truly voluntary. The culmination was the decision in *Miranda* v. *Arizona* (1966), which stipulated that any evidence, including material obtained by the police in pretrial "custodial interrogation," will be admissible only if the police have told the defendant that she has a right to remain silent, that anything she says can be used against her, that she has a right to have her attorney present during the questioning, that if she cannot afford an attorney one will be provided for her, and that she has the right to terminate the police interrogation at any time.

The Miranda decision evoked a storm of protest from law enforcement officials. They noted that about 90 percent of all criminal convictions result from guilty pleas, which, they argued, means that pretrial interrogation and investigation are critical stages in law enforcement. The Court's restrictions, they declared, would make convicting criminals enormously difficult and thus seriously cripple the police in their war against crime. The 1968 Crime Control Act authorized the trial judge to investigate the circumstances in which a confession is made, determine whether or not it is voluntary, and instruct the jury to decide what weight should be given to it. In making his determination, the judge need not be bound by any single factor of those stipulated in the Miranda decision but can take the whole situation into account.

This law was also a major victory for the police-powers side, but in the United States, as in other constitutional democracies, the courts, and especially the Supreme Court, have the last word about whether any particular defendant has been coerced into confessing and unjustly convicted as a result.

Sometimes investigators and prosecutors determine that they would rather have a witness reveal his knowledge about a large body of crimes than convict him for relatively minor criminal acts—a strategy that received much publicity in 1987 when the congressional committees investigating the "Irangate" scandals agreed to give Lt. Col. Oliver North and Admiral John Poindexter immunity from having anything they said in their testimony to the committees used against them in any future criminal prosecutions. After immunity has been granted, the witness has no further constitutional right to refuse to testify.

The exclusionary rule.   As we have seen, the courts have specified a considerable number of things that the police may not do in the course of arresting, questioning, and gathering evidence on criminal suspects. For example, they may not tap a suspect's telephone, torture him to force a confession, question him without an attorney present if he requests one, or fail to inform him of his right to remain silent. But what if the police cut some corners on these restrictions and, as a result, get evidence that proves his guilt and use it in court to convict him? Or, to put it another way, what can the courts do to ensure that the police obey court rules in gathering evidence for prosecutors?

The answer is that in trying cases against persons accused of crime, the courts use the **exclusionary rule** first laid down in *Mapp* v. *Ohio* (1961). This rule stipulates that *evidence obtained in violation of a defendant's constitutional rights must be excluded from the trial.* Under this rule the appellate courts will overturn any conviction resulting from a trial in which illegally obtained evidence has been used. The defendant may be tried again and convicted in a trial in which such evidence is not used, but he can never be convicted in any trial in which it is used.

Some critics say that it is foolish to let criminals go free because the police misbehave. Why not let the courts examine all the evidence, including the misbehavior of the police, and make their decisions after weighing all the relevant facts? For that matter, why not punish the police—not the general public—if the police misbehave?

In some recent decisions the Supreme Court has somewhat relaxed the exclusionary rule. Some people have urged that when the police believe "in objective good faith" that they have obtained evidence in a constitutional manner, the evidence should be admitted even if they have slipped up on a point or two. The Court has not yet gone quite that far, but in two 1984 cases it ruled that where a police officer has obtained a search warrant from a magistrate, the evidence obtained thereby is admissible even if the magistrate lacked probable cause to issue the warrant (*U.S.* v. *Leon*) or the warrant was technically defective (*Massachusetts* v. *Sheppard*). Even so, the Court has not yet held that evidence gained entirely without a search warrant can be used if the police were acting "in objective good faith." Until it does, the exclusionary rule—which clearly tips the scales in favor of defendants' rights over the suppression of crime—remains a prime guiding principle in American criminal justice.

CONFLICT OVER THE STATUS OF WOMEN

SEXISM: MEANING AND MANIFESTATIONS

With the dubious exception of the legendary Amazons, in almost all societies in almost all periods of history, women have been treated in many ways as men's inferiors. Typically, women have been barred from owning property, from holding any but menial service jobs, from holding public office, even from voting. This discrimination has often been embodied in laws and even more often in social customs. It has been rooted in most men's—and many women's—

views about the appropriate social and legal consequences of women's unique biological function of bearing and nursing children and of men's generally greater physical size and strength. The child-bearing trait has inclined societies to impose—and women to accept—the prime obligation of caring for children from birth to adulthood upon women. Women's relative physical weakness has helped men to keep in their inferior roles even those few women who have rebelled against them.

Sex discrimination has been particularly prominent in politics. History tells of a few powerful queens—Elizabeth I, Anne, and Victoria of England, Catherine the Great of Russia, Christina of Sweden. But in most nations of the old order, the Salic law excluded women from succeeding to the throne, and so they could play political roles only as wives and mothers (Catherine de Medici, Anne of Austria) or mistresses (Diane de Poitiers, Nell Gwyn) of kings.

The twentieth century has thus far seen more improvement in the status of women, at least in the developed nations, than in all previous history. Most Western nations, including the United States, gave women the right to vote around the time of World War I. In the 1920s the new Soviet regime placed women in many jobs they had never held before (for example, bus drivers, airline pilots, even combat soldiers), and in the 1950s the new communist regime in China followed suit. In both Communist systems, however, women are still very far from achieving political or economic equality: For example, only about 10 to 20 percent of the members of the all-powerful Communist parties are women, no woman has yet been the head of either nation's government or held one of its top positions, and women are disproportionately employed in lower-paying jobs and are paid less than men who do the same jobs. And in the non-Communist nations of the West, this century's modest social and political gains for women seem to many to highlight not so much how far they have come as how far they still have to go. We will therefore examine their present economic and political status in the United States, where the movement for women's rights is one of the most powerful in the world.

In Employment and Pay

In 1986, women constituted 51.3 percent of the population of the United States, but 39.6 percent of its full-time workers and 67.4 percent of its part-time workers. Even so, this proportion had increased markedly from the 28.1 percent figure for full-time workers in 1947. Of the over 40 million new jobs added to the labor force from 1960 to 1986, 61 percent went to women (for example, 75 percent of the new bus drivers and over 50 percent of the new newspaper reporters were women). But women's continuing underrepresentation in the labor force doubtless reflects in part their responsibilities for rearing children. In 1970, of all women with children under the age of six (when most children start attending school full time), only 30 percent were employed, compared with nearly half of the women with older children or no children. In

1985 the figures were 41 percent for women with children under six and 52 percent for women with older children or no children—so not only have the two figures risen rapidly in recent years but the gap between them has narrowed. More women are working today than ever before in American history, and the proportion is bound to rise still further.

But the proportion of women with jobs of some kind tells only part of the story. Another part is the inferior status of women in the types of jobs they hold and in their rates of pay. In 1986 the median pay for all women working full time was $16,232 per year, compared with $25,256 for men working full time—or only 64 percent as much. Women employed by state and local governments did best: Their median income was 71 percent as high as men working in similar jobs, whereas in the private sector women's median income was only 56 percent as high as men's in similar jobs.

My own field of political science has certainly been no exception, though things have improved considerably for women since the early 1970s. In college and university departments of political science in 1972, 82 percent of the men were on "tenure track" appointments, compared to 63 percent of the women. In 1987 the figures were 95 percent for men and 90 percent for women. The median salary of full-time male college teachers of political science in all ranks in 1972 was $15,200, compared with $12,720 for their female colleagues. In 1987 the figures for full professors were $43,500 for male teachers and $39,500 for female teachers; for associate professors it was $32,500 for both men and women; and for assistant professors it was $25,500 for men and $24,500 for women.[2] It is not surprising, therefore, that the women's rights movement still puts a high priority on the goals of equal job opportunities and equal pay for equal work.

In Politics and Government

In 1988, women constituted 52.6 percent of the voting-age population in the United States, but a far smaller proportion of the political elite. Neither major party has ever nominated a woman for the presidency (although several minor parties have), and in 1984 Democratic Representative Geraldine Ferraro became the first woman ever nominated by a major party for the vice presidency, a precedent not followed by either party in 1988. Equally striking is the small number of women candidates for Congress. In 1988, for example, there were 66 major-party candidates for the U.S. Senate, of whom two were women (compared with 9 in 1986), and neither was elected. In 1978 Nancy Landon Kassebaum, Republican of Kansas, became the first woman ever to be elected to the Senate without having been preceded in Congress by her husband; in 1980 Paula Hawkins, Republican of Florida, became the second (she was defeated for re-election in 1986); and in 1986 Barbara Mikulski, Democrat of Maryland, became the third. In 1988 there were 793 major-party candidates for the House of Representatives, of whom 61 (7.7 percent) were women. Twenty-five were elected, so women constituted 2 percent of the members of the Senate and 7.5 percent of the members of the House. Three of the 50 state governors were women: Rose Mofford, Democrat of Arizona; Kay Orr, Republican of Nebraska; and Madeleine Kunin, Democrat of Vermont. Perhaps most striking of all, in 1981 Sandra Day O'Connor became the first woman ever appointed to the U.S. Supreme Court.

Women in other democratic nations have fared little or no better. For example, in the 1987 British general election, a grand total of 2,327 candidates stood for Parliament, and 327 (14 percent) were women. A total of 41 women were elected, and they comprised 6 percent of the total of 650 MPs—not very much, but still the highest proportion in British history.[3]

American women have made somewhat greater progress in getting elected to state and local offices. In 1975, for example, only 8 percent of the members of all state legislatures were women, but in 1987 the figure had nearly doubled to 15.5 percent. In 1975, 456 women were members of county governing bodies, and in 1987 the number had increased over threefold, to 1,566.[4]

The main political advance for women in recent years has resulted from the efforts of both major parties, but particularly the Democrats, to increase the proportions of women among the delegates to their national nominating conventions. In 1972 the Democrats used a semiquota system; in 1976 they modified it to an affirmative action policy; and in 1978 the Democratic National Committee adopted a rule that henceforth at least half of every delegation to the convention must be composed of women—an explicit mandatory quota system. The results are shown in Table 16.2.

It could be argued that the increased proportion of women delegates in both parties shown in Table 16.2 represented no great victory for women's interests, since the powers of the national conventions have in recent years been reduced to registering the decisions made by the voters in presidential primary elections. Even so, it was clear that for some time to come women would continue to hold a higher proportion of official positions in the major parties' national conventions than in any other level of American politics and government.

TABLE 16.2.   **Women Delegates in National Nominating Conventions, 1968–88**

Party	(Percentage of Women Among All Delegates)					
	1968	1972	1976	1980	1984	1988
Democratic	13	40	33	49	51	52
Republican	16	29	31	29	46	37

Source: Barbara G. Farah, "Delegate Polls, 1944 to 1984," *Public Opinion,* August/September 1984, Table 1, p. 44. Copyright American Enterprise Institute. The figures for 1988 are taken from *The New York Times,* July 17, 1988, p. 11; and August 14, 1988, p. 14.

THE WOMEN'S RIGHTS MOVEMENT

Ever since the eighteenth century there have been occasional feminist movements to improve the status of women by political action. Among the most successful were the suffragette movements of the late nineteenth and early twentieth centuries, which played major roles in securing women's rights to vote in a number of Western nations. New Zealand was the first to establish women's suffrage in 1893, followed by Norway in 1913, Great Britain in 1918, and the United States in 1920. France and Italy did not give women the right to vote until 1946, and Switzerland—though often said to be a model democracy—did not do so until 1971!

Organization and Objectives

The American women's rights (or women's liberation or "women's lib") movement has been in high gear since the 1970s, and it has surpassed the suffragette movement of the early 1900s as the most active and powerful feminist movement the world has yet seen. Like most protest movements (see, for example, the African-American civil rights movement, discussed in a moment), the women's rights movement has no universally agreed-upon list of demands or beliefs. It has its radicals (who say that men are incurably hostile and oppressive to women, and women should always deal with them as potential or active enemies), its moderates (who say that women should have the same basic rights and opportunities as men, and right-thinking men can and will help women achieve them), and its conservatives (who say that women will and should always be primarily wives and mothers, though perhaps they deserve a somewhat better break politically and economically than they have had).

The women's movement also has no one dominant organization. Among its leading pressure groups are the National Organization for Women (NOW), the Women's Equity Action League, the Women's National Abortion Rights Action League, and the Women's Political Caucus. The prime objectives sought by these and other women's organizations include the elimination of all gender-based discrimination in employment opportunities, pay, and advancement; liberalized birth control and abortion laws; expanded children's day-care programs; liberalized tax deductions for child-care expenses; more women candidates and public office holders; and the repeal of all laws that in any way give women a legal status inferior to men's.

The women's organizations, with some help from male allies, have used most of the broad range of pressure-group tactics (see Chapter 1) to persuade or force the national and state governments and political parties to adopt policies and platforms promoting these goals. Like other protest movements, they have won a few and lost a few; but compared with most such movements, they have done well and are likely to do even better, as is evident from some recent developments.

The National Organization For Women (NOW) in Action. (Source: AP/Wide World Photos.)

The Equal Rights Amendment (ERA)

Many leaders of the women's movement believe that their cause must rest on firmer ground than the vagaries of administrators' plans and judges' interpretations, and for decades their central strategy was to amend the U.S. Constitution so as to prohibit gender-based discrimination in all forms once and for all. The first of several such amendments was introduced in Congress as early as 1923, but none got anywhere until 1971, when Congress approved and sent to the states for ratification the equal rights amendment (ERA), which read as follows:

> *Equality of rights under the law shall not be denied or abridged by the United States or by any state on account of sex.*

The Constitution requires that all amendments be ratified by at least three-quarters of the states (38 of 50), and the ERA got off to a fast start.

Twenty-two states ratified it in 1972, 8 more followed suit in 1973, and it looked as though the remaining 8 would come through in 1974. However, a militant opposition movement was formed by noted conservative activist Phyllis Schlafly. The opposition argued that the amendment would deprive women of the legal protections they now enjoy, force them to be drafted for military combat service, outlaw separate sanitary facilities, deprive divorced women of their alimony, and so on. Many added that women are by nature primarily wives and mothers, that they should be protected as such, and that the price for such protection is to preserve the role of men as husbands, fathers, soldiers, and breadwinners. The amendment's supporters, especially NOW, retorted that these alleged protections have helped women very little, that they have served mainly as masks and justifications for discrimination, and that reasonable gender-based legal distinctions—as opposed to the sexist discrimination that now prevails—could still be made.

The battle between the two sides was joined with increasing heat in the unratified states, and the ERA's progress slowed sharply: In 1974 only 3 states ratified; in 1975, only 1; in 1976, none; and in 1977, only 1 more. The amendment's terms required that it be ratified by 1979, and as that fateful year approached, the total of ratifying states was stuck at 35, and the prospects for getting 3 more by 1979 looked bleak. However, highly effective lobbying by the women's movement induced Congress to allow 39 additional months for ratification, so the deadline was moved back to June 30, 1982. The extra time did not help, however: No additional states ratified the ERA, and it finally died on the appointed day in 1982.

Undaunted by this failure, a coalition of pro-ERA members of Congress introduced an identical new amendment in February 1983; but in November 1983 it failed by 6 votes to get the necessary two-thirds approval in the House of Representatives, and many advocates of women's rights concluded that the ERA was dead and that a new strategy had to be adopted.

After ERA

Since the ERA's 1983 failure, the women's rights movement has focused on a number of specific policy changes and has pursued them by the classical tactics of lobbying, electioneering, and litigation. They have pressed for such measures as federal funding of abortions for poor women, expanded publicly funded day-care programs to make it easier for women to work, liberalized leaves of absence from work for women to bear and care for babies, and the barring of all discrimination in life insurance premiums and benefits based on the fact that on the average women live longer than men (78 years for women, 71 years for men).

In the 1980s, however, the women's movement has increasingly concentrated its efforts on promoting the idea of "comparable worth"—the proposition that workers in jobs of comparable social value should be paid the same regardless of whether they are held mainly by women or men.

But how is a job's social worth to be determined? How do we decide whether a librarian's work is worth more, less, or the same as an auto mechanic's? No procedure has been approved in every detail, but many advocates of comparable worth suggest that a representative committee in each industry and government agency should identify *and weight* all the major variables that should be involved in determining rates of pay—for example, education, experience, manual and intellectual skills, and physical strength. The committee will then assign to each job a number representing the sum of all the job's scores on all the weighted variables, and the law will require that jobs with similar numbers will receive similar wages regardless of who holds them.

"Comparable worth" has aroused a storm of opposition. Its opponents say that any "job-worth" number is bound to be highly arbitrary, that determining it will become a political test of strength rather than a scientific or economic judgment, that the cost of leveling wage rates up (no one expects them to be leveled down) will be staggering, and that in the end wage rates will continue to be determined, as they always have been, by the relative needs of employers for certain kinds of skills and by how much they are willing to pay to get such skills in competition with other employers in the labor market.

American public opinion on comparable worth is mixed. On the one hand, an overwhelming 97 percent of the population, men and women alike, agree with the statement that "men and women should be paid equally for jobs of comparable worth." But when asked, "do you think it is possible to compare jobs that are quite different—such as a secretary and an electrician—using some kind of rating or evaluation system, and then set fair salaries or pay rates as a result," 65 percent agree with the statement that "such comparisons would be too difficult to do and, therefore, not fair." And when asked, "to the extent that comparable worth is a good idea, who do you think should decide if two jobs really are of comparable worth and thus merit the same pay," 19 percent say that the government should decide, 18 percent say that the courts should decide, and 41 percent say that private employers should decide.[5]

It is too early to tell whether comparable worth will fare better than ERA, but it is likely to become one of the main battlegrounds for the women's rights movement in the 1990s.

CONFLICT OVER THE STATUS OF AFRICAN-AMERICANS

BLACK AMERICA, YESTERDAY AND TODAY

Racial discrimination *imposes handicaps on all members of a particular race solely because of their race and without regard to their individual merits.* For example, barring any African-American, no matter how intelligent or well prepared, from attending a particular school is a form of racial discrimination;

prohibiting a Vietnamese refugee, no matter how pleasant and neighborly, from buying a house in a particular neighborhood is another form. Racial discrimination is one of the oldest and most frequently encountered aspects of man's inhumanity to man. Wherever people of different races (and sometimes ethnic groups) have been thrown together in the same society, at least some members of the dominant group have attempted to discriminate against members of another group or groups—gentiles against Jews, whites against blacks, Africans against Indians, Anglo-Saxons against Latins, Occidentals against Orientals, Japanese against Koreans, and so on. In most societies, conflicts over discrimination sooner or later become political: groups favoring discrimination try to have their views incorporated into law, and antidiscrimination groups try to get the discriminations outlawed.

The United States, as we will see, certainly has no monopoly on race discrimination, public or private. But discrimination against African-Americans in this country has, justly or not, received more attention and comment both here and abroad than has discrimination in any other nation, with the possible exception of the policy of *apartheid* (racial separation and white supremacy) in the Republic of South Africa (to be discussed in a moment).

The people whom we call "African-Americans" in this book have been know by a variety of names. After their emancipation from slavery in 1865, they were widely called "colored people," as is illustrated by the fact that the first major organization, formed in 1909, to advance their interests called itself the National Association for the Advancement of Colored People. They were also widely called "Negroes."

This changed after World War II, however. Many members of the new civil rights movement made a point of calling themselves "blacks," for reasons given by the authors of a book prominent in the movement: "There is growing resentment of the word 'Negro' ... because the term is an invention of our oppressor; it is his image of us that he describes. Many blacks are now calling themselves African-Americans, Afro-Americans, or black people because that is *our* image of ourselves."[6] Since most of the members of the race who were most active politically called themselves "blacks," that is the usage we employed in earlier editions of this book.

However, the Reverend Jesse Jackson and many other leaders of what used to be called "blacks" have recently said that they prefer to be called African-Americans. As Rev. Jackson said in 1988, "To be called African-Americans has cultural integrity. It puts us in our proper historical context. Every ethnic group in this country has a reference to some land base, some historical cultural base. African-Americans have hit that level of cultural maturity."[7]

Accordingly, in the current edition we have adopted the new usage wherever appropriate.

The problem of the status of African-Americans has plagued American society and government for more than three centuries. By the 1780s enough African slaves had been imported so that questions of what to do about slavery and how to count slaves for purposes of congressional representation sharply divided the Constitutional Convention of 1787. The question of whether slavery should be extended, maintained, or abolished was the main cause of our Civil War (1861–65), the bloodiest war in American history. The war resulted in the legal emancipation of the slaves, but for a century after Appomattox, African-Americans remained second-class citizens in every way.

Since 1945 the struggle over the status of African-Americans has greatly intensified. It has become one of the most divisive domestic political issues of our time, and there is still no end in sight. It involves the status of only 12.2 percent of our population—but that means over 31 million human beings. African-Americans are not only the most numerous and visible of our nation's depressed minorities; they are also politically the most significant. They differ sharply from the white majority in appearance, history, culture, and other respects, some of which are shown in Table 16.3.

Table 16.3 makes it clear that compared with whites, African-Americans today are more concentrated in the inner cities of our large metropolitan areas, have a higher proportion of families headed by mothers, have lower life expectancies, have less formal education, work disproportionately in the lower-status and lower-paid occupations, make less money, have more unemployment and more persons below the poverty line, and vote in smaller proportions. Indeed, many of the toughest problems American governments face—the "urban problem," poverty, undereducation, unemployment, and so on—are largely manifestations of the underlying problem of the status of African-Americans. Let us begin our examination of that problem by reviewing the history of the issues and the contending forces in this long-standing conflict.

THE CIVIL RIGHTS MOVEMENT: A BRIEF HISTORY

White Supremacy and Legally Forced Segregation

Until the 1950s the status of African-Americans in the United States was determined largely by a powerful group of whites who believed in racial segregation and white supremacy. Their belief in racial segregation was based on the doctrine that whites and African-Americans should conduct most of their activities in all-white and all-black situations—that there should be racially segregated schools, housing, transportation, athletic contests, public accommodations, recreation facilities, churches, jobs, and so on. Above all, there should be no interracial marriage. Their belief in white supremacy meant that whites should dominate both parts of the segregated society by deciding what areas of life would be segregated and the conditions in which each race would live and work. The people who believed in racial segregation and white supremacy held that both should be enforced by the kind of "Jim Crow" compulsory segregation

TABLE 16.3.   African-Americans and Whites in the United States, 1986 (in percentages)

Characteristics	African-Americans	Whites
Householder		
Married couple	54	82
Male householder	4	5
Female householder	42	13
	100	100
Residence		
Metropolitan central cities	60	27
Metropolitan outside central cities	22	47
Nonmetropolitan	18	26
	100	100
Life Expectancy in Years at Birth		
Male	67.6	72.0
Female	75.1	78.9
Education		
Mean school years completed by age 25	12.3	12.6
Percent high school graduates	62.0	76.0
Percent some college	27.0	37.0
Employment Status		
Percent employed	91	96
Percent unemployed	9	4
	100	100
Occupation		
Managerial and professional	16	28
Technical, sales, and admin. support	26	30
Service	22	12
Precision production, craft and repair	10	13
Operators, fabricators and laborers	24	14
Farming, forestry, and fishing	2	3
	100	100
Median family income	$16,786	$29,152
Percent of persons below poverty line	31	11
Voting turnout percent		
1980 election	51	61
1982 election	43	50
1984 election	56	60
1986 election	43	47
1988 election	52	59

Source: Statistical Abstract of the United States, 1988 (Washington, D.C.: Bureau of the Census, 1988).

laws that were so common before the 1950s. The most prominent advocates of racial segregation and white supremacy were whites living in the South, probably because that is where most African-Americans lived. Many whites in the North, Midwest, and West felt the same way, but few African-Americans lived in their areas, and the issues of race relations were less prominent.

Martin Luther King, Jr.
(Source: UPI/Bettmann Newsphotos.)

Roy Wilkins
(Source: AP/Wide World Photos.)

Joseph Lowery.
(Source: AP/Wide World Photos.)

Jesse Jackson.
(Source AP/Wide World Photos.)

Leaders of the African-American Civil Rights Movement.

The Struggle against Discrimination: Organizations and Leaders

What history has come to call the civil rights movement began to emerge and gather strength in the 1930s. It was led by a number of organizations, most of them multiracial in membership but predominantly African-American in leadership. The most influential were the following:

The National Association for the Advancement of Colored People (NAACP). The oldest of the organizations in the civil rights movement, the NAACP, founded in 1909, has consistently emphasized pressure on Congress and constitutional challenges to discrimination in the federal courts and has won many notable legislative and judicial victories. Its emphasis on acting within the system, its occasional acceptance of whites in positions of leadership, and its strong resistance to the hatred of all whites expressed by some African-Americans have won it the reputation of being the conservative wing of the civil rights movement.

The National Urban League. Founded in 1910, this organization has stressed interracial educational programs in local communities aimed at breaking segregation and discrimination, particularly in housing and employment. It has operated as actively in the North as in the South. Its directors, first Whitney M. Young, Jr. and then Vernon Jordan, have been generally regarded as among the leading moderates in the African-American rights movement.

The Southern Christian Leadership Conference (SCLC). The SCLC was founded in 1957 by perhaps the greatest single leader of the civil rights movement, Dr. Martin Luther King, Jr. He headed the organization until his murder in 1968, and he is the only African-American leader who, in addition to his Nobel Peace Prize, has had the nation honor his birthday as a national holiday. Under his leadership the SCLC pioneered the use of Gandhian nonviolent resistance (see Chapter 2) and won major victories over discrimination against African-Americans in the 1960s. In recent years, under the leadership first of Ralph D. Abernathy and then of Joseph Lowery, the SCLC has joined with impoverished whites and Hispanic Americans to press for greater government efforts to end poverty, but it has been beset by internal conflict between those who want to put more emphasis on protest activities and those, including President Lowery, who prefer to emphasize the funding of social-welfare projects and lobbying Congress and the administration for larger appropriations for jobs for African-Americans.

The Congress of Racial Equality (CORE). At one time the most militant of the civil rights organizations, CORE was founded in 1941 by James Farmer. It pioneered the use of such direct-action techniques as picketing, demonstrations, sit-ins, and boycotts. In 1969 Farmer, to the consternation of some of his colleagues, accepted an appointment in the Nixon administration as assistant secretary for administration of the Department of Health, Education, and Welfare. In 1976 the organization split between a group that recruited African-American Vietnam War veterans to fight in the Angolan civil war in Africa and an older group who felt that this was going too far outside the organization's basic purposes. CORE's internal divisions, like those of the SCLC, weakened its position in the civil rights movement.

People United to Save Humanity (PUSH).   From the mid-1970s on, one of the most dynamic and visible leaders of the African-American rights movement has been the Reverend Jesse Jackson of Chicago. He founded PUSH mainly to encourage African-American parents and African-American children to work hard in school and equip themselves to compete successfully with whites in the business and educational worlds. In 1984 Jackson entered the contest for the Democratic party's presidential nomination. He was widely and fervently supported by African-American voters in the primaries, and his participation in the contest stimulated a record number of African-Americans to register and vote. In the end he won over 3 million votes in the primaries (18.6 percent of all the votes cast) and finished a solid third behind the winner, Walter Mondale, and his chief challenger, Gary Hart.

In 1988 Jackson did even better: He again sought the Democratic presidential nomination and not only attracted over 90 percent of all African-American votes but substantially increased his support among white voters. He won a total of over 6.5 million votes (29 percent of all the votes cast), and finished second to the eventual winner, Michael Dukakis. Most observers felt that the two campaigns had established Jackson not only as the first serious African-American contender for the presidency but also as the most prominent and powerful leader of African-Americans in the 1990s.

From these brief sketches it is clear that there have been some disagreements both among and within these organizations. But far more important is the fact that for decades they fought side by side in many battles and won many victories in the struggle to end the many forms of legal and extralegal discrimination against African-Americans.

The Struggle against Discrimination: Areas and Issues

From the 1930s to the 1970s, the main objective of most people in the civil rights movement was to end all forms of segregation and discrimination against African-Americans, and most of them looked forward to the day when the United States would at last become truly "color blind"—a society in which people's educations, jobs, incomes, residences, and social statuses would be determined solely by their abilities and achievements, not by the color of their skin. The main struggles took place in the following areas of concern:

> *I have a dream that my four little children will one day live in a nation where they will not be judged by the color of their skin, but by the content of their character.*
>
> *Martin Luther King, Jr.*[8]

Voting.   After the post–Civil War Reconstruction period ended in the late 1870s, southern whites tried to keep the newly emancipated African-Americans from exercising the voting rights granted to them by the Fifteenth Amendment to the U.S. Constitution. They used such devices as poll taxes, selectively administered literacy tests, "white primaries," and physical violence and intimidation. Their success is shown by the fact that even as late as the 1940s, only about 12 percent of southern African-Americans of voting age were registered to vote, and well less than half of even that handful bothered—or dared—to go to the polls.

That situation changed radically in the 1960s, and in the 1980s this form of discrimination has been almost entirely abolished. The Twenty-Fourth Amendment, ratified in 1964, outlawed all state requirements for the payment of poll taxes as a precondition for voting. Even more important was the passage of the Voting Rights Act of 1965. This act requires the U.S. attorney general to determine whether or not an unusually low voting turnout in any of the nation's counties results from racial discrimination. If he determines that it does, he is empowered to send federal registrars into any such county with authority to register all qualified voters, regardless of what the local officials may or may not do. Furthermore, the federal representatives must ignore any local laws that discriminate against African-Americans and must supervise the conduct of elections to make sure that no registered voter is in any way inhibited from voting.

Such registrars have been sent into a number of southern counties, and in other areas local registrars have voluntarily given up trying to keep African-Americans from voting. As a result, the percentage of voting-age African-Americans registered to vote in the eleven southern (ex-Confederate) states rose from 12 percent in 1947 to 61 percent in 1986. The Bureau of the Census estimates that in the 1984 presidential election, 51 percent of voting-age African-Americans in the South actually voted, compared with 44 percent in 1964 and 28 percent in 1960.

Education.   For many years people in both North and South who believed in maintaining racial segregation and white supremacy insisted that under no circumstances should African-Americans be permitted to attend the same schools as whites, arguing that African-Americans' genetic mental inferiority would be a drag on the educational development of white children. Immediately after the Civil War, most states adopted constitutional or statutory prohibitions of racial integration in public schools. In the succeeding decades, however, most states outside the South repealed them, and 22 states adopted provisions specifically prohibiting racial segregation.

The great turning point came in 1954. In that year a total of 19 states (4 of them outside the South) and the District of Columbia legally required racial segregation in their public schools. On several occasions these laws had been challenged in the Supreme Court as violations of the clause in the Fourteenth Amendment that provides, "No State shall ... deny to any person within its jurisdiction the equal protection of the laws." However, the Court consistently upheld the segregation laws, following the separate-but-equal rule first laid down in the case of *Plessy* v. *Ferguson* (1896). According to this rule, segregation in itself is not a denial of equal protection as long as equal facilities are provided for both races (see Chapter 14).

In the early 1950s, however, the NAACP, under the leadership of its chief constitutional lawyer, Thurgood Marshall (who later became the first African-American justice of the Supreme Court), again challenged the constitutionality of state school-segregation laws. This time, in a unanimous opinion written by Chief Justice Earl Warren in *Brown* v. *Board of Education* (1954), the Court reversed the *Plessy* decision and ruled that racial segregation *in itself* is a denial of equal protection, regardless of the facilities provided; and in 1955 the Court ordered the federal district courts to proceed "with all deliberate speed" to see that local school boards complied with the ruling.

For the next 10 years desegregation proceeded very slowly in some areas, especially in the states of Alabama, Georgia, Louisiana, Mississippi, and South Carolina. In 1964, however, Congress—under the leadership of Senator Hubert Humphrey and the relentless prodding of President Lyndon Johnson of Texas, the first southerner to be president since the Civil War—passed the most far-reaching federal civil rights legislation since Reconstruction. We will observe the impact of this legislation in other areas, but we note here that Title VI authorizes the Office (now Department) of Education to cut off federal financial aid to any school district that refuses to pursue an acceptable program of desegregation. That speeded up desegregation considerably, but in the 1970s and 1980s the conflict over desegregation became overshadowed by the conflict over integration by busing; and it was soon clear that desegregation and integration are not the same thing.

As it was originally conceived by the civil rights movement, desegregation meant an end to all laws and practices forcing African-American children to attend exclusively African-American schools. As we have just seen, the first mortal blow to legally forced segregation was delivered by the decision in *Brown* v. *Board of Education,* and the final blow was given by the enforcement procedures in Title VI of the Civil Rights Act of 1964. But in the early 1970s the issue became *integration*—that is, ensuring that all public schools are racially mixed, that every school has both African-American pupils and white pupils.

The problem of converting desegregation into integration arises from the fact that in most cities in all parts of the country, most neighborhoods are de facto racially segregated; that is, most African-Americans live in exclusively African-American areas, most whites live in exclusively white areas, and only a few neighborhoods are racially mixed. Moreover, one of the oldest and most admired traditions everywhere is the tradition of neighborhood schools—that is, the belief that schools should be located in particular neighborhoods and attended by children living in those neighborhoods. Clearly, then, if residential neighborhoods are de facto racially segregated, they are bound to result in schools that are racially segregated.

Many people in the civil rights movement who believe that the goal is not mere desegregation but full integration of the schools have proposed a number of plans to overcome the difficulty. The method most often used and most controversial is busing—the practice of assigning African-American children living in African-American neighborhoods to schools in white neighborhoods, assigning white children living in white neighborhoods to schools in African-American neighborhoods, and carrying out the assignments by requiring many children of both races to travel in buses to schools miles from their homes.

The controversy over this policy first became a major issue in the early 1970s, when a number of federal district judges decided that desegregation really means integration, that all public schools must have certain minimum percentages of both African-American and white children (for example, a judge in Richmond, Virginia, ruled that every school must have from 20 to 40 percent African-American pupils), and that busing is an appropriate way to fill the racial quotas.

School integration and busing converted what was mainly a southern controversy into a national controversy. Busing aroused intense opposition by large numbers of white parents in Boston, Denver, Louisville, Detroit, Indianapolis, and many other non-southern cities. Some opponents have expressed their opposition by obstructing the movement of school buses, and others by taking their children out of public schools and putting them into mostly white private schools. Congress has adopted a number of resolutions intended to prohibit busing for racial integration, but the Supreme Court has approved busing as a tool that judges can constitutionally use in certain circumstances. The Court's general rule is this: If it finds that the schools in a school district are segregated as the result of the school board's deliberate policy to keep schools segregated, it will uphold a lower court's order to require busing to integrate the schools. On the other hand, if it finds that de facto racial segregation in a school district results from racial housing patterns and not from a deliberate policy to keep the schools segregated, it will not uphold lower-court orders to bus children across school district lines.

Housing.   For many years African-Americans (and, to a lesser extent, Jews) have been denied equal opportunities for housing by means of "restrictive covenants"—that is, by agreements among white and gentile property owners not to sell their houses to African-American or Jewish buyers, thus preserving all-white and all-gentile neighborhoods. These covenants used to be inserted in formal contracts among property owners. An owner who violated such a covenant by selling to an African-American or a Jew could be sued in the courts for breach of contract. In 1948, however, the Supreme Court struck a powerful (though not mortal) blow at restrictive covenants by ruling that, though they are not in themselves unlawful, they cannot be enforced by any court, state or federal; for such enforcement would make the courts parties to the covenants, in violation of the Fourteenth Amendment.

But this decision was at best a negative sanction, and many restrictive covenants continued to be made and effectively enforced as unwritten "gentlemen's agreements." Finally, in 1968, after years of battle over the issue, Congress passed a major open-housing law that prohibits racial discrimination in the sale or rental of most of the nation's housing. It applies to all public housing and urban-renewal projects, all private multiple-unit dwellings except those of no more than four units that are occupied by their owners, all single-family houses not owned by private individuals, and all privately owned single family houses that are sold or rented by real-estate agents or brokers. About the only exemptions are privately owned homes whose owners sell or rent them without the services of real-estate brokers or agents. The act is thus estimated to apply to about 80 percent of all the nation's housing units.

Public accommodations.   Segregationists have long sought to keep African-Americans from using the same public services and accommodations as whites—riding in the same parts of trains and buses; sitting in the same parts of theaters; using the same restaurants, golf courses, swimming pools, barbershops, rest rooms, and drinking fountains. In 1954 more than 20 states had Jim Crow laws requiring such segregation, but they were deemed unconstitutional after the Brown decision threw out the old separate-but-equal formula. Another 20 states adopted laws prohibiting racial discrimination by private businesses offering public accommodations or by any publicly owned and operated facility. But many of these laws were enforced minimally or not at all, African-Americans were commonly refused service, and civil rights leaders came to believe that only positive action by the federal government would guarantee truly equal rights in this area.

They achieved their goal in the Civil Rights Act of 1964. Title II forbids racial discrimination in all publicly owned or operated facilities. It also prohibits racial discrimination in serving customers by all private businesses providing public accommodations—hotels, motels, restaurants, gasoline stations, theaters, sports arenas, and the like. As a result, racial discrimination in these areas has almost entirely disappeared, even in the small towns and rural areas of the deep South.

Employment.   African-Americans have long been the most economically depressed ethnic group in the United States, although they are better off today than they were 20 years ago. The figures in Table 16.3 show that the median income of African-American families in 1986 was only 58 percent as high as the median income of white families—and not by chance. For many decades after the end of slavery, many white employers and white-dominated labor unions made sure that the only jobs open to most African-Americans were the lowest paying, and most African-Americans worked as unskilled industrial and farm laborers and domestic servants. Even in 1986, as Table 16.3 shows, 48 percent of all working African-Americans were employed in the lower- paying service, manual labor, and farm labor jobs, compared with only 29 percent of all working whites.

Accordingly, most African-American leaders, whatever their differences may be on other issues, give top priority to ensuring that African-Americans get better jobs and more pay. One of the top demands of the civil rights movement up to the 1970s was that qualified African-Americans must have as good a chance at desirable jobs as qualified whites. The leaders also urged the government to provide massive programs for training African-Americans in the knowledge and skills that will enable them to perform well in the more demanding and better-paying jobs.

Before 1964 some states had adopted fair-employment-practice laws, but many had not. Here again the federal Civil Rights Act was a major turning point. Title VII forbids private employers to practice racial discrimination in hiring or promotion. It also prohibits labor unions from excluding any applicant for membership because of his or her race. The rules are enforced by a five-person Equal Employment Opportunity Commission (EEOC), which is empowered to hear and investigate charges of discrimination against employers and unions and to ask the U.S. attorney general to force compliance when efforts at persuasion fail.

As a result, there has been considerable progress toward not only equal employment rights for African-Americans but toward all of the other objectives of the original civil rights movement as well. In the 1970s, however, some deep fissures began to appear in the movement, and conflict over the status of African- Americans in the 1990s has become a good deal more complicated than it was in the period from the 1930s to the 1970s. The deepest of these fissures has been the increasingly bitter disagreement among different parts of the old civil rights movement over the issue of affirmative action. Let us examine that dispute in some detail.

AFRICAN-AMERICAN RIGHTS IN THE 1980s: ANTIDISCRIMINATION OR AFFIRMATIVE ACTION?

Antidiscrimination

The civil rights movement's 30-year fight against racial discrimination had the objective of achieving a society in which the competition for the good things of life, such as well-paying jobs, decent houses in decent neighborhoods, and good educations, is truly open and fair. In such a society African-Americans would in no way be handicapped in the competition by the color of their skins, and whites would in no way be advantaged because of the color of theirs. The competition's results would thus be determined by the individual merits of the competing persons, not by their race. Able and hard-working African-Americans would get every bit as much, but no more, of life's good things as equally able and hard-working whites. To be sure, the competition, like all free competitions, would produce unequal results: Some AfricanAmericans and whites would win more of the good things than other African-Americans and whites. But African-Americans would have just as good a chance as whites to be winners.

In short, the old civil rights movement wanted a truly "color-blind society"—one in which persons would be judged, in Martin Luther King's famous words, "not by the color of their skin, but by the content of their character." To achieve this noble goal, the movement sought to eradicate every kind of handicap imposed on African-Americans by government or private agencies so as to achieve truly fair "color- blind" competition. Most who fought for that goal also believed that if poor education in underfunded ghetto schools kept African-American children from taking advantage of the new opportunities for fair competition, that handicap too should be removed by special remedial education and training programs such as the preschool Head Start program begun by the federal government in 1965. But the ultimate goal of those who believe in antidiscrimination is equality of *opportunity,* not equality of *result.*

Affirmative Action

Some members of the old civil rights movement have come to believe that while ending discrimination against African-Americans is certainly desirable, the goal of fair competition is not enough. For three centuries, they declare, white America has either made African-Americans into slaves or allowed them only a few crumbs from its table even after the formal end of slavery. This monstrous injustice cannot be remedied today merely by dumping modern African-Americans into a competition in which, because of those centuries of slavery and discrimination, they have no fair chance to win. The Reverend Jesse Jackson puts the argument in terms of a much-used analogy:

> *Two world-class distance runners begin the grueling human test of trying to run a sub-four-minute mile. Two minutes into the race, officials observe that one runner, falling far behind, still has running weights on his ankles. They stop the race and hold both runners in their tracks. The weights are removed from the runner far behind, the officials re-fire the starting gun, and both runners continue from the points where they were when the race was stopped. Not surprisingly, the runner who ran the entire race without the ankle weights comes in with a sizable lead.*[9]

Clearly such a competition would be unfair. But what is the best way to make it fair? Start the race over with both runners unshackled at the starting line? That might be the way for future generations, Reverend Jackson says, but it will not do for this one. Give the previously shackled runner some kind of special advantage to compensate for his previous unfair treatment? But what kind of advantage, and how much? Fix the races so that the previously shackled competitors win 12.2 percent of the time? Fifty percent of the time? Over 50 percent of the time? And at what point does "fairness" to the previously shackled runner become "unfairness" to the the runner who was never shackled but did not himself do any shackling of his competitors?

One widely proposed remedy is what some people call "compensatory racial preferences," others call "reverse discrimination," and the Reverend Jackson calls "racial reparations." This remedy requires that since the proportion of African-Americans in the general population is 12.2 percent, then it should be mandatory that at least 12.2 percent of the students entering colleges, law schools, and medical schools should be African-Americans; 12.2 percent of the persons holding the high-paying skilled craft jobs should be African-Americans; 12.2 percent of top-level government workers should be African-Americans; and so on. Only when all traces *and consequences* of past discrimination against African-Americans have been wiped out can we justly return to "fair competition" as the prime objective in dealing with the status of African-Americans.

People who, like Reverend Jackson, want racial reparations for African-Americans through guaranteed results rather than nondiscriminatory competition believe that the best way to get the reparations is to install **affirmative action programs**—*programs designed to remedy the effects of past discrimination by increasing the proportions of women, African-Americans, and other racial minorities in desirable social and economic positions.*

Many women's groups insist that affirmative action programs should also guarantee proper proportions of such benefits for women. For both African-Americans and women, proper proportions and appropriate shares mean proportions close to their proportions in the general population—12.2 percent for African-Americans and 51.3 percent for women.

The two watchwords for those who favor affirmative action programs are *goals* and *timetables*. The ultimate goal of each program is full proportional equality in the numbers of African-Americans and women both in initial hirings and in promotion to higher positions. A timetable is a firm commitment to achieve the goal by a stipulated time in the not-too-distant future.

The great trouble with affirmative action, say its opponents, is that such goals are in fact nothing more than *quotas*—that is, minimum numbers of places that must be reserved for African-Americans because they are African-American and for women because they are female, without regard to their individual qualifications compared to those of individual whites and men. Reserving some of the limited number of places available for African-Americans and women will inevitably mean, opponents believe, that some whites and some males will be denied places for which they are better qualified than the African-Americans and women who get the reserved places. Hence, they say, affirmative action amounts to reverse discrimination, which replaces the old

The first great test of whether affirmative action programs are constitutional came in one of the most-discussed Supreme Court cases in recent years: *University of California Regents* v. *Bakke,* 438 U.S. 265 (1978). The Medical School of the University of California at Davis (UCDMS) admitted only 100 applicants each year, but instituted an affirmative action program setting aside 16 of those places to be filled exclusively by African-Americans, Hispanics, and members of other minority groups. In August 1973 a total of 3,737 persons applied for admission to UCDMS, including Allan Bakke, a 32-year-old white man. Bakke's undergraduate grades were above the average of those of the persons admitted, and his aptitude test scores were well above the average. Nevertheless, he was denied admission. In June 1974 he sued UCDMS for admission, claiming that some of the persons admitted under the affirmative action program had lower scores than he and that the program had therefore racially discriminated against him and other qualified whites in violation of both the Civil Rights Act of 1964 and the Fourteenth Amendment to the U.S. Constitution.

The case eventually went to the Supreme Court. The basic issue was whether it is constitutionally permissible for a tax supported institution, the UCDMS, to compensate African-Americans and other minority groups for past discrimination against them by guaranteeing a certain number of places for them but not for white males. This issue was highly important not only to Allan Bakke but to many other people and groups not directly parties to the case. A total of 57 organizations filed "amicus curiae" briefs supporting one side or the other; for example, UCDMS was supported by the NAACP, the National Association of Minority Contractors, the Association of American Medical Colleges, and a number of labor unions. Bakke was supported by a number of Jewish organizations, the American Federation of Teachers, and the U.S. Chamber of Commerce.

The Court handed down its decision in June 1978. It was extremely complicated, with no fewer than six of the nine justices writing separate opinions. But it boiled down to a three-way split: Four justices (Warren Burger, William Rehnquist, John Paul Stevens, and Potter Stewart) held that the UCDMS special admissions program and all programs like it constitute racial discrimination against whites and are therefore unconstitutional. Four other justices (Harry Blackmun, William Brennan, Thurgood Marshall, and Byron White) held that the UCDMS program and all like it are constitutionally permissible as ways of compensating minority groups whose forebears were victims of discrimination in the past. The swing vote was cast by Justice Lewis Powell, who held that while the UCDMS program was unconstitutional because it used a specific numerical quota, other programs that take race into account (without quotas) along with other factors in admitting applicants to universities or jobs are constitutional.

The upshot was that nobody won a total victory or suffered a total defeat. Bakke was admitted to UCDMS (he later graduated and received his medical degree); numerical racial quotas were outlawed; but affirmative action programs giving special help to minority applicants continue to operate under Powell's formula.

sin of discrimination against African-Americans and women with the new sin of discrimination against whites and males.

This difficult and hotly disputed issue has deeply divided the old civil rights movement. Since the Supreme Court first gave its complex ruling in the 1978 Bakke case (see the box), subsequent decisions in 1979, 1980, 1984, and 1986 still have not settled the fate of affirmative action plans once and for all, but many observers believe that the Court has clearly accepted a certain amount of tilting the scales in favor of women, African-Americans, and other minorities today in order to remedy the damage done by past tilting of the scales against them. Even so, many people still believe that any kind of "reverse discrimination" that *guarantees* more good things for African-Americans and women than their individual merits justify is just as wrong as the original discrimination that denied them the good things that their merits deserved. Consequently, affirmative action programs that guarantee preferential treatment are likely to be as highly controversial in the 1990s as they have been in the 1970s and 1980s.

RACIAL SEPARATION AND DISCRIMINATION IN SOUTH AFRICA

The United States is by no means the only modern nation in which powerful political groups have pressed for a government policy of segregation and white supremacy. Most Australians, for example, long regarded their nation as "a white island in an Asiatic sea," and for many years after its independence from Great Britain in 1900, Australia followed the "white Australia" policy of prohibiting all but a trickle of nonwhite immigration and giving the native aborigine population less-than-equal status. Even Great Britain, long considered a model of racial equality, has had its troubles. The great influx of Pakistanis and West Indians in the 1950s and 1960s led to the creation of racial ghettos and even race riots in several big cities. It also led to the passage in 1961 of the Commonwealth Immigrants Act, which ended the free entry of West Indians and Pakistanis but did not end the tensions between whites and coloreds and angry complaints by coloreds about discrimination and poor treatment.

However, the drive for governmentally enforced segregation and white supremacy has come closest to total victory in the Republic of South Africa.

THE BACKGROUND

The Republic of South Africa presently has a population of over 33 million, of whom 18 percent are of pure European descent, 10 percent are "colored" (of mixed native and European descent), 3 percent are Asian (mainly Indian), and 69 percent are of pure native descent (the whites call them *Bantus,* the Zulu word for men, but the blacks consider the label demeaning). Most of the Europeans are highly conscious of their status as a small white minority among a large native majority, and their consciousness is reinforced by the knowledge that on the whole continent of Africa there are only about 8 million Europeans compared with nearly 400 million natives.

From the time of the earliest white settlements, most Europeans in South Africa—the Afrikaners (settlers of Dutch descent) and the British-descended settlers alike—have been acutely conscious of the *swart gevaar* ("black menace" in Afrikaans, the language of the Dutch-descended Boers) and have resolved to maintain the *baaskap* (literally, "boss- ship") of whites over blacks.

THE POLICY OF APARTHEID

For many years the white rulers of South Africa have pursued the policy of *apartheid* ("separation"). The long-range goal of this policy is complete separation of the natives from the Europeans, with each race living in its own special areas but with ultimate government power over all areas and races held exclusively by whites. However, most white South Africans regard the achievement of this goal as centuries away. So as a short-range policy, apartheid means substantial segregation of the races in most activities, especially residence and work, and white supremacy in all aspects of life, especially political participation and power. Among its leading legal manifestations are the following.

Apartheid in Action. South African police search a "Bantu." (Source: Reuters/ Bettmann Newsphotos.)

Separation

The Population Registration Act of 1950 provides for the classification and registration of the entire South African population into three categories: European, native, and colored (mixed). Each person must carry an identification card showing to which of the three races he belongs. The Group Areas Act of 1950 empowers the government to designate particular areas for exclusive occupancy by particular races, and the Native Resettlement Act authorizes the forcible relocation of natives from their present living areas to native "reserves." Every native must carry an identification card, and if he wishes to travel or work outside his reserve he must shown a pass authorizing him to do so. Since 1950 the government has actually moved several hundred thousand natives in accordance with this legislation, but at present fewer than half the natives live in reserves. Those who do are required by the government to follow their ancient forms of tribal government and chieftainship, even though many believe that these forms are outmoded and wish to adopt more modern systems.

Education

The South African government controls all native education and teaches only what it finds appropriate for the traditionally primitive culture and technology of the blacks. Before 1957 a few coloreds and blacks attended South Africa's universities. The Separate Universities Education Act of 1957 ended that; all nonwhites are barred from attending any of the regular universities, and a Bantu college has been established for each nonwhite tribal group. None of these colleges is independent; all are administered directly by government departments to make sure that the "right" things are taught.

Political Participation

In only one of five provinces, Cape Province, have natives and coloreds ever been allowed to vote for members of the national Parliament. The Representation of Natives Act of 1936 confined the natives to voting for only seven members of Parliament, each of whom had to be a European. In 1960 Cape Province natives and coloreds were deprived of even these rights, and the native representatives were abolished. In 1983 South Africa adopted a new three-chamber Parliament: the House of Assembly for whites, the House of Representatives for Coloreds, and the House of Delegates for Asians. The blacks have no chamber and no representation. The House of Assembly continues to have the final say on everything, but some people regard the creation of special representation for coloreds and Asians as a modest step in the right direction. The first elections were held in 1984, and the turnout by coloreds and Asians was very low, but the representatives elected took their seats and the two new chambers are now in operation.

Occupations

Natives in South Africa have long been informally barred from engaging in any occupation higher or better paid than domestic service and unskilled labor. The Industrial Conciliation Act of 1954 placed the power of the government behind this discrimination by authorizing the Minister of Labor to determine at his own discretion which occupations will be open to members of the various races. On occasion he has used it to admit natives to some new occupations, such as druggists and clerks in certain kinds of stores, but no native has any chance at a managerial or professional position.

Public Accommodations

Complete racial segregation in such areas as transportation, hospitals, cemeteries, restaurants, and theaters has long been practiced by the private individuals who manage them. The Separate Amenities Act of 1953 made such segregation compulsory. Since 1978 the government has moderated the policy a bit by allowing all races to use the same public transportation, to attend the same churches, to participate in the same sports, and to attend a total of 26 integrated theaters. But most of the essentials of the long-standing policies of racial segregation and white supremacy remain in full force.

POLITICAL CONFLICT

The overwhelmingly dominant political party in South Africa is the National party, which in 1985 held 79 percent of the seats in the House of Assembly. It is now led by President Pieter W. Botha. The far-distant second party is the Progressive Federal party, which has 16 percent of the seats, and the third party is the New Republic party, which has 5 percent. The National party came to power in the general election of 1948, and since then it has pressed for apartheid at an even more rapid pace than the other white parties have thought desirable. The Nationalists have controlled Parliament since 1948, and in their resolute effort to establish apartheid and stamp out all opposition to it they have sometimes pushed the nation along the road to totalitarianism, although not yet all the way. There have been several milestones in this effort: In 1951 the Nationalist government forced through the Suppression of Communism Act, which not only empowers the government to jail all Communists and suppress all Communist doctrines, but also defines communism as *any* doctrine or scheme "which aims at bringing about any political, industrial, or economic change within the [nation] by the promotion of disturbance or by the threat of such acts" or "which aims at the encouragement of feelings of hostility between the European and non-European races"—rather different from the definition of communism we have been using in this book (see Chapter 4).

In 1951 the Nationalist government also enacted a bill to strike the coloreds from the common roll of voters in Cape Province, but the five-man

Supreme Court of Appeals unanimously declared it unconstitutional. The Nationalists then passed a bill making Parliament itself the high court, with final authority to interpret the Constitution; the Supreme Court also declared this law unconstitutional. After three years of searching for ways of getting around the Court, the Nationalists found one: In 1955 they enacted a law enlarging the Court from 5 to 11 members; the Nationalist prime minister appointed as the six new judges men known to be faithful supporters of the Nationalist program. Thereafter the Court caused no trouble.

In the years following, the Nationalists enacted the "90- day" law, which empowers the government to arrest anyone it wishes and hold that person in house or village arrest for 90 days without having to bring him to trial. In 1962 the Nationalists also enacted the General Law Amendment (Sabotage) Act, which gives a broad definition of sabotage and makes it punishable by death. Most observers believe that there is now no legal barrier in the path of any policy of apartheid the Nationalists may wish to adopt.

THE "BANTUSTANS"

In 1959 the Nationalist government enacted the Promotion of Bantu Self-Government Act, which proposed to establish four exclusively native areas, use them for the massive relocation of blacks from the Republic itself, and eventually give them the power of self-government under South African supervision. In 1963 the government announced that self-government had been granted to the Transkei; in 1977 they made a similar announcement about Bophuthatswana, in 1979 one concerning Venda, and in 1981 one concerning Ciskei. South Africa remains the only nation that recognizes any of the four Bantu republics as independent nations. The main problem seems to be the government's policy, announced in 1959, that any funds spent on the development of the "Bantustans" would have to come from the natives themselves. And since there seems to be no possibility that the natives can ever provide from their own resources anything remotely approaching what is needed for true development and independence, all four areas will remain parts of South Africa for a long time to come, and apartheid will continue to mean governmentally enforced racial segregation and white supremacy rather than the complete separation of the races.

South Africa has become something of a pariah nation in the world: It has been repeatedly condemned in resolutions by the United Nations and by most individual nations as well. Since the mid-1980s there has been increasingly violent resistance to apartheid by blacks in South Africa, growing protests by other nations, and many demands that government agencies and private institutions should sever all economic relations with South Africa. In 1986 the United States joined the growing number of nations imposing sanctions when Congress, over President Reagan's veto, imposed a limited economic boycott. How effective such measures will be in ending apartheid remains to be seen.

For the time being it is clear that South Africa will continue to show how far policies of racial segregation and white supremacy can go in a modern nation.

FOR FURTHER READING

POLICE POWERS AND DEFENDANTS' RIGHTS

*LEWIS, ANTHONY. *Gideon's Trumpet.* New York: Random House, 1964. Dramatic account of a famous Supreme Court decision on defendants' right to counsel.

PRITCHETT, C. HERMAN. *Constitutional Civil Liberties.* Englewood Cliffs, NJ: Prentice-Hall, 1984. Authoritative account of current civil liberties issues, with emphasis on Supreme Court interpretations.

*WILSON, JAMES Q. *Varieties of Police Behavior.* New York: Atheneum, 1970. Study of police behavior in selected communities.

*———. *Thinking about Crime,* rev. ed.. New York: Basic Books, 1982. Thoughtful analysis of causes, detection, and punishment of crime in a free society.

THE STATUS OF WOMEN

*AARON, HENRY J., and Cameron Lougy. *The Comparative Worth Controversy.* Washington, D.C.: Brookings Institution, 1986. Analysis of what has become one of the leading issues in the conflict over women's rights.

CONOVER, PAMELA JOHNSTON, and VIRGINIA GRAY. *Feminism and the New Right: Conflict over the American Family.* New York: Praeger, 1983. Account of conflict over the ERA and the abortion issue.

DECTER, MIDGE. *The New Chastity.* New York: Coward McCann & Geoghan, 1972. Strongest attack by a woman on the radical feminist position.

*FRIEDAN, BETTY. *The Feminine Mystique.* New York: W. W. Norton, 1968. The book that, more than any other, launched the contemporary women's rights movement.

*GELB, JOYCE, and Marian Lief Palley. *Women and Public Policies.* Princeton, NJ: Princeton University Press, 1982. Study of the women's

rights movement, with special emphasis on its internal politics and its approach to other groups.

KIRKPATRICK, JEANE J. *Political Woman.* New York: Basic Books, 1974. Instructive study of prominent women state legislators as examples of woman who, like the author, have been successful in politics.

KLEIN, ETHEL. *Gender Politics.* Cambridge: Harvard University Press, 1984. Account of the rise and impact of feminist political movements from the late 1960s to the 1980s.

LOVENDUSKI, JONI. *Women in European Politics.* Amherst, MA: University of Massachusetts Press, 1987. Survey of the role of women and women's political movements in Western European nations.

MANSBRIDGE, JANE J. *Why We Lost the ERA.* Chicago: University of Chicago Press, 1986. Account of the politics of the women's movement in the context of the struggle over the ERA.

THE STATUS OF AFRICAN-AMERICANS

BURSTEIN, PAUL. *Discrimination, Jobs, and Politics.* Chicago: University of Chicago Press, 1985. Study of efforts to mandate equal employment opportunities for blacks since 1945.

GLAZER, NATHAN. *Affirmative Discrimination.* New York: Basic Books, 1976. Scholarly argument against affirmative action programs.

GOLDMAN, ALAN H. *Justice and Reverse Discrimination.* Princeton, NJ: Princeton University Press, 1979. Scholarly argument against affirmative action programs.

*HOCHSCHILD, JENNIFER L. *The New American Dilemma: Liberal Democracy and School Desegregation.* New Haven, CT: Yale University Press, 1984. Analysis of current state of racial desegregation and integration of schools, with discussion of busing and other methods and their impact on the quality of education.

KIRP, DAVID L. *Just Schools: The Idea of Racial Equality in American Education.* Berkeley: University of California Press, 1982. Study of problems and conflicts in school desegregation and integration.

O'NEIL, ROBERT M. *Discrimination against Discrimination.* Bloomington: Indiana University Press, 1975. Scholarly defense of affirmative action.

REYNOLDS, FARLEY. *Blacks and Whites: Narrowing the Gap.* Cambridge: Harvard University Press, 1984. Analysis of impact of civil rights legislation of the 1960s and 1970s on the social and economic status of African-Americans in the 1980s.

*SINDLER, ALLAN P. *Bakke, DeFunis, and Minority Admissions: The Quest for Equal Opportunity.* New York: Longman, 1978. Thoughtful analysis of the issues involved in affirmative action programs for admission to graduate and professional schools.

SNIDERMAN, PAUL M., and MICHAEL GRAY HAGEN. *Race and Inequality: A Study in American Values.* Chatham, NJ: Chatham House, 1986. Survey-based study of Americans' changing attitudes on race and equality.

THOMPSON, LEONARD. *The Political Mythology of Apartheid.* New Haven, CT: Yale University Press, 1986. Analysis of theory and practice of apartheid in South Africa.

NOTES

[1]*Black's Law Dictionary,* 4th ed., (St. Paul: West, 1951), p. 445.

[2]*1986–87 Survey of Departments* (Washington, D.C.: American Political Science Association, 1987), pp. 1, 5.

[3]Walter S. G. Kohn in the *British Politics Group Newsletter,* Summer 1987.

[4]*Statistical Abstract of the United States, 1988* (Washington, D.C.: Bureau of the Census, 1988), Table 417, p. 248.

[5]*Public Opinion,* September/October 1986, pp. 34–35.

[6]Stokely Carmichael and Charles V. Hamilton, *Black Power: The Politics of Liberation in America* (New York: Vintage Books, 1967), p. 37. Copyright Random House, Inc.

[7]*The New York Times,* December, 21, 1988, p. A12.

[8]Speech to the Civil Rights March on Washington, August 28, 1963.

[9]Jesse Jackson, "Reparations Are Justified for Blacks," *Regulation,* September/October 1978, pp. 17–28. Copyright American Enterprise Institute.

17 Politics Among Nations

After World War I the German novelist Erich Maria Remarque wrote a scene in *All Quiet on the Western Front* that must strike a responsive chord in anyone who has ever crouched in a slit trench, peered out of a bomber at bursting flak, or huddled in a bomb shelter during a raid—or in all who think that one day they might have to do so. In this scene a group of German soldiers are in a rest area behind the lines, and the following conversation takes place after one of them, Tjaden, has asked what causes wars. His comrade Albert Kropp replies:

"Mostly by one country badly offending another,"...
Then Tjaden pretends to be obtuse. "A country? I don't follow. A mountain in Germany cannot offend a mountain in France. Or a river, or a wood, or a field of wheat."
"Are you really as stupid as that, or are you just pulling my leg?" growls Kropp. "I don't mean that at all. One people offends the other——"
"Then I haven't any business here at all," replies Thaden. "I don't feel myself offended."
"Ach, man! he means the people as a whole, the State——" exclaims Muller. "State, State——" Tjaden snaps his fingers contemptuously. "Gendarmes, police, taxes, that's your State;——if that's what you are talking about, no thank you."
"That's right," says Kat, "you've said something for once, Tjaden. State and home-country, there's a big difference."
"But they go together," insists Kropp, "without the State there wouldn't be any home-country."
"True, but just you consider, almost all of us are simple folk. And in France, too, the majority of men are labourers, workmen, or poor clerks. Now just why would a

French blacksmith or a French shoemaker want to attack us? No, it is merely the rulers. I had never seen a Frenchman before I came here, and it will be just the same with the majority of Frenchmen as regards us. They weren't asked about it any more than we were."

And one of the soldiers proposes a solution that would surely be endorsed by a great many GIs, Tommies, *poilus,* and Ivans.

Kropp on the other hand is a thinker. He proposes that a declaration of war should be a kind of popular festival with entrance-tickets and bands, like a bull fight. Then in the arena the ministers and generals of the two countries, dressed in bathing-drawers and armed with cubs, can have it out among themselves. Whoever survives, his country wins. That would be much simpler and more just than this arrangement, where the wrong people do the fighting.[1]

The questions that these fictional soldiers—and so many real soldiers and their sweethearts, parents, and friends—have asked are among the most difficult and urgent facing anyone concerned with the impact of politics on modern life: What causes wars? How can they be prevented?

In this and the following chapter I cannot hope to answer either of these questions fully and satisfactorily. I can, however, set forth some of the more prominent factors that political scientists believe must be taken into account in the search for answers.

THE BASIC STRUCTURE: THE STATE SYSTEM

The first and most important thing to understand is that in the 1990s, as in centuries past, politics among nations is conducted in a basic framework that political scientists call the **state system**—*the division of the world's population into nations, each of which has complete legal authority within its particular territory and none of which acknowledges a government legally superior to its own.* We begin by explaining just what this means and noting some of its consequences for the nature of international politics.

THE NATURE OF NATIONS

The dominance of world politics by the state system means that the main actors in international politics are not races, or classes, or genders, but *nations.* As of January 1, 1989 there were 167 political units generally accorded the legal status of nationhood (for a complete list, see Table 16.1 in Chapter 16). There are, of course, enormous differences among them on many dimensions—population size, natural resources, economic productivity, military power, and so on. But they all share the following five common characteristics:

Many Loyalties, Many Nations.
Opening ceremonies of the Olympic
Games, Los Angeles, 1984. (Source:
Tom McHugh, Photo Researchers.)

Particular Territory

Each of the world's nations is located on a particular area of the earth's surface and has definite, generally recognized boundaries that do not overlap those of any other nation. To be sure, the exact locations of mutual boundaries are sometimes disputed by adjoining nations, as they were by China and India in the 1960s; but the *principle* of definite boundaries is accepted by all nations.

Definite Population

Each nation regards only certain people as its citizens and all others as aliens. A **citizen** is *a person who has the legal status of being a full member of a particular nation.* This status includes giving loyalty to the nation, receiving its protection, and enjoying the right to participate in its political processes. By the same token, each nation regards any noncitizen as an **alien**—*a person who is neither a citizen nor a national of the nation in which he or she is present.*

Government

Each nation has an officially designated set of persons and institutions authorized to make and enforce laws for all people within its territory.

Formal Independence

Each nation has **sovereignty**—*the full and exclusive legal power to make and enforce laws for a particular people in a particular territory.* This means that each nation, large or small, strong or weak, has supreme legal authority over its own affairs and in that respect each nation is fully equal to every other nation. Note that this is a purely *legal* principle, and it is known in international law as "the principle of the sovereign equality of nations." In actuality, of course, some nations are more subject to influence by foreign nations than others. If the Soviet Union strongly suggests that Poland adopt a certain policy, Poland is more likely to accept the suggestion than the Soviet Union would be to act on a similar suggestion put to it by Poland. *Legally* speaking, however, Poland has as much right to make decisions for Poland as the Soviet Union has to make decisions for the Soviet Union.

Nationalism

The state system is rooted in **nationalism**—*the psychological attachment to a particular nation, based upon a common history, common language and literature, common culture, and a desire for political independence.* For many of the world's inhabitants, especially those in the long-established nations, nationalism is the highest allegiance: They are more loyal to their nations than to their churches, their social classes, their races, even their families. The most striking evidence of nationalism's power over human thought and behavior is that in modern times, wars, the supreme test of people's loyalties, are fought mainly among nations, not among races or churches or social classes, as they once were. When the United States has fought with Germany, American workers, capitalists, Roman Catholics, and Lutherans have killed and been killed by German workers, capitalists, Roman Catholics, and Lutherans.

Some commentators feel that nationalism and national sovereignty are old-fashioned and downright dangerous in a modern, highly interdependent world in which a number of nations have nuclear weapons. Be that as it may, the fact is that nationalism has never been stronger than it is right now. Of the 167 generally recognized nations today, no fewer than 117—well over half—have achieved their independence since the end of World War II in 1945. Indeed, 94—or 56 percent—have come into existence just since 1960. By far the greatest number of new nations have been created in Africa, where 44 of the 48 nations have achieved independence since 1945. The world's newest nations, Brunei on the island of Borneo in Asia and St. Kitts and Nevis in the Caribbean, became independent in 1983.

Thus, like it or not, modern international politics is conducted in the framework of the state system. What difference does it make? Let us see.

THE NATURE OF INTERNATIONAL POLITICS

What we have previously learned about domestic politics can tell us a lot about international politics. We begin by noting the principal similarities and differences between the two.

SIMILARITIES TO DOMESTIC POLITICS

International politics resembles domestic politics in several important respects. First, it consists of conflict among people, acting mainly in groups, whose values and interests differ and are to some extent incompatible. If some values are satisfied, then other values must go unsatisfied, and it is impossible to satisfy *all* groups equally.

Second, each group to some extent and in some manner *acts* to achieve its values as fully as possible, which inevitably brings it into conflict with other groups holding contrary values. In international as in domestic politics, *conflict* among individuals and groups is thus not an unfortunate but avoidable aberration from what is normal; it is the very essence of politics and human life itself. International politics, no less than domestic politics, is a perpetual struggle over "who gets what, when, and how."

Third, international conflict is not much more cumulative than domestic conflict. We observed in Chapter 2 that conflict in domestic politics tends to be noncumulative in the sense that when one issue replaces another in the center of the political stage, there is always some reshuffling of the conflicting individuals and groups. Some pros and cons on issue A remain associated on issue B, but some former allies find themselves on opposite sides, some old partisans are indifferent to the new issue, and some who were indifferent on issue A become partisans on issue B. The hostilities generated by one issue are thus not fully reinforced on each new issue; they are to some extent redirected and moderated by the succession of new issues.

International conflict is also relatively noncumulative, for the shuffling and reshuffling of allies and enemies is as frequent as it is in domestic politics. From 1941 to 1945, for example, Great Britain and the United States were allied with the Soviet Union and China in a gigantic war against Germany and Japan. From 1945 to the 1980s, Great Britain and the United States relied heavily on the support of their former enemies, West Germany and Japan, in their "cold war" with their former allies, the Soviet Union and China. From 1949 to the late 1950s, the Soviet Union and the People's Republic of China (PRC) stood shoulder to shoulder in a worldwide struggle against the Western powers. Since then, however, the two Communist giants have had their own cold war with each other, and the relations of both the Soviet Union and the PRC with Western nations, including the United States, have warmed considerably. Some onlookers may regard this kind of shifting about as evidence of the mendacity and hypocrisy of the great powers, but others may find it merely an indication that politics is politics whatever the arena. In fact, unless we long for an Armageddon in which the good nations wipe out the bad ones once and for all, perhaps we should view this international reshuffling as fortunate.

Finally, in both international and domestic politics, competing groups sometimes use violence to achieve their goals (see Chapter 2). The horrors of international war sometimes make us forget that more people have been killed in civil wars than in international wars.[2] Americans should know this very well, because more of us were killed in our Civil War (1861–65) than in all of our international wars put together, including the undeclared wars in Korea in the 1950s and Vietnam in the 1960s. Yet domestic violence is very different from international war. Internal political conflict is often nasty, expensive, and sometimes violent; but unlike international conflict, there is no possibility that it will escalate into full-scale thermonuclear war and the extermination of large parts of the human race. Domestic conflicts such as those between the prolife and prochoice factions in the United States or the Catholics and Protestants in Northern Ireland, bitter and sometimes violent though they may be, are not likely to be settled by one side dropping a hydrogen bomb on the other. But no one can predict with confidence that the disagreements between the United States and the Soviet Union, or between Israel and the Arab nations, will not be settled that way. The differences between international and domestic politics, therefore, are at least as significant as the similarities.

DIFFERENCES FROM DOMESTIC POLITICS

International politics differs from domestic politics mainly in the kinds of groups among which conflicts take place and the legal, social, and political framework in which those conflicts are fought out.

Little Overlapping Membership

The main contestants in domestic politics are individuals and interest groups. The main contestants in international politics are nations. They differ from the domestic political interest groups we have discussed in previous chapters mainly in that there is far less overlapping membership among them. Within any nation, as we noted in Chapter 2, each person is a member, formally or not, of many different groups; one can, for example, be simultaneously white, of Irish extraction, a Roman Catholic, a Democrat, a graduate of Berkeley, and an officer of a union. Among nations, however, the situation is different. Although a few people have dual citizenship (two or more nations claim them as citizens) and a few others are stateless (no nation claims them as citizens), nearly every one of the world's 5.3 billion inhabitants (as of 1990) is legally a citizen of one nation only. Moreover, very few think of themselves as equally Americans and Russians or Israelis and Egyptians—or, for that matter, as "citizens of the world."

Absence of a Government

In domestic politics, as we have seen many times, political interest groups try to achieve their ends solely or mainly by inducing their nation's government to make and enforce policies that the groups favor. Every government makes authoritative and binding rules, and politics is a contest among the nation's groups to shape those rules.

There is no world government with the power to make and enforce policies binding upon all peoples and all nations, however. (We will see in detail in Chapter 18 how far short the United Nations falls of being a world government.) Each nation therefore seeks to achieve its goals by inducing other nations, both allies and antagonists, to act as it wishes. A nation's power is thus measured by its success in this effort and not by its success in influencing the policy decisions of a nonexistent world government.

Accordingly, international politics is like domestic politics in that the essence of both is conflict among human groups to determine who gets what, when, and how. It differs from domestic politics mainly in that its contesting groups are nations with little or no overlapping membership and in the lack of a government with effective authority over all nations. And these differences arise from the fact that international politics is conducted within the state system, not within some system of world government.

The fact is that the international political system constitutes the nearest thing the world knows to true anarchy—a political system in which there is no government or other agency with the legal right or physical power to force people to do what they do not wish to do. Some political theorists argue that anarchy is the ideal form of political organization. Under anarchy, they say, people would participate in cooperative activities only by the free and independent consent of each, never by orders from a popular majority or a ruling class or a monarch. We noted in Chapter 1 that no human society has ever deliberately adopted anarchy as its organizing principle, although governments have from time to time broken down and lost their power to make authoritative rules—but usually only for brief periods of time.

Yet the state system, in both legal principle and political reality, comes very close to being true anarchy. Its basic legal principle is "the sovereign equality of nations," which means that every nation has the legal right to make and enforce laws without interference from outside; and that means that no international law that a nation has not accepted voluntarily is binding upon it. Nations may, and sometimes do, cooperate with other nations, but they do so because they think it is in their national interest, not because of some moral commitment to cooperation for its own sake.

There is no world legislature to make laws binding upon all nations, no world executive and police force to make sure that world laws are obeyed, and no world judiciary to adjudicate violations of the law and punish the violators. The United Nations General Assembly is, to be sure, a pseudolegislature, the United Nations Security Council is a pseudoexecutive, and the International Court of Justice is a pseudo–supreme court. But as we will see in Chapter 18, none of these institutions has any real power beyond what the individual member nations give them—and can withhold or withdraw whenever they choose.

The state system, in short, means that international politics is conducted within a framework of both legal and political anarchy. That is the basic fact shaping the nature of international conflict.

CHARACTERISTICS OF INTERNATIONAL CONFLICT

For many years after 1945, many Americans thought that the only international conflict that mattered was the cold war between the constitutional
democracies, led by the United States, and the Communist nations, led by the
Soviet Union. But as we have sometimes been pained to learn, most other
nations rarely see things this way. India and Pakistan, for example, have been
much more concerned with the status of Bengal and went to war over the
independence of Bangladesh. The Arab nations of the Middle East and Israel
have had no doubt that their hot-and-cold war is the crucial contest. Iran and
Iraq fought a bloody war from 1981 to 1988. And so on.

In the 1990s many Americans are no longer sure that there is a *single*
international conflict dividing the whole world into two great camps. They see,
instead, many divisions cutting across one another. Americans are currently
involved in no shooting war with any nation, but there are other conflicts
aplenty: Arabs v. Israelis, India v. Pakistan, Vietnam v. the PRC, and—potentially the most important of all—the PRC v. the Soviet Union. Each of these
conflicts has its own constellation of issues and contestants, and is in some
respects different from all other international conflicts. Yet most political
scientists believe that all past and present international conflicts under the
state system are alike to at least some degree and that understanding what
they have in common will help us understand what is involved in any particular conflict, including those in which our own country is most involved.

In this section, accordingly, we will examine what political scientists
generally believe to be the enduring characteristics of all international conflict
under the state system.

SOME GOALS OF NATIONS' FOREIGN POLICIES

Every nation's foreign policy is the product of its policy makers' answers to
these questions: What should be our national goals? Since some are bound to be
incompatible with others, which are the most important? What are our *vital*
interests? Of what kinds of international actions are we capable? Which are
best calculated to achieve our most important national goals?

National foreign policies thus originate in national goals. Although these
goals vary considerably from one nation to another, the most common can be
classified under five headings: security, markets and prosperity, territorial
expansion, defending and spreading ideology, and peace. Let us look at each.

✗ Security

The first goal of every nation, and the one to which all other goals are
usually sacrificed if necessary, is security. It has two main aspects. The first is

the preservation of the nation's legal right and practical ability to rule its own affairs. The second is the creation and maintenance of a state of affairs in which the nation can be relatively free of fear for its survival and independence. There is no such thing as absolute security or complete freedom from fear, of course. Consequently, each nation strives for the degree of security its leaders think they can reasonably attain. Even this minimum level of security is by no means the nation's only goal, however, and it sometimes conflicts with some of its other goals.

Markets and Prosperity

Every nation wishes to maintain and improve its citizens' standard of living. In foreign policy this goal affects a wide variety of matters, including tariffs and trade agreements, currency exchange rates, giving or receiving economic aid, and so on. One illustration known only too well by most Americans is our continuing (and increasingly urgent) efforts to improve our "international balance of payments"—that is, to get other nations, especially Japan, to buy as many or more of our products as we buy of theirs.

Some Marxist analysts (see Chapter 4) declare that aggression, imperialism, and war are entirely the products of capitalism and thus can be eliminated only by overthrowing capitalism and establishing socialism the world over. Capitalism, according to them, produces surplus capital and goods; domestic markets cannot absorb the surpluses; so the capitalists direct the government, which of course they "own," to embark on imperialist ventures for the purpose of gaining control of new markets; these ventures involve nations in wars with natives of the areas to be conquered and with other capitalist-imperialist nations trying to conquer the same areas for the same reasons. The United States is thus said to have precipitated World War II, the Korean War in the 1950s, and the Vietnam War in the 1960s to protect old markets and to gain new ones; Israel is said to have invaded Egypt in 1956 and 1967 for the same reason; and so on.

This analysis is appealing in its simplicity and its clear identification of heroes and villains, but most political scientists believe that it has little scientific validity. Among other deficiencies, it does not explain aggressive behavior by socialist nations, of which there has been plenty: for example, the Soviet Union's conquest and annexation of Estonia, Latvia, and Lithuania in the 1930s and its invasion of Hungary in 1956, Czechoslovakia in 1968, and Afghanistan in 1979; the invasion of Communist Vietnam by the Communist PRC in 1976; the invasion of Communist Kampuchea by Communist Vietnam in 1978; and so on. Since some socialist nations war with other socialist nations, then evidently the capitalist drive for markets is not the *only* force that drives nations to make war. Most political scientists therefore continue to believe that expanding markets and promoting economic prosperity are only two of several goals of foreign policy.

Territorial Expansion

Few diplomats unabashedly proclaim that their nations want more territory, but just about every nation has at one time or another tried to get more. They have followed expansionist—or, as they are sometimes called, imperialist—policies for various reasons: to obtain economic advantages expected from controlling new mineral and other resources and opening up new markets; to provide more living space for their people; and to realize their "manifest destiny" to rule (which characterized American western expansion in the nineteenth century).

Defending and Spreading Ideology

Political scientists have long argued about the proper role of political and economic interests on the one hand and moral ideals on the other in the formation of foreign policy. Some analysts, such as Hans J. Morgenthau and George F. Kennan, have contended that the real goal of any nation's foreign policy is to defend and promote its national interest, conceived mainly as its most advantageous power position for preserving and improving its military, territorial, and economic security and well-being. All the palaver about political ideals and moral values, they say, is at most a way of disguising and promoting the nation's underlying *real* interests. But if the policy makers forget the true nature and purpose of such talk and begin to take it seriously, their naivete will only plunge the nation into serious trouble.

The opposing position, advanced by such scholars as Frank Tannenbaum and Malcolm Moos, holds that one of the main purposes of a democratic nation's foreign policy is—or should be—to promote such moral values as freedom, democracy, and human rights for all people everywhere. Otherwise, they say, foreign policy and international politics become merely a global chess game, hideous because it is played with human lives and meaningless because it lacks any higher purpose.

In my opinion this debate is about a false issue, that of ideology *versus* other national interests, as though the two were incompatible and one had to be totally sacrificed to the other. There is every reason to believe that *both* ideology *and* other national interests are goals of every nation's foreign policy. We have already noted some of the other goals. Let us examine ideology for a moment.

Most Americans wish to preserve the independence and security of the United States and to defend and promote its national interests. But let us ask ourselves *why* preserving the United States is important enough to justify risking even thermonuclear war. Some people will reply, "It isn't!" But many more will insist that it is necessary to preserve our independence and save our way of life. That way of life includes not only a high standard of physical wealth and comfort but also some cherished ideals, such as freedom of speech and religion, democracy, and due process of law.

TABLE 17.1.   How the People of Different Countries View the Causes
of International Tensions (in percentages)

Question (1982): "Which of the following things do you feel are most responsible for current international tensions?"

	France	Germany	Great Britain	Italy	United States
The Soviet military buildup	21	55	33	37	27
The U.S. military buildup	14	39	15	20	11
U.S. interest rates and role of the dollar	45	28	7	19	19
Extension of Soviet influence	19	28	19	16	22
Superpower activities in the third world	29	26	16	15	17
Insufficient unity in Western Europe	26	36	17	24	18
U.S. aggressive policies toward the USSR	15	28	24	26	10

Source: Humphrey Taylor in *Public Opinion,* August/September 1983, Table 1, p. 17.

The same is true of other peoples in other nations. After 1933, for example, many Germans left Germany because they could not bear to live under the totalitarian regime of Adolf Hitler. Most of them later fought with the Allies in the war against Germany (1939–45). To many Germans, therefore, the Germany of Hitler was not worth preserving. How many of us would feel the same about the United States if it came to be ruled by a Fascist or Communist dictator?

Such attitudes among ordinary people—who, let us remember, make up the nation—help to account for some, though by no means all, of the foreign policies pursued by nations. In 1939, for example, a strong argument could have been made that the clash of American and British interests in the western hemisphere made Great Britain more dangerous to the United States than Germany. Yet we lined up with and ultimately fought beside Great Britain against Germany. Why? Surely one powerful reason was that the British, like ourselves, were committed to democratic ideals and were therefore defending values that we also held dear, whereas aggressively Fascist Germany was seeking to destroy them.

I am not arguing here that a democratic nation does or should always support all other democratic nations and oppose all dictatorial regimes in all circumstances. After all, from 1941 to 1945 the United States and Great Britain gladly accepted the Soviet Union's help against the Germans; both nations now accept help from authoritarian regimes of both Left (the PRC) and Right (Pakistan) in their conflict with the Soviet Union. Furthermore, the United States did little to help democratic rebellions in Hungary in 1956, Czechoslovakia in 1968, or Poland in the 1980s. In the latter instances we held off because three presidents, one moderate Democrat (Carter) and two conservative Republicans (Nixon and Reagan), thought that no American interest involved was vital enough to risk World War III. The point is that defending and spreading its ideology constitutes *one* of the goals of every nation, including the United States. Like every goal of foreign policy, it is sometimes in conflict with other goals and must compete with them for priority in deciding what to do. To overlook or slight the significance of ideology as a factor in foreign policy and international politics is therefore just as unrealistic as to give it the leading role.

Peace

Judging by what their leaders say, all nations and all peoples of the world cherish peace, regard war as the greatest of evils, and condemn those who cause wars as the worst of villains. The Charter of the United Nations declares that the organization's first purpose is "to maintain international peace and security," requires its members to "settle their international disputes by peaceful means," and opens membership to "all other peace-loving states." In most international conflicts, all sides strive constantly to portray themselves—and perhaps even think of themselves—as the true lovers and defenders of peace and their antagonists as aggressors and warmongers.

Ordinary people feel the same. If we take a poll among our friends on the question, "Do you want the United States to go to war with the Soviet Union?" only a handful will say yes. A comparable poll taken in Moscow would undoubtedly produce the same results.

So just about every person and every nation wants peace—and, we should add, sincerely wants it. Thus the accusation, often heard at the United Nations and elsewhere, that this or that nation "wants war" (because it loves war for its own sake?) is nonsense. But despite this universal love for peace, it is difficult to find a single year in world history in which no wars were fought anywhere. And even though just about every person and nation in the world today abhors the prospect of thermonuclear World War III, most of them believe that it is a serious possibility. So we are faced with this great paradox: Everyone wants peace, yet wars are more normal than peace and have been for a long time. How can this be?

Perhaps the following line of reasoning provides the answer: Peace is the absence of war, and it takes at least two nations to make a war. If the United States (or the Soviet Union or any other nation) *really* wants peace, let it announce to all the world today that under no conditions whatever will it fight another war and that it is dumping all its weapons into the ocean immediately. This policy is absolutely guaranteed to bring peace, and anyone who *really* wants peace at any price should urge immediate unilateral disarmament on the president and Congress and on the Soviet Politburo.

But, many would say, that is ridiculous: If we disarmed ourselves, the Communists (or the capitalists) would simply move in and take over. Others would say that unilateral disarmament would render us helpless to support our friends against their enemies—for example, Israel against the Arabs. Either or both may be true—but do we or do we not want peace? The answer, I think, is that we do—but not at any price. For most people agree with the famous maxim of Mexican leader Emiliano Zapata, that "It is better to die on your feet than to live on your knees."

The solution to the paradox is that people and nations genuinely want peace—but peace is only one of the things they want. Sometimes the desire for peace conflicts with other things they want, such as winning independence from colonial masters, preserving independence already won, or advancing the cause of social justice or democracy or human rights. When that happens, people and nations must choose which goals they want most and be prepared to sacrifice those that they want less. Such choices are the very essence of making foreign policy.

MAKING FOREIGN POLICY

CHOOSING GOALS, METHODS, AND CAPABILITIES

Making foreign policy in any nation involves making at least three kinds of choices. First is the choice of goals—deciding what should be the nation's general objectives in international politics and its particular objectives in particular situations. As we have noted, this choice often involves sacrificing or risking some goals in order to pursue other, more cherished goals.

Second, once the goals and their order of priority are set, the next step is to select and put into operation the methods most likely to achieve the goals. We will survey the most commonly used methods in a moment.

Third, capabilities must be assessed. Both of the first two choices must necessarily be influenced by the policy makers' judgment of what the nation can and cannot do relative to the capabilities of the other nations involved. For example, Cuba is a small nation, militarily more powerful than most other nations in the Western Hemisphere but not as powerful as the United States. If Fidel Castro dreamed of dominating the whole hemisphere he would be well advised not to pursue his goal by launching a military attack on the United States. Like any other nation, Cuba can successfully pursue only the goals and employ only the methods within its powers and capabilities. If it ventures beyond them, it is likely to end up worse off than it began. Even the world's "superpowers," the United States and the Soviet Union, have learned—for example, in Vietnam and Afghanistan—that being "global policemen" is beyond their capabilities.

We should not, however, picture the making of any nation's foreign policy as a process in which steel-nerved and far-seeing diplomats coolly survey an infinite range of possibilities and unerringly choose those best calculated to promote the national interest. Many people who have actually engaged in making foreign policy have testified that the decisions are made by all-too-fallible human beings subject to a variety of pressures from other government agencies, pressure groups, public opinion, and the mass communications media. In a democracy, foreign policy can never be made in complete isolation from the demands of domestic policy. Moreover, the makers of foreign policy are subject to internal doubts and hesitations, for they are hemmed in by real-life circumstances in which the possibilities do not seem nearly as numerous as they may appear to critics in college seminars and opposition parties. They have to make the best choices possible within limits imposed by their individual abilities and the circumstances in which they find themselves. The eminent British diplomat and historian Sir Harold Nicolson, who knew firsthand what it is like to make foreign policy, has given us something of the feel in this illuminating passage:

> *Nobody who has not watched "policy" expressing itself in day-to-day action can realize how seldom is the course of events determined by deliberately planned purpose, or how often what in retrospect appears to have been a fully conscious intention was at the same time governed and directed by that most potent of all factors—"the chain of circumstance." Few indeed are the occasions on which any statesman sees his objective clearly before him and marches towards it with undeviating stride; numerous indeed are the occasions when a decision or an event, which at one time seemed wholly unimportant, leads almost fortuitously to another decision which is no less incidental, until, link by link, the chain of circumstance is forged.*[3]

AGENCIES AND OFFICIALS

In almost every modern nation the government agencies most directly and exclusively concerned with making and conducting foreign policy are directed by the head of government, although in none of the democracies does the executive have a total monopoly over foreign policy (see Chapter 12). The principal agency working under his direction is a department specializing in foreign affairs, called variously the Department of State (United States), the Foreign Office (Great Britain), the Ministere des Affaires Étrangères (France), the Minindel (Soviet Union), and so on. The head of this department—the secretary of state or the foreign minister—is generally regarded as the number-two person in the executive and often succeeds to the top position.

The top career civil servants under the foreign minister's direction are generally known as the foreign service, which in most nations was one of the first administrative agencies to be put under the merit system (see Chapter 13). Foreign-service officers perform one of two types of activities: consular and diplomatic. The consular activities are the older but today the less important. Consuls in various foreign cities concentrate mainly on reporting economic information about their host countries and promoting the sale of the home country's products; they also perform some services for the home country's citizens traveling abroad.

Diplomatic officials, whether stationed in the foreign-affairs office at home or in the nation's various embassies abroad (most nations rotate their foreign-service officers from home duty to foreign duty and back to home duty), have four main functions:

1. *Communication and negotiation:* transmission and reception of all official communications with foreign nations and negotiations of international treaties and agreements.
2. *Intelligence:* the study of current and probable future events in foreign nations likely to affect their foreign policies and reporting conclusions to the home office. In many nations military services also conduct intelligence operations, and in the United States we have an additional major agency performing this function, the Central Intelligence Agency.
3. *Policy recommendations:* although the authority to make foreign-policy decisions belongs to the foreign secretary, the chief executive, and the legislature, subordinate officers and some employees of the foreign-affairs department are expected to make recommendations in their particular areas of concern. For reasons discussed in Chapter 13, these recommendations often become policy.
4. *Services:* awarding passports and visas, assisting citizens who have encountered legal trouble in foreign nations, and so on.

SOME METHODS OF FOREIGN POLICY

Diplomacy and Recognition

Diplomacy is *the conduct of international relations by negotiations among nations' official representatives.* Basic formal relations between any two nations are established through the exchange of official diplomatic missions—composed

Bilateral Diplomacy at the Top. Soviet General Secretary Gorbachev, U.S. President Reagan, and U.S. Vice-president Bush meet in 1988. (Source: The White House/David Valdez.)

of a top envoy known as an ambassador, minister, or chargé d'affaires, and a number of subordinate aides, secretaries, attachés, and so on. In deciding whether to receive officially some particular foreign diplomatic mission, each nation determines whether it formally "recognizes" the people who send the envoys as the foreign nation's legitimate rulers. A nation or a set of rulers whose envoys are not recognized by any other nation is in great trouble, for it cannot conclude formal international treaties or agreements, provide legal protection for its citizens traveling abroad, or engage in any of the legal relations that are basic to being recognized as a legitimate part of the state system.

The decision on whether or not to recognize a particular foreign regime can thus become a major issue in any nation's foreign policy. The basic question is whether to recognize all governments that are in fact in full control of their particular nations or only those that pass certain minimum standards of moral and political respectability. Some nations have attempted to answer these questions by extending de jure recognition to governments of which they approve and de facto recognition to those of which they disapprove. The United States, however, has occasionally refused formal recognition to regimes that were in full control. Notable instances include the communist governments of China (from 1949 to 1978), Cuba (since 1961), and Vietnam (since 1975).

Short of going to war, perhaps the most extreme way in which a nation can show its displeasure with a foreign nation is to sever diplomatic relations by withdrawing its diplomatic mission and ordering the other nation's mission to leave, as most Arab nations did to Egypt after the signing of the Egypt–Israel peace treaty in 1979 and as the United States did to Iran after the seizure of the American hostages in 1979. On the other hand, the quick recognition of Israel by the United States in 1948 shortly after it had proclaimed itself to be an independent sovereign nation helped considerably in establishing its status as such, though the Arab nations (except Egypt), the Soviet Union, and other Communist countries have never recognized Israel.

From the beginning of the state system until the outbreak of World War I in 1914, professional diplomats in foreign missions played significant parts in the formation and conduct of foreign policy. Their official titles as ambassadors and ministers plenipotentiary (meaning "with full power") were accurate descriptions of their powers, for the difficulty and loss of time involved in communicating with officials at home necessarily gave them wide discretion in negotiating and concluding agreements with their host nations. Since World War I, however, professional diplomats have lost much of their power of independent negotiation and agreement and have become mainly cultivators of good will, reporters of developments in their host nations, and advisors to the top policy makers back home. Most important negotiations are conducted by foreign secretaries, special envoys, or even heads of government in "summit" meetings.

Regardless of who conducts it, diplomacy can be used for different purposes, each of which can be illustrated from cold-war diplomatic relations since 1945.

First, diplomacy can be used to seek genuine agreements, as in 1987 when

Multilateral Diplomacy at the Summit. The "economic summit" of 1987 among the leaders of (clockwise) Great Britain, the United States, Canada, France, West Germany, Italy, the European Economic Community, and Japan. (Source: AP/Wide World Photos.)

the United States and the Soviet Union negotiated an agreement to limit the number of intermediate ballistic missiles in Europe.

Second, it can be used as a propaganda device to embarrass the nation's opponents. For example, if nation A has twice as many intercontinental ballistic missiles as nation B and nation A proposes an immediate freeze on the testing, manufacture, and deployment of such weapons, it puts nation B in an awkward diplomatic position. If it accepts the proposal, it guarantees permanent military superiority for nation A. If it rejects the proposal, it is denounced as a "warmonger" dead set on "escalating the arms race," while nation A preempts the desirable label of "peace-loving nation."

Finally, diplomacy can be used to play for time while awaiting improvement in the military situation. An example is the lengthy peace talks between the Chinese Communists and United Nations representatives in Korea in 1952 and 1953, in which the Chinese threw up one negotiating roadblock after another for more than a year while continuing intermittent military offensives. Only when the Chinese became convinced that their military situation would not markedly improve did they begin to negotiate seriously; once they did, a truce was concluded in a mere two months.

Trade Policies and Foreign Aid

Most nations use trade restrictions such as tariffs, import quotas and licenses, export controls, regulation of rates and conditions of international currency exchange, and even barter to control their economic relations with other nations. Many have also entered into agreements, such as the American reciprocal trade agreements and the European Economic Community, to give one another preferential treatment under such controls.

For a long time the main purpose of trade policies was to promote the economic prosperity of the nation pursuing them, but since World War I increasing numbers of nations have used them for political purposes as well. For instance, they have been used to promote the economic health of friendly nations or to damage that of unfriendly nations. In many nations, indeed, the economic and political purposes of trade policies often conflict.

For example, in the 1980s the balance of trade between Japan and the United States has tilted sharply in favor of Japan: In 1986 Japan sold $82 billion worth of its goods to the United States but bought only $27 billion from the United States. The imbalance was particularly great in electronics, automobiles, and steel. This resulted in growing pressure by Congress to put import quotas or heavy tariffs, or both, on Japanese goods coming into the United States unless the Japanese did a lot more to increase sales of American goods in Japan. President Reagan and his advisers resisted these pressures, partly on the ground that free trade is the best economic policy and partly on the ground that the Japanese are our most important allies in the Far East and we should not jeopardize our friendly relations with them. In the 1990s many Americans continue to see the clash as a conflict between the economic and the political interests of the United States, and no clear-cut choice for one over the other has yet emerged.

Foreign aid has been an important tool of foreign policy for the United States only since 1945. It became important in 1947 with the creation of the famous Marshall Plan to assist the economic recovery of the European nations after the devastation of World War II, and it has subsequently become a major foreign policy instrument not only for the United States but also for the Soviet Union, Great Britain, France, and other nations.

Foreign aid is generally intended to accomplish two main goals: to strengthen the economies and military capabilities of friendly nations so as to ensure their continuing strength and political support; and to strengthen the economies and military capabilities of neutral nations so as to increase their support. These goals are pursued through outright grants of money, food, machinery, and other goods; through technical assistance, mainly in the form of expert advice on how to increase productivity; and through supplying military weapons, materiel, and advisers. In 1986, for example, the United States gave a total of $13 billion in foreign aid, $4.1 billion of which was in military aid and the remaining $8.7 billion in nonmilitary aid. The biggest recipients were Israel ($4 billion), Egypt ($2.7 billion), and the Philippines ($449 million). The most controversial issue in foreign aid in the 1980s was a series of proposals by the Reagan administration to give massive aid, both military and nonmilitary, to the Nicaraguan *contras*—the forces who were trying to overthrow the Castroite government of Nicaragua.

Foreign Aid and Foreign Policy. U.S. aid to Ethiopia, 1986.
(Source: Carl Frank/Photo Researchers.)

The United States, of course, is by no means the only nation that gives foreign aid, though it gives far more than any other nation. The Soviet Union gives about $1 billion a year, with $700 million going to other Communist nations (Cuba is the leading recipient) and $300 million going to countries in the Third World.

There has never been general agreement on how effective foreign aid is as a device for winning friends among the neutral nations, and it seems that in the United States each year, the requested appropriation for foreign aid is harder to get through Congress. That results in part from the fact that of all the things on which the federal government spends money, foreign aid is the least popular with the general public (see Table 17.2), and it is therefore especially vulnerable to cuts. Still, as long as our adversaries are dispensing aid, it seems unlikely that the United States or any other major power will abandon it altogether; so it seems likely to remain a major weapon of foreign policy—at least for relatively rich nations— for some time to come.

Propaganda and Subversion

Diplomacy and foreign aid are direct efforts to induce the public officials of other nations to act in the desired manner. Propaganda and subversion are indirect efforts in that they are intended to change political conditions in the target nations in such a way that their officials will be forced to adopt the desired policies.

Propaganda in this context means the use of mass communications to influence the target nation's general public so that they will insist that their officials act as the propagandizing nation wishes. Most major powers use propaganda for these purposes. The United States, for example, maintains the U.S. Information Agency to organize broadcasts, libraries, film showings, and other programs in friendly and neutral foreign nations, in order to present the American point of view in the most favorable light. The Voice of America beams radio broadcasts to the other side of the iron curtain, and Radio Marti broadcasts to Cuba. The Soviet Union has long used posters, films, and radio broadcasts to spread accusations that the United States has used germ warfare in Korea and Vietnam, that it is conspiring to overthrow other governments, and that it is preparing to start World War III. The technological improvement of mass communications and the increasing importance of public opinion (see Chapters 6 and 7) have made propaganda of this sort far more common than it was before World War I.

Sometimes nations try to influence the policies of other nations by **subversion**—*covert action designed to overthrow an established government.* Such action can take many forms, including secret financial and military help to rebel forces in the target nation and efforts to damage the reputations and popularity of the target government's leaders. The built-in secrecy of these operations makes it difficult to obtain accurate data and analyze them in a

TABLE 17.2.   Public Opinion on Foreign Aid v. Other Kinds of Spending

Question: ''We are faced with many problems in this country, none of which can be solved easily or inexpensively. I'm going to name some of these problems, and for each one I'd like you to tell me whether you think we're spending too much money on it, too little money, or about the right amount.''

	Percentage Saying Government is Spending		
Spending on	Too Much	About Right	Too Little
Handling rising crime rate	4	23	68
Improving the nation's education system	6	34	56
Increasing the nation's energy supply	7	37	45
Improving and protecting the environment	10	37	47
Welfare	45	26	22
Foreign aid	76	15	3

Source: Roper Poll, reported in *Public Opinion,* April/May 1983, p. 27.

scholarly way, and so much of what is written on subversion today is journalistic, often sensational, and impossible to verify. Nevertheless, it is now well established that in the 1920s and 1930s the Soviet Union, operating through the Communist International (Comintern), carried on a program of espionage, sabotage, infiltration of other nations' governments, and even assassination in order to promote Soviet foreign policy objectives.

Most students of subversion also agree that a classic instance was Nazi Germany's campaign in the 1930s to overthrow the government of Austria and replace it with a pro-Nazi government, a campaign that achieved complete success in 1938 when the Austrian Nazi party took power, invited in German troops, and brought about the *anschluss*—the complete absorption of Austria into the Third Reich. More recent instances have been the secret efforts of the Communist government of Cuba to aid rebel forces in Bolivia, Peru, El Salvador, and Guatemala; and the quasi-secret efforts of the United States to support the contra rebels against the Communist-leaning government of Nicaragua. In short, distasteful though subversion may be compared with such respectable techniques as diplomacy and foreign aid, it seems likely that some nations will use it some of the time to pursue their foreign-policy goals.

Terrorism

In the 1980s Americans have become acutely conscious of another method of foreign policy: **terrorism**—*the systematic use of violence or the threat of violence against individuals to achieve political objectives.* The term is taken from the "reign of terror" in the French Revolution (1793–94), when the Committee of Public Safety, led by Maximilien Robespierre, sought to eliminate the opposition by using mass executions to terrify and intimidate all those who opposed them. (In just over a year, over 300,000 persons were arrested and over 17,000 were sent to the guillotine.)

Terrorism is used by nations and political groups that cannot accomplish their objectives by diplomacy and are too weak to use conventional military force. Its immediate targets are ordinary, unsuspecting people such as passengers on airliners, patrons of airports, or diners at restaurants. Its techniques are to harm or threaten to harm its victims by seizing them as hostages or killing them with guns and bombs. And its object is to terrify the people and the officials of the target government so that they will alter their policies as the terrorists wish.

There is no shortage of recent examples of terrorism. Perhaps Americans are most conscious of the use of terror by various Muslim groups in the Middle East—especially the Shi'ite Muslims of Lebanon—to force the United States to end its support of Israel and get out of the area altogether. For instance, in 1979 Iranian Shi'ites, with the full approval of the Ayatollah Khomeini's Iranian government, stormed the American embassy in Teheran and held 60 diplomatic employees prisoner for over a year before they were finally released. In April 1983, a car filled with explosives was detonated at the American embassy in Beirut, Lebanon, killing over 50 persons. In October, an explosive-laden truck crashed into the compound of the American marines serving in the multinational peace-keeping force in Beirut and killed over 200. In February 1984, President Reagan ordered the marines to withdraw, and the peace-keeping force soon dissolved. And in June 1985, Shi'ite Muslim terrorists hijacked an American airliner and held over 70 passengers hostage, demanding that Israel release 700 Shi'ites being held in Israeli jails.

Americans have by no means been the only targets of terrorists. In 1983 the Provisional Irish Republican Army (IRA), a terrorist organization seeking to force the removal of British troops and influence from Northern Ireland, exploded a bomb at Harrod's, one of London's leading department stores. And in 1983 the IRA exploded a bomb in a hotel in Brighton, where the Conservative party's annual conference was being held, killing 4 people, wounding 32, and narrowly missing Prime Minister Margaret Thatcher. In 1986 terrorists exploded a bomb in a Paris cafe, killing 8 people and wounding over 200.

Terrorism is perpetrated in extreme secrecy by small numbers of terrorists, and so it is usually difficult or impossible to specify exactly which governments are using terrorism as a matter of policy. Even so, American and NATO intelligence agencies have concluded that a number of nations—especially Libya, Iran, Cuba, Syria, North Korea, and the Soviet Union—have given training, weapons, and money to terrorists and have sometimes deliberately used them as instruments of foreign policy. Whether directed by governments or not, terrorism is extremely difficult for the target nations to deal with. They would like to reject all terrorist demands, and yet the consequence might well be the murder of innocent hostages. They would like to take swift and devastating military reprisals against the terrorists, but usually they cannot be sure precisely who the terrorists are or who supports them; and as President Reagan said in 1985, if in taking reprisals against terrorists the United States were to kill innocent nonterrorists, "we would become terrorists ourselves."

So far terrorism has not won any major political victories comparable to those won by diplomacy or victory in war. But for those nations with no scruples about using it, terrorism is a low-cost, low-risk technique, and the odds are that it will be used more rather than less in the years ahead.

War

War has long been regarded by most people as perhaps the worst disease in the whole grim pathology of human affairs—and for good reason. Even before the advent of nuclear weapons, wars exacted a price in death and suffering too enormous for the imagination to grasp. It is estimated, for example, that in World War I (1914–18), an incomprehensible total of 37 million human beings died either on the battlefield or as a direct result of the famine and disease brought on by the struggle. In World War II (1939–45), another 22 million perished. Wars have also damaged the human race in other ways. Not only have the volunteers and first casualties been some of the finest of the nations' youths and potential leaders, but the moral, social, and economic deterioration that infects both winners and losers after most wars has also left the world much poorer. Paying for past, present, and future wars is by far the greatest single economic burden borne by any large modern nation. All these things were true of war before nuclear weapons were available; what the costs of war are likely to be now that many nations have such weapons we can only guess.

Yet scarcely any generation in the history of any modern nation has lived out its time in peace, and many generations in many nations have endured as many as two or three major wars. Thus we all have to face the fact that, terrible though they may be, wars continue to happen. Wars, in fact, are as normal as peace in the modern world. Consequently, one of the most baffling and increasingly urgent questions confronting students of governing is, How can something so terrible happen so often?

Some theologians believe that war is a divine punishment laid on humanity for its sins, and so it may be. However, social scientists must proceed from the assumption that war is not imposed on people by forces outside themselves, but is an activity in which they engage voluntarily for purposes of their own. Most political scientists regard war much as did the great Prussian student of war, Karl von Clausewitz, who declared, "War is a political instrument, a continuation of political relations, a carrying out of the same by other means."[4]

To the political scientist, then, war has to be seen as one of the methods that nations use to achieve their ends. For most nations its tremendous costs and great risks make it the method of last resort. Most nations turn to war only when one of their most cherished goals—such as preserving their independence or protecting their basic institutions—appears to be in mortal danger and all other means of achieving their goal seem to have failed. Only such a goal in such circumstances can justify the costs and risks of war.

Yet we cannot talk *only* of the costs and risks of war, for the fact is that many nations have won highly valued goals through war when they might not have done so by other means. The United States and Israel, for example, established their very national existence by fighting and winning wars of independence. Great Britain and the United States may not have made the world "safe for democracy" by fighting World War II, but at least they preserved their independence, helped to end Hitler's Third Reich, a regime that as a matter of deliberate policy had murdered 6 million Jews in the never-to-be-forgotten Holocaust, and helped to save the world from Hitler's demonic plans for the future. Many of the world's great religions—notably Christianity and Islam—have been spread among the heathen and defended against infidels and heretics largely by the sword. We are clearly not justified in calling *all* wars futile and barren of accomplishment. One of the most eminent students of war sums it up as follows:

> War, then, has been the instrument by which most of the great facts of political national history have been established and maintained. ... The map of the world today has been largely determined upon the battlefield. The maintenance of civili-

zation itself has been, and still continues to be, underwritten by the insurance of an army and navy ready to strike at any time where danger threatens.[5]

Great questions face all nations in the nuclear age: Is war still a thinkable instrument of national policy, or do nuclear weapons mean that war will destroy everything and achieve nothing for any nation? Can it be avoided or limited? Or are we all done for? In several senses, these are truly the final questions in a study of governing in the modern world, and we will consider them in our next and final chapter.

FOR FURTHER READING

*BEITZ, CHARLES. *Political Theory and International Relations*. Princeton, NJ: Princeton University Press, 1979. Survey of leading theories of international politics.

*BEST, GEOFFREY. *Humanity in Warfare*. New York: Columbia University Press, 1980. Analysis of the causes and consequences of war.

DUCHACEK, IVO D. *The Territorial Dimension of Politics: Within, Among, and Across Nations*. Boulder, CO: Westview Press, 1986. A defense of the state system and national sovereignty as a rational organizing principle for world politics.

*FROMKIN, DAVID. *The Independence of Nations*. New York: Praeger, 1981. Analysis of the differences between domestic and international politics, with emphasis on the consequences of the state system.

*GILPIN, ROBERT. *War and Change in World Politics*. Cambridge: Cambridge University Press, 1981. Study of the impact of war on societies and international relations.

*HALPERIN, MORTON H. *Bureaucratic Politics and Foreign Policy*. Washington, D.C.: Brookings Institution, 1974. Study of foreign-policy processes from standpoint of bureaucratic infighting.

*HOWARD, MICHAEL. *The Causes of War*. Cambridge, MA: Harvard University Press, 1983. Innovative analysis of what causes wars.

KISSINGER, HENRY. *White House Years*. Boston: Little, Brown, 1979. Reflective memoirs by a scholar who became a key maker of foreign policy.

*LIEBER, ROBERT J. *No Common Power: Understanding International Relations*. Glenview, IL: Scott, Foresman/Little, Brown, 1988. Survey of the structure and processes of world politics.

MACFARLANE, S. NEIL. *Superpower Rivalry and Third World Radicalism*. Baltimore: Johns Hopkins University Press, 1985. Analysis of the relationship between Third World national liberation movements and the relations between the United States and the Soviet Union.

MORGENTHAU, HANS J., and Kenneth W. Thompson. *Politics Among Nations*, 6th ed. New York: Knopf, 1985. Most recent version of influential survey of international politics.

RUSSETT, BRUCE M., and HARVEY STARR, *World Politics: The Menu for Choice*, 2nd ed. New York: St. Martin's Press, 1985. General survey of international politics.

TREVERTON, GREGORY F. *Covert Action: The Limits of Intervention in the Postwar World*. New York: Basic Books, 1987. Critical study of the use of covert actions in peacetime international politics.

WALTZ, KENNETH N. *Theory of International Politics*. Reading, MA.: Addison-Wesley, 1979. Innovative conceptualization and explanation of international politics.

NOTES

[1]Excerpts from *All Quiet on the Western Front* by Erich Maria Remarque, "im Westen Nichts Neues," copyright 1928 by Ullstein E.G.; Copyright renewed 1956 by Erich Maria Remarque; "All Quiet on the Western Front," copyright 1929, 1930 by Little, Brown; Copyright renewed 1957, 1958 by Erich Maria Remarque.

[2]See Lewis F. Richardson, *Statistics of Deadly Quarrels* (Pittsburgh: Boxwood Press, 1960), pp. 32–50.

[3]Harold Nicolson, *The Congress of Vienna* (New York: Harcourt Brace Jovanovich, 1946), pp. 19–20.

[4]Karl von Clausewitz, *On War* (London: Routledge and Kegal Paul, 1940), vol. 3, p. 122.

[5]James T. Shotwell, *War as an Instrument of National Policy* (New York: Harcourt Brace Jovanovich, 1929), p. 15.

18 The Quest for Peace in the Thermonuclear Age

There is such a thing as a man being too proud to fight. (1915)
But the right is more precious than peace, and we shall fight for the things which we have always carried nearest our hearts. ... (1917)

Woodrow Wilson

Older men declare war. But it is youth that must fight and die. And it is youth who must inherit the tribulation, the sorrow, and the triumphs that are the aftermath of war.

Herbert Hoover

Unconditional war can no longer lead to unconditional victory. It can no longer serve to settle disputes. It can no longer be of concern to great powers alone. For a nuclear disaster, spread by winds and waters and fear, could well engulf the great and the small, the rich and the poor, the committed and the uncommitted alike. Mankind must put an end to war or war will put an end to mankind.

John F. Kennedy

As long as there are sovereign nations possessing great power, war is inevitable.

Albert Einstein

If it comes, what will World War III be like? Figure 18.1, which shows the damage range of a hypothetical thermonuclear bomb detonated over the center of Washington, D.C., suggests part of the answer. According to data from official tests, on which the figure is based, *one* 20-megaton thermonuclear bomb (1 megaton equals the destructive force of 1 million tons of TNT) is more

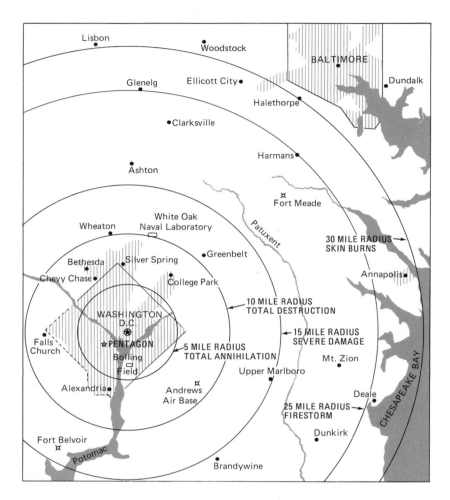

FIGURE 18.1.   The damage range of a thermonuclear bomb

powerful than *all* the bombs dropped on Germany and Japan in World War II put together. One 10-megaton bomb obliterates everything within a radius of 5 miles around the blast point and leaves only a poisonously radioactive crater more than 500 feet deep. The blast sets off a suffocating fire storm for a radius of 25 miles or more. More than 200 different radioactive compounds are created and attached to particles of debris, which are swept into the air and form the familiar mushroom cloud. These deadly particles float back to earth at varying speeds, depending upon their weight and, if spread uniformly, produce lethal levels of radioactivity over about 5,000 square miles.[1]

But that is only what one bomb can do. What about the 150 or more bombs that might be delivered in an all-out attack? In 1959 the Joint Congressional Committee on Atomic Energy tried to answer this question. Its members heard testimony from military, scientific, and medical experts about the probable effects of a 1,500-megaton attack on the United States. They concluded (and their conclusions have been confirmed and extended by later studies published by the U.S. Arms Control and Disarmament Agency) that 25 million people would die the first day, another 25 million would be fatally injured, and still another 20 million would be injured but not fatally.

Some experts estimate that a 20,000-megaton attack with "dirty" bombs (those with high-fission yield) would, within 60 days, kill by fallout every American who had survived the original blasts and fire storms. Others believe that "only" 70 percent of the population would be killed.[2] Many scientists believe that even worse would be the long-range effects of the "nuclear winter" that would follow: They predict that after a major nuclear attack, much of the earth would be covered with a cloud of radioactive soot that would block the sun, push temperatures far below freezing, and prevent the growing of most kinds of food. Others fear still more the breakdown of the ozone layer that now protects the earth from the full power of the sun's rays; the nuclear cloud would destroy the ozone, and when the cloud cleared there would be no protection against death from sunburn and skin cancer. Still others fear most of all the long-range genetic effects of the exposure to radiation poisoning, which, by massively altering the genes of humans and animals, might produce generations of mutants, with unpredictable consequences.

Some commentators believe that such predictions are far worse than the reality will be—that with proper measures for bomb shelters and first aid, preattack evacuation from cities, and postattack medical assistance, millions of people would survive. No cne knows for sure.

Only two atomic bombs have so far been exploded in warfare, both by the Americans against the Japanese in 1945: The 12.5-kiloton bomb (1 kiloton equals the force of 1,000 tons of TNT) dropped on Hiroshima killed 70,000 persons, and the 35-kiloton bomb dropped on Nagasaki killed 35,000. But those bombs were very primitive by present-day standards: Modern intercontinental ballistic missiles (ICBMs) are "MIRVed" (an acronym for "multiple independently targeted reentry vehicle"); that is, each can carry a number of nuclear warheads, each of which is independently guided to a separate target. But no matter how much they may disagree on the likely total damage from a nuclear attack, all experts believe that a thermonuclear war would be by far the greatest catastrophe ever experienced by the human race.

The London-based International Institute for Strategic Studies estimated that in 1984 the Soviet Union had deployed about 1,400 land-based and 981 sea-based ICBMs, while the United States had deployed about 1,000 land-based and 590 sea-based missiles.[3] If thermonuclear bombs are delivered as the warheads of ICBMs launched from deep and indestructible concrete "silos," there is no known way to prevent them from reaching their targets. In 1984, however, President Reagan proposed that the United States study the feasibility of building and deploying a system of satellite-based laser weapons to destroy incoming missiles before they can reach their targets—a proposal Reagan called the strategic defense initiative (SDI) and some opponents dubbed the "Star Wars" defense.

We do not yet know whether such a system is technically feasible and economically affordable, but at best it is years in the future. At present, however, no nation can hope to defend itself against thermonuclear attack; it can only retaliate by sending its own ICBMs against the aggressor—and hope that the fear of mutual assured destruction (MAD) will deter any potential aggressor from launching an attack. This is why a nation's nuclear weapons are often called its *deterrent*.

For these reasons, then, no one doubts that in the ICBM with a thermonuclear warhead we have at last found "the absolute weapon" with which we can literally exterminate humanity and most other living things on the planet. Everyone recognizes that the thermonuclear age may very well be our last—if we decide to fight World War III with thermonuclear weapons. The grim fact dominating our time is that the quest for peace has become a quest for the means of sheer physical survival for all people in all nations.

It is further complicated by the "*n*th-country problem." At present the United States and the Soviet Union are by far the biggest nuclear powers, but at least four other nations—Great Britain, France, the People's Republic of China (PRC), and India—also have thermonuclear weapons and some means of delivering them. And many other nations (for example, West Germany, Japan, Israel, Pakistan, and Sweden) have the scientific knowledge and the engineering capability necessary to make nuclear weapons. If the possession of such weapons by the United States and the Soviet Union makes us a bit nervous, how about their possession by, say, Libya and Israel, or Iran and Iraq, or India and Pakistan? For World War III might be touched off not by the original nuclear powers, but by the *n*th country to possess the Bomb.

Precisely this apprehension induced the Soviet Union and the United States to take the lead in drawing up and pressing for the adoption of the general Nuclear Nonproliferation Treaty in 1968. The treaty provides, first, that nations now possessing nuclear weapons will not transfer them to any other nation; second, that non-nuclear nations will not manufacture or acquire nuclear weapons; third, that the International Atomic Energy Authority is authorized to conduct inspections in the various participating nations to ensure compliance; and, fourth, that all signatory nations will have access to information about peaceful uses of atomic energy. By early 1970 a total of 97 nations had signed the treaty. However, they included only three of the six members of the "nuclear club," for France, the PRC, and India refused to sign. Israel, a potential nuclear power, also refused to sign, and so the treaty is far from being a complete solution to the *n*th-country problem. But at least it gives us some hope that the problem will eventually be brought under control.

What, then, are our chances of survival? Some analysts believe that they depend upon our ability to keep World War III from being fought with thermonuclear weapons and to confine nations to the use of non-nuclear "conventional" weapons, which, however destructive, do not have the capacity to wipe out all life on earth. These analysts believe that there is a strong possibility that nations will refrain from using thermonuclear weapons by mutual consent. Other analysts argue that our best chance lies in keeping all future wars limited, in geographic area as well as in the number of nations involved, as those in Korea, Indochina, the Persian Gulf, the South Atlantic, and the Middle East have been limited since 1945. Still others insist that, because limiting wars is risky at best—if we fail just once we lose the whole game—our only real chance for survival is to find a way to prevent *all* international wars, limited or general.

Whatever the policies they think we should adopt, however, all present-day students of international affairs believe that the thermonuclear age has transformed the ancient quest for peace from a search for a utopia of tranquility into a hunt for the minimum conditions of human survival. This hunt, moreover, must take place in an age in which nuclear power makes it urgent while the political fission characteristic of the state system may still prevent people—as it has prevented them for centuries—from finding a way to eliminate war.

War, as we noted in Chapter 17, has always been both costly and risky for any nation, and few nations' leaders have ever engaged in it for its own sake

Do Nuclear Weapons Make War Obsolete? A hydrogen bomb in the Pacific, 1954. (Source: AP/Wide World Photos.)

because they thought it would be fun, or it would improve their nations' moral character. Yet under the state system just about every nation has fought wars when its leaders and people came to believe that not fighting would bring even greater disasters than the horrors of war. We have no reason to be confident that the enormously greater costs of thermonuclear war have basically altered this historic general attitude toward international violence.

As Albert Einstein, the great physicist whose letter to President Franklin D. Roosevelt in 1939 launched the creation of the first nuclear weapons, said: "The unleashed power of the atom has changed everything except our modes of thinking."[4]

If peace is to prevail in our time, it will come either because modern nations do not desire *any* national goal enough to go to war for it or because they believe they can achieve their goals by means other than war. The quest for peace in our age is thus a search for a world political structure that will incline peoples and leaders to adopt either or both attitudes toward war.

In this final chapter, we will accordingly examine the nature and record of some of the more prominent approaches to conducting international political conflict without war that have already been tried or considered.

APPROACHES TO PEACE WITHIN THE STATE SYSTEM

The state system, as we learned in Chapter 17, is deeply rooted in the fact that most people give their basic political loyalties to their nations rather than to their races, sexes, economic classes, churches, or other group affiliations. Although the leaders of nations have long sought ways of achieving national goals without resorting to war, most have had no desire or hope of eliminating such basic features of the state system as the sovereign independence of nations and the legal right of each nation to make its policies without interference from outside. Our first category of approaches to peace therefore includes those that assume the continuation of the state system and rely on the voluntary actions of independent sovereign nations as they now exist.

Each of the approaches in this category, moreover, rests upon a set of ideas about what causes wars and how to alleviate or eliminate those causes. Accordingly, we will consider the rationale as well as the record of each suggested approach to peace within the existing state system.

BALANCE OF POWER

A Description and an Approach to Peace

The term *balance of power* is used in several different senses by analysts of international affairs. In a purely descriptive sense it simply means the distribution of power among nations at any given moment and carries no necessary connotation of equal shares. As an approach to peace, however,

balance of power means *a distribution of power among nations that is sufficiently equal to maintain security and peace.* And following a policy of balance of power means striving for such a distribution. The balance-of-power approach to peace is based on the assumption that war results when a particular nation feels sufficiently stronger than its antagonists to believe that it can threaten or attack them with assurance of success—or feels sufficiently weaker to require it to strike now while it still has a chance. The adherents of this approach propose to keep the peace by preventing any nation from feeling that much stronger or weaker than any of its rivals.

Methods

Many nations have sought both to protect their national interests and to avoid war by pursuing balance-of-power policies calculated to keep themselves and their allies strong enough to prevent opposing nations or combinations of nations from becoming too strong. Among the traditional methods have been *domestic measures,* such as building up their armaments and strengthening their military organizations; *alliances,* including both acquiring allies for themselves and splitting off their opponents' allies in the ancient strategy of divide and conquer; *compensations,* including dividing up colonial areas among the great powers so that they will be satisfied and thus diverted from aggression against other great powers; and *war,* used as a last resort to prevent the opposing nation or bloc of nations from becoming too powerful. A classic example of a balance-of-power policy is that followed by Great Britain for centuries, in which it put its weight against whatever was the single most powerful nation in Europe—first Spain, then the Netherlands, then France, then Germany, and now the Soviet Union.

Evaluation

Most political scientists believe that, whatever balance-of-power policies may have done for the interests of individual nations, they have not kept the peace. Their failure has resulted partly from the impossibility of measuring accurately what the distribution of power actually is, which means that no nation can ever be sure when power is sufficiently "balanced" and when it is not. Another deficiency is that most nations believe that prudence requires them to leave a margin for error in their calculations; they therefore build up their armaments and their alliances to a level higher than what they estimate is the necessary minimum. Their antagonists feel the same need for a margin of safety, however, and they in turn build up *their* armaments to a level beyond that of the rival nations. And so on in a process familiarly known as an arms race.

The whole idea of a balance of power thus rests upon an oversimplified and mechanical conception of international relations. It assumes that relative national power can be calculated precisely, and it assumes that all nations wish only to maintain their existing situations, not to improve them. Both assumptions are wrong. Balance of power has never succeeded in keeping the peace in the past, and it seems likely that even its modern version, called by some commentators the "balance of terror," will not succeed either, despite the possibility that fear of thermonuclear weapons may make nations more hesitant than in the past to resort to war. Always before in history, some nation or group of nations has sooner or later come to believe that the only way to restore the balance is to go to war before it is too late. Is there any good reason to suppose that the present balance of power will work any better?

COLLECTIVE SECURITY

Meaning and Rationale

As we have seen, those who seek peace through balance-of-power methods assume that no nation will launch an attack on any other nation unless it is confident that it has the preponderance of power necessary for victory. Peace can be maintained, they reason, by keeping any nation from acquiring enough extra power to feel that kind of confidence.

A major extension and reorientation of this point of view is the concept of **collective security**—*an arrangement by which nations agree in advance to take collective action against any nation that breaks the peace by committing aggression.* Thus the collective-security approach seeks peace by making it clear *in advance* to any would-be aggressor that its contemplated aggression will be met with overwhelming force and therefore cannot possibly succeed. It has been one of the most widely approved of all approaches to peace within the state system, and, as we will see, it is one of the main elements in the United Nations approach to peace.

Collective security is sometimes confused with defensive military alliances such as the North Atlantic Treaty Organization (NATO) and the East European communist nations' Warsaw Pact. These alliances differ from true collective-security arrangements, however, in that they are not intended to be universal in their membership, while universality is a goal of all genuine collective-security agreements. The NATO and Warsaw alliances are examples of a type of defensive military alliance that nations often form as part of a balance-of-power strategy. The nearest approximations to a genuine collective-security system in the twentieth century have been embodied in certain articles of the Covenant of the League of Nations and the Charter of the United Nations (UN), both of which we will consider later.

Preconditions

The collective-security approach to peace does not propose any alteration in the formal structure of the state system, in the sense of establishing a global government with the legal and physical power to *make* nations come to one another's defense whether they want to or not. Rather, it depends upon their willingness to do so voluntarily. It does, however, require a number of drastic changes in the attitudes of nations and the makers of their foreign policies. For, if collective security is to work as intended, most people in most nations must fully accept at least the idea of "the indivisibility of peace"—the notion that their destinies are inextricably intertwined with the security and welfare of all nations, not just their own. Furthermore, the people and the policy makers of each nation must put the general requirements and obligations of collective security before their own national interests. Finally, each nation must voluntarily surrender to some kind of international body a considerable portion of its power over its own foreign policy.

To illustrate the differences between balance-of-power and collective-security arrangements for meeting aggression, let us consider the case of American policy toward Korea in the early 1950s. When North Korea attacked South Korea in 1950, the UN, under American leadership, declared North Korea the aggressor and called for all member nations to come to South Korea's defense. The United States, which had already started to fight the North Koreans, complied with the resolution by sending large numbers of troops, although many other UN members did not. The United States thus acted just as every member of a collective-security agreement should.

But let us suppose that some time in the future, anti-Communist South Korea attacks Communist North Korea. Let us suppose, further, that the UN brands South Korea the aggressor and calls upon all member nations to go to the Communists' defense. What would we do? What *should* we do? On the one hand, many Americans feel that any aggression *by* Communists is dangerous to American security, whereas any aggression *against* Communists is helpful. On the other hand, under a collective-security agreement, we would be bound to help the Communists just as diligently as we helped the anti-Communists in the early 1950s. If we were to honor our collective-security commitments, American troops would stand shoulder to shoulder with Communists, killing non-Communists. If such a situation were actually to arise, it is not likely that the United States would join in any collective-security defense of Communism, and we know that in 1950 the Soviet Union not only did not join the collective-security defense of an anti-Communist victim of aggression but actively opposed what the UN was doing.

Hans J. Morgenthau and Kenneth W. Thompson have neatly summed up the difference between the national attitudes required by genuine collective security and those that actually prevail under the state system:

> *Collective security as an ideal is directed against all aggression in the abstract; foreign policy can only operate against a particular concrete aggressor. The only question collective security is allowed to ask is, "Who has committed aggression?" Foreign policy cannot help asking, "What interest do I have in opposing this particular aggressor, and what power do I have with which to oppose him?"*[5]

Until such time as the United States can be counted upon to rush to the defense of Communists against anti-Communist aggression and the Soviet

Union to fight Communist aggression against non-Communists, no global collective-security system in the strict sense can exist, for the good and sufficient reason that the attitudinal prerequisites for it do not exist. We will return to this problem in our discussion of the UN.

DISARMAMENT

Rationale

Disarmament is *the reduction or elimination of the personnel and/or equipment of national armed forces.* Closely associated concepts are *arms limitation*—a degree of mutual disarmament agreed to by two or more nations; and *arms control agreements,* which are agreements among nations for certain mutual arms limitations.

Since the end of the Napoleonic wars in 1815, every major nation has occasionally publicly declared itself in favor of some kind of disarmament. Nations advance such proposals for various reasons. One is their desire to reduce the heavy economic burdens of large military establishments. Another is their wish to reduce the destructiveness of war if it should come. A third is their wish to polish up their images as "peace-loving nations" and pinning the

Bilateral Arms Reduction Sometimes Works. President Reagan and General Secretary Gorbachev signing the 1987 treaty limiting the number and deployment of intermediate-range nuclear weapons in Europe. (Source: UPI/Bettmann Newsphotos.)

label of "warmongers" on their antagonists. The motive for disarmament proposals that concerns us here, however, is the desire to prevent war.

The theory of disarmament as an approach to peace is based upon the assumption that if there is no restriction on how heavily the major powers are armed, they will inevitably engage in arms races; and as national leaders simply cannot be trusted not to use huge military establishments if they have them, sooner or later arms races bring on wars. Thus one way of approaching peace, not necessarily the only way but often complementary to other ways, is to persuade all nations either to limit the total quantities of their weapons or to forswear the use of certain weapons (for example, poison gas, bacterial bombs, thermonuclear weapons), or both.

Record

Since 1815 many attempts have been made at both general and local disarmament. There have been a few successes with local disarmament: The best known is the Rush-Bagot Agreement of 1817 between Canada and the United States, which limits naval forces on the Great Lakes and has come by informal extension to mean the demilitarization of the entire Canadian-American border—which, at 3,000 miles, is the longest undefended international boundary in the world.

The most notable efforts at general disarmament have been the Holy Alliance of the immediate post-Napoleonic period in the 1820s, the Hague peace conferences of 1899 and 1907, the Washington naval conference of 1922, the world disarmament conference of 1932, and the many efforts made by the disarmament commissions of the League of Nations and the UN. Generally speaking, such efforts have failed to accomplish anything remotely approaching their stated objectives, for reasons we will review in a moment.

Nuclear Weapons: Disarmament and Control

We noted earlier in this chapter that the development of thermonuclear weapons has forced the age-old quest for peace into a brand-new atmosphere of great urgency; and much the same can be said for the problem of disarmament, which since 1945 has centered mainly upon the problem of reducing or abolishing nuclear weapons and the control of materials and facilities for nuclear fission and fusion. A brief review of these negotiations illuminates not only the special difficulties in nuclear disarmament but also the continuing difficulties of any effort at general disarmament under the state system.

Most of the efforts have centered on what are generally called strategic weapons rather than tactical weapons. The distinction between them is made largely in terms of their geographic reach: a **strategic weapon** is *a weapon capable of striking over long distances,* such as an intercontinental ballistic missile or a long-range bomber; whereas a **tactical weapon** is one *capable of striking only over relatively short distances,* such as artillery or small arms.

In 1946 the United States—which at that time had a world monopoly on nuclear weapons—laid before the Atomic Energy Commission of the UN a proposal that an international atomic-development authority be created as a body affiliated with, but independent of, the UN. This agency would be given a worldwide monopoly on the ownership and operation of all mines and plants producing fissionable materials and of all research and testing of nuclear weapons. It would also be empowered to license nations to use nuclear materials for peaceful purposes and would make unrestricted inspections of all nations' scientific and industrial establishments to detect illicit supplies of fissionable materials and misuse of licenses for their peaceful use. When such an authority was established and working to American satisfaction, the United States would surrender to the authority its national stockpiles of atomic bombs and fissionable materials.

The Soviet Union found the proposal unacceptable, however. It insisted that the establishment of any international control of atomic energy must be preceded by the legal prohibition of all nuclear weapons and by the United States' destruction of its stocks of such weapons. It also insisted that the proposed international authority should have no power to own, operate, or license atomic facilities and that even the authority's rather vague inspecting functions should operate in clear subordination to the Security Council, over whose operations the Soviet Union and the other great powers have a veto.

In 1948 the General Assembly approved a somewhat revised version of the American plan, but the Soviets were so hostile to it that no serious attempt has ever been made to implement it. Since 1948 there has been seemingly endless haggling in the UN's Disarmament Commission and Atomic Energy Commission, and many dramatic speeches have been made in the Security Council and the General Assembly—but very little effective agreement has been reached.

Several rays of hope have occasionally appeared. The first came in 1963, when the United States and the Soviet Union signed a treaty to end the testing of nuclear weapons in the atmosphere, outer space, and under water; and more than one hundred other nations also signed the treaty. But it provided for no system of inspection (which was considered unnecessary because the development of sensitive detection devices has made it almost impossible to conduct such tests without the other signatories' knowledge), and France and the PRC—both of which had just developed their own nuclear weapons—refused to sign it. The second hopeful development was the 1968 launching of the Nuclear Nonproliferation Treaty, also boycotted by France and the PRC.

Since 1969 the United States and the Soviet Union have engaged in on-again-off-again bilateral negotiations called the "strategic arms limitation talks" but better known by the acronym SALT. In 1972 the two nations signed a treaty, known as SALT I, which limited each nation to deploying only two antiballistic missile systems (ABMs), which was later reduced to one each; and it was understood that compliance with the agreement would be monitored by the earth-orbiting surveillance satellites of both nations. There were also accompanying executive agreements freezing for five years the deployment of strategic missile launchers and establishing a Standing Consultative Commission to formulate procedures for destroying or dismantling weapons in excess of the agreements or replacing old weapons with newer, improved weapons (which were allowed by the agreements).

SALT I was generally thought to be a major achievement in arms limitation, and the negotiations continued. In 1979 the two nations signed SALT II, a treaty limiting the number of each nation's launchers for ICBMs, sea-launched ballistic missiles (SLBMs), and heavy bombers. However, the treaty aroused strong opposition in the United States. Led by Ronald Reagan, the treaty's opponents argued that it endorsed and preserved the existing Soviet superiority in strategic weapons. Any chances SALT II had for ratification by the Senate disappeared when the Soviets invaded Afghanistan, and President Jimmy Carter withdrew it from formal consideration. SALT II has never been ratified, but both the Carter and Reagan administrations decided to observe its provisions as long as the Soviets did not exceed its limits (a pledge Reagan renewed in 1985).

Perhaps the greatest arms control achievement since World War II has been the 1987 agreement between the two great nuclear superpowers limiting the number and deployment of intermediate nuclear missiles (those with ranges between 315 and 3,125 miles). In 1982 the Soviet Union and the United States began talks in Geneva, Switzerland, on the possibilities of limiting the number of intermediate-range missiles deployed in Europe by the NATO and Warsaw Pact forces. The negotiations experienced several major setbacks: In 1983 the Soviets withdrew from the talks because the United States, with support from its NATO partners, refused to halt the deployment of additional missiles intended to even the balance in Europe. The talks resumed in 1985, but this time the major problem was the Soviets' insistence that no agreement could be reached until President Reagan gave up his plan to develop and deploy a new and advanced ABM system known as the strategic defense initiative (SDI, or, as some of its opponents called it, "star wars"), which was intended to use laser-armed satellites to destroy ICBMs before they could penetrate American defenses.

In 1987, however, under the new leadership of Mikhail Gorbachev, the Soviet Union dropped its insistence on the discontinuation of SDI development, and a treaty was negotiated in which the Soviets agreed to destroy about 400 SS-20 missiles aimed at Western Europe and the United States agreed to destroy about 325 Pershing II missiles aimed at the Soviet Union. In another major departure from past policies, each nation agreed to permit inspectors from the other to oversee and verify the destruction of the missiles. The treaty was signed by Gorbachev and Reagan at a summit meeting in Washington in December 1987, and ratified by a 93 to 5 vote by the U.S. Senate in 1988. The actual destruction of the weapons in both countries, watched by inspectors from the other countries, began in September 1988.

INTERNATIONAL LAW

As an Approach to Peace

The peculiar nature and problems of international law are suggested by the fact that legal theorists and political scientists disagree about whether or not it is really law. This dispute turns on the question of whether or not "real law" must emanate from an authoritative legislative source, be enforced by an authoritative executive, and be applied by authoritative courts, so we need not linger over it. Certainly international law is not law in exactly the same sense as domestic law is (see Chapters 1 and 14), yet it plays some role in international relations. Thus for our purposes, **international law** may be defined as *the body of rules and principles that nations usually accept as binding in their relations with one another.*

Before World War I, war was entirely legal under international law, and the law was useful as an approach to establishing peace only in the sense that it provided a body of rules and principles for the settlement of international disputes and therefore helped to avoid or limit war. Since 1918, however, war—at least war waged for any purpose other than self-defense—has become illegal in international law. The Covenant of the League of Nations severely restricted the circumstances in which its members could legally go to war; nearly all the nations in the world ratified the Kellogg-Briand Pact of 1928, which declared that all the nations "condemn recourse to war for the solution of international controversies and renounce it as an instrument of national policy"; and the Charter of the UN requires that all its members "shall settle their international disputes by peaceful means" and "refrain ... from the threat or use of force against the territorial integrity or political independence of any other state" (Article 2). Thus international law now seeks to prevent war by making it illegal as well as by providing rules and procedures for settling the disputes that lead to war.

Scope and Content

The rules of international law fall into four main categories: (1) The *law of peace* includes rules such as those affecting the legal creation of sovereign nations and their recognition by other nations, the definition of national boundaries, the extent of nations' legal jurisdictions over their territories, the status of alien persons and property, and so on. (2) The *law of war* regulates the declaration and termination of war; the conduct of hostilities; the treatment of enemy civilians and their property, prisoners of war, and spies; exclusion of certain weapons (such as poison gas); and so on. (3) The *law of neutrality* includes the definition and protection of the mutual rights and obligations of neutral and belligerent nations in time of war. And (4) the *laws concerning resort to war,* as we have noted, now consist of prohibitions against war except for purposes of self-defense.

Structure

The differences between domestic and international law, all of which relate to the utility of the latter as an approach to peace, are most clearly shown by examining the legislative, judicial, and executive structure of international law.

International legislation.   The rules of international law arise from two principal sources. Some come from customs, which are regular ways of handling certain types of situations, usually followed by nations over a long period of time (such as the custom that one nation will not arrest, try, or imprison official diplomatic representatives from another nation). Other rules arise from treaties—formal international agreements between two or more nations. It is important to note that *no* rule of international law is formally binding upon any nation that has not voluntarily accepted it, and no custom is binding unless the nation voluntarily adheres to it. For example, from 1979 to 1981, Iran did not let the diplomatic-immunity rule deter it from capturing the U.S. embassy in Teheran and holding over 60 American diplomats hostage for well over a year. Furthermore, no treaty is legally binding on a nation unless it has been

The International Court of Justice in Session (Source: Alain Mingam Gamma-Liaison.)

officially ratified by that nation. Thus no new rule of international law can legally be forced upon a nation by any outside agency—for that would violate its sovereignty (see Chapter 17).

Once a nation has accepted a custom or ratified a treaty, how binding are its rules *legally?* Two equally valid but quite contradictory legal maxims apply: *pacta sunt servanda* ("agreements are to be observed"), which means that a nation cannot legally free itself at will from treaty obligations; and *rebus sic stantibus* ("in this state of affairs"), meaning that treaties cease to be legally binding as soon as the conditions under which they were negotiated and signed have substantially changed. Who, then, is to say which treaty obligations are binding upon a nation and which are not? Who is authorized to interpret international law? There is only one realistic answer: Each nation interprets the law *for itself.* But if it wishes, it may submit questions of disputed interpretation to an international judicial body.

International adjudication.   Some nations sometimes submit disputed legal questions to *arbitration,* in which they agree to have some third party settle their dispute. But the only body that resembles an international court is the International Court of Justice (ICJ). This tribunal sits at The Hague in the Netherlands and consists of 15 judges, each selected from a different nation for a 9-year term by concurrent action of the UN Security Council and General Assembly.

The ICJ, however, is a pale image of a "world supreme court." It has no compulsory jurisdiction; that is, there is no legal way in which it can compel any nation to come before it. The Statute of the Court declares in Article 36 that its jurisdiction covers "all cases which the parties refer to it." The statute's often-mentioned "optional clause," to be sure, allows the parties to a dispute to make unilateral declarations "that they recognize as compulsory *ipso facto* and without special agreement, in relation to any other state accepting the same obligation, the jurisdiction of the Court" in certain kinds of cases. Yet over half of the members of the UN (including the Soviet Union) have not made such declarations, and most that have (including the United States and Great Britain) have hedged their declarations with so many qualifications and reservations that they are legally quite free to refuse to participate in any kind of dispute before the Court—as the United States did, with full legality, in 1984 when it refused to appear before the Court and answer a charge brought by Nicaragua that it was illegally trying to overthrow the Nicaraguan government. The ICJ cannot legally compel any nation to appear before it, nor can any nation legally "arraign" another nation against its desires. This lack of any effective compulsory jurisdiction sharply differentiates the ICJ from the domestic courts of any nation.

Execution.   The execution of international law is also decentralized and feeble, and for the most part the rules are enforced only by the voluntary compliance of nations. Before World War I the only way in which a nation could legally be compelled to obey international law was through the breaking of diplomatic relations, boycotts, blockades, and even military intervention. The collective-security provisions of the League of Nations Covenant and the UN Charter permit the use of collective sanctions for the enforcement of international law, but, as we have seen, they have been little used for this purpose. For the most part, accordingly, the enforcement of international law depends upon the willingness of nations to abide by it rather than upon compulsion by any international police force.

Record

There is a widespread popular impression that international law is a kind of political joke and that nations ignore it all the time as a matter of course. However, this impression is inaccurate, for, as J. L. Brierly has pointed out:

> *[International] law is normally observed because ... the demands that it makes on states are generally not exacting, and on the whole states find it convenient to observe it; but this fact receives little notice because the interest of most people in international law is not in the ordinary routine of international legal business, but in the occasions, rare but generally sensational, on which it is flagrantly broken. Such breaches generally occur either when some great political issue has arisen between states, or in that part of the system which professes to regulate the conduct of war.*[6]

The rules of international law that apply to technical and nonpolitical matters are thus usually observed by nations for the excellent reason that they find such observance to be in their self-interest; and these rules constitute the great bulk of international law. This service to mankind, as Brierly correctly points out, should not be overlooked or undervalued.

By the same token, however, the few areas in which international law is largely impotent are precisely those in which conflicts generally lead to war. International law in the current state of world politics thus makes many valuable contributions but is of little use as a barrier against war. The value and limitations of its contribution have been well summed up by Gaetano Anzilotti, a former justice of the ICJ.

> *The interests protected by international law are not those which are of major weight in the life of states. It is sufficient to think of the great political and economic rivalries to which no juridical formula applies, in order to realize the truth of this statement. International law develops its true function in a sphere considerably circumscribed and modest, not in that in which there move the great conflicts of interest which induce states to stake their very existence in order to make them prevail.*[7]

Perhaps that is why the often-heard charge that the United States' participation in the Vietnam War and its aid to the Nicaraguan contras were "illegal" had no effect on ending either activity—and why, by the same token, the United States' alleged violations of international law in its border disputes with Mexico in the 1970s were settled so amicably out of court.

APPROACHES TO PEACE THROUGH THE UNITED NATIONS

The UN, like its predecessor, the League of Nations (1919–46), is not intended to achieve world peace by abolishing the state system. Its charter explicitly states that "the Organization is based on the principle of the sovereign equality of all its Members" (Article 2), which, as we noted in Chapter 17, is the basic legal principle of the state system. The UN is clearly not, as the term is used in this book, a world *government*.

What is it, then? Perhaps the most accurate answer is that the UN is an international *organization* that tries to do two things. First, it tries to draw together in one world organization the various agencies and efforts for seeking peace *within* the state system just outlined, so that they can be used with maximum effectiveness. Second, it tries to encourage and administer international cooperation on many largely nonpolitical matters. The UN is not committed to any one approach to peace, but attempts to further all approaches that do not involve basic alterations of the state system.

The UN is thus an international organization, not a world government. In this discussion we will not attempt to examine all of its many and varied organs and activities but will concentrate mainly on the nature and results of those charter provisions and organs most directly related to efforts to maintain peace and security.

ESTABLISHMENT

The label "united nations" was first applied to a loose association of the nations fighting against Germany and Japan in World War II (1939–45), all of which on or after January 1, 1942, signed the Declaration of the United Nations—a document that proclaimed some general war aims and pledged the signatories not to make a separate peace with the enemy. Preliminary plans for a permanent peacetime organization of these nations were drawn up at two conferences in Washington, D.C., in 1944. The Charter of the United Nations was written at the UN conference on international organization in San Francisco in 1945. The UN was launched in 1946, when the first General Assembly and Security Council met in London. Since 1950 the organization has had its permanent headquarters in New York City.

STRUCTURE

Membership

The UN consists of the 51 nations that originally signed the charter and the nations that have subsequently applied and been admitted by votes of the General Assembly upon recommendations by the Security Council. As of 1989 there were 159 members, including almost all of the nations of the world and a few regions (for example, the Soviet republics of the Ukraine and Byelorussia) that are not full-fledged nations. Only one nation (Indonesia) has withdrawn (it later rejoined), and one (the Chinese Nationalist government of Taiwan) has been expelled.

Organs

According to the charter (Article 7) the UN has six principal organs: the General Assembly, Security Council, Secretariat, Economic and Social Council, International Court of Justice, and Trusteeship Council (see Figure 18.2). We will consider only the first three here.

General Assembly.   The General Assembly is the only organ of the UN that includes all its members, and it holds annual sessions. Each nation has one vote, although it can send a delegation of up to five members. The General Assembly exercises powers and functions that may be called *deliberative* (discussing any matters within the scope of the charter); *supervisory* (controlling and regulating other organs—receiving annual reports from them and establishing certain administrative procedures for them to follow); *financial* (making up the UN budget and apportioning expenses among the members); *elective* (admitting new members and choosing members for the other organs); and *constituent* (proposing amendments to the Charter). Several of these powers, as we will see, are exercised jointly with the Security Council. It decides "important questions" (as defined in Article 18) by two-thirds majorities of the members present and voting and decides all other matters by simple majorities.

Security Council.   The Security Council is composed of 15 member nations, divided into two classes: 5 permanent members (the PRC, France, the Soviet Union, Great Britain, and the United States); and 10 nonpermanent members, which are elected for 2-year terms by the General Assembly. The terms of the elected members are staggered so that 5 new members are elected each year, and no nonpermanent member may serve two consecutive terms. The Security Council was originally intended to bear the main responsibility for and control over UN machinery for maintaining peace and security, but it has come to share a good deal of its power in this area with the General Assembly.

The most noteworthy feature of the Security Council is its voting procedure, which provides for a veto by any one of the five permanent members. Article 27 of the charter stipulates the following:

> *1. Each member of the Security Council shall have one vote. 2. Decisions of the Security Council on procedural matters shall be made by an affirmative vote of nine members. 3. Decisions of the Security Council on all other matters shall be made by an affirmative vote of nine members* including the concurring votes of the permanent members. ...

Thus the Security Council, which is supposed to be the UN's main organ, cannot act unless the 5 permanent members unanimously agree that it should

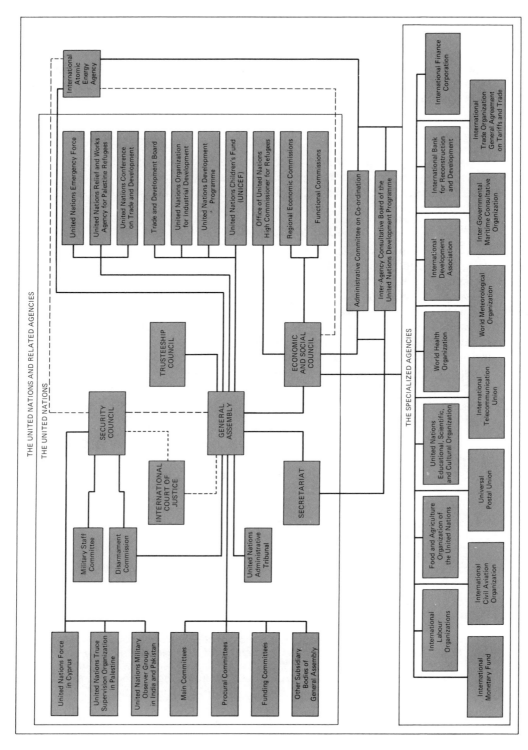

FIGURE 18.2. The Structure of the United Nations

act (or at least abstain from voting no). This veto provision and its frequent use, especially by the Soviet Union and the United States, are often blamed for the failure of the organization to live up to its promise, but it simply accords with the facts of international life. No resolution *for action* adopted by the UN could possibly be effective if either of the two "superpowers," the Soviet Union and the United States, believed that such action would threaten its vital interests and strongly opposed it. In short, the veto does not create the present nature of world politics; it merely reflects it.

Secretariat and Secretary-General. The UN Secretariat is the organization's civil service and performs many secretarial, research, and other administrative chores for the various agencies. It is headed by the secretary-general, who is appointed by the General Assembly on the recommendation of the Security Council. In addition to acting as the organization's chief administrative officer, the secretary-general plays a significant political role. Article 99 of the charter authorizes him to "bring to the attention of the Security Council any matter which in his opinion may threaten international peace and security." All occupants of the office to date—from Trygve Lie (1946–54) to Javier Perez de Cuellar (1982–)—have made full use of this power, and the office of secretary-general has come to be one of the most powerful agencies in the whole UN structure, exercising a major influence on its operations.

These, then, are the UN's principal organs for maintaining international peace and security. Let us now review the charter's provisions for handling such matters and see how they have worked out in practice.

MAINTAINING INTERNATIONAL PEACE AND SECURITY

The Charter of the United Nations incorporates many of the approaches to peace we have been considering. The General Assembly and Security Council are forums in which international issues can be discussed and "world public opinion" can be expressed. The Economic and Social Council and affiliated specialized agencies provide opportunities for many kinds of cooperation on nonpolitical and technical matters so as to benefit most nations. Although all of the UN's trust territories have now achieved independence, the Trusteeship Council formerly provided a means for the enlightened administration of non-self-governing territories and has also sought to eliminate quarrels over colonies as a cause of war. The UN also has agencies for the mediation and conciliation of international disputes, the adjudication of international legal controversies (the ICJ), and the reduction and regulation of armaments.

However, the UN relies upon collective security as its main approach to preventing war. The relevant provisions are stated mainly in Chapter VII, Articles 39 through 51, of the charter, and may be briefly summarized as follows: The Security Council is charged with determining "the existence of any threat to the peace, breach of the peace, or act of aggression" and with deciding what measures will be taken when such threats arise (Article 39). It may decide to adopt measures not involving the use of armed force and may call upon the members to apply them. "These may include complete or partial interruption of economic relations and of rail, sea, air, postal, telegraphic, radio, and other means of communication, and the severance of diplomatic relations" (Article 41). If the Security Council decides that these measures are inadequate, it may adopt others "to maintain or restore international peace and security. Such action may include demonstrations, blockades, and other operations by air, sea, or land forces of Members of the United Nations" (Article 42). And the members are obligated to respond to the Security Council's requests that they take such action (Articles 48–50).

These charter provisions are clearly intended to create a strong collective-security system centered upon the Security Council as the decision-making body. How have they worked out in practice?

The United Nations General Assembly in Session (Source: United Nations.)

THE CHANGING UNITED NATIONS

Ever since the UN began functioning in 1946, the basic fact of international life has been the "cold war" between the United States and its allies on the one hand, and the Soviet Union and its allies on the other. The fundamental prerequisite for the successful operation of the UN collective- security system—unanimity among the permanent members of the Security Council—has thus rarely been present. In those instances of aggression or breaches of the peace in which the Soviet Union and the United States have favored different sides, the Security Council has been unable to act at all because one or the other superpower has used or threatened to use its veto, and on occasion the other permanent members have done the same.

The most notable exception to this generalization was the Korean action of 1950. In June of that year Communist North Korea launched an armed invasion of non-Communist South Korea—a clear instance of aggression in violation of the charter. By an ironic twist of fate the Soviets at that moment were boycotting the UN in protest against its failure to admit the PRC, and the American-sponsored resolution in the Security Council to invoke Article 42 against North Korea was passed. The Soviets returned too late to veto it. However, the response of the member nations to the Security Council's call for troops to help repel the invasion was somewhat less than unanimous enthusiastic cooperation. Of the 60 member nations, only 16 sent armed forces of any kind, and only the United States, Great Britain, Canada, and Turkey sent more than token forces. Most members sat on the sidelines, some (such as the Latin American nations) cheering the UN "team" on, others (India, for instance) wringing their hands over the whole unfortunate affair, and still others (the Communist bloc) denouncing the action as illegal, imperialistic, warmongering, and so on.

The Korean War came to an end in 1953 with an uneasy truce, and the whole episode represented neither a total collapse nor a great success for the UN's collective-security system. Certainly it was possible at all only because the Soviet Union was boycotting the UN when the aggression took place. Otherwise the Security Council would have been prevented from taking action just as it has been in most other instances of aggression and war since 1946.

On several other occasions the UN has sent small peace-keeping forces or truce-supervising teams into some of the world's trouble spots to observe, report, and try to prevent violations of truce agreements among warring factions or nations—but only when the Soviet Union and the United States agreed that they should be sent or when the General Assembly acted to bypass the Security Council. The contributions of the UN peace-keeping forces received their greatest recognition by being awarded the Nobel Peace Prize in 1988.

The fact is that the UN in the 1990s is a very different organization from the one created in the 1940s, and its changing nature has had a lot to do with the considerable fluctuations in its importance as an agency for maintaining peace and security. Its history has so far seen three main phases. The basic facts about each phase are shown in Table 18.1, and the story of each is as follows.

Decline of the Security Council, Rise of the General Assembly, 1946–54

In its first decade the membership of the UN was little changed, and most of its proceedings were dominated by a coalition led by the United States. On most issues the United States could count on the support of the Western European, British Commonwealth, and Latin American nations. In the Security Council the Soviet Union often vetoed actions proposed by the United States, but in the General Assembly the United States–led coalition could usually muster 39 of the 60 members, and this majority enabled it to carry most of the resolutions it wished. By far the most notable of these was the uniting-for-peace resolution passed over Soviet opposition in 1950, which provided that in instances in which there appear to be threats to peace or acts of aggression and in which the Security Council, because of a veto by one of its permanent members, fails to recommend action under Articles 41 and 42, the General Assembly will immediately consider the matter. If two-thirds of the members agree, the General Assembly will recommend that the member nations use whatever measures, including armed force, seem appropriate to maintain or restore international peace and security.

Thus the General Assembly assumed a good deal of the power and action in the collective-security area that was originally reserved for the Security Council, and it has been used several times since 1950. In 1960, for example, the General Assembly, over strong Soviet-bloc opposition, sent 23,000 troops

TABLE 18.1.   Changing Membership of the United Nations, 1945–88

Blocs of Member Nations	By Period of Admission				
	Before 1955	Percentage of Votes	1955 to 1964	1965 to 1988	Total 1988	Percentage of Votes
Afro-Asian	10	17.0	35	27	72	45.3
Communist	6	10.2	5	2	13	8.2
U.S. and Western Europe	12	20.3	6	1	19	11.9
British Commonwealth	4	6.8	1	7	12	7.5
Latin America	19	32.2	1	4	24	15.1
Middle East (Muslim)	6	10.2	2	5	13	8.2
Other	2	3.3	4	—	6	3.8
Totals	59	100	54	56	159	100

Source: The World Almanac and Book of Facts 1988 (New York: Newspaper Enterprise Association, 1988), p. 744.

from UN members to the Congo to prevent expansion of the civil war in that newly independent nation, and Secretary-General Dag Hammarskjold was killed in the crash of a UN plane flying a reconnaissance mission over the fighting area. In 1956 the UN sent an emergency force of 6,000 to the Middle East to supervise the armistice lines established after the war between Egypt and Israel. The force remained in place for years afterward but was unable to prevent the outbreak in 1967 of the "Six-Day War" between Israel and the Arab nations and later was unable to prevent violations of the postwar cease-fire agreements, and a new war broke out in 1973.

However, the international peace-keeping forces sent to Lebanon in 1982 to supervise the truce between Israel, Syria, and the various Lebanese factions were organized and sent by the United States, Great Britain, France, and Italy by mutual agreements made outside the UN machinery. In short, the UN's peace-keeping operations, originally made possible by the rise of the General Assembly and the bypassing of vetoes in the Security Council in the early 1950s, have had only modest success.

Third-World Dominance, 1955–64

The first two decades after World War II saw the breakup of most of the prewar colonial empires, particularly the British, French, and Dutch. The result was a great expansion in the number of independent sovereign nations, almost of all which applied for membership in the UN. The dam burst in 1955 and 1956, when the UN admitted 20 new members; and over the next nine years it added 34 more. Thus by 1964 the UN had 113 members, compared with the original 59, and the organization's politics changed radically. The United States added only 4 new members to its coalition and the Soviet Union added only a dozen or so. The great gainers were the countries, mainly in Africa and Asia, called "Third World" because they claimed to be politically as well as geographically and economically separate from the Western bloc and the Communist bloc.

At first, with the Security Council still stymied by the superpowers' vetoes, most issues were fought out mainly in the General Assembly. By the early 1960s the Western bloc could regularly muster a coalition of only about one-third of the members, the Soviet bloc could do about the same, and the remaining third consisted of the new nations. Both the Western and Soviet blocs sought the Third World bloc's support, and each won a few and lost a few.

In 1964, however, the General Assembly's new ascendence received a major setback. By a two-thirds vote under the uniting-for-peace resolution it ordered UN peace-keeping forces into the Congo in Africa and the Gaza Strip in the Middle East. Both France and the Soviet Union denounced these moves and refused to pay the special assessments voted by the General Assembly to support the UN forces. The consequences seemed perfectly clear: The ICJ ruled that the operations were lawful and that all members were obligated to pay. Article 19 of the charter provides that any member nation more than two years in arrears of its financial obligations as voted by the General Assembly will be deprived of its vote in the UN. But when it came time to enforce this rule, the General Assembly—and most of the Third World countries—backed down. In its 1964 session no formal votes were taken at all,[8] France and the Soviet Union were not expelled, and the principle was established that in fact the General Assembly cannot force a major power to abide by any of its decisions calling for action unless that nation volunteers to do so—in short, a quasi-veto power came to operate in the General Assembly as well as in the Security Council.

Much Talk, Little Action, 1965–

Since 1965, as Table 18.1 shows, the UN has admitted 46 new members, 27 of which are located in Africa and Asia. In the 1990s the Afro-Asian nations constitute nearly half of the entire membership, and Third World nations as a group control well over two-thirds of the votes in the General Assembly. Of course the Third World nations do not vote together on all questions, and they are split into several caucuses—the Afro-Asian caucus, the African caucus, the Latin American caucus, the "nonaligned nations" caucus, and so on. They regularly unite on resolutions condemning Israel, South Africa, U.S. actions in Central America, and indeed any resolution dealing with what they regard as the vestiges of colonialism; the Soviet bloc invariably joins them on such resolutions, and the Western bloc is usually a small minority. Occasionally many Third World nations join the Western bloc in resolutions criticizing the Soviet Union; for example, a 1980 resolution condemned Soviet armed intervention in Afghanistan, and a 1983 resolution condemned the Soviets for shooting down a South Korean civilian airliner. They can also get near-unanimous support (since they are joined by both the Western and Soviet blocs) urging warring nations, such as Iran and Iraq, to cease fire and settle their differences by peaceful means. But the General Assembly can get a two-thirds vote for a resolution calling for real action under the uniting-for-peace precedent only when it is not strongly opposed by either the Western or the Soviet bloc; and that does not happen very often.

As a result, the UN's record in preventing or stopping major wars since 1965 has not been impressive. As we have seen, it did play a minor role in monitoring a truce between Israel and Egypt after their war in 1973, but it played no role of any significance in the wars between the United States and North Vietnam (1964–73), India and Pakistan (1971), Israel and Syria in Lebanon (1978–85), Ethiopia and Somalia (1978–), Libya and Chad (1979–81), or Great Britain and Argentina (1982), or in the Soviet invasion of Afghanistan (1979–89) and the seemingly endless conflicts in Central America (1979–). Perhaps the UN's greatest role in ending a major war came in 1988, when Secretary General Perez de Cuellar played a key role in mediating the end of the long (1980–88) and bloody war between Iran and Iraq.

Of course, this does not mean that the UN has made no contribution whatever to human betterment. Most observers believe that the organization has done good things in many *nonpolitical* areas, such as improving health, combatting illiteracy, bringing self-government to the trust territories, and helping refugees.

However, the UN has done only a little to move the world toward international peace and security. How could it be otherwise? As we have seen, in both legal theory and political fact, the UN is founded on total acceptance of the state system. As long as its member nations and their leaders and citizens continue to prefer national independence and self-determination to truly supernational government, the UN cannot become a significantly stronger force for peace than it is now. Eliminating the veto from the Security Council or enforcing Article 19 or any other institutional tinkering cannot change this fact. As long as powerful nations like the Soviet Union and the United States—and less powerful nations like Israel and Syria, India and Pakistan—refuse to submit what they regard as their vital national interests to control by the UN or any other outside agency, the UN cannot be expected to bring world peace.

In short, the UN is part of the state system. If the state system is, as some

TABLE 18.2.   **Public Opinion Toward the United Nations (in percentages)**

Question (1985): "In general, do you feel the United Nations is doing a good job or a poor job in trying to solve the problems it has had to face?"

Nation	Good Job	Poor Job	No Opinion
Australia	49	34	17
Argentina	32	32	36
Belgium	34	17	49
Brazil	27	23	50
Canada	36	39	26
Greece	31	36	33
West Germany	25	31	44
Japan	16	28	56
Netherlands	66	23	12
Philippines	64	15	21
Portugal	17	14	69
South Africa	13	65	22
Switzerland	49	24	27
Turkey	22	43	35
Uruguay	25	49	27
United Kingdom	26	47	27
United States	28	54	18

Question (1981): "Are you strongly in favor of the United States being a member of the United Nations, or moderately in favor of it, or not very much in favor of it, or not at all in favor of it?"

In favor	77
Not in favor	15
Don't know	8

Source: For 1985 questions, the Gallup Poll, *Public Opinion 1985* (Wilmington, DE: Scholarly Resources, 1985), pp. 84, 229. For 1981 question, *Public Opinion*, June/July 1982, pp. 35–37.

believe, the basic cause of international war, then the UN is powerless to prevent it. But if even within the state system there is some real hope of preventing World War III, then the organization has made some contribution, however modest, to keeping that hope alive.

DOES HUMANITY HAVE A FUTURE?

In the present state of political science, there are many questions that cannot be answered with any degree of confidence beyond that of the educated guess. The most important of all is certainly an example: Does humanity have a future?

Political scientists usually regret their inability to make reliable predictions on such matters, but perhaps in this instance we should be glad. For if the answer is that thermonuclear world war is inevitable and humanity has no future, most of us would prefer not to know it until we have to. In any case, the most that political scientists—or anyone else—can answer is: maybe.

Political scientists *can* predict with confidence at least some of the short-term prospects for world politics. Most analysts of international affairs agree that in the immediate future the essentials of the state system will remain unchanged, although the atomistic nationalism and unilateral national actions characteristic of world politics before 1914 will be increasingly replaced by the work of regional associations of nations with common interests and similar ideologies, such as NATO, the European Economic Community, the Organization of American States, the Warsaw Pact, and the Arab League.

The UN will continue to have its greatest successes in nonpolitical and technical activities, such as combatting illiteracy and disease, and most of its political efforts to prevent aggression and maintain peace through collective security, disarmament, and peaceful settlement of disputes will have little success.

Thermonuclear weapons will continue to be made, stockpiled, and held in readiness by the United States, the Soviet Union, France, Great Britain, and the PRC—and also by India, Israel, Pakistan, and other nations (Libya?) that are now developing nuclear capabilities. The means of delivering such weapons over intercontinental distances will continue to be improved, and just possibly the means of defending against them will also be improved.

Finally, the burden of preventing international conflict from erupting into thermonuclear World War III will continue to be borne, if at all, by the rickety old structures and processes of the state system.

On balance, then, we must all accept the fact that for some time to come we will live in a world in which the possibility of thermonuclear warfare is always present and in which smaller, less devastating wars will occur from time to time, always posing the danger of becoming general and unlimited wars.

Even so, the record is not entirely disheartening. After all, there have been at least 15 major wars and over 30 lesser wars since the end of World War

II in 1945. Yet after all those decades it is still true that the only nuclear weapons ever used in combat were the bombs dropped on Hiroshima and Nagasaki by the Americans in 1945. Since then nuclear war has always been a very real and frightening possibility—but it has not happened, at least not yet. Consequently, no concerned and realistic person can expect either physical security or psychic ease for some time to come. We can all expect to live for many decades, perhaps all our lives, in what some observers have called—with grim accuracy—"the age of anxiety."

That much the political scientist can foretell. Does humanity have a future? Perhaps fortunately, neither I nor anyone else can say for sure. I personally am an optimist. But as thermonuclear-age humor has it, "An optimist is one who believes that the future is uncertain."

FOR FURTHER READING

INTERNATIONAL POLITICS

CLAUDE, INIS L., JR. *Swords into Plowshares: The Problems and Progress of International Organizations,* 4th ed. New York: Random House, 1981. Analysis of theories and results of various approaches to peace within the state system.

*FARLEY, LAWRENCE T. *Change and Process in International Organizations.* Cambridge, MA.: Schenckman, 1982. Short description of changing nature of international organizations, mainly outside the UN.

JACOBSON, HAROLD K. *Networks of Interdependence,* 2nd ed. New York: Knopf, 1984. Calm and balanced survey of governmental and nongovernmental international organizations, and their achievements, limitations, and problems.

*LEVI, WERNER. *The Coming End of War.* Beverly Hills, CA.: Sage, 1981. Argument that the changing ecological conditions of the world are slowly transforming the international order so as to diminish the chances of war.

BALANCE OF POWER

DEHIO, LUDWIG. *The Precarious Balance.* New York: Knopf, 1962. Analysis of balance-of-power policies in modern conditions.

GULICK, EDWARD V. *Europe's Classical Balance of Power.* Ithaca, NY: Cornell University Press, 1955. Study of balance-of-power policies in Europe prior to World War II.

RIKER, WILLIAM H. *The Theory of Political Coalitions.* New Haven, CT: Yale University Press, 1962. Leading formal- theory study of political coalitions, with many applications to international power relations.

COLLECTIVE SECURITY

BEATON, LEONARD. *The Reform of Power: A Proposal for an International Security System.* New York: Viking Press, 1972. Argument in favor of collective security as the main path to peace.

BROWN, HAROLD. *National Security.* Boulder, CO: Westview Press, 1983. Analysis of national

security requirements by former secretary of defense.

GADDIS, JOHN LEWIS. *Strategies of Containment.* New York: Oxford University Press, 1982. Analysis of collective-security arrangements to check the Soviet Union's expansionism without risking war.

DISARMAMENT

EPSTEIN, WILLIAM. *The Last Chance: Nuclear Proliferation and Arms Control.* New York: Free Press, 1976. Study of nuclear disarmament, with special attention to the *n*th-country problem.

GRAY, COLIN S. *The Soviet-American Arms Race.* Lexington, MA: Lexington Books, 1976. Description of arms buildups and efforts at limitation.

Harvard Nuclear Study Group. *Living with Nuclear Weapons.* New York: Bantam Books, 1983. Widely read study of problems and possibilities for nuclear disarmament.

WIESELTIER, LEON. *Nuclear War, Nuclear Peace.* New York: Holt, Rinehart & Winston, 1983. Study of consequences of nuclear war and of possibilities for nuclear arms management and control.

INTERNATIONAL LAW

BRIERLY, J. L. *The Law of Nations,* 6th ed. New York: Oxford University Press, 1963. A leading survey of the nature, principles, and applications of international law.

O'BRIEN, WILLIAM V. *The Conduct of Just and Limited War.* New York: Praeger, 1981. Study of

philosophical attitudes toward war and international law.

VON GLAHN, GERHARD. *Law Among Nations,* 5th ed. New York: Macmillan, 1986. Updated version of a standard text on international law.

THE UNITED NATIONS

ALGER, CHADWICK F., and BRUCE M. RUSSETT. *World Politics in the General Assembly.* New Haven, CT: Yale University Press, 1965. Study of shifting political alignments and power in the General Assembly after the uniting-for-peace resolution.

GATI, TOBY T., ed. *The U.S., the U.N., and the Management of Global Change.* New York: New York University Press, 1983. Essays by various authors on the changing nature of the UN, its place in American foreign policy, and its future problems and possibilities.

MURPHY, JOHN P. *The United Nations and the Control of International Violence.* Totowa, NJ: Allanheld, Osmun, 1983. Mainly legal analysis of UN authority to prevent international violence and descriptions of main instances in which the power has been used.

PETERSON, M. J. *The General Assembly in World Politics.* Winchester, MA: Allen & Unwin, 1986. Study of the Third-World's domination of the UN General Assembly.

NOTES

[1]The authoritative public account is still Samuel Glasstone, ed., *The Effect of Nuclear Weapons,* rev. ed. (Washington, D.C.: U.S. Atomic Energy Commission, 1962).

[2]Harrison Brown and James Real, *Community of Fear* (Santa Barbara, CA: Center for the Study of Democratic Institutions, 1960), pp. 14–20.

[3]*The World Almanac and Book of Facts,* 1985 (New York: Newspaper Enterprise Association, 1985), p. 339.

[4]Quoted in Ralph E. Lapp, "The Einstein Letter that Started it All," *New York Times Magazine,* August 2, 1964.

[5]Hans J. Morgenthau and Kenneth W. Thompson, *Politics Among Nations: The Struggle for Power and Peace,* 6th ed. (New York: Knopf, 1985), p. 454.

[6]J. L. Brierly, *The Law of Nations,* 6th ed. (New York: Oxford University Press, 1963), pp. 71–72.

[7]Quoted in H. Lauterpacht, *The Function of Law in the International Community* (New York: Oxford University Press, 1933), p. 169.

[8]When an issue had to be decided, General Assembly President Alex Quaison-Sackley of Ghana would invite the members to give him their opinions privately, after which he would announce the Assembly's consensus.

Index